THE SEVENTH
Garfield
Fat Cat 3-Pack

JIM DAVIS

Ballantine Books • New York

GARFIELD HANGS OUT copyright © 1990 by Paws, Incorporated
GARFIELD TAKES UP SPACE copyright © 1990 by Paws, Incorporated
GARFIELD SAYS A MOUTHFUL copyright © 1991 by Paws, Incorporated
GARFIELD Comic Strips copyright 1989, 1990 by Paws, Incorporated

All rights reserved under International and Pan-American Copyright
Conventions. Published in the United States by Ballantine Books, a
division of Random House, Inc., New York, and simultaneously in
Canada by Random House of Canada Limited, Toronto.

http://www.randomhouse.com

Library of Congress Catalog Card Number: 96-95449

ISBN: 0-345-41449-7

Manufactured in the United States of America

First Edition: April 1997

10 9 8 7 6 5 4 3 2 1

Garfield hangs out

BY: JIM DAVIS

PET PICKS & PANS

PET EXPERT GARFIELD ON CATS AND THEIR COMPETITION

RABBITS: BUY TWO CHOCOLATE ONES AND HOPE THEY MULTIPLY.

HAMSTERS: BIG DUMB COUSINS OF MICE.

GOLDFISH: NEAT, QUIET, DON'T NEED WALKING, AND IN A PINCH THEY MAKE A TASTY HORS D'OEUVRE.

SPIDERS: THAT'S NOT A PET; THAT'S A NIGHTMARE.

MICE: SURE, THEY'RE CUTE, BUT THEY ONLY LOVE YOU FOR YOUR CHEESE.

BOA CONSTRICTORS: RIGHT. NOTHING LIKE A PET THAT WILL HUG YOU, THEN EAT YOU.

PARROTS: PRETTY BIRDS. A GOOD ACCESSORY WITH AN EYE PATCH AND PEG LEG.

DOGS: LOVING, LOYAL, OBEDIENT, AND BREATH THAT WOULD STUN A YAK.

CATS: NATURE'S MOST PERFECT PET. NEED I SAY MORE?

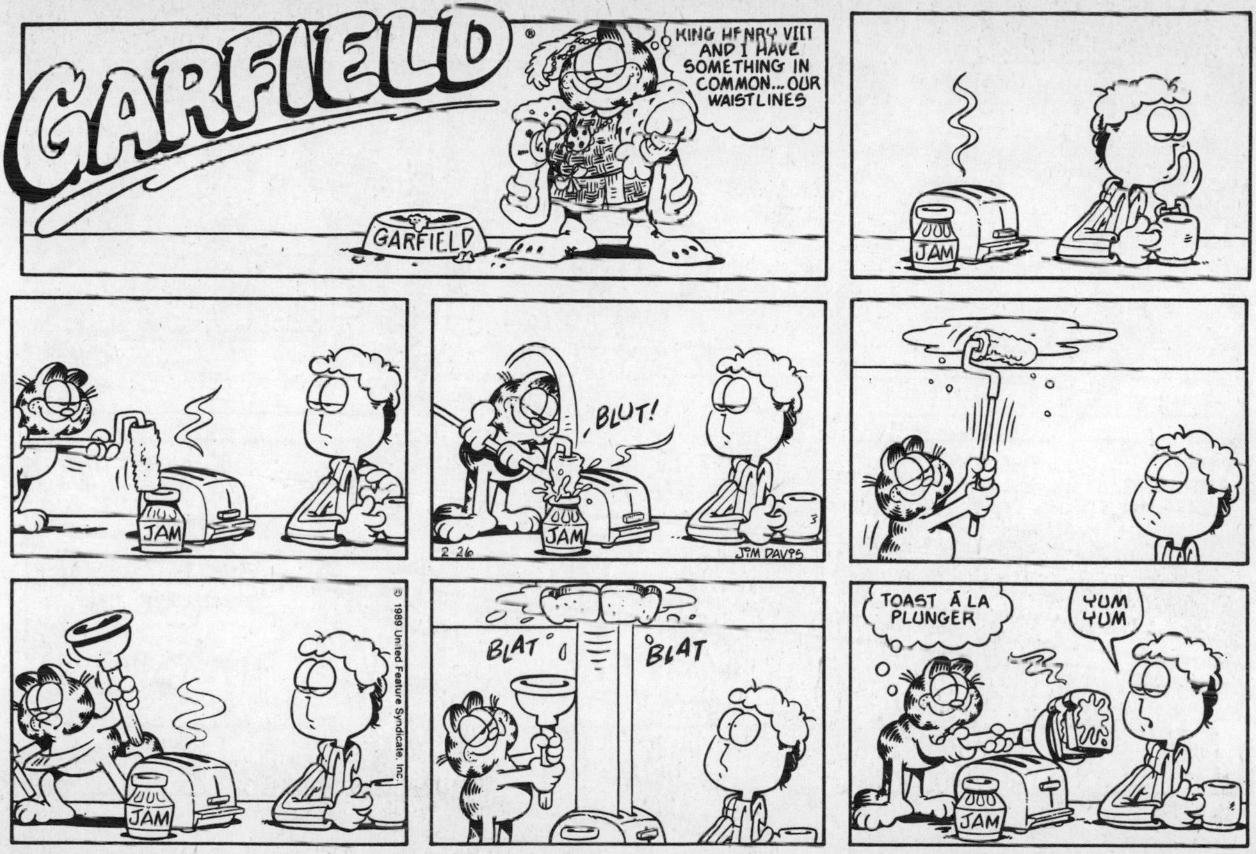
GARFIELD
KING HENRY VIII AND I HAVE SOMETHING IN COMMON... OUR WAISTLINES
GARFIELD
JAM
JAM
BLUT!
JAM
2-26
JIM DAVIS
© 1989 United Feature Syndicate, Inc.
JAM
BLAT
BLAT
TOAST Á LA PLUNGER
YUM YUM
JAM

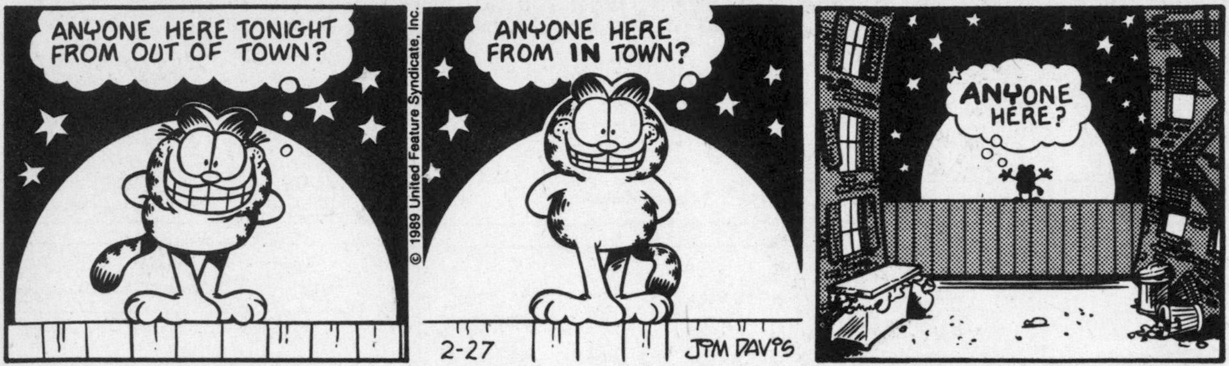
ANYONE HERE TONIGHT FROM OUT OF TOWN?
© 1989 United Feature Syndicate, Inc.
ANYONE HERE FROM IN TOWN?
2-27
JIM DAVIS
ANYONE HERE?

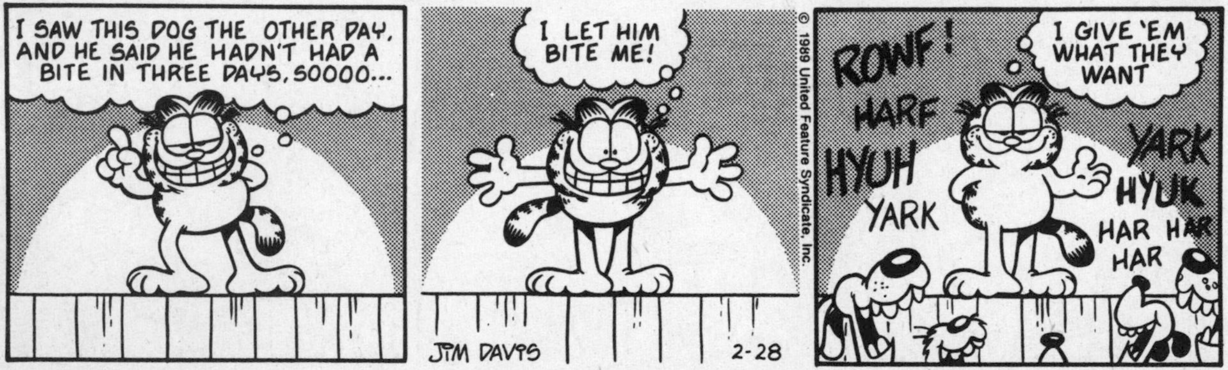
I SAW THIS DOG THE OTHER DAY, AND HE SAID HE HADN'T HAD A BITE IN THREE DAYS, SOOOO...
I LET HIM BITE ME!
JIM DAVIS
2-28
© 1989 United Feature Syndicate, Inc.
RONF!
HARF
HYUH
YARK
I GIVE 'EM WHAT THEY WANT
YARK
HYUK
HAR HAR
HAR

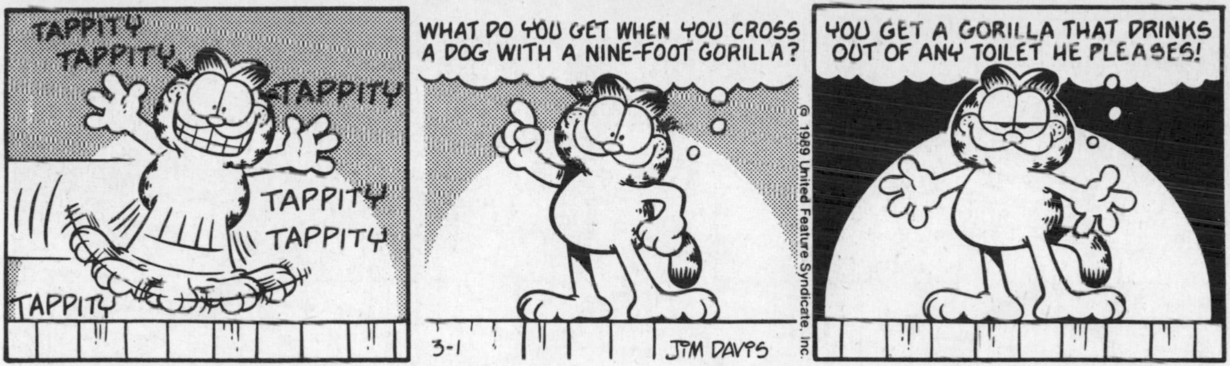
TAPPITY
TAPPITY
TAPPITY
TAPPITY
TAPPITY
TAPPITY
WHAT DO YOU GET WHEN YOU CROSS A DOG WITH A NINE-FOOT GORILLA?
3-1
JIM DAVIS
© 1989 United Feature Syndicate, Inc.
YOU GET A GORILLA THAT DRINKS OUT OF ANY TOILET HE PLEASES!

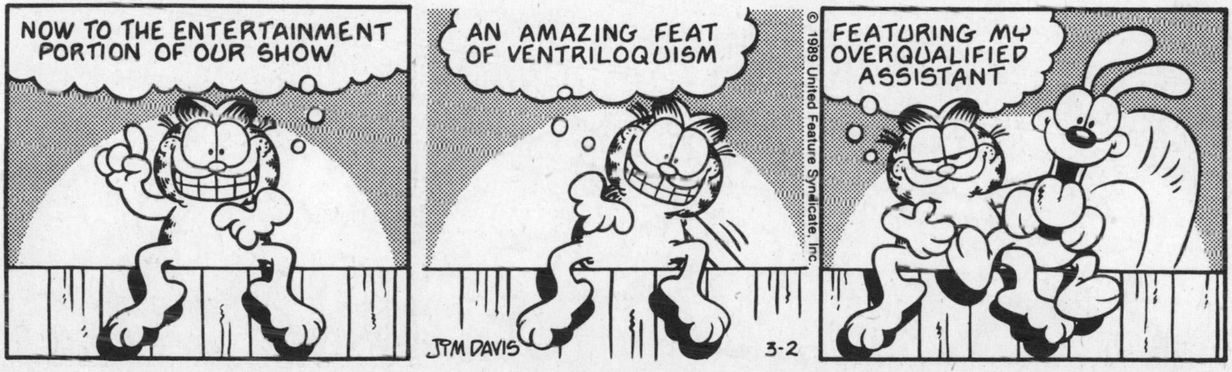
NOW TO THE ENTERTAINMENT PORTION OF OUR SHOW
AN AMAZING FEAT OF VENTRILOQUISM
JIM DAVIS
3-2
© 1989 United Feature Syndicate, Inc.
FEATURING MY OVERQUALIFIED ASSISTANT

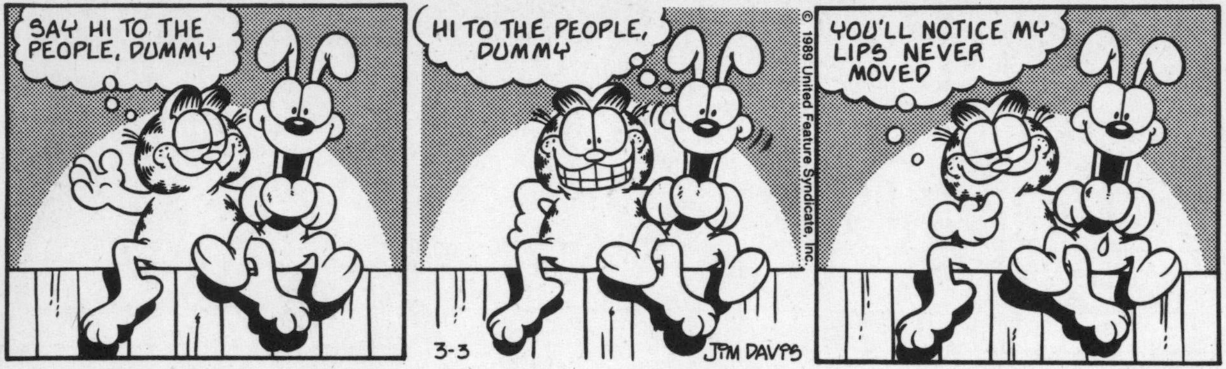
SAY HI TO THE PEOPLE, DUMMY
HI TO THE PEOPLE, DUMMY
YOU'LL NOTICE MY LIPS NEVER MOVED
© 1989 United Feature Syndicate, Inc.
3-3
JIM DAVIS

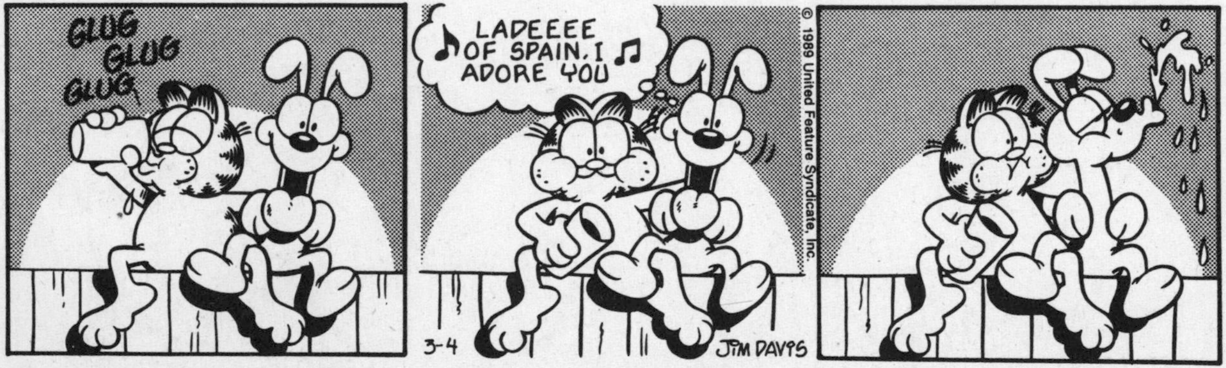
GLUG GLUG GLUG
LADEEEE OF SPAIN, I ADORE YOU
© 1989 United Feature Syndicate, Inc.
3-4
JIM DAVIS

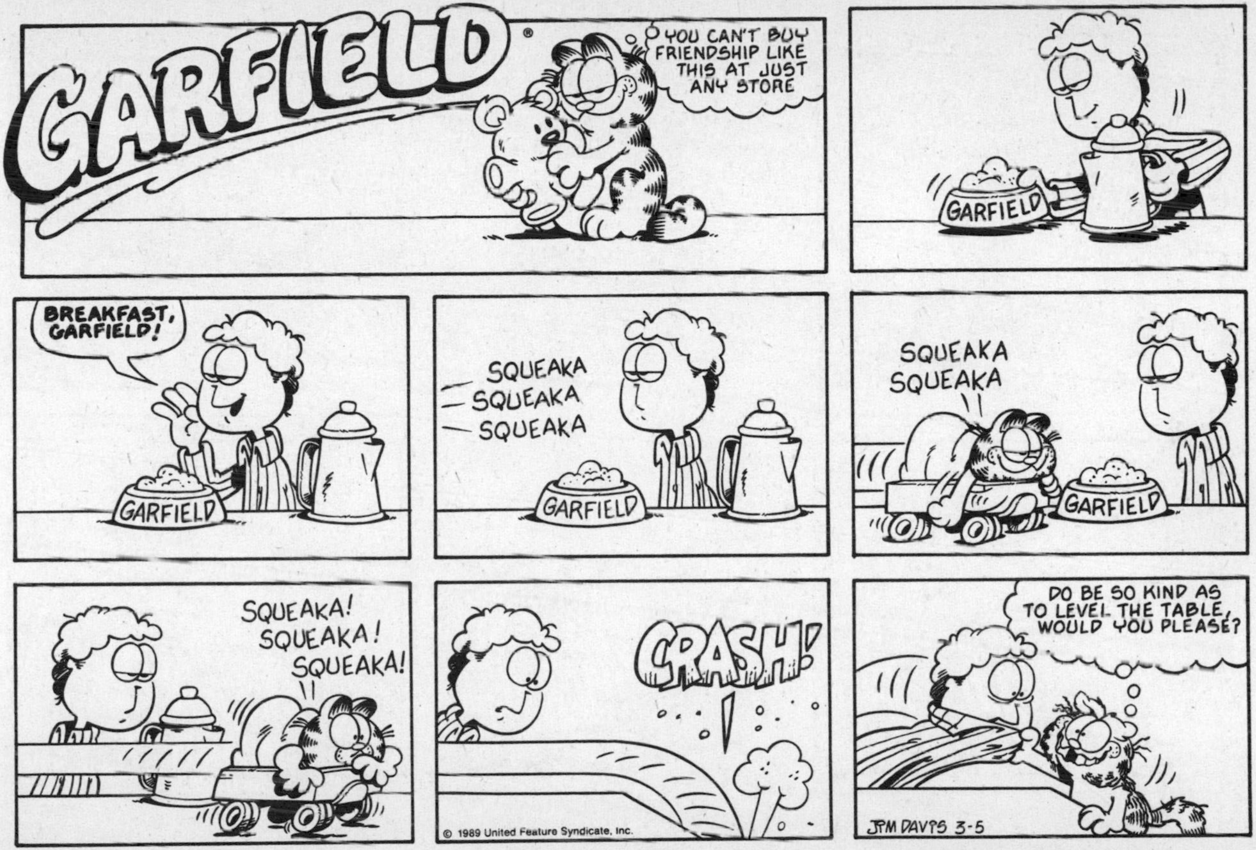
GARFIELD®
YOU CAN'T BUY FRIENDSHIP LIKE THIS AT JUST ANY STORE
GARFIELD
BREAKFAST, GARFIELD!
GARFIELD
SQUEAKA SQUEAKA SQUEAKA
GARFIELD
SQUEAKA SQUEAKA
GARFIELD
SQUEAKA! SQUEAKA! SQUEAKA!
CRASH!
© 1989 United Feature Syndicate, Inc.
DO BE SO KIND AS TO LEVEL THE TABLE, WOULD YOU PLEASE?
JIM DAVIS 3-5

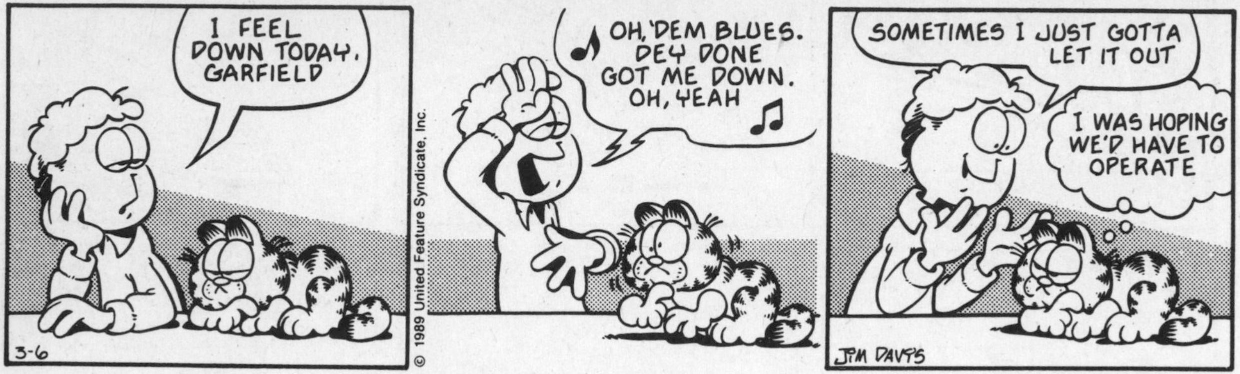
I FEEL DOWN TODAY, GARFIELD
OH, 'DEM BLUES. DEY DONE GOT ME DOWN. OH, YEAH
SOMETIMES I JUST GOTTA LET IT OUT
I WAS HOPING WE'D HAVE TO OPERATE
3-6
© 1989 United Feature Syndicate, Inc.
JIM DAVIS

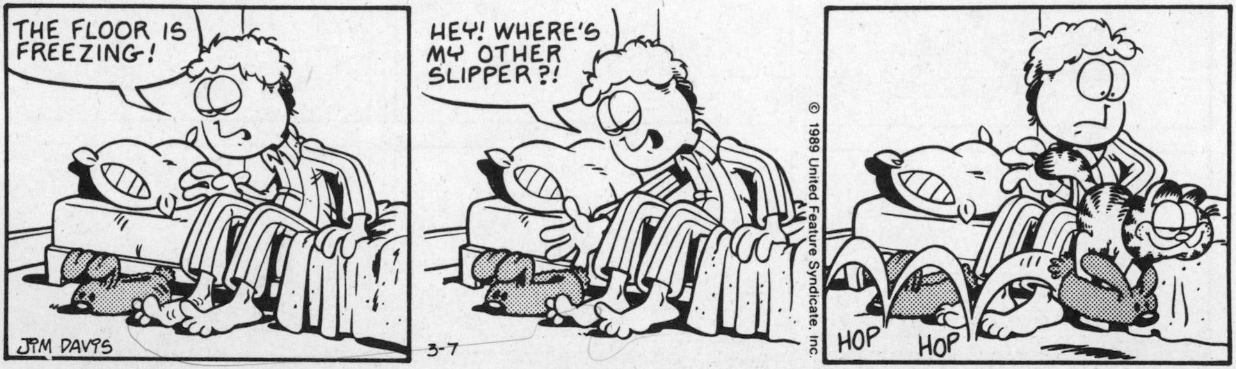
THE FLOOR IS FREEZING!
HEY! WHERE'S MY OTHER SLIPPER?!
HOP
HOP
JIM DAVIS
3-7
© 1989 United Feature Syndicate, Inc.

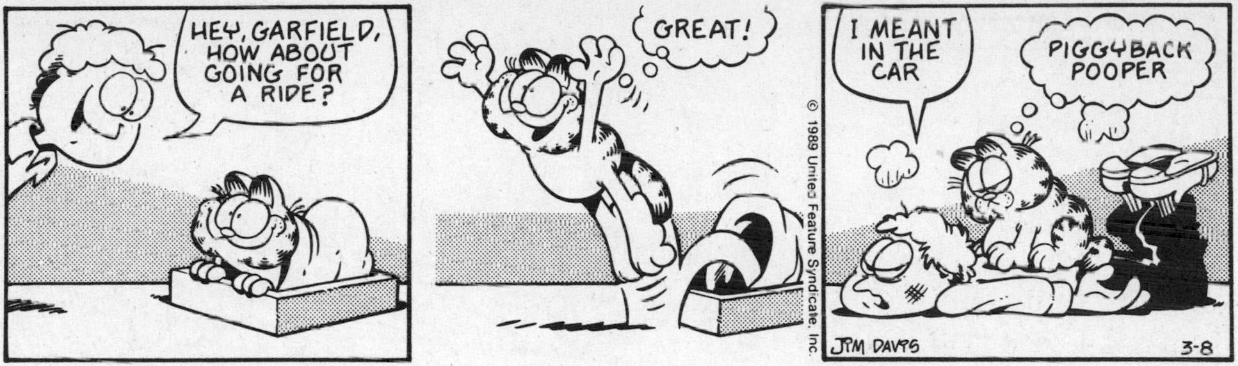
HEY, GARFIELD, HOW ABOUT GOING FOR A RIDE?
GREAT!
I MEANT IN THE CAR
PIGGYBACK POOPER
JIM DAVIS
3-8
© 1989 United Feature Syndicate, Inc.

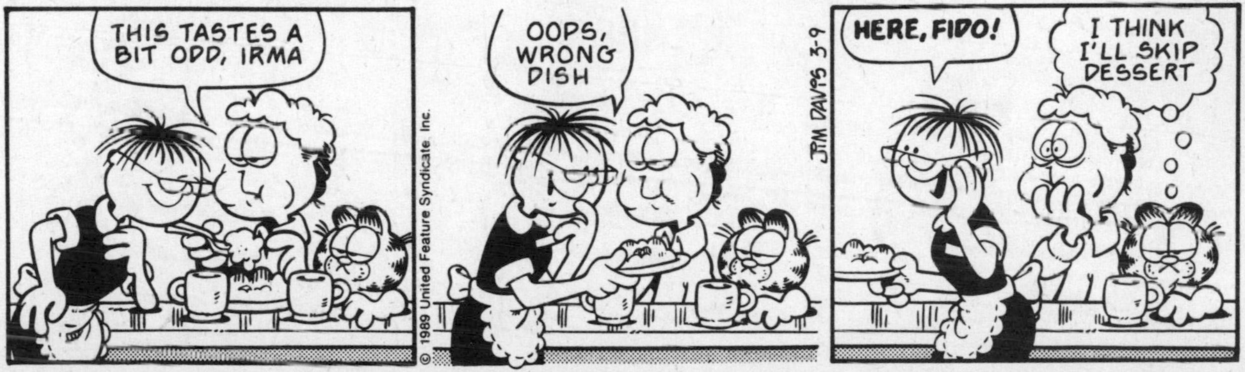
THIS TASTES A BIT ODD, IRMA
OOPS, WRONG DISH
HERE, FIDO!
I THINK I'LL SKIP DESSERT
JIM DAVIS 3-9
© 1989 United Feature Syndicate, Inc.

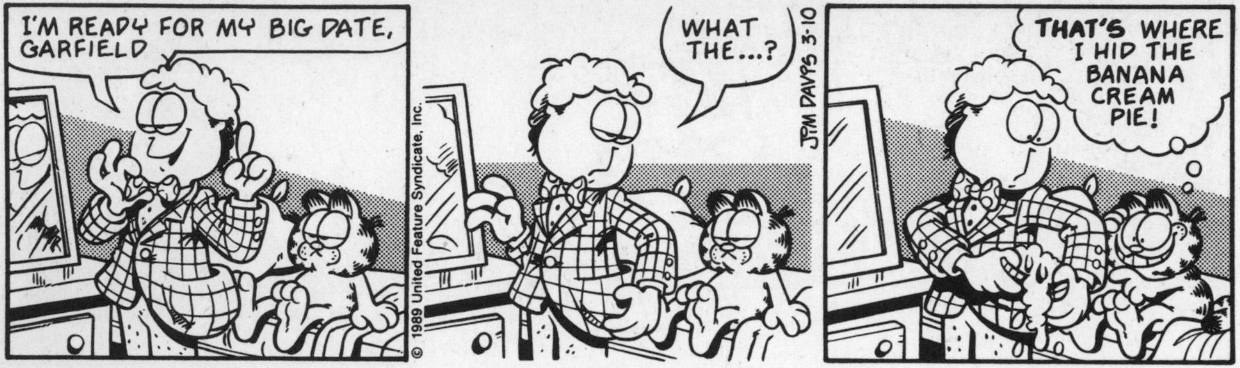
I'M READY FOR MY BIG DATE, GARFIELD
WHAT THE...?
THAT'S WHERE I HID THE BANANA CREAM PIE!
JIM DAVIS 3-10
© 1989 United Feature Syndicate, Inc.

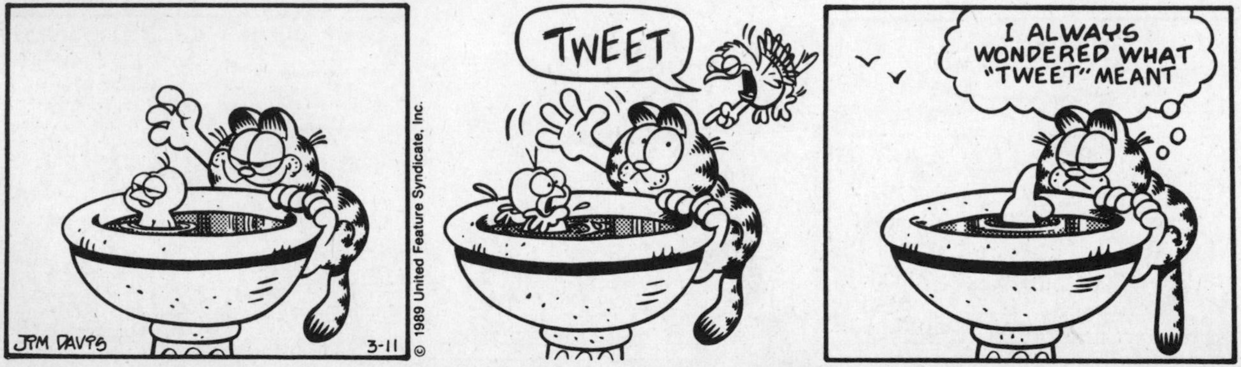
JIM DAVIS
3-11
© 1989 United Feature Syndicate, Inc.
TWEET
I ALWAYS WONDERED WHAT "TWEET" MEANT

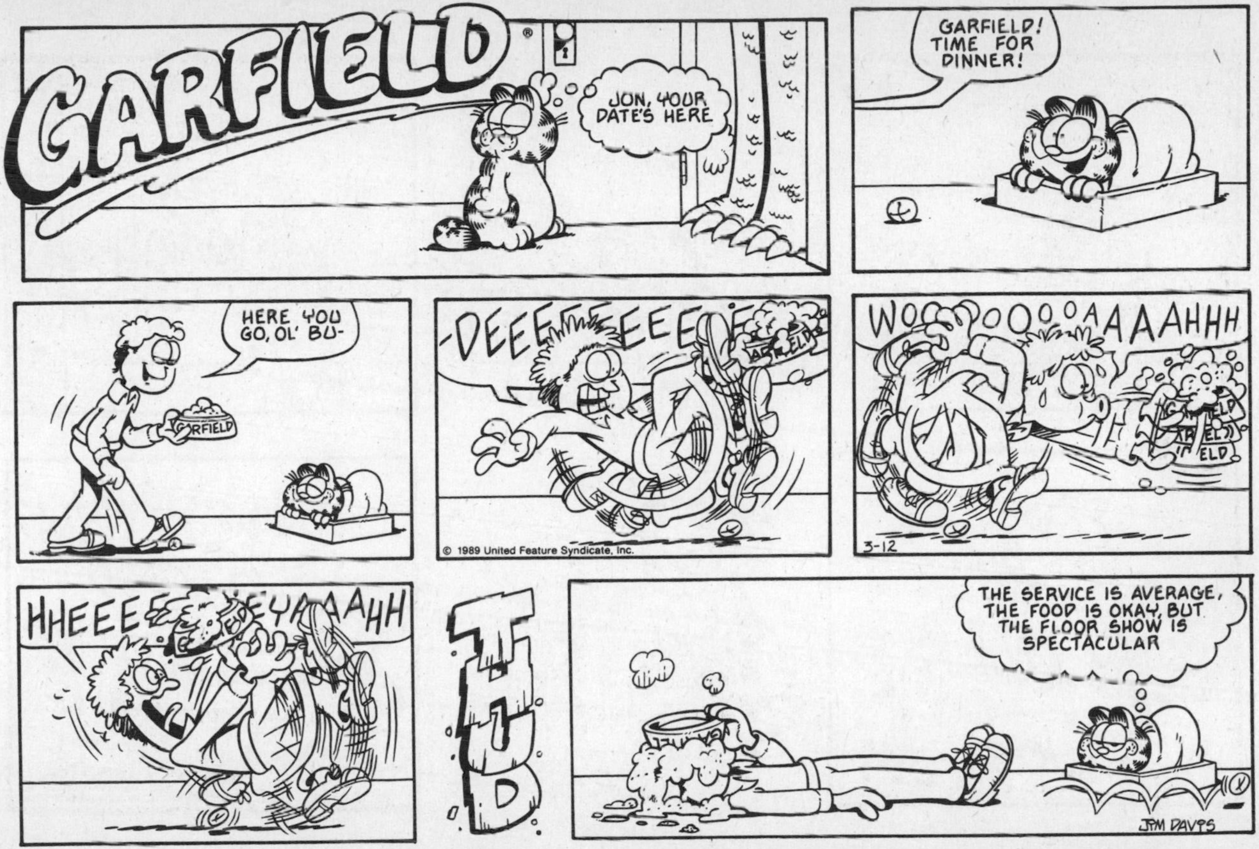
GARFIELD®
JON, YOUR DATE'S HERE
GARFIELD! TIME FOR DINNER!
HERE YOU GO, OL' BU-
GARFIELD
-DEEEEEEEEEE
© 1989 United Feature Syndicate, Inc.
WOOOOOOOOAAAAHHH
3-12
HHEEEEEEYAAAHH
THUD
THE SERVICE IS AVERAGE, THE FOOD IS OKAY, BUT THE FLOOR SHOW IS SPECTACULAR
JIM DAVIS

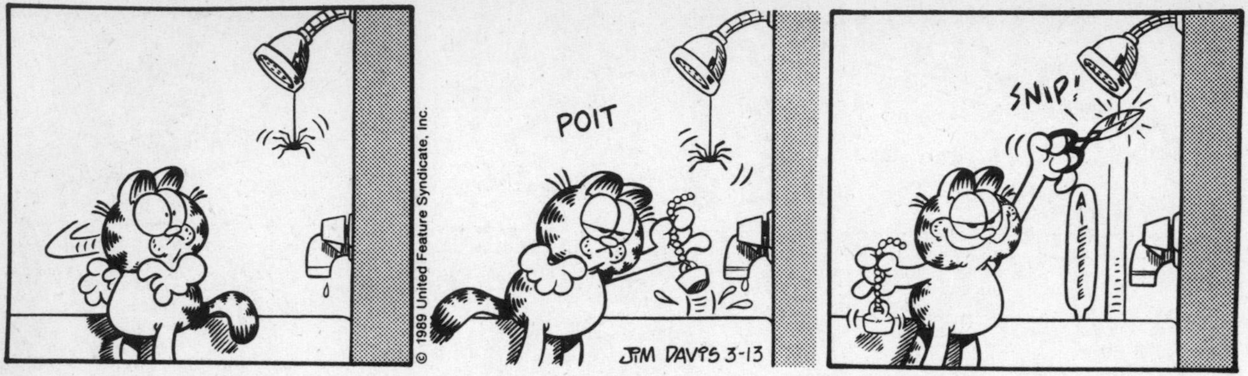
POIT
SNIP!
AIEEEEEE
JIM DAVIS 3-13
© 1989 United Feature Syndicate, Inc.

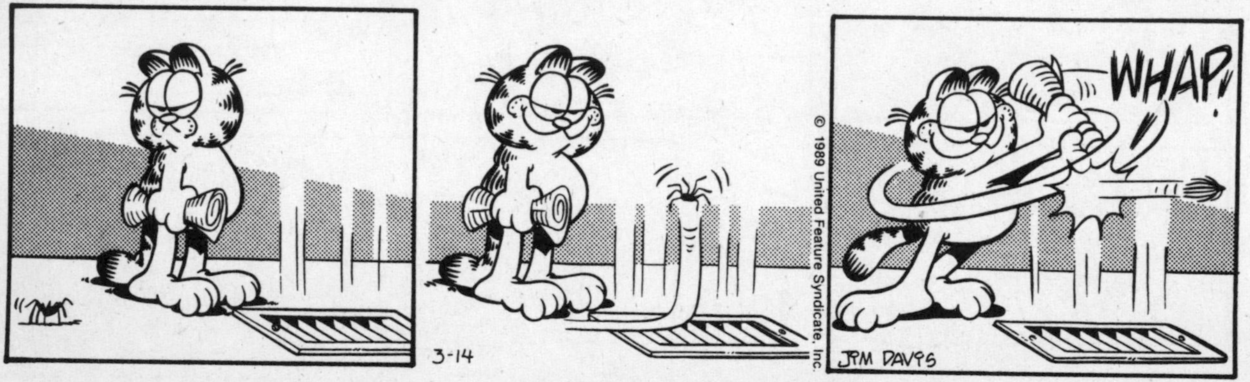
WHAP!
3-14
JIM DAVIS
© 1989 United Feature Syndicate, Inc.

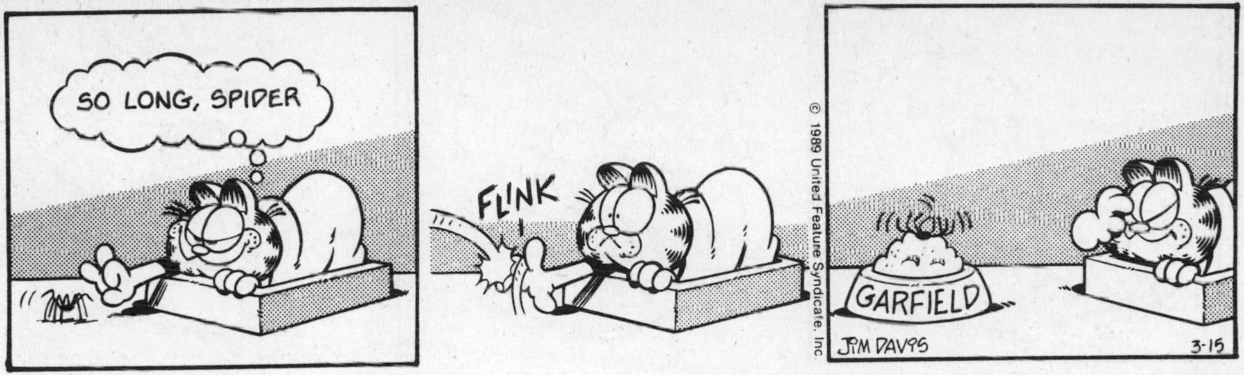
SO LONG, SPIDER
FLINK
GARFIELD
© 1989 United Feature Syndicate, Inc.
JIM DAVIS
3-15

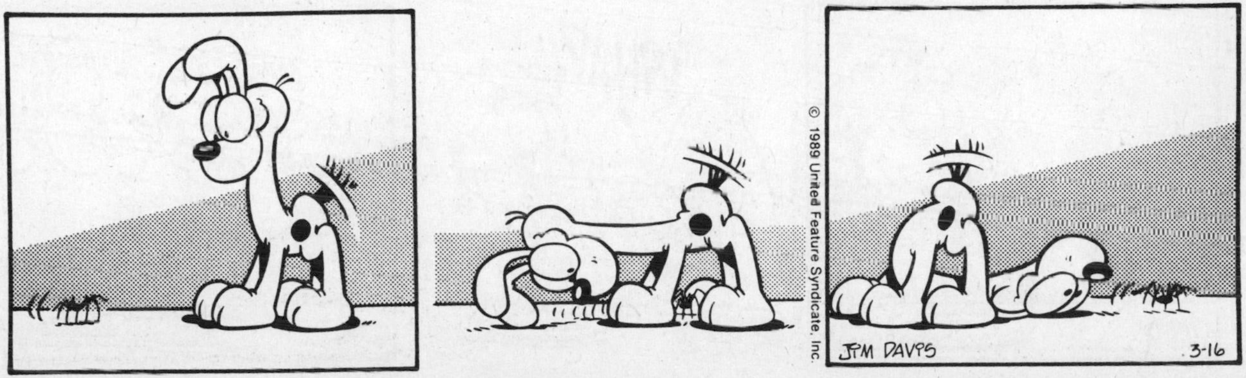
© 1989 United Feature Syndicate, Inc.
JIM DAVIS
3-16

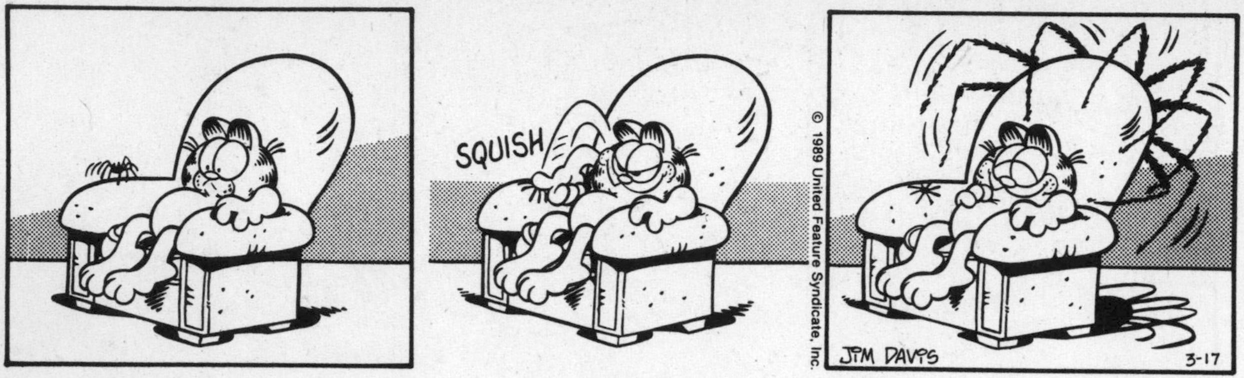
SQUISH
© 1989 United Feature Syndicate, Inc.
JIM DAVIS
3-17

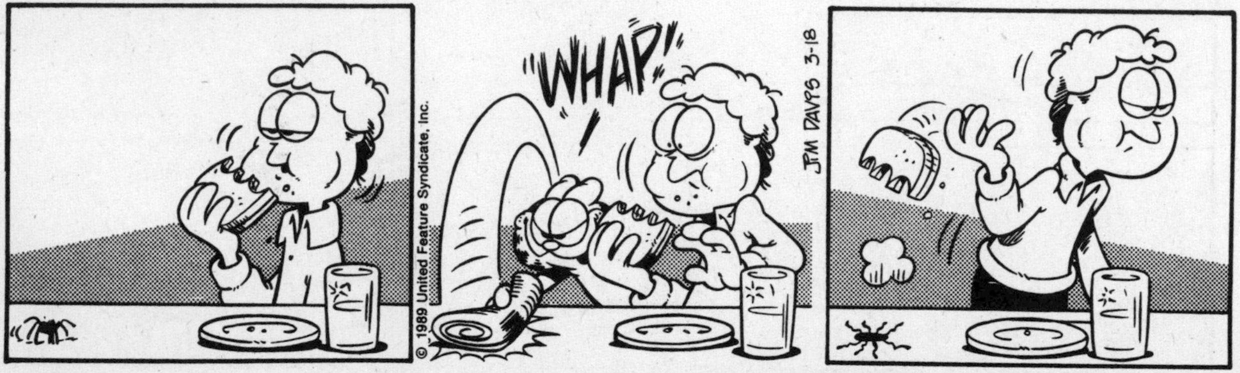
WHAP!
© 1989 United Feature Syndicate, Inc.
JIM DAVIS 3-18

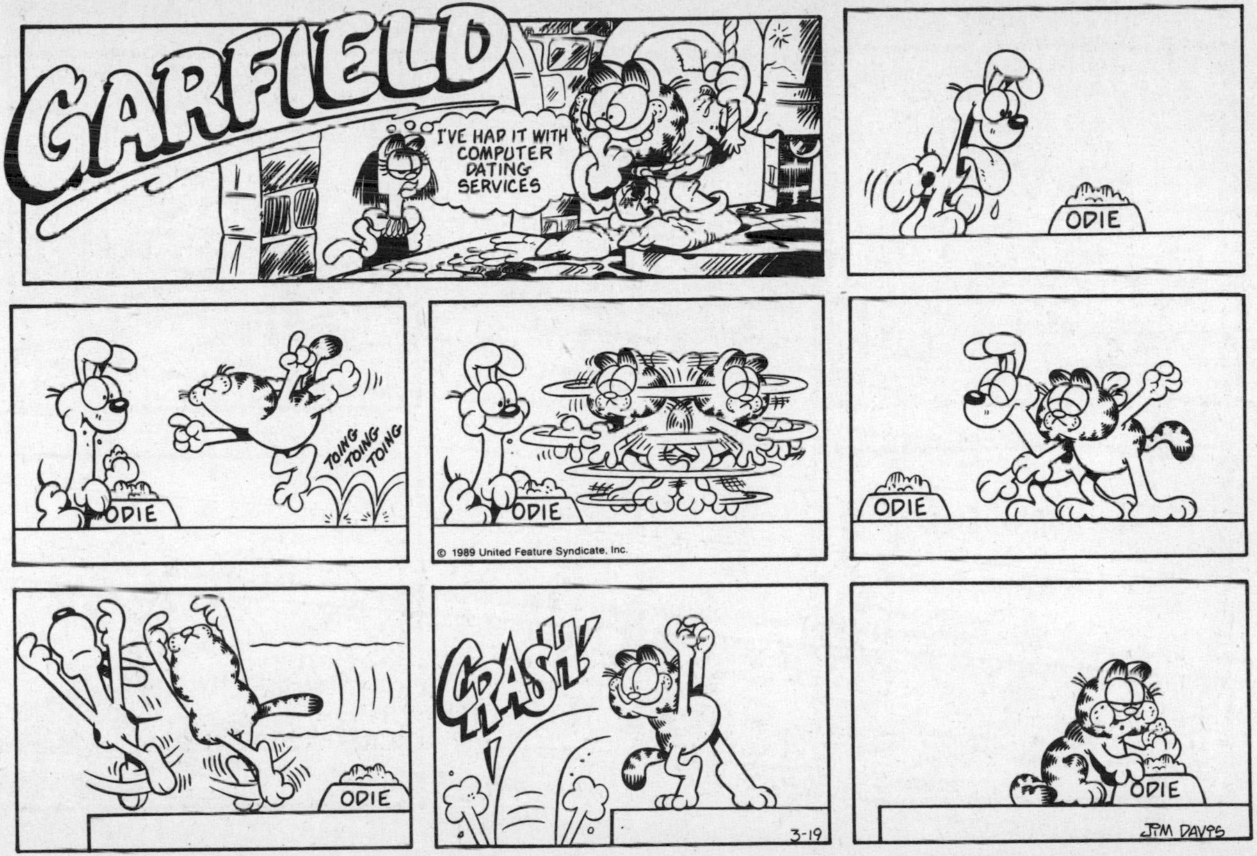
GARFIELD
I'VE HAD IT WITH COMPUTER DATING SERVICES
ODIE
ODIE
TOING TOING TOING
ODIE
© 1989 United Feature Syndicate, Inc.
ODIE
ODIE
CRASH
3-19
ODIE
JIM DAVIS

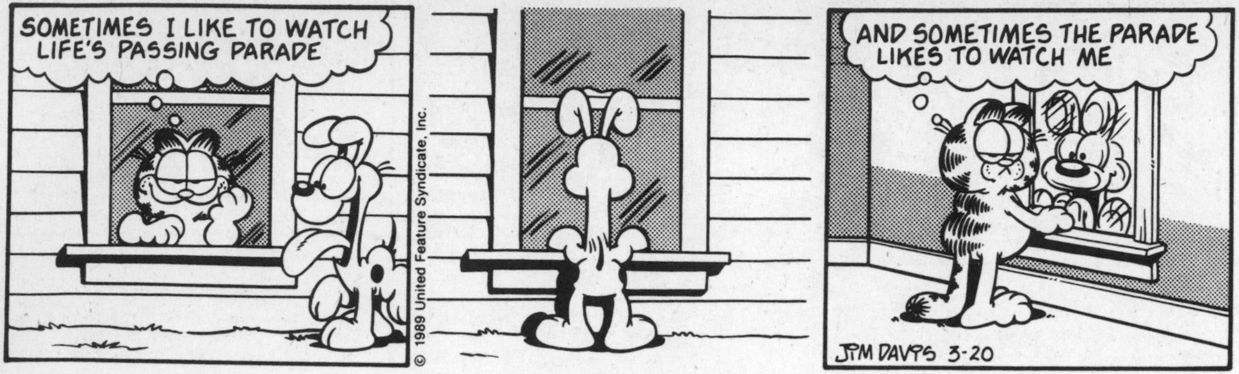
SOMETIMES I LIKE TO WATCH LIFE'S PASSING PARADE
© 1989 United Feature Syndicate, Inc.
AND SOMETIMES THE PARADE LIKES TO WATCH ME
JIM DAVIS 3-20

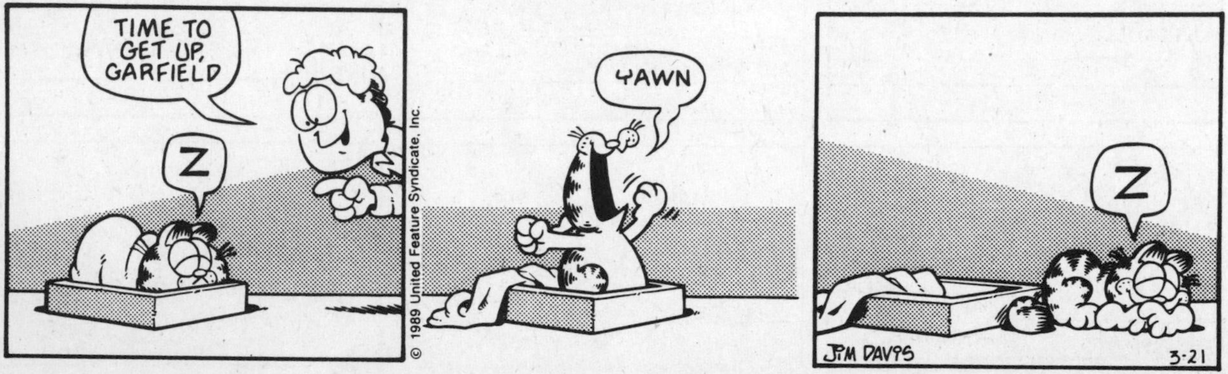
TIME TO GET UP, GARFIELD
Z
© 1989 United Feature Syndicate, Inc.
YAWN
Z
JIM DAVIS
3-21

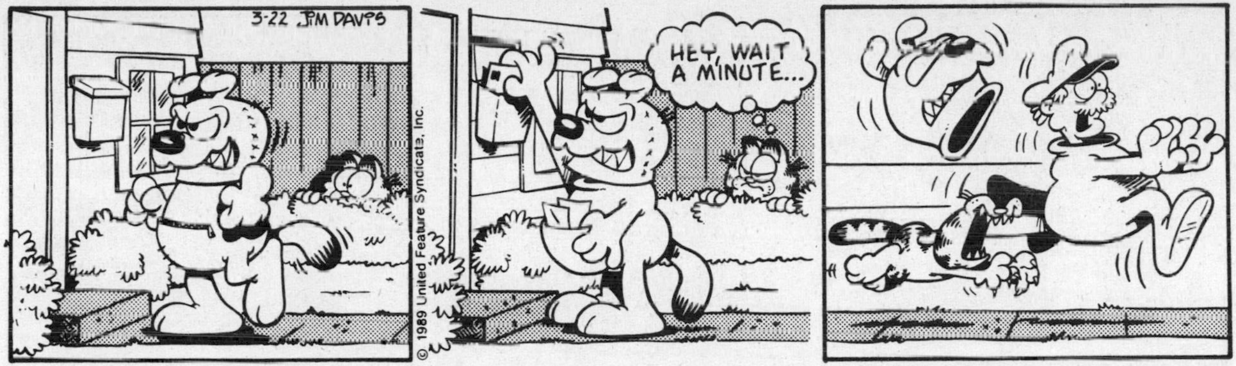
3-22 JIM DAVIS
HEY, WAIT A MINUTE...
© 1989 United Feature Syndicate, Inc.

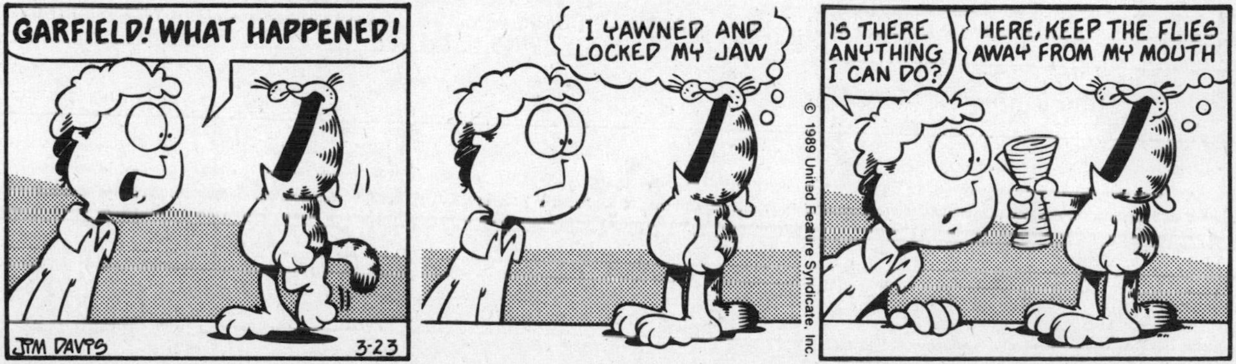
GARFIELD! WHAT HAPPENED!
JIM DAVIS
3-23
I YAWNED AND LOCKED MY JAW
IS THERE ANYTHING I CAN DO?
HERE, KEEP THE FLIES AWAY FROM MY MOUTH
© 1989 United Feature Syndicate, Inc.

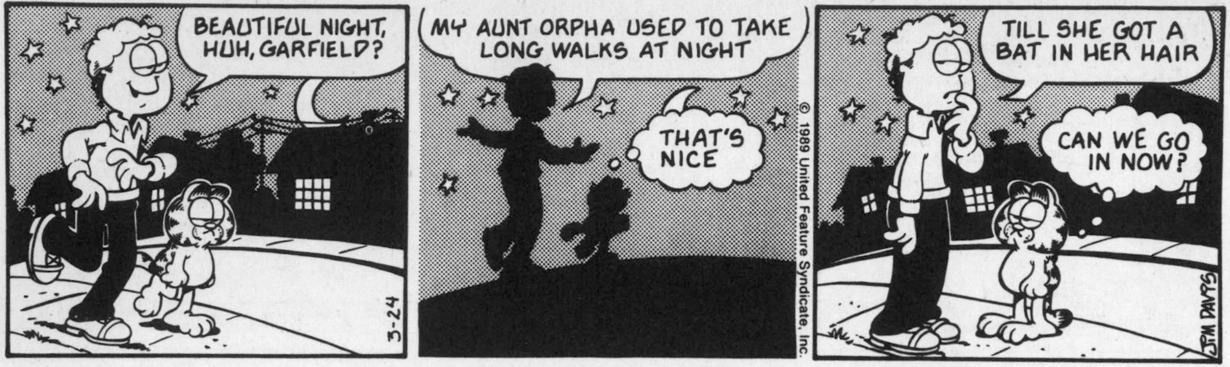
BEAUTIFUL NIGHT, HUH, GARFIELD?
3-24
MY AUNT ORPHA USED TO TAKE LONG WALKS AT NIGHT
THAT'S NICE
© 1989 United Feature Syndicate, Inc.
TILL SHE GOT A BAT IN HER HAIR
CAN WE GO IN NOW?
JIM DAVIS

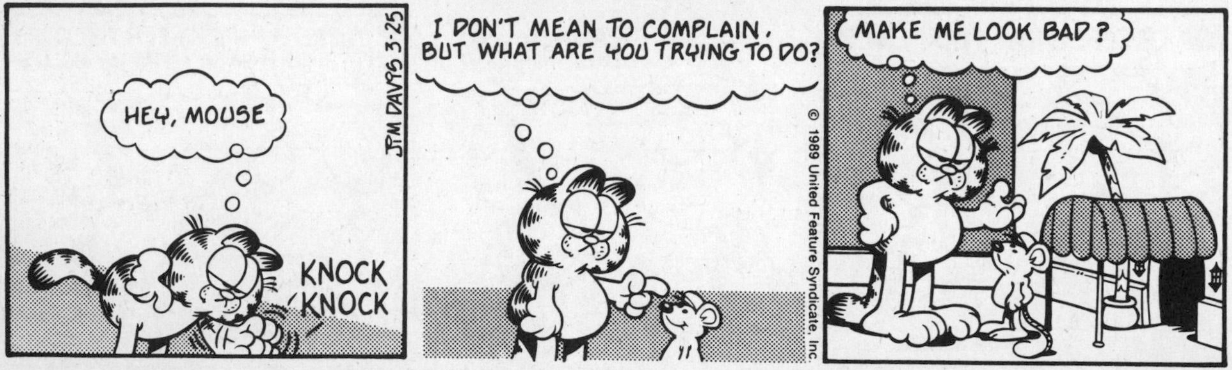
JIM DAVIS 3-25
HEY, MOUSE
KNOCK KNOCK
I DON'T MEAN TO COMPLAIN, BUT WHAT ARE YOU TRYING TO DO?
© 1989 United Feature Syndicate, Inc.
MAKE ME LOOK BAD?

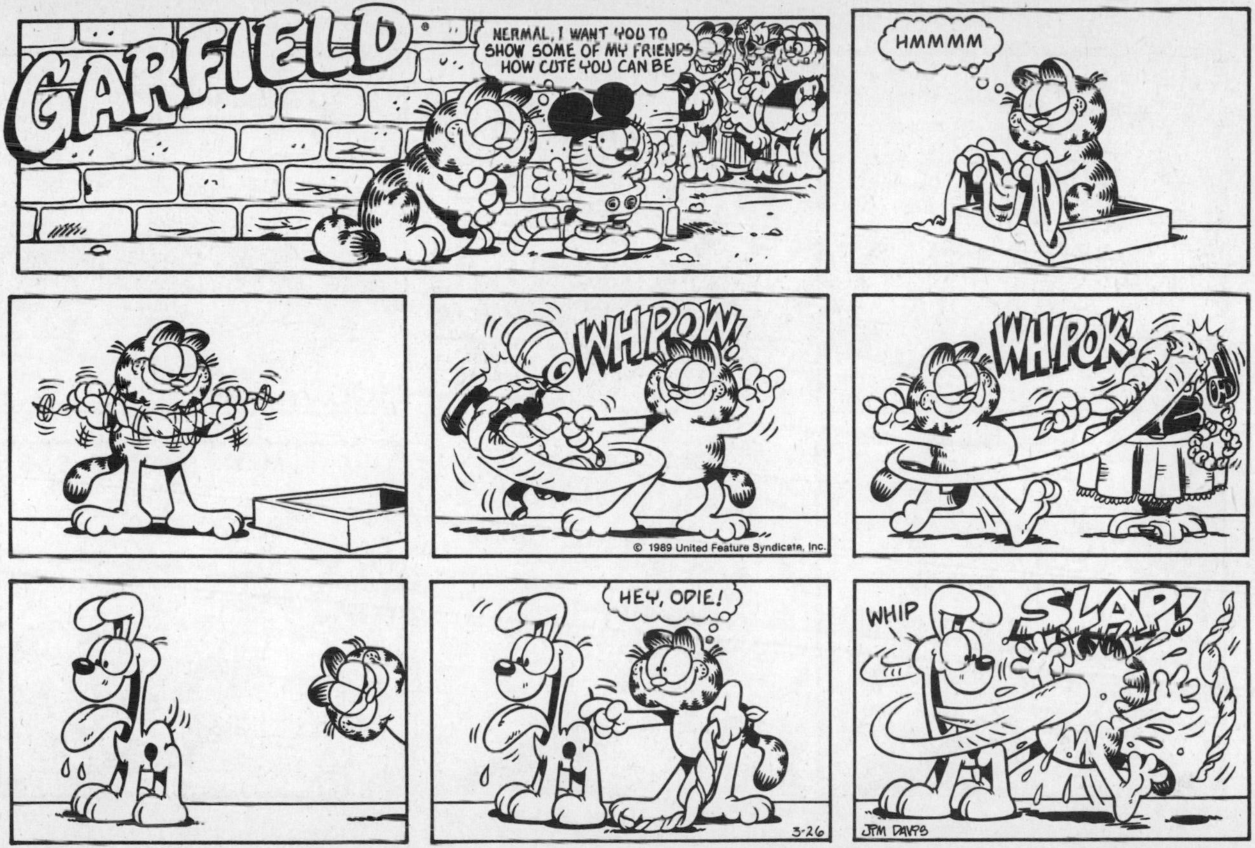
GARFIELD
NERMAL, I WANT YOU TO SHOW SOME OF MY FRIENDS HOW CUTE YOU CAN BE
HMMMM
WHPOW!
WHPOK!
© 1989 United Feature Syndicate, Inc.
HEY, ODIE!
3-26
WHIP
SLAP!
JIM DAVIS

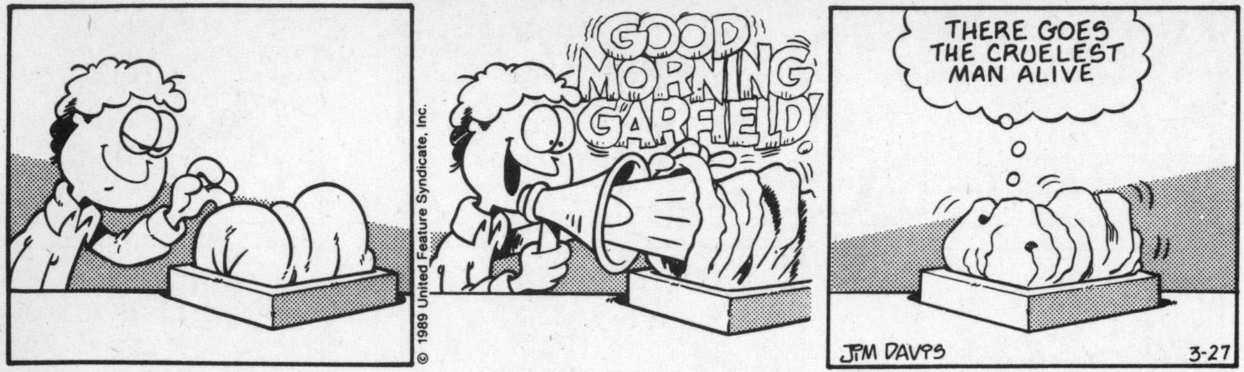
GOOD MORNING GARFIELD
THERE GOES THE CRUELEST MAN ALIVE
© 1989 United Feature Syndicate, Inc.
JIM DAVIS
3-27

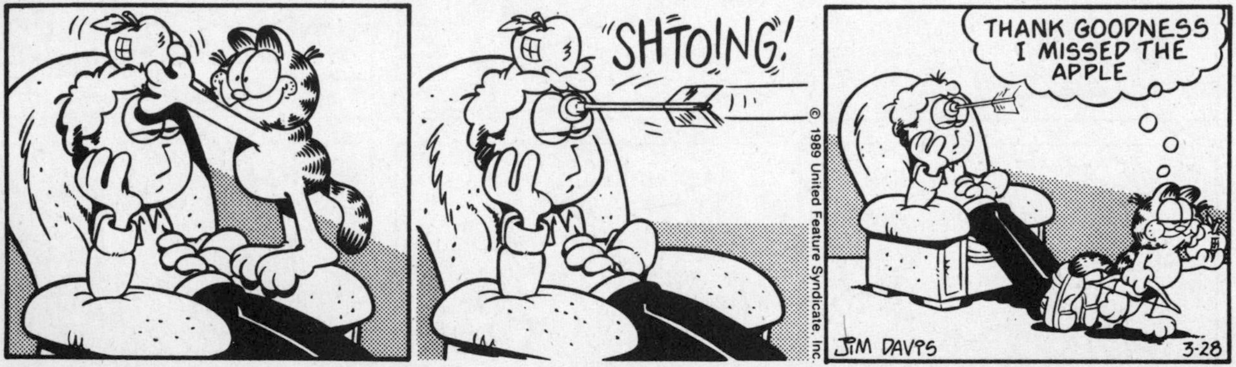
SHTOING!
THANK GOODNESS I MISSED THE APPLE
© 1989 United Feature Syndicate, Inc.
JIM DAVIS
3-28

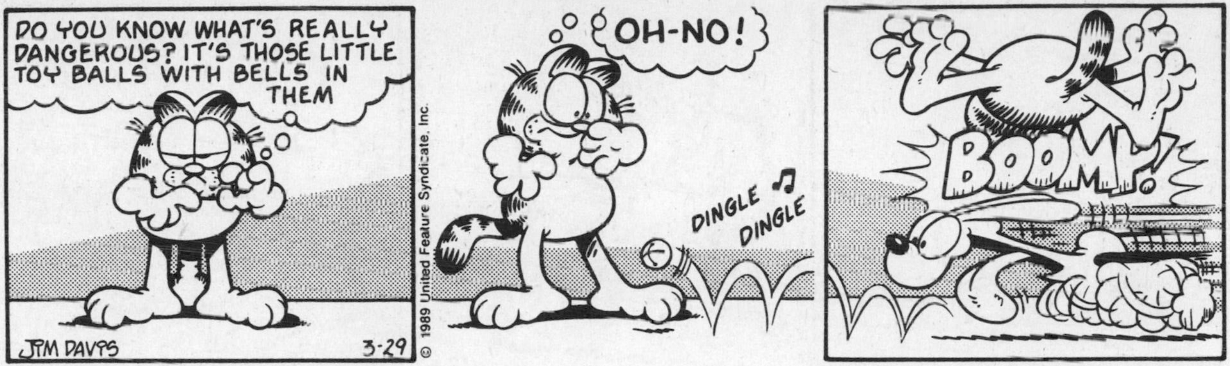
DO YOU KNOW WHAT'S REALLY DANGEROUS? IT'S THOSE LITTLE TOY BALLS WITH BELLS IN THEM
JIM DAVIS
3-29
© 1989 United Feature Syndicate, Inc.
OH-NO!
DINGLE DINGLE
BOOM!

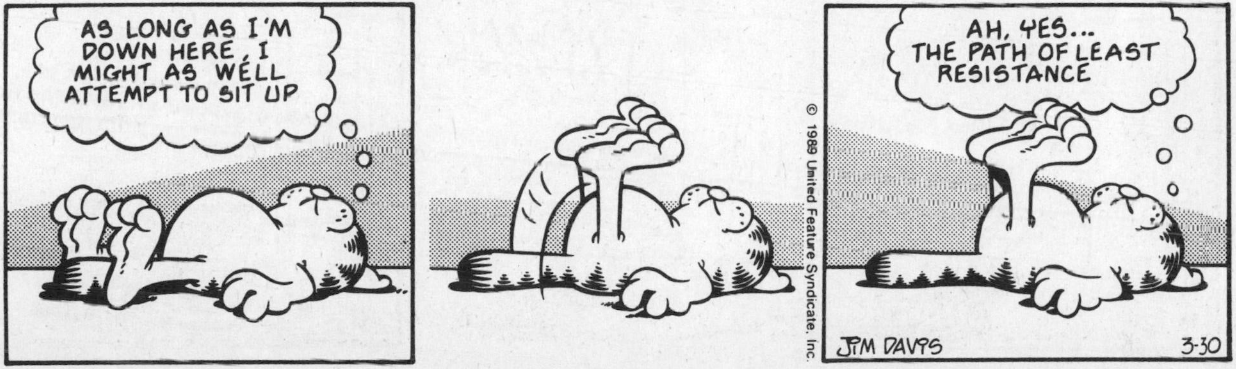
AS LONG AS I'M DOWN HERE, I MIGHT AS WELL ATTEMPT TO SIT UP
© 1989 United Feature Syndicate, Inc.
AH, YES... THE PATH OF LEAST RESISTANCE
JIM DAVIS
3-30

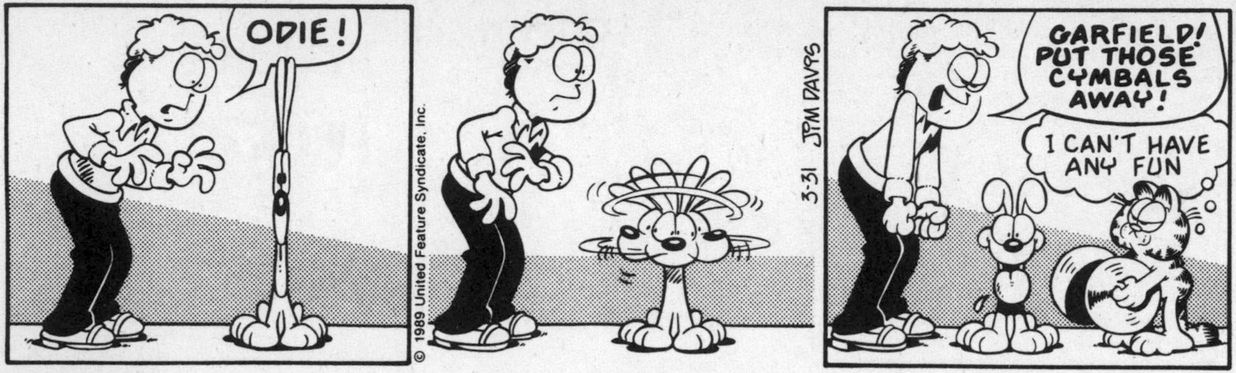
ODIE!
© 1989 United Feature Syndicate, Inc.
JIM DAVIS 3-31
GARFIELD! PUT THOSE CYMBALS AWAY!
I CAN'T HAVE ANY FUN

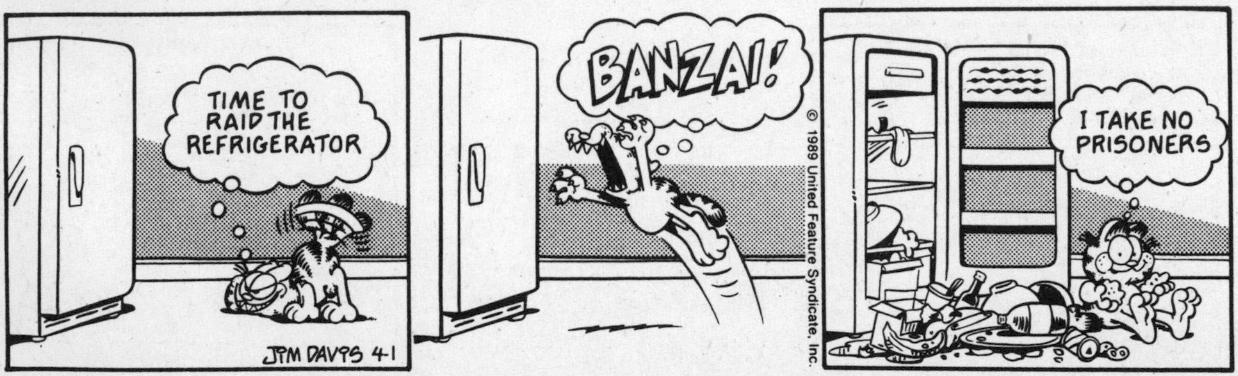
TIME TO RAID THE REFRIGERATOR
JIM DAVIS 4-1
BANZAI!
© 1989 United Feature Syndicate, Inc.
I TAKE NO PRISONERS

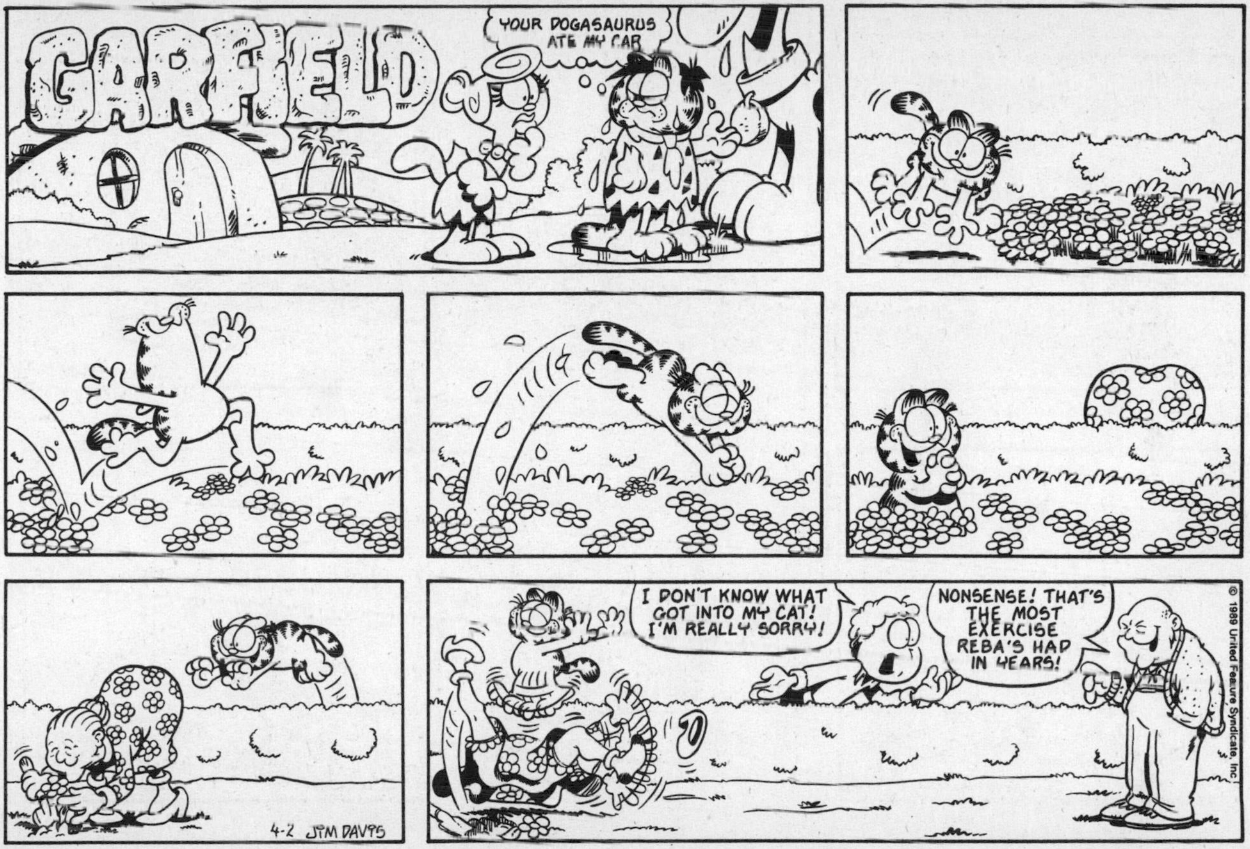
GARFIELD
YOUR DOGASAURUS ATE MY CAR
I DON'T KNOW WHAT GOT INTO MY CAT! I'M REALLY SORRY!
NONSENSE! THAT'S THE MOST EXERCISE REBA'S HAD IN YEARS!
4-2 JIM DAVIS
© 1989 United Feature Syndicate, Inc.

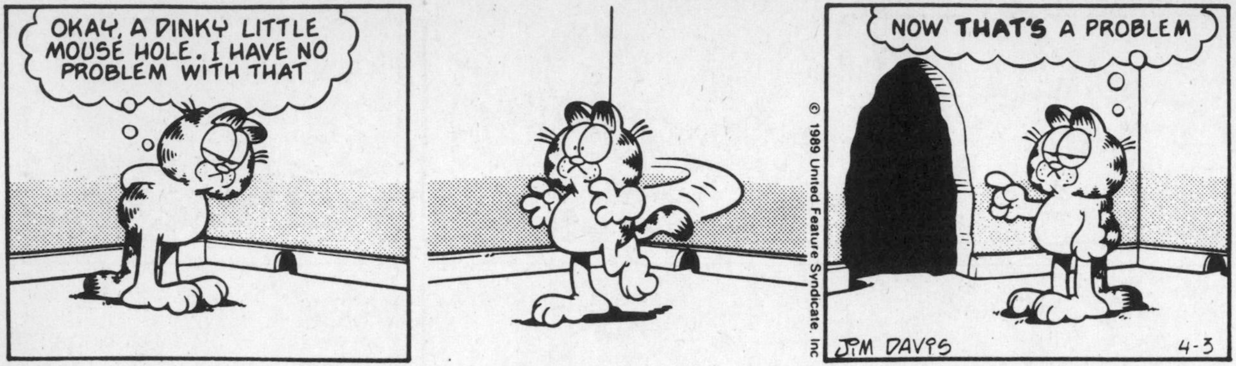
OKAY, A DINKY LITTLE MOUSE HOLE. I HAVE NO PROBLEM WITH THAT
NOW THAT'S A PROBLEM
© 1989 United Feature Syndicate, Inc
JIM DAVIS
4-3

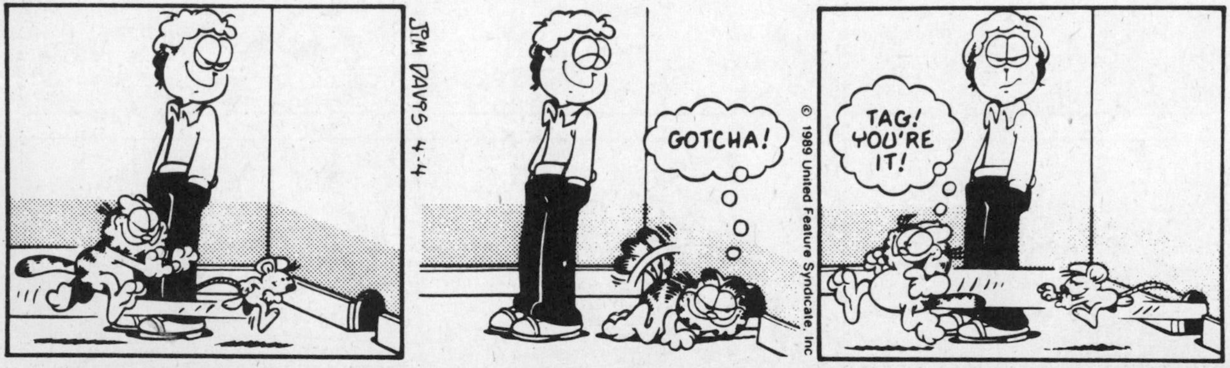
JIM DAVIS 4-4
GOTCHA!
© 1989 United Feature Syndicate, Inc
TAG! YOU'RE IT!

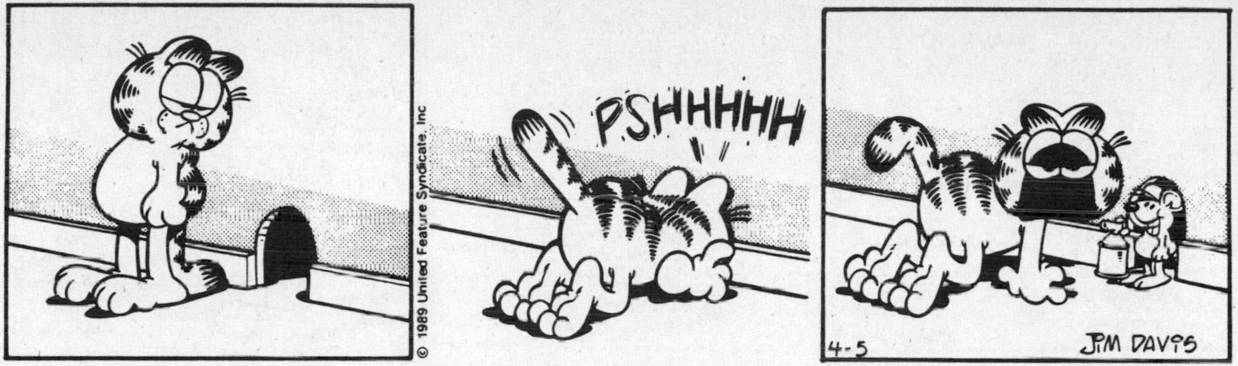
PSHHHHH
© 1989 United Feature Syndicate, Inc.
4-5
JIM DAVIS

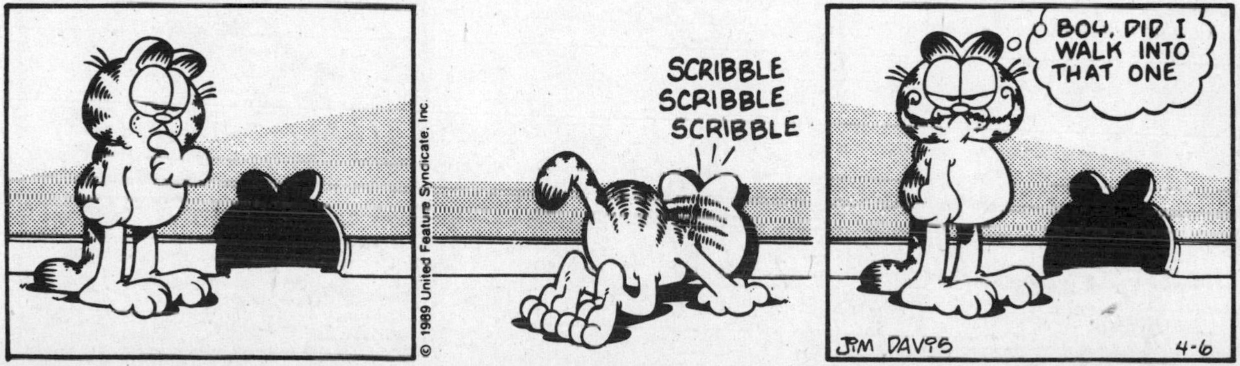
SCRIBBLE
SCRIBBLE
SCRIBBLE
BOY, DID I WALK INTO THAT ONE
© 1989 United Feature Syndicate, Inc.
JIM DAVIS
4-6

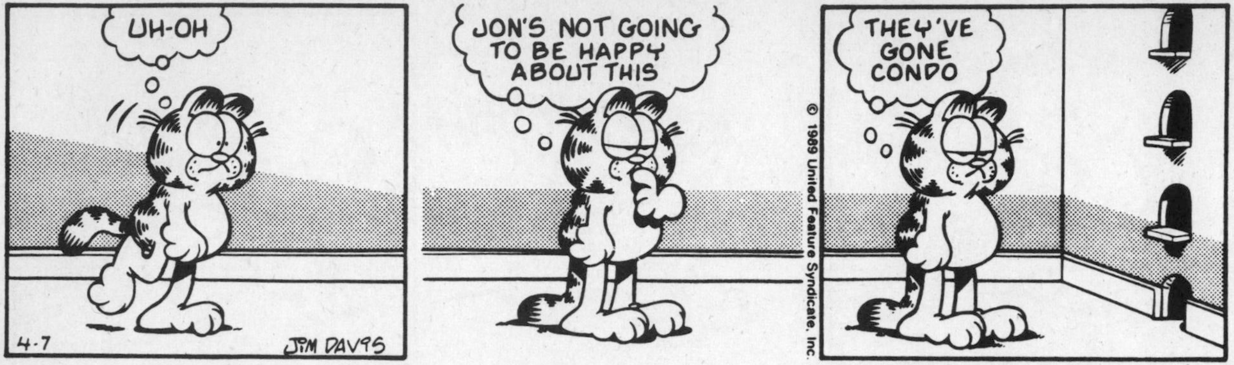
UH-OH
4-7
JIM DAVIS
JON'S NOT GOING TO BE HAPPY ABOUT THIS
© 1989 United Feature Syndicate, Inc.
THEY'VE GONE CONDO

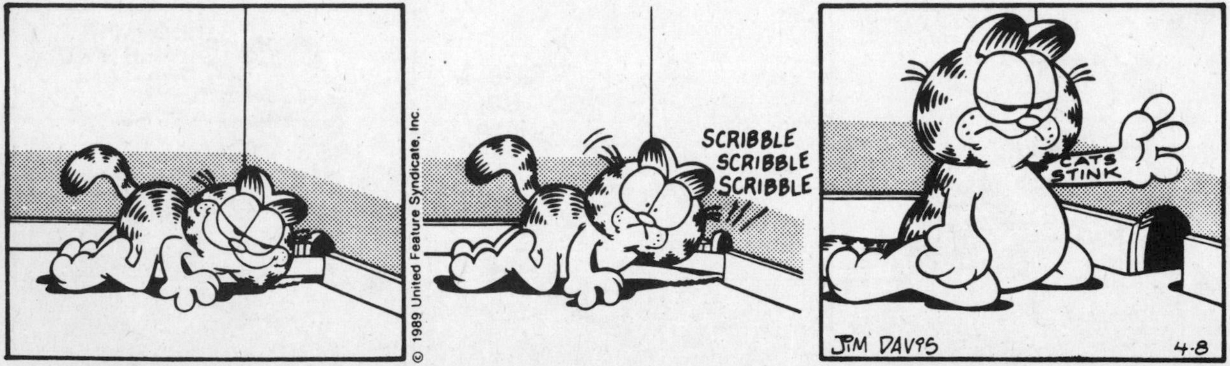
© 1989 United Feature Syndicate, Inc.
SCRIBBLE
SCRIBBLE
SCRIBBLE
CATS STINK
JIM DAVIS
4-8

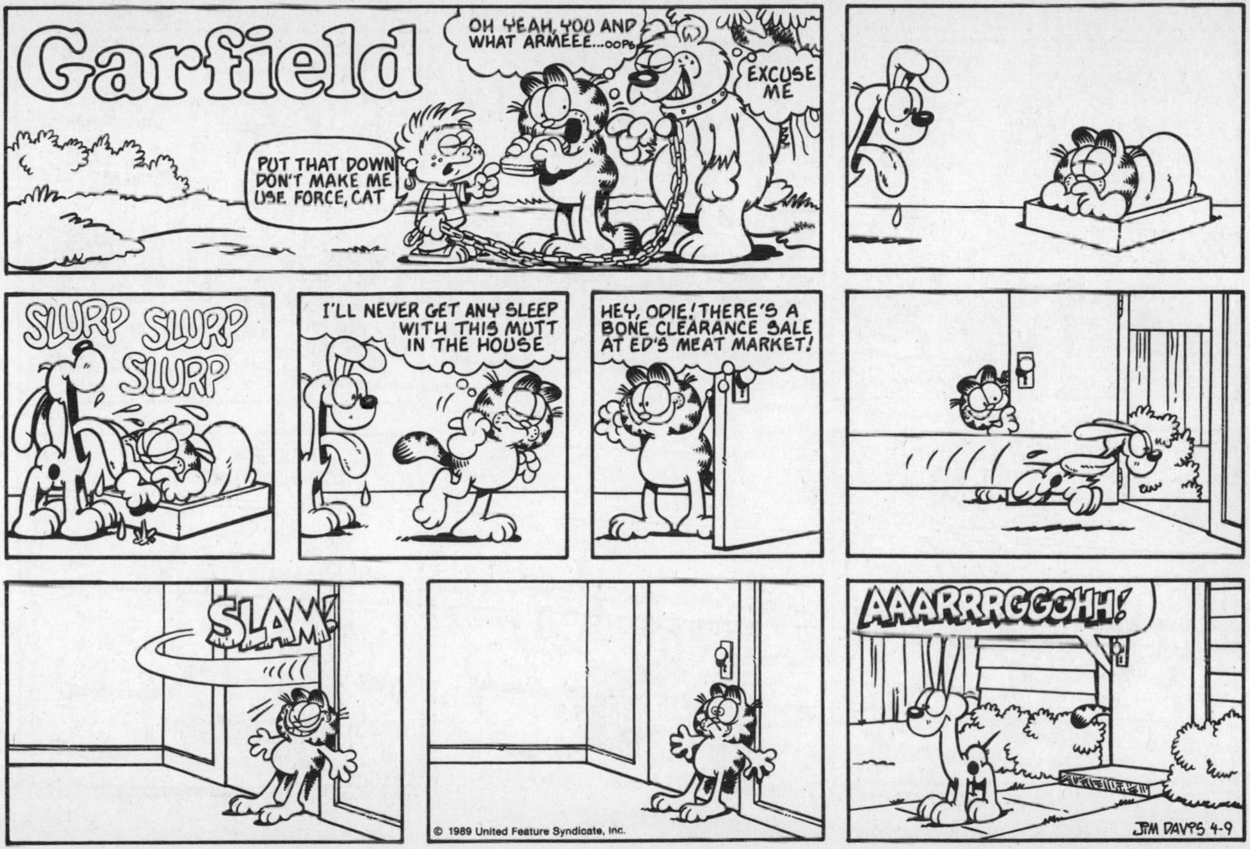
Garfield
OH YEAH, YOU AND WHAT ARMEEE...OOPS
EXCUSE ME
PUT THAT DOWN DON'T MAKE ME USE FORCE, CAT
SLURP SLURP SLURP
I'LL NEVER GET ANY SLEEP WITH THIS MUTT IN THE HOUSE
HEY, ODIE! THERE'S A BONE CLEARANCE SALE AT ED'S MEAT MARKET!
SLAM!
© 1989 United Feature Syndicate, Inc.
AAARRRGGGHH!
JIM DAVIS 4-9

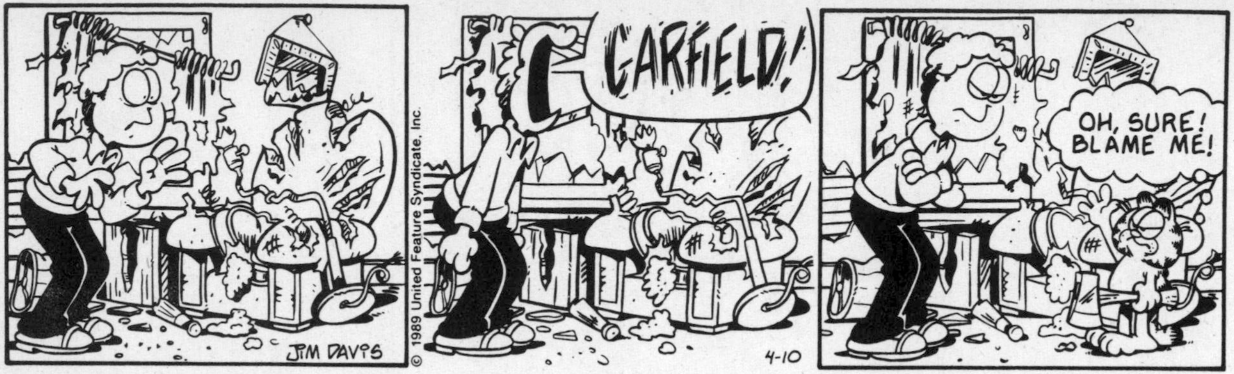
JIM DAVIS
© 1989 United Feature Syndicate, Inc.
GARFIELD!
4-10
OH, SURE! BLAME ME!

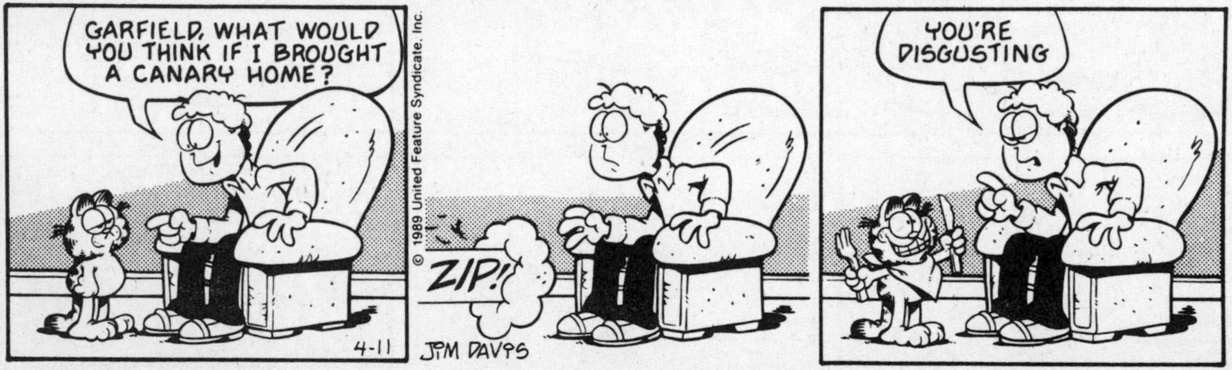
GARFIELD, WHAT WOULD YOU THINK IF I BROUGHT A CANARY HOME?
4-11
© 1989 United Feature Syndicate, Inc.
ZIP!
JIM DAVIS
YOU'RE DISGUSTING

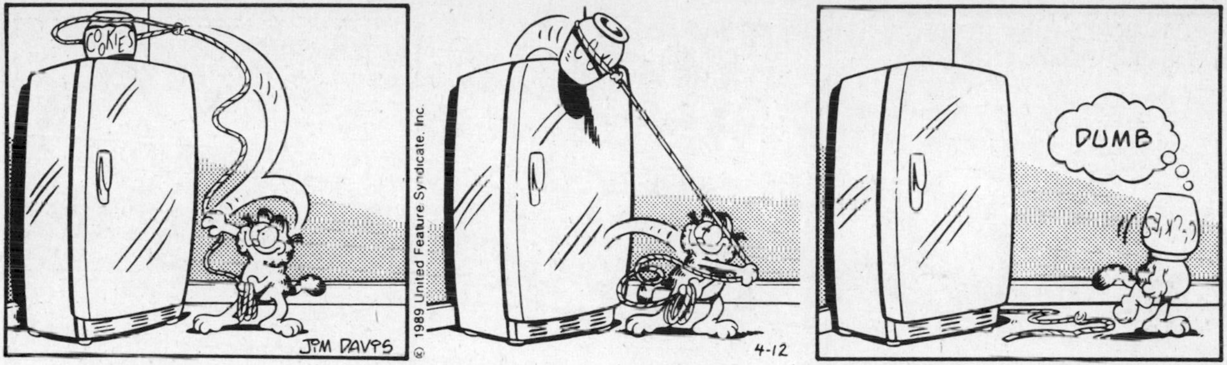
COOKIES
JIM DAVIS
© 1989 United Feature Syndicate, Inc.
4-12
DUMB

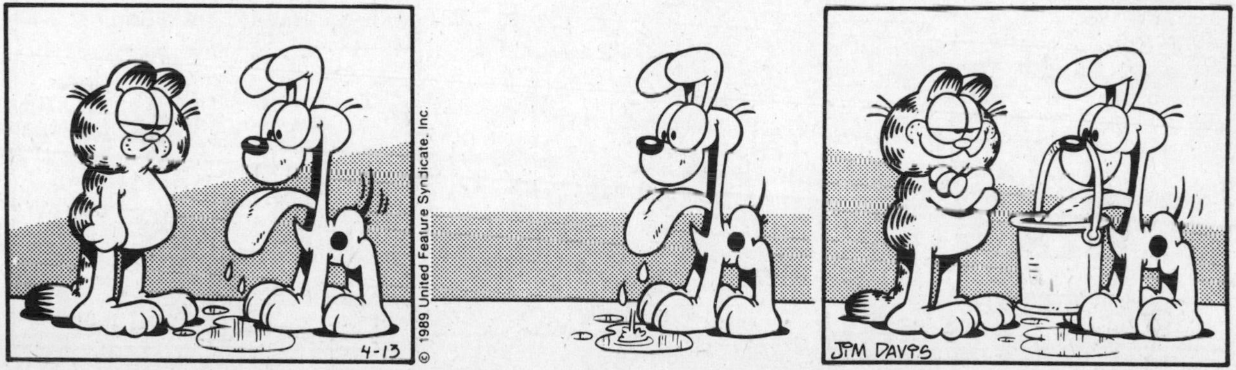
© 1989 United Feature Syndicate, Inc.
4-13
JIM DAVIS

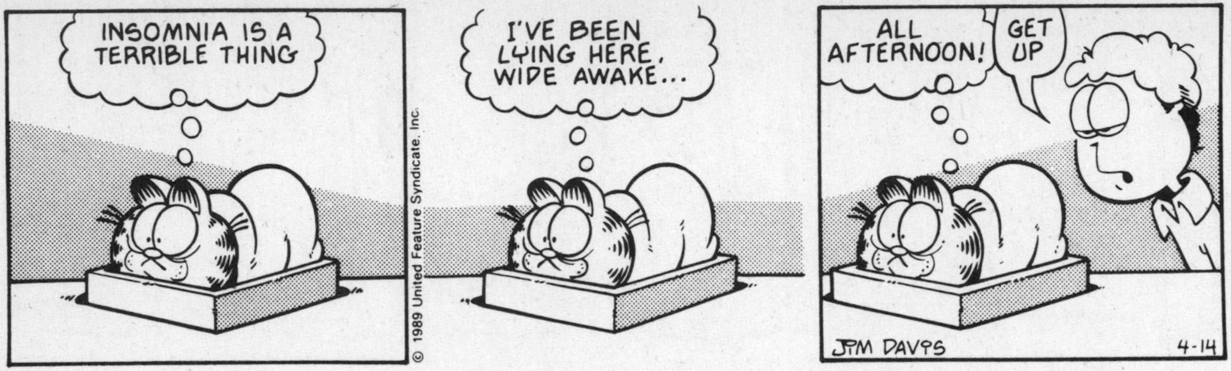
INSOMNIA IS A TERRIBLE THING
I'VE BEEN LYING HERE, WIDE AWAKE...
ALL AFTERNOON!
GET UP
© 1989 United Feature Syndicate, Inc.
JIM DAVIS
4-14

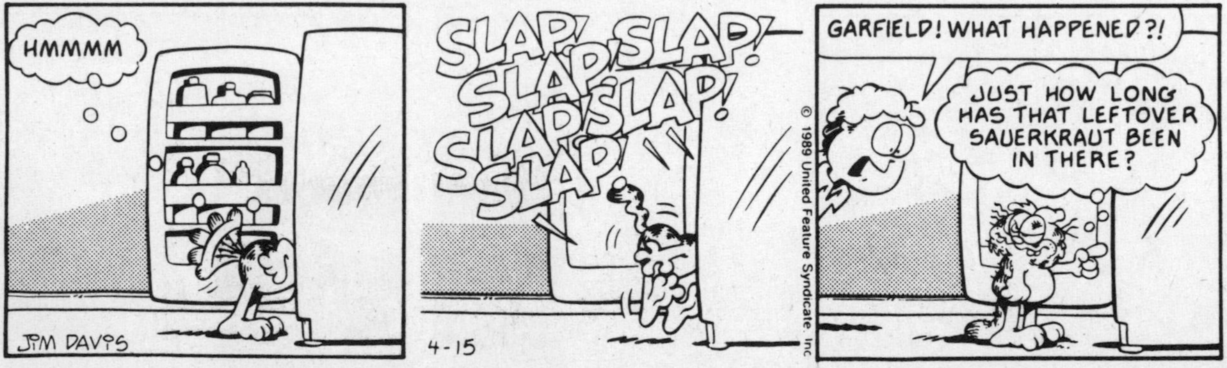
HMMMM
SLAP! SLAP! SLAP! SLAP! SLAP! SLAP! SLAP! SLAP!
GARFIELD! WHAT HAPPENED?!
JUST HOW LONG HAS THAT LEFTOVER SAUERKRAUT BEEN IN THERE?
© 1989 United Feature Syndicate, Inc.
JIM DAVIS
4-15

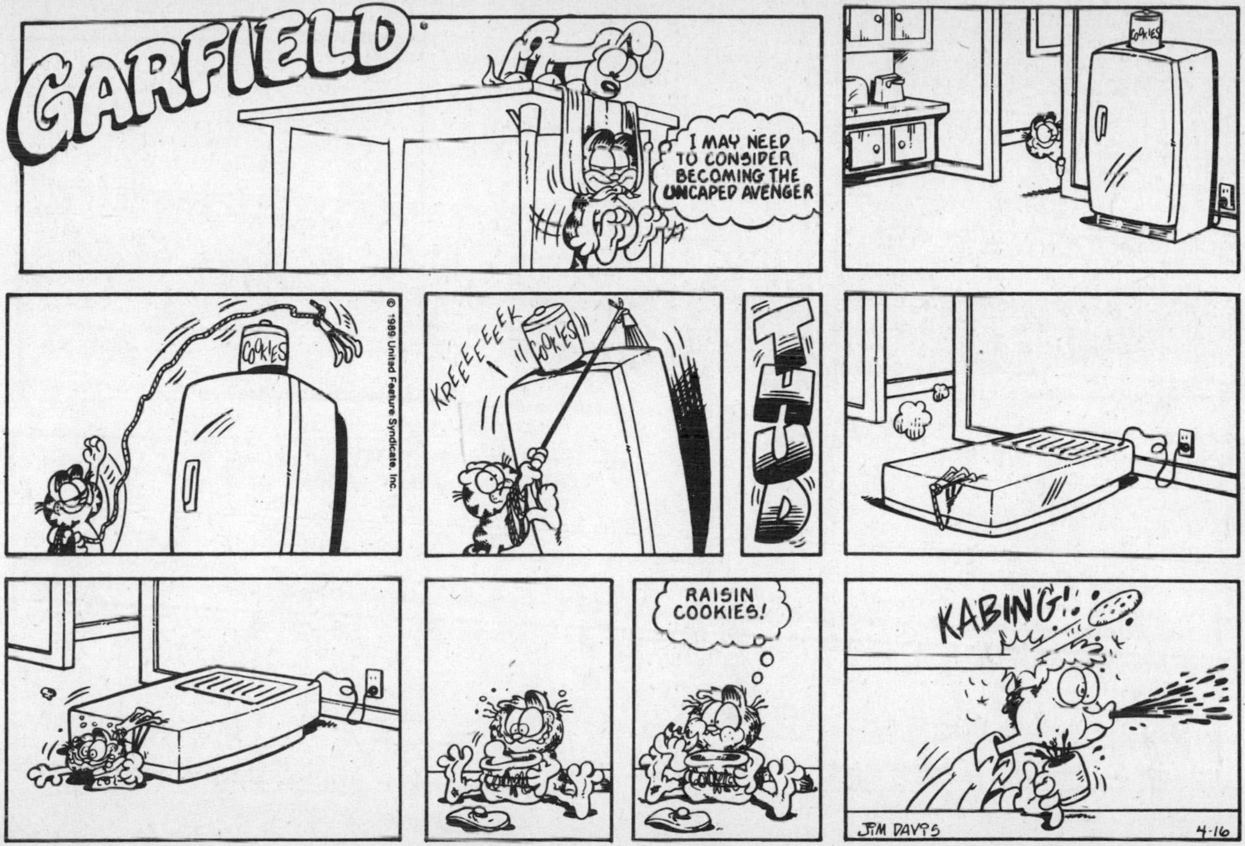
GARFIELD
I MAY NEED TO CONSIDER BECOMING THE UNCAPED AVENGER
COOKIES
© 1989 United Feature Syndicate, Inc.
KREEEEEEEK
THUD
RAISIN COOKIES!
KABING!
JIM DAVIS
4-16

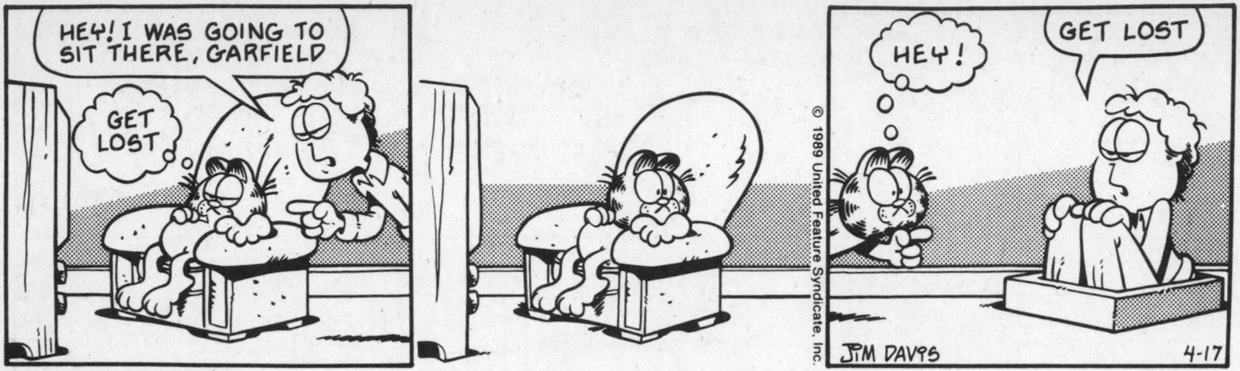
HEY! I WAS GOING TO SIT THERE, GARFIELD
GET LOST
HEY!
GET LOST
© 1989 United Feature Syndicate, Inc.
JIM DAVIS
4-17

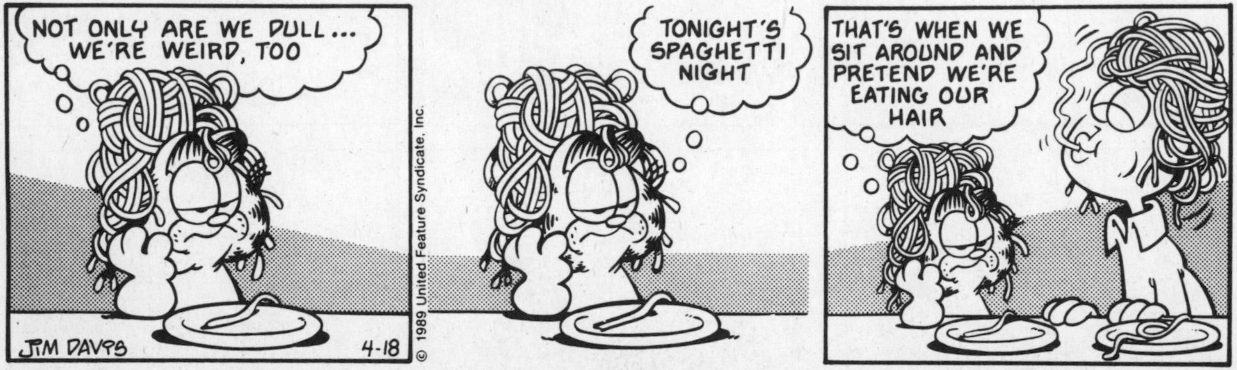
NOT ONLY ARE WE DULL... WE'RE WEIRD, TOO
TONIGHT'S SPAGHETTI NIGHT
THAT'S WHEN WE SIT AROUND AND PRETEND WE'RE EATING OUR HAIR
© 1989 United Feature Syndicate, Inc.
JIM DAVIS
4-18

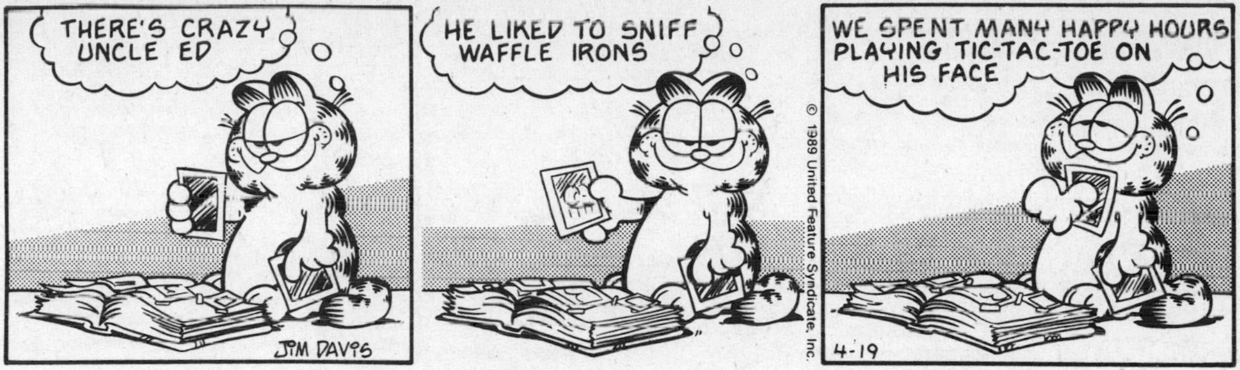
THERE'S CRAZY UNCLE ED
JIM DAVIS
HE LIKED TO SNIFF WAFFLE IRONS
© 1989 United Feature Syndicate, Inc.
WE SPENT MANY HAPPY HOURS PLAYING TIC-TAC-TOE ON HIS FACE
4-19

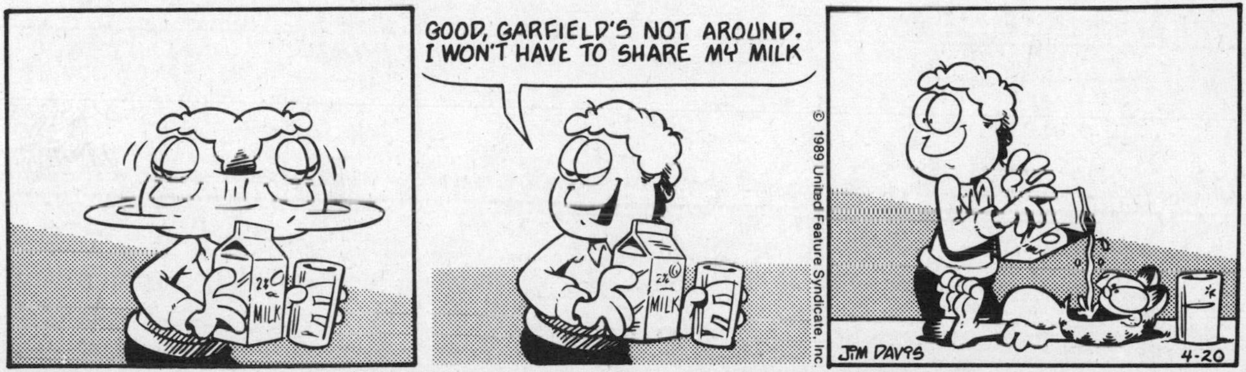
2%
MILK
GOOD, GARFIELD'S NOT AROUND. I WON'T HAVE TO SHARE MY MILK
© 1989 United Feature Syndicate, Inc.
JIM DAVIS
4-20

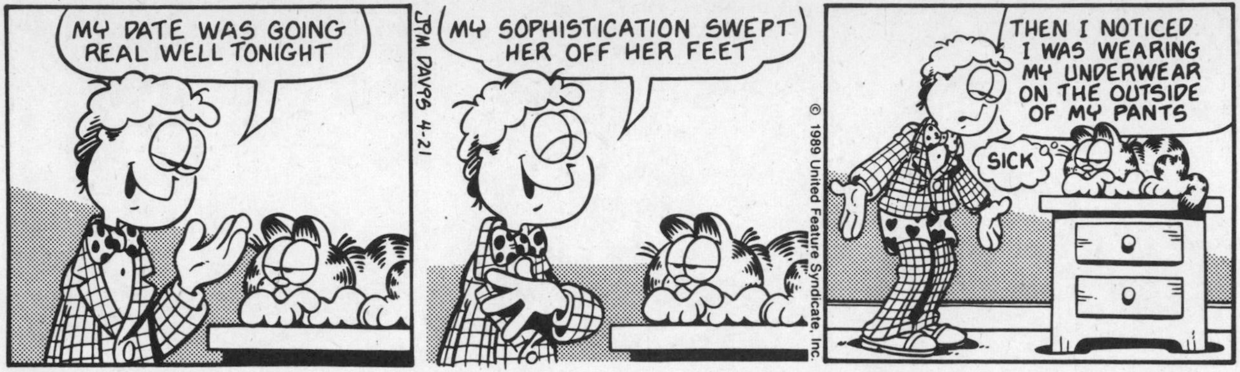
MY DATE WAS GOING REAL WELL TONIGHT
JIM DAVIS 4-21
MY SOPHISTICATION SWEPT HER OFF HER FEET
© 1989 United Feature Syndicate, Inc.
THEN I NOTICED I WAS WEARING MY UNDERWEAR ON THE OUTSIDE OF MY PANTS
SICK

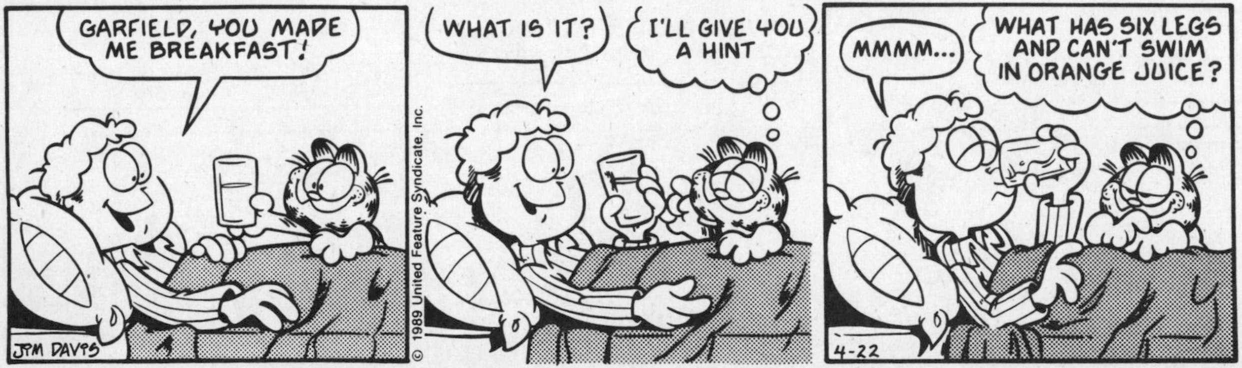
GARFIELD, YOU MADE ME BREAKFAST!
JIM DAVIS
© 1989 United Feature Syndicate, Inc.
WHAT IS IT?
I'LL GIVE YOU A HINT
MMMM...
WHAT HAS SIX LEGS AND CAN'T SWIM IN ORANGE JUICE?
4-22

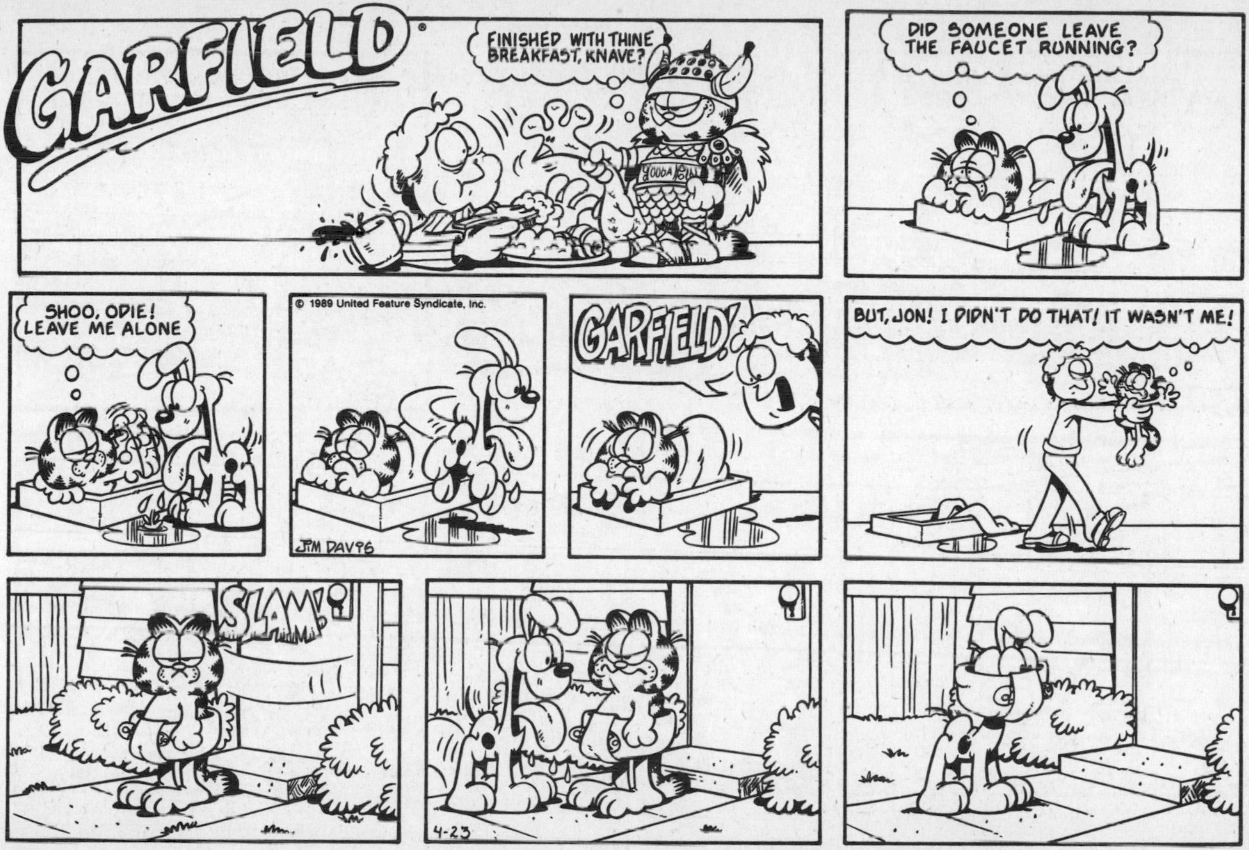
GARFIELD®
FINISHED WITH THINE BREAKFAST, KNAVE?
OOGA
DID SOMEONE LEAVE THE FAUCET RUNNING?
SHOO, ODIE! LEAVE ME ALONE
© 1989 United Feature Syndicate, Inc.
JIM DAVIS
GARFIELD!
BUT, JON! I DIDN'T DO THAT! IT WASN'T ME!
SLAM!
4-23

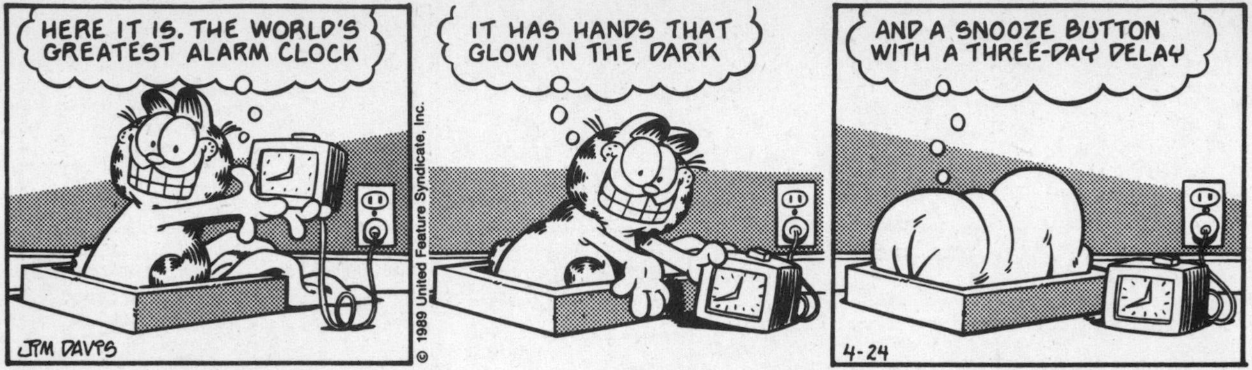
HERE IT IS. THE WORLD'S GREATEST ALARM CLOCK
IT HAS HANDS THAT GLOW IN THE DARK
AND A SNOOZE BUTTON WITH A THREE-DAY DELAY
JIM DAVIS
© 1989 United Feature Syndicate, Inc.
4-24

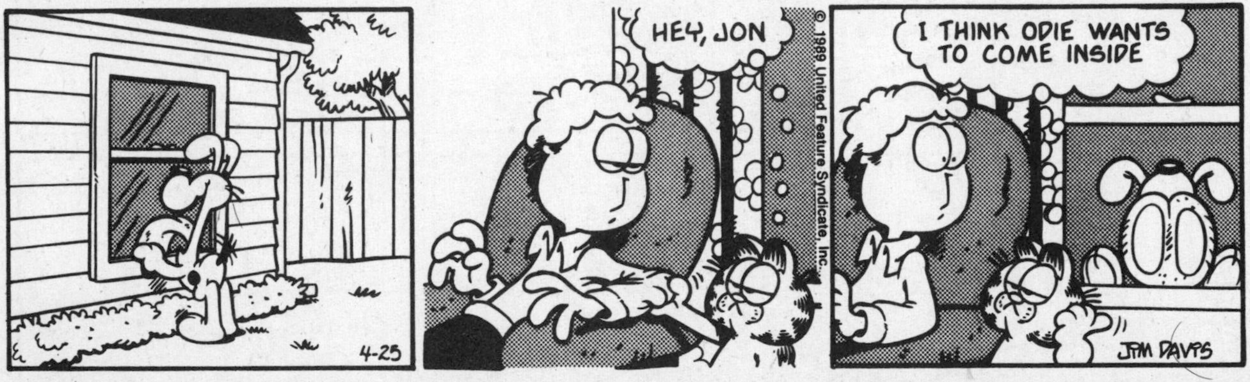
HEY, JON
I THINK ODIE WANTS TO COME INSIDE
4-25
© 1989 United Feature Syndicate, Inc.
JIM DAVIS

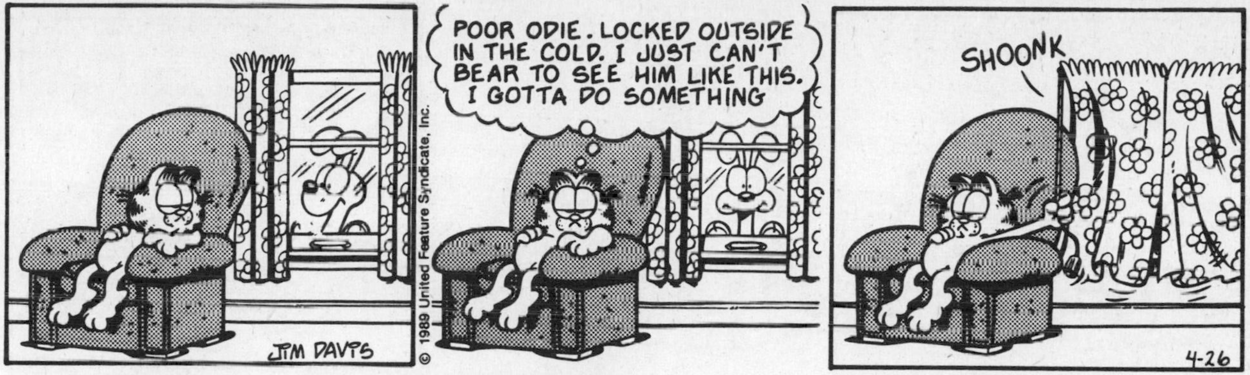
JIM DAVIS
© 1989 United Feature Syndicate, Inc.
POOR ODIE. LOCKED OUTSIDE IN THE COLD. I JUST CAN'T BEAR TO SEE HIM LIKE THIS. I GOTTA DO SOMETHING
SHOONK
4-26

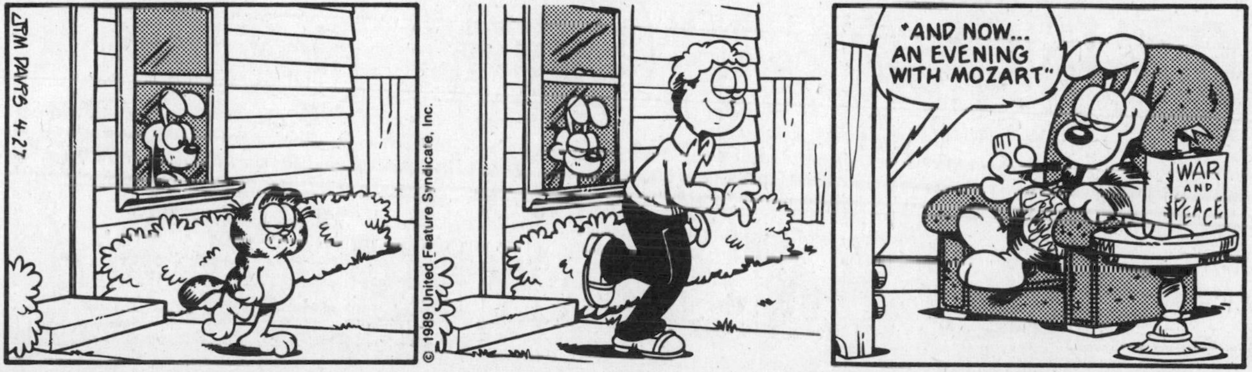
JIM DAVIS 4-27
© 1989 United Feature Syndicate, Inc.
"AND NOW... AN EVENING WITH MOZART"
WAR AND PEACE

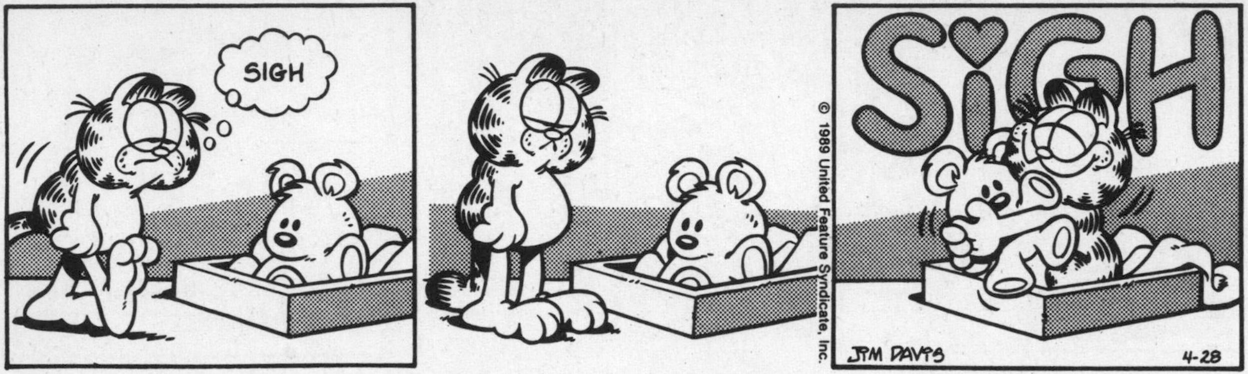
SIGH
SIGH
JIM DAVIS
4-28
© 1989 United Feature Syndicate, Inc.

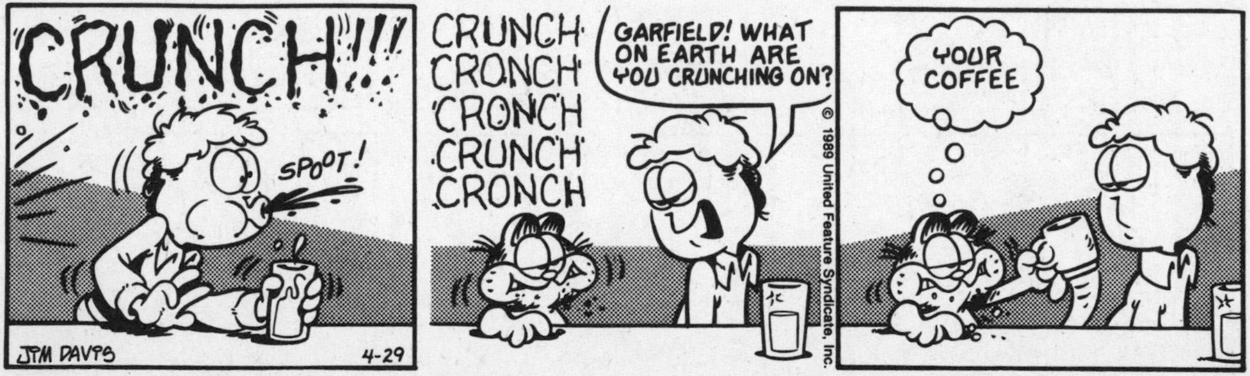
CRUNCH!!!
SPOOT!
JIM DAVIS
4-29
CRUNCH
CRONCH
CRONCH
CRUNCH
CRONCH
GARFIELD! WHAT ON EARTH ARE YOU CRUNCHING ON?
YOUR COFFEE
© 1989 United Feature Syndicate, Inc.

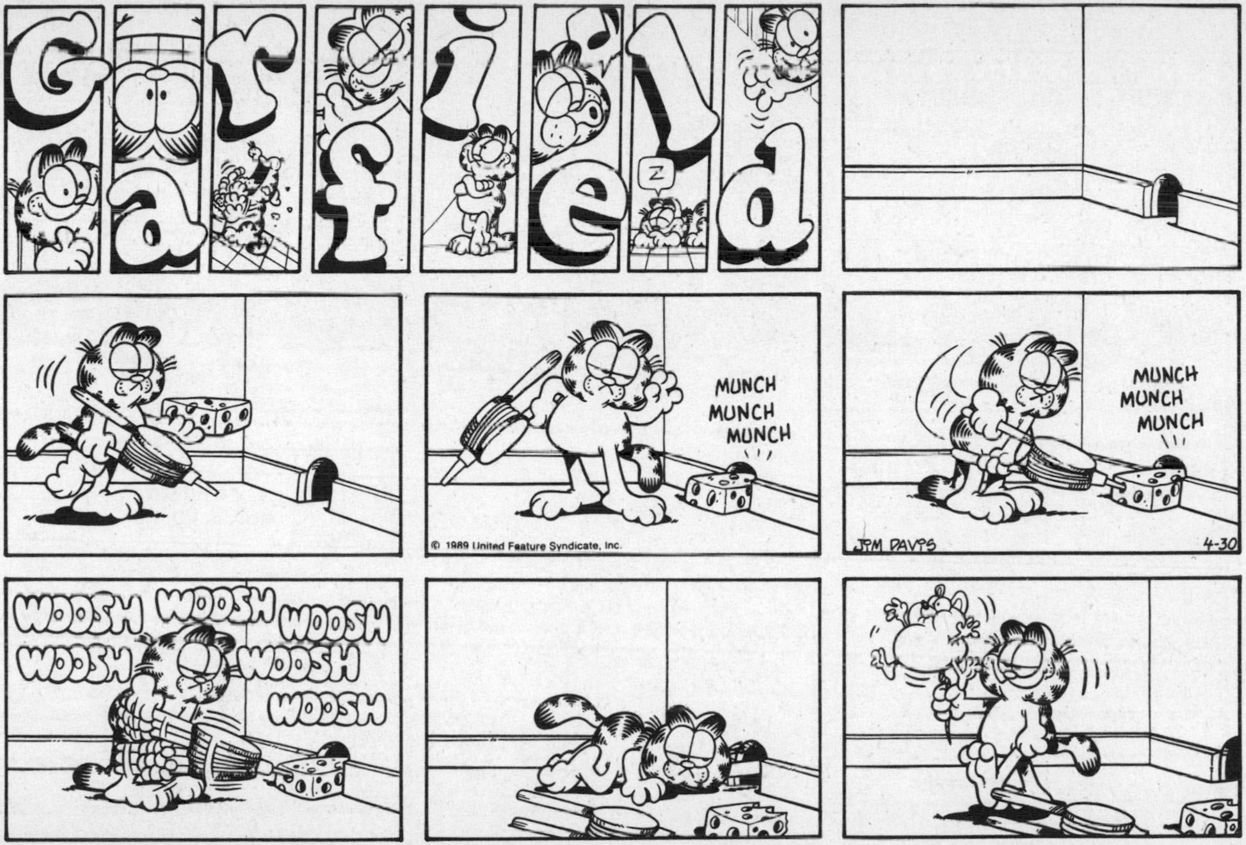
Garfield
MUNCH
MUNCH
MUNCH
© 1989 United Feature Syndicate, Inc.
MUNCH
MUNCH
MUNCH
JIM DAVIS
4-30
WOOSH WOOSH WOOSH
WOOSH WOOSH
WOOSH

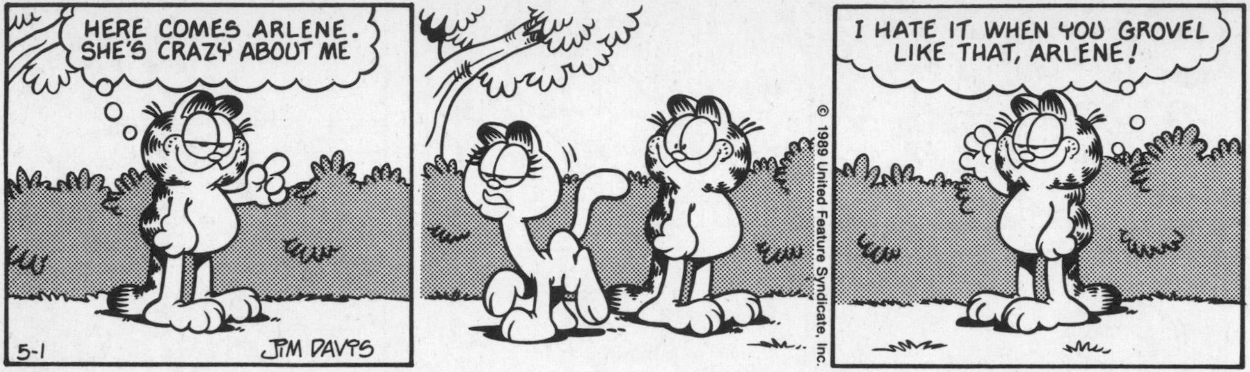
HERE COMES ARLENE. SHE'S CRAZY ABOUT ME
5-1
JIM DAVIS
© 1989 United Feature Syndicate, Inc.
I HATE IT WHEN YOU GROVEL LIKE THAT, ARLENE!

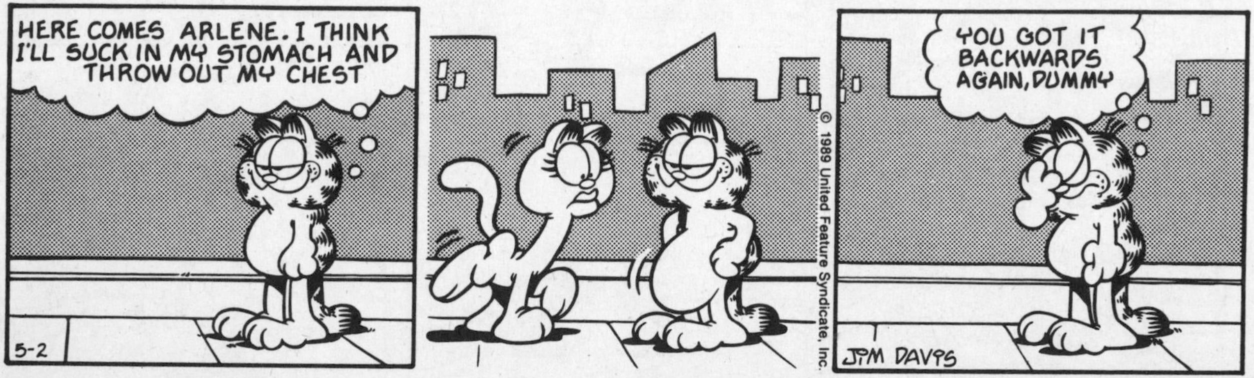
HERE COMES ARLENE. I THINK I'LL SUCK IN MY STOMACH AND THROW OUT MY CHEST
5-2
© 1989 United Feature Syndicate, Inc.
YOU GOT IT BACKWARDS AGAIN, DUMMY
JIM DAVIS

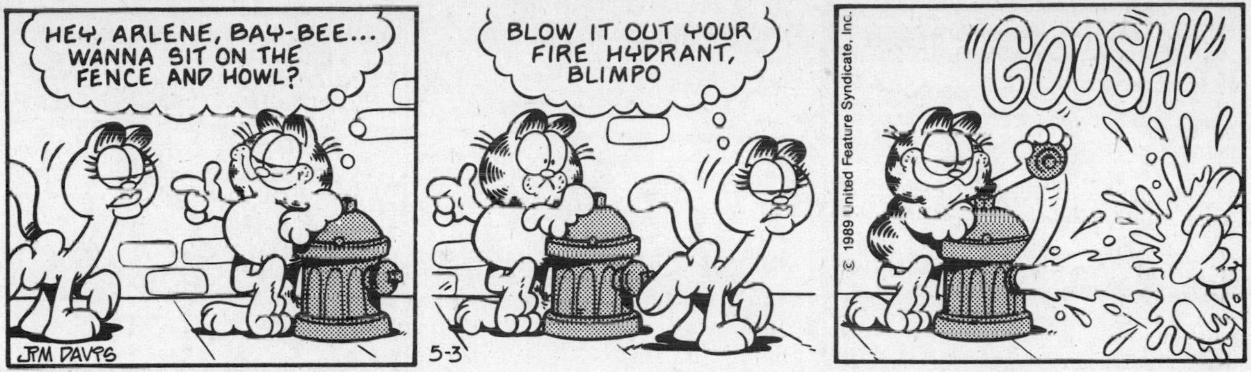
HEY, ARLENE, BAY-BEE... WANNA SIT ON THE FENCE AND HOWL?
JIM DAVIS
BLOW IT OUT YOUR FIRE HYDRANT, BLIMPO
5-3
© 1989 United Feature Syndicate, Inc.
GOOSH!

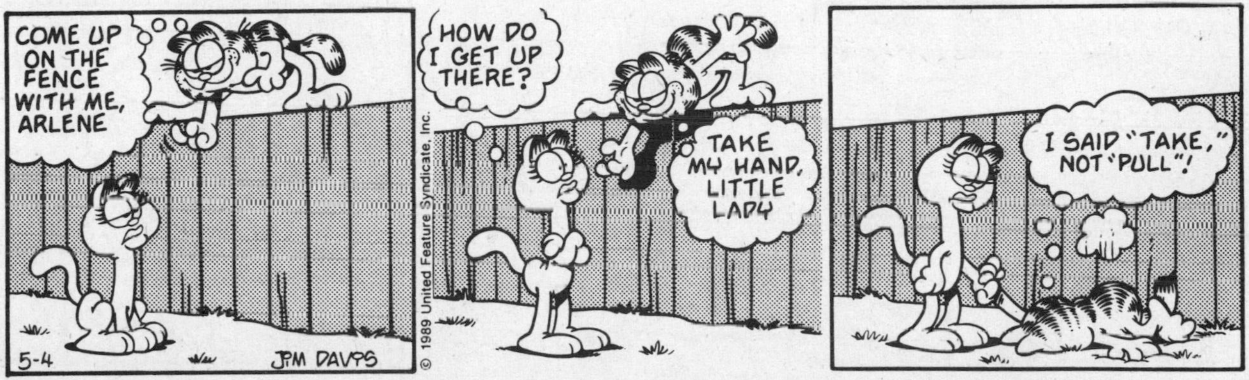
COME UP ON THE FENCE WITH ME, ARLENE
5-4
JIM DAVIS
© 1989 United Feature Syndicate, Inc.
HOW DO I GET UP THERE?
TAKE MY HAND, LITTLE LADY
I SAID "TAKE," NOT "PULL"!

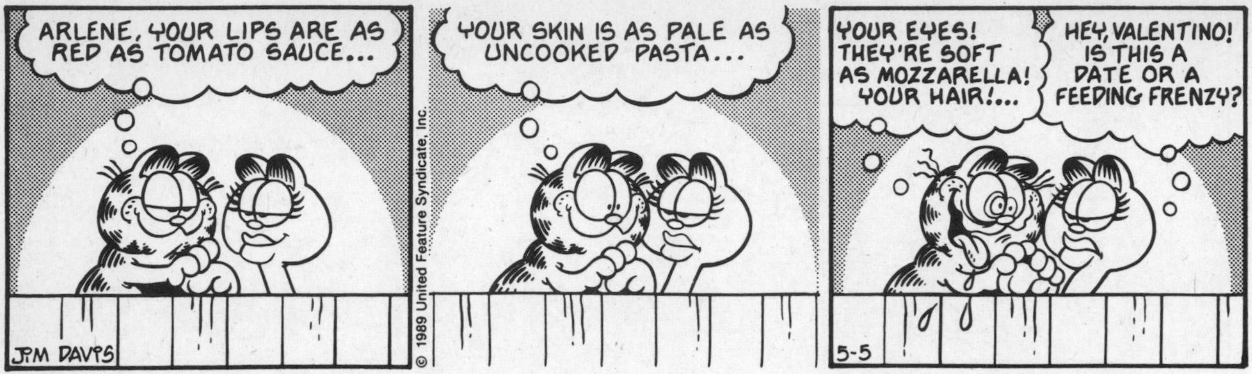
ARLENE, YOUR LIPS ARE AS RED AS TOMATO SAUCE...
YOUR SKIN IS AS PALE AS UNCOOKED PASTA...
YOUR EYES! THEY'RE SOFT AS MOZZARELLA! YOUR HAIR!...
HEY, VALENTINO! IS THIS A DATE OR A FEEDING FRENZY?
JIM DAVIS
© 1989 United Feature Syndicate, Inc.
5-5

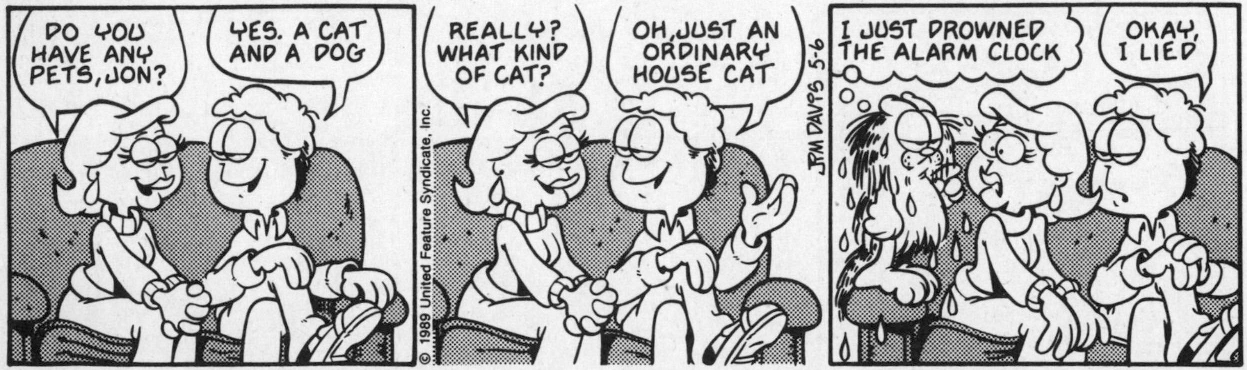
DO YOU HAVE ANY PETS, JON?
YES. A CAT AND A DOG
REALLY? WHAT KIND OF CAT?
OH, JUST AN ORDINARY HOUSE CAT
I JUST DROWNED THE ALARM CLOCK
OKAY, I LIED
© 1989 United Feature Syndicate, Inc.
JIM DAVIS 5-6

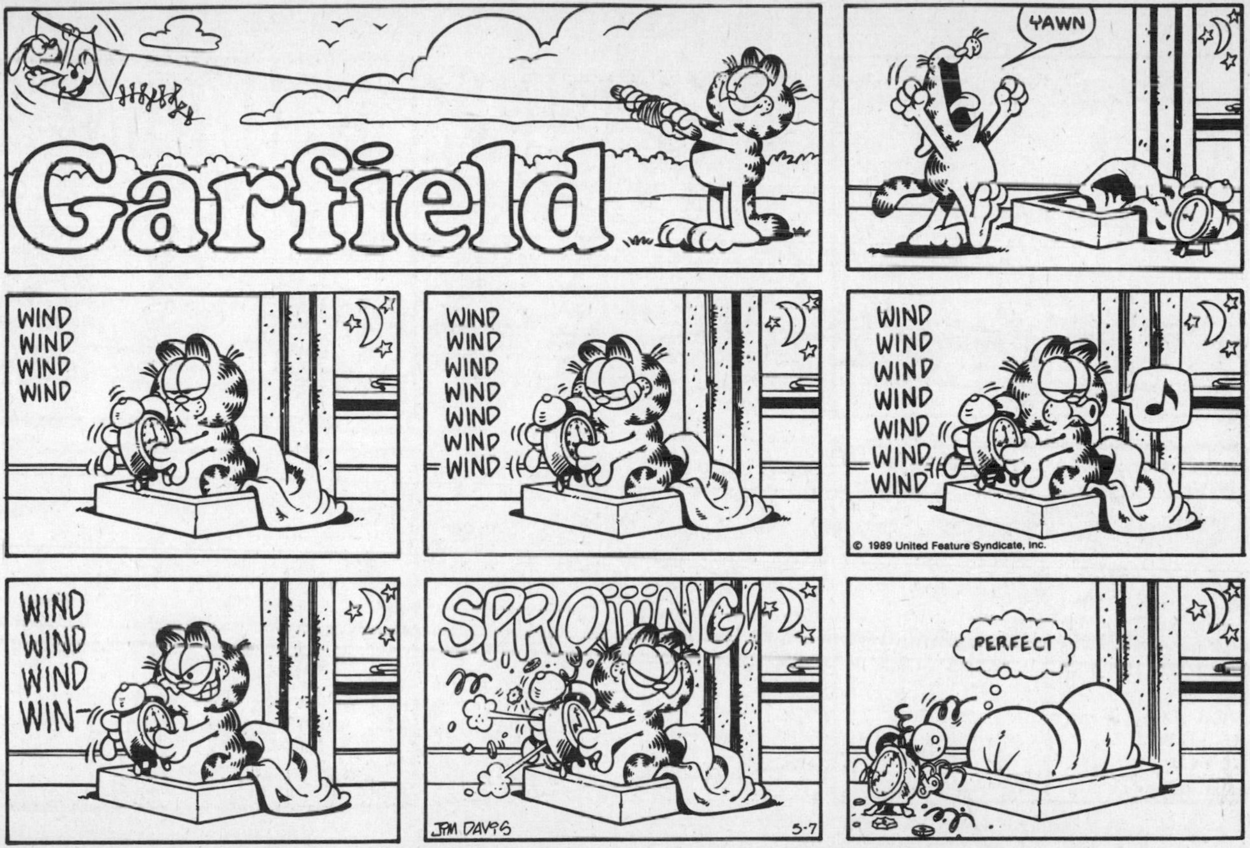
Garfield
YAWN
WIND
WIND
WIND
WIND
WIND
WIND
WIND
WIND
WIND
WIND
WIND
WIND
WIND
WIND
WIND
WIND
WIND
WIND
© 1989 United Feature Syndicate, Inc.
WIND
WIND
WIND
WIN-
SPROIIING!
JIM DAVIS
5-7
PERFECT

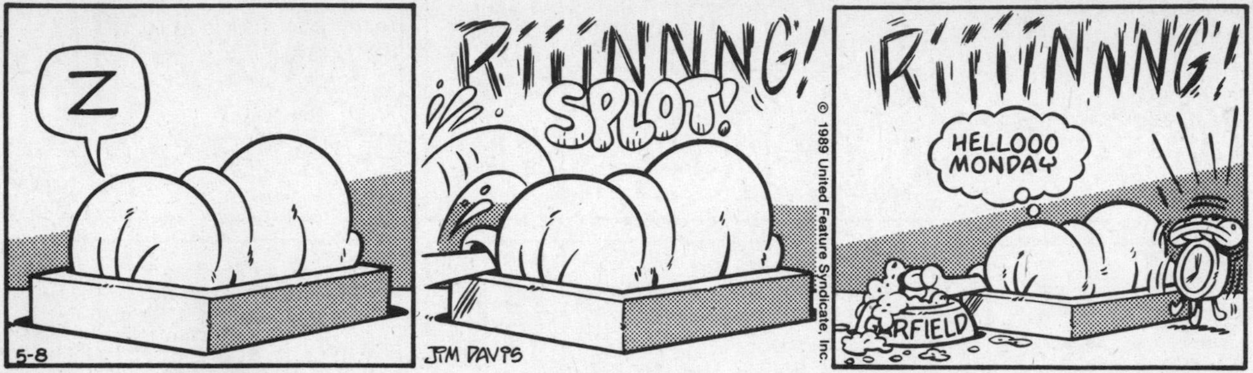
Z
RIIINNNG!
SPLOT!
JIM DAVIS
© 1989 United Feature Syndicate, Inc.
RIIIINNNG!
HELLOOO MONDAY
RFIELD
5-8

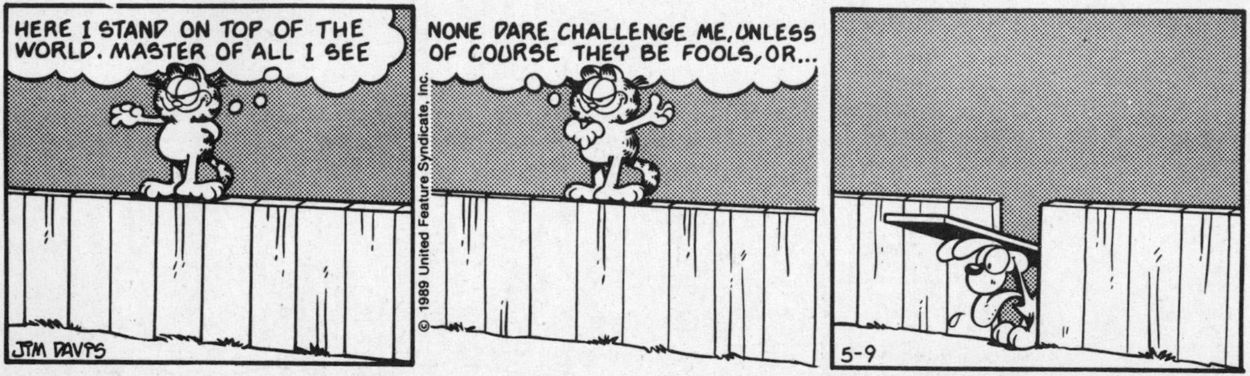
HERE I STAND ON TOP OF THE WORLD. MASTER OF ALL I SEE
JIM DAVIS
© 1989 United Feature Syndicate, Inc.
NONE DARE CHALLENGE ME, UNLESS OF COURSE THEY BE FOOLS, OR...
5-9

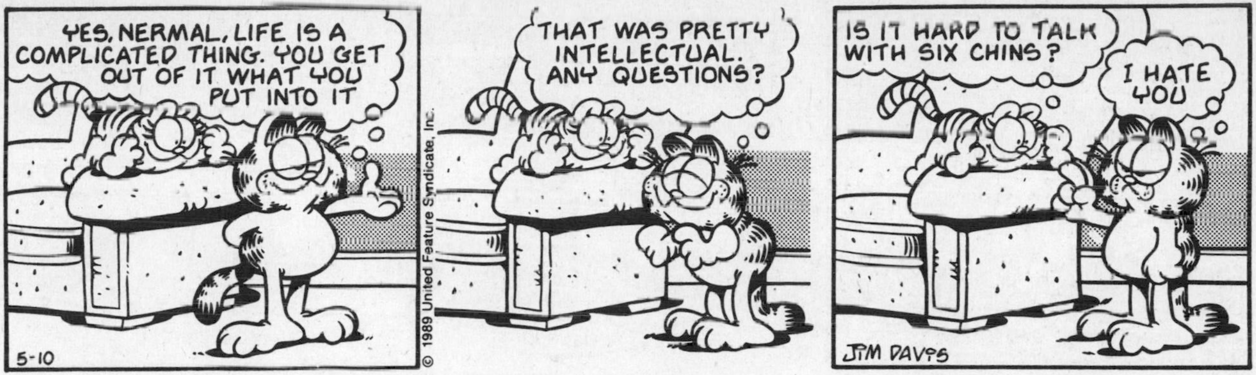
YES, NERMAL, LIFE IS A COMPLICATED THING. YOU GET OUT OF IT WHAT YOU PUT INTO IT
THAT WAS PRETTY INTELLECTUAL. ANY QUESTIONS?
IS IT HARD TO TALK WITH SIX CHINS?
I HATE YOU
5-10
© 1989 United Feature Syndicate, Inc.
JIM DAVIS

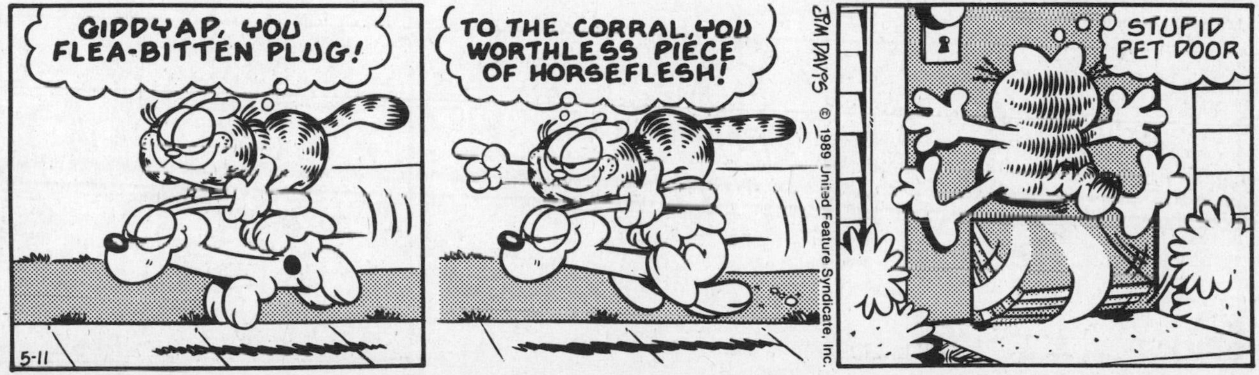
GIDDYAP, YOU FLEA-BITTEN PLUG!
TO THE CORRAL, YOU WORTHLESS PIECE OF HORSEFLESH!
STUPID PET DOOR
5-11
JIM DAVIS
© 1989 United Feature Syndicate, Inc.

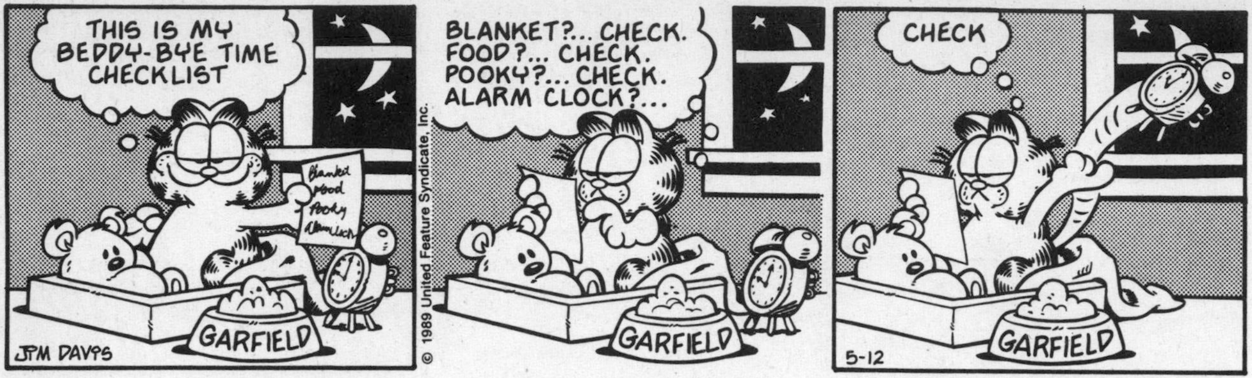
THIS IS MY BEDDY-BYE TIME CHECKLIST
Blanket
food
Pooky
Alarm clock
GARFIELD
JIM DAVIS
BLANKET?... CHECK.
FOOD?... CHECK.
POOKY?... CHECK.
ALARM CLOCK?...
GARFIELD
CHECK
GARFIELD
5-12

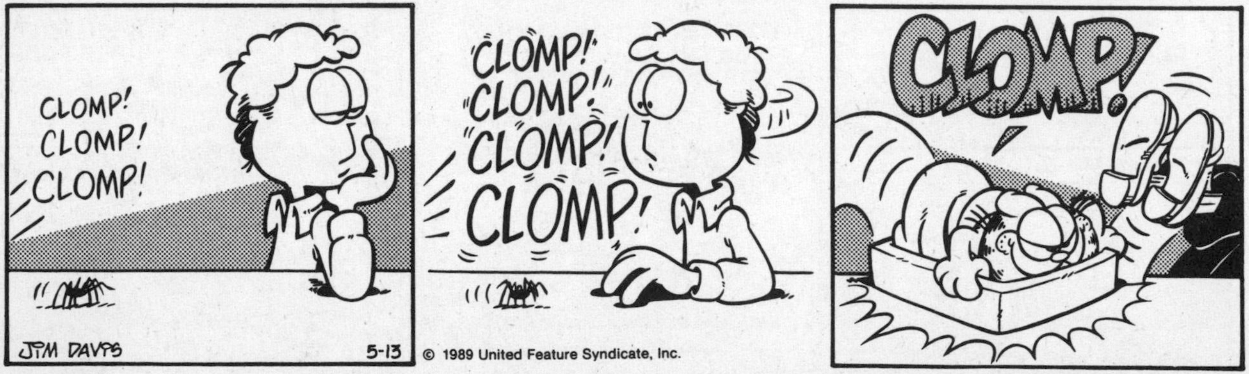
CLOMP!
CLOMP!
CLOMP!
JIM DAVIS
5-13
CLOMP!
CLOMP!
CLOMP!
CLOMP!
CLOMP!

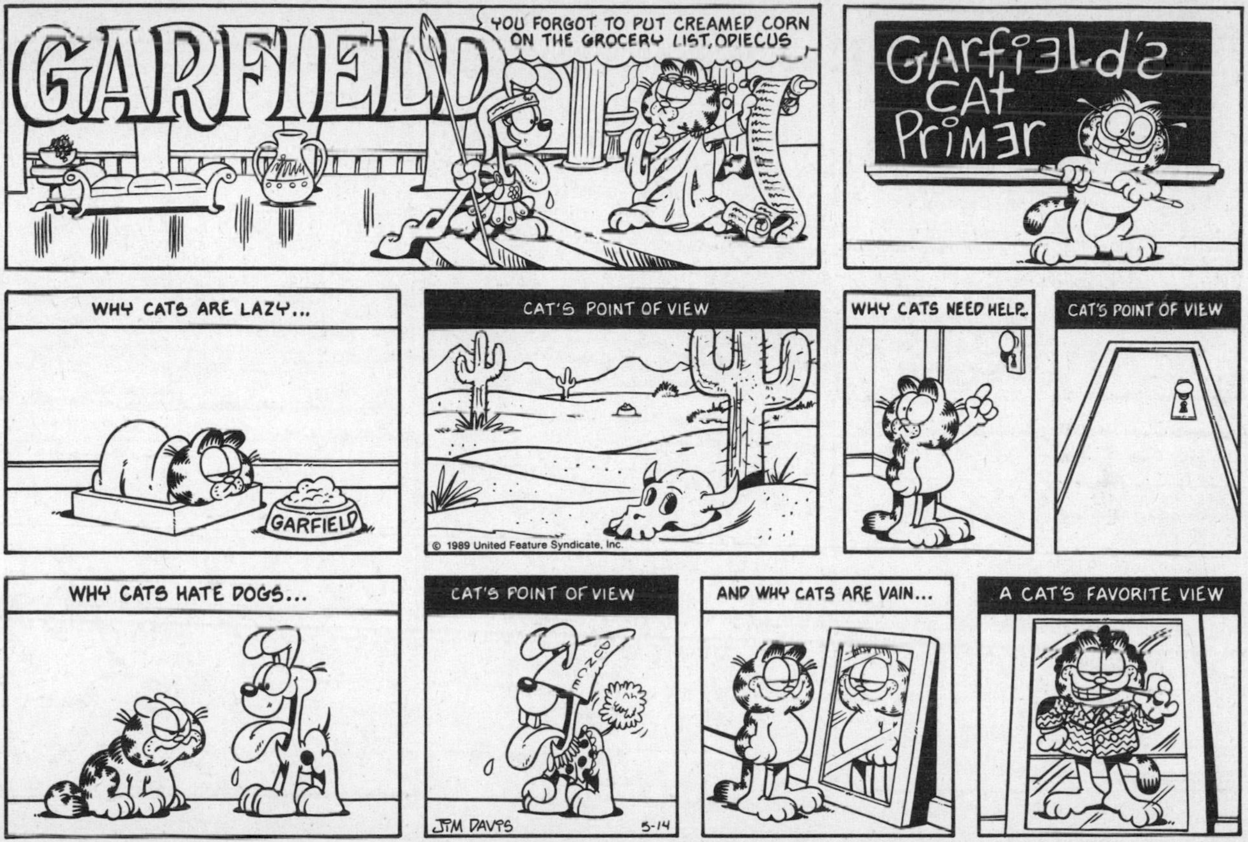
GARFIELD
YOU FORGOT TO PUT CREAMED CORN ON THE GROCERY LIST, ODIECUS
GARFIELD'S CAT PRIMER
WHY CATS ARE LAZY...
GARFIELD
CAT'S POINT OF VIEW
© 1989 United Feature Syndicate, Inc.
WHY CATS NEED HELP...
CAT'S POINT OF VIEW
WHY CATS HATE DOGS...
CAT'S POINT OF VIEW
JIM DAVIS
5-14
AND WHY CATS ARE VAIN...
A CAT'S FAVORITE VIEW

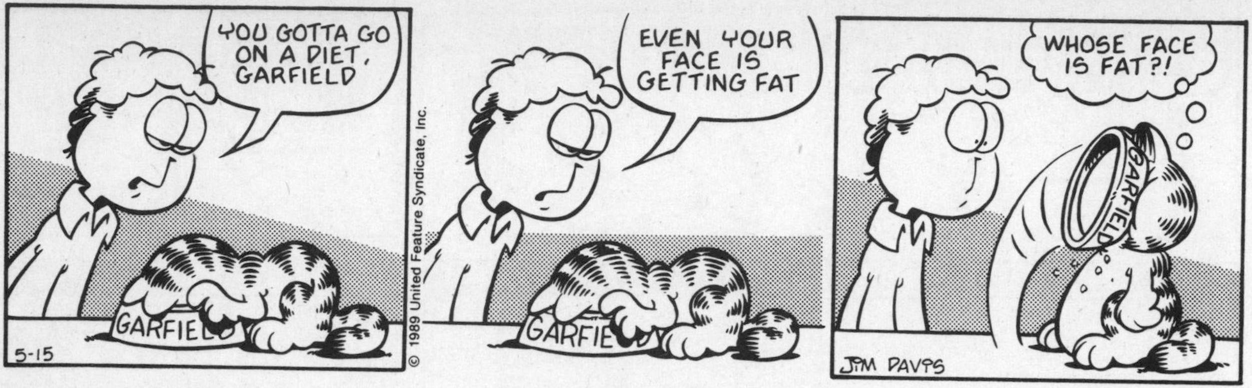
YOU GOTTA GO ON A DIET, GARFIELD
GARFIELD
5-15
EVEN YOUR FACE IS GETTING FAT
GARFIELD
WHOSE FACE IS FAT?!
GARFIELD
JIM DAVIS

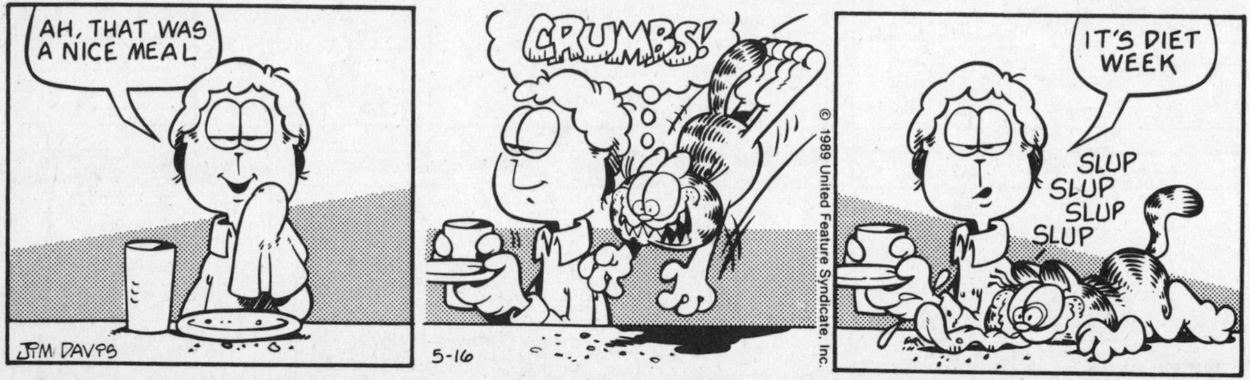
AH, THAT WAS A NICE MEAL
JIM DAVIS
CRUMBS!
5-16
IT'S DIET WEEK
SLUP
SLUP
SLUP
SLUP

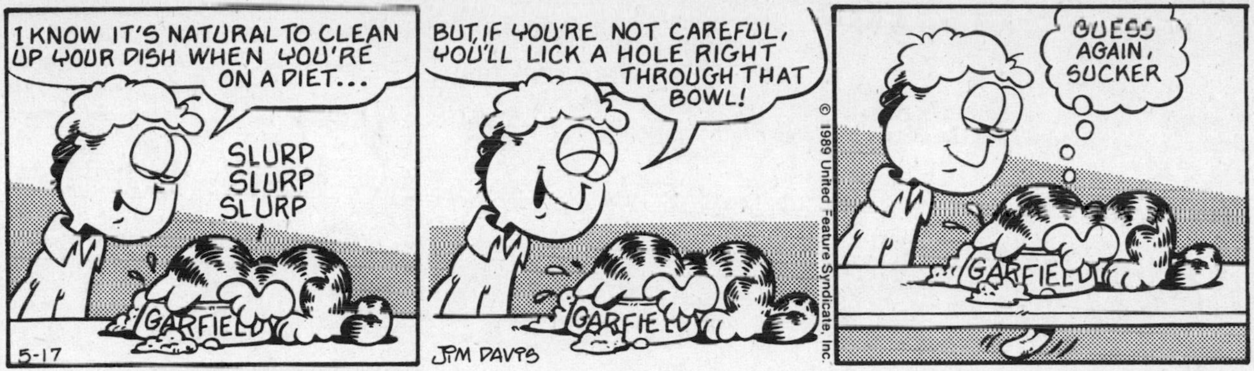
I KNOW IT'S NATURAL TO CLEAN UP YOUR DISH WHEN YOU'RE ON A DIET...
SLURP SLURP SLURP
5-17
BUT, IF YOU'RE NOT CAREFUL, YOU'LL LICK A HOLE RIGHT THROUGH THAT BOWL!
JIM DAVIS
GARFIELD
© 1989 United Feature Syndicate, Inc.
GUESS AGAIN, SUCKER

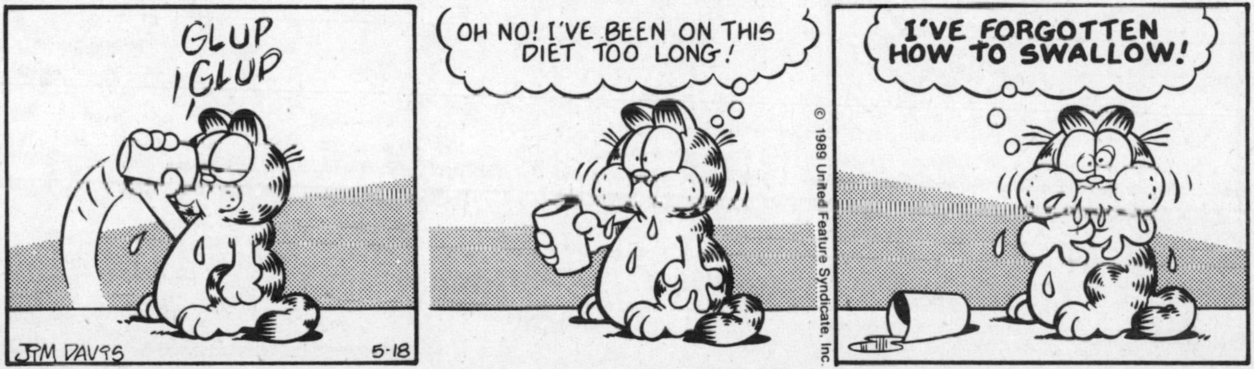
GLUP GLUP
JIM DAVIS
5-18
OH NO! I'VE BEEN ON THIS DIET TOO LONG!
© 1989 United Feature Syndicate, Inc.
I'VE FORGOTTEN HOW TO SWALLOW!

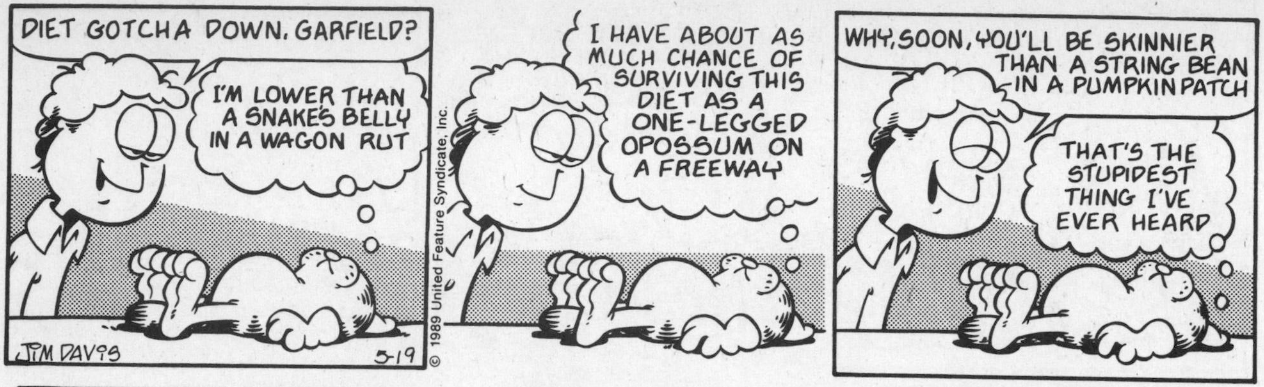
DIET GOTCHA DOWN, GARFIELD?
I'M LOWER THAN A SNAKE'S BELLY IN A WAGON RUT
I HAVE ABOUT AS MUCH CHANCE OF SURVIVING THIS DIET AS A ONE-LEGGED OPOSSUM ON A FREEWAY
WHY, SOON, YOU'LL BE SKINNIER THAN A STRING BEAN IN A PUMPKIN PATCH
THAT'S THE STUPIDEST THING I'VE EVER HEARD
JIM DAVIS
5-19
© 1989 United Feature Syndicate, Inc.

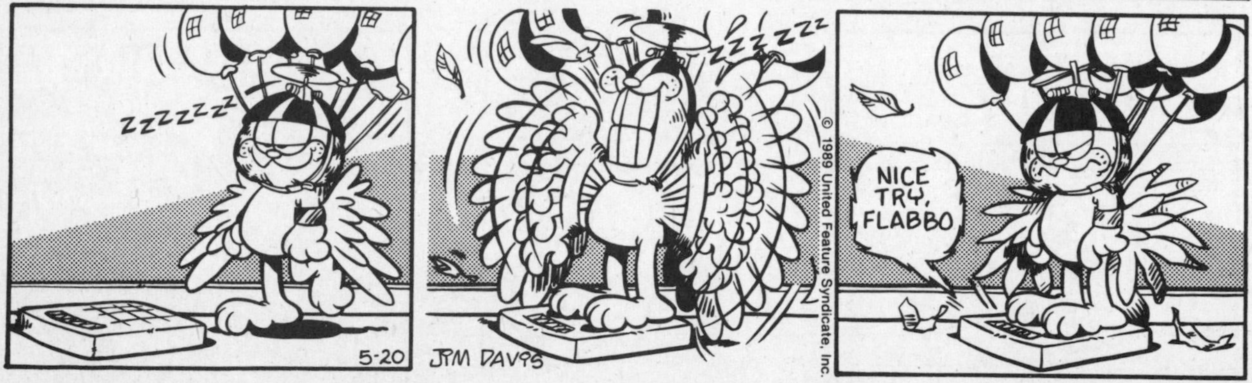
ZZZZZZZ
5-20
ZZZZZZZ
JIM DAVIS
© 1989 United Feature Syndicate, Inc.
NICE TRY, FLABBO

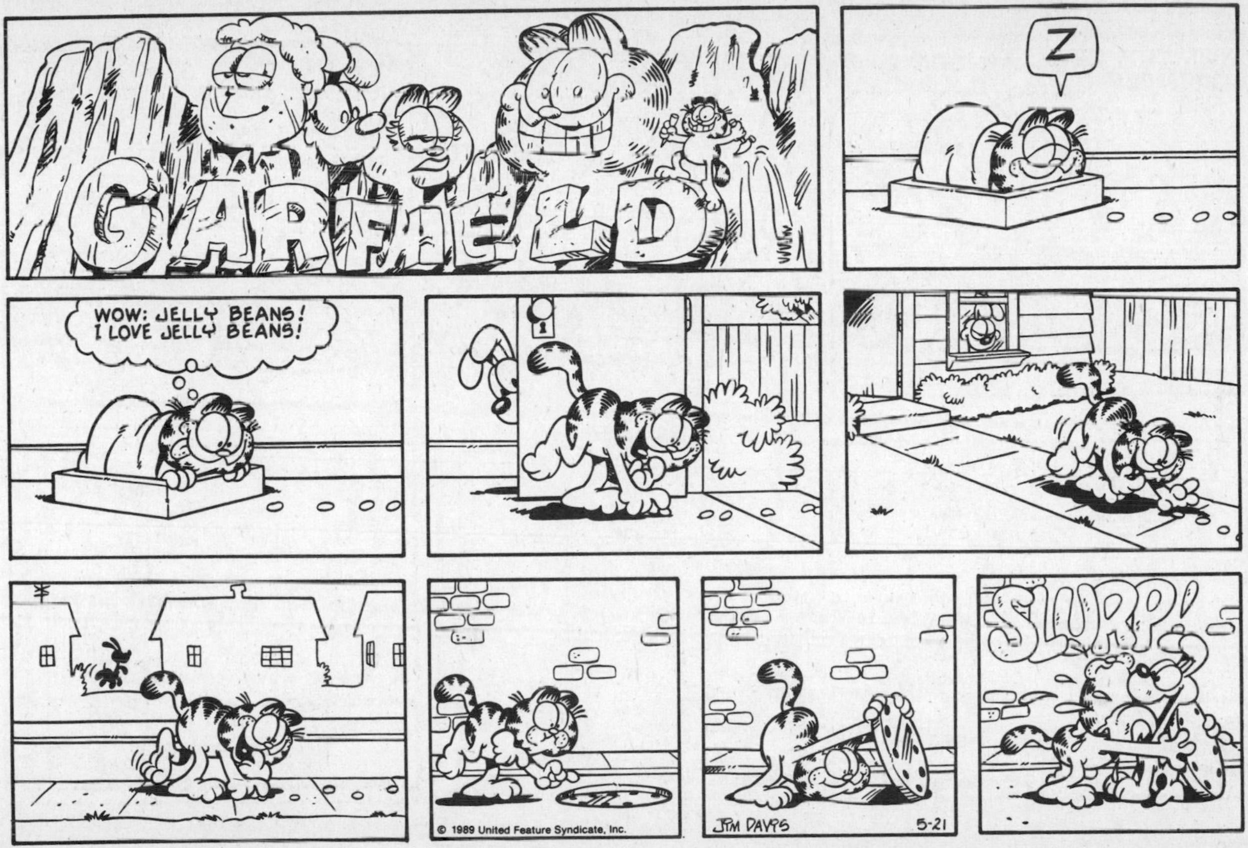
GARFIELD
Z
WOW: JELLY BEANS! I LOVE JELLY BEANS!
© 1989 United Feature Syndicate, Inc.
JIM DAVIS
5-21
SLURP!

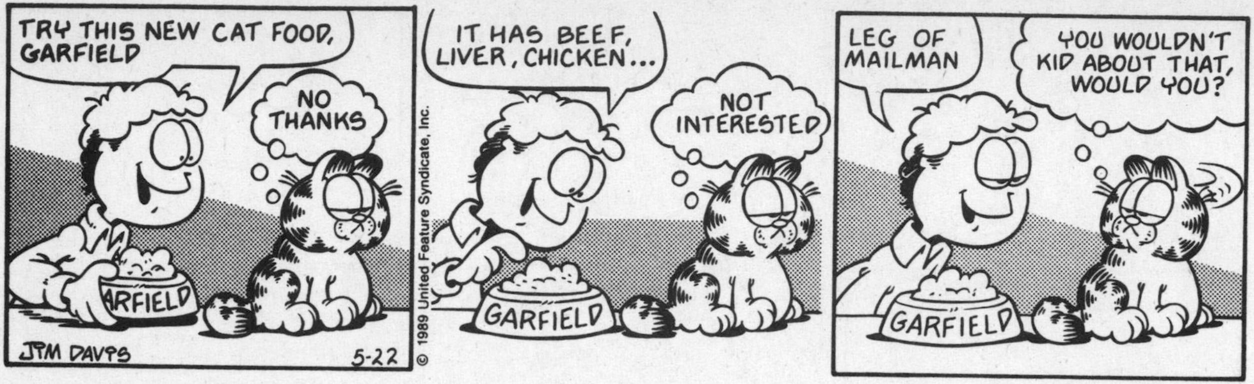
TRY THIS NEW CAT FOOD, GARFIELD
NO THANKS
JIM DAVIS
5-22
© 1989 United Feature Syndicate, Inc.
IT HAS BEEF, LIVER, CHICKEN...
NOT INTERESTED
GARFIELD
LEG OF MAILMAN
YOU WOULDN'T KID ABOUT THAT, WOULD YOU?
GARFIELD

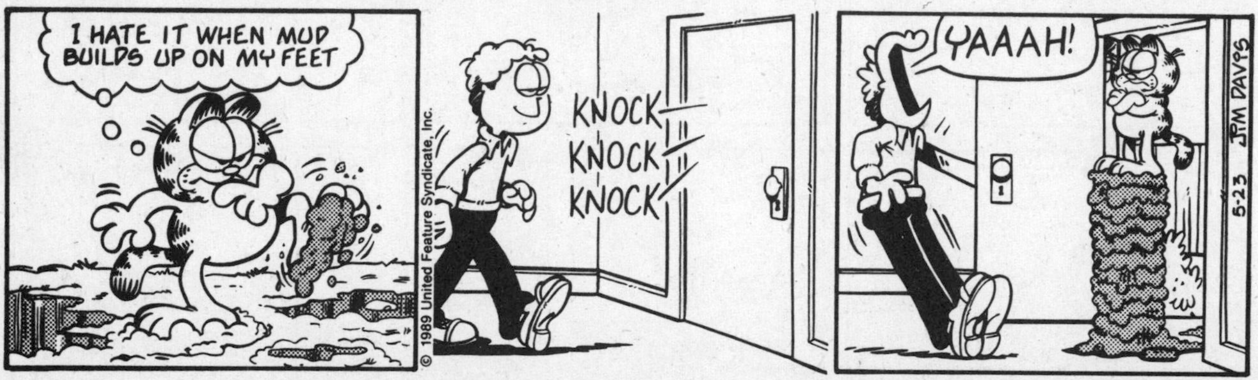
I HATE IT WHEN MUD BUILDS UP ON MY FEET
© 1989 United Feature Syndicate, Inc.
KNOCK
KNOCK
KNOCK
YAAAH!
JIM DAVIS
5-23

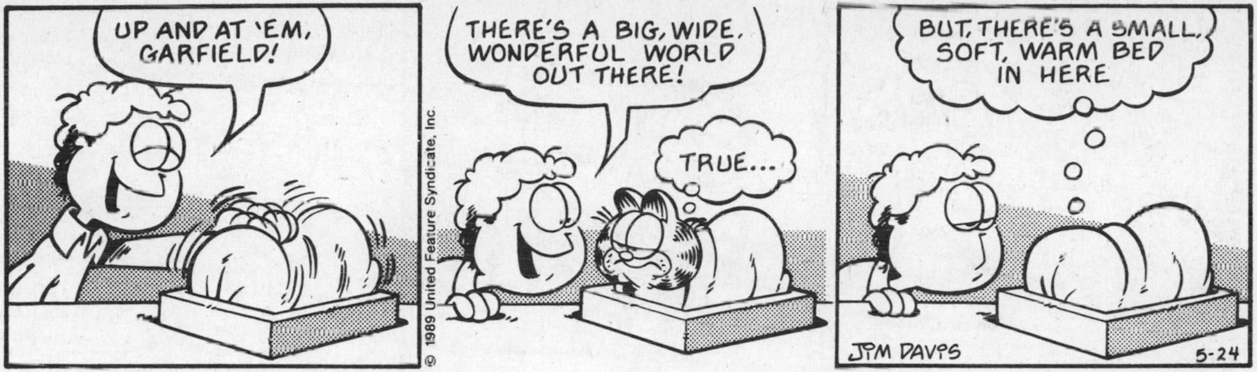
UP AND AT 'EM, GARFIELD!
THERE'S A BIG, WIDE, WONDERFUL WORLD OUT THERE!
TRUE...
BUT, THERE'S A SMALL, SOFT, WARM BED IN HERE
JIM DAVIS
5-24
© 1989 United Feature Syndicate, Inc.

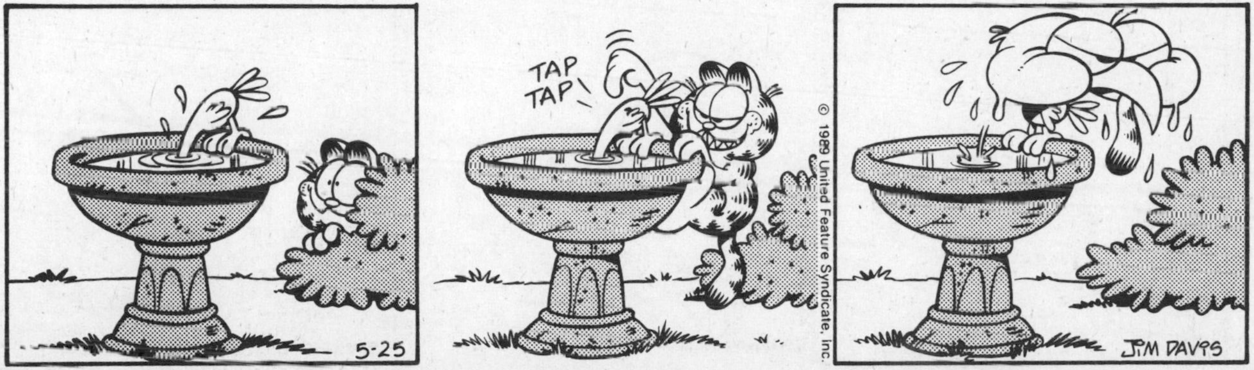
5-25
TAP TAP!
JIM DAVIS
© 1989 United Feature Syndicate, Inc.

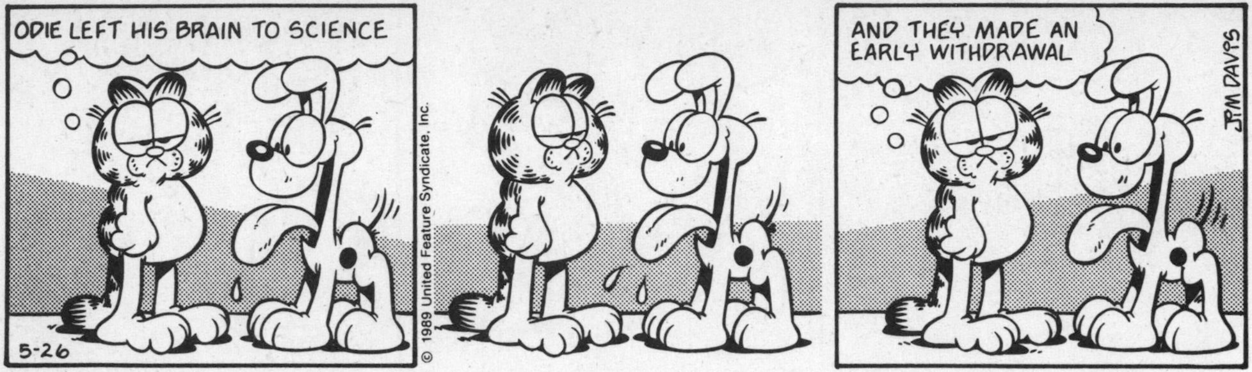
ODIE LEFT HIS BRAIN TO SCIENCE
AND THEY MADE AN EARLY WITHDRAWAL
JIM DAVIS
5-26
© 1989 United Feature Syndicate, Inc.

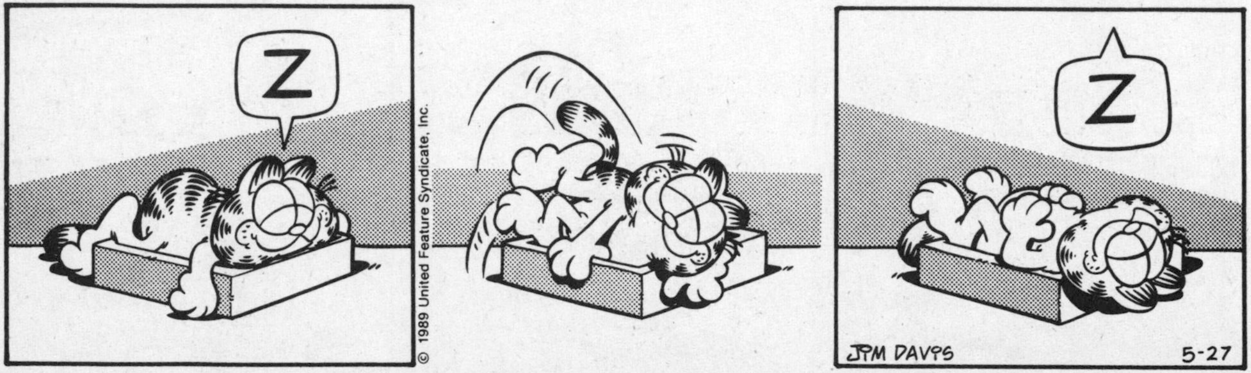
Z
Z
JIM DAVIS
5-27
© 1989 United Feature Syndicate, Inc.

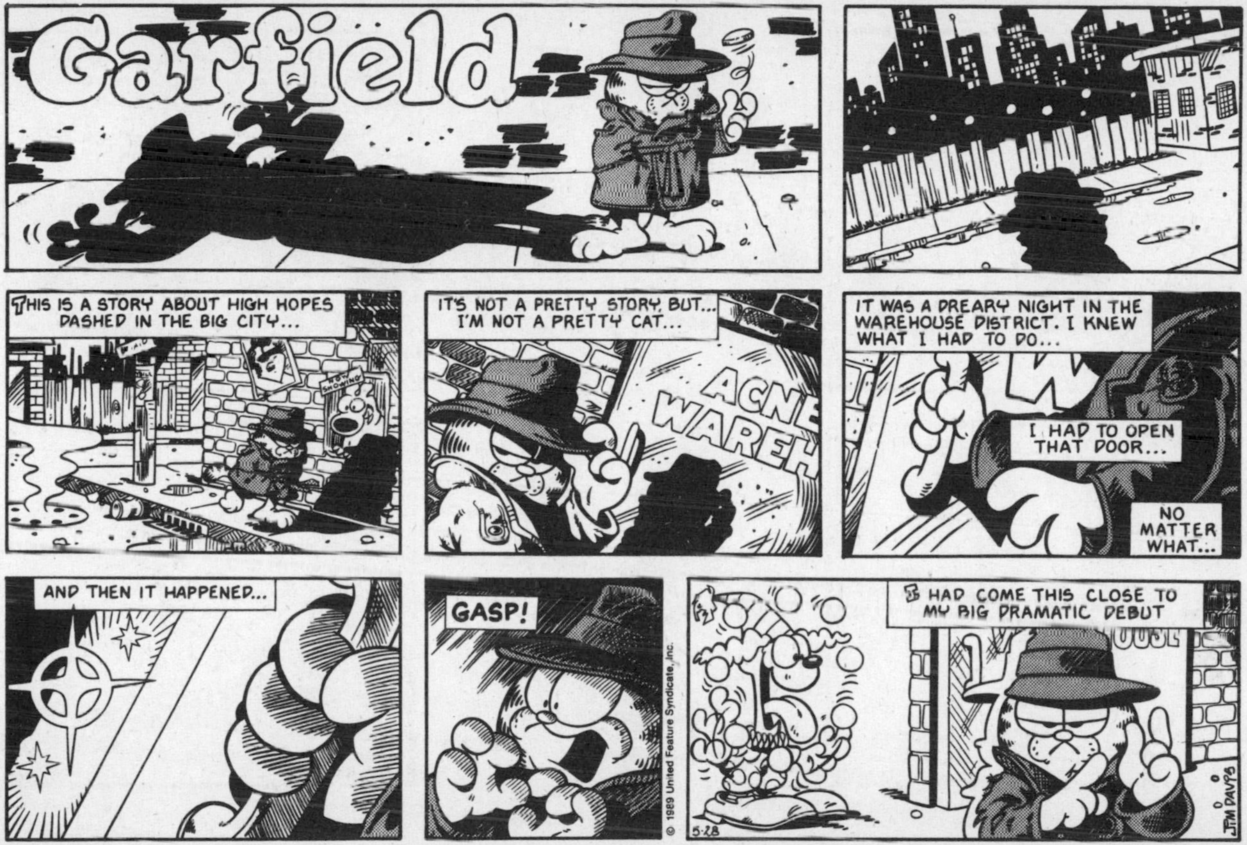
Garfield
THIS IS A STORY ABOUT HIGH HOPES DASHED IN THE BIG CITY...
NOW SHOWING
IT'S NOT A PRETTY STORY, BUT... I'M NOT A PRETTY CAT...
ACNE WAREH
IT WAS A DREARY NIGHT IN THE WAREHOUSE DISTRICT. I KNEW WHAT I HAD TO DO...
I HAD TO OPEN THAT DOOR...
NO MATTER WHAT...
AND THEN IT HAPPENED...
GASP!
© 1989 United Feature Syndicate, Inc.
5-28
I HAD COME THIS CLOSE TO MY BIG DRAMATIC DEBUT
JIM DAVIS

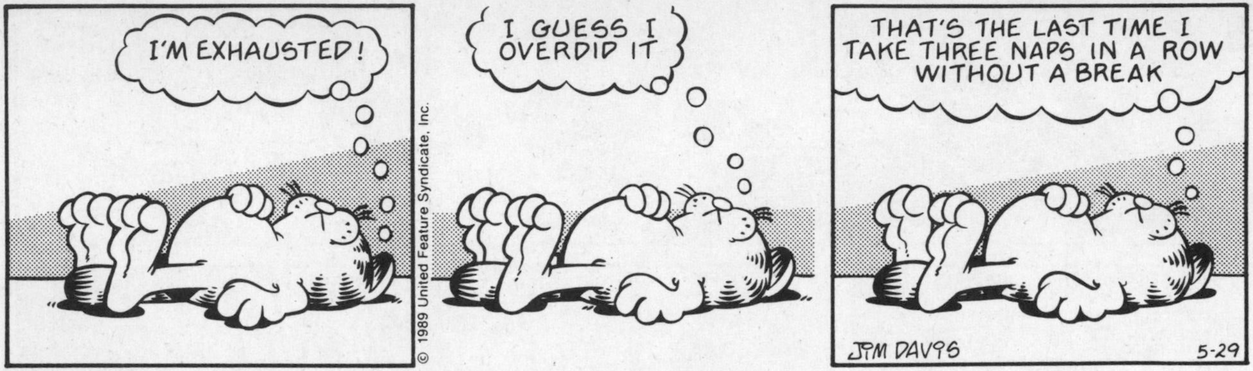
I'M EXHAUSTED!
I GUESS I OVERDID IT
THAT'S THE LAST TIME I TAKE THREE NAPS IN A ROW WITHOUT A BREAK
JIM DAVIS
5-29
© 1989 United Feature Syndicate, Inc.

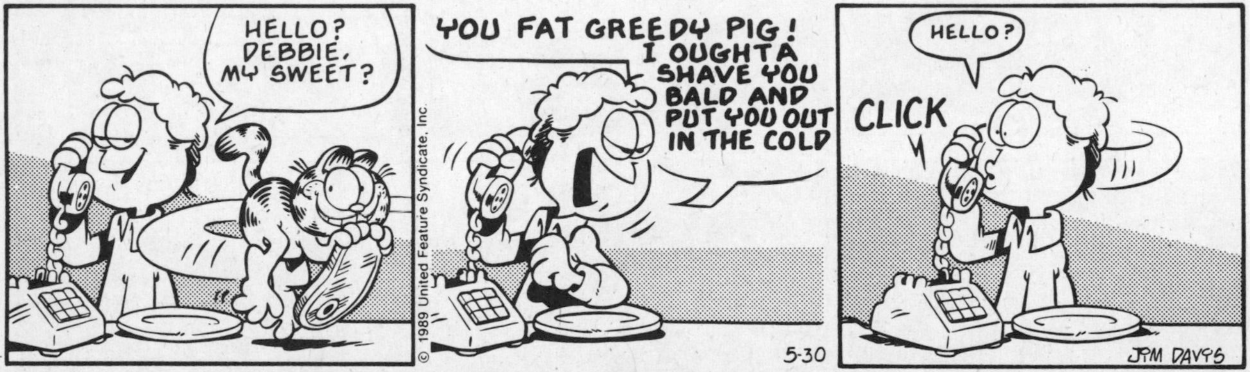
HELLO? DEBBIE, MY SWEET?
YOU FAT GREEDY PIG! I OUGHTA SHAVE YOU BALD AND PUT YOU OUT IN THE COLD
5-30
CLICK
HELLO?
JIM DAVIS
© 1989 United Feature Syndicate, Inc.

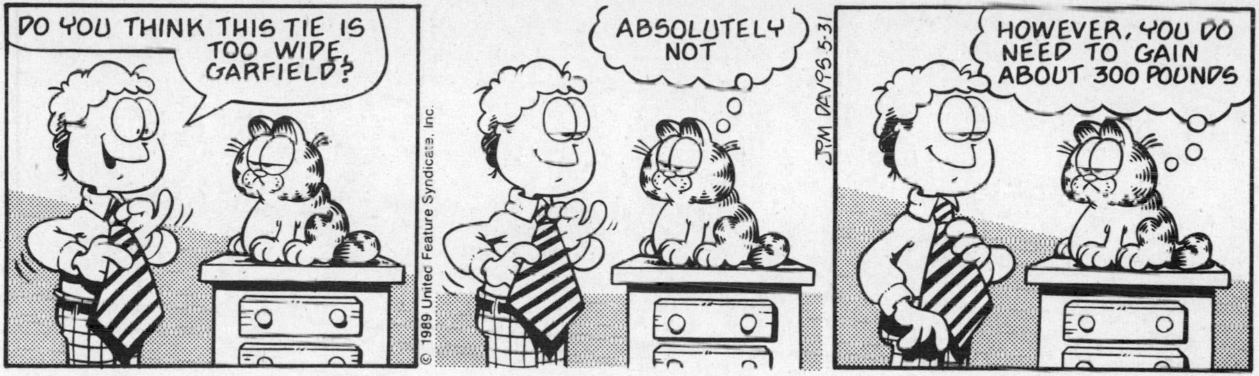
DO YOU THINK THIS TIE IS TOO WIDE, GARFIELD?
ABSOLUTELY NOT
HOWEVER, YOU DO NEED TO GAIN ABOUT 300 POUNDS
© 1989 United Feature Syndicate, Inc.
JIM DAVIS 5-31

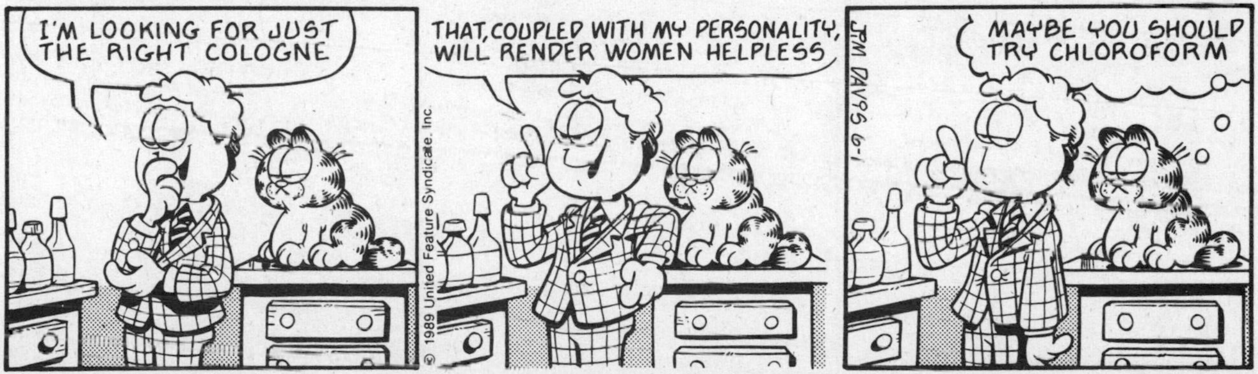
I'M LOOKING FOR JUST THE RIGHT COLOGNE
THAT, COUPLED WITH MY PERSONALITY, WILL RENDER WOMEN HELPLESS
MAYBE YOU SHOULD TRY CHLOROFORM
© 1989 United Feature Syndicate, Inc.
JIM DAVIS 6-1

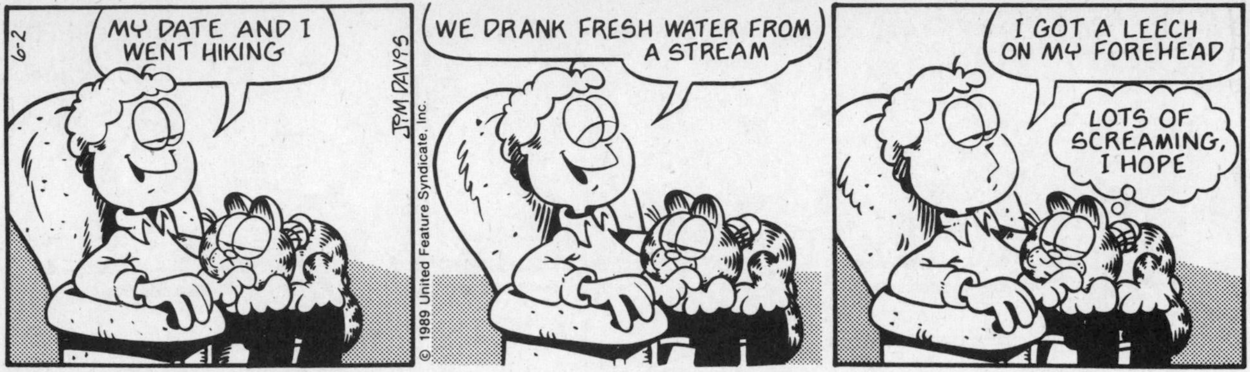
6-2
MY DATE AND I WENT HIKING
JIM DAVIS
© 1989 United Feature Syndicate, Inc.
WE DRANK FRESH WATER FROM A STREAM
I GOT A LEECH ON MY FOREHEAD
LOTS OF SCREAMING, I HOPE

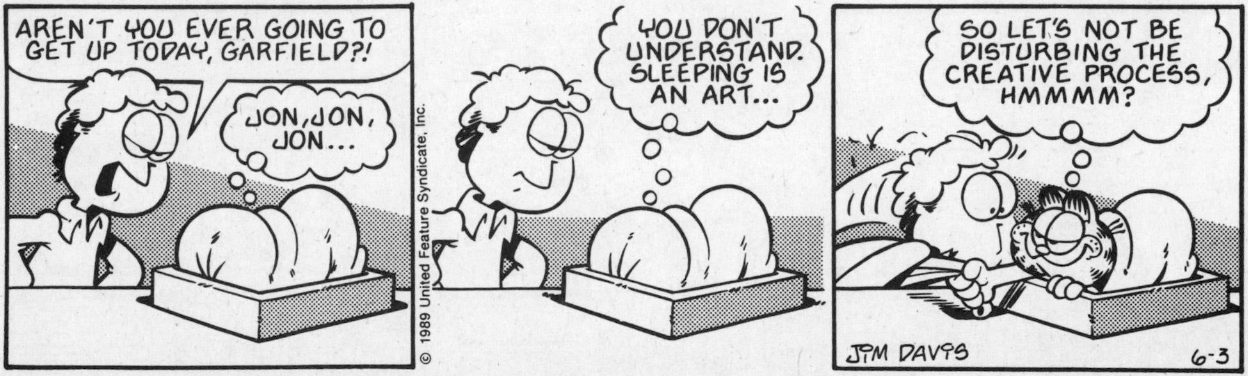
AREN'T YOU EVER GOING TO GET UP TODAY, GARFIELD?!
JON, JON, JON...
© 1989 United Feature Syndicate, Inc.
YOU DON'T UNDERSTAND. SLEEPING IS AN ART...
SO LET'S NOT BE DISTURBING THE CREATIVE PROCESS, HMMMM?
JIM DAVIS
6-3

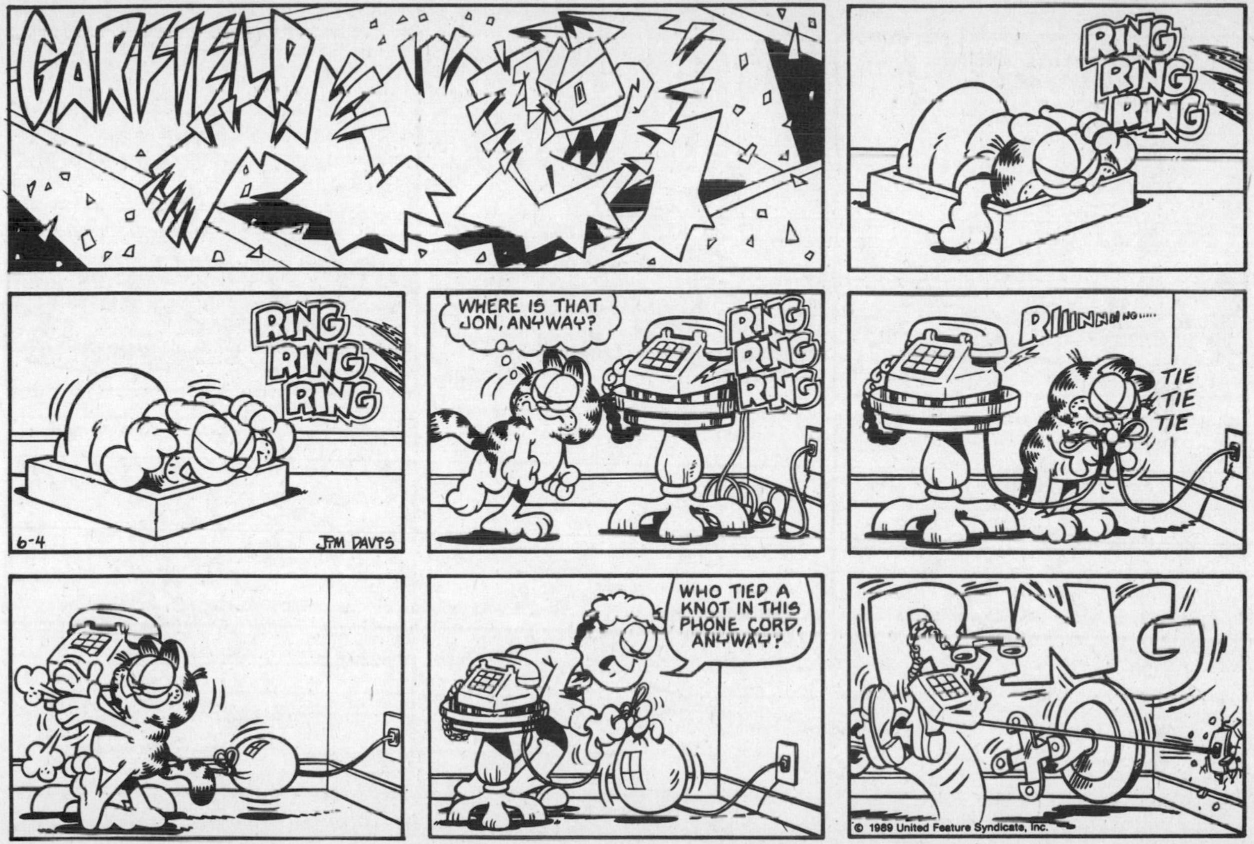
GARFIELD
RING RING RING
RING RING RING
WHERE IS THAT JON, ANYWAY?
RING RING RING
RIIINNNNG.....
TIE TIE TIE
WHO TIED A KNOT IN THIS PHONE CORD, ANYWAY?
RING
6-4
JIM DAVIS
© 1989 United Feature Syndicate, Inc.

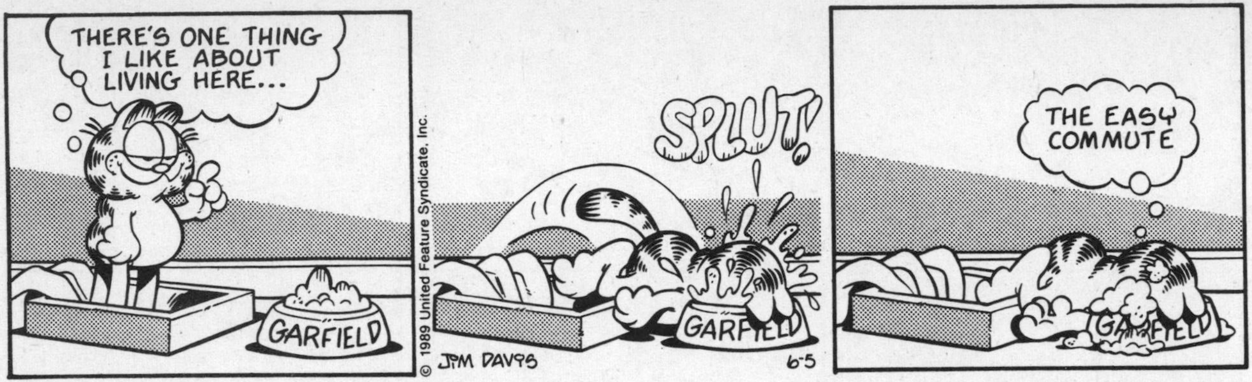
THERE'S ONE THING I LIKE ABOUT LIVING HERE...
SPLUT!
THE EASY COMMUTE
© 1989 United Feature Syndicate, Inc.
JIM DAVIS
6-5

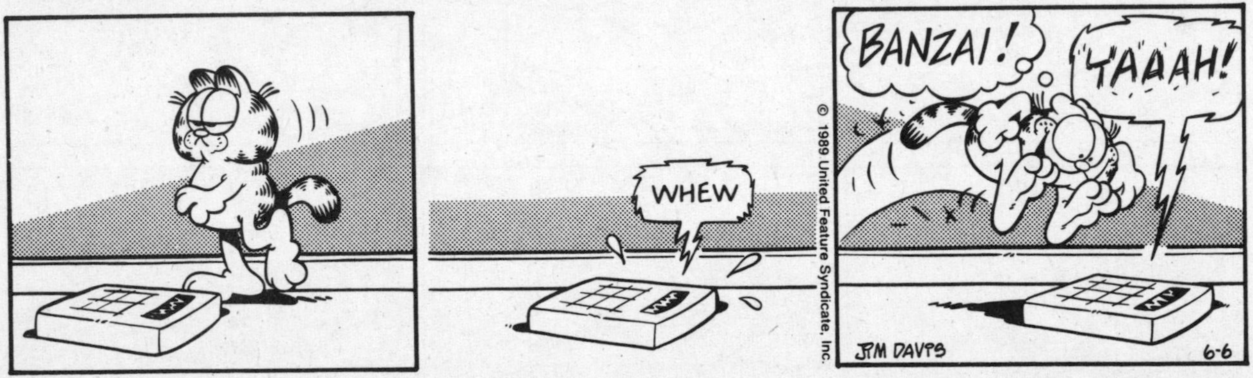
WHEW
BANZAI!
YAAAH!
© 1989 United Feature Syndicate, Inc.
JIM DAVIS
6-6

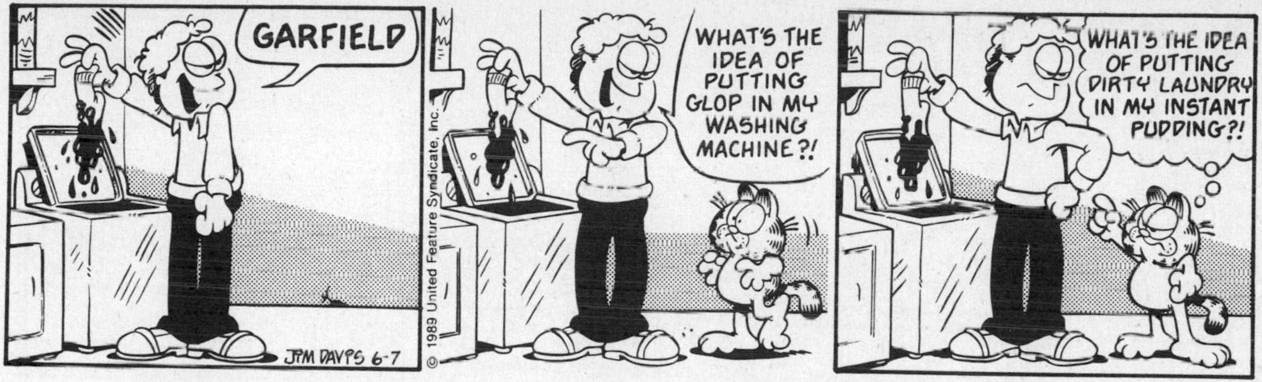
GARFIELD
JIM DAVIS 6-7
© 1989 United Feature Syndicate, Inc.
WHAT'S THE IDEA OF PUTTING GLOP IN MY WASHING MACHINE?!
WHAT'S THE IDEA OF PUTTING DIRTY LAUNDRY IN MY INSTANT PUDDING?!

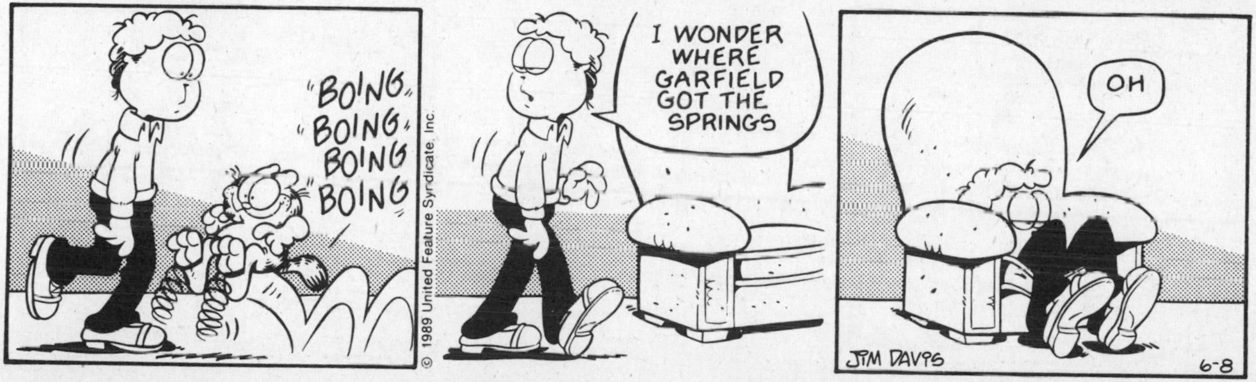
"BOING" "BOING" BOING BOING
© 1989 United Feature Syndicate, Inc.
I WONDER WHERE GARFIELD GOT THE SPRINGS
OH
JIM DAVIS
6-8

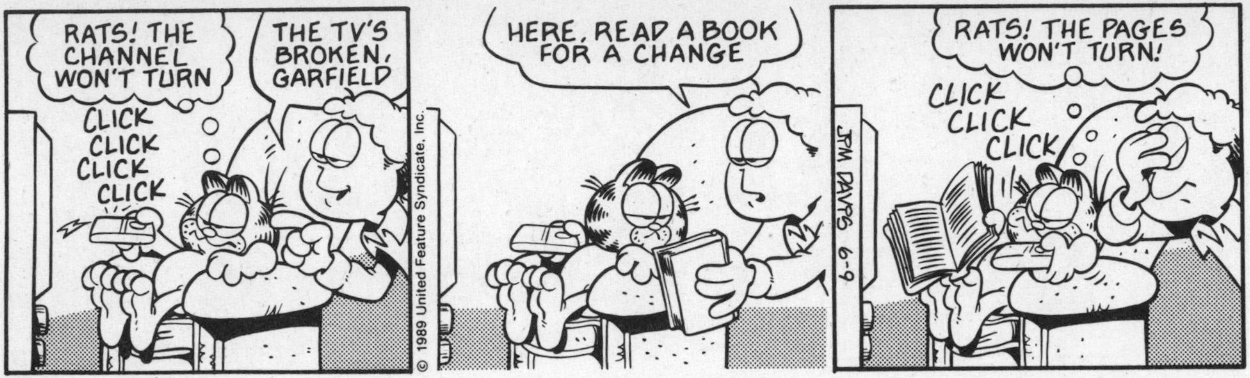
RATS! THE CHANNEL WON'T TURN
CLICK CLICK CLICK CLICK
THE TV'S BROKEN, GARFIELD
© 1989 United Feature Syndicate, Inc.
HERE, READ A BOOK FOR A CHANGE
JIM DAVIS 6-9
RATS! THE PAGES WON'T TURN!
CLICK CLICK CLICK

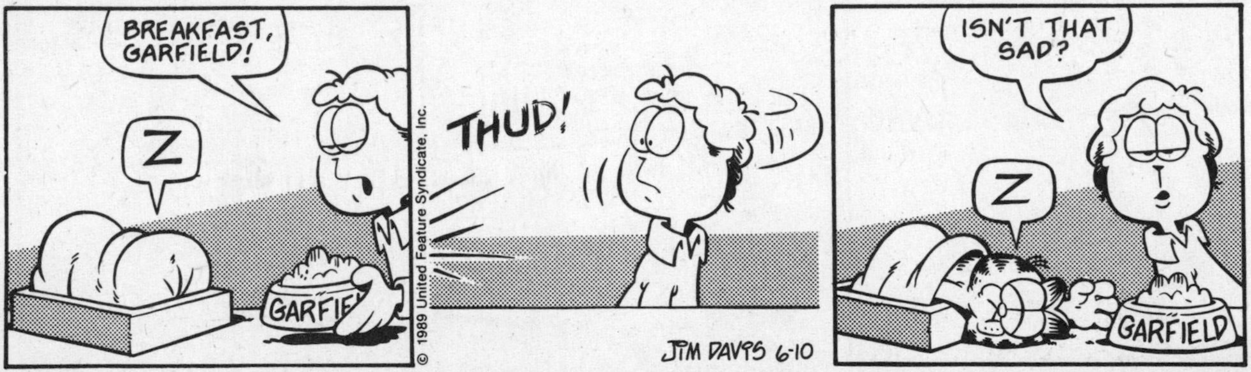
BREAKFAST, GARFIELD!
Z
GARFIELD
© 1989 United Feature Syndicate, Inc.
THUD!
JIM DAVIS 6-10
ISN'T THAT SAD?
Z
GARFIELD

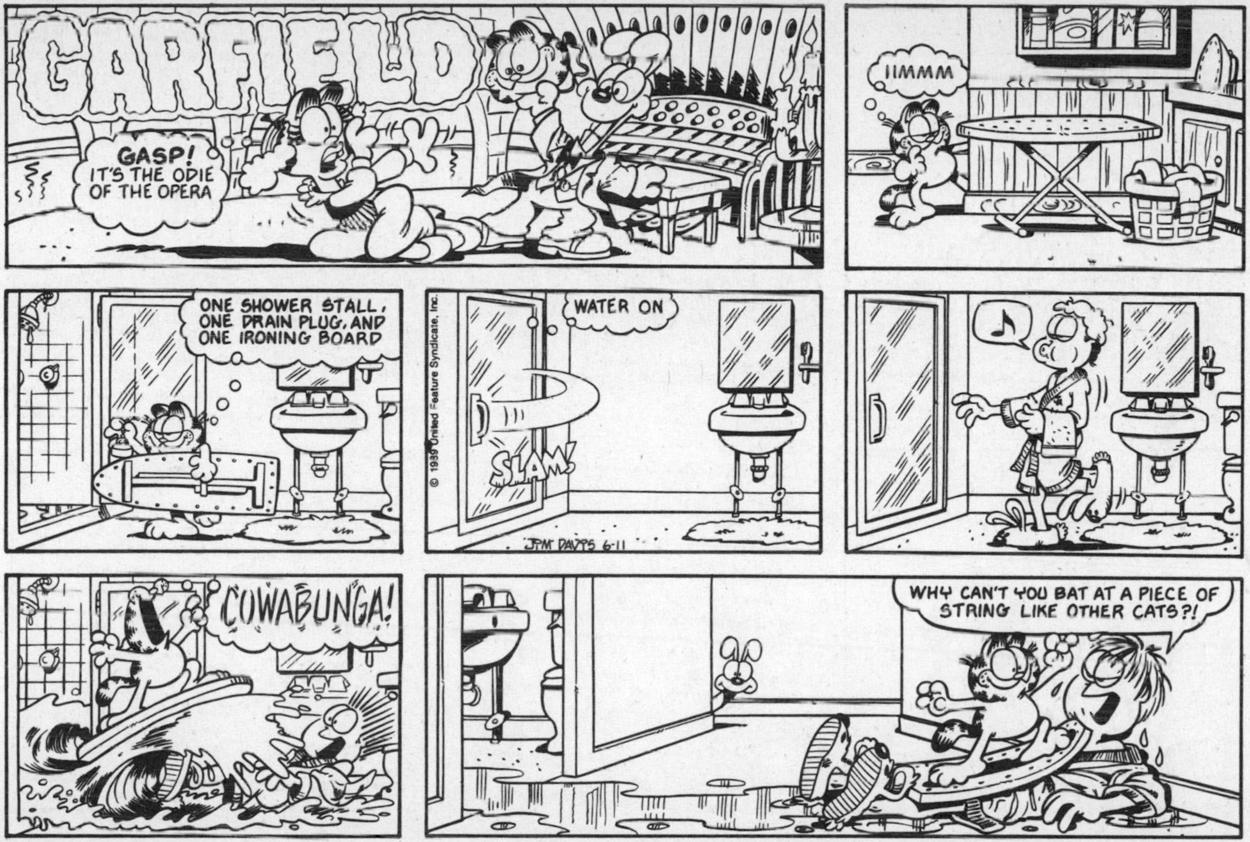
GARFIELD
GASP! IT'S THE ODIE OF THE OPERA
IIMMM
ONE SHOWER STALL, ONE DRAIN PLUG, AND ONE IRONING BOARD
© 1939 United Feature Syndicate, Inc.
WATER ON
SLAM!
JPM DAVPS 6-11
COWABUNGA!
WHY CAN'T YOU BAT AT A PIECE OF STRING LIKE OTHER CATS?!

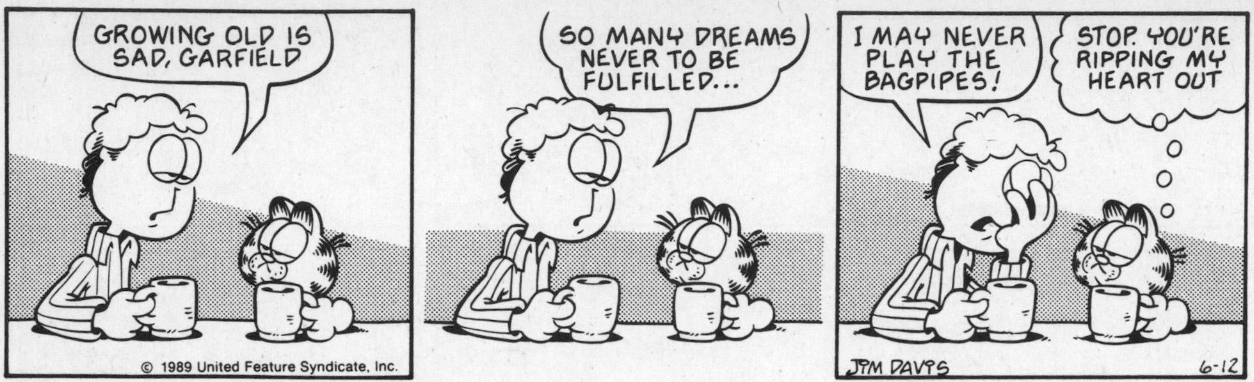
GROWING OLD IS SAD, GARFIELD
© 1989 United Feature Syndicate, Inc.
SO MANY DREAMS NEVER TO BE FULFILLED...
I MAY NEVER PLAY THE BAGPIPES!
STOP. YOU'RE RIPPING MY HEART OUT
JIM DAVIS
6-12

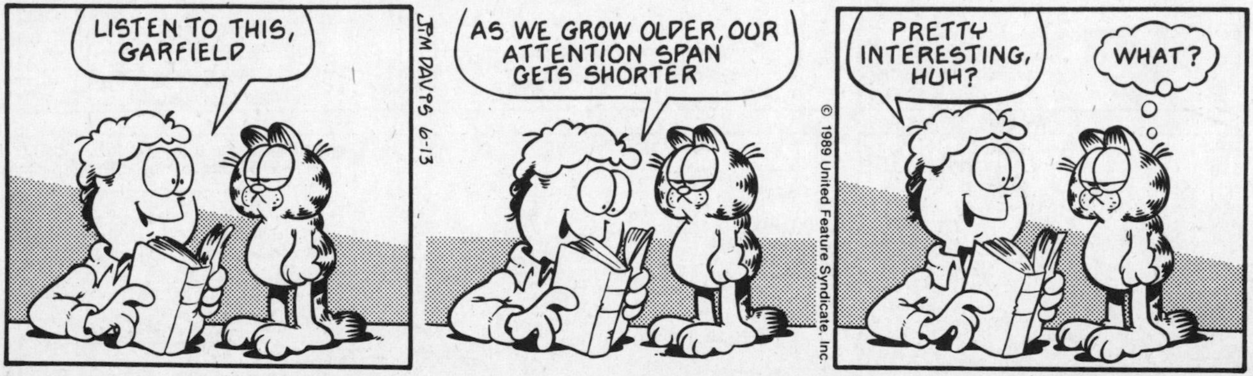
LISTEN TO THIS, GARFIELD
JIM DAVIS 6-13
AS WE GROW OLDER, OUR ATTENTION SPAN GETS SHORTER
© 1989 United Feature Syndicate, Inc.
PRETTY INTERESTING, HUH?
WHAT?

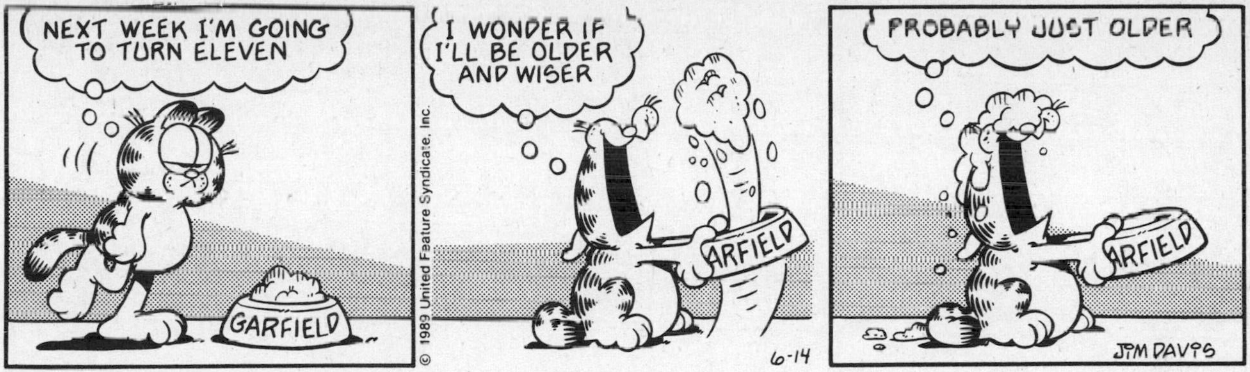
NEXT WEEK I'M GOING TO TURN ELEVEN
I WONDER IF I'LL BE OLDER AND WISER
GARFIELD
© 1989 United Feature Syndicate, Inc.
PROBABLY JUST OLDER
6-14
JIM DAVIS

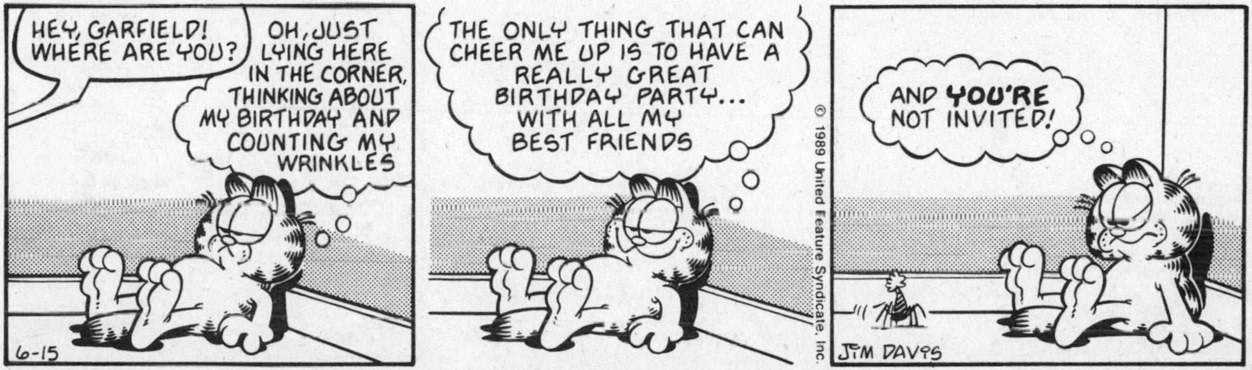
HEY, GARFIELD! WHERE ARE YOU?
OH, JUST LYING HERE IN THE CORNER, THINKING ABOUT MY BIRTHDAY AND COUNTING MY WRINKLES
6-15
THE ONLY THING THAT CAN CHEER ME UP IS TO HAVE A REALLY GREAT BIRTHDAY PARTY... WITH ALL MY BEST FRIENDS
© 1989 United Feature Syndicate, Inc.
AND **YOU'RE** NOT INVITED!
JIM DAVIS

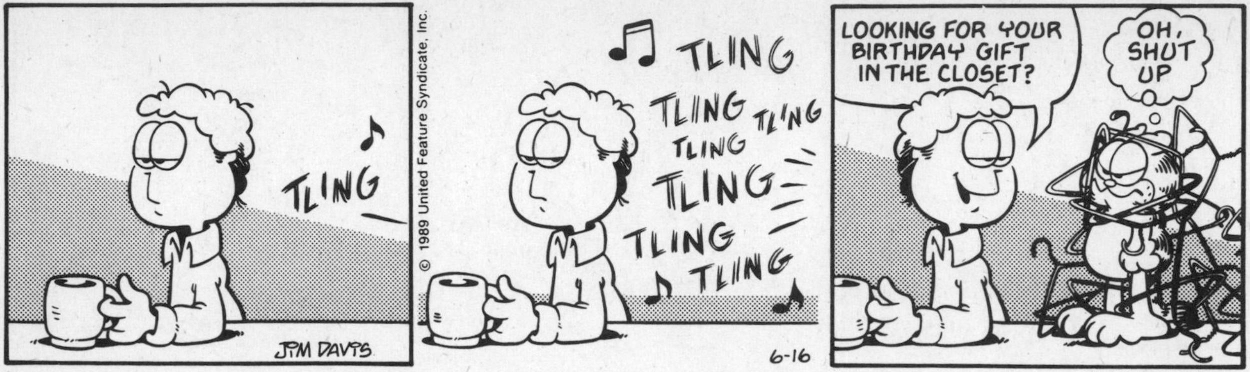
TLING
© 1989 United Feature Syndicate, Inc.
JIM DAVIS
TLING
TLING
TL'NG
TLING
TLING
TLING
TLING
6-16
LOOKING FOR YOUR BIRTHDAY GIFT IN THE CLOSET?
OH, SHUT UP

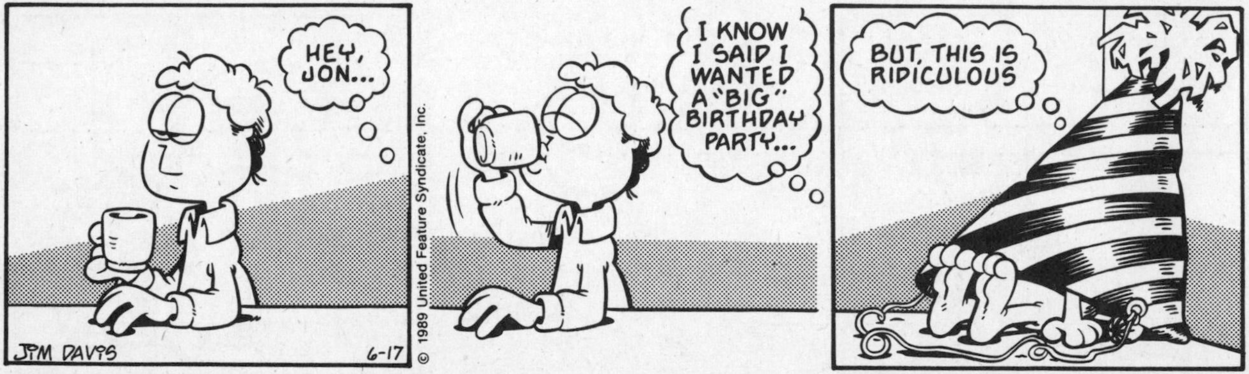
HEY, JON...
JIM DAVIS
6-17
© 1989 United Feature Syndicate, Inc.
I KNOW I SAID I WANTED A "BIG" BIRTHDAY PARTY...
BUT, THIS IS RIDICULOUS

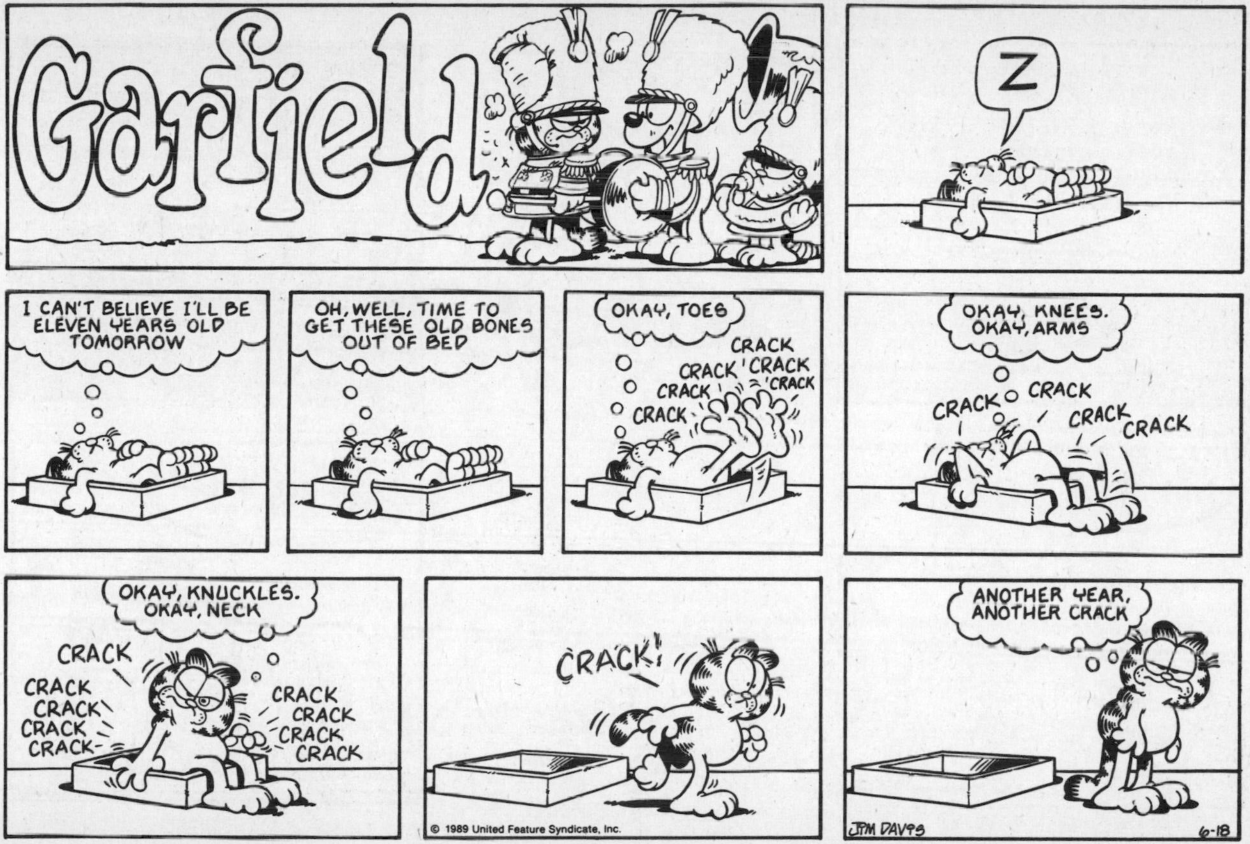
Garfield
Z
I CAN'T BELIEVE I'LL BE ELEVEN YEARS OLD TOMORROW
OH, WELL, TIME TO GET THESE OLD BONES OUT OF BED
OKAY, TOES
CRACK
CRACK
CRACK
CRACK
CRACK
CRACK
OKAY, KNEES. OKAY, ARMS
CRACK
CRACK
CRACK
CRACK
OKAY, KNUCKLES. OKAY, NECK
CRACK
CRACK
CRACK
CRACK
CRACK
CRACK
CRACK
CRACK
CRACK
CRACK
CRACK!
© 1989 United Feature Syndicate, Inc.
ANOTHER YEAR, ANOTHER CRACK
JIM DAVIS
6-18

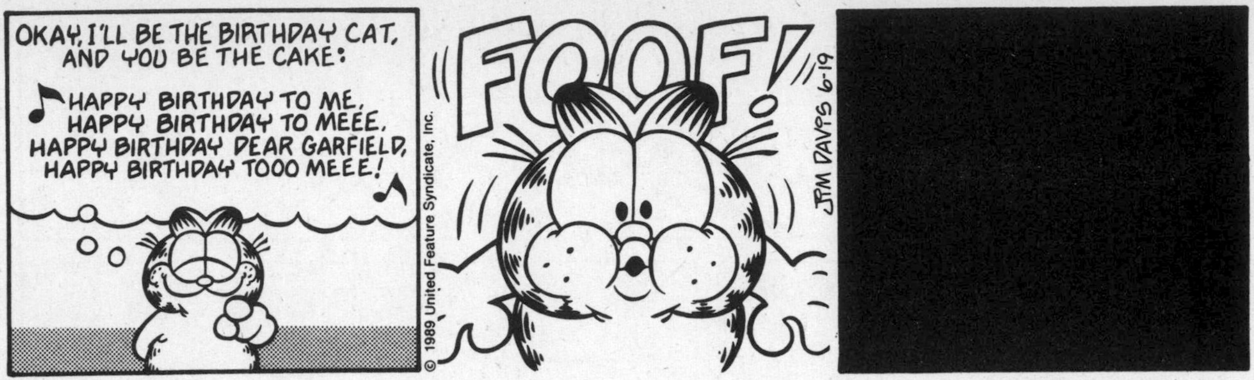
OKAY, I'LL BE THE BIRTHDAY CAT, AND YOU BE THE CAKE:
HAPPY BIRTHDAY TO ME, HAPPY BIRTHDAY TO MEEE, HAPPY BIRTHDAY DEAR GARFIELD, HAPPY BIRTHDAY TOOO MEEE!
© 1989 United Feature Syndicate, Inc.
FOOF!
JIM DAVIS 6-19

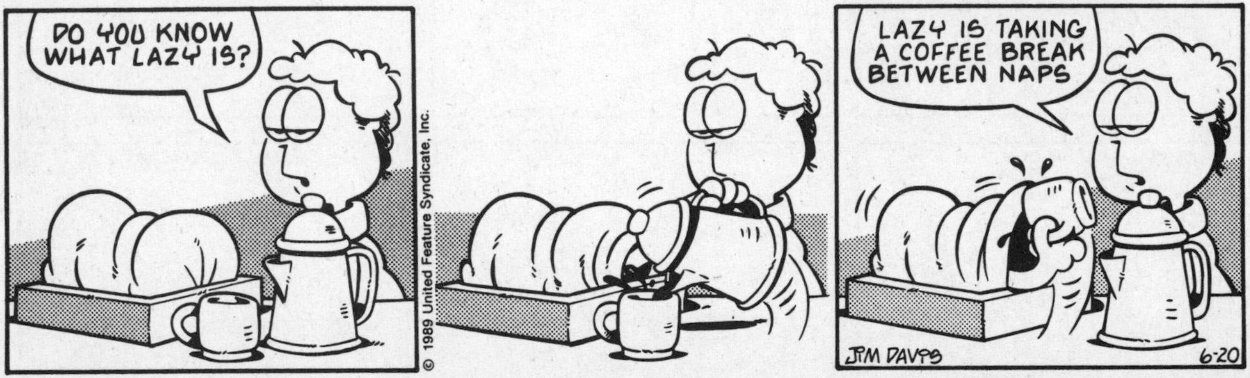
DO YOU KNOW WHAT LAZY IS?
© 1989 United Feature Syndicate, Inc.
LAZY IS TAKING A COFFEE BREAK BETWEEN NAPS
JIM DAVIS
6-20

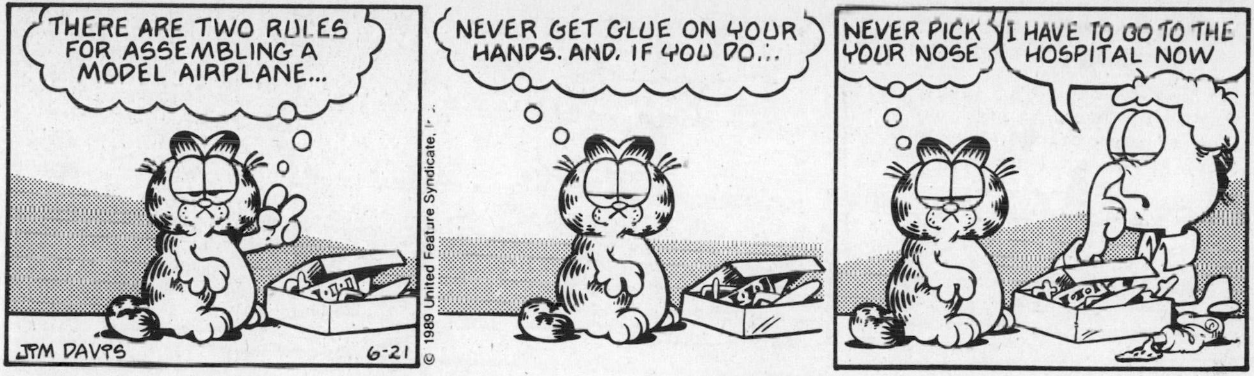
THERE ARE TWO RULES FOR ASSEMBLING A MODEL AIRPLANE...
JIM DAVIS
6-21
© 1989 United Feature Syndicate, I
NEVER GET GLUE ON YOUR HANDS. AND, IF YOU DO...
NEVER PICK YOUR NOSE
I HAVE TO GO TO THE HOSPITAL NOW

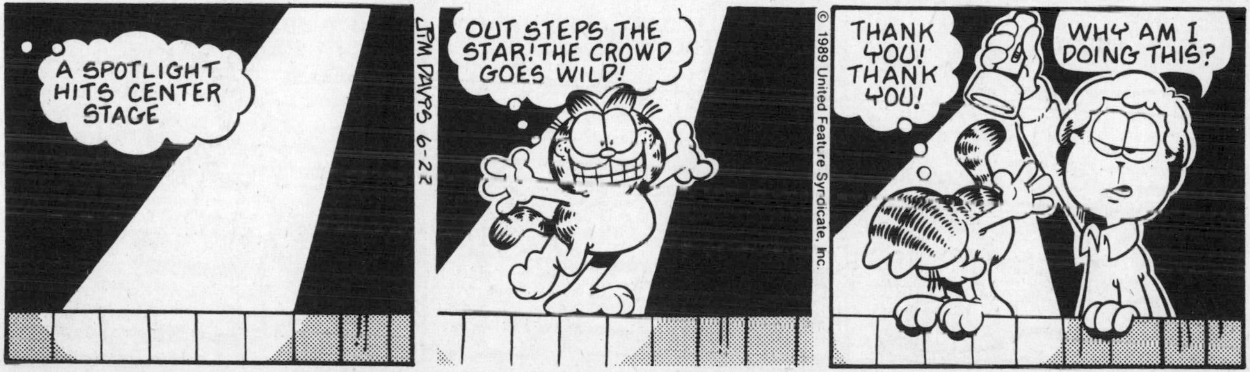
A SPOTLIGHT HITS CENTER STAGE
JIM DAVIS 6-22
OUT STEPS THE STAR! THE CROWD GOES WILD!
© 1989 United Feature Syndicate, Inc.
THANK YOU! THANK YOU!
WHY AM I DOING THIS?

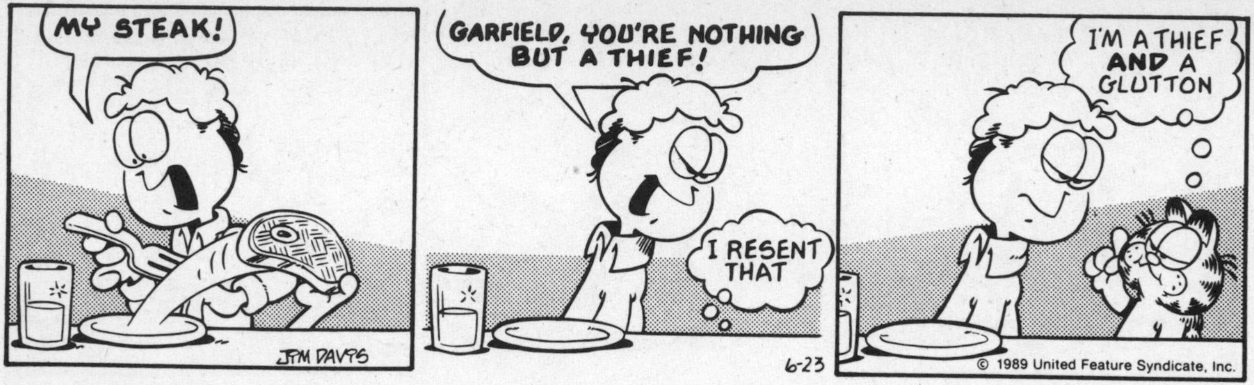
MY STEAK!
JIM DAVIS
GARFIELD, YOU'RE NOTHING BUT A THIEF!
I RESENT THAT
6-23
I'M A THIEF AND A GLUTTON
© 1989 United Feature Syndicate, Inc.

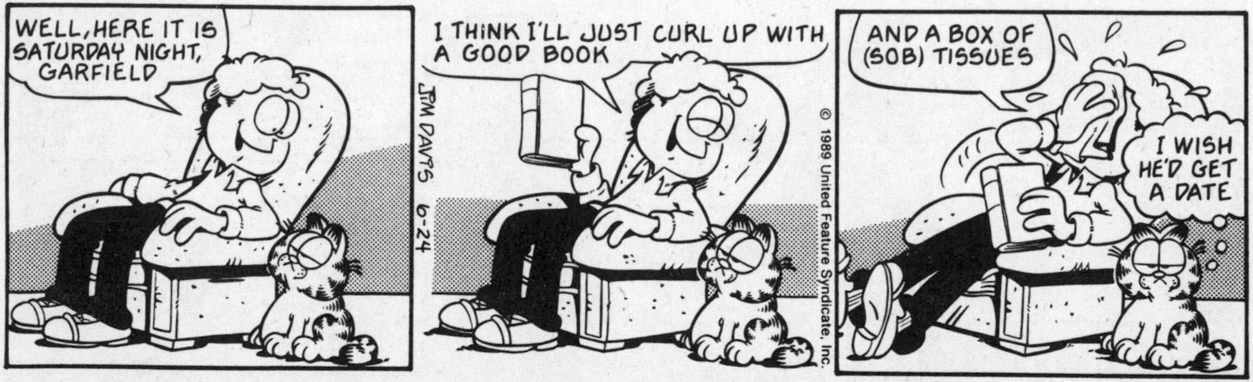
WELL, HERE IT IS SATURDAY NIGHT, GARFIELD
JIM DAVIS 6-24
I THINK I'LL JUST CURL UP WITH A GOOD BOOK
© 1989 United Feature Syndicate, Inc.
AND A BOX OF (SOB) TISSUES
I WISH HE'D GET A DATE

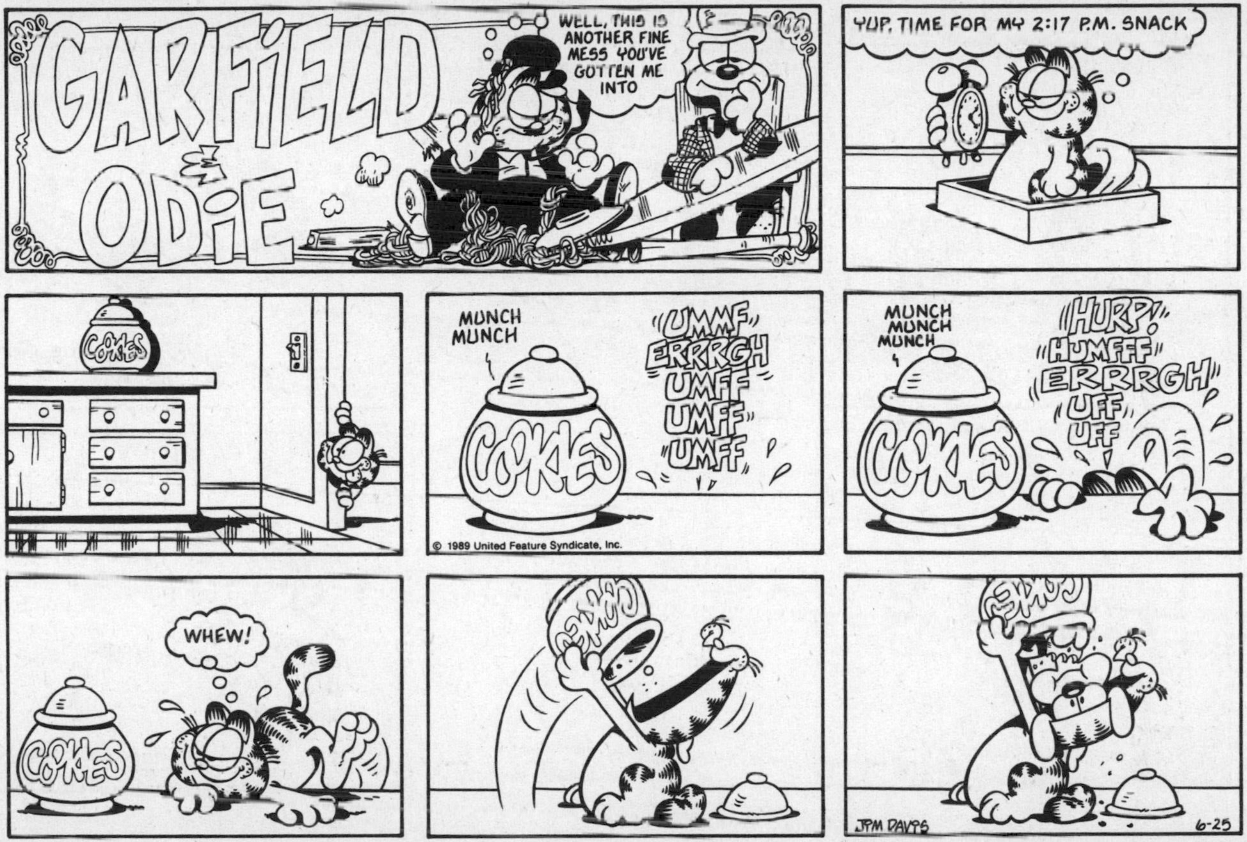
GARFIELD & ODIE
WELL, THIS IS ANOTHER FINE MESS YOU'VE GOTTEN ME INTO
YUP, TIME FOR MY 2:17 P.M. SNACK
COOKIES
MUNCH MUNCH
UMMF ERRRGH UMFF UMFF UMFF
MUNCH MUNCH MUNCH
HURP! HUMFFF ERRRGH UFF UFF
WHEW!
© 1989 United Feature Syndicate, Inc.
JPM DAVPS
6-25

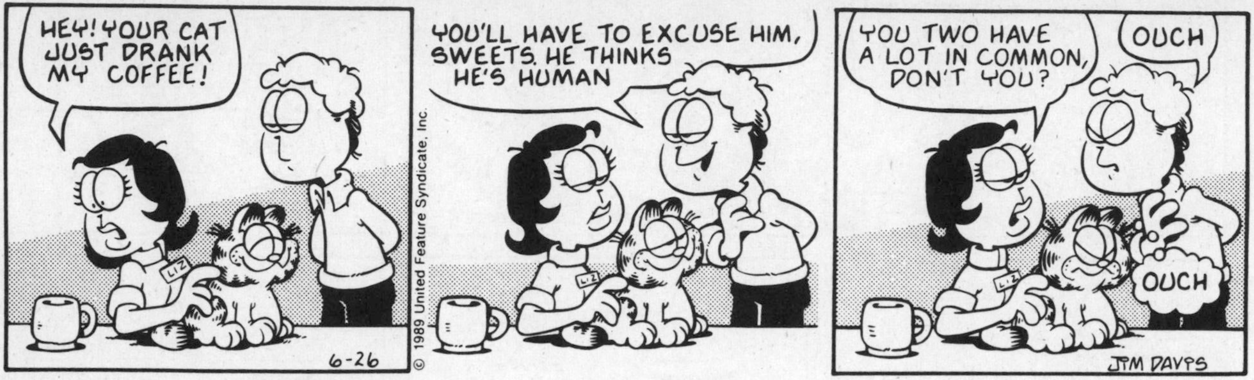
HEY! YOUR CAT JUST DRANK MY COFFEE!
6-26
© 1989 United Feature Syndicate, Inc.
YOU'LL HAVE TO EXCUSE HIM, SWEETS. HE THINKS HE'S HUMAN
YOU TWO HAVE A LOT IN COMMON, DON'T YOU?
OUCH
OUCH
JIM DAVIS

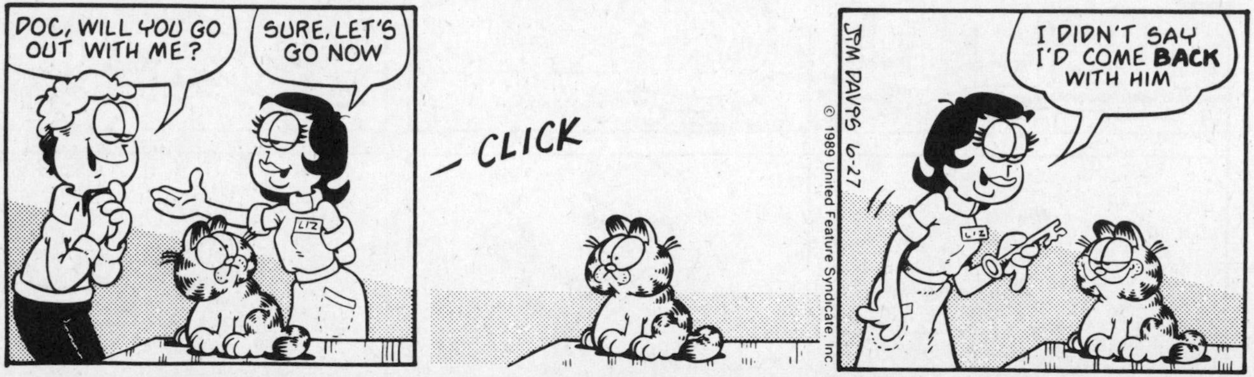
DOC, WILL YOU GO OUT WITH ME?
SURE, LET'S GO NOW
— CLICK
JIM DAVIS 6-27
© 1989 United Feature Syndicate, Inc.
I DIDN'T SAY I'D COME **BACK** WITH HIM

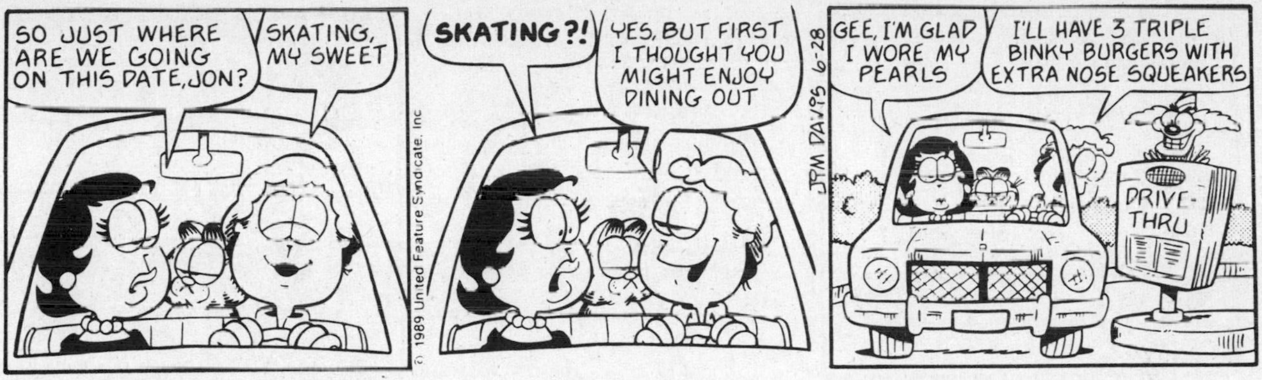
SO JUST WHERE ARE WE GOING ON THIS DATE, JON?
SKATING, MY SWEET
SKATING?!
YES, BUT FIRST I THOUGHT YOU MIGHT ENJOY DINING OUT
GEE, I'M GLAD I WORE MY PEARLS
I'LL HAVE 3 TRIPLE BINKY BURGERS WITH EXTRA NOSE SQUEAKERS
DRIVE-THRU
JIM DAVIS 6-28
© 1989 United Feature Syndicate, Inc

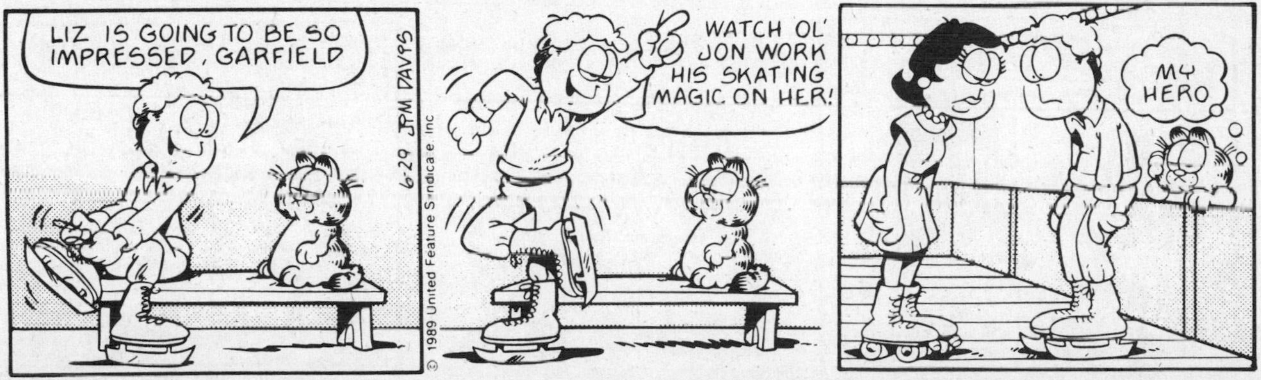
LIZ IS GOING TO BE SO IMPRESSED, GARFIELD
WATCH OL' JON WORK HIS SKATING MAGIC ON HER!
MY HERO
JIM DAVIS 6-29
© 1989 United Feature Syndicate, Inc

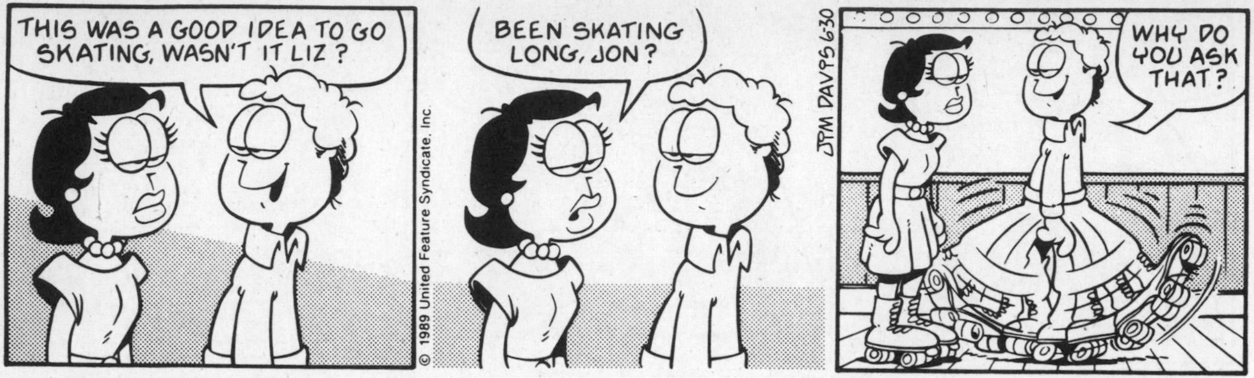
THIS WAS A GOOD IDEA TO GO SKATING, WASN'T IT LIZ?
BEEN SKATING LONG, JON?
WHY DO YOU ASK THAT?
JIM DAVIS 6-30
© 1989 United Feature Syndicate, Inc.

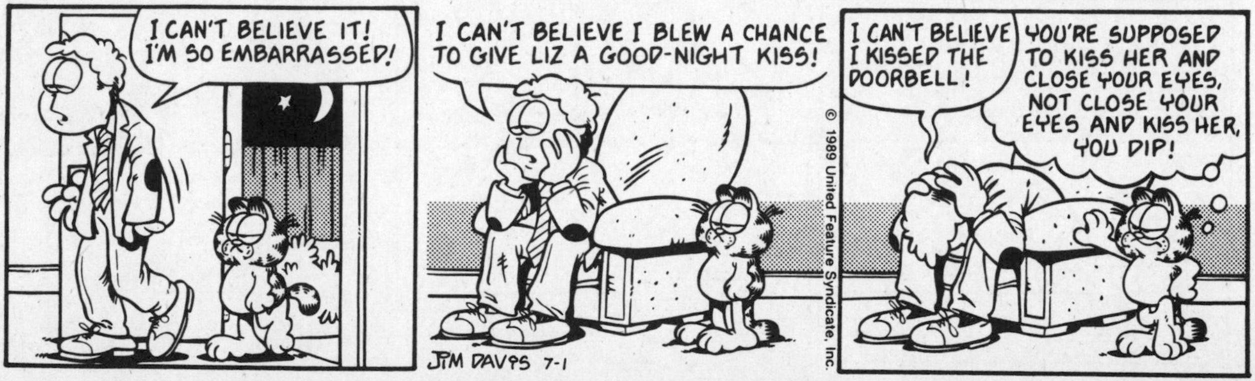
I CAN'T BELIEVE IT! I'M SO EMBARRASSED!
I CAN'T BELIEVE I BLEW A CHANCE TO GIVE LIZ A GOOD-NIGHT KISS!
I CAN'T BELIEVE I KISSED THE DOORBELL!
YOU'RE SUPPOSED TO KISS HER AND CLOSE YOUR EYES, NOT CLOSE YOUR EYES AND KISS HER, YOU DIP!
JIM DAVIS 7-1
© 1989 United Feature Syndicate, Inc.

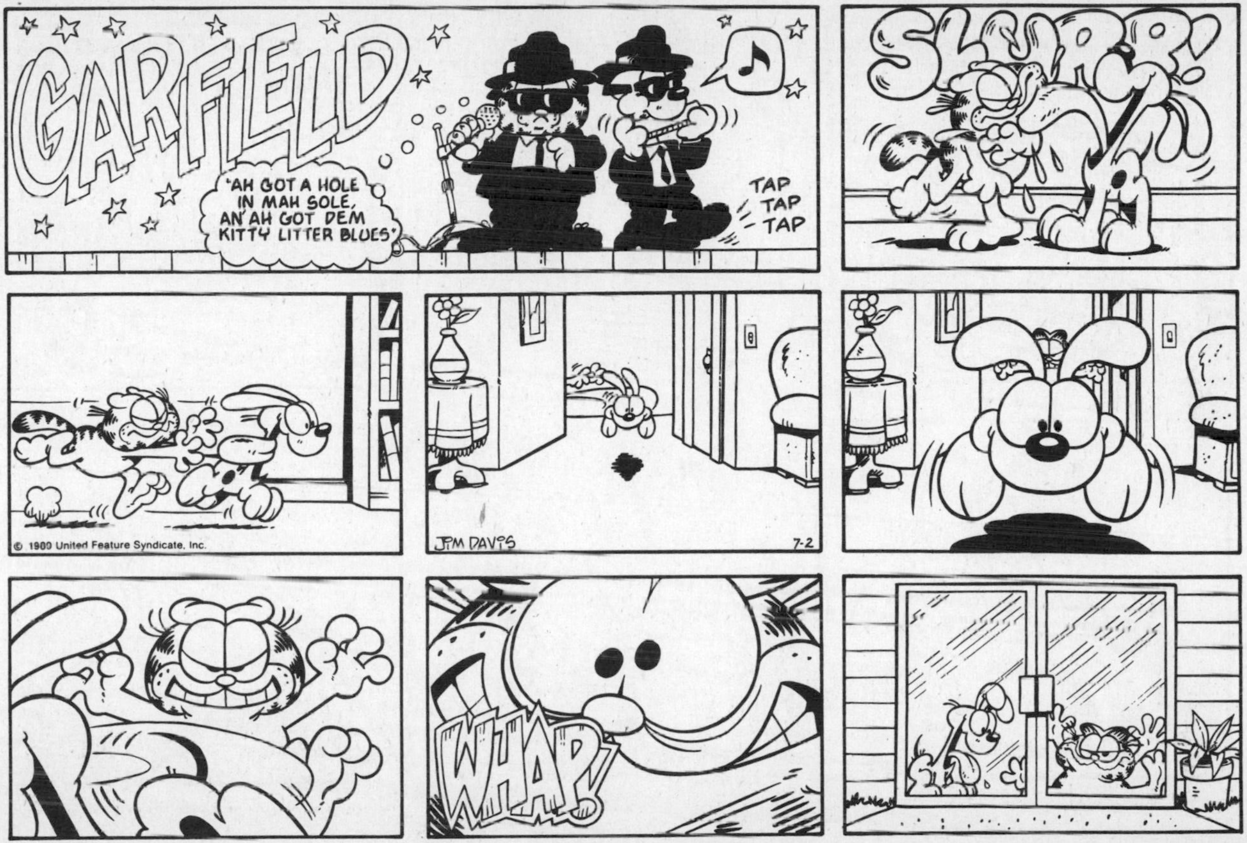
GARFIELD
"AH GOT A HOLE IN MAH SOLE, AN' AH GOT DEM KITTY LITTER BLUES"
TAP TAP TAP
SLURP!
© 1980 United Feature Syndicate, Inc.
JIM DAVIS 7-2
WHAP!

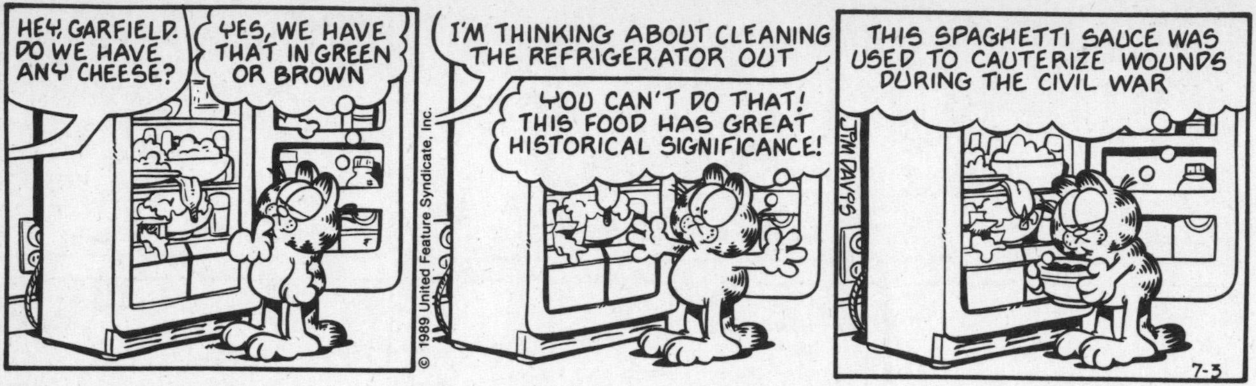
HEY, GARFIELD. DO WE HAVE ANY CHEESE?
YES, WE HAVE THAT IN GREEN OR BROWN
I'M THINKING ABOUT CLEANING THE REFRIGERATOR OUT
YOU CAN'T DO THAT! THIS FOOD HAS GREAT HISTORICAL SIGNIFICANCE!
THIS SPAGHETTI SAUCE WAS USED TO CAUTERIZE WOUNDS DURING THE CIVIL WAR
JIM DAVIS
7-3
© 1989 United Feature Syndicate, Inc.

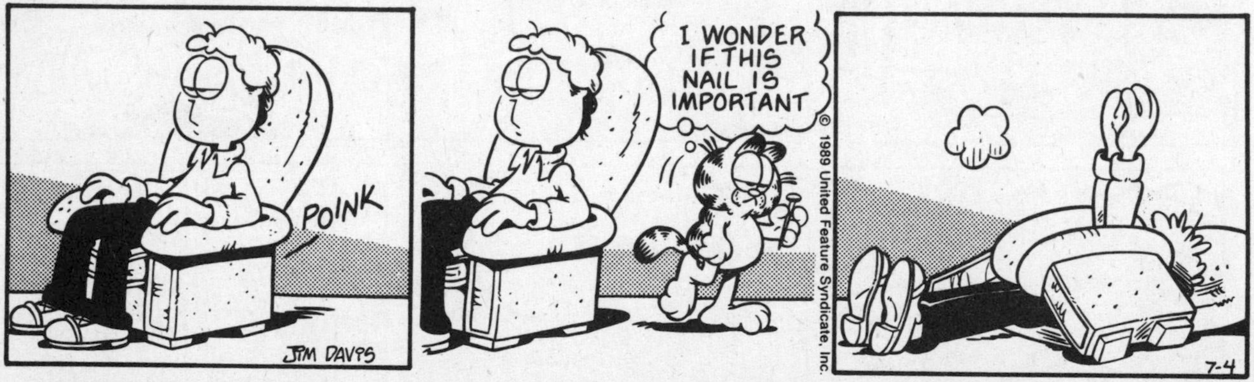
POINK
JIM DAVIS
I WONDER IF THIS NAIL IS IMPORTANT
7-4
© 1989 United Feature Syndicate, Inc.

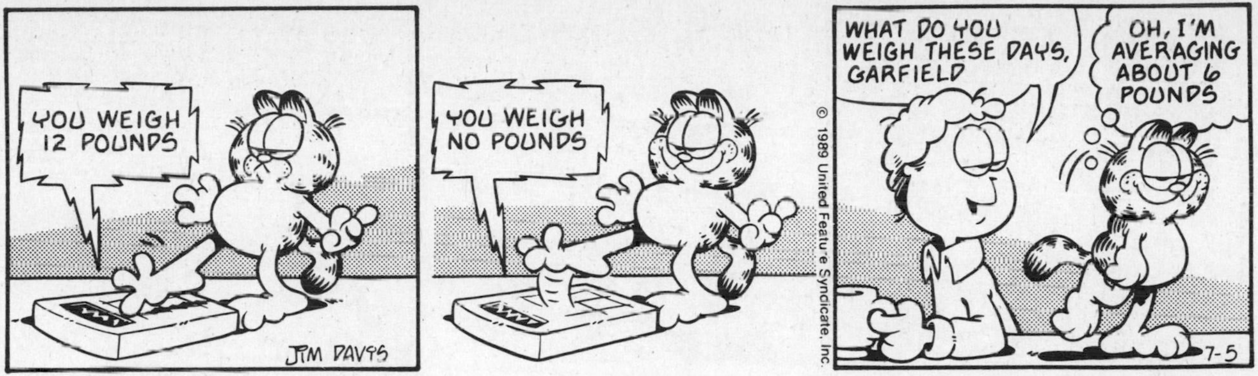
YOU WEIGH 12 POUNDS
JIM DAVIS
YOU WEIGH NO POUNDS
© 1989 United Feature Syndicate, Inc.
WHAT DO YOU WEIGH THESE DAYS, GARFIELD
OH, I'M AVERAGING ABOUT 6 POUNDS
7-5

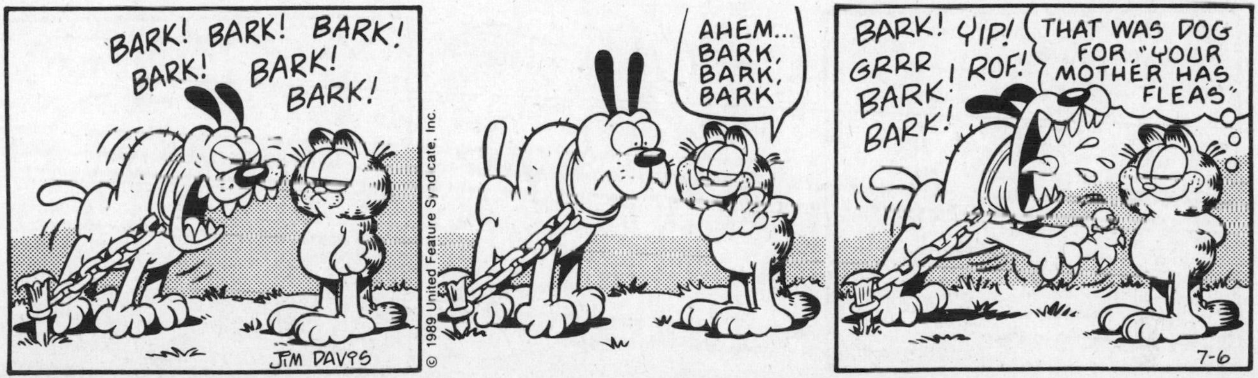
BARK! BARK! BARK! BARK! BARK! BARK!
JIM DAVIS
© 1989 United Feature Syndicate, Inc.
AHEM... BARK, BARK, BARK
BARK! YIP! GRRR ROF! BARK! BARK!
THAT WAS DOG FOR "YOUR MOTHER HAS FLEAS"
7-6

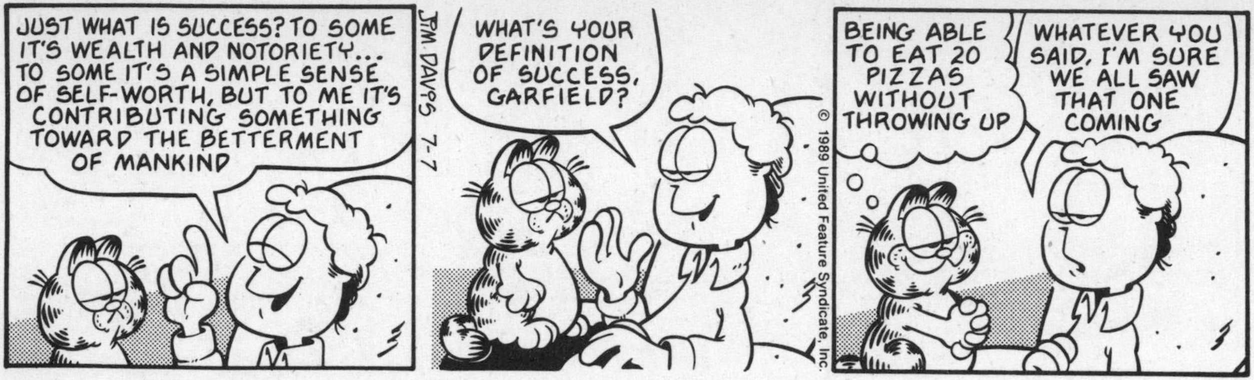
JUST WHAT IS SUCCESS? TO SOME IT'S WEALTH AND NOTORIETY... TO SOME IT'S A SIMPLE SENSE OF SELF-WORTH, BUT TO ME IT'S CONTRIBUTING SOMETHING TOWARD THE BETTERMENT OF MANKIND
JIM DAVIS 7-7
WHAT'S YOUR DEFINITION OF SUCCESS, GARFIELD?
© 1989 United Feature Syndicate, Inc.
BEING ABLE TO EAT 20 PIZZAS WITHOUT THROWING UP
WHATEVER YOU SAID, I'M SURE WE ALL SAW THAT ONE COMING

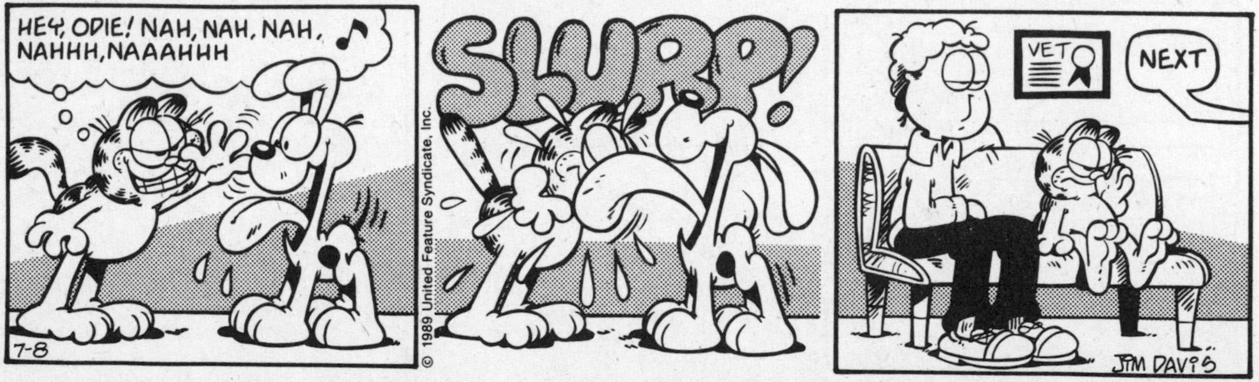
HEY, ODIE! NAH, NAH, NAH, NAHHH, NAAAHHH ♪
7-8
© 1989 United Feature Syndicate, Inc.
SLURP!
VET
NEXT
JIM DAVIS

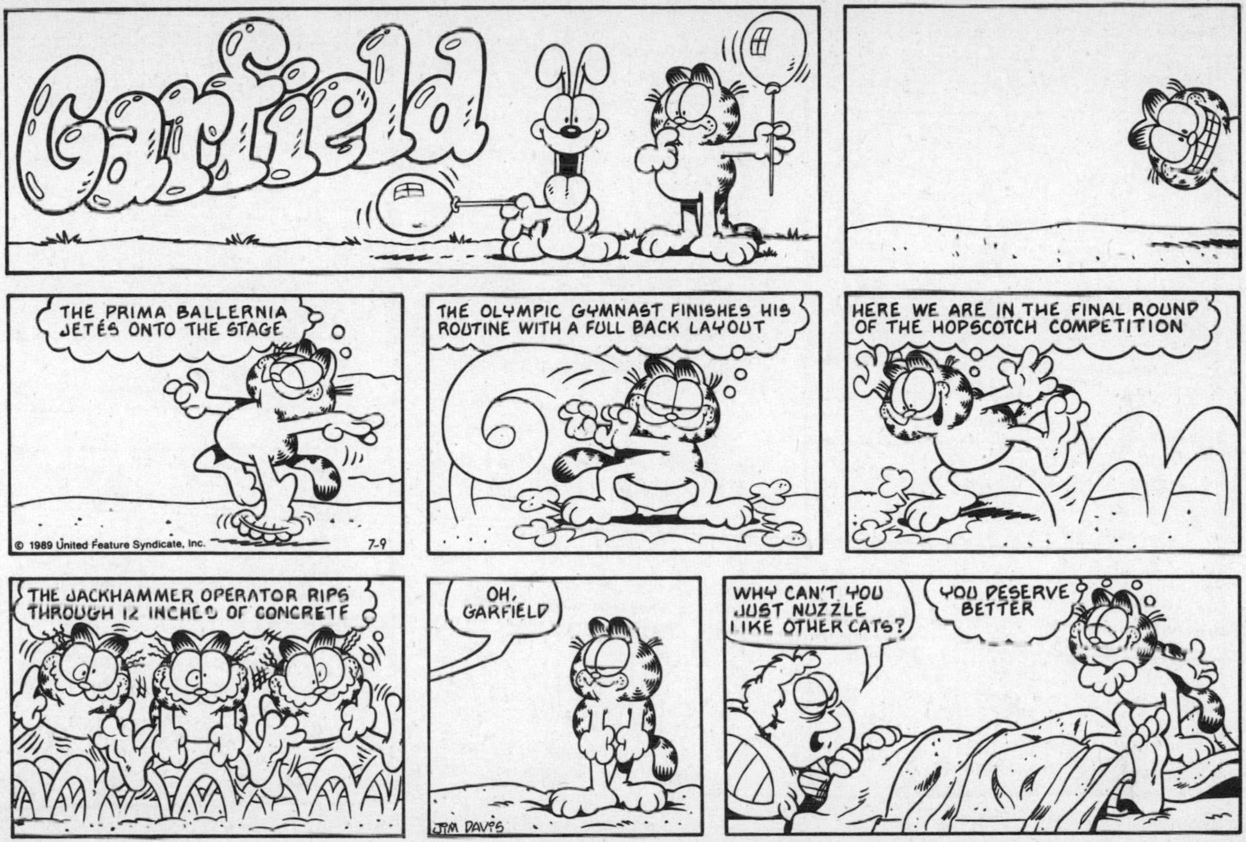
Garfield
THE PRIMA BALLERNIA JETÉS ONTO THE STAGE
© 1989 United Feature Syndicate, Inc.
7-9
THE OLYMPIC GYMNAST FINISHES HIS ROUTINE WITH A FULL BACK LAYOUT
HERE WE ARE IN THE FINAL ROUND OF THE HOPSCOTCH COMPETITION
THE JACKHAMMER OPERATOR RIPS THROUGH 12 INCHES OF CONCRETE
OH, GARFIELD
JIM DAVIS
WHY CAN'T YOU JUST NUZZLE LIKE OTHER CATS?
YOU DESERVE BETTER

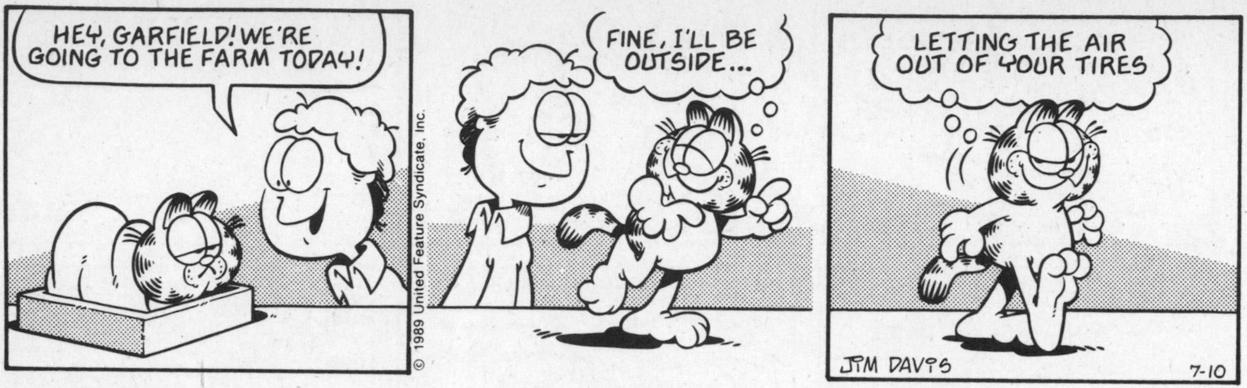

HEY, GARFIELD! WE'RE GOING TO THE FARM TODAY!
© 1989 United Feature Syndicate, Inc.
FINE, I'LL BE OUTSIDE...
LETTING THE AIR OUT OF YOUR TIRES
JIM DAVIS
7-10

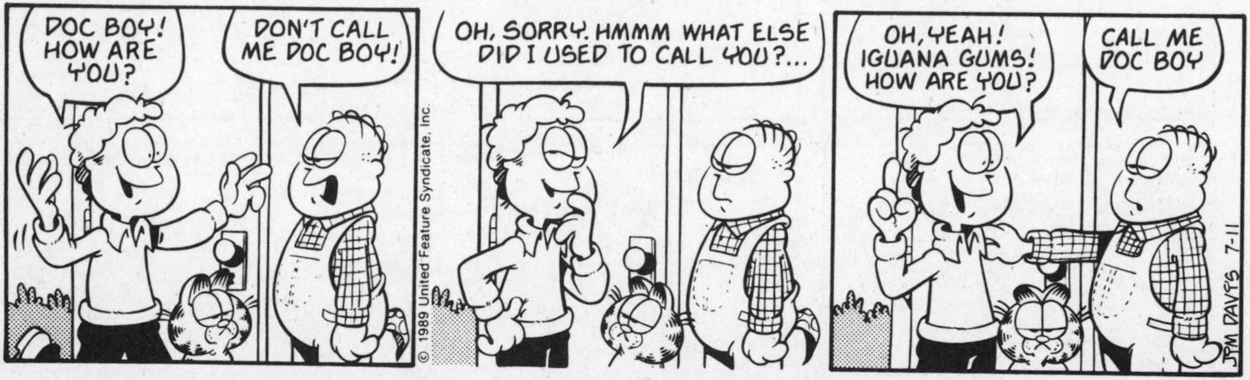

DOC BOY! HOW ARE YOU?
DON'T CALL ME DOC BOY!
© 1989 United Feature Syndicate, Inc.
OH, SORRY. HMMM WHAT ELSE DID I USED TO CALL YOU?...
OH, YEAH! IGUANA GUMS! HOW ARE YOU?
CALL ME DOC BOY
JIM DAVIS
7-11

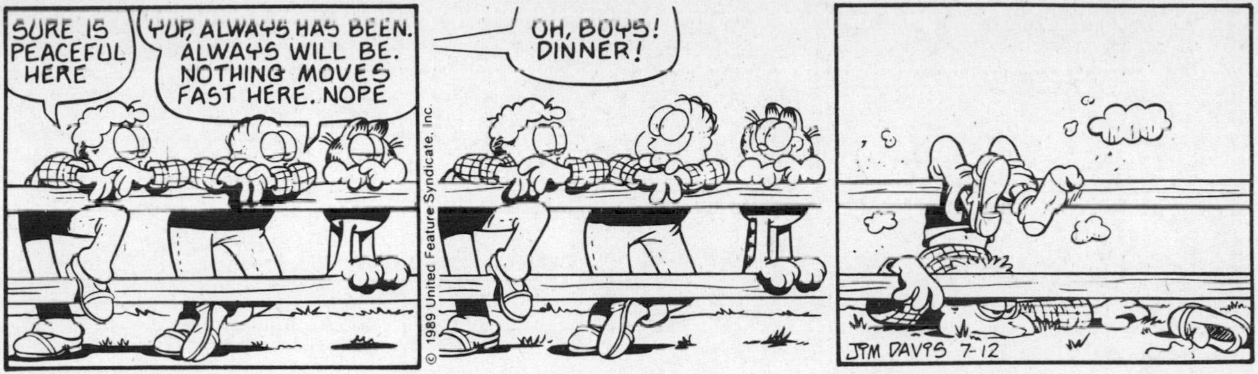
SURE IS PEACEFUL HERE
YUP, ALWAYS HAS BEEN. ALWAYS WILL BE. NOTHING MOVES FAST HERE. NOPE
© 1989 United Feature Syndicate, Inc.
OH, BOYS! DINNER!
JIM DAVIS 7-12

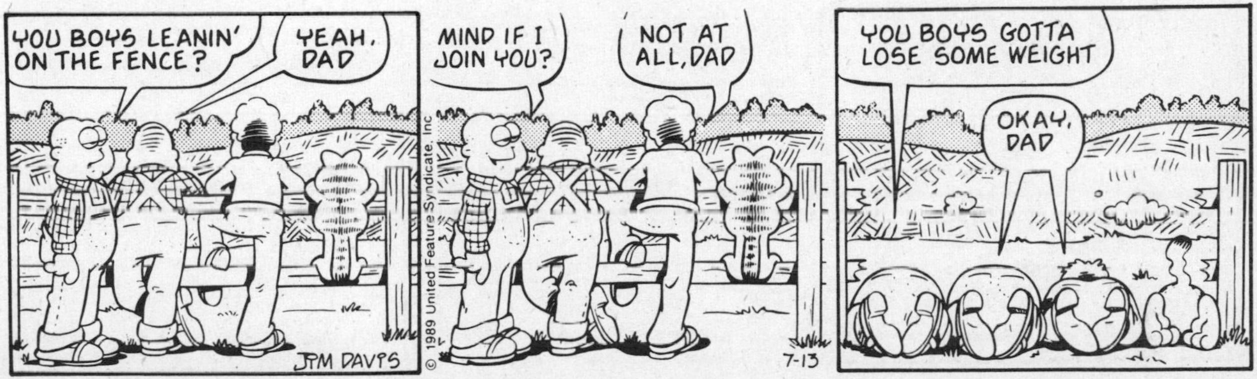
YOU BOYS LEANIN' ON THE FENCE?
YEAH, DAD
JIM DAVIS
© 1989 United Feature Syndicate, Inc.
MIND IF I JOIN YOU?
NOT AT ALL, DAD
7-13
YOU BOYS GOTTA LOSE SOME WEIGHT
OKAY, DAD

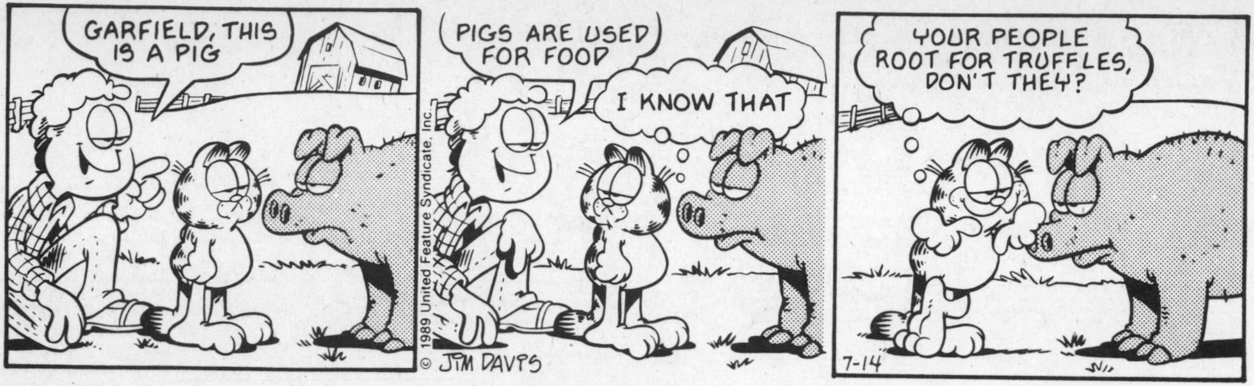
GARFIELD, THIS IS A PIG
PIGS ARE USED FOR FOOD
I KNOW THAT
YOUR PEOPLE ROOT FOR TRUFFLES, DON'T THEY?
© 1989 United Feature Syndicate, Inc.
JIM DAVIS
7-14

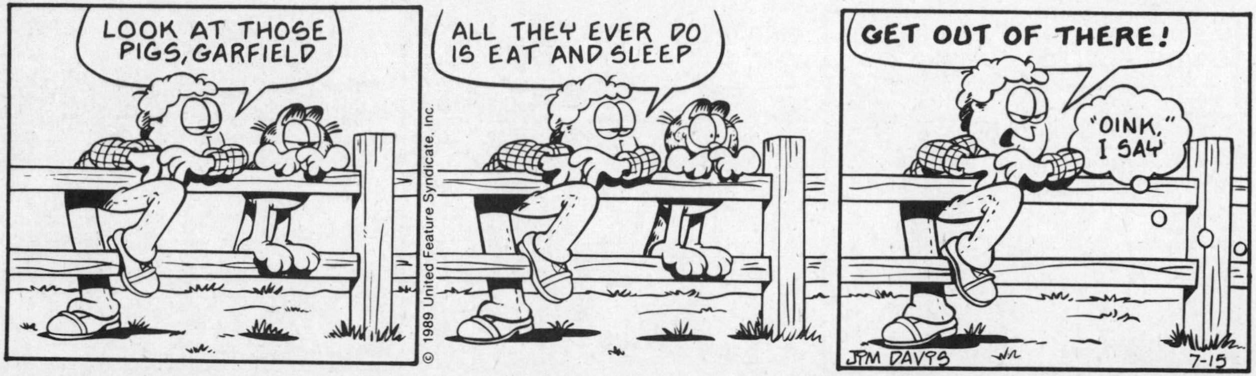
LOOK AT THOSE PIGS, GARFIELD
ALL THEY EVER DO IS EAT AND SLEEP
GET OUT OF THERE!
"OINK," I SAY
© 1989 United Feature Syndicate, Inc.
JIM DAVIS
7-15

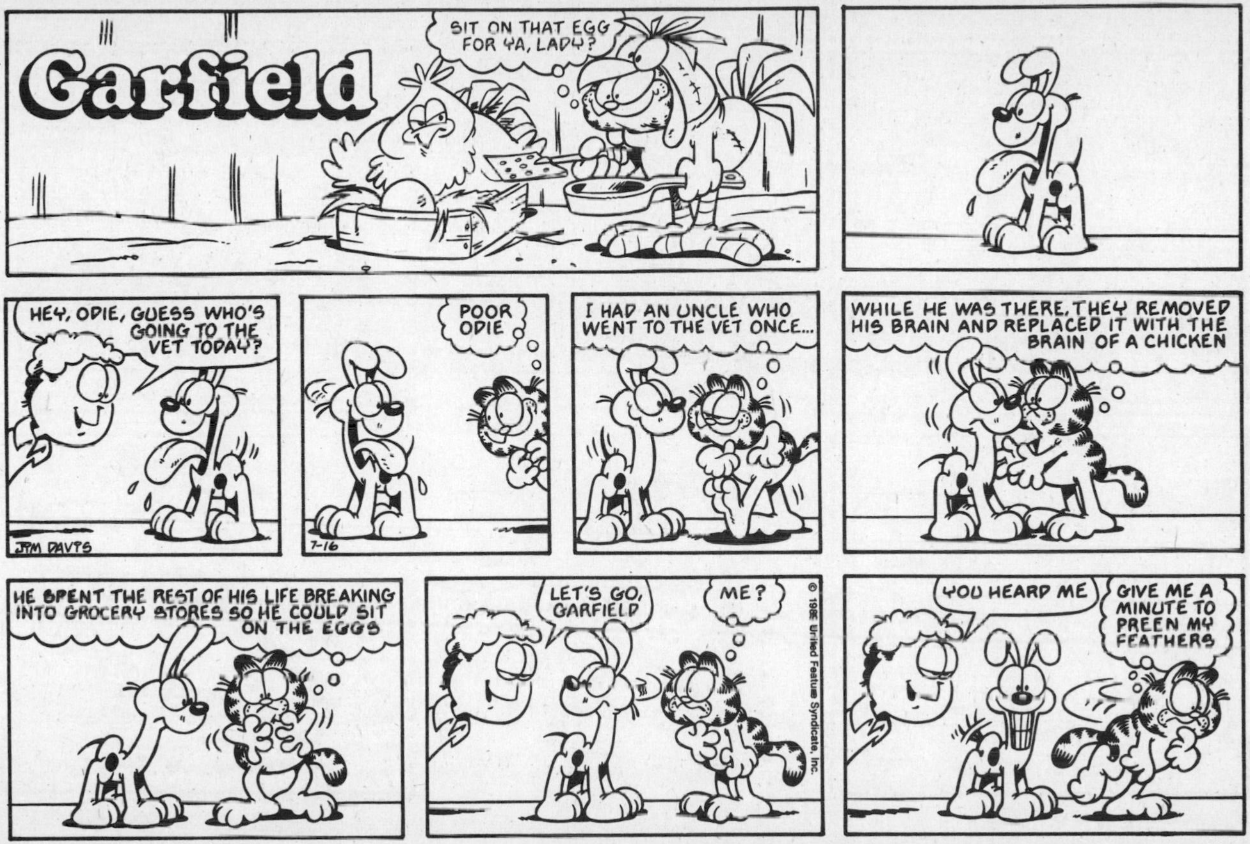
Garfield
SIT ON THAT EGG FOR YA, LADY?
HEY, ODIE, GUESS WHO'S GOING TO THE VET TODAY?
JPM DAVPS
POOR ODIE
7-16
I HAD AN UNCLE WHO WENT TO THE VET ONCE...
WHILE HE WAS THERE, THEY REMOVED HIS BRAIN AND REPLACED IT WITH THE BRAIN OF A CHICKEN
HE SPENT THE REST OF HIS LIFE BREAKING INTO GROCERY STORES SO HE COULD SIT ON THE EGGS
LET'S GO, GARFIELD
ME?
© United Feature Syndicate, Inc.
YOU HEARD ME
GIVE ME A MINUTE TO PREEN MY FEATHERS

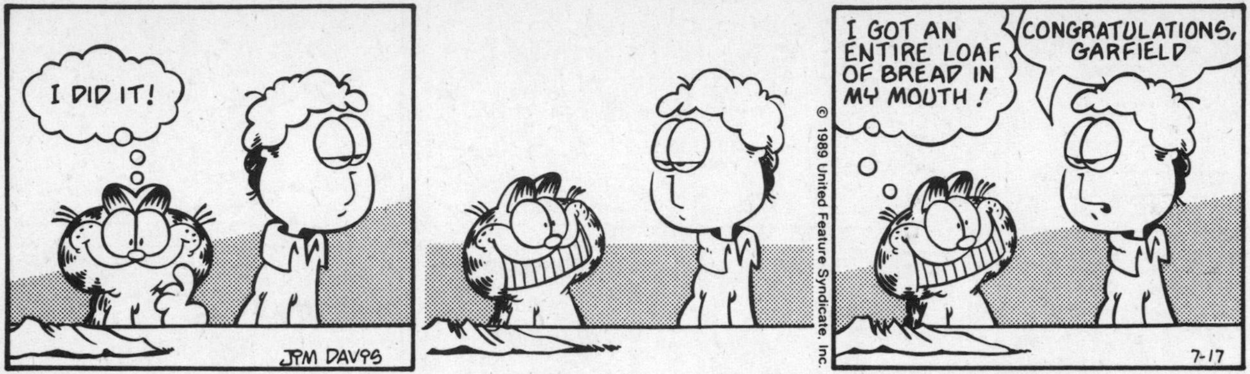
I DID IT!
JIM DAVIS
I GOT AN ENTIRE LOAF OF BREAD IN MY MOUTH!
CONGRATULATIONS, GARFIELD
7-17

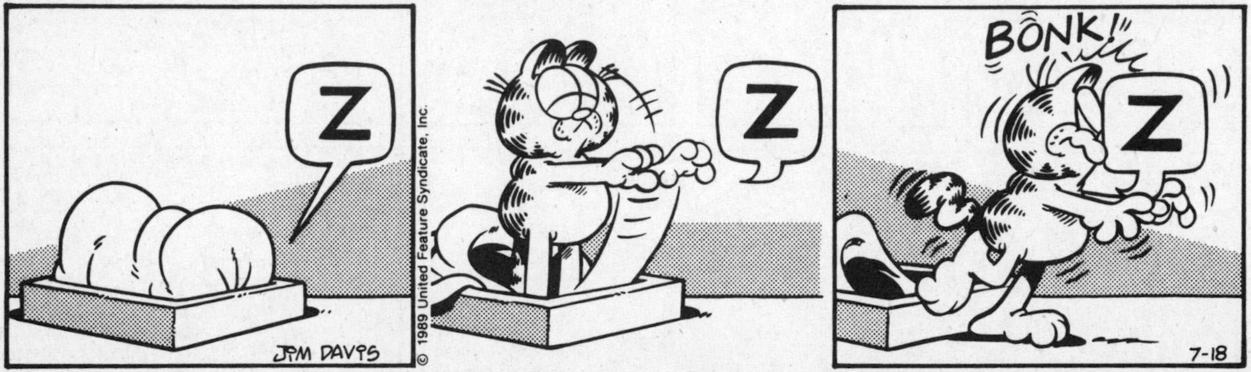
Z
JIM DAVIS
Z
BONK!
Z
7-18

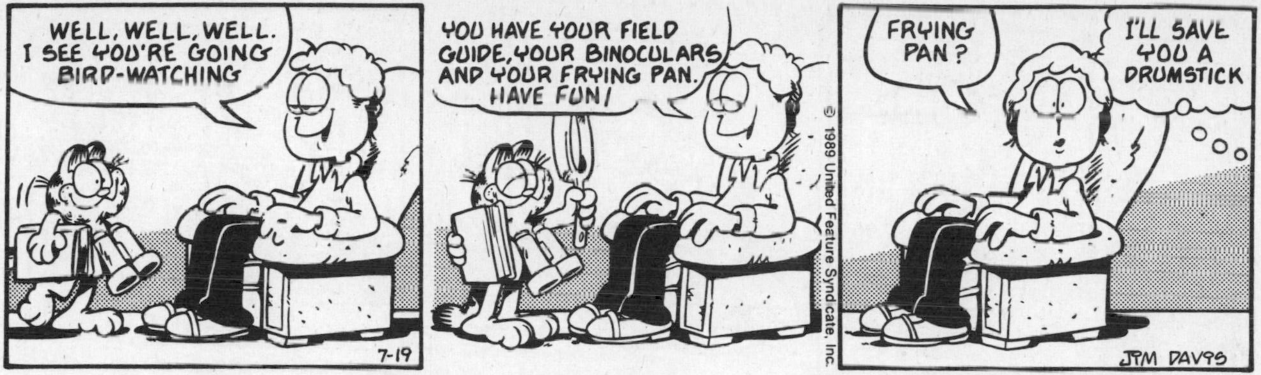
WELL, WELL, WELL. I SEE YOU'RE GOING BIRD-WATCHING
YOU HAVE YOUR FIELD GUIDE, YOUR BINOCULARS AND YOUR FRYING PAN. HAVE FUN!
FRYING PAN?
I'LL SAVE YOU A DRUMSTICK
7-19
JIM DAVIS

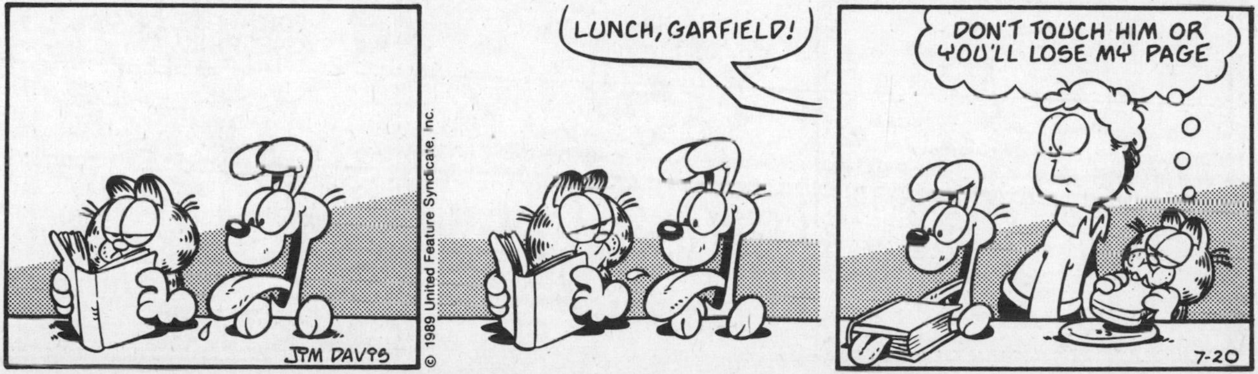
JIM DAVIS
LUNCH, GARFIELD!
DON'T TOUCH HIM OR YOU'LL LOSE MY PAGE
7-20

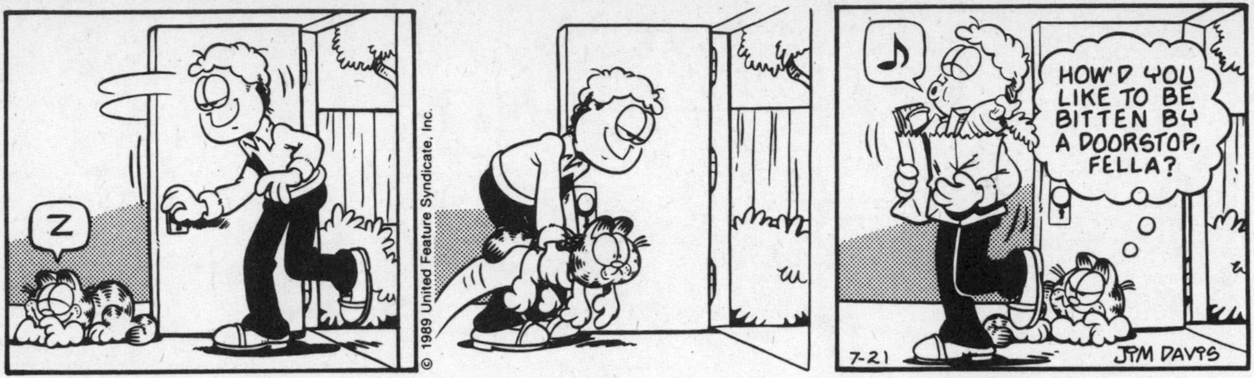
Z
♪
HOW'D YOU LIKE TO BE BITTEN BY A DOORSTOP, FELLA?
7-21
JIM DAVIS

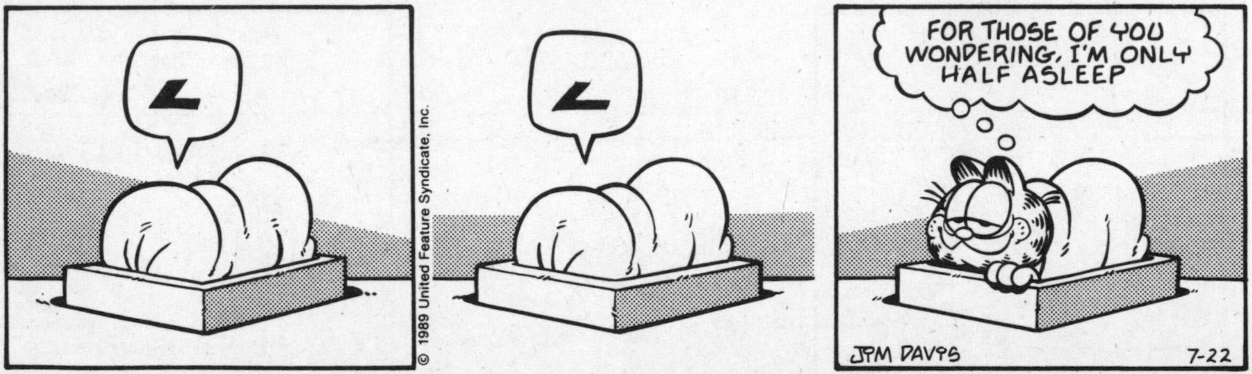
FOR THOSE OF YOU WONDERING, I'M ONLY HALF ASLEEP
JIM DAVIS
7-22

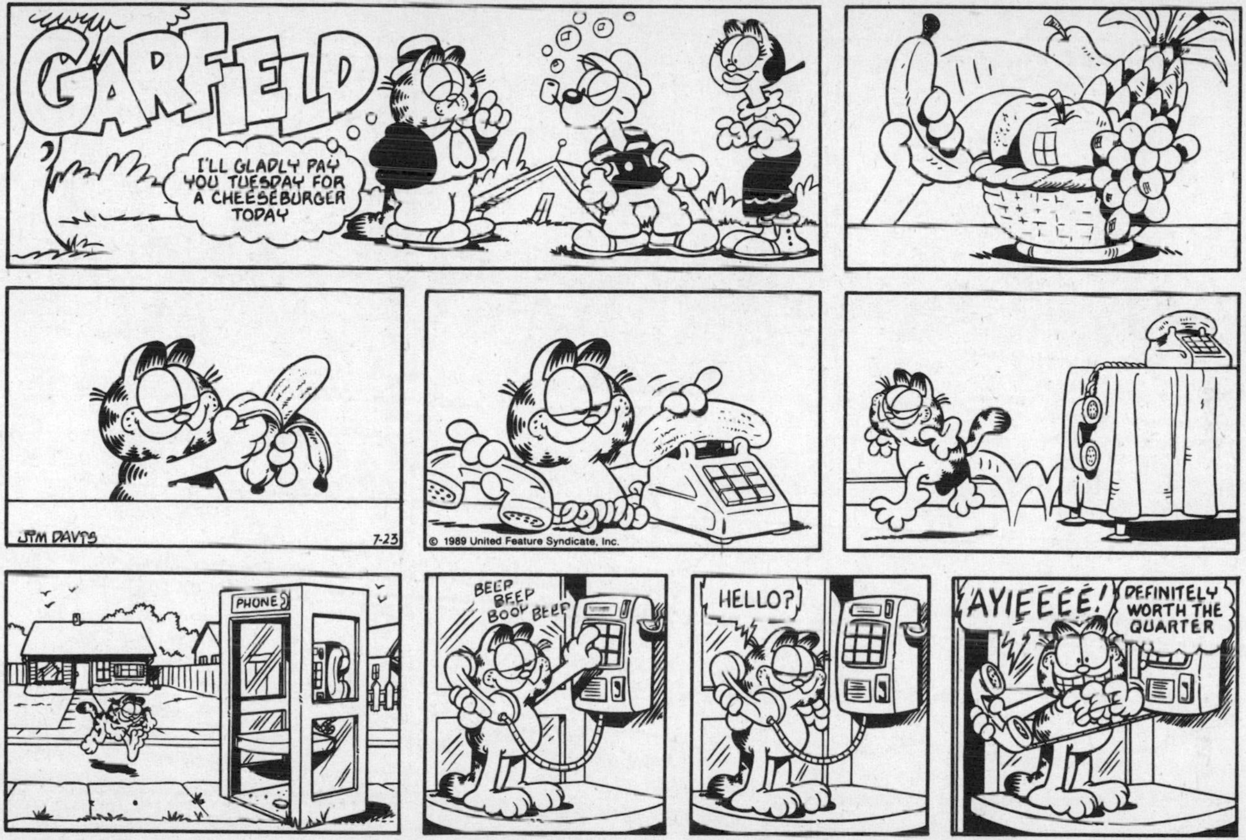
GARFIELD
I'LL GLADLY PAY YOU TUESDAY FOR A CHEESEBURGER TODAY
JIM DAVIS
7-23
© 1989 United Feature Syndicate, Inc.
PHONE
BEEP BEEP BOOP BEEP
HELLO?
AYIEEEE!
DEFINITELY WORTH THE QUARTER

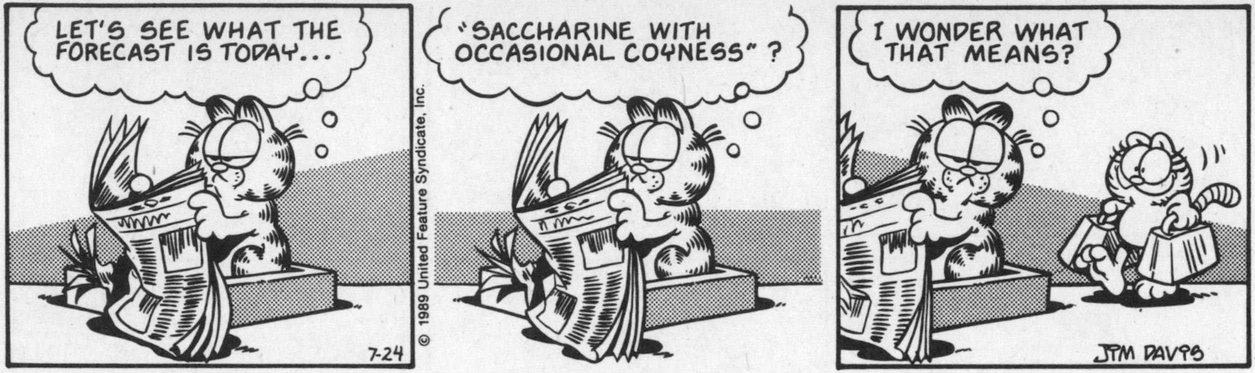
LET'S SEE WHAT THE FORECAST IS TODAY...
7-24
© 1989 United Feature Syndicate, Inc.
"SACCHARINE WITH OCCASIONAL COYNESS"?
I WONDER WHAT THAT MEANS?
JIM DAVIS

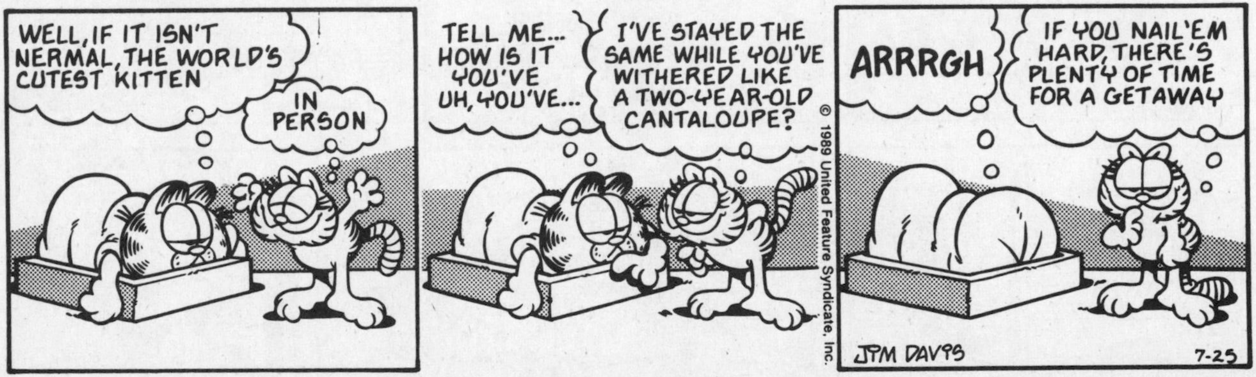
WELL, IF IT ISN'T NERMAL, THE WORLD'S CUTEST KITTEN
IN PERSON
TELL ME... HOW IS IT YOU'VE UH, YOU'VE...
I'VE STAYED THE SAME WHILE YOU'VE WITHERED LIKE A TWO-YEAR-OLD CANTALOUPE?
© 1989 United Feature Syndicate, Inc.
ARRRGH
IF YOU NAIL 'EM HARD, THERE'S PLENTY OF TIME FOR A GETAWAY
JIM DAVIS
7-25

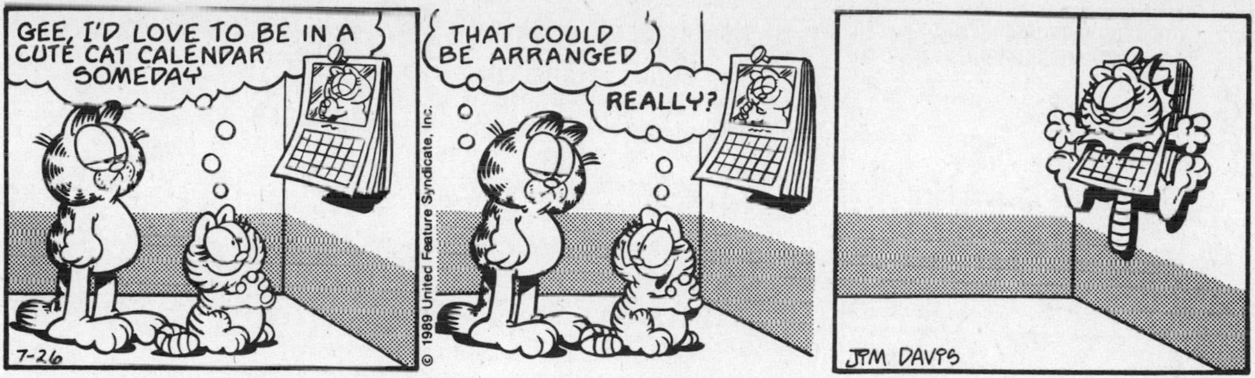
GEE, I'D LOVE TO BE IN A CUTE CAT CALENDAR SOMEDAY
7-26
© 1989 United Feature Syndicate, Inc.
THAT COULD BE ARRANGED
REALLY?
JIM DAVIS

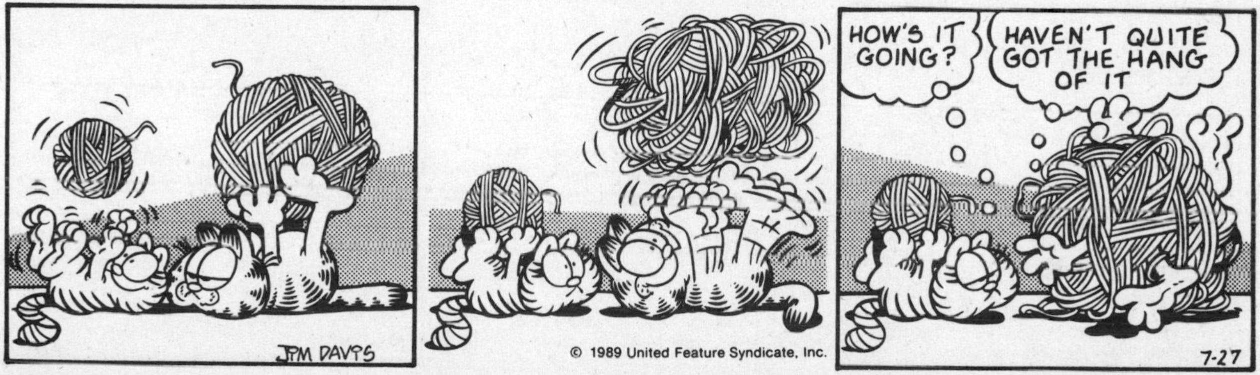
JIM DAVIS
© 1989 United Feature Syndicate, Inc.
HOW'S IT GOING?
HAVEN'T QUITE GOT THE HANG OF IT
7-27

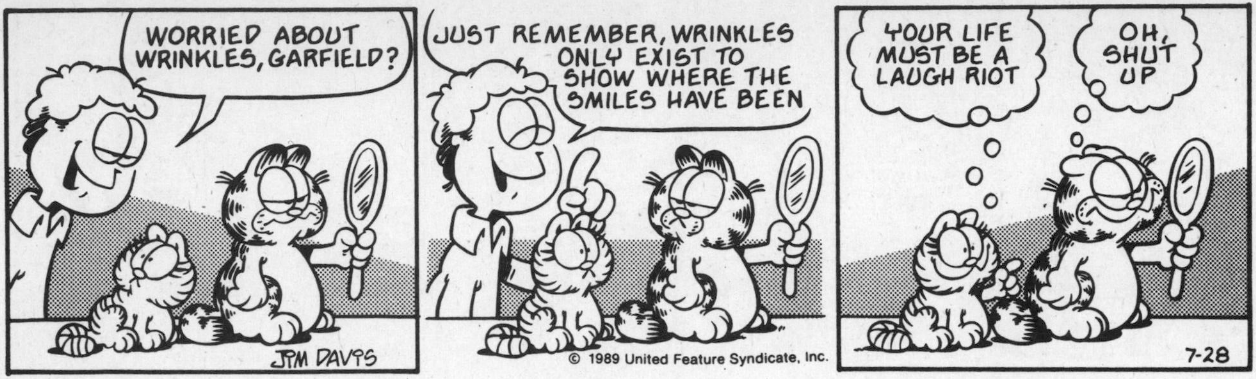
WORRIED ABOUT WRINKLES, GARFIELD?
JUST REMEMBER, WRINKLES ONLY EXIST TO SHOW WHERE THE SMILES HAVE BEEN
YOUR LIFE MUST BE A LAUGH RIOT
OH, SHUT UP
JIM DAVIS
© 1989 United Feature Syndicate, Inc.
7-28

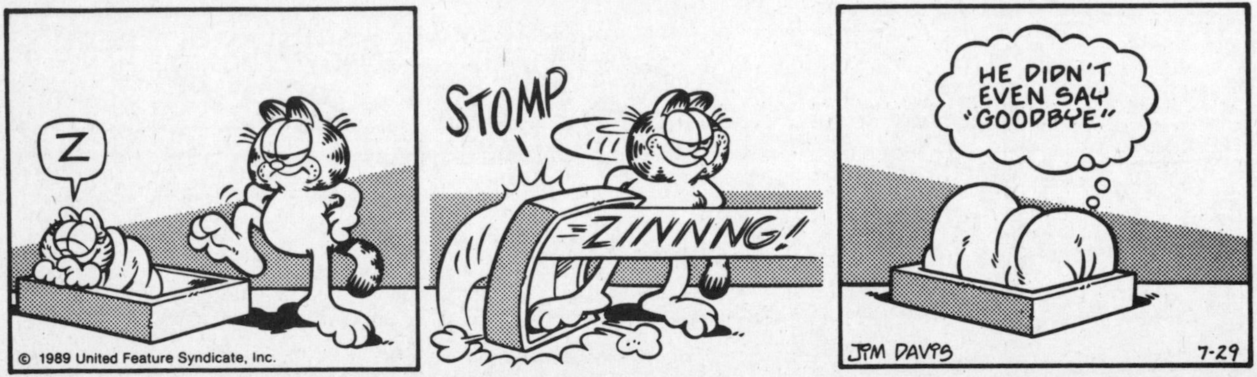
Z
STOMP
ZINNNG!
HE DIDN'T EVEN SAY "GOODBYE"
© 1989 United Feature Syndicate, Inc.
JIM DAVIS
7-29

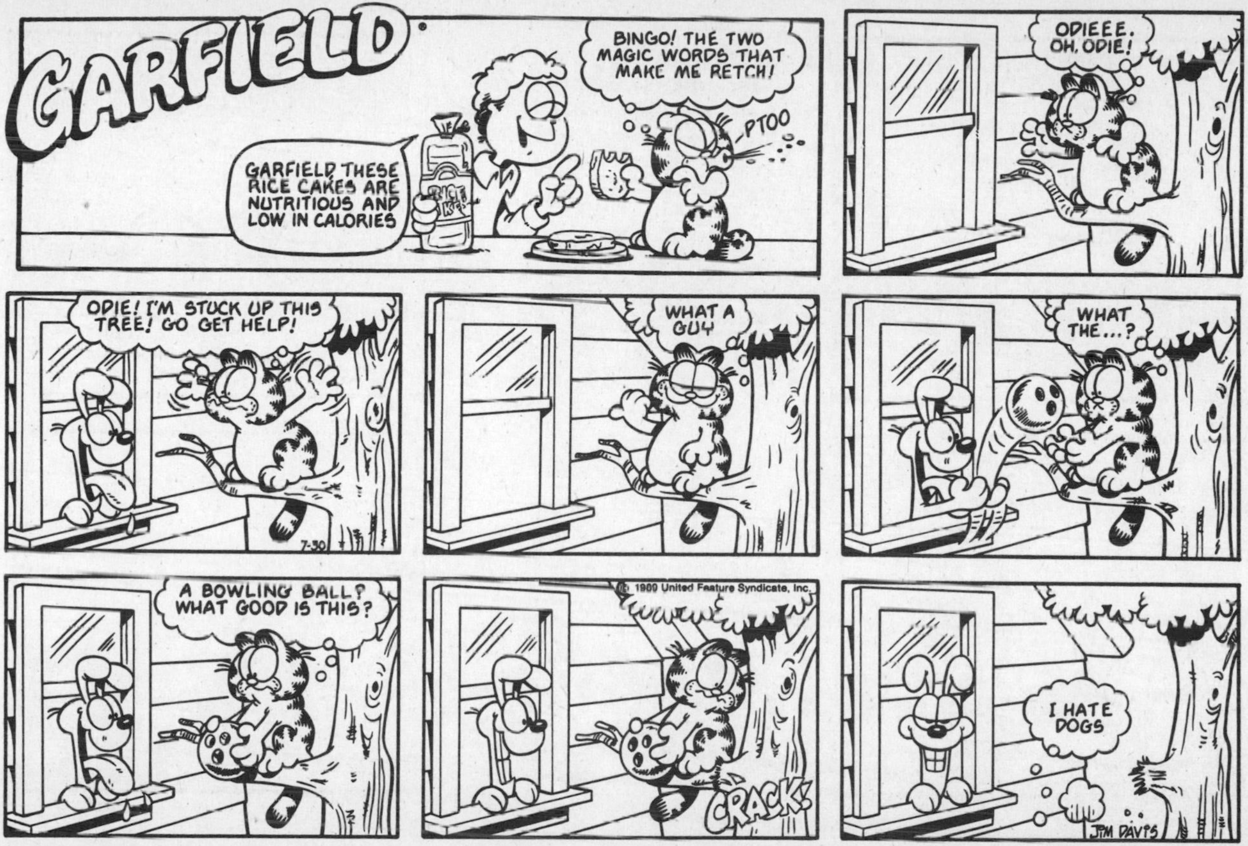
GARFIELD
GARFIELD THESE RICE CAKES ARE NUTRITIOUS AND LOW IN CALORIES
BINGO! THE TWO MAGIC WORDS THAT MAKE ME RETCH!
PTOO
ODIEEE. OH, ODIE!
ODIE! I'M STUCK UP THIS TREE! GO GET HELP!
7-30
WHAT A GUY
WHAT THE...?
A BOWLING BALL? WHAT GOOD IS THIS?
© 1989 United Feature Syndicate, Inc.
CRACK!
I HATE DOGS
JIM DAVIS

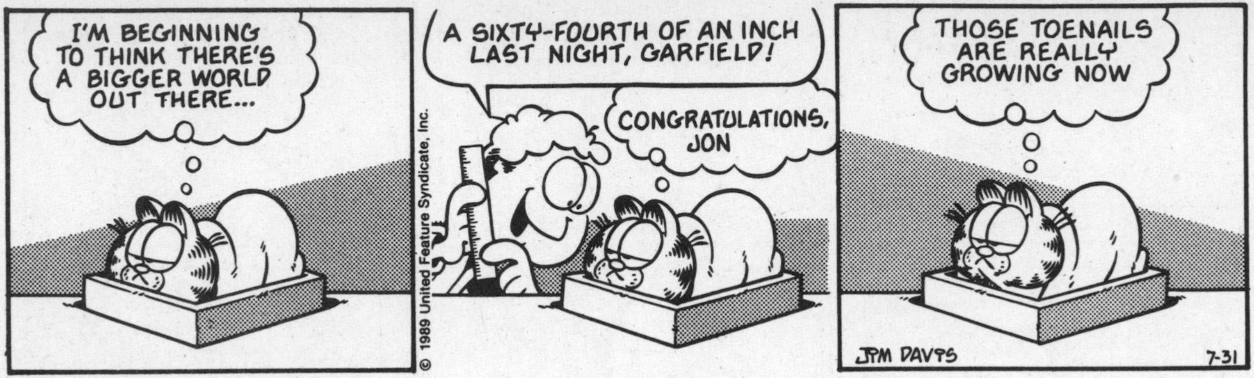
I'M BEGINNING TO THINK THERE'S A BIGGER WORLD OUT THERE...
© 1989 United Feature Syndicate, Inc.
A SIXTY-FOURTH OF AN INCH LAST NIGHT, GARFIELD!
CONGRATULATIONS, JON
THOSE TOENAILS ARE REALLY GROWING NOW
JIM DAVIS
7-31

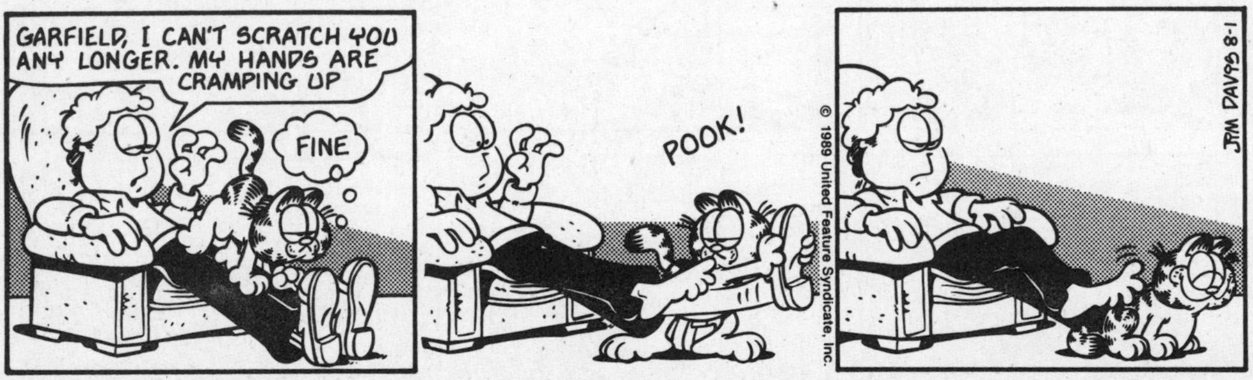
GARFIELD, I CAN'T SCRATCH YOU ANY LONGER. MY HANDS ARE CRAMPING UP
FINE
POOK!
© 1989 United Feature Syndicate, Inc.
JIM DAVIS 8-1

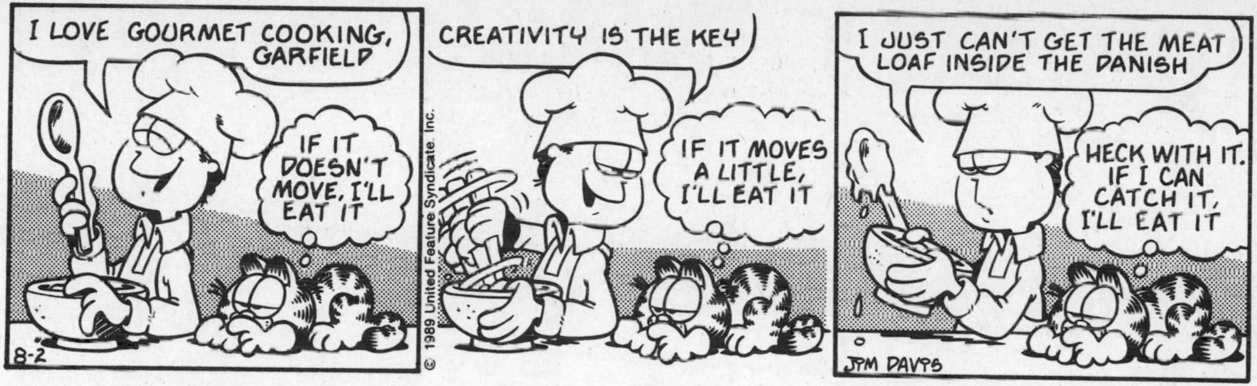
I LOVE GOURMET COOKING, GARFIELD
IF IT DOESN'T MOVE, I'LL EAT IT
8-2
© 1989 United Feature Syndicate, Inc.
CREATIVITY IS THE KEY
IF IT MOVES A LITTLE, I'LL EAT IT
I JUST CAN'T GET THE MEAT LOAF INSIDE THE DANISH
HECK WITH IT. IF I CAN CATCH IT, I'LL EAT IT
JIM DAVIS

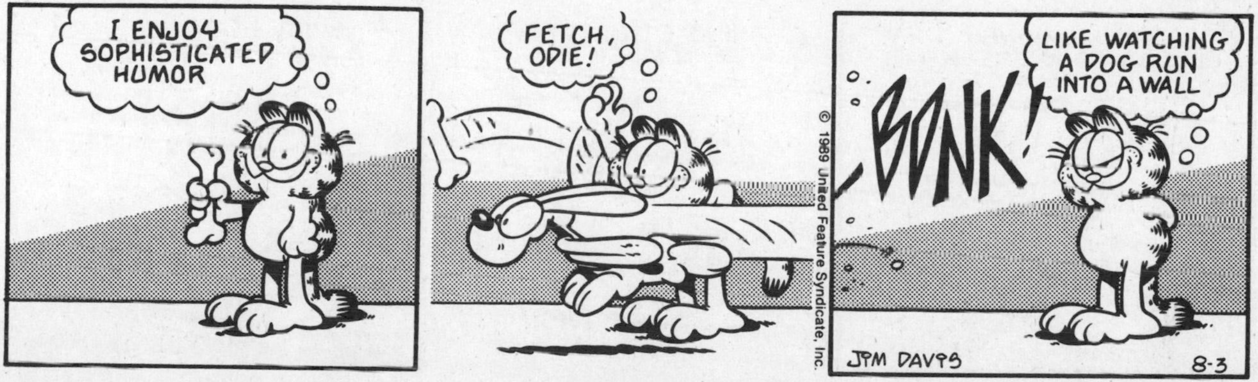
I ENJOY SOPHISTICATED HUMOR
FETCH, ODIE!
© 1989 United Feature Syndicate, Inc.
BONK!
LIKE WATCHING A DOG RUN INTO A WALL
JIM DAVIS
8-3

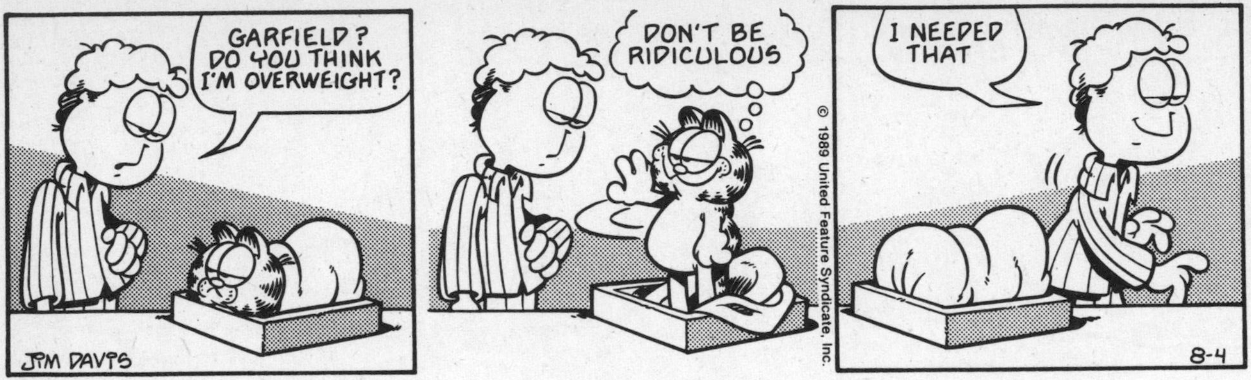
GARFIELD? DO YOU THINK I'M OVERWEIGHT?
JIM DAVIS
DON'T BE RIDICULOUS
© 1989 United Feature Syndicate, Inc.
I NEEDED THAT
8-4

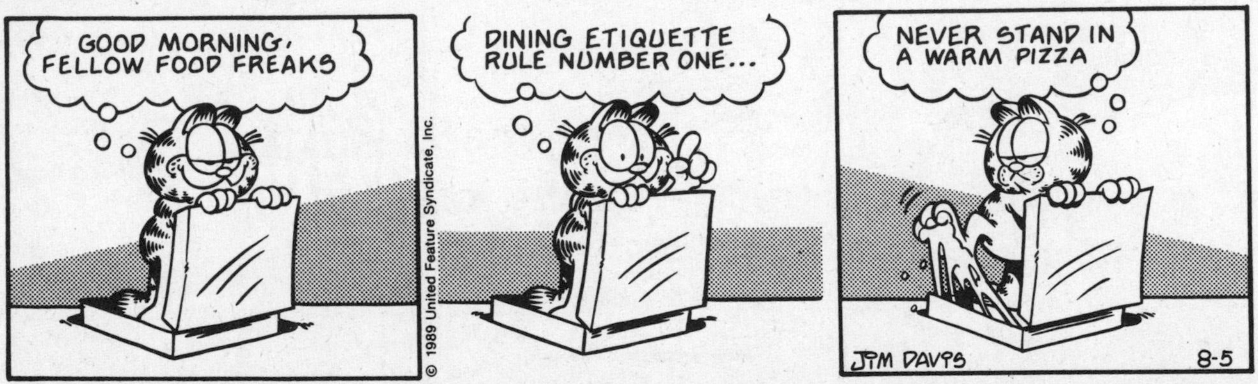
GOOD MORNING, FELLOW FOOD FREAKS
© 1989 United Feature Syndicate, Inc.
DINING ETIQUETTE RULE NUMBER ONE...
NEVER STAND IN A WARM PIZZA
JIM DAVIS
8-5

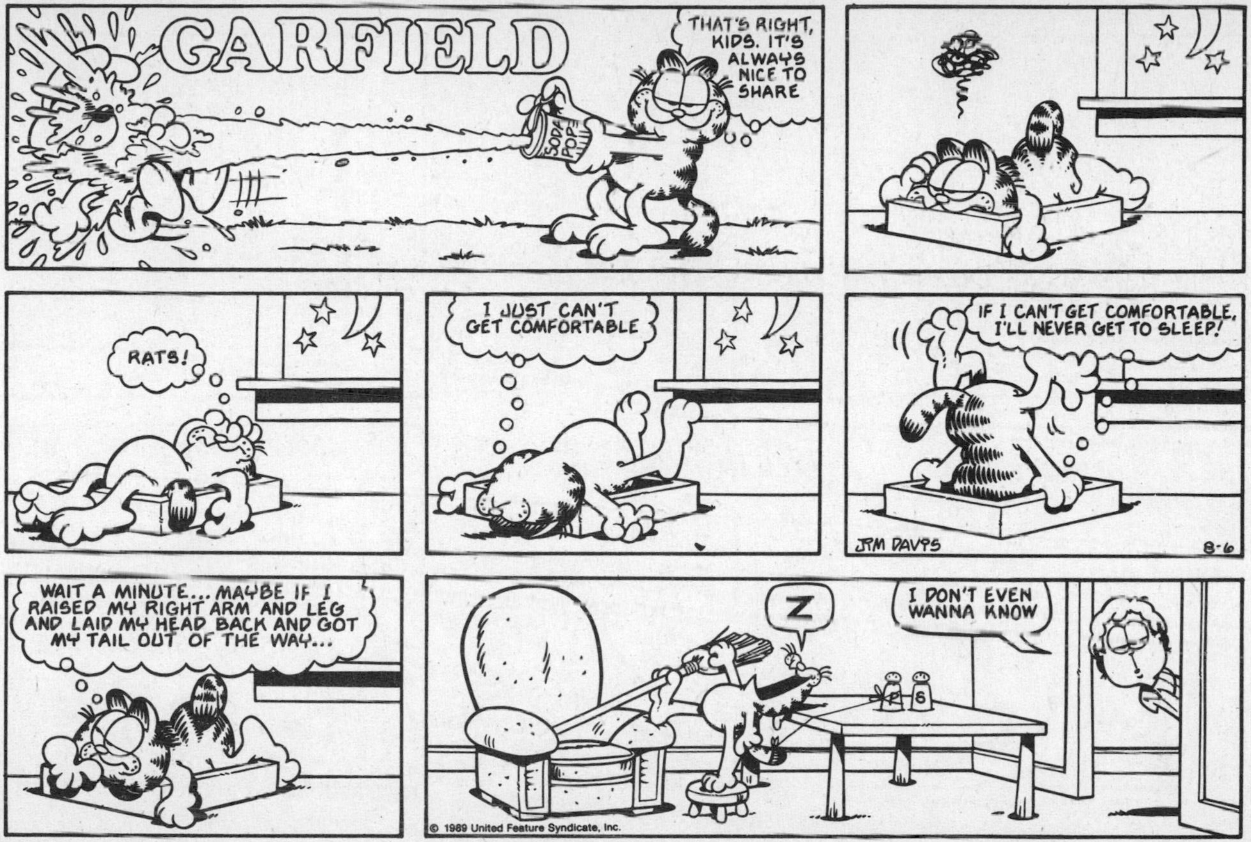
GARFIELD
THAT'S RIGHT, KIDS. IT'S ALWAYS NICE TO SHARE
SODA POP
RATS!
I JUST CAN'T GET COMFORTABLE
IF I CAN'T GET COMFORTABLE, I'LL NEVER GET TO SLEEP!
JIM DAVIS
8-6
WAIT A MINUTE... MAYBE IF I RAISED MY RIGHT ARM AND LEG AND LAID MY HEAD BACK AND GOT MY TAIL OUT OF THE WAY...
Z
I DON'T EVEN WANNA KNOW
P
S
© 1989 United Feature Syndicate, Inc.

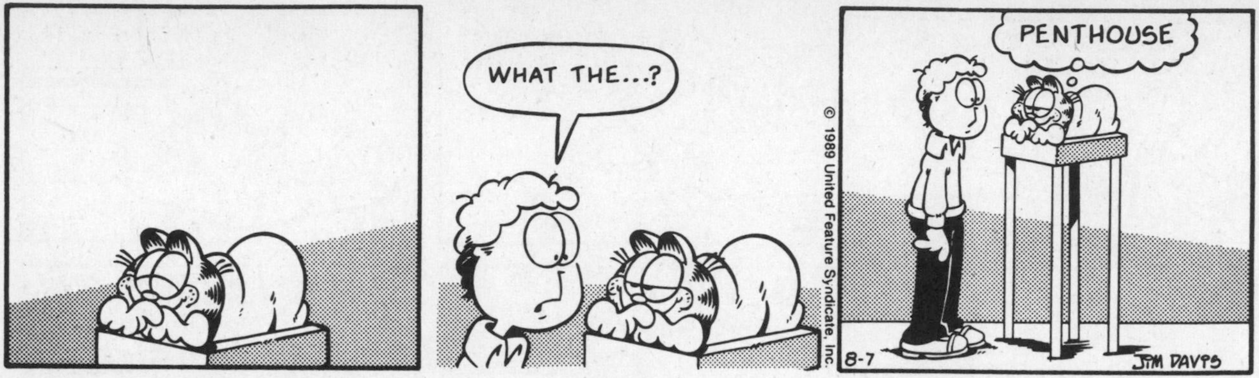
WHAT THE...?
© 1989 United Feature Syndicate, Inc.
PENTHOUSE
8-7
JIM DAVIS

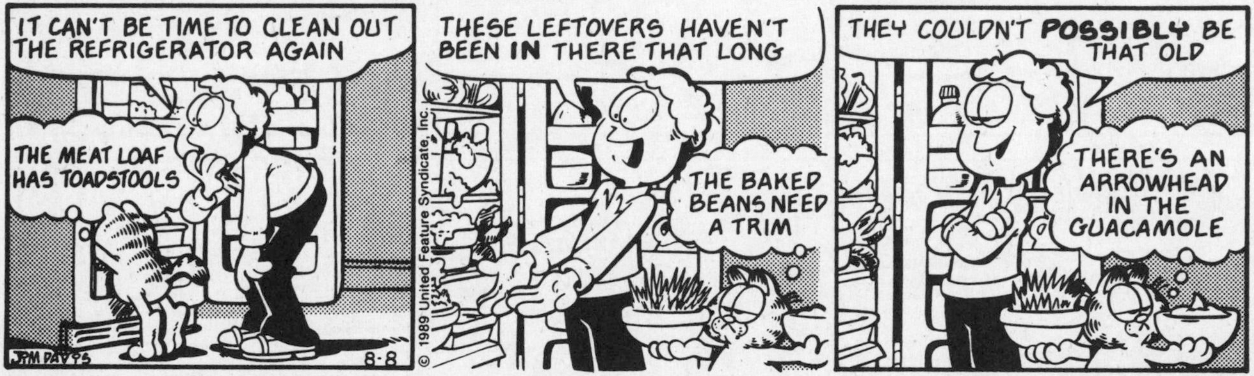
IT CAN'T BE TIME TO CLEAN OUT THE REFRIGERATOR AGAIN
THE MEAT LOAF HAS TOADSTOOLS
JIM DAVIS
8-8
© 1989 United Feature Syndicate, Inc.
THESE LEFTOVERS HAVEN'T BEEN IN THERE THAT LONG
THE BAKED BEANS NEED A TRIM
THEY COULDN'T POSSIBLY BE THAT OLD
THERE'S AN ARROWHEAD IN THE GUACAMOLE

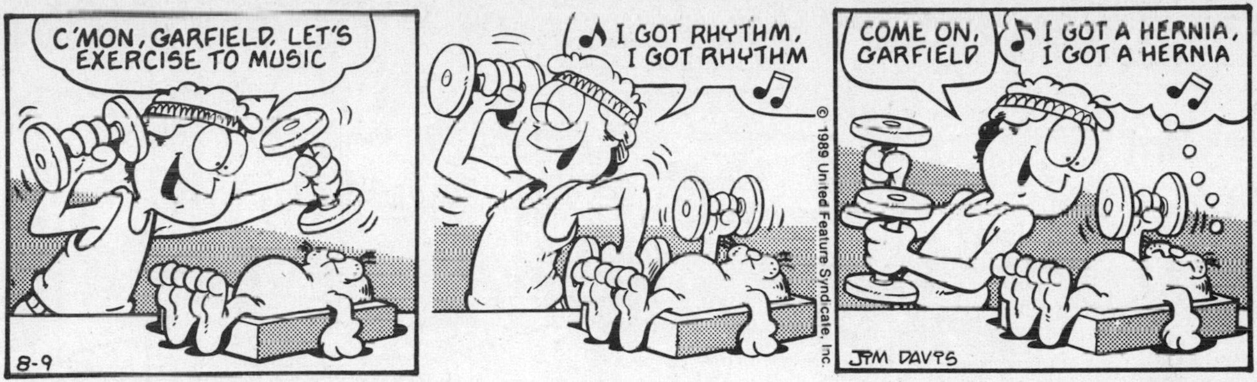
C'MON, GARFIELD. LET'S EXERCISE TO MUSIC
I GOT RHYTHM, I GOT RHYTHM
COME ON, GARFIELD
I GOT A HERNIA, I GOT A HERNIA
8-9
JIM DAVIS
© 1989 United Feature Syndicate, Inc.

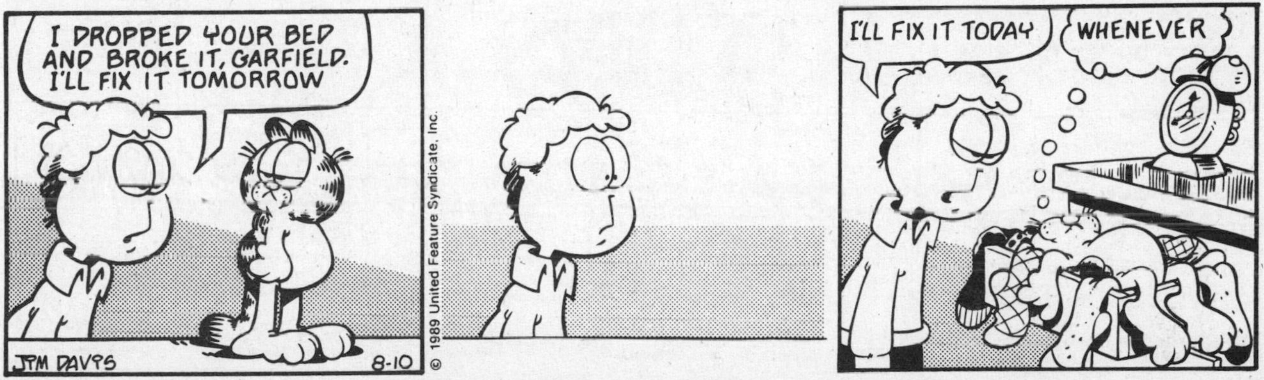
I DROPPED YOUR BED AND BROKE IT, GARFIELD. I'LL FIX IT TOMORROW
I'LL FIX IT TODAY
WHENEVER
JIM DAVIS
8-10
© 1989 United Feature Syndicate, Inc.

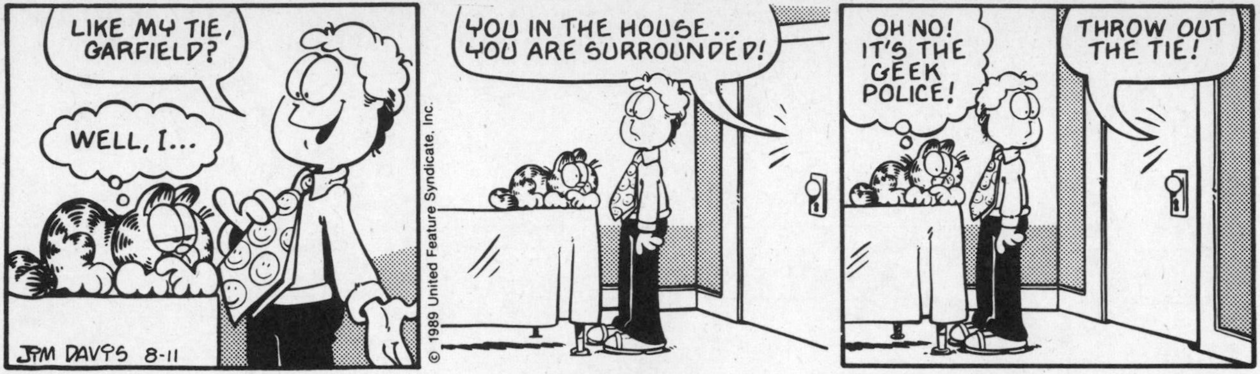
LIKE MY TIE, GARFIELD?
WELL, I...
JIM DAVIS 8-11
© 1989 United Feature Syndicate, Inc.
YOU IN THE HOUSE... YOU ARE SURROUNDED!
OH NO! IT'S THE GEEK POLICE!
THROW OUT THE TIE!

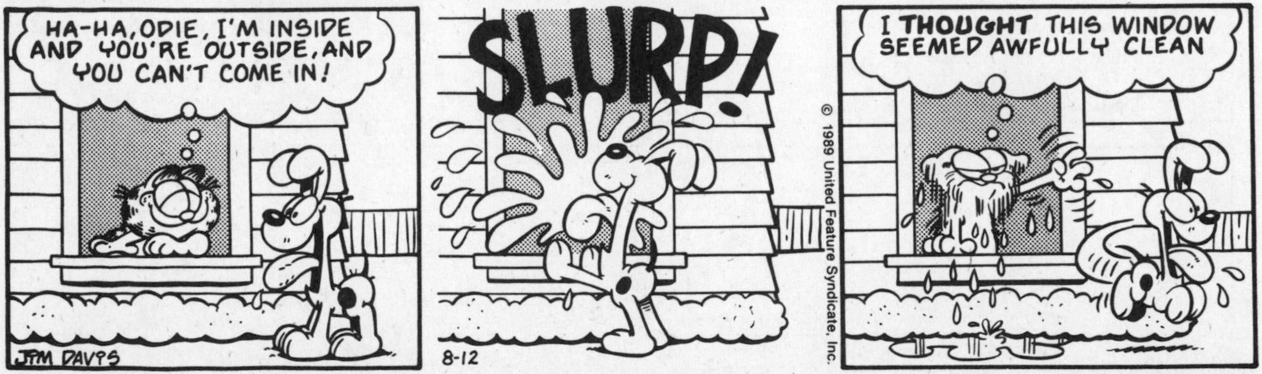
HA-HA, ODIE, I'M INSIDE AND YOU'RE OUTSIDE, AND YOU CAN'T COME IN!
JIM DAVIS
SLURP!
8-12
© 1989 United Feature Syndicate, Inc.
I THOUGHT THIS WINDOW SEEMED AWFULLY CLEAN

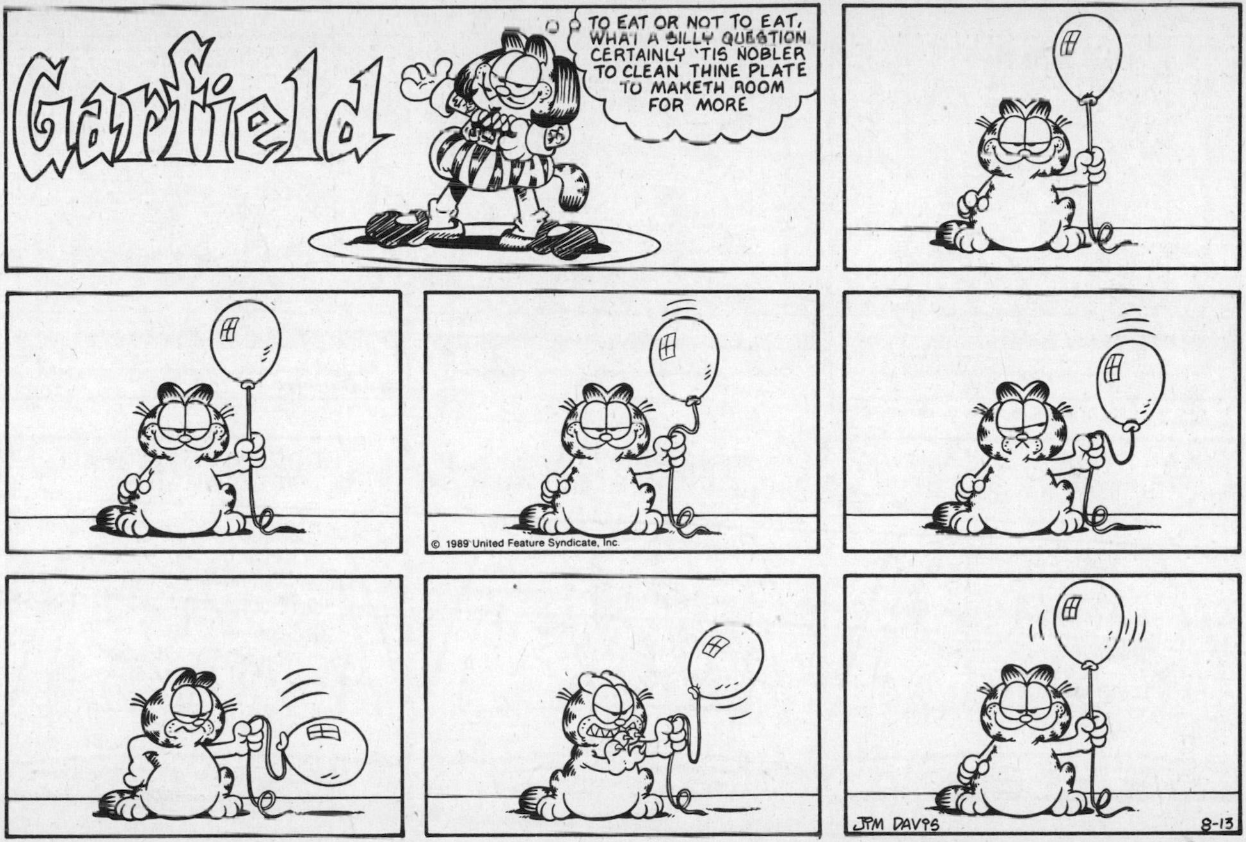
Garfield
TO EAT OR NOT TO EAT, WHAT A SILLY QUESTION CERTAINLY 'TIS NOBLER TO CLEAN THINE PLATE TO MAKETH ROOM FOR MORE
© 1989 United Feature Syndicate, Inc.
JPM DAVIS
8-13

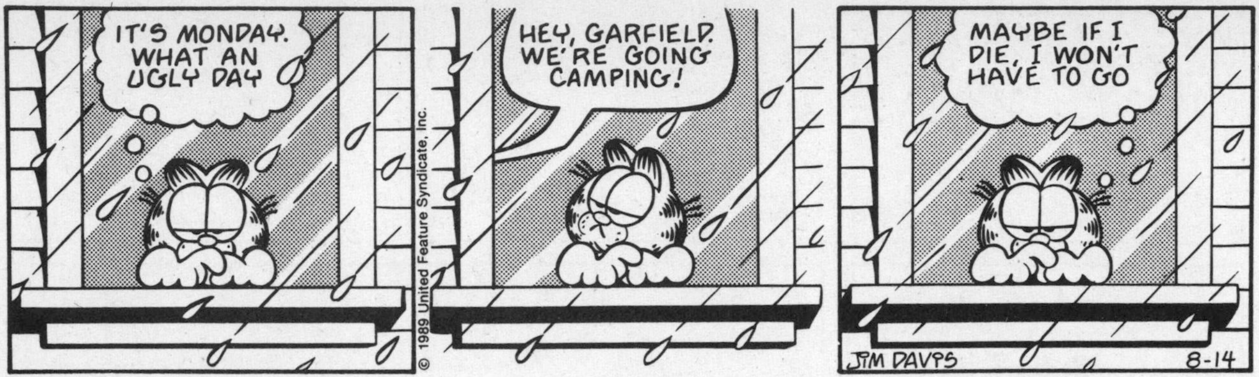
IT'S MONDAY. WHAT AN UGLY DAY
HEY, GARFIELD. WE'RE GOING CAMPING!
MAYBE IF I DIE, I WON'T HAVE TO GO
© 1989 United Feature Syndicate, Inc.
JIM DAVIS 8-14

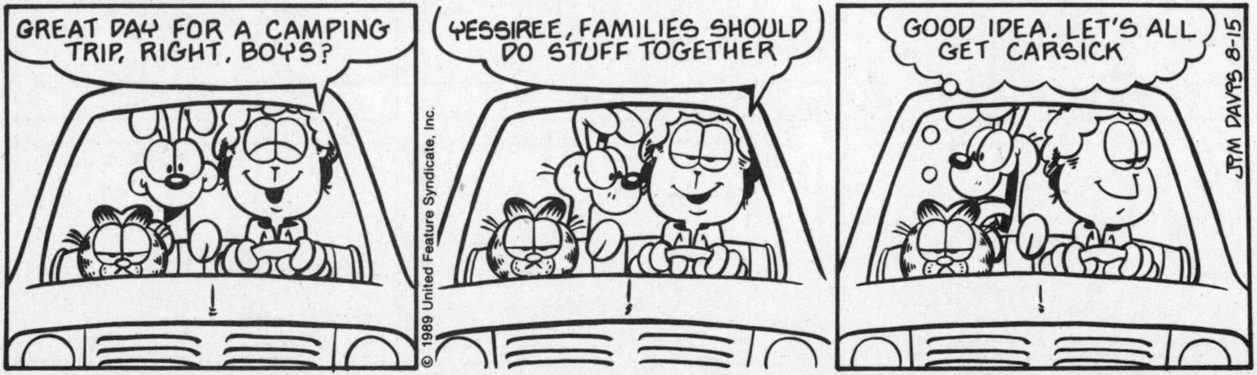
GREAT DAY FOR A CAMPING TRIP, RIGHT, BOYS?
YESSIREE, FAMILIES SHOULD DO STUFF TOGETHER
GOOD IDEA. LET'S ALL GET CARSICK
© 1989 United Feature Syndicate, Inc.
JIM DAVIS 8-15

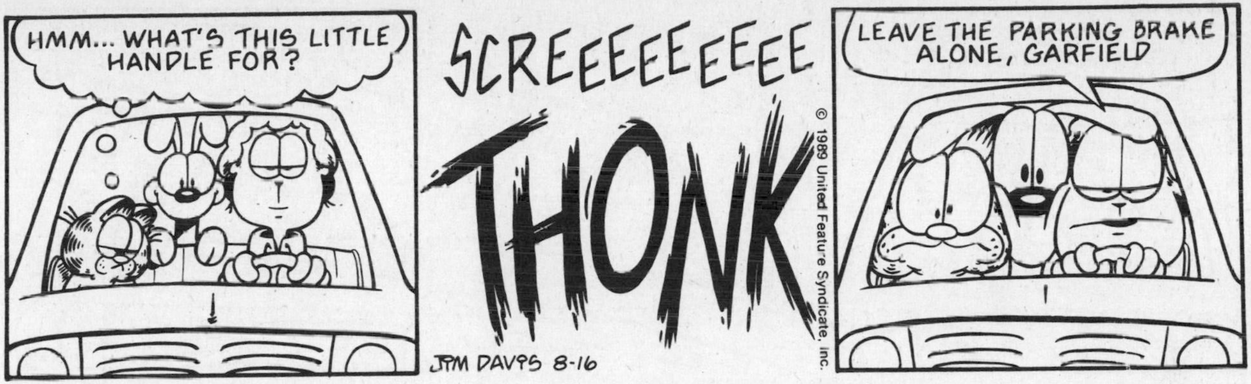

HMM... WHAT'S THIS LITTLE HANDLE FOR?
SCREEEEEEEEE
THONK
JPM DAVPS 8-16
© 1989 United Feature Syndicate, Inc.
LEAVE THE PARKING BRAKE ALONE, GARFIELD

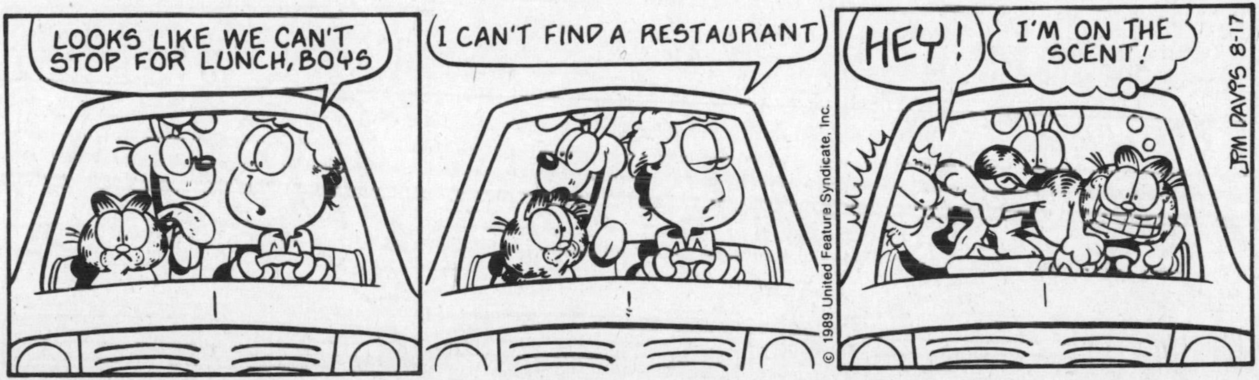

LOOKS LIKE WE CAN'T STOP FOR LUNCH, BOYS
I CAN'T FIND A RESTAURANT
© 1989 United Feature Syndicate, Inc.
HEY!
I'M ON THE SCENT!
JPM DAVPS 8-17

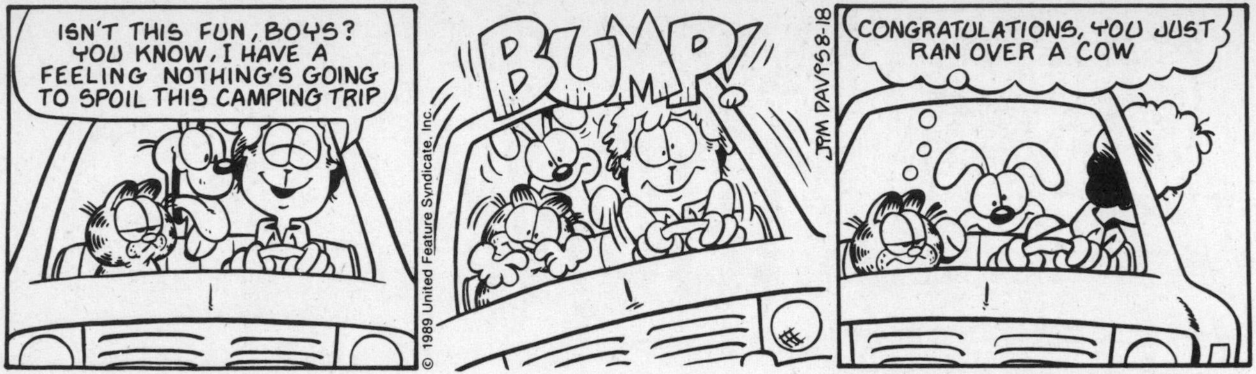
ISN'T THIS FUN, BOYS? YOU KNOW, I HAVE A FEELING NOTHING'S GOING TO SPOIL THIS CAMPING TRIP
BUMP
CONGRATULATIONS, YOU JUST RAN OVER A COW
© 1989 United Feature Syndicate, Inc.
JPM DAVPS 8-18

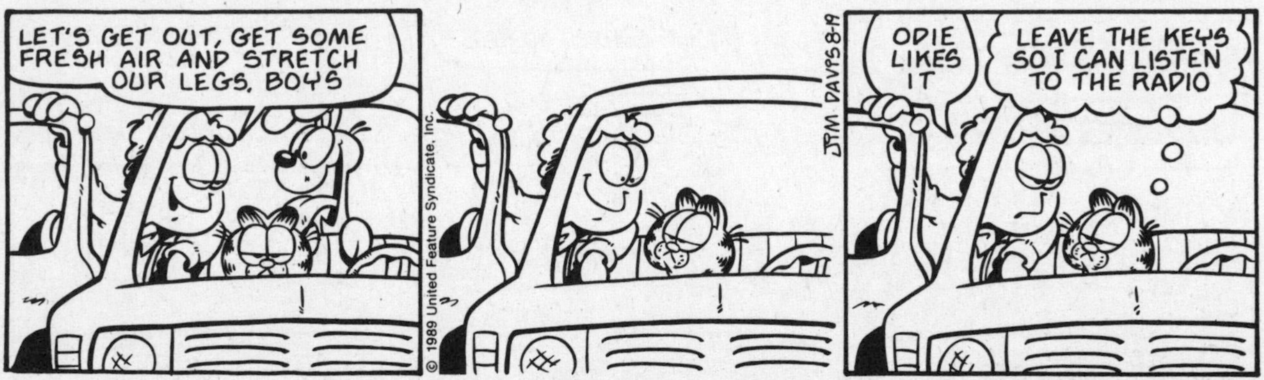
LET'S GET OUT, GET SOME FRESH AIR AND STRETCH OUR LEGS, BOYS
ODIE LIKES IT
LEAVE THE KEYS SO I CAN LISTEN TO THE RADIO
© 1989 United Feature Syndicate, Inc.
JPM DAVPS 8-19

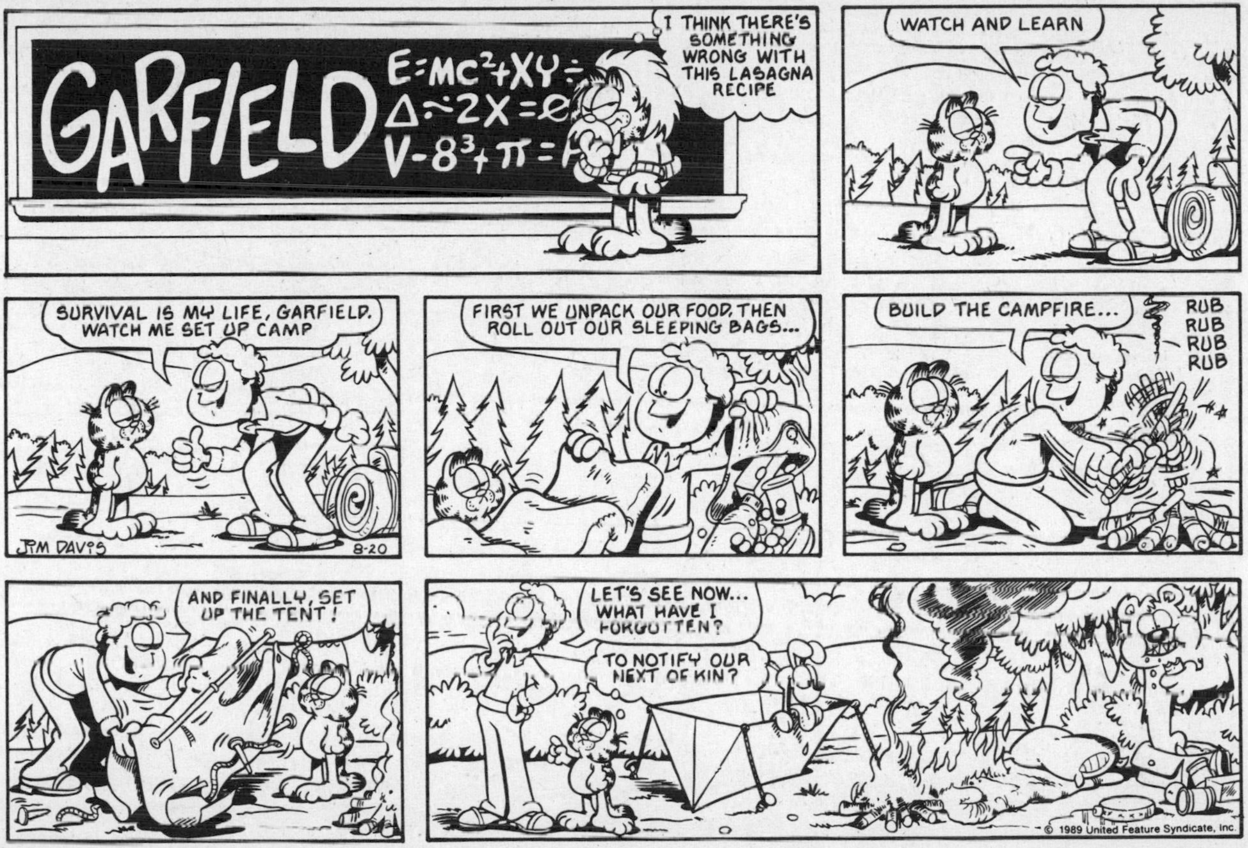
GARFIELD
E=MC²+XY=
Δ≈2X=e
V-8³+π=
I THINK THERE'S SOMETHING WRONG WITH THIS LASAGNA RECIPE
WATCH AND LEARN
SURVIVAL IS MY LIFE, GARFIELD. WATCH ME SET UP CAMP
JIM DAVIS
8-20
FIRST WE UNPACK OUR FOOD, THEN ROLL OUT OUR SLEEPING BAGS...
BUILD THE CAMPFIRE...
RUB RUB RUB RUB
AND FINALLY, SET UP THE TENT!
LET'S SEE NOW... WHAT HAVE I FORGOTTEN?
TO NOTIFY OUR NEXT OF KIN?
© 1989 United Feature Syndicate, Inc.

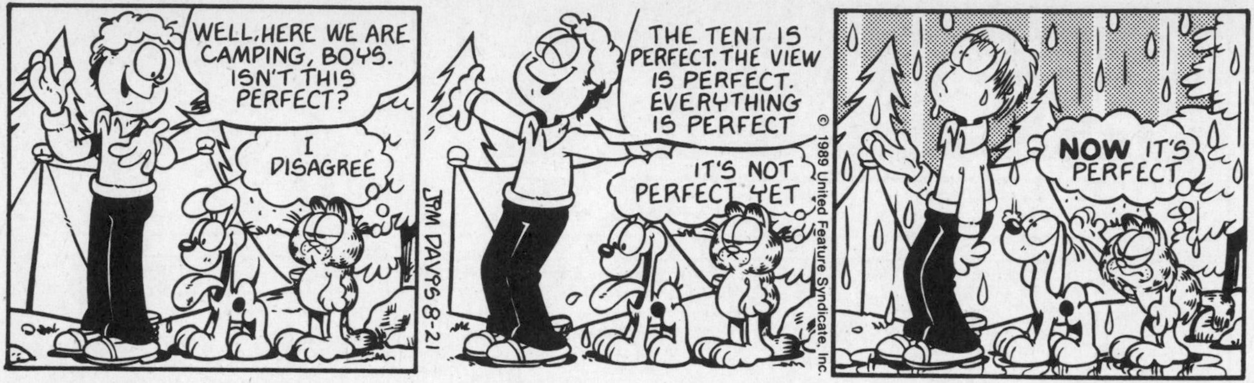
WELL, HERE WE ARE CAMPING, BOYS. ISN'T THIS PERFECT?
I DISAGREE
JIM DAVIS 8-21
THE TENT IS PERFECT. THE VIEW IS PERFECT. EVERYTHING IS PERFECT
IT'S NOT PERFECT YET
© 1989 United Feature Syndicate, Inc.
NOW IT'S PERFECT

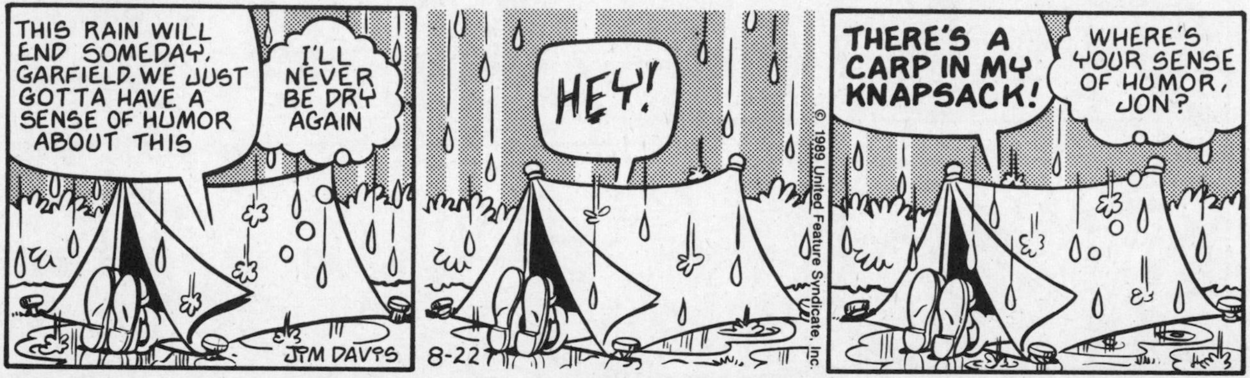
THIS RAIN WILL END SOMEDAY, GARFIELD. WE JUST GOTTA HAVE A SENSE OF HUMOR ABOUT THIS
I'LL NEVER BE DRY AGAIN
JIM DAVIS
HEY!
8-22
© 1989 United Feature Syndicate, Inc.
THERE'S A CARP IN MY KNAPSACK!
WHERE'S YOUR SENSE OF HUMOR, JON?

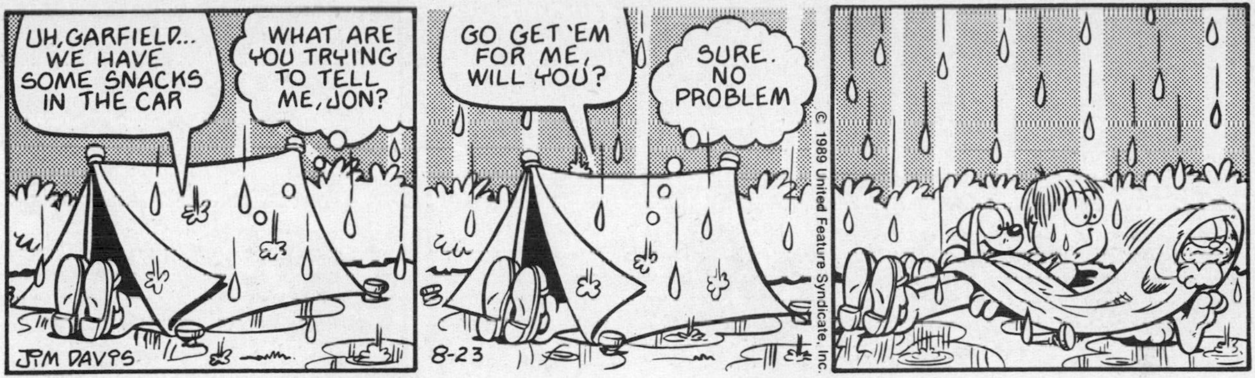
UH, GARFIELD... WE HAVE SOME SNACKS IN THE CAR
WHAT ARE YOU TRYING TO TELL ME, JON?
GO GET 'EM FOR ME, WILL YOU?
SURE. NO PROBLEM
JIM DAVIS
8-23
© 1989 United Feature Syndicate, Inc.

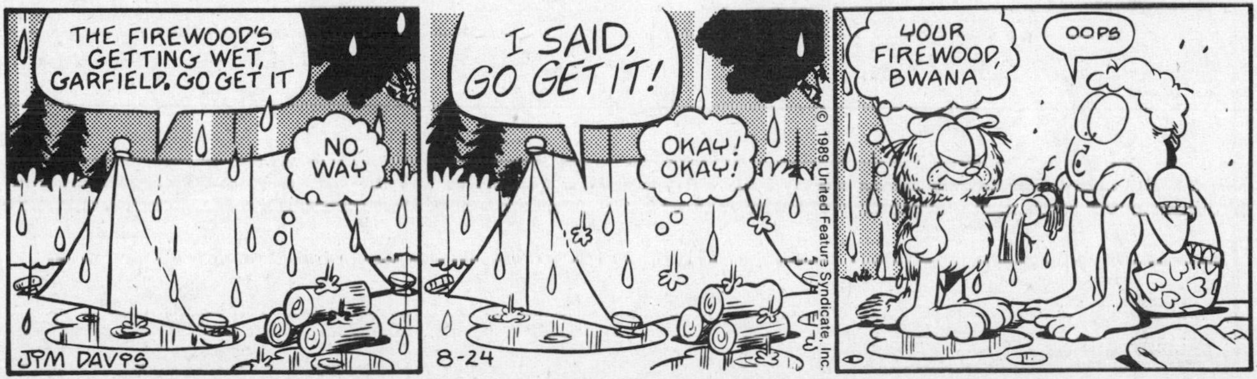
THE FIREWOOD'S GETTING WET, GARFIELD. GO GET IT
NO WAY
I SAID, GO GET IT!
OKAY! OKAY!
YOUR FIREWOOD, BWANA
OOPS
JIM DAVIS
8-24
© 1989 United Feature Syndicate, Inc.

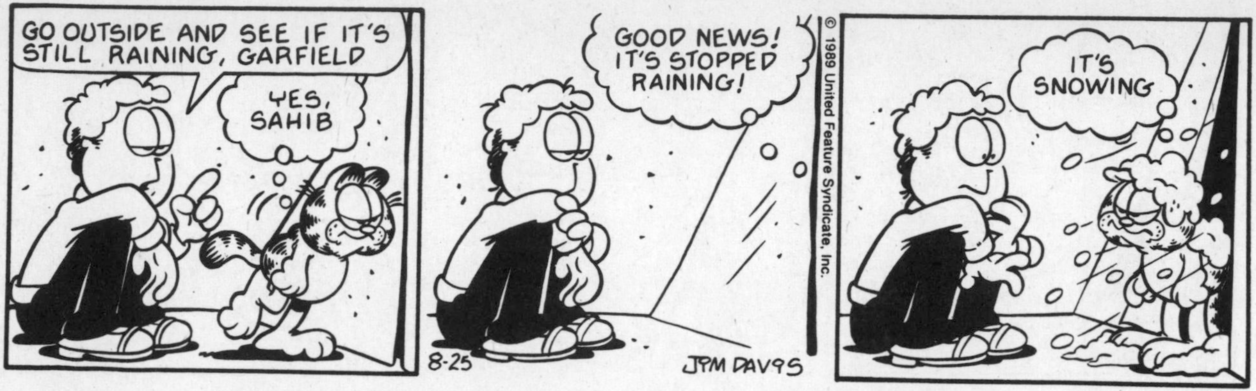
GO OUTSIDE AND SEE IF IT'S STILL RAINING, GARFIELD
YES, SAHIB
GOOD NEWS! IT'S STOPPED RAINING!
8-25
JIM DAVIS
© 1989 United Feature Syndicate, Inc.
IT'S SNOWING

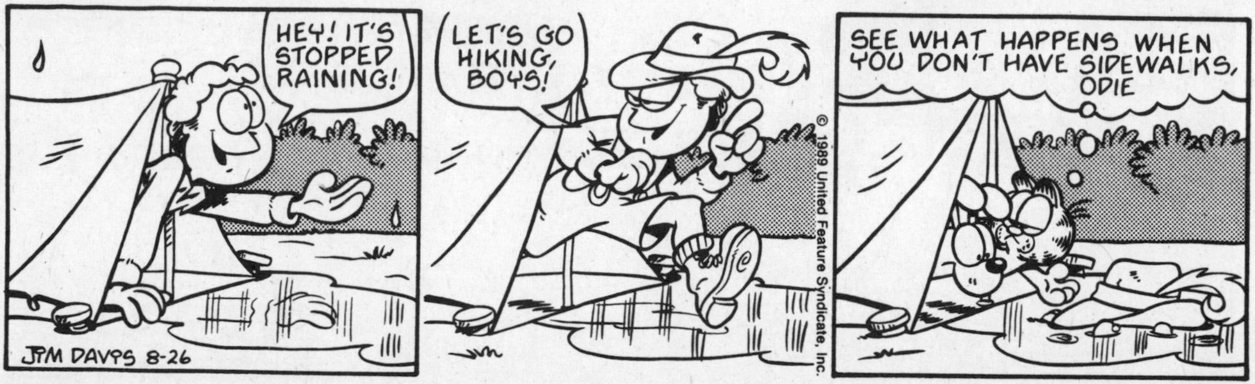
HEY! IT'S STOPPED RAINING!
JIM DAVIS 8-26
LET'S GO HIKING, BOYS!
© 1989 United Feature Syndicate, Inc.
SEE WHAT HAPPENS WHEN YOU DON'T HAVE SIDEWALKS, ODIE

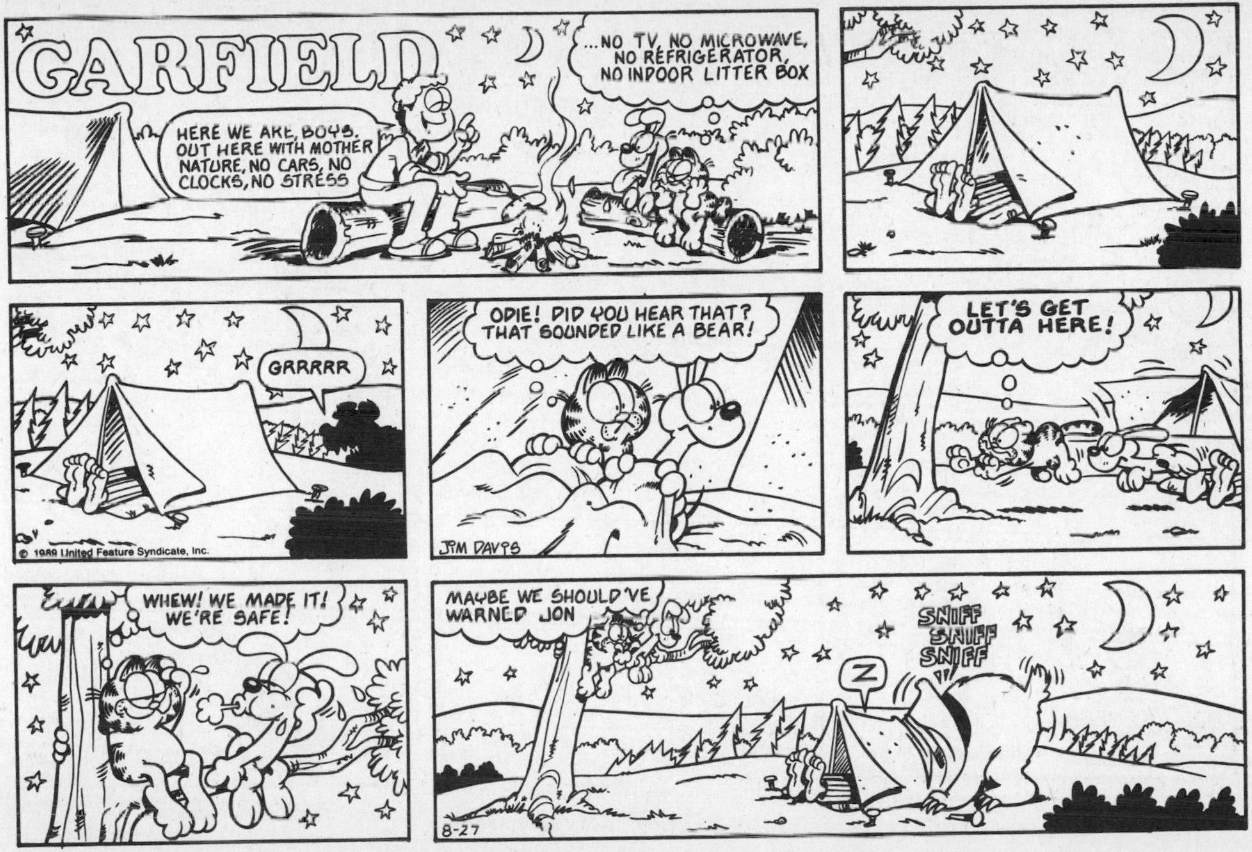
GARFIELD
HERE WE ARE, BOYS. OUT HERE WITH MOTHER NATURE, NO CARS, NO CLOCKS, NO STRESS
...NO TV, NO MICROWAVE, NO REFRIGERATOR, NO INDOOR LITTER BOX
GRRRRR
© 1989 United Feature Syndicate, Inc.
ODIE! DID YOU HEAR THAT? THAT SOUNDED LIKE A BEAR!
JIM DAVIS
LET'S GET OUTTA HERE!
WHEW! WE MADE IT! WE'RE SAFE!
MAYBE WE SHOULD'VE WARNED JON
Z
SNIFF
SNIFF
SNIFF
8-27

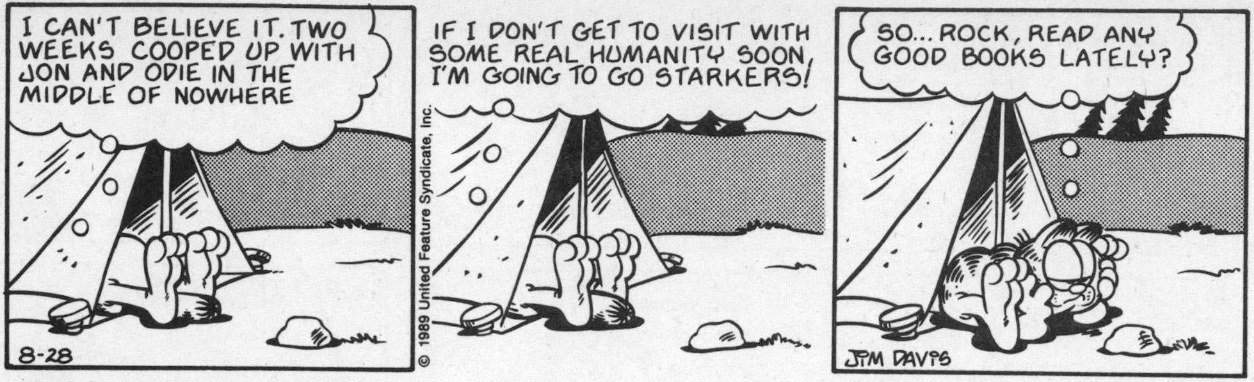
I CAN'T BELIEVE IT. TWO WEEKS COOPED UP WITH JON AND ODIE IN THE MIDDLE OF NOWHERE
IF I DON'T GET TO VISIT WITH SOME REAL HUMANITY SOON, I'M GOING TO GO STARKERS!
SO... ROCK, READ ANY GOOD BOOKS LATELY?
8-28
© 1989 United Feature Syndicate, Inc.
JIM DAVIS

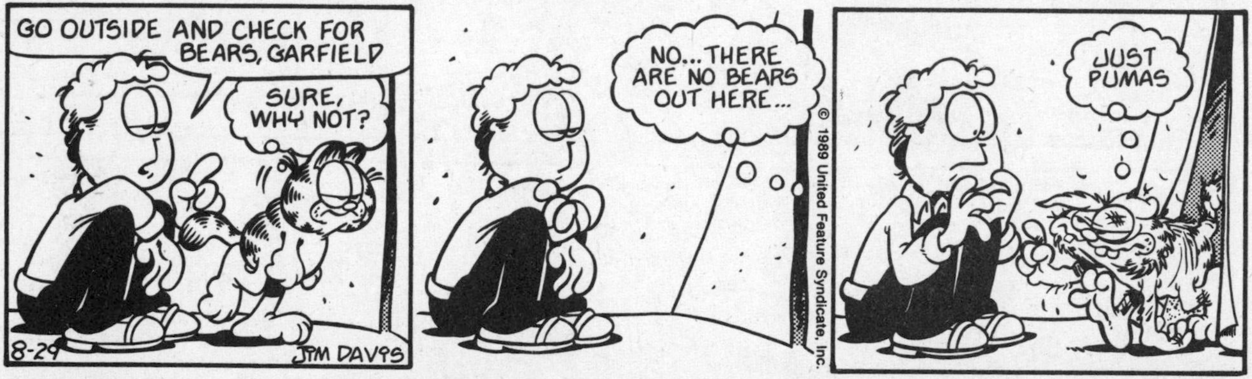
GO OUTSIDE AND CHECK FOR BEARS, GARFIELD
SURE, WHY NOT?
NO... THERE ARE NO BEARS OUT HERE...
JUST PUMAS
8-29
JIM DAVIS
© 1989 United Feature Syndicate, Inc.

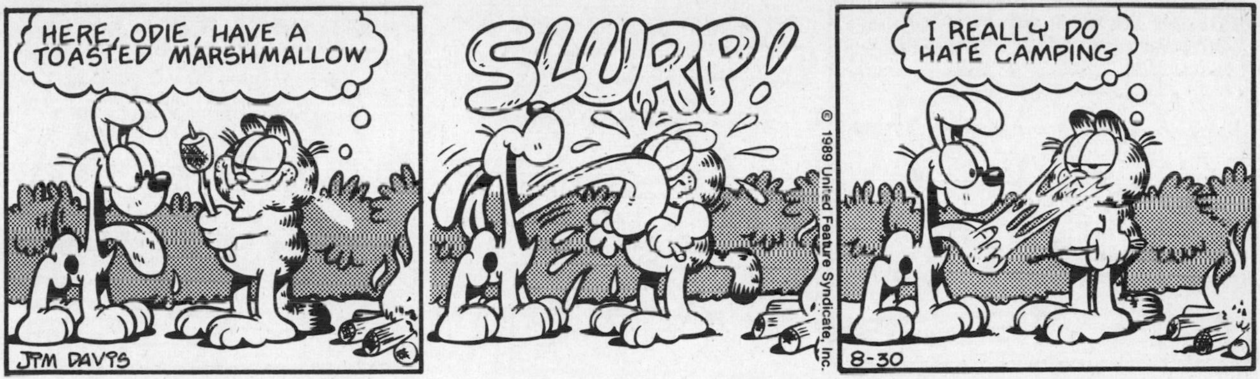
HERE, ODIE, HAVE A TOASTED MARSHMALLOW
SLURP!
I REALLY DO HATE CAMPING
JIM DAVIS
8-30
© 1989 United Feature Syndicate, Inc.

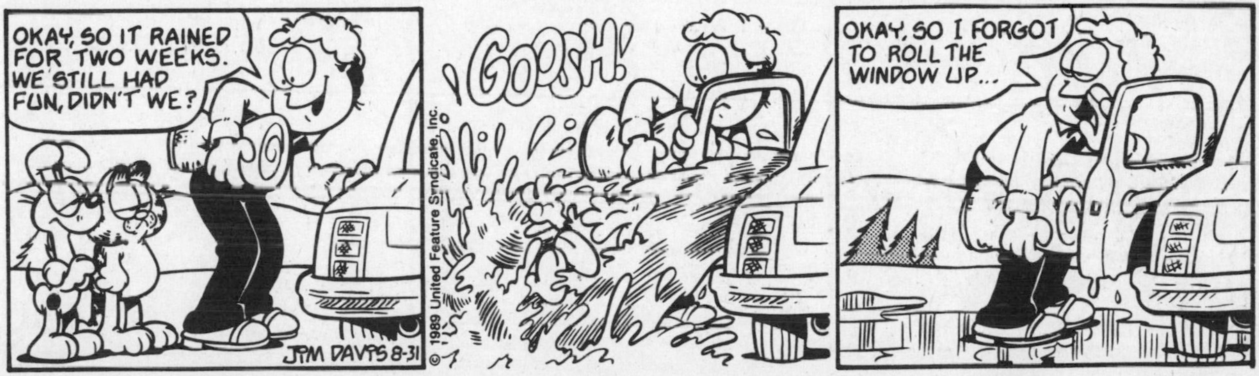
OKAY, SO IT RAINED FOR TWO WEEKS. WE STILL HAD FUN, DIDN'T WE?
GOOSH!
OKAY, SO I FORGOT TO ROLL THE WINDOW UP...
JIM DAVIS 8-31
© 1989 United Feature Syndicate, Inc.

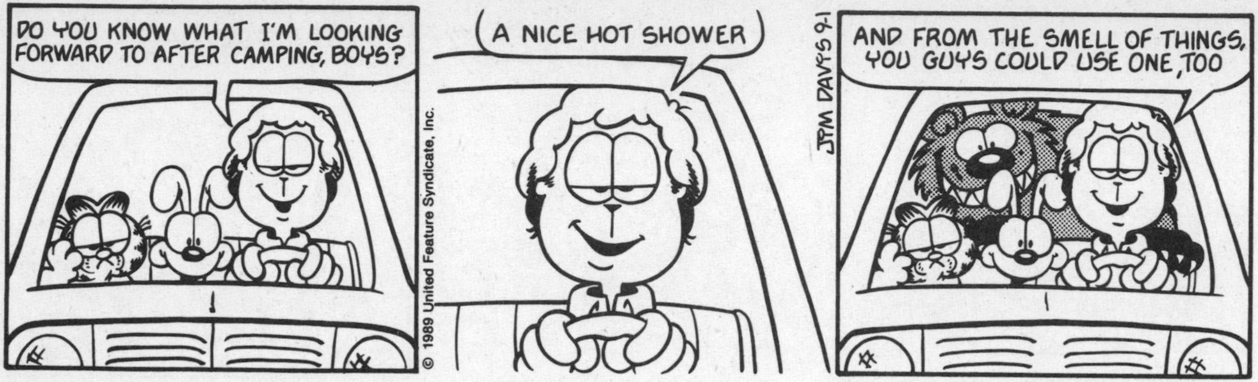
DO YOU KNOW WHAT I'M LOOKING FORWARD TO AFTER CAMPING, BOYS?
A NICE HOT SHOWER
AND FROM THE SMELL OF THINGS, YOU GUYS COULD USE ONE, TOO
© 1989 United Feature Syndicate, Inc.
JIM DAVIS 9-1

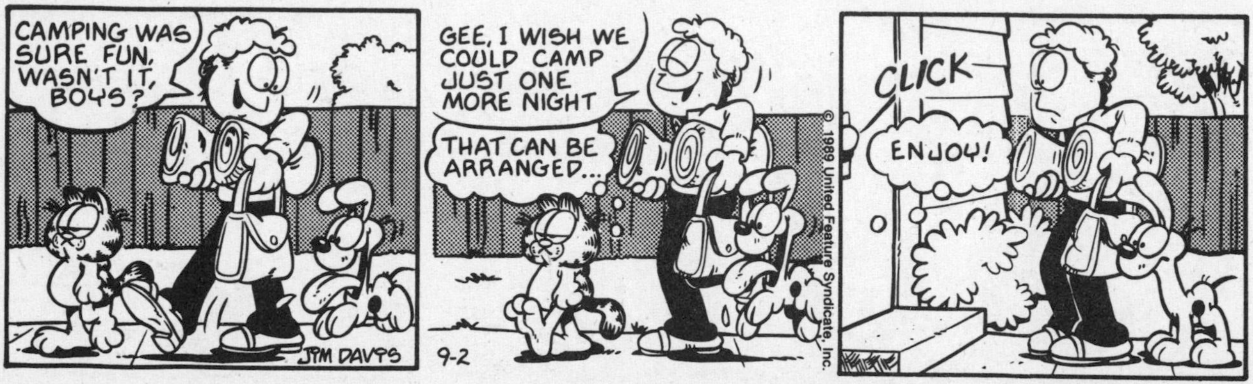
CAMPING WAS SURE FUN, WASN'T IT, BOYS?
JIM DAVIS
9-2
GEE, I WISH WE COULD CAMP JUST ONE MORE NIGHT
THAT CAN BE ARRANGED...
CLICK
ENJOY!
© 1989 United Feature Syndicate, Inc.

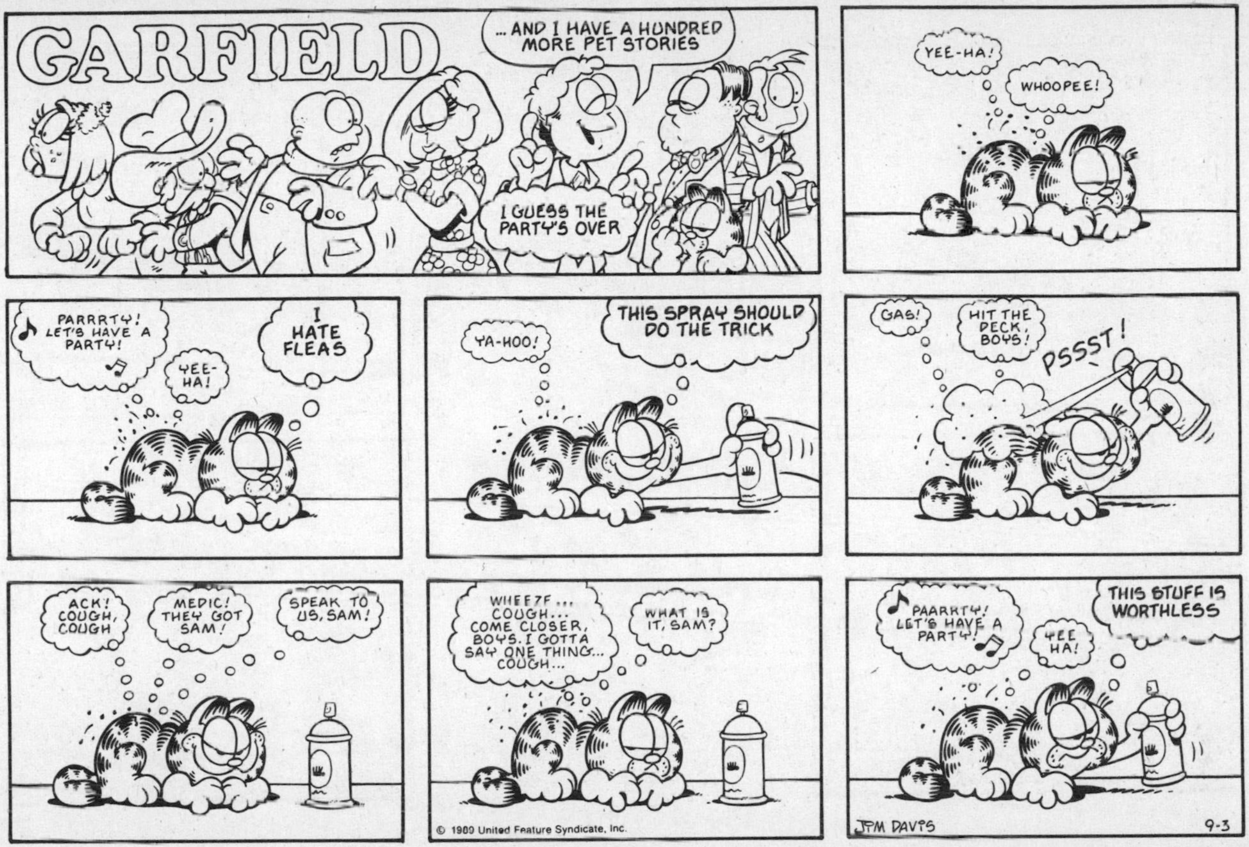
GARFIELD
... AND I HAVE A HUNDRED MORE PET STORIES
I GUESS THE PARTY'S OVER
YEE-HA!
WHOOPEE!
PARRRTY! LET'S HAVE A PARTY!
YEE-HA!
I HATE FLEAS
YA-HOO!
THIS SPRAY SHOULD DO THE TRICK
GAS!
HIT THE DECK, BOYS!
PSSST!
ACK! COUGH, COUGH
MEDIC! THEY GOT SAM!
SPEAK TO US, SAM!
WHEEZE... COUGH... COME CLOSER, BOYS. I GOTTA SAY ONE THING... COUGH...
WHAT IS IT, SAM?
PAARRTY! LET'S HAVE A PARTY!
YEE HA!
THIS STUFF IS WORTHLESS
JIM DAVIS
9-3

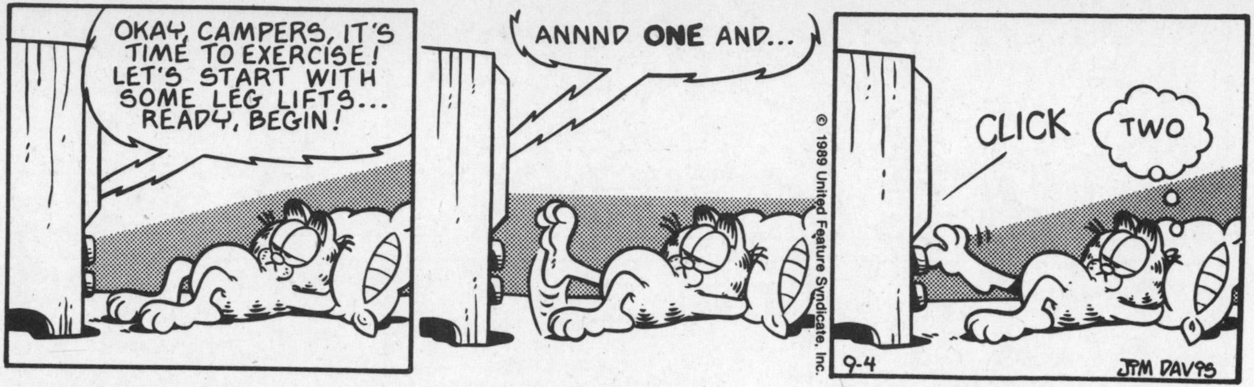
OKAY, CAMPERS, IT'S TIME TO EXERCISE! LET'S START WITH SOME LEG LIFTS... READY, BEGIN!
ANNND **ONE** AND...
CLICK
TWO
© 1989 United Feature Syndicate, Inc.
9-4
JIM DAVIS

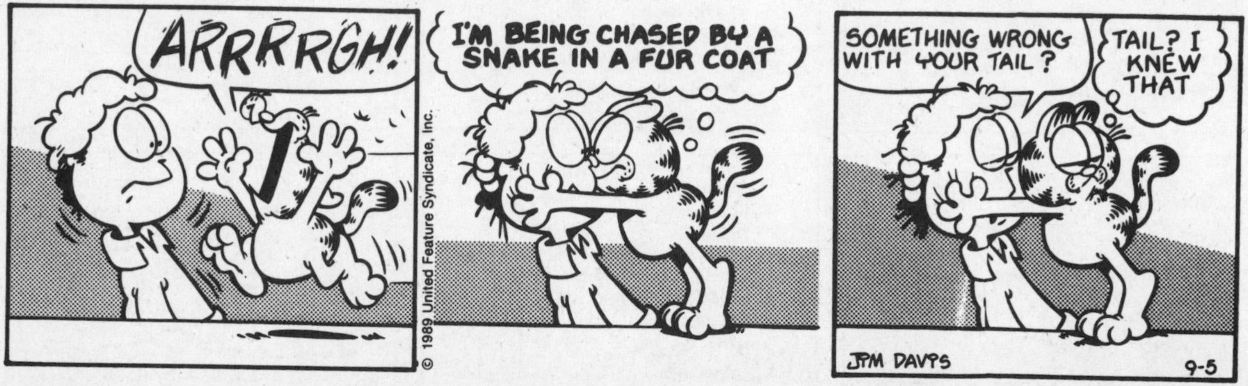
ARRRRGH!
© 1989 United Feature Syndicate, Inc.
I'M BEING CHASED BY A SNAKE IN A FUR COAT
SOMETHING WRONG WITH YOUR TAIL?
TAIL? I KNEW THAT
JIM DAVIS
9-5

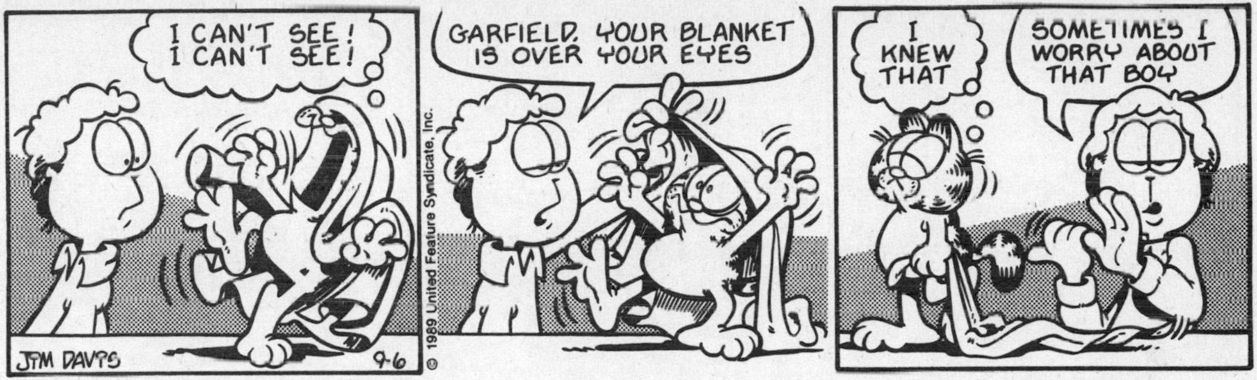
I CAN'T SEE! I CAN'T SEE!
JIM DAVIS
9-6
© 1989 United Feature Syndicate, Inc.
GARFIELD, YOUR BLANKET IS OVER YOUR EYES
I KNEW THAT
SOMETIMES I WORRY ABOUT THAT BOY

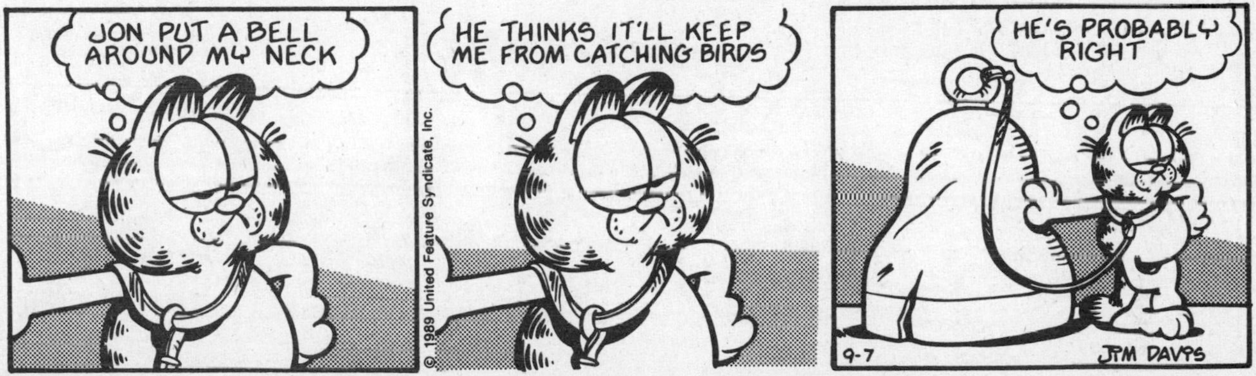
JON PUT A BELL AROUND MY NECK
© 1989 United Feature Syndicate, Inc.
HE THINKS IT'LL KEEP ME FROM CATCHING BIRDS
HE'S PROBABLY RIGHT
9-7
JIM DAVIS

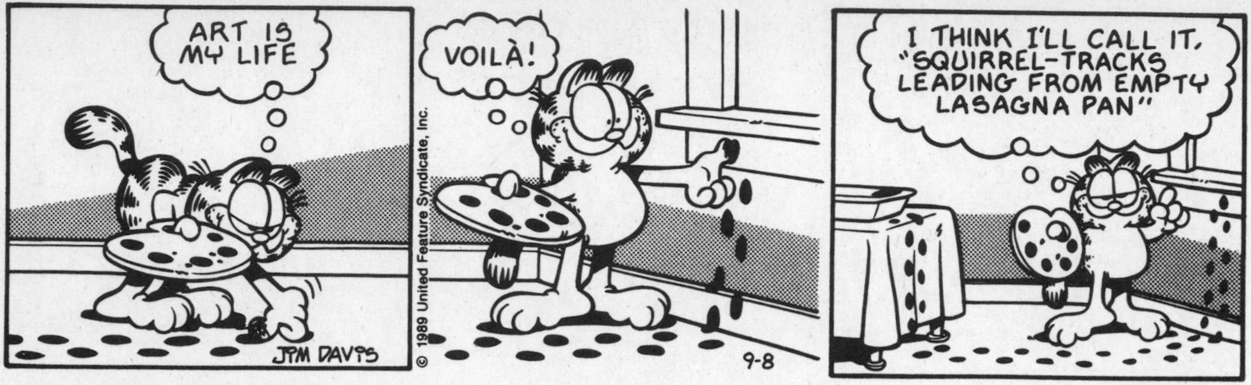
ART IS MY LIFE
VOILÀ!
I THINK I'LL CALL IT, "SQUIRREL-TRACKS LEADING FROM EMPTY LASAGNA PAN"
JIM DAVIS
© 1989 United Feature Syndicate, Inc.
9-8

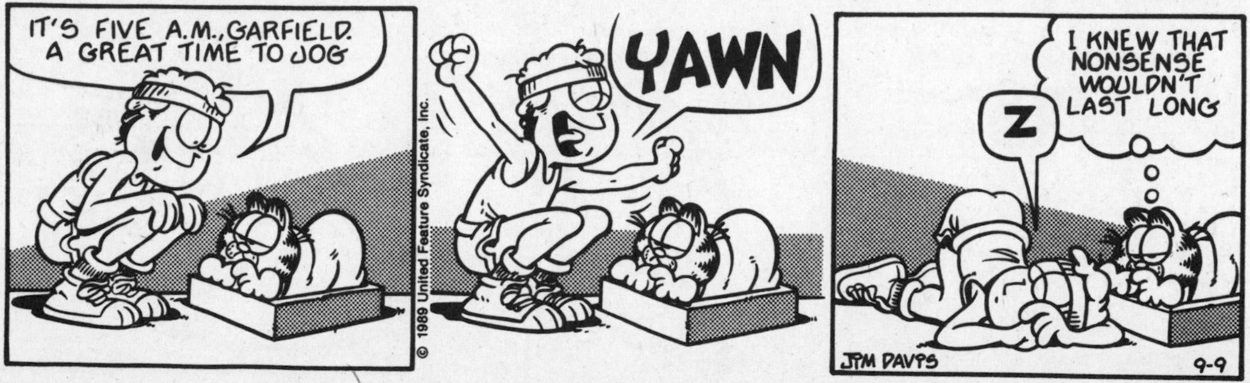
IT'S FIVE A.M., GARFIELD. A GREAT TIME TO JOG
YAWN
Z
I KNEW THAT NONSENSE WOULDN'T LAST LONG
JIM DAVIS
© 1989 United Feature Syndicate, Inc.
9-9

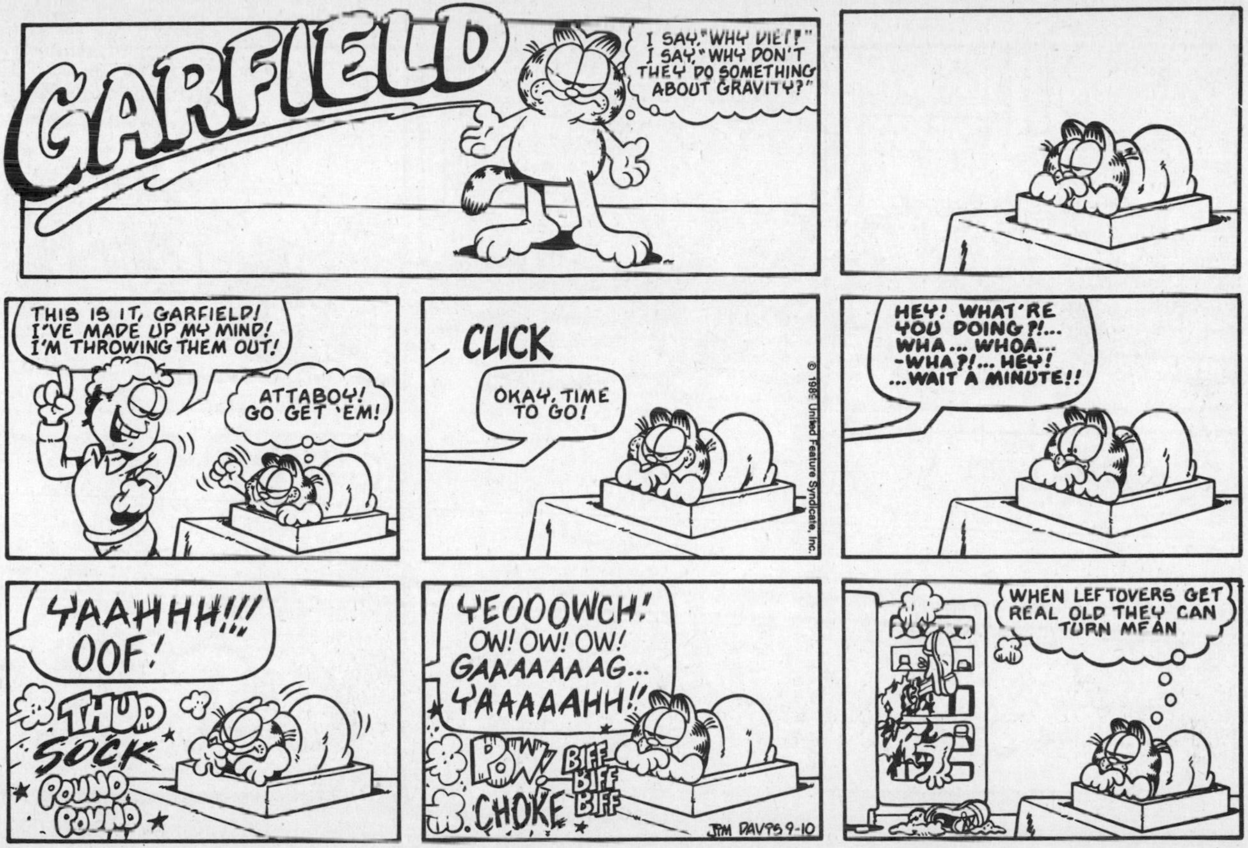
GARFIELD
I SAY, "WHY DIET?" I SAY, "WHY DON'T THEY DO SOMETHING ABOUT GRAVITY?"
THIS IS IT, GARFIELD! I'VE MADE UP MY MIND! I'M THROWING THEM OUT!
ATTABOY! GO GET 'EM!
CLICK
OKAY, TIME TO GO!
HEY! WHAT'RE YOU DOING?!... WHA... WHOA... -WHA?!... HEY! ...WAIT A MINUTE!!
YAAHHH!!! OOF!
THUD
SOCK
POUND POUND
YEOOOWCH! OW! OW! OW! GAAAAAAAG... YAAAAAHH!!
POW!
BIFF BIFF BIFF
CHOKE
JIM DAVIS 9-10
WHEN LEFTOVERS GET REAL OLD THEY CAN TURN MEAN

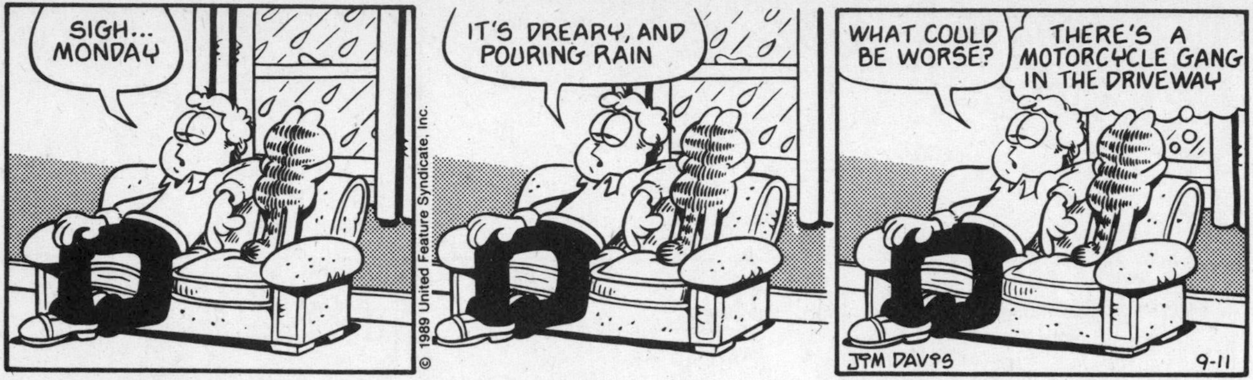
SIGH... MONDAY
IT'S DREARY, AND POURING RAIN
WHAT COULD BE WORSE?
THERE'S A MOTORCYCLE GANG IN THE DRIVEWAY
© 1989 United Feature Syndicate, Inc.
JIM DAVIS
9-11

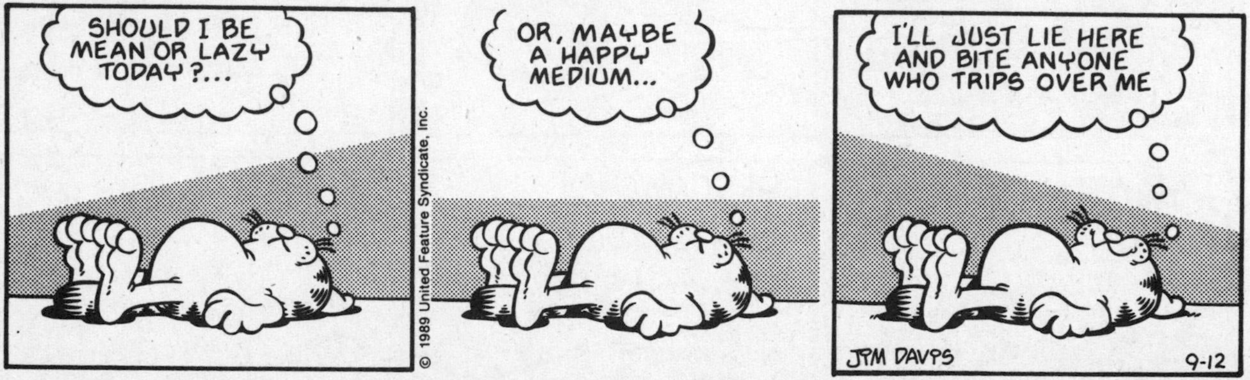
SHOULD I BE MEAN OR LAZY TODAY?...
OR, MAYBE A HAPPY MEDIUM...
I'LL JUST LIE HERE AND BITE ANYONE WHO TRIPS OVER ME
© 1989 United Feature Syndicate, Inc.
JIM DAVIS
9-12

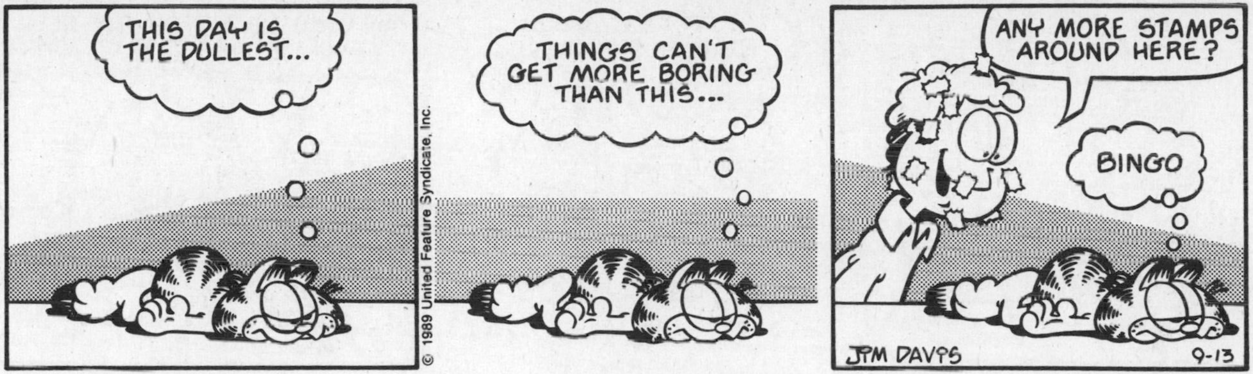
THIS DAY IS THE DULLEST...
THINGS CAN'T GET MORE BORING THAN THIS...
ANY MORE STAMPS AROUND HERE?
BINGO
JIM DAVIS
9-13
© 1989 United Feature Syndicate, Inc.

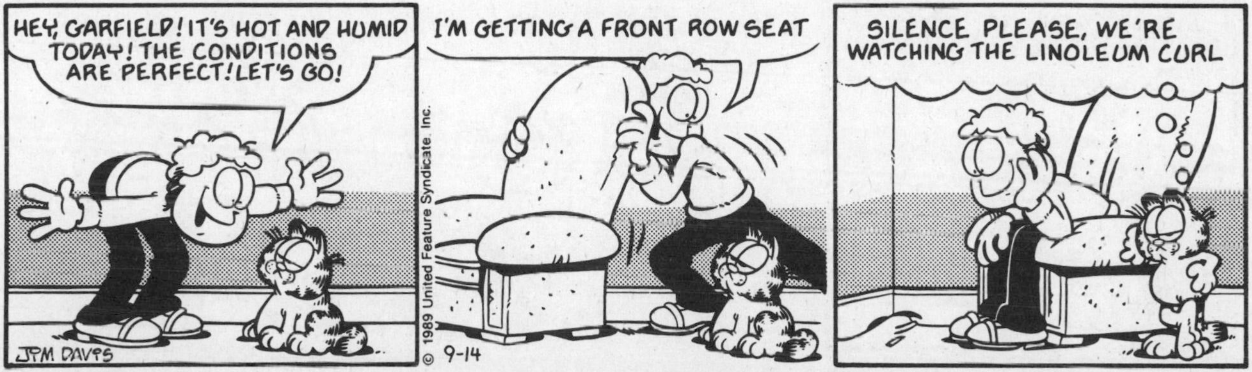
HEY, GARFIELD! IT'S HOT AND HUMID TODAY! THE CONDITIONS ARE PERFECT! LET'S GO!
JIM DAVIS
I'M GETTING A FRONT ROW SEAT
SILENCE PLEASE, WE'RE WATCHING THE LINOLEUM CURL
9-14
© 1989 United Feature Syndicate, Inc.

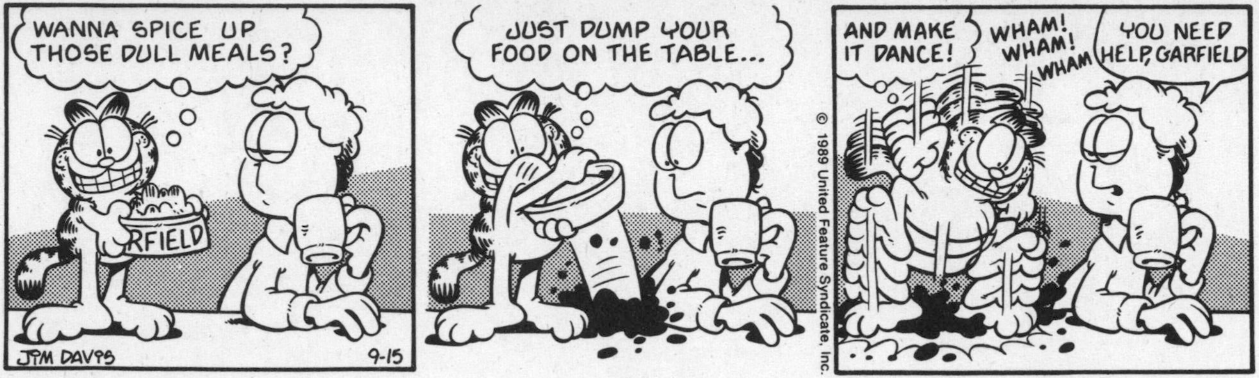
WANNA SPICE UP THOSE DULL MEALS?
RFIELD
JIM DAVIS
9-15
JUST DUMP YOUR FOOD ON THE TABLE...
© 1989 United Feature Syndicate, Inc.
AND MAKE IT DANCE!
WHAM! WHAM! WHAM
YOU NEED HELP, GARFIELD

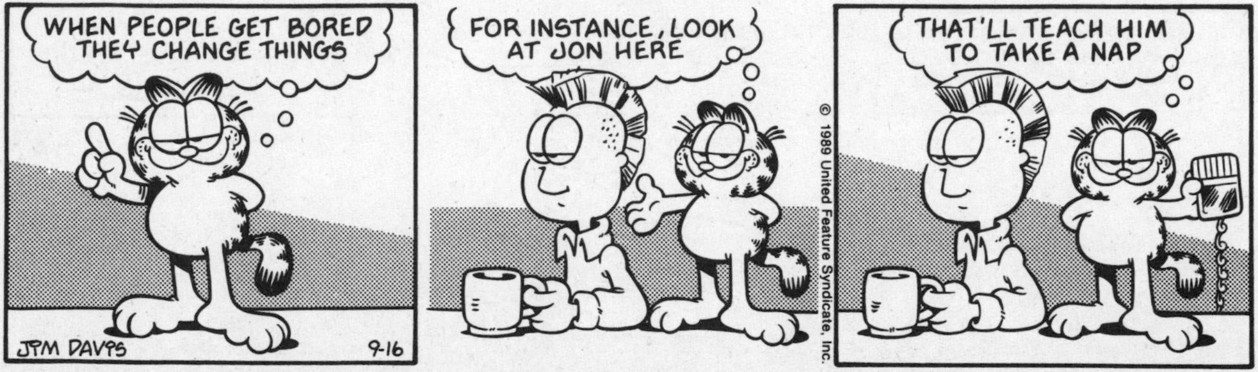
WHEN PEOPLE GET BORED THEY CHANGE THINGS
JIM DAVIS
9-16
FOR INSTANCE, LOOK AT JON HERE
© 1989 United Feature Syndicate, Inc.
THAT'LL TEACH HIM TO TAKE A NAP

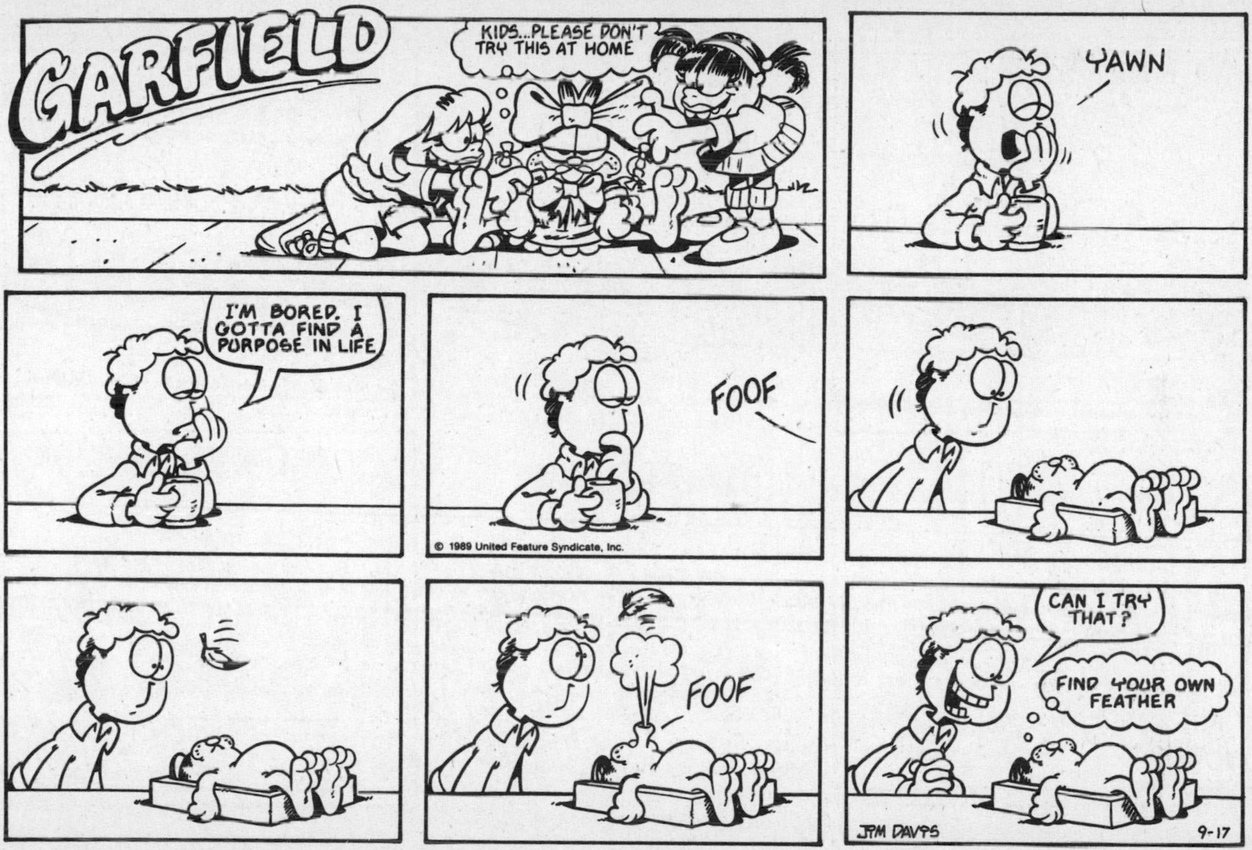
GARFIELD
KIDS...PLEASE DON'T TRY THIS AT HOME
YAWN
I'M BORED. I GOTTA FIND A PURPOSE IN LIFE
FOOF
© 1989 United Feature Syndicate, Inc.
FOOF
CAN I TRY THAT?
FIND YOUR OWN FEATHER
JIM DAVIS
9-17

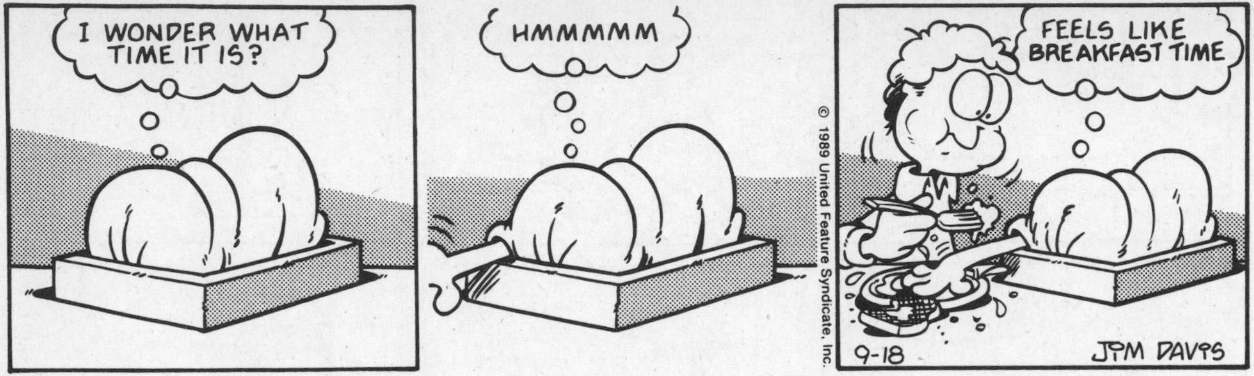
I WONDER WHAT TIME IT IS?
HMMMMM
FEELS LIKE BREAKFAST TIME
© 1989 United Feature Syndicate, Inc.
9-18
JIM DAVIS

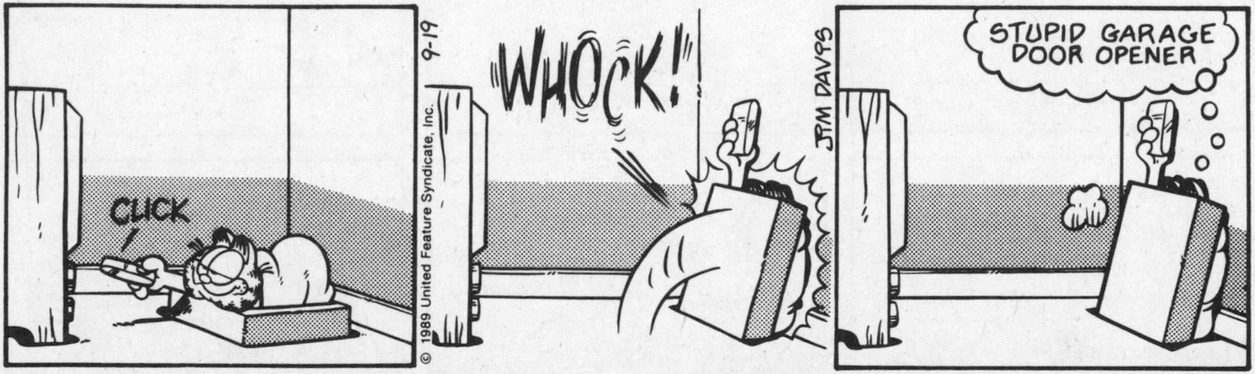
CLICK
9-19
© 1989 United Feature Syndicate, Inc.
WHOCK!
JIM DAVIS
STUPID GARAGE DOOR OPENER

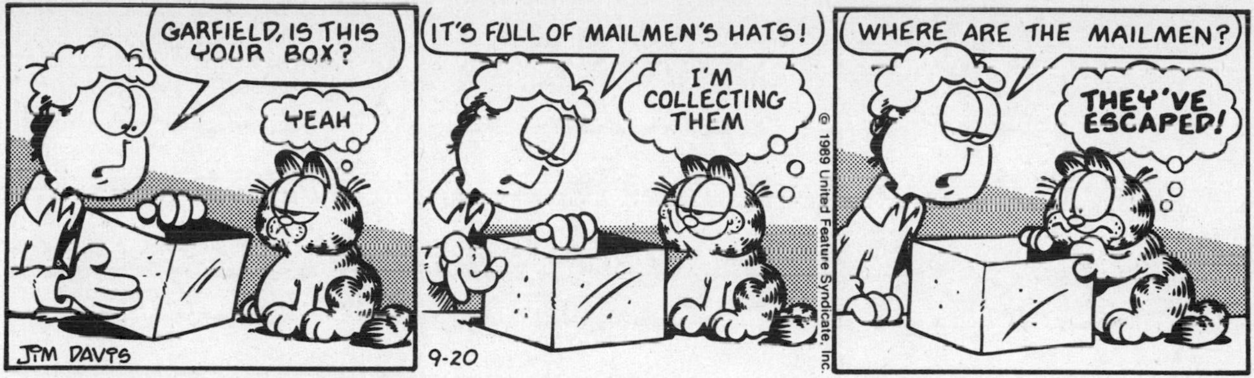
GARFIELD, IS THIS YOUR BOX?
YEAH
IT'S FULL OF MAILMEN'S HATS!
I'M COLLECTING THEM
WHERE ARE THE MAILMEN?
THEY'VE ESCAPED!
JIM DAVIS
9-20
© 1989 United Feature Syndicate, Inc.

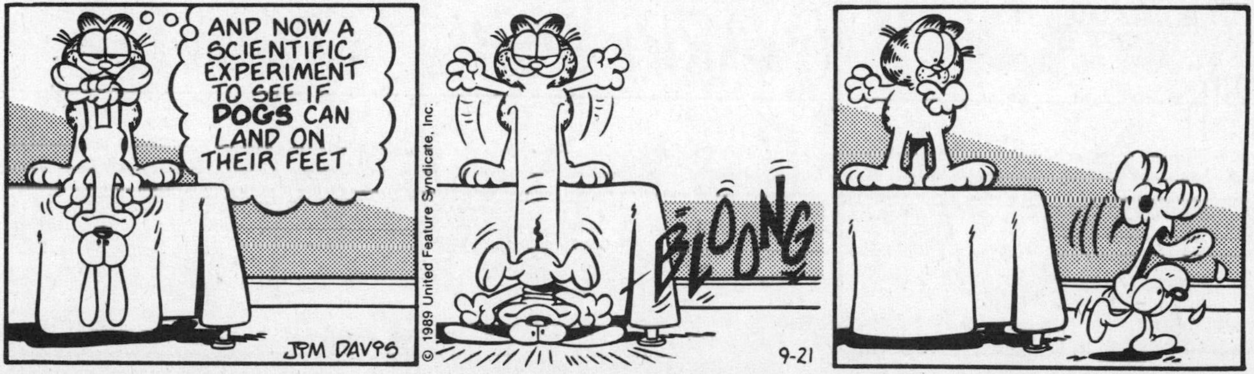
AND NOW A SCIENTIFIC EXPERIMENT TO SEE IF **DOGS** CAN LAND ON THEIR FEET
BLOONG
JIM DAVIS
9-21
© 1989 United Feature Syndicate, Inc.

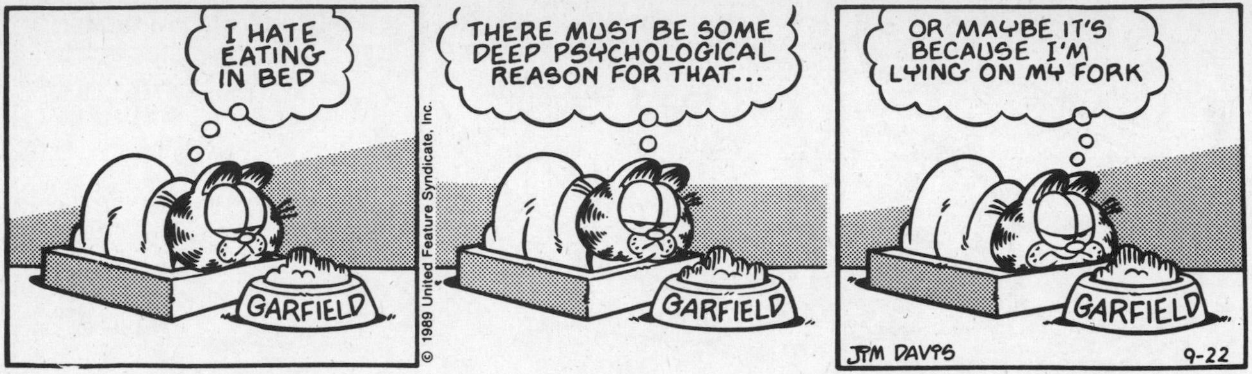
I HATE EATING IN BED
GARFIELD
THERE MUST BE SOME DEEP PSYCHOLOGICAL REASON FOR THAT...
GARFIELD
OR MAYBE IT'S BECAUSE I'M LYING ON MY FORK
GARFIELD
© 1989 United Feature Syndicate, Inc.
JIM DAVIS
9-22

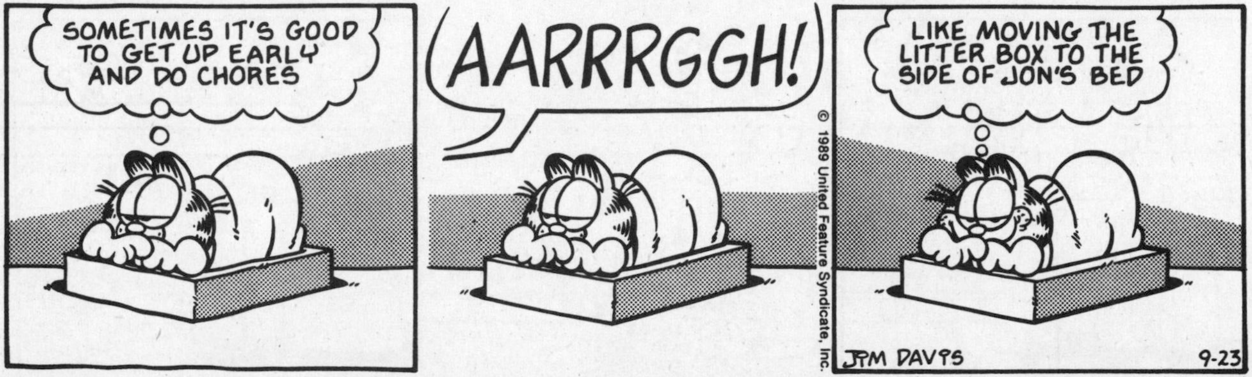
SOMETIMES IT'S GOOD TO GET UP EARLY AND DO CHORES
AARRRGGH!
LIKE MOVING THE LITTER BOX TO THE SIDE OF JON'S BED
© 1989 United Feature Syndicate, Inc.
JIM DAVIS
9-23

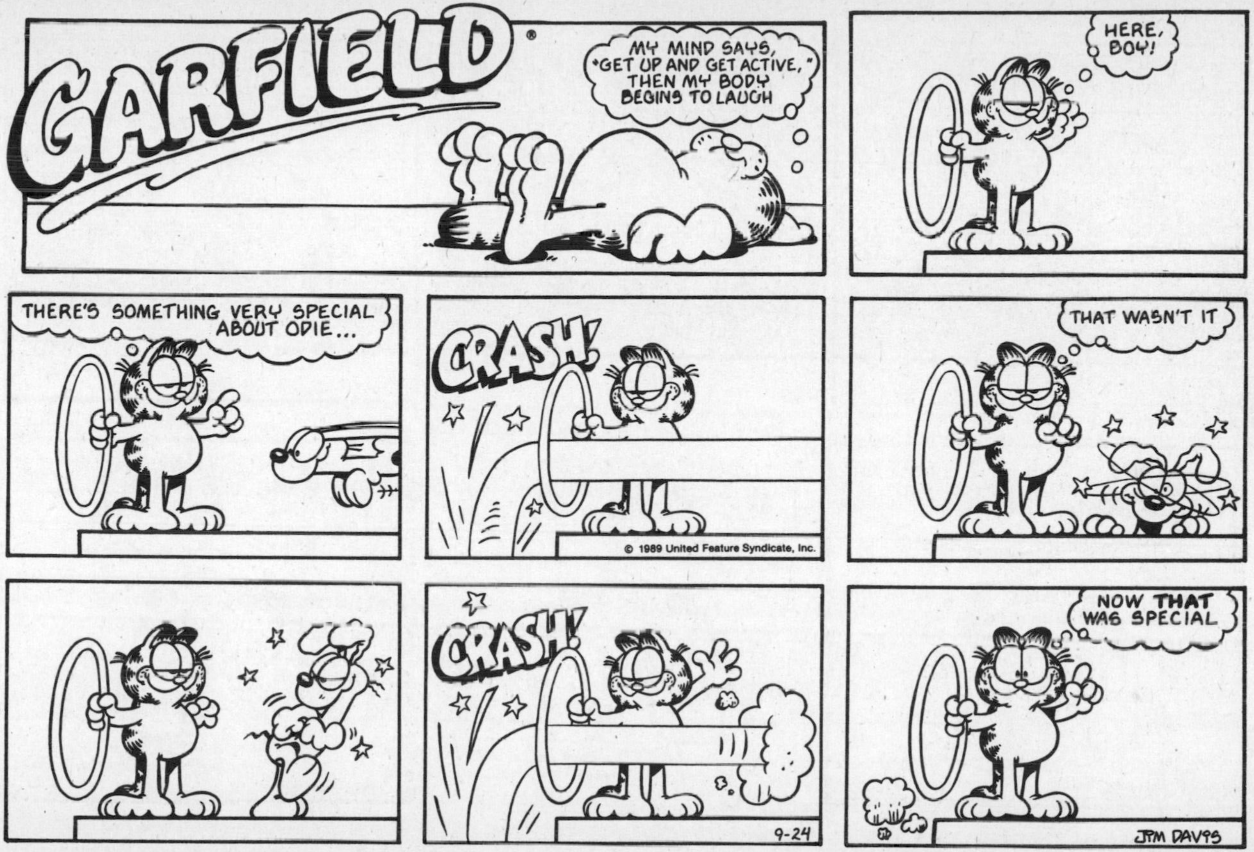
GARFIELD®
MY MIND SAYS, "GET UP AND GET ACTIVE," THEN MY BODY BEGINS TO LAUGH
HERE, BOY!
THERE'S SOMETHING VERY SPECIAL ABOUT ODIE...
CRASH!
© 1989 United Feature Syndicate, Inc.
THAT WASN'T IT
CRASH!
9-24
NOW THAT WAS SPECIAL
JIM DAVIS

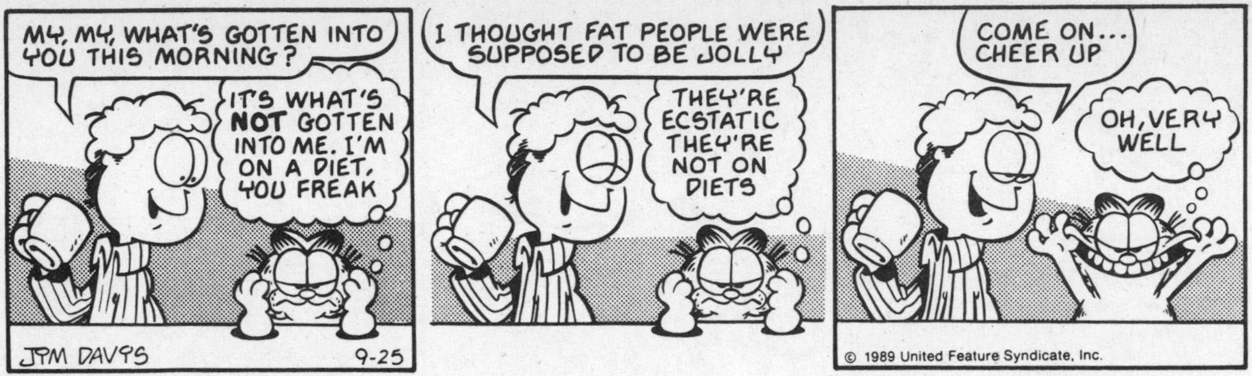
MY, MY, WHAT'S GOTTEN INTO YOU THIS MORNING?
IT'S WHAT'S NOT GOTTEN INTO ME. I'M ON A DIET, YOU FREAK
I THOUGHT FAT PEOPLE WERE SUPPOSED TO BE JOLLY
THEY'RE ECSTATIC THEY'RE NOT ON DIETS
COME ON... CHEER UP
OH, VERY WELL
JIM DAVIS
9-25
© 1989 United Feature Syndicate, Inc.

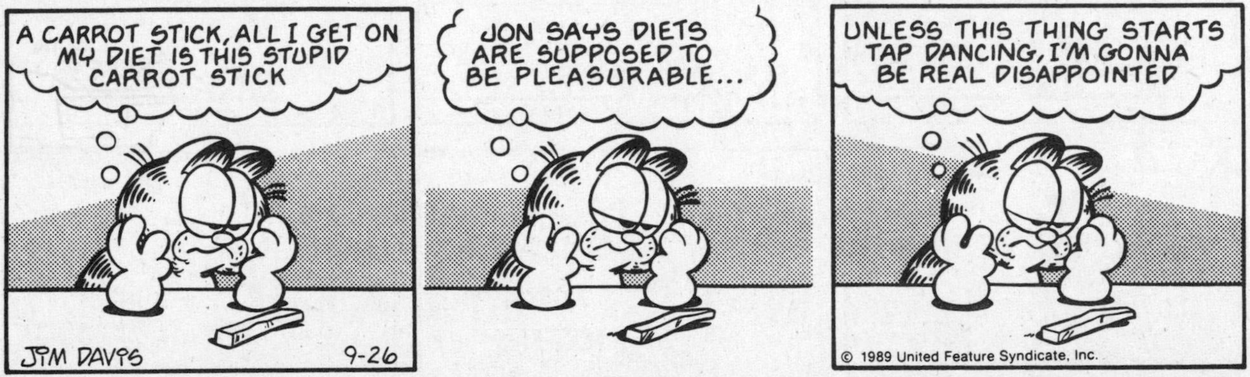
A CARROT STICK, ALL I GET ON MY DIET IS THIS STUPID CARROT STICK
JON SAYS DIETS ARE SUPPOSED TO BE PLEASURABLE...
UNLESS THIS THING STARTS TAP DANCING, I'M GONNA BE REAL DISAPPOINTED
JIM DAVIS
9-26
© 1989 United Feature Syndicate, Inc.

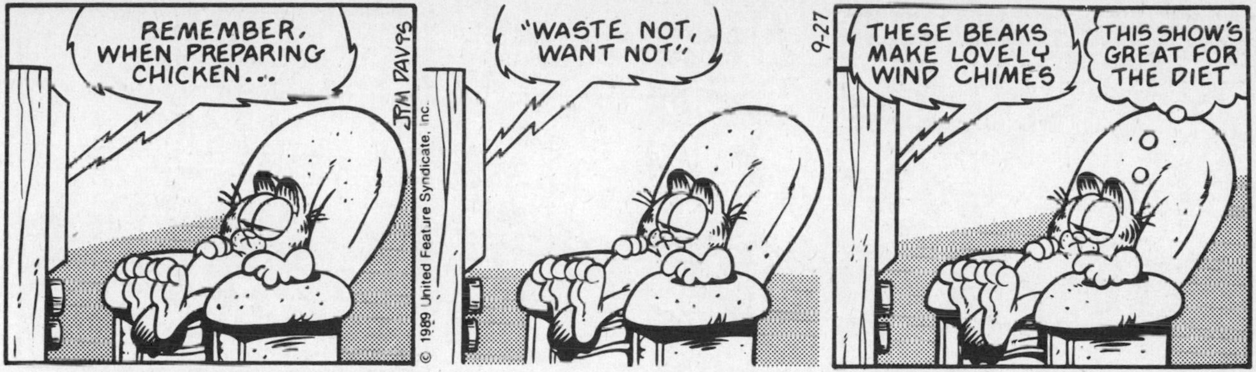
REMEMBER, WHEN PREPARING CHICKEN...
"WASTE NOT, WANT NOT"
THESE BEAKS MAKE LOVELY WIND CHIMES
THIS SHOW'S GREAT FOR THE DIET
JIM DAVIS
© 1989 United Feature Syndicate, Inc.
9-27

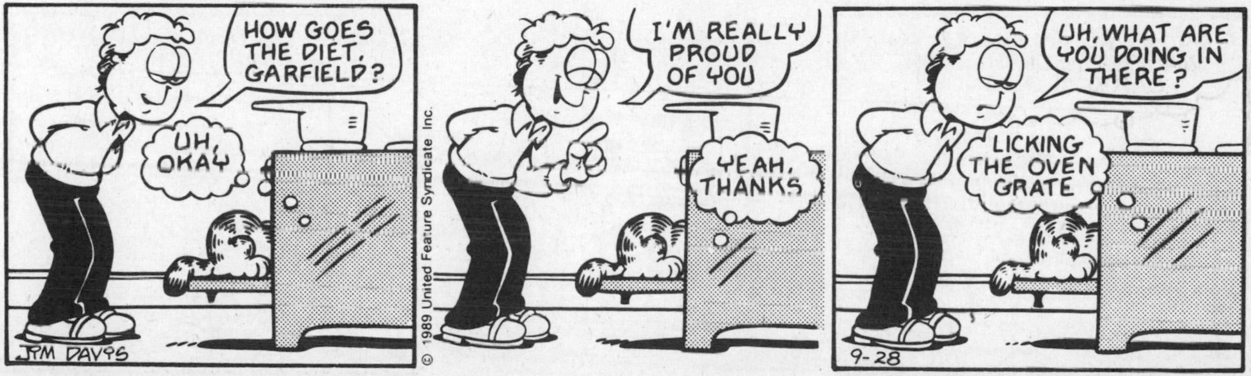
HOW GOES THE DIET, GARFIELD?
UH, OKAY
I'M REALLY PROUD OF YOU
YEAH, THANKS
UH, WHAT ARE YOU DOING IN THERE?
LICKING THE OVEN GRATE
JIM DAVIS
© 1989 United Feature Syndicate Inc.
9-28

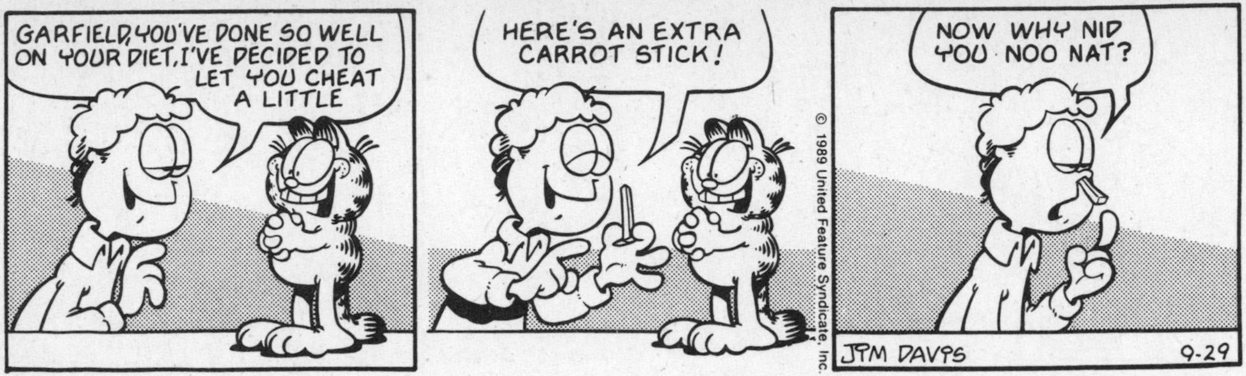
GARFIELD, YOU'VE DONE SO WELL ON YOUR DIET, I'VE DECIDED TO LET YOU CHEAT A LITTLE
HERE'S AN EXTRA CARROT STICK!
© 1989 United Feature Syndicate, Inc.
NOW WHY NID YOU NOO NAT?
JIM DAVIS
9-29

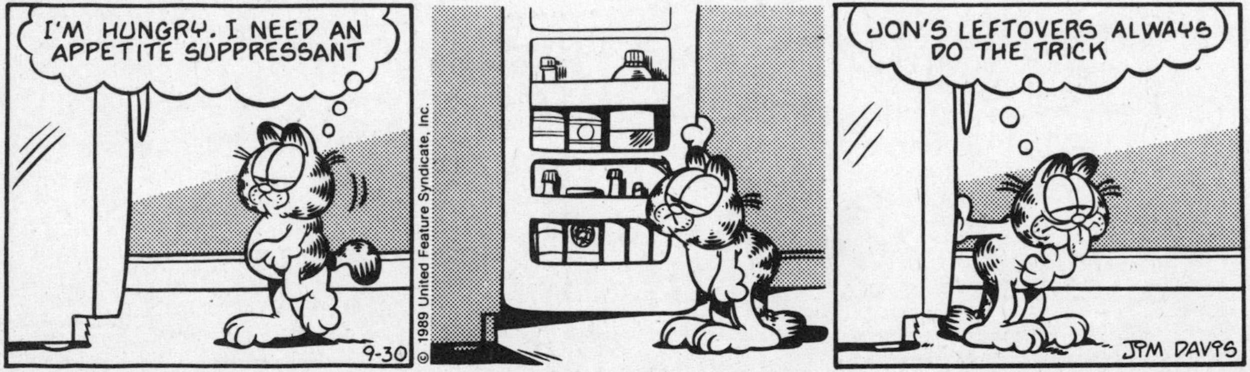
I'M HUNGRY. I NEED AN APPETITE SUPPRESSANT
9-30
© 1989 United Feature Syndicate, Inc.
JON'S LEFTOVERS ALWAYS DO THE TRICK
JIM DAVIS

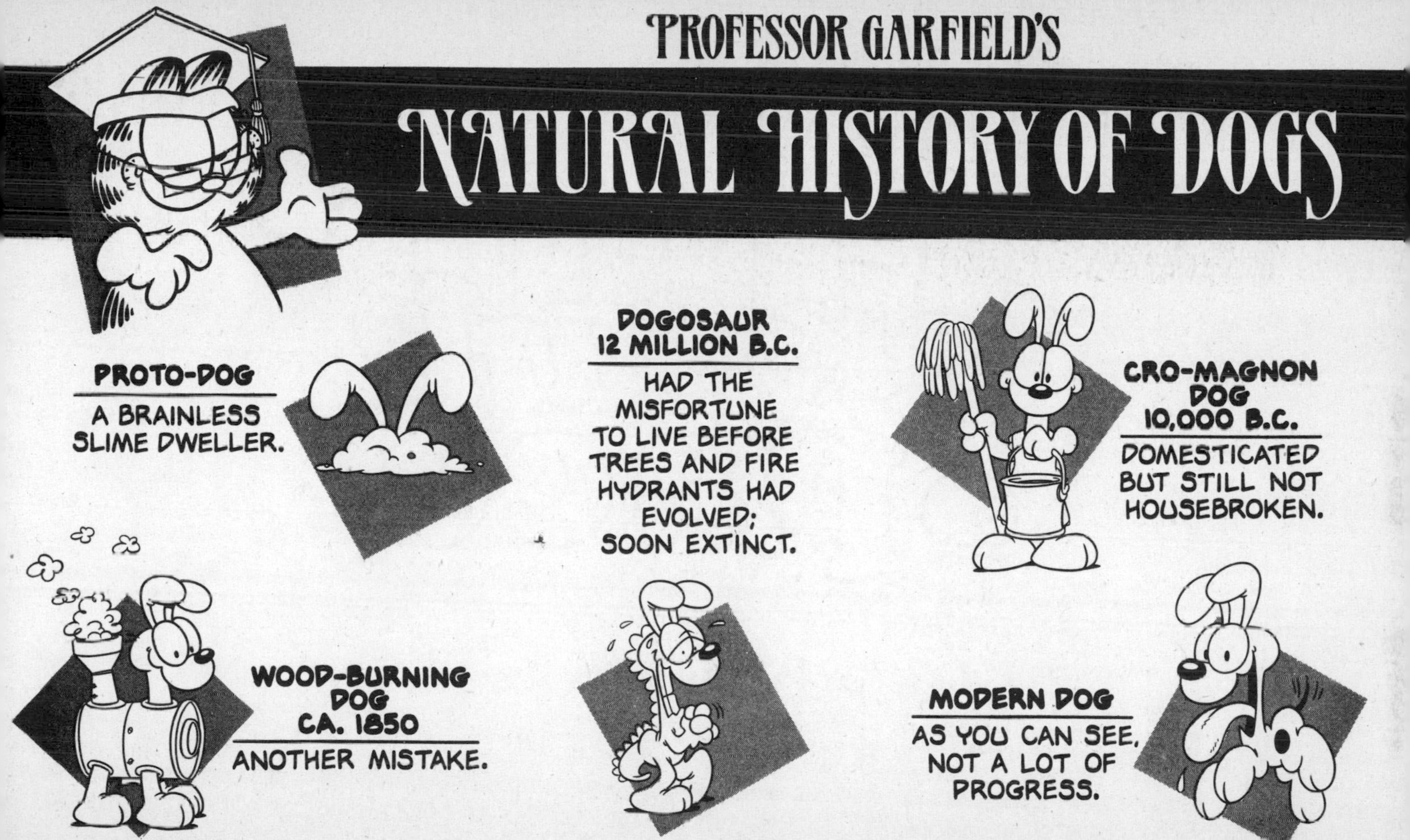
PROFESSOR GARFIELD'S
NATURAL HISTORY OF DOGS
PROTO-DOG
A BRAINLESS SLIME DWELLER.
DOGOSAUR 12 MILLION B.C.
HAD THE MISFORTUNE TO LIVE BEFORE TREES AND FIRE HYDRANTS HAD EVOLVED; SOON EXTINCT.
CRO-MAGNON DOG 10,000 B.C.
DOMESTICATED BUT STILL NOT HOUSEBROKEN.
WOOD-BURNING DOG CA. 1850
ANOTHER MISTAKE.
MODERN DOG
AS YOU CAN SEE, NOT A LOT OF PROGRESS.

Garfield takes up space

BY: JIM DAVIS

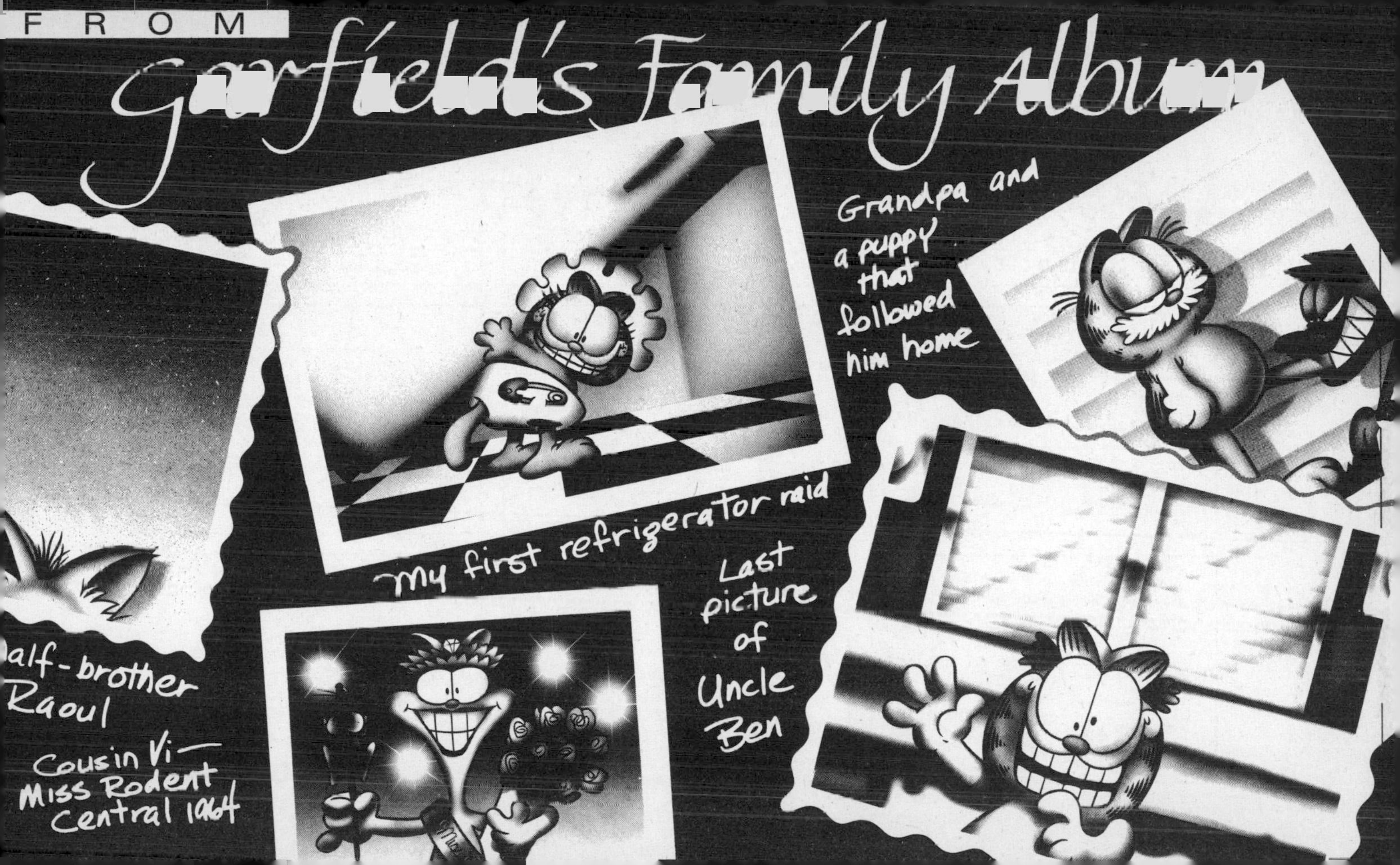

FROM
Garfield's Family Album
My first refrigerator raid
Grandpa and a puppy that followed him home
alf-brother Raoul
Cousin Vi— Miss Rodent Central 1964
Last picture of Uncle Ben

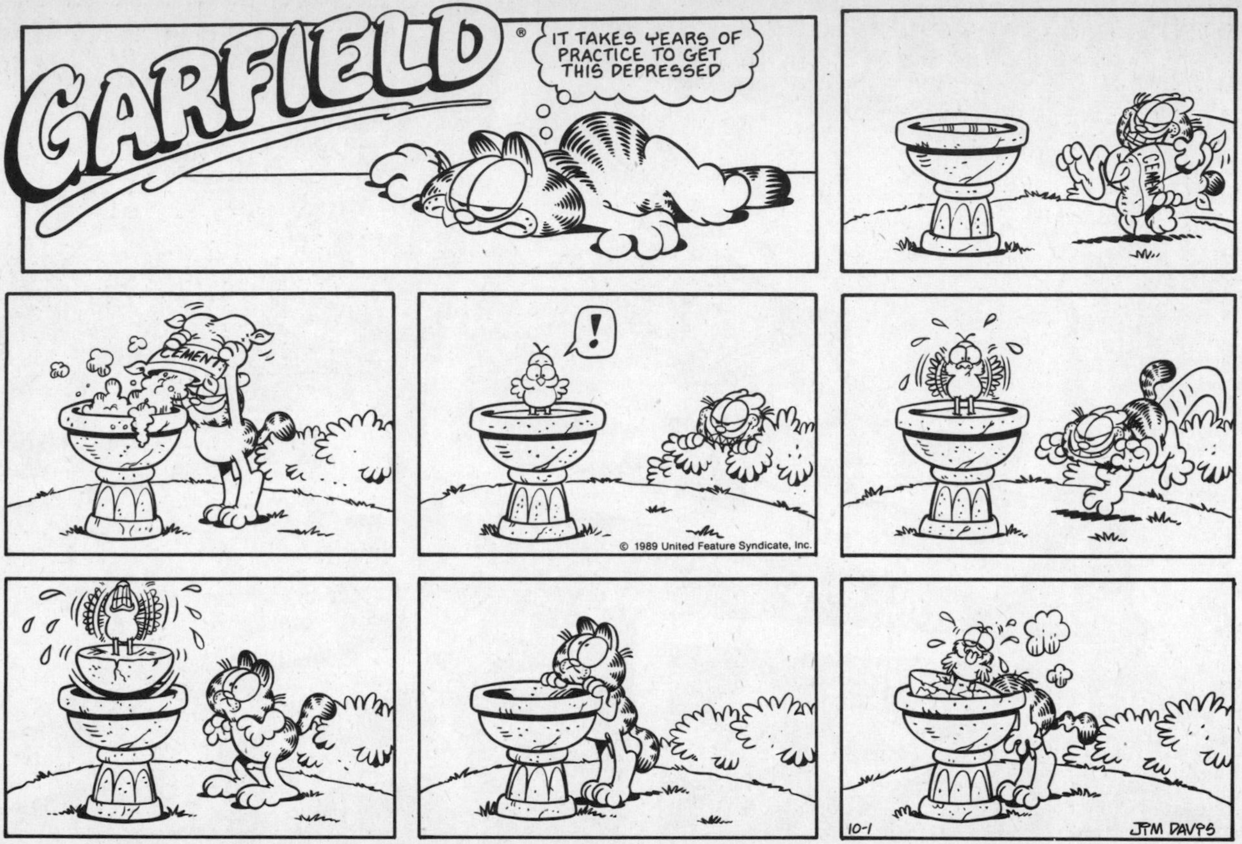
GARFIELD®
IT TAKES YEARS OF PRACTICE TO GET THIS DEPRESSED
CEMENT
CEMENT
!
© 1989 United Feature Syndicate, Inc.
10-1
JIM DAVIS

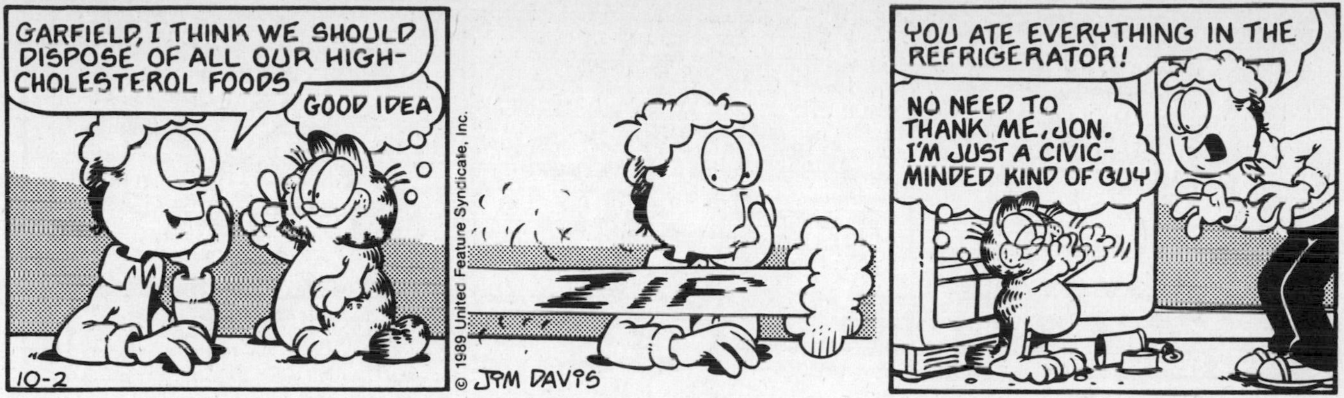
GARFIELD, I THINK WE SHOULD DISPOSE OF ALL OUR HIGH-CHOLESTEROL FOODS
GOOD IDEA
10-2
© 1989 United Feature Syndicate, Inc.
JIM DAVIS
ZIP
YOU ATE EVERYTHING IN THE REFRIGERATOR!
NO NEED TO THANK ME, JON. I'M JUST A CIVIC-MINDED KIND OF GUY

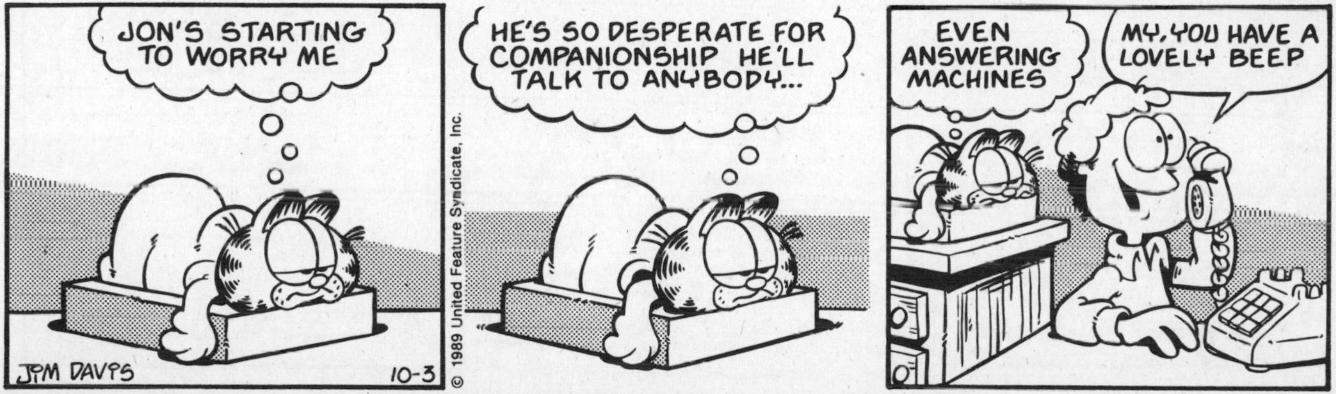
JON'S STARTING TO WORRY ME
JIM DAVIS
10-3
© 1989 United Feature Syndicate, Inc.
HE'S SO DESPERATE FOR COMPANIONSHIP HE'LL TALK TO ANYBODY...
EVEN ANSWERING MACHINES
MY, YOU HAVE A LOVELY BEEP

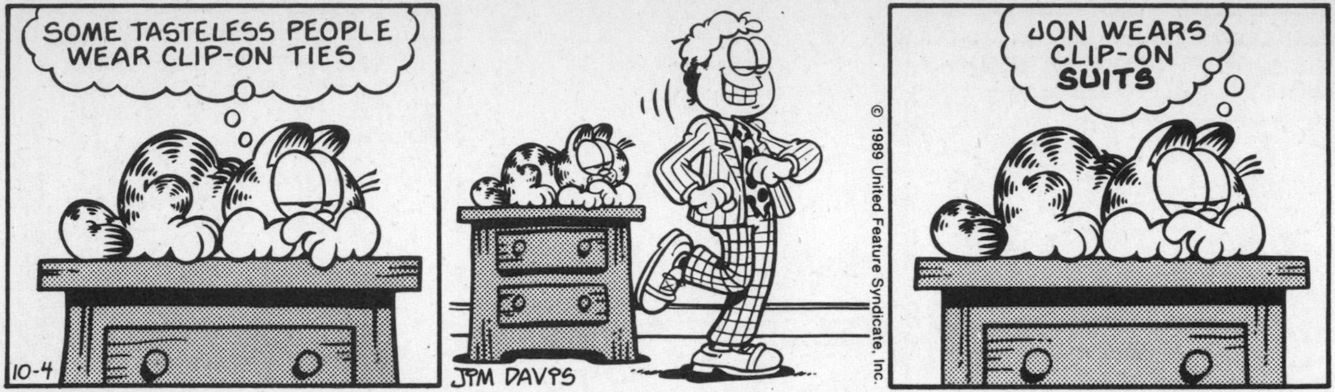
SOME TASTELESS PEOPLE WEAR CLIP-ON TIES
10-4
JIM DAVIS
© 1989 United Feature Syndicate, Inc.
JON WEARS CLIP-ON **SUITS**

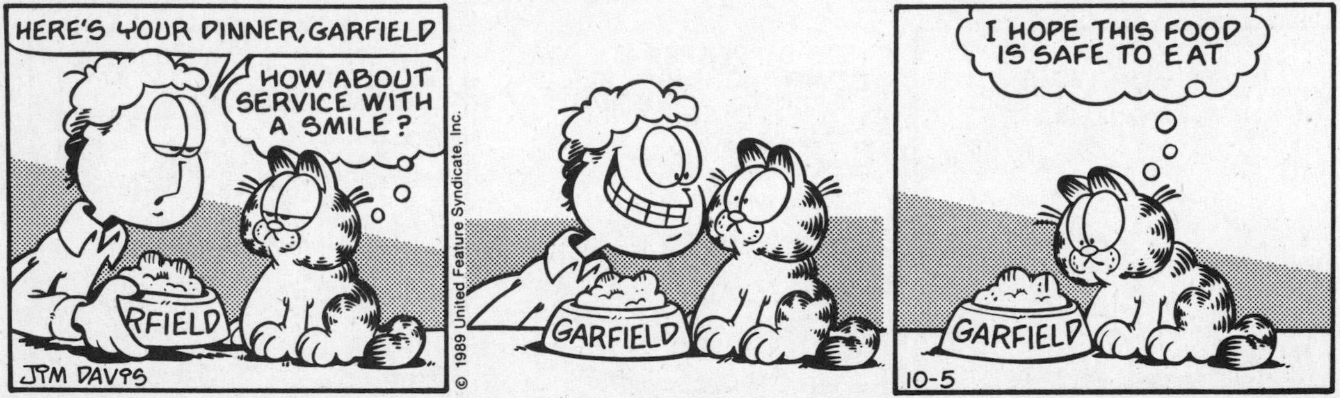
HERE'S YOUR DINNER, GARFIELD
HOW ABOUT SERVICE WITH A SMILE?
RFIELD
JIM DAVIS
© 1989 United Feature Syndicate, Inc.
GARFIELD
I HOPE THIS FOOD IS SAFE TO EAT
GARFIELD
10-5

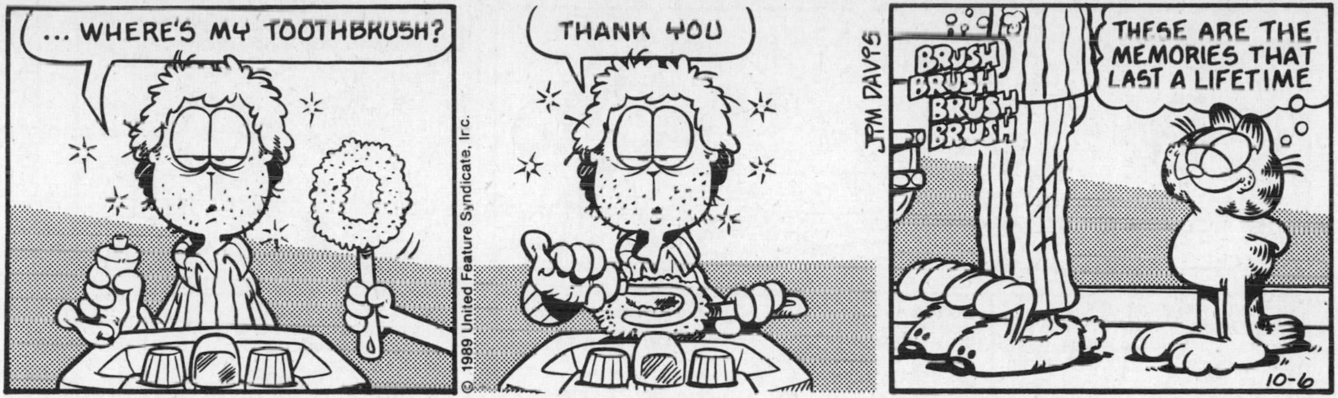

... WHERE'S MY TOOTHBRUSH?
THANK YOU
© 1989 United Feature Syndicate, Inc.
JIM DAVIS
BRUSH
BRUSH
BRUSH
BRUSH
THESE ARE THE MEMORIES THAT LAST A LIFETIME
10-6

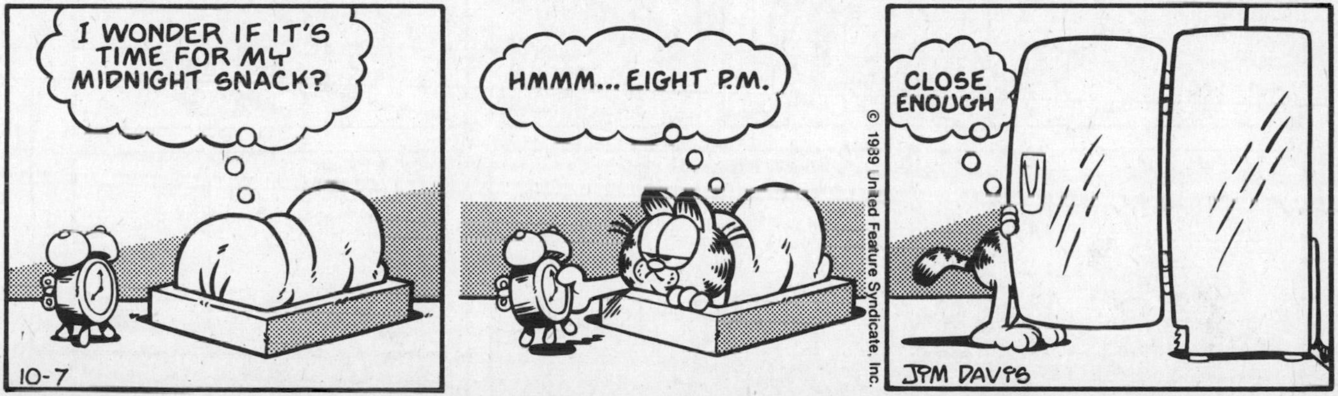

I WONDER IF IT'S TIME FOR MY MIDNIGHT SNACK?
10-7
HMMM... EIGHT P.M.
© 1989 United Feature Syndicate, Inc.
CLOSE ENOUGH
JIM DAVIS

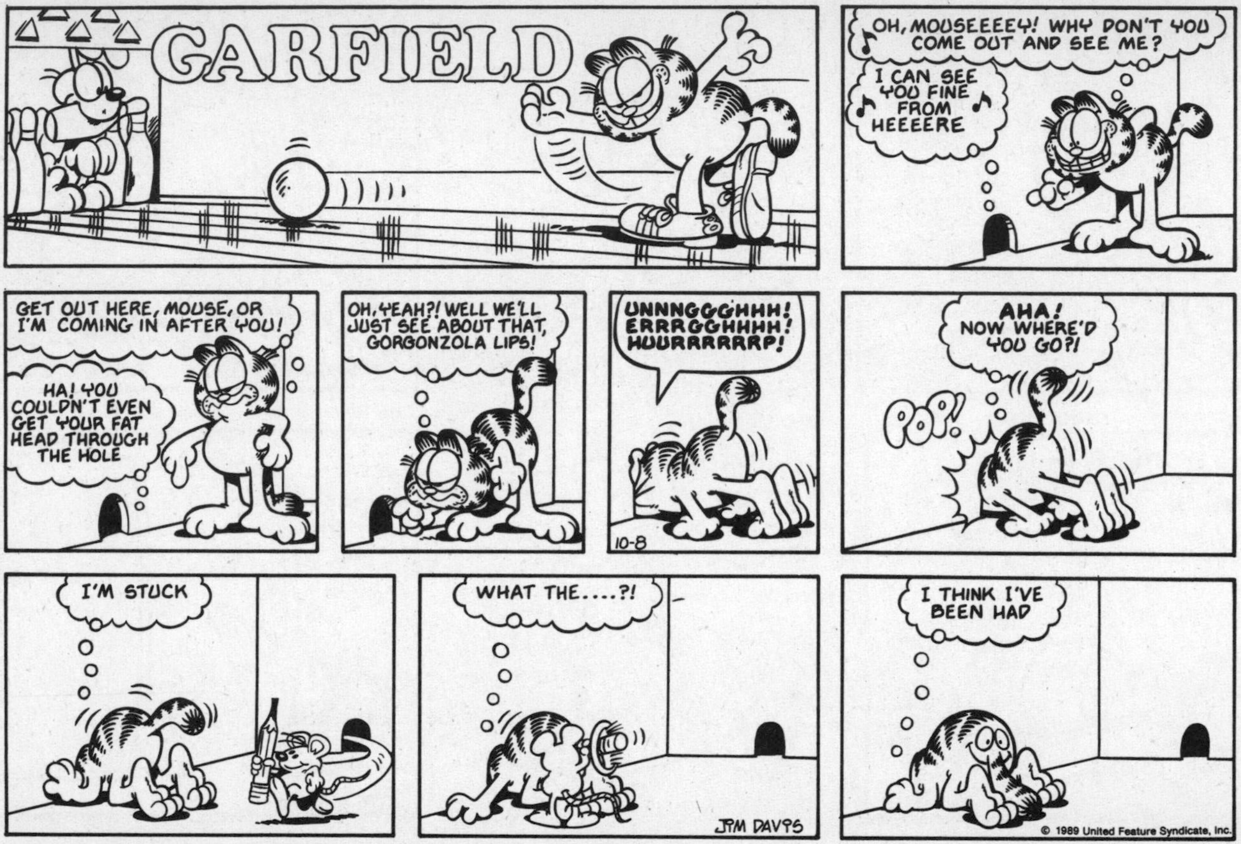

GARFIELD
OH, MOUSEEEEY! WHY DON'T YOU COME OUT AND SEE ME?
I CAN SEE YOU FINE FROM HEEEERE
GET OUT HERE, MOUSE, OR I'M COMING IN AFTER YOU!
HA! YOU COULDN'T EVEN GET YOUR FAT HEAD THROUGH THE HOLE
OH, YEAH?! WELL WE'LL JUST SEE ABOUT THAT, GORGONZOLA LIPS!
UNNNGGGHHH! ERRRGGHHHH! HUURRRRRRP!
10-8
AHA! NOW WHERE'D YOU GO?!
POP!
I'M STUCK
WHAT THE....?!
JIM DAVIS
I THINK I'VE BEEN HAD
© 1989 United Feature Syndicate, Inc.

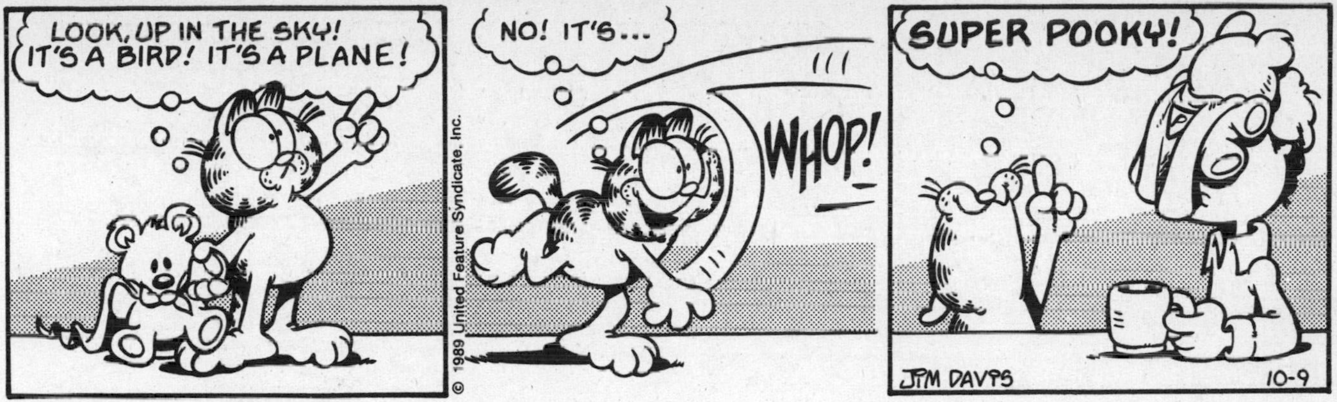
LOOK, UP IN THE SKY! IT'S A BIRD! IT'S A PLANE!
NO! IT'S...
WHOP!
SUPER POOKY!
© 1989 United Feature Syndicate, Inc.
JIM DAVIS
10-9

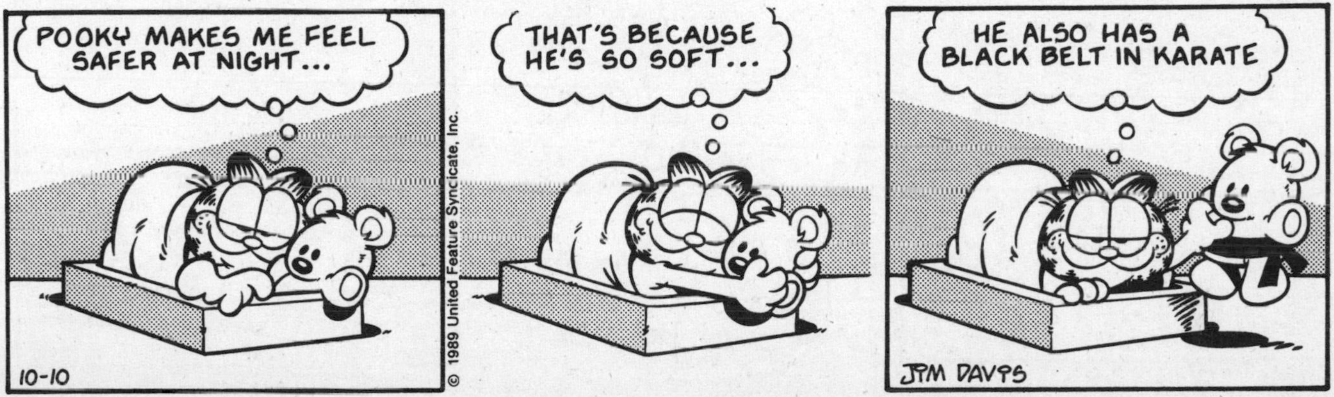
POOKY MAKES ME FEEL SAFER AT NIGHT...
THAT'S BECAUSE HE'S SO SOFT...
HE ALSO HAS A BLACK BELT IN KARATE
© 1989 United Feature Syncicate, Inc.
10-10
JIM DAVIS

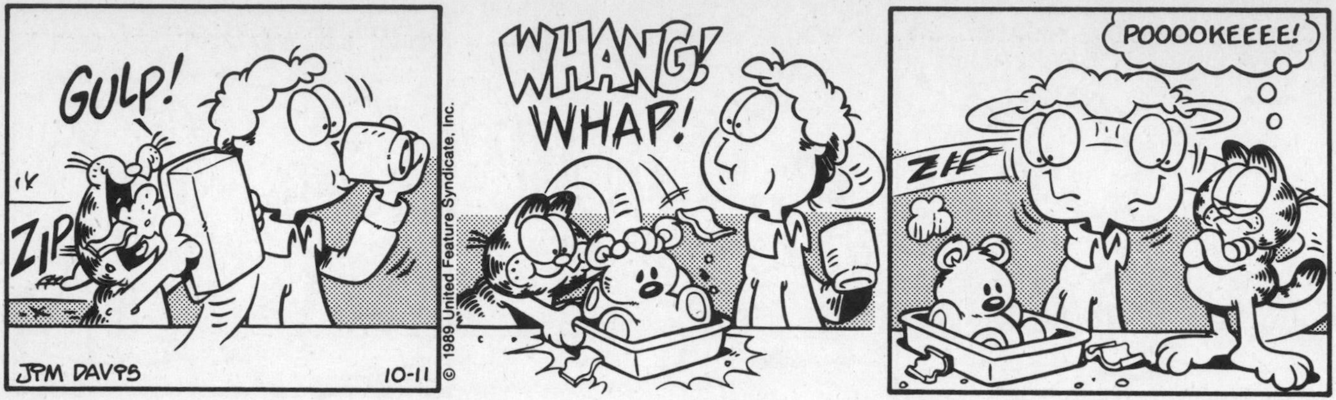
GULP!
ZIP
JIM DAVIS
10-11
© 1989 United Feature Syndicate, Inc.
WHANG!
WHAP!
POOOOKEEEE!
ZIP

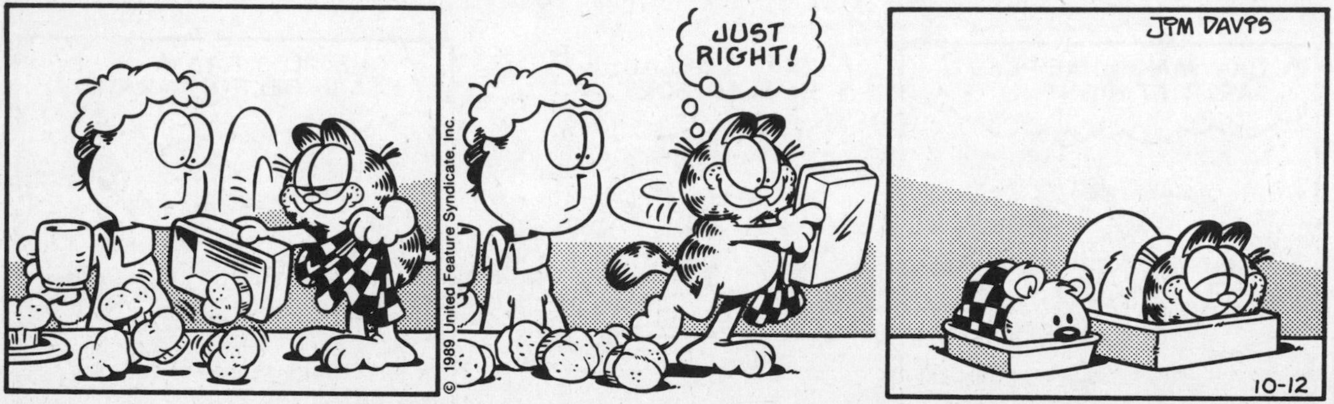
© 1989 United Feature Syndicate, Inc.
JUST RIGHT!
JIM DAVIS
10-12

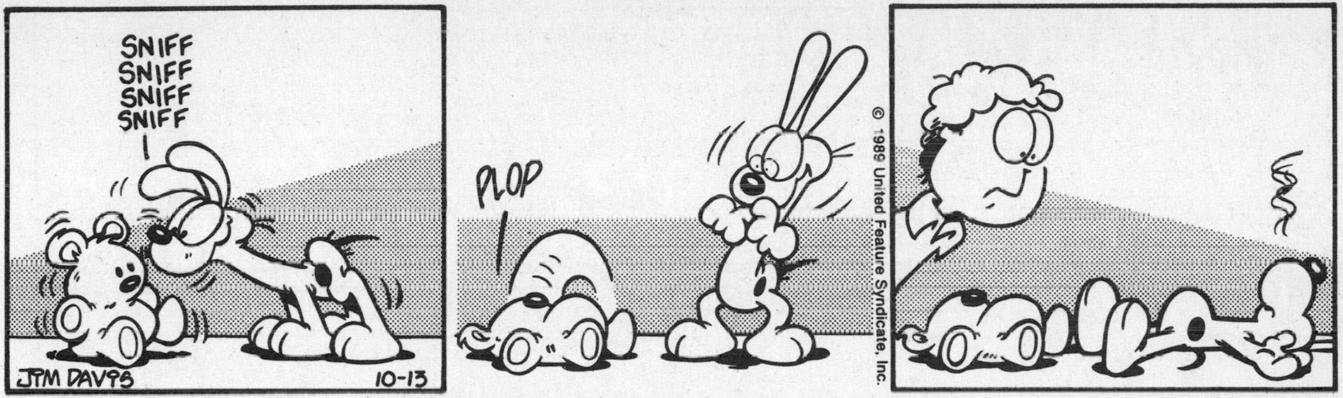
SNIFF
SNIFF
SNIFF
SNIFF
PLOP
JIM DAVIS
10-13
© 1989 United Feature Syndicate, Inc.

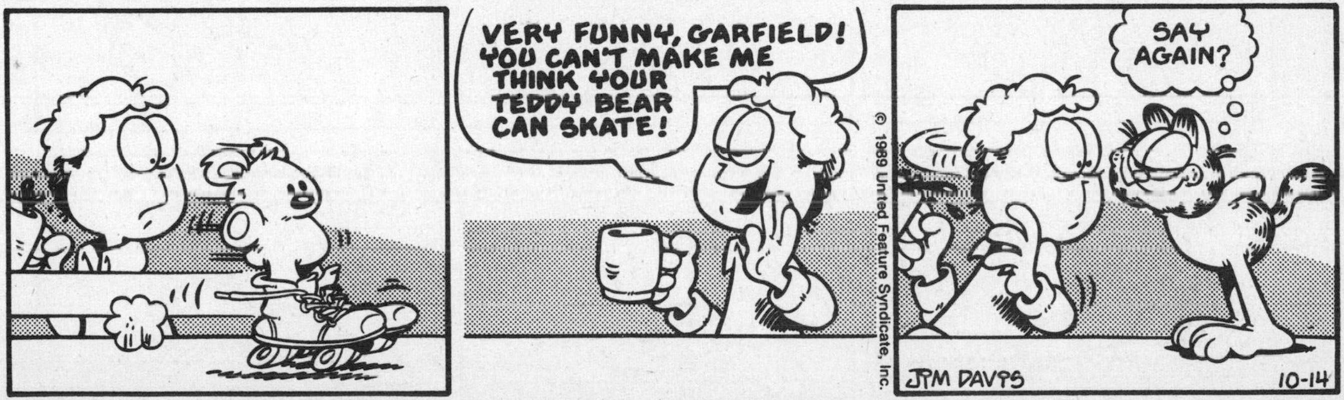
VERY FUNNY, GARFIELD! YOU CAN'T MAKE ME THINK YOUR TEDDY BEAR CAN SKATE!
SAY AGAIN?
JIM DAVIS
10-14
© 1989 United Feature Syndicate, Inc.

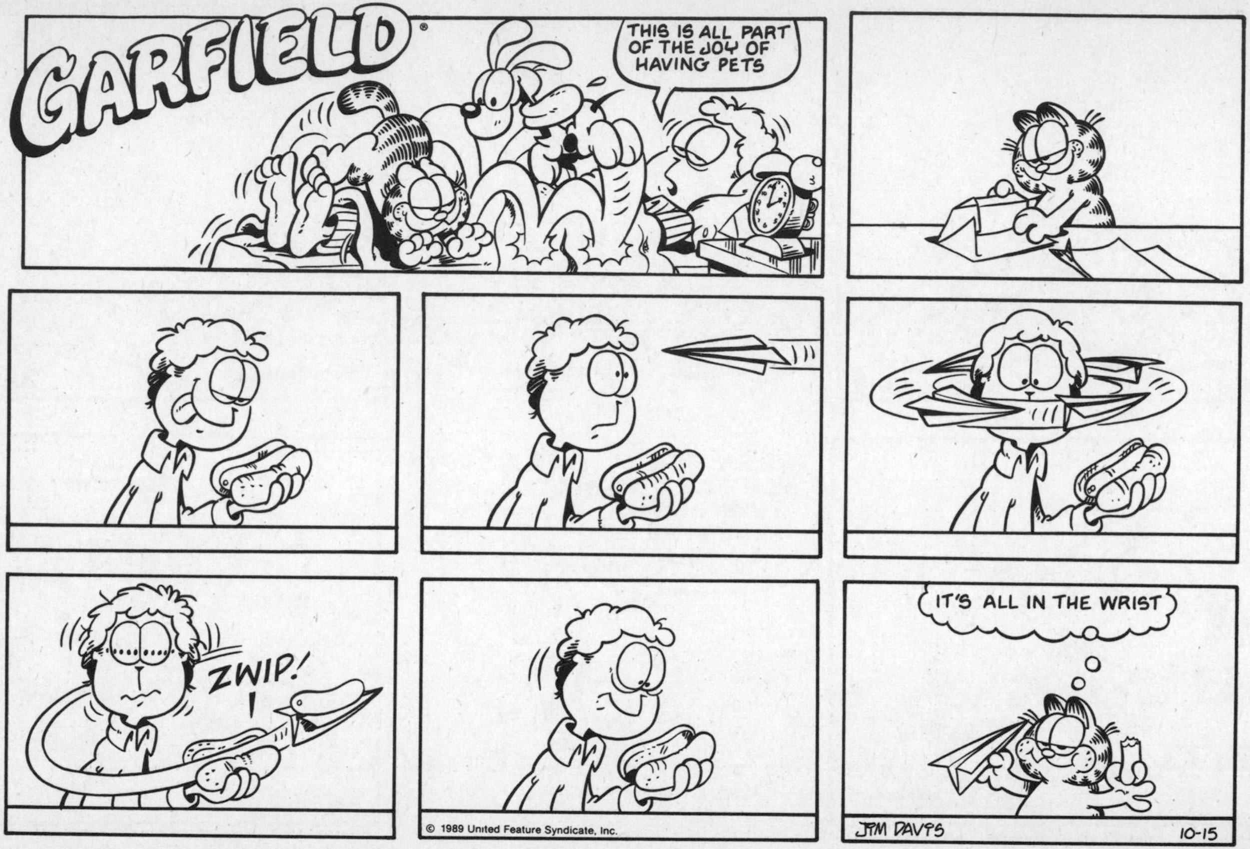
GARFIELD
THIS IS ALL PART OF THE JOY OF HAVING PETS
ZWIP!
IT'S ALL IN THE WRIST
© 1989 United Feature Syndicate, Inc.
JIM DAVIS
10-15

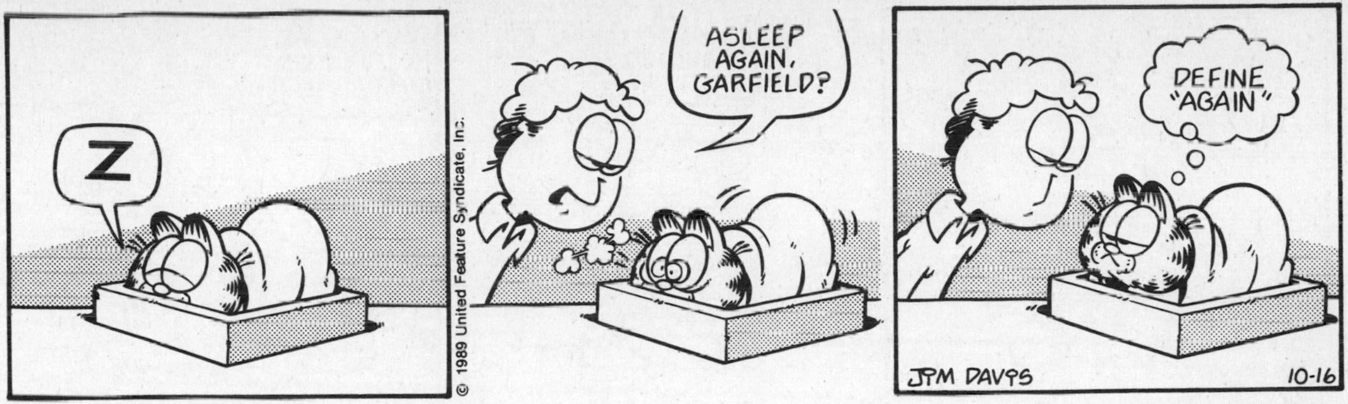
Z
ASLEEP AGAIN, GARFIELD?
DEFINE "AGAIN"
© 1989 United Feature Syndicate, Inc.
JIM DAVIS
10-16

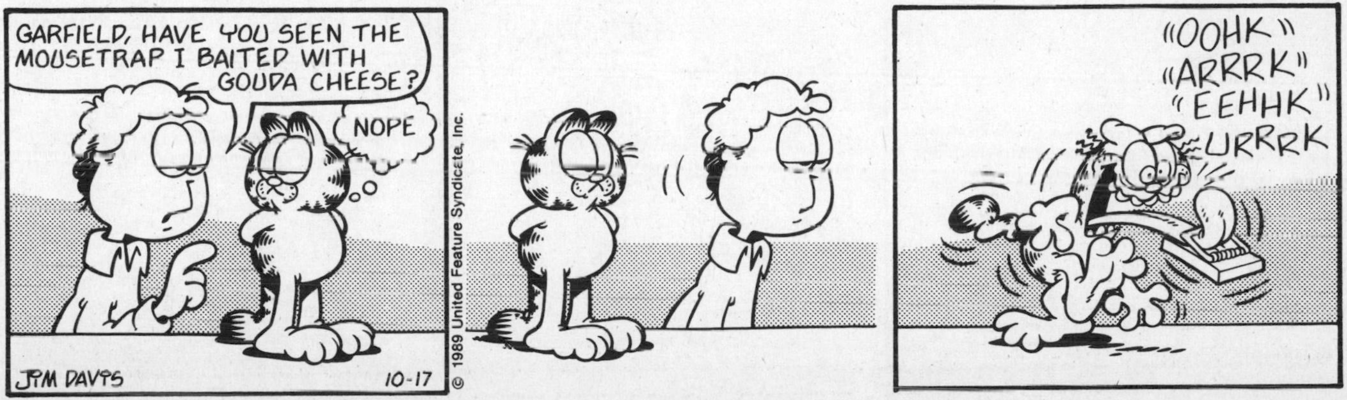
GARFIELD, HAVE YOU SEEN THE MOUSETRAP I BAITED WITH GOUDA CHEESE?
NOPE
© 1989 United Feature Syndicate, Inc.
"OOHK"
"ARRRK"
"EEHHK"
URRRK
JIM DAVIS
10-17

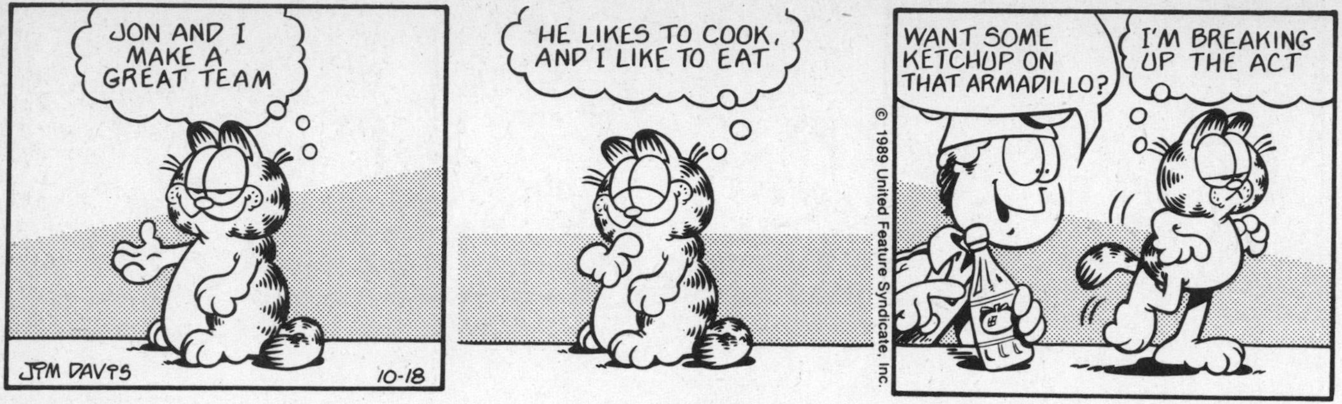
JON AND I MAKE A GREAT TEAM
JIM DAVIS
10-18
HE LIKES TO COOK, AND I LIKE TO EAT
WANT SOME KETCHUP ON THAT ARMADILLO?
I'M BREAKING UP THE ACT
© 1989 United Feature Syndicate, Inc.

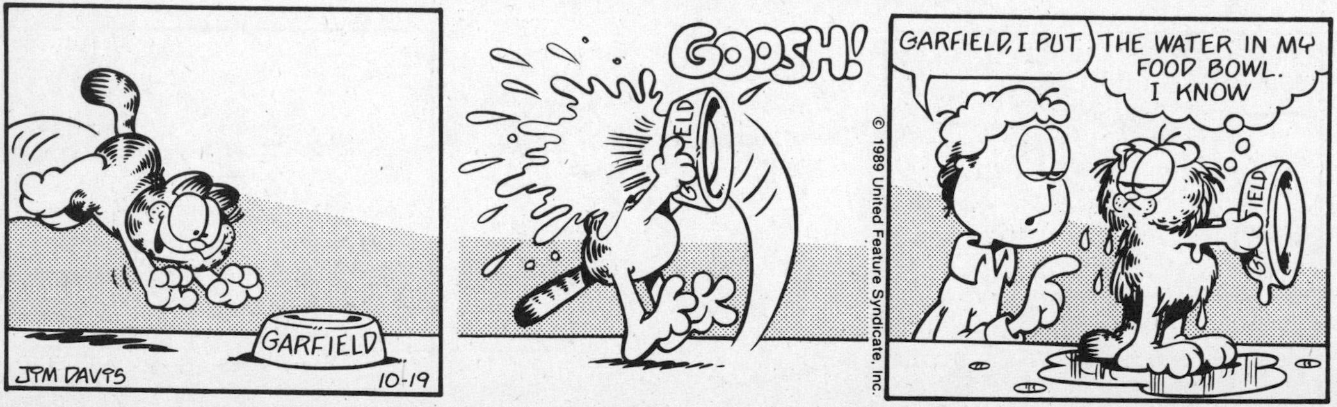
JIM DAVIS
GARFIELD
10-19
GOOSH!
GARFIELD, I PUT
THE WATER IN MY FOOD BOWL. I KNOW
© 1989 United Feature Syndicate, Inc.

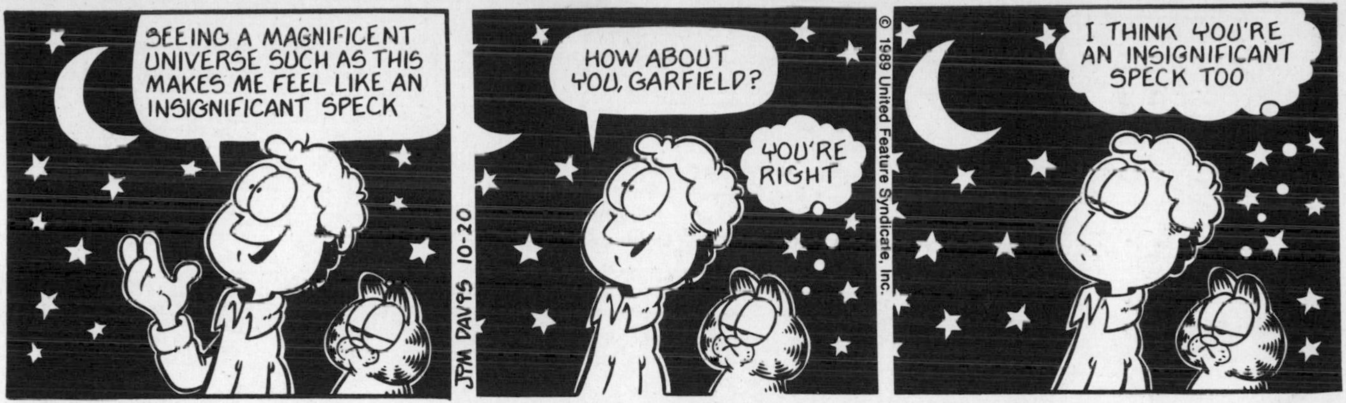
SEEING A MAGNIFICENT UNIVERSE SUCH AS THIS MAKES ME FEEL LIKE AN INSIGNIFICANT SPECK
JIM DAVIS 10-20
HOW ABOUT YOU, GARFIELD?
YOU'RE RIGHT
© 1989 United Feature Syndicate, Inc.
I THINK YOU'RE AN INSIGNIFICANT SPECK TOO

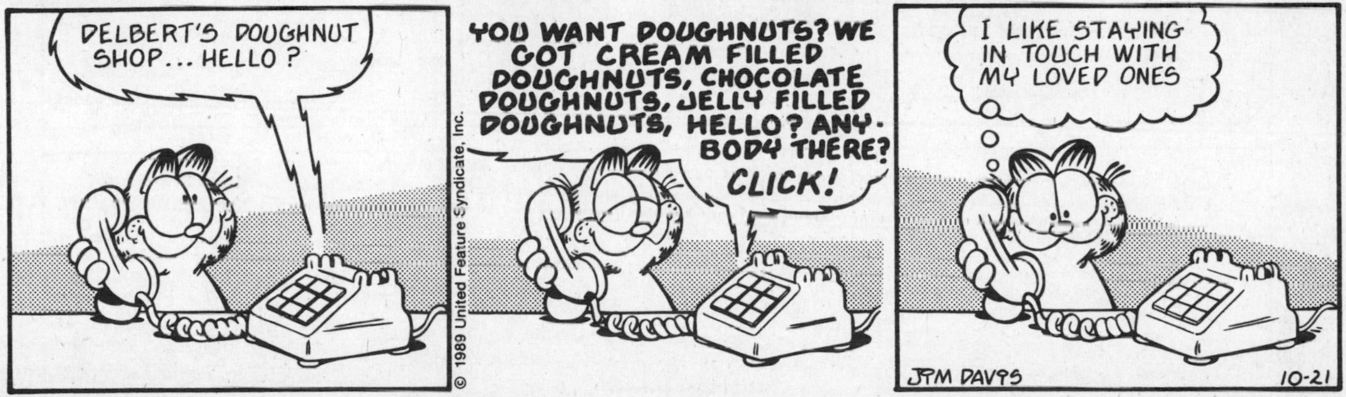
DELBERT'S DOUGHNUT SHOP... HELLO?
© 1989 United Feature Syndicate, Inc.
YOU WANT DOUGHNUTS? WE GOT CREAM FILLED DOUGHNUTS, CHOCOLATE DOUGHNUTS, JELLY FILLED DOUGHNUTS, HELLO? ANY-BODY THERE?
CLICK!
I LIKE STAYING IN TOUCH WITH MY LOVED ONES
JIM DAVIS
10-21

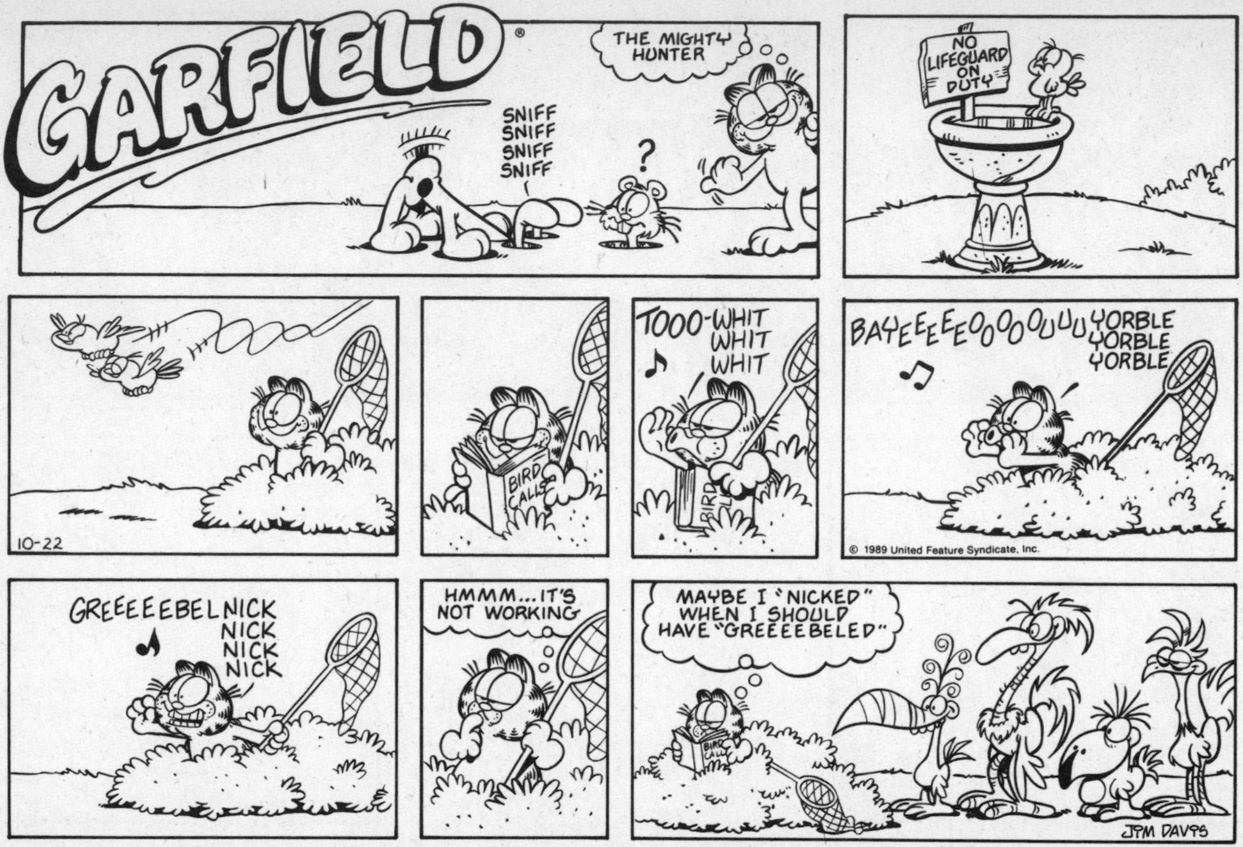
GARFIELD
THE MIGHTY HUNTER
SNIFF SNIFF SNIFF SNIFF
?
NO LIFEGUARD ON DUTY
10-22
BIRD CALLS
TOOO-WHIT WHIT WHIT
BAYEEEEEOOOOOUUU YORBLE YORBLE YORBLE
© 1989 United Feature Syndicate, Inc.
GREEEEEBELNICK NICK NICK NICK
HMMM... IT'S NOT WORKING
MAYBE I "NICKED" WHEN I SHOULD HAVE "GREEEEBELED"
JIM DAVIS

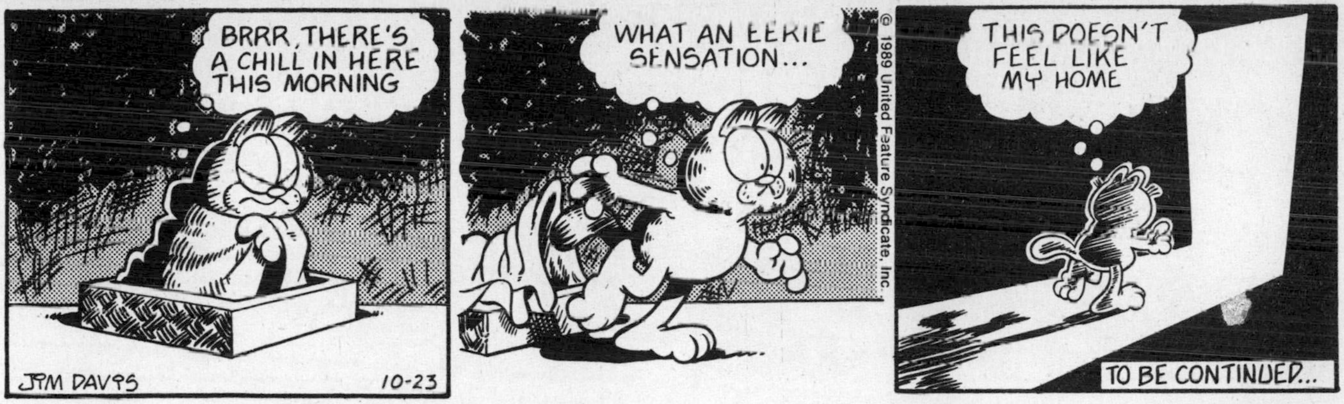
BRRR, THERE'S A CHILL IN HERE THIS MORNING
JIM DAVIS
10-23
WHAT AN EERIE SENSATION...
© 1989 United Feature Syndicate, Inc.
THIS DOESN'T FEEL LIKE MY HOME
TO BE CONTINUED...

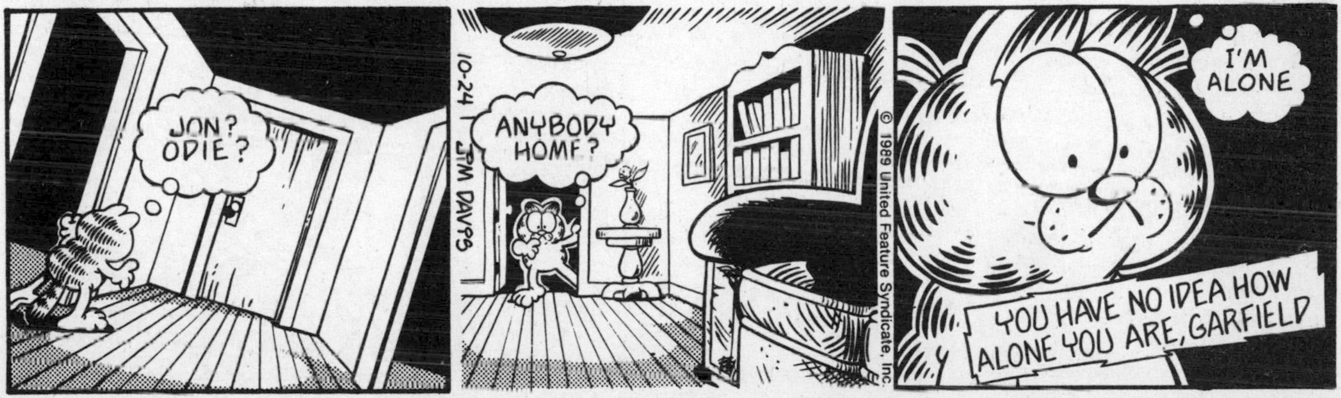
JON? ODIE?
10-24
JIM DAVIS
ANYBODY HOME?
© 1989 United Feature Syndicate, Inc.
I'M ALONE
YOU HAVE NO IDEA HOW ALONE YOU ARE, GARFIELD

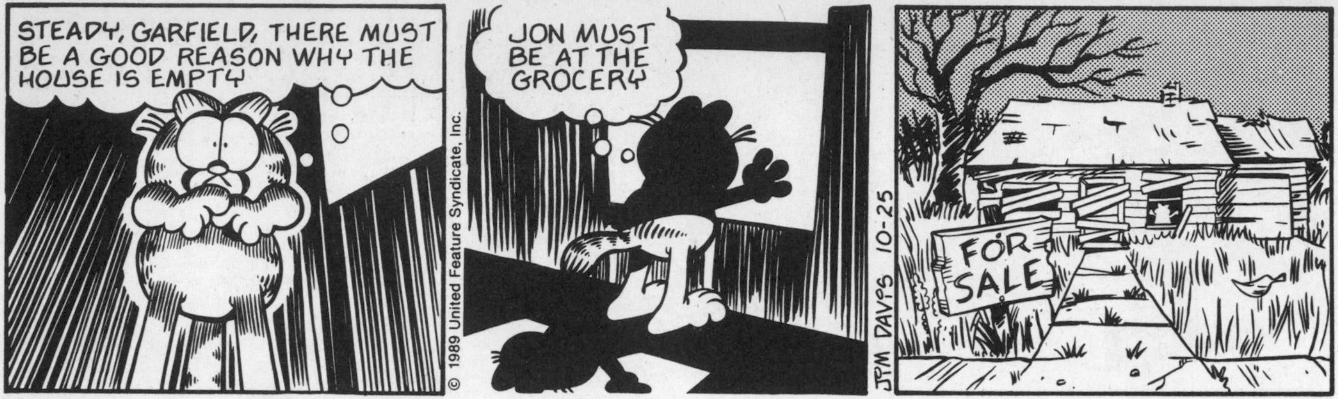
STEADY, GARFIELD, THERE MUST BE A GOOD REASON WHY THE HOUSE IS EMPTY
© 1989 United Feature Syndicate, Inc.
JON MUST BE AT THE GROCERY
JIM DAVIS 10-25
FOR SALE

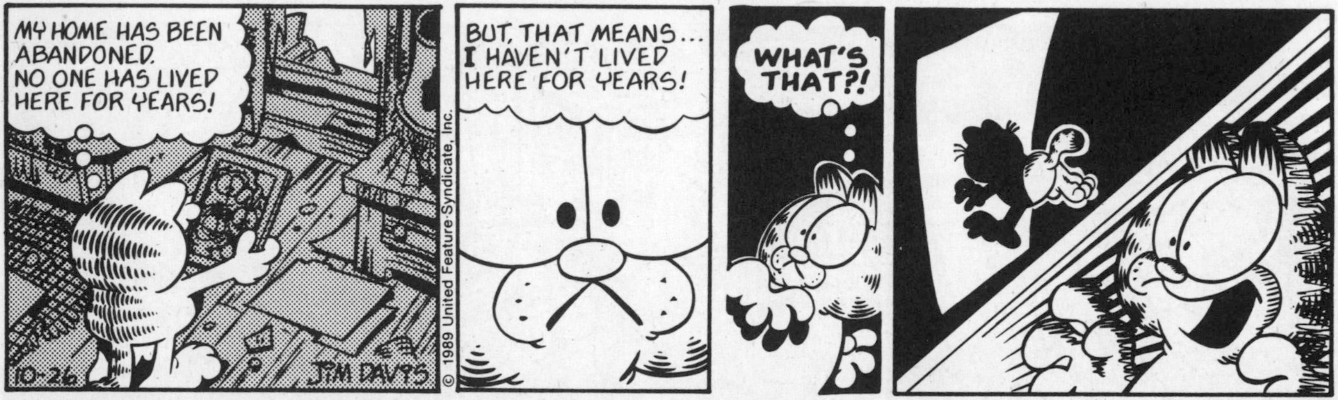
MY HOME HAS BEEN ABANDONED. NO ONE HAS LIVED HERE FOR YEARS!
10-26
JIM DAVIS
© 1989 United Feature Syndicate, Inc.
BUT, THAT MEANS... I HAVEN'T LIVED HERE FOR YEARS!
WHAT'S THAT?!

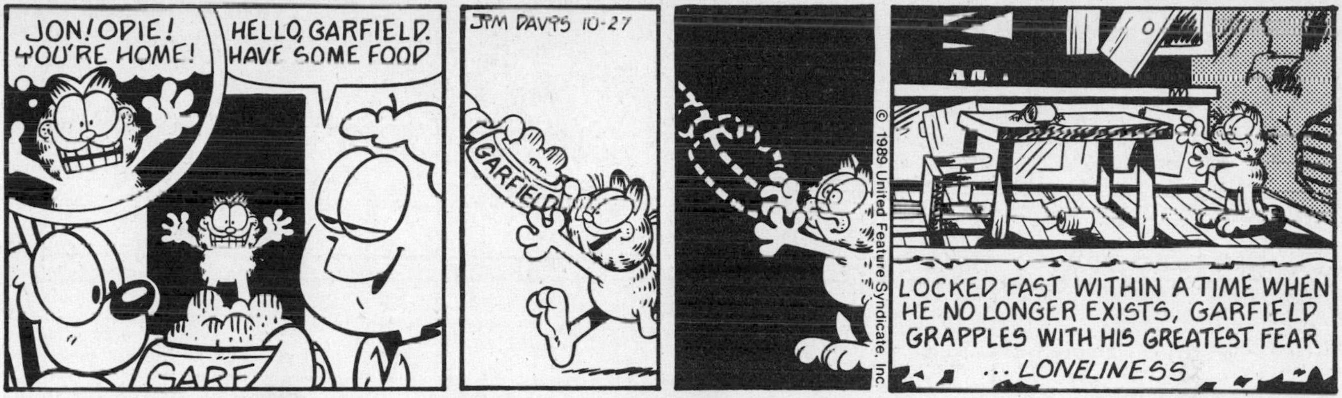
JON! OPIE! YOU'RE HOME!
HELLO, GARFIELD. HAVE SOME FOOD
GARF
JIM DAVIS 10-27
GARFIELD
© 1989 United Feature Syndicate, Inc.
LOCKED FAST WITHIN A TIME WHEN HE NO LONGER EXISTS, GARFIELD GRAPPLES WITH HIS GREATEST FEAR
...LONELINESS

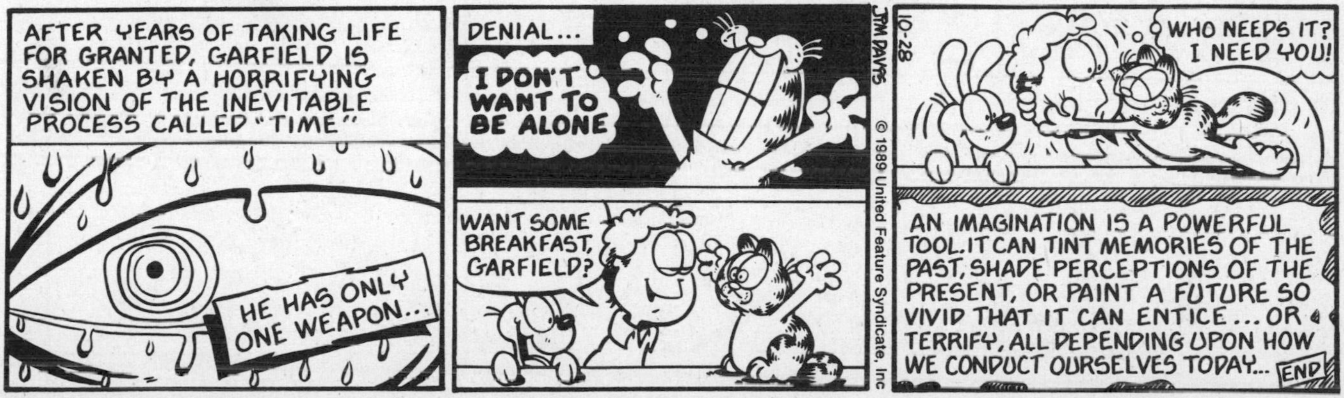
AFTER YEARS OF TAKING LIFE FOR GRANTED, GARFIELD IS SHAKEN BY A HORRIFYING VISION OF THE INEVITABLE PROCESS CALLED "TIME"
HE HAS ONLY ONE WEAPON...
DENIAL...
I DON'T WANT TO BE ALONE
WANT SOME BREAKFAST, GARFIELD?
JIM DAVIS 10-28
© 1989 United Feature Syndicate, Inc.
WHO NEEDS IT? I NEED YOU!
AN IMAGINATION IS A POWERFUL TOOL. IT CAN TINT MEMORIES OF THE PAST, SHADE PERCEPTIONS OF THE PRESENT, OR PAINT A FUTURE SO VIVID THAT IT CAN ENTICE... OR TERRIFY, ALL DEPENDING UPON HOW WE CONDUCT OURSELVES TODAY...
END

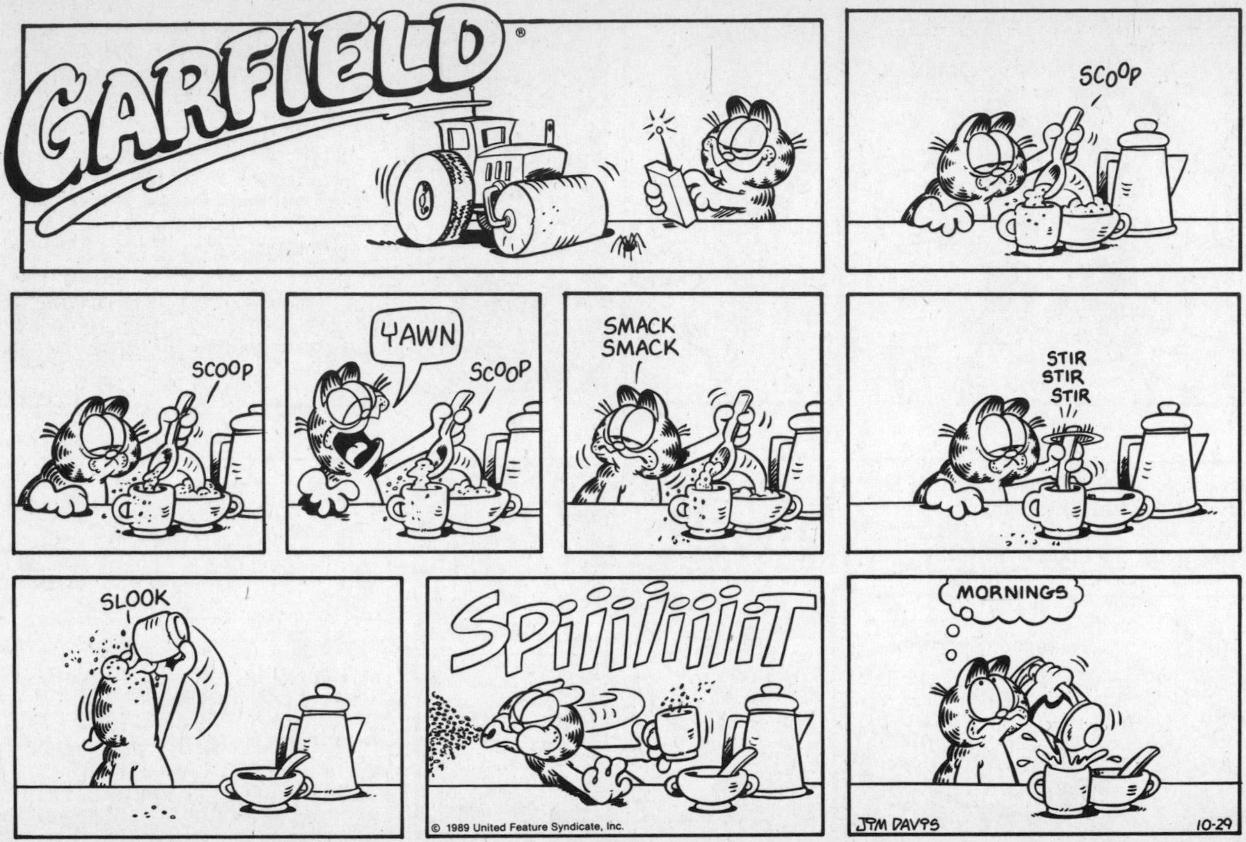
GARFIELD®
SCOOP
SCOOP
YAWN
SCOOP
SMACK SMACK
STIR STIR STIR
SLOOK
SPIIIIIIIT
MORNINGS
© 1989 United Feature Syndicate, Inc.
JIM DAVIS
10-29

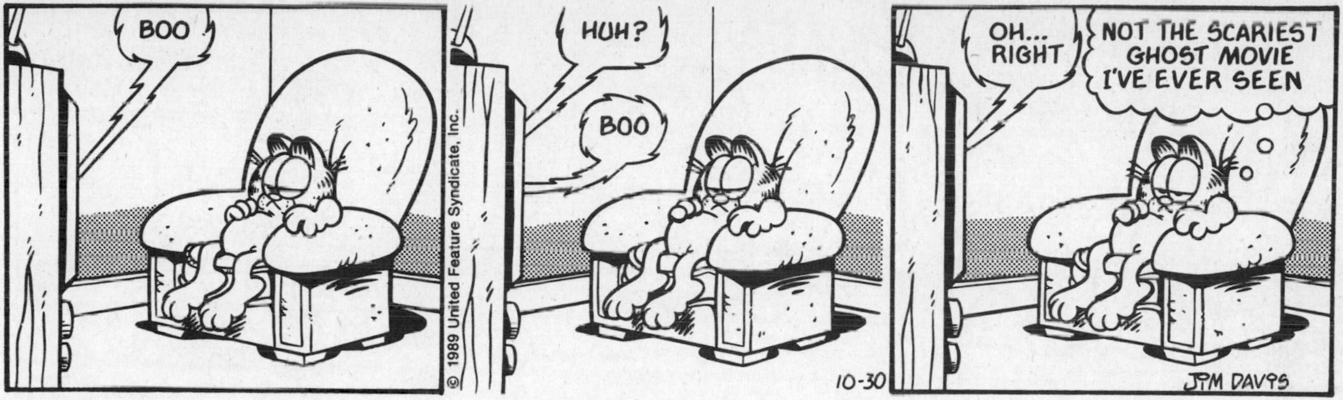
BOO
HUH?
BOO
OH... RIGHT
NOT THE SCARIEST GHOST MOVIE I'VE EVER SEEN
© 1989 United Feature Syndicate, Inc.
10-30
JIM DAVIS

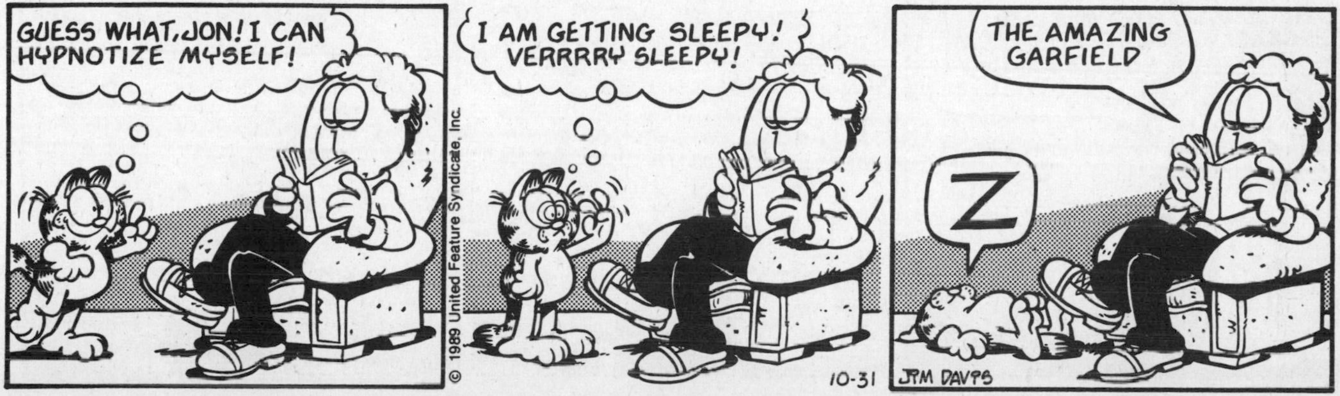
GUESS WHAT, JON! I CAN HYPNOTIZE MYSELF!
I AM GETTING SLEEPY! VERRRRY SLEEPY!
Z
THE AMAZING GARFIELD
© 1989 United Feature Syndicate, Inc.
10-31
JIM DAVIS

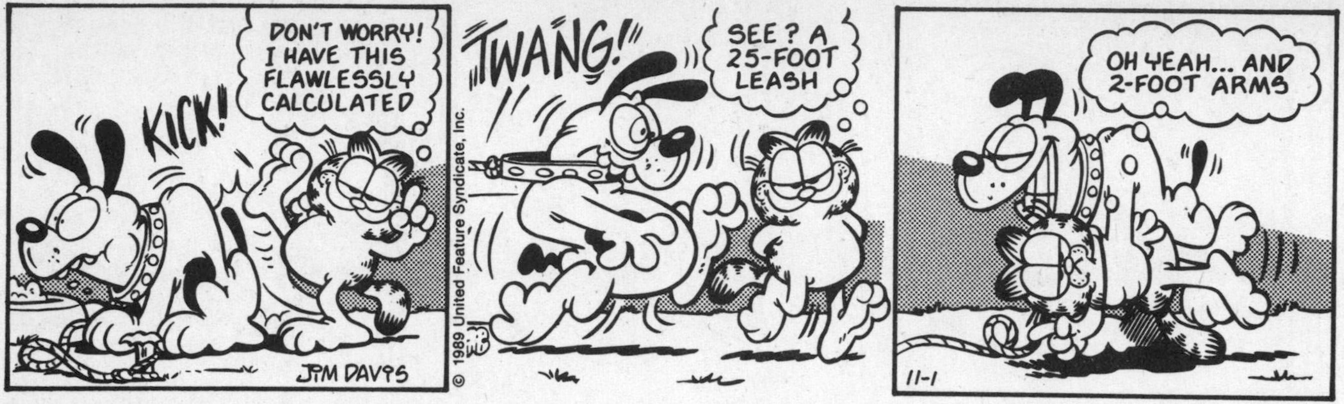
KICK!
DON'T WORRY! I HAVE THIS FLAWLESSLY CALCULATED
JIM DAVIS
© 1989 United Feature Syndicate, Inc.
TWANG!
SEE? A 25-FOOT LEASH
OH YEAH... AND 2-FOOT ARMS
11-1

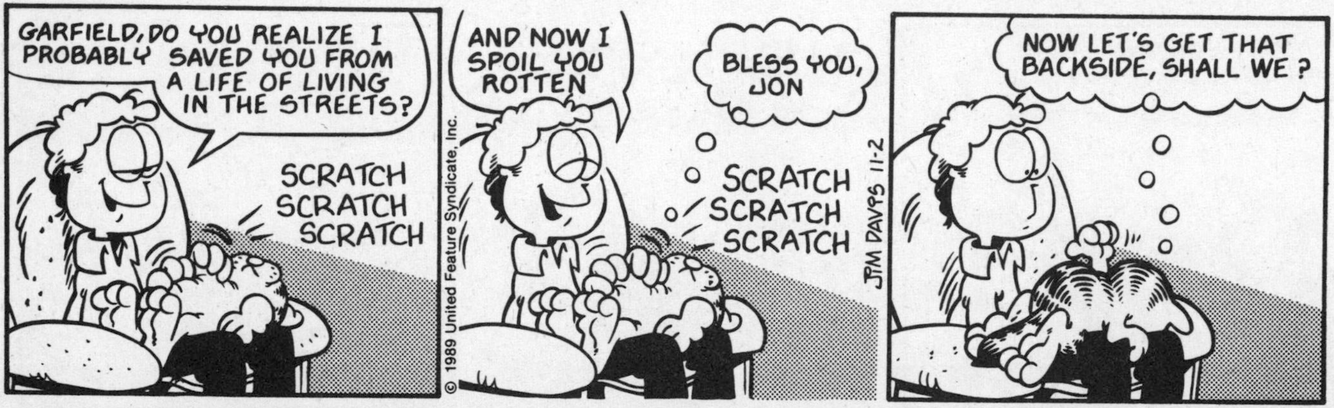
GARFIELD, DO YOU REALIZE I PROBABLY SAVED YOU FROM A LIFE OF LIVING IN THE STREETS?
SCRATCH SCRATCH SCRATCH
© 1989 United Feature Syndicate, Inc.
AND NOW I SPOIL YOU ROTTEN
BLESS YOU, JON
SCRATCH SCRATCH SCRATCH
JIM DAVIS 11-2
NOW LET'S GET THAT BACKSIDE, SHALL WE?

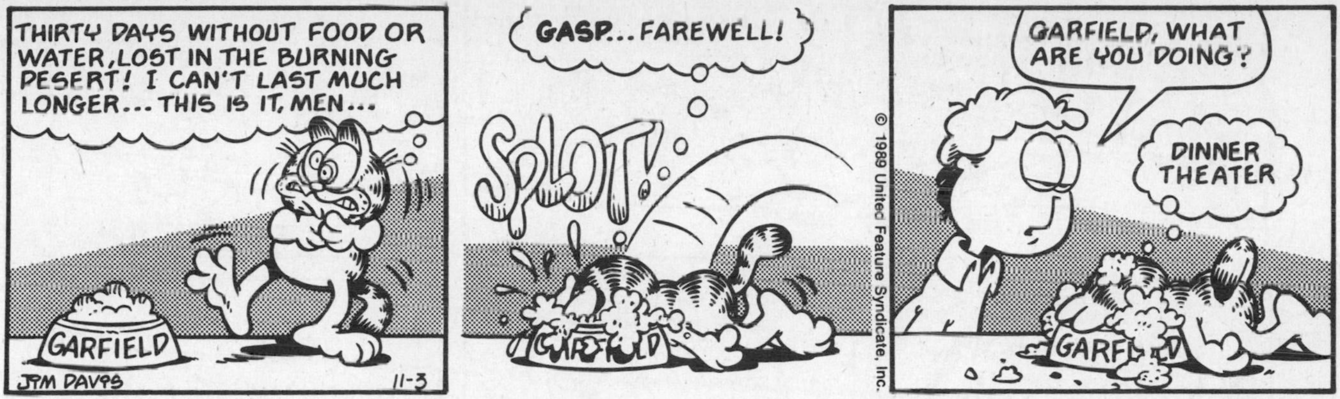
THIRTY DAYS WITHOUT FOOD OR WATER, LOST IN THE BURNING DESERT! I CAN'T LAST MUCH LONGER... THIS IS IT, MEN...
JIM DAVIS
11-3
GASP... FAREWELL!
SPLOT!
© 1989 United Feature Syndicate, Inc.
GARFIELD, WHAT ARE YOU DOING?
DINNER THEATER

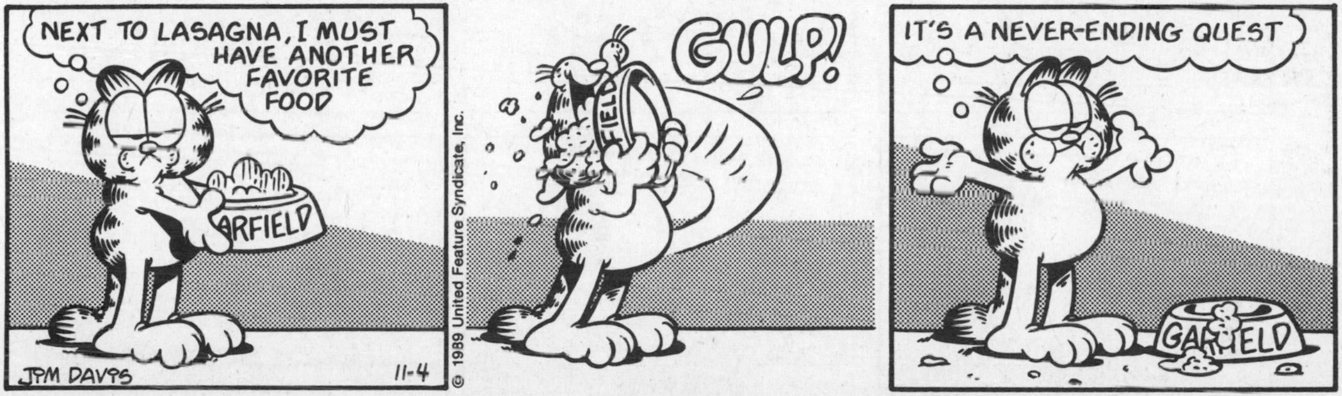
NEXT TO LASAGNA, I MUST HAVE ANOTHER FAVORITE FOOD
JIM DAVIS
11-4
© 1989 United Feature Syndicate, Inc.
GULP!
IT'S A NEVER-ENDING QUEST

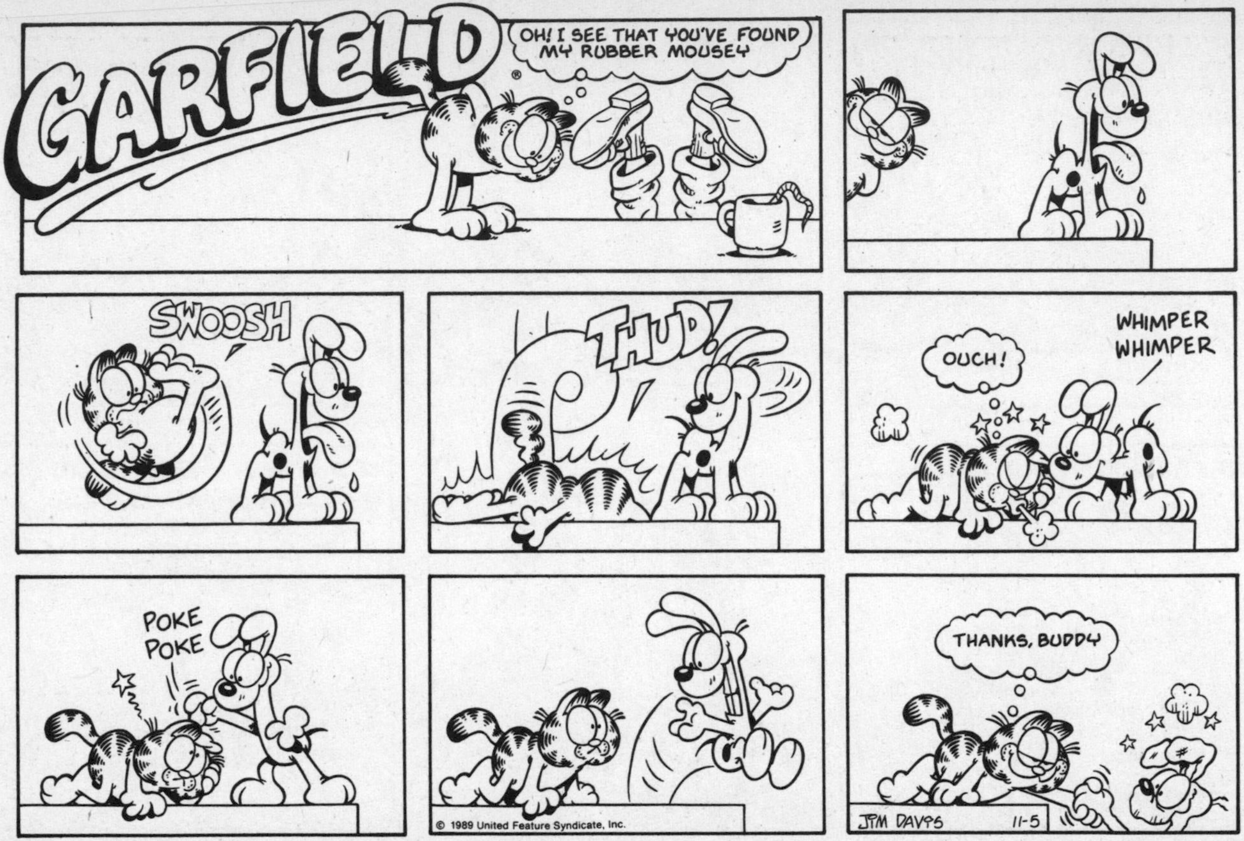
GARFIELD®
OH! I SEE THAT YOU'VE FOUND MY RUBBER MOUSEY
SWOOSH
THUD!
OUCH!
WHIMPER WHIMPER
POKE POKE
THANKS, BUDDY
© 1989 United Feature Syndicate, Inc.
JIM DAVIS 11-5

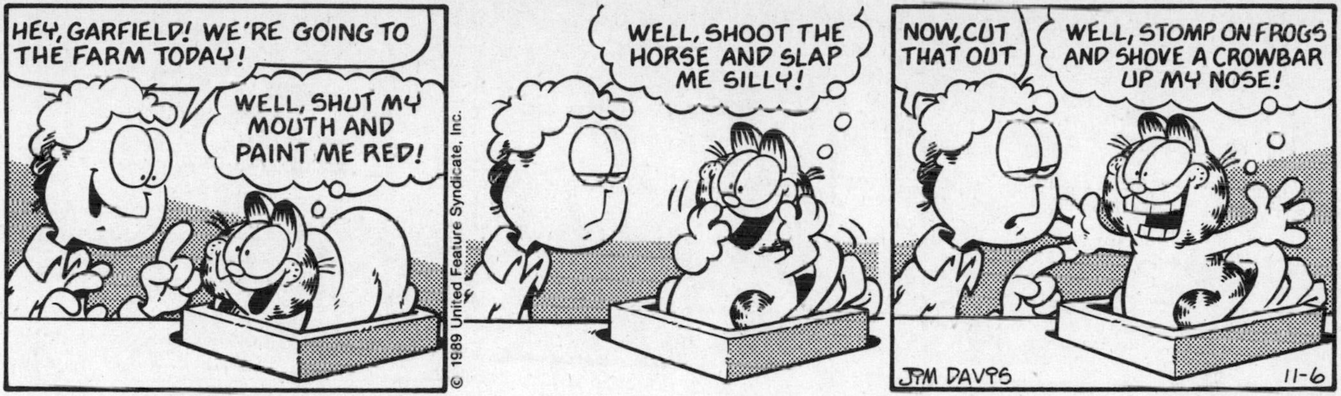
HEY, GARFIELD! WE'RE GOING TO THE FARM TODAY!
WELL, SHUT MY MOUTH AND PAINT ME RED!
© 1989 United Feature Syndicate, Inc.
WELL, SHOOT THE HORSE AND SLAP ME SILLY!
NOW, CUT THAT OUT
WELL, STOMP ON FROGS AND SHOVE A CROWBAR UP MY NOSE!
JIM DAVIS
11-6

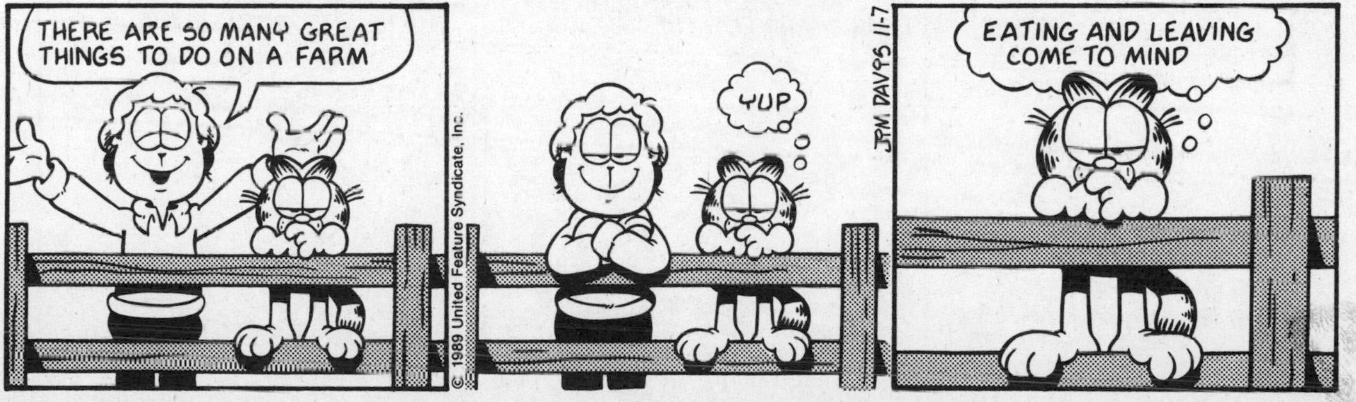
THERE ARE SO MANY GREAT THINGS TO DO ON A FARM
© 1989 United Feature Syndicate, Inc.
YUP
JIM DAVIS 11-7
EATING AND LEAVING COME TO MIND

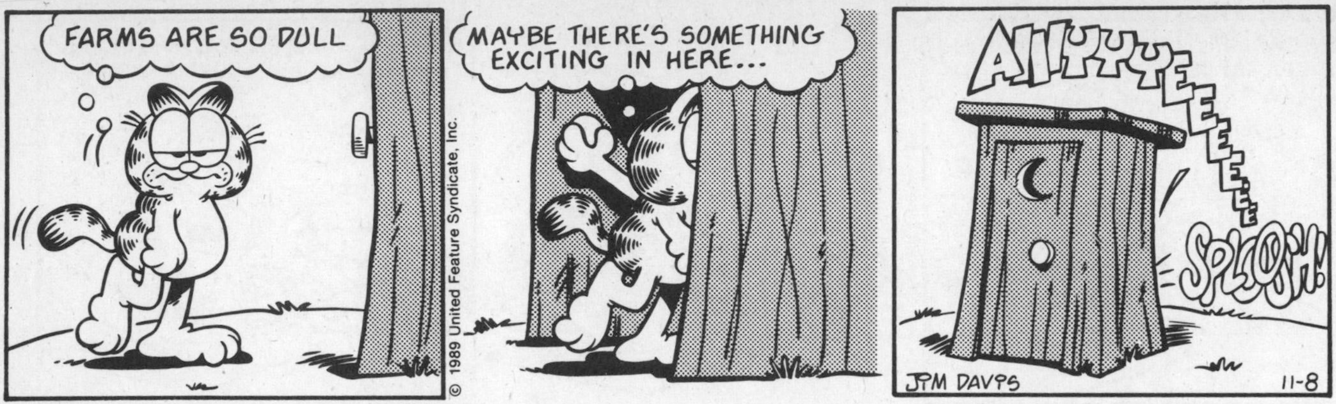
FARMS ARE SO DULL
© 1989 United Feature Syndicate, Inc.
MAYBE THERE'S SOMETHING EXCITING IN HERE...
AIIIYYYEEEEEEE
SPLOOSH!
JIM DAVIS
11-8

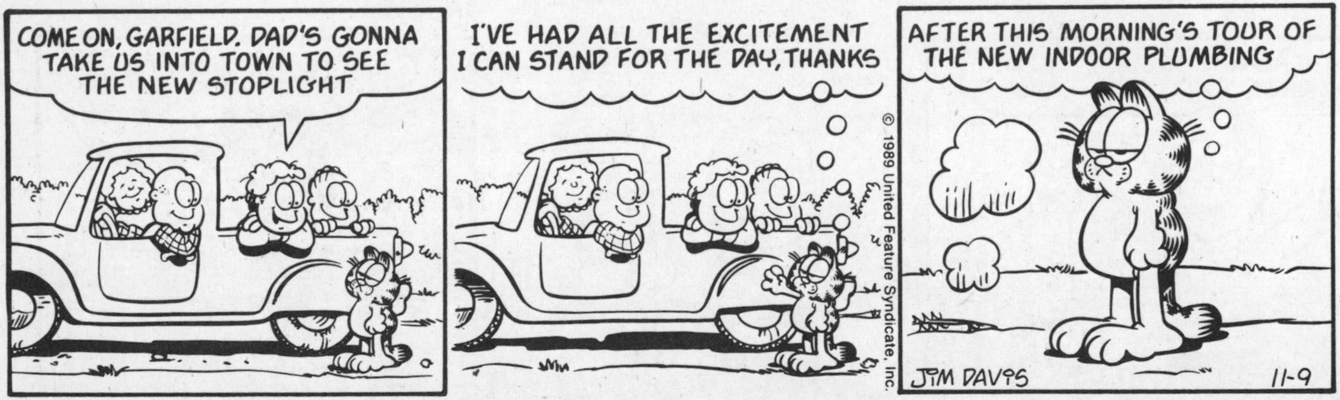
COME ON, GARFIELD. DAD'S GONNA TAKE US INTO TOWN TO SEE THE NEW STOPLIGHT
I'VE HAD ALL THE EXCITEMENT I CAN STAND FOR THE DAY, THANKS
© 1989 United Feature Syndicate, Inc.
AFTER THIS MORNING'S TOUR OF THE NEW INDOOR PLUMBING
JIM DAVIS
11-9

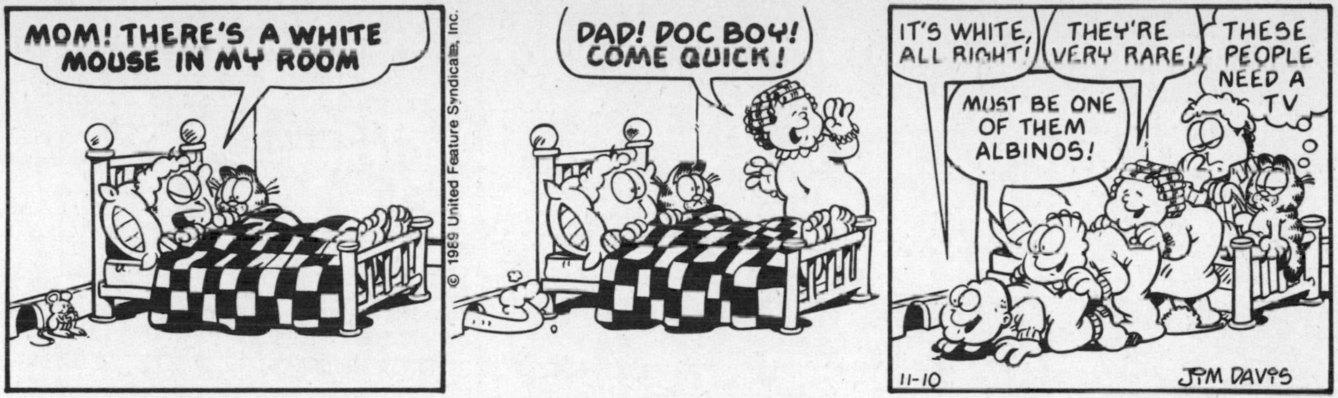
MOM! THERE'S A WHITE MOUSE IN MY ROOM
DAD! DOC BOY! COME QUICK!
IT'S WHITE, ALL RIGHT!
THEY'RE VERY RARE!
MUST BE ONE OF THEM ALBINOS!
THESE PEOPLE NEED A TV
11-10
JIM DAVIS
© 1989 United Feature Syndicate, Inc.

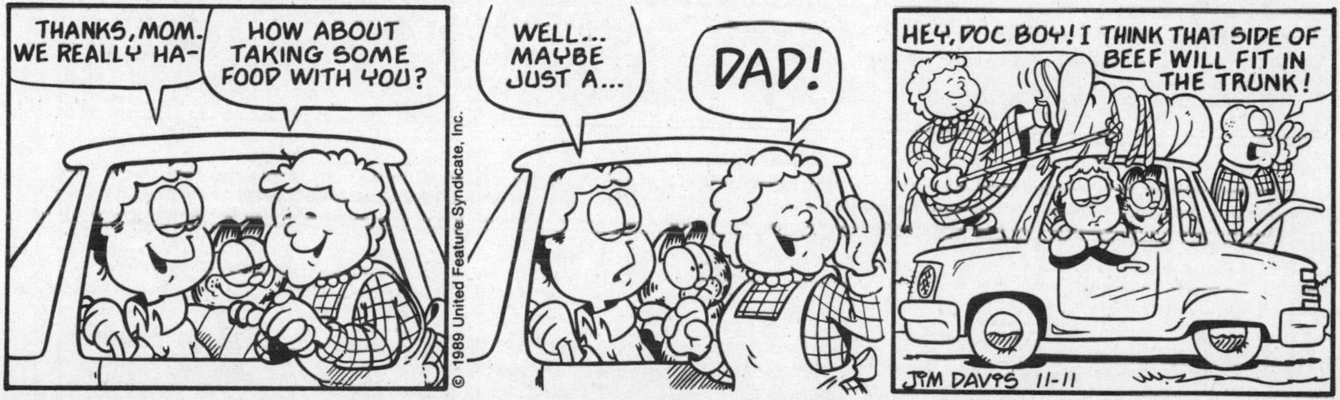
THANKS, MOM. WE REALLY HA-
HOW ABOUT TAKING SOME FOOD WITH YOU?
WELL... MAYBE JUST A...
DAD!
HEY, DOC BOY! I THINK THAT SIDE OF BEEF WILL FIT IN THE TRUNK!
JIM DAVIS 11-11
© 1989 United Feature Syndicate, Inc.

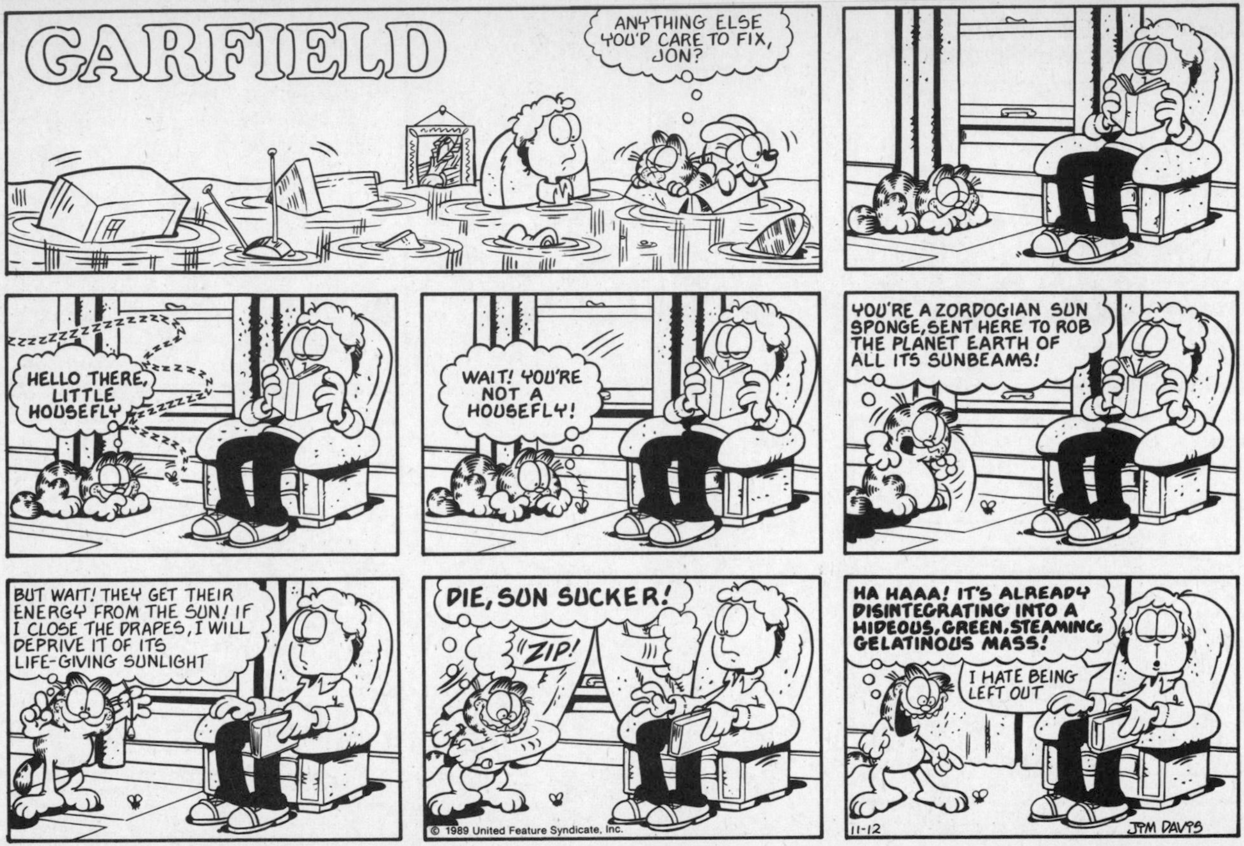
GARFIELD
ANYTHING ELSE YOU'D CARE TO FIX, JON?
HELLO THERE, LITTLE HOUSEFLY
WAIT! YOU'RE NOT A HOUSEFLY!
YOU'RE A ZORDOGIAN SUN SPONGE, SENT HERE TO ROB THE PLANET EARTH OF ALL ITS SUNBEAMS!
BUT WAIT! THEY GET THEIR ENERGY FROM THE SUN! IF I CLOSE THE DRAPES, I WILL DEPRIVE IT OF ITS LIFE-GIVING SUNLIGHT
DIE, SUN SUCKER!
ZIP!
HA HAAA! IT'S ALREADY DISINTEGRATING INTO A HIDEOUS, GREEN, STEAMING, GELATINOUS MASS!
I HATE BEING LEFT OUT
© 1989 United Feature Syndicate, Inc.
11-12
JIM DAVIS

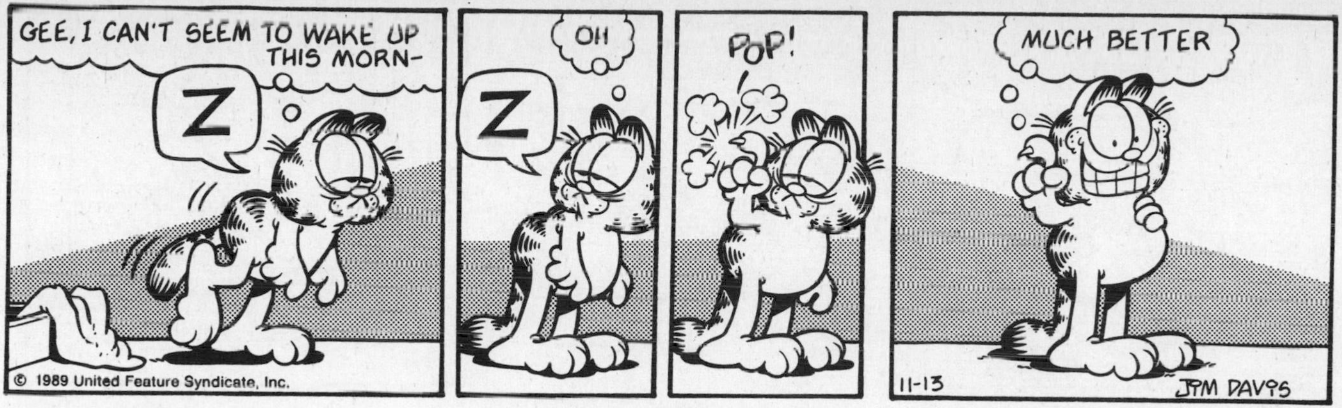
GEE, I CAN'T SEEM TO WAKE UP THIS MORN-
Z
Z
OH
POP!
MUCH BETTER
© 1989 United Feature Syndicate, Inc.
11-13
JIM DAVIS

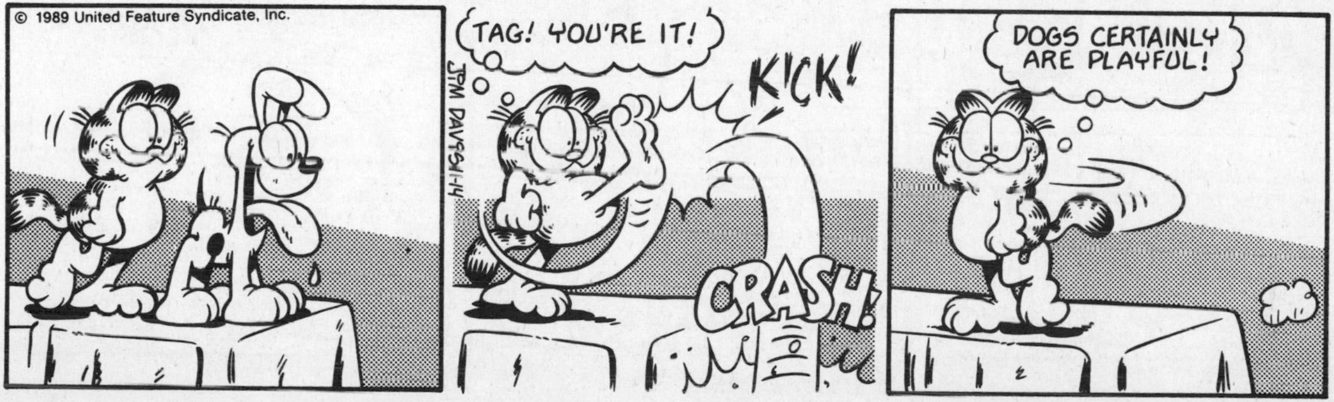
© 1989 United Feature Syndicate, Inc.
JIM DAVIS 11-14
TAG! YOU'RE IT!
KICK!
CRASH!
DOGS CERTAINLY ARE PLAYFUL!

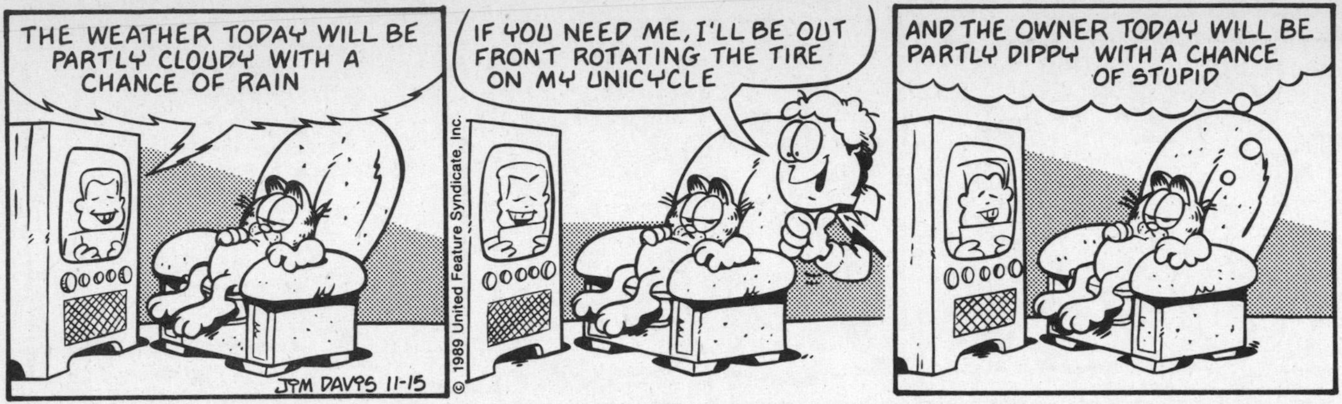
THE WEATHER TODAY WILL BE PARTLY CLOUDY WITH A CHANCE OF RAIN
JIM DAVIS 11-15
IF YOU NEED ME, I'LL BE OUT FRONT ROTATING THE TIRE ON MY UNICYCLE
© 1989 United Feature Syndicate, Inc.
AND THE OWNER TODAY WILL BE PARTLY DIPPY WITH A CHANCE OF STUPID

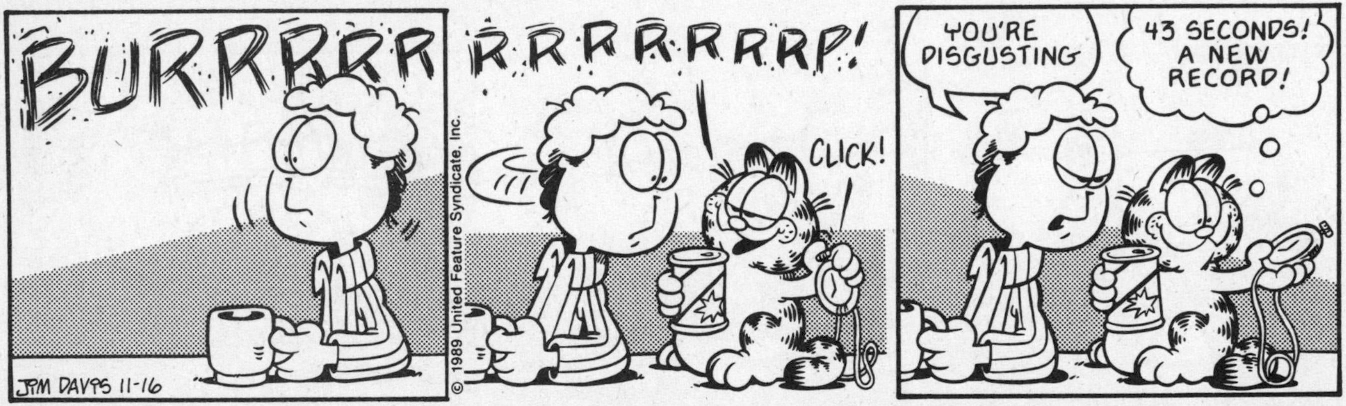
BURRRRR RRRRRRRRP!
JIM DAVIS 11-16
CLICK!
© 1989 United Feature Syndicate, Inc.
YOU'RE DISGUSTING
43 SECONDS! A NEW RECORD!

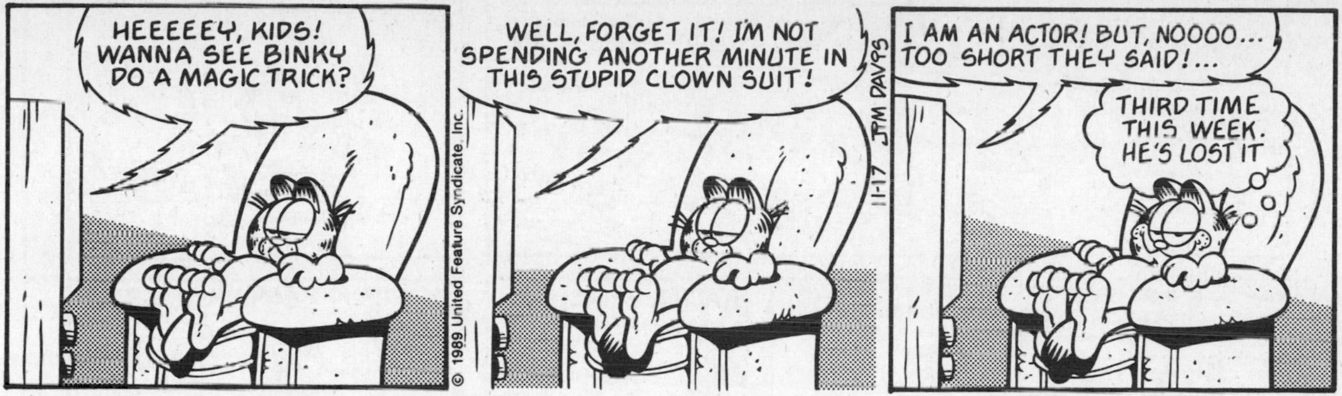
HEEEEEY, KIDS! WANNA SEE BINKY DO A MAGIC TRICK?
© 1989 United Feature Syndicate, Inc.
WELL, FORGET IT! I'M NOT SPENDING ANOTHER MINUTE IN THIS STUPID CLOWN SUIT!
JIM DAVIS 11-17
I AM AN ACTOR! BUT, NOOOO... TOO SHORT THEY SAID!...
THIRD TIME THIS WEEK. HE'S LOST IT

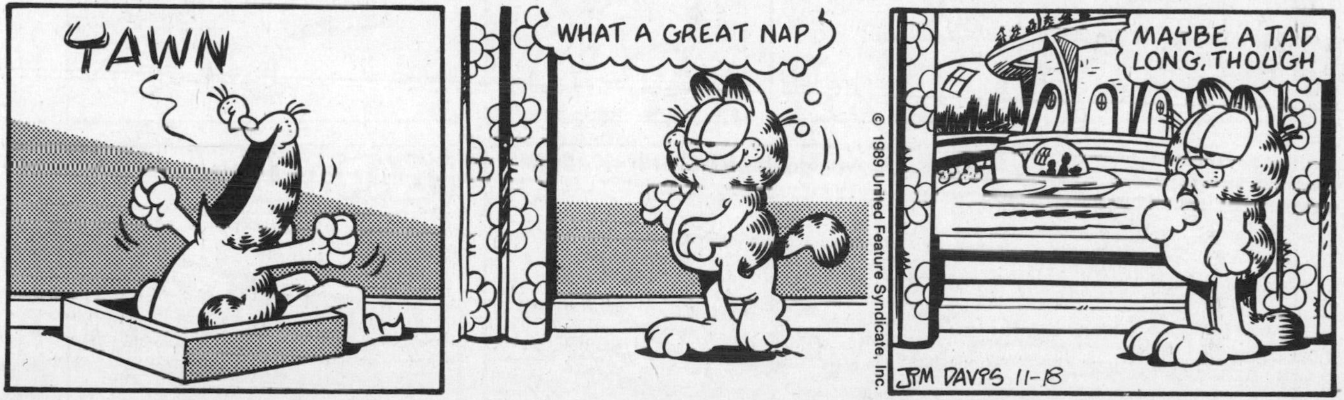
YAWN
WHAT A GREAT NAP
© 1989 United Feature Syndicate, Inc.
MAYBE A TAD LONG, THOUGH
JIM DAVIS 11-18

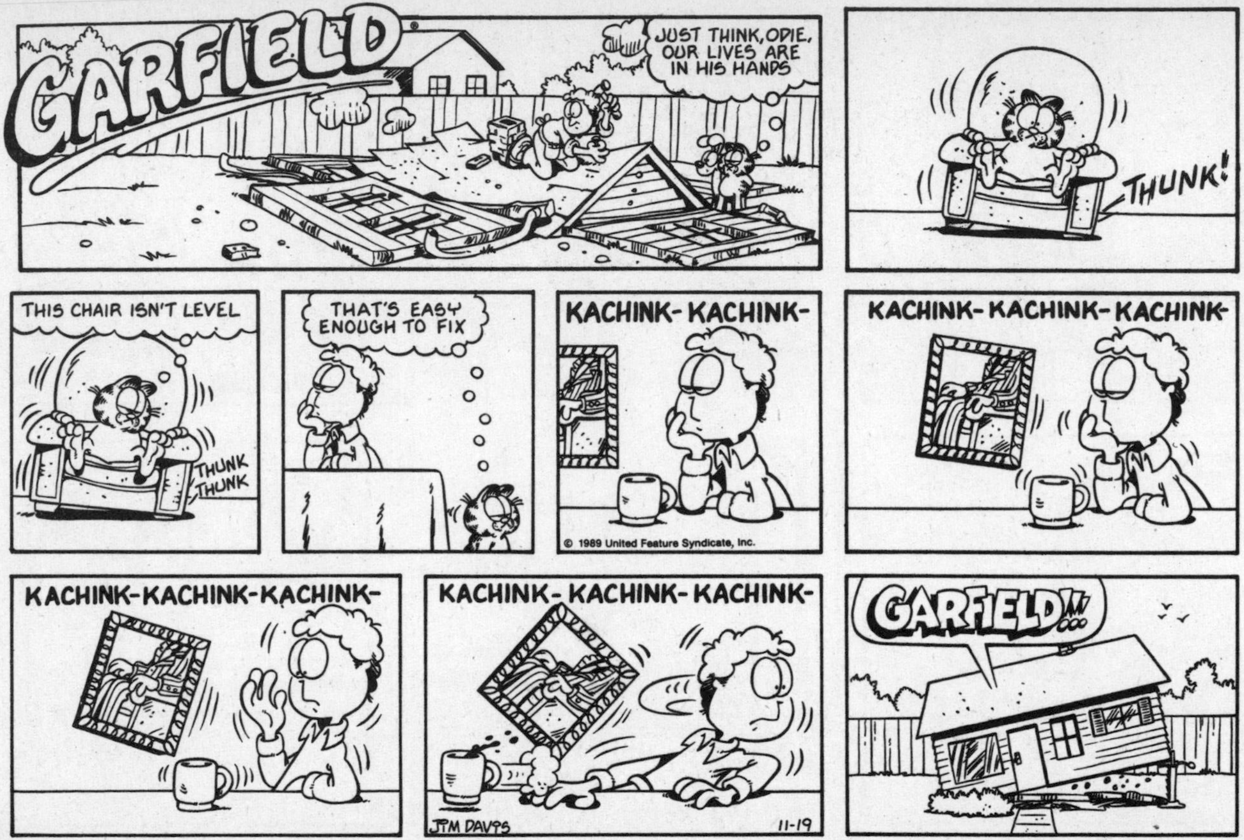
GARFIELD
JUST THINK, ODIE, OUR LIVES ARE IN HIS HANDS
THUNK!
THIS CHAIR ISN'T LEVEL
THUNK THUNK
THAT'S EASY ENOUGH TO FIX
KACHINK- KACHINK-
© 1989 United Feature Syndicate, Inc.
KACHINK- KACHINK- KACHINK-
KACHINK-KACHINK-KACHINK-
KACHINK- KACHINK- KACHINK-
JIM DAVIS
11-19
GARFIELD!!

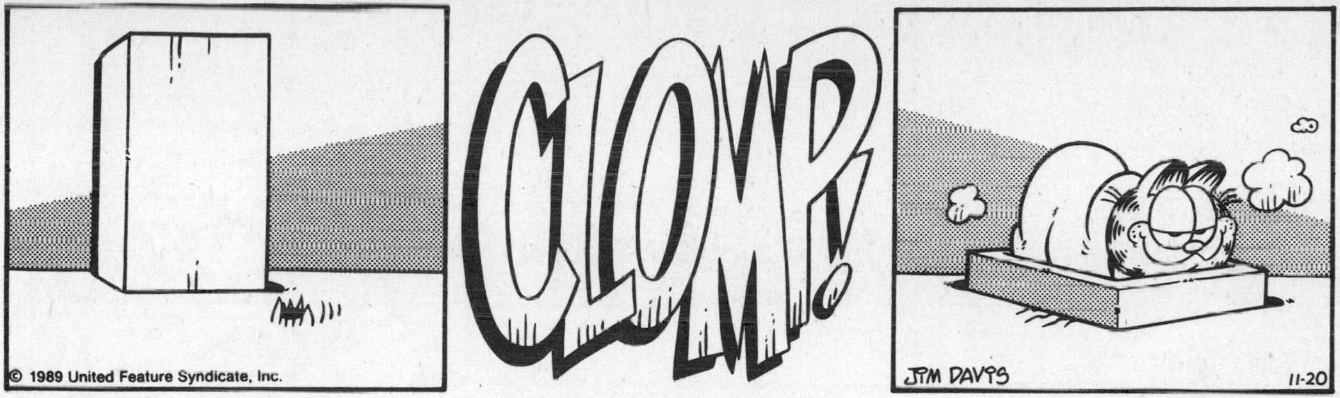

© 1989 United Feature Syndicate, Inc.
CLOMP!
JIM DAVIS
11-20

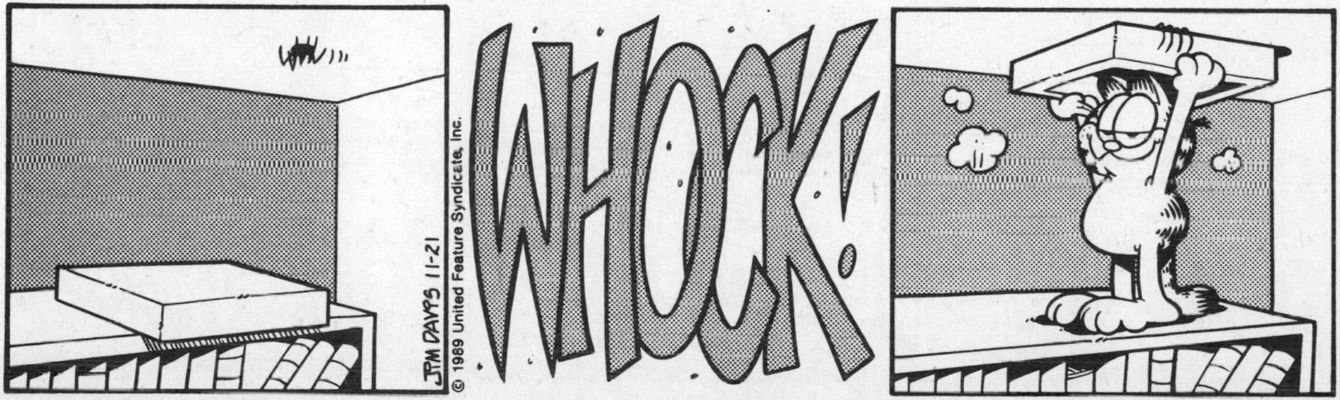

JIM DAVIS 11-21
© 1989 United Feature Syndicate, Inc.
WHOCK!

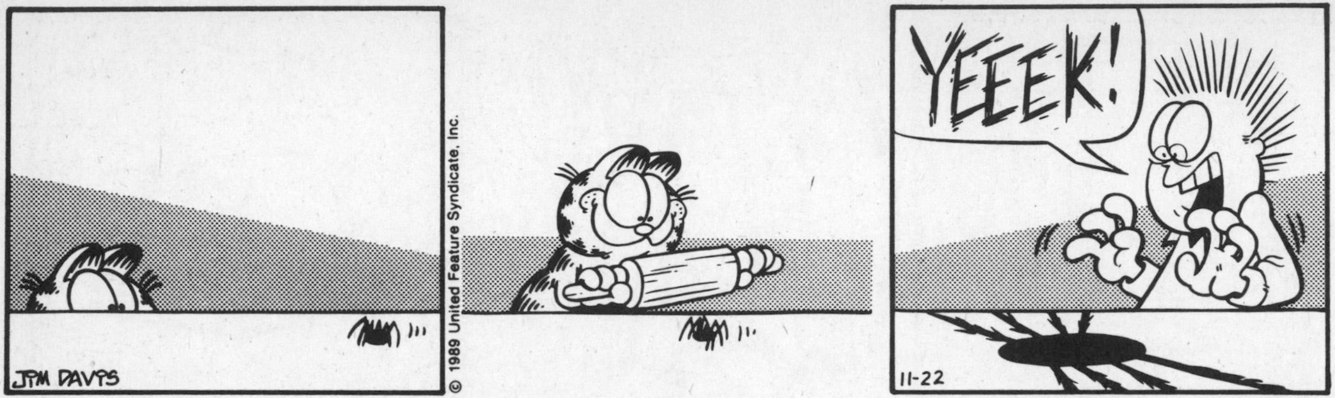
JIM DAVIS
© 1989 United Feature Syndicate, Inc.
YEEEK!
11-22

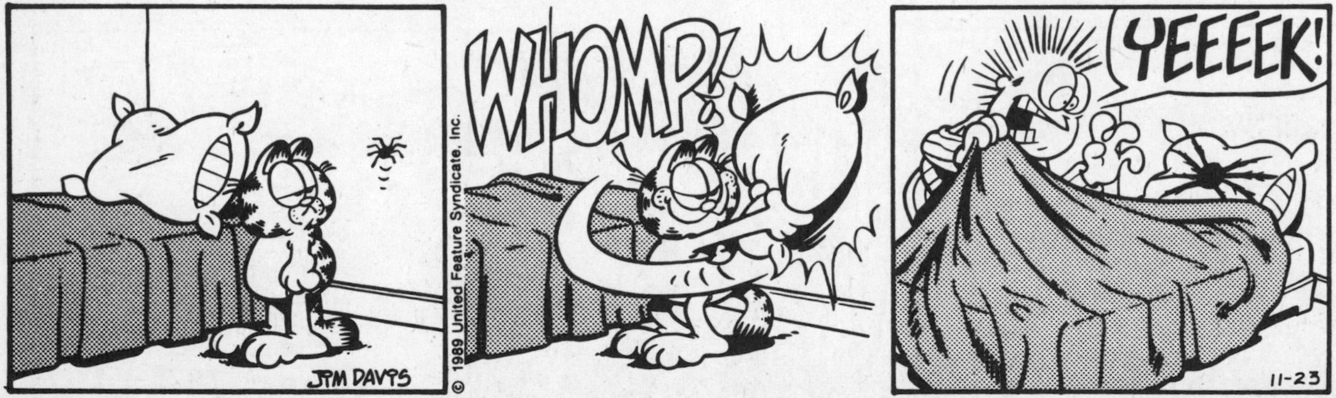
JIM DAVIS
© 1989 United Feature Syndicate, Inc.
WHOMP!
YEEEEK!
11-23

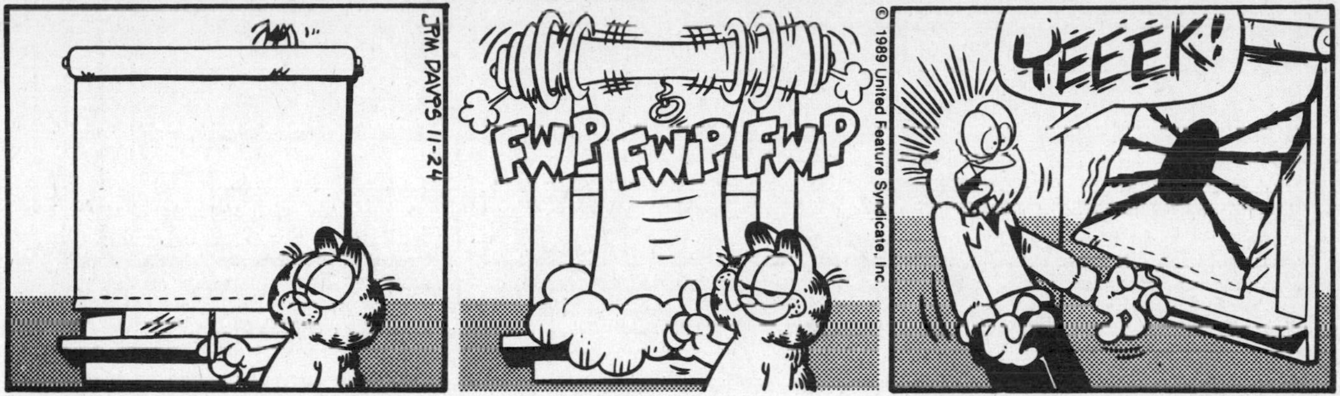
JIM DAVIS 11-24
FWIP FWIP FWIP
© 1989 United Feature Syndicate, Inc.
YEEEK!

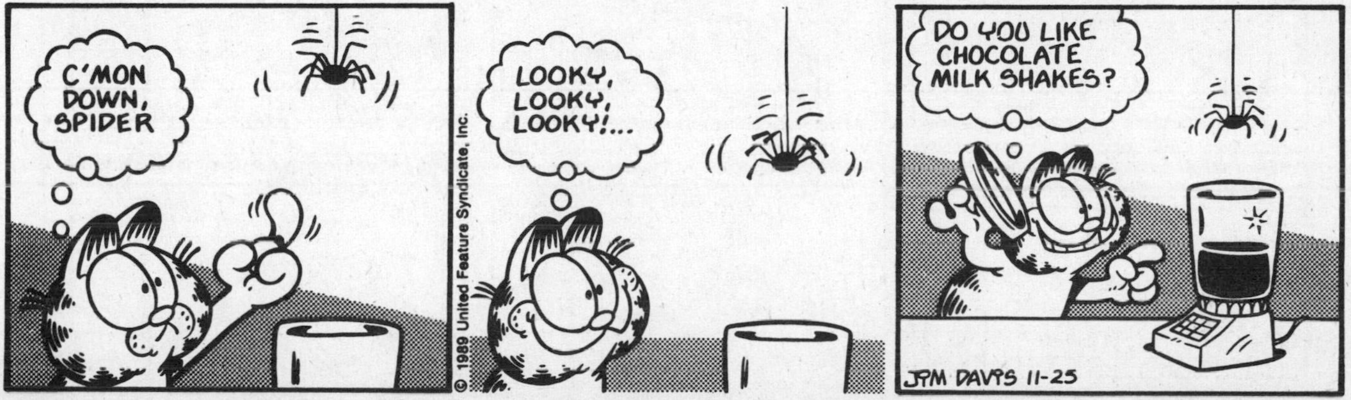
C'MON DOWN, SPIDER
© 1989 United Feature Syndicate, Inc.
LOOKY, LOOKY, LOOKY!...
DO YOU LIKE CHOCOLATE MILK SHAKES?
JIM DAVIS 11-25

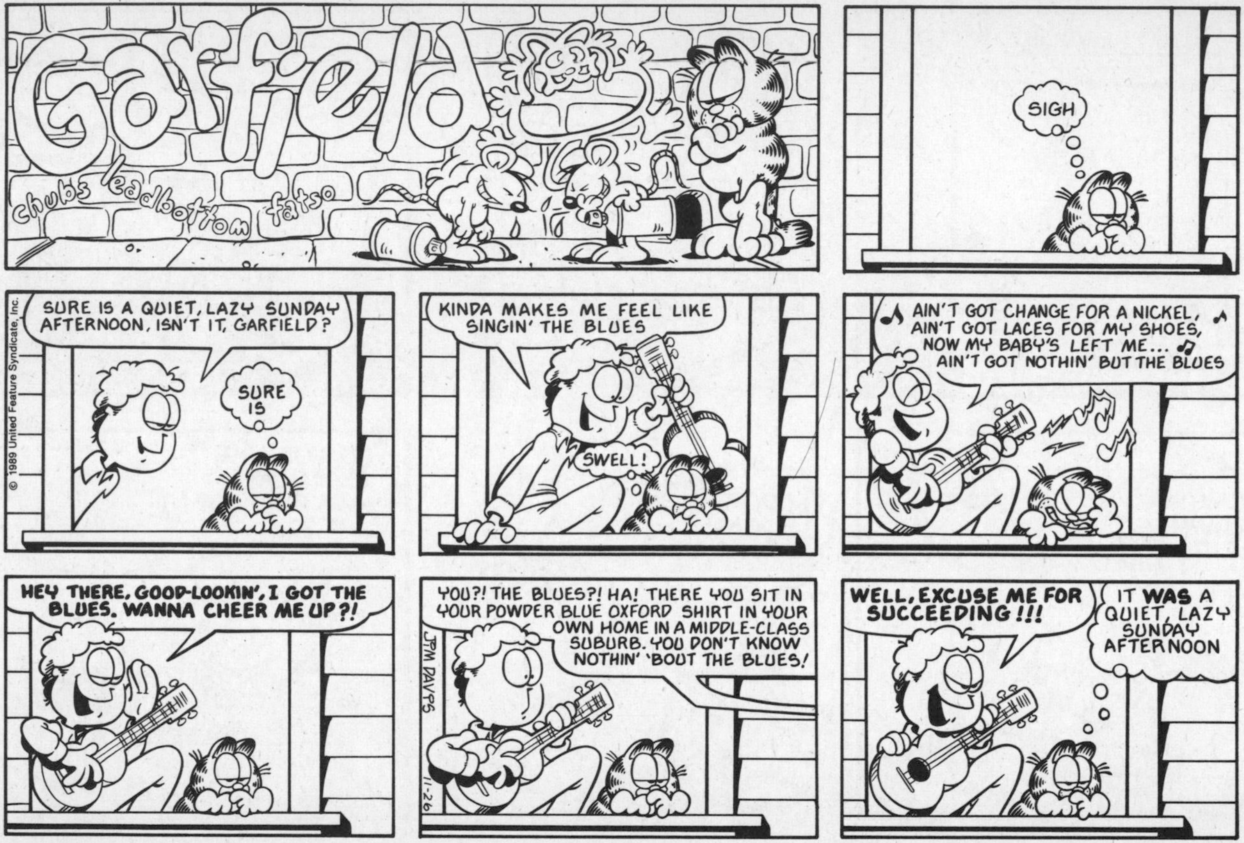
Garfield
chubbs leadbottom fatso
SIGH
SURE IS A QUIET, LAZY SUNDAY AFTERNOON, ISN'T IT, GARFIELD?
SURE IS
KINDA MAKES ME FEEL LIKE SINGIN' THE BLUES
SWELL!
AIN'T GOT CHANGE FOR A NICKEL, AIN'T GOT LACES FOR MY SHOES, NOW MY BABY'S LEFT ME... AIN'T GOT NOTHIN' BUT THE BLUES
HEY THERE, GOOD-LOOKIN', I GOT THE BLUES. WANNA CHEER ME UP?!
YOU?! THE BLUES?! HA! THERE YOU SIT IN YOUR POWDER BLUE OXFORD SHIRT IN YOUR OWN HOME IN A MIDDLE-CLASS SUBURB. YOU DON'T KNOW NOTHIN' 'BOUT THE BLUES!
JIM DAVIS
11-26
WELL, EXCUSE ME FOR SUCCEEDING!!!
IT WAS A QUIET, LAZY SUNDAY AFTERNOON

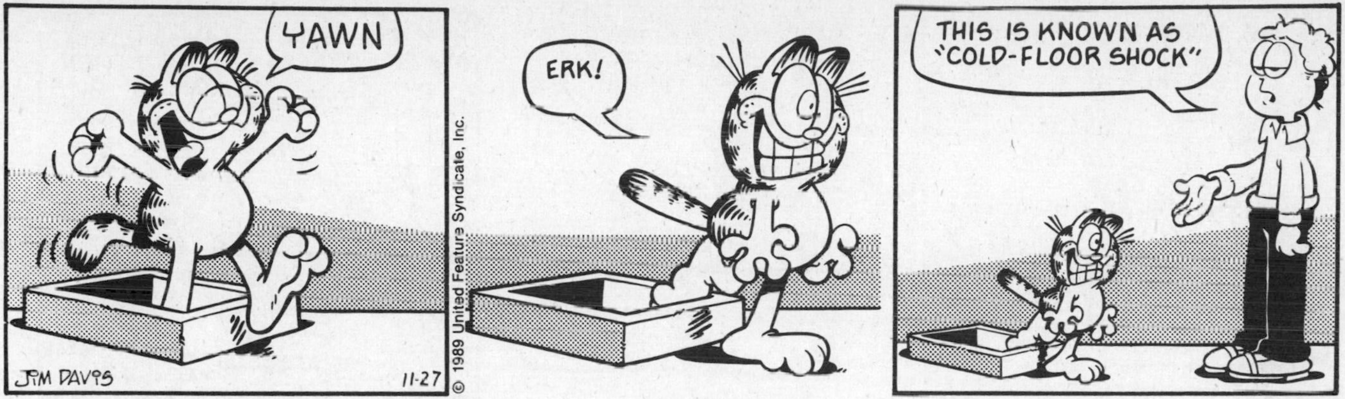

YAWN
JIM DAVIS
11-27
© 1989 United Feature Syndicate, Inc.
ERK!
THIS IS KNOWN AS "COLD-FLOOR SHOCK"

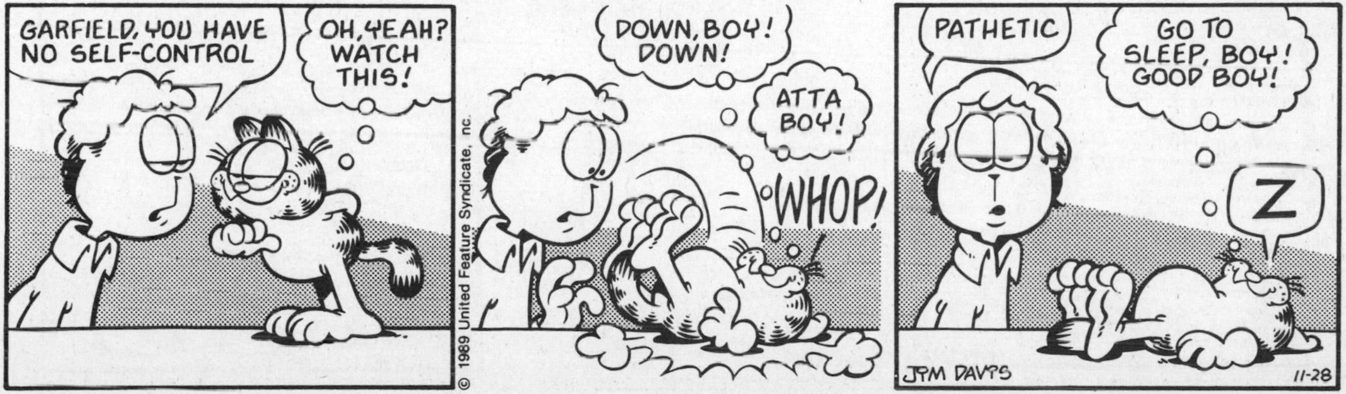

GARFIELD, YOU HAVE NO SELF-CONTROL
OH, YEAH? WATCH THIS!
© 1989 United Feature Syndicate, Inc.
DOWN, BOY! DOWN!
ATTA BOY!
WHOP!
PATHETIC
GO TO SLEEP, BOY! GOOD BOY!
Z
JIM DAVIS
11-28

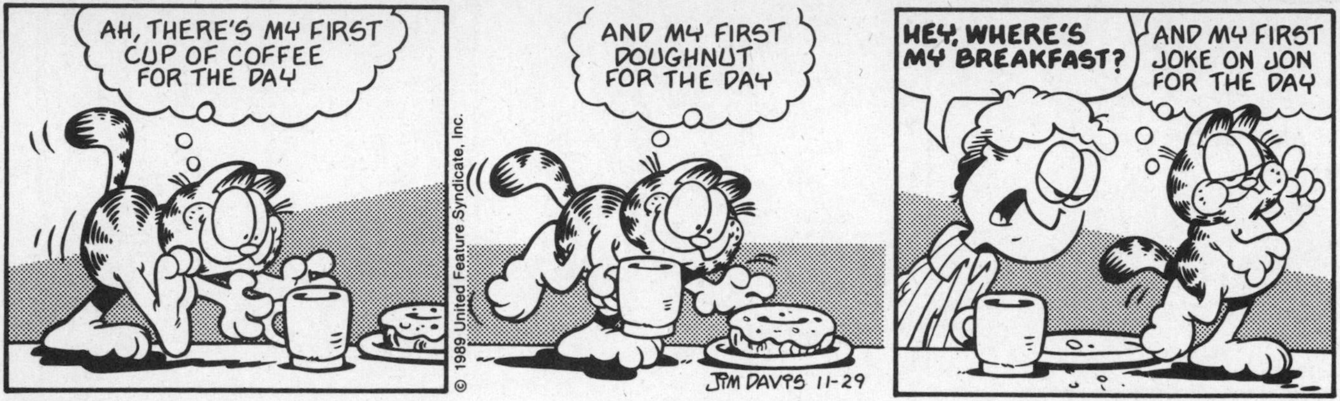
AH, THERE'S MY FIRST CUP OF COFFEE FOR THE DAY
AND MY FIRST DOUGHNUT FOR THE DAY
HEY, WHERE'S MY BREAKFAST?
AND MY FIRST JOKE ON JON FOR THE DAY
JIM DAVIS 11-29
© 1989 United Feature Syndicate, Inc.

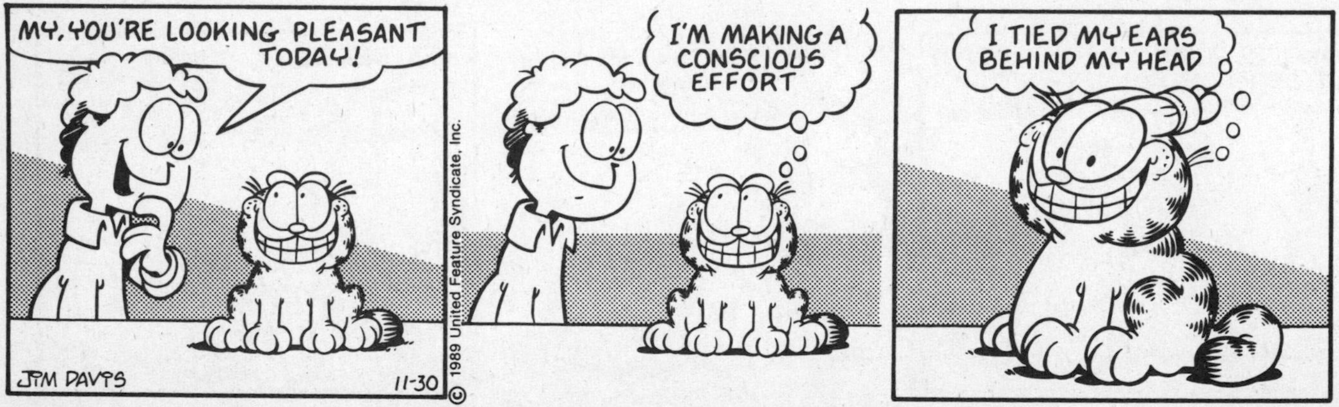
MY, YOU'RE LOOKING PLEASANT TODAY!
I'M MAKING A CONSCIOUS EFFORT
I TIED MY EARS BEHIND MY HEAD
JIM DAVIS 11-30
© 1989 United Feature Syndicate, Inc.

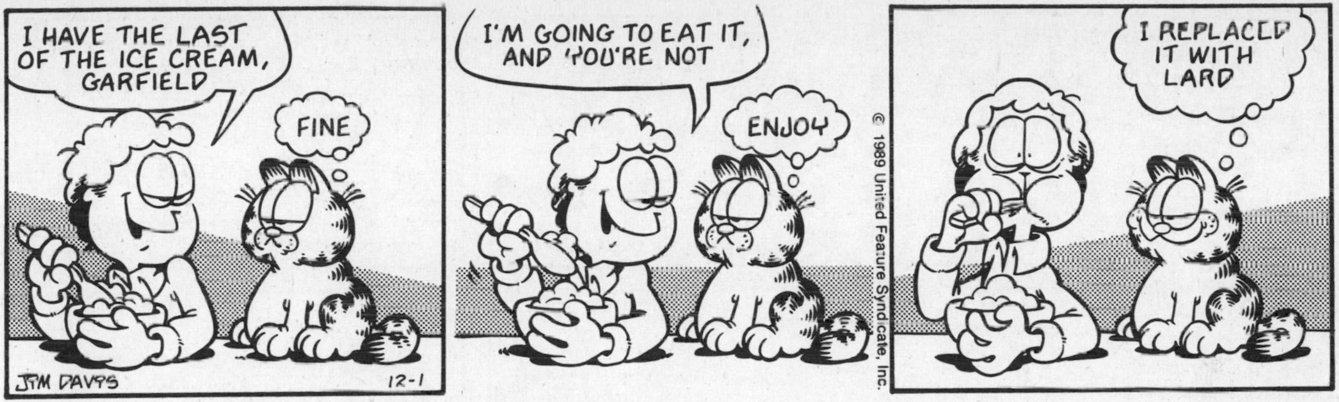
I HAVE THE LAST OF THE ICE CREAM, GARFIELD
FINE
JIM DAVIS
12-1
I'M GOING TO EAT IT, AND YOU'RE NOT
ENJOY
© 1989 United Feature Syndicate, Inc.
I REPLACED IT WITH LARD

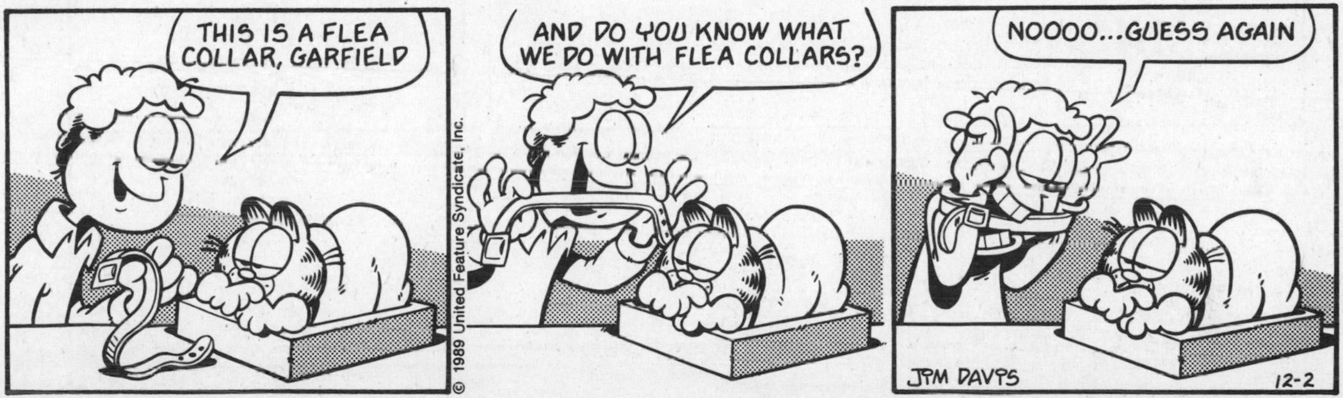
THIS IS A FLEA COLLAR, GARFIELD
© 1989 United Feature Syndicate, Inc.
AND DO YOU KNOW WHAT WE DO WITH FLEA COLLARS?
NOOOO...GUESS AGAIN
JIM DAVIS
12-2

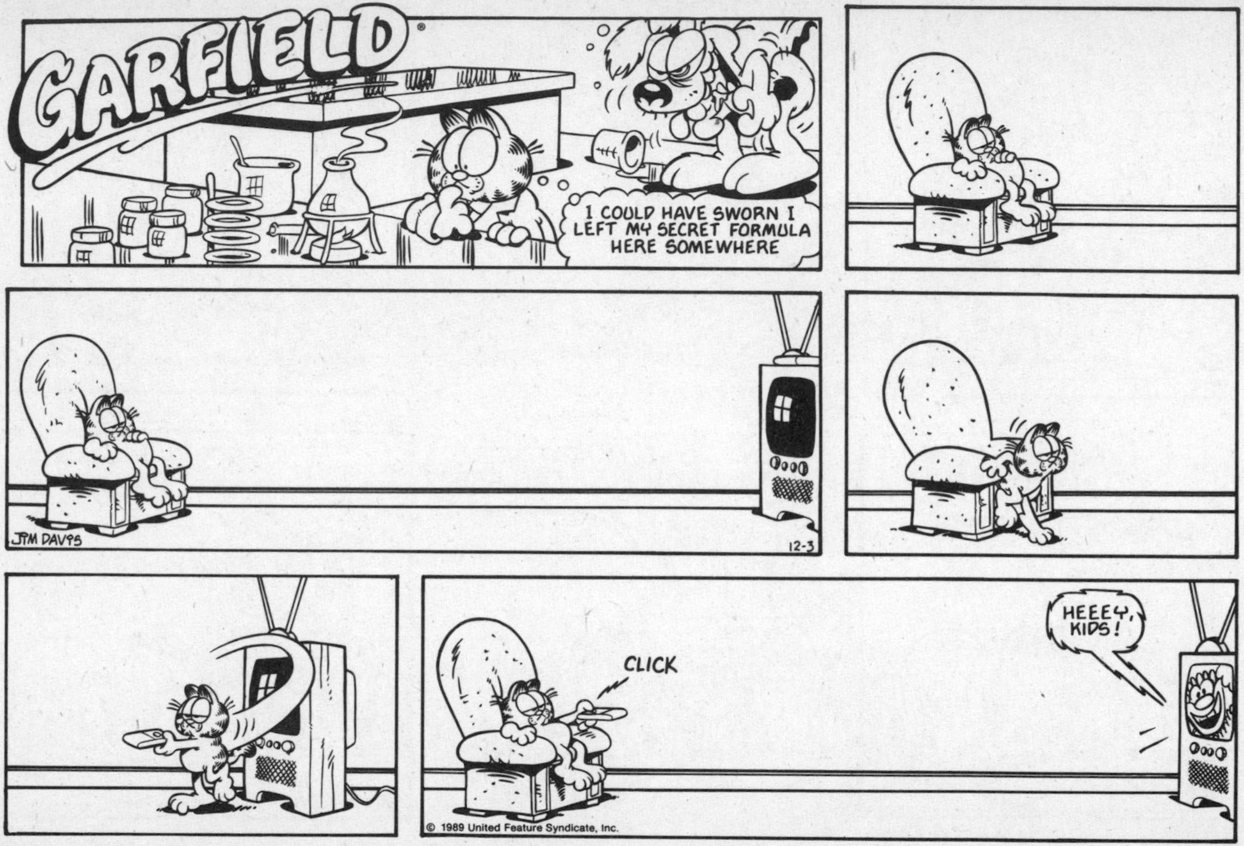
GARFIELD
I COULD HAVE SWORN I LEFT MY SECRET FORMULA HERE SOMEWHERE
JIM DAVIS
12-3
CLICK
HEEEY, KIDS!
© 1989 United Feature Syndicate, Inc.

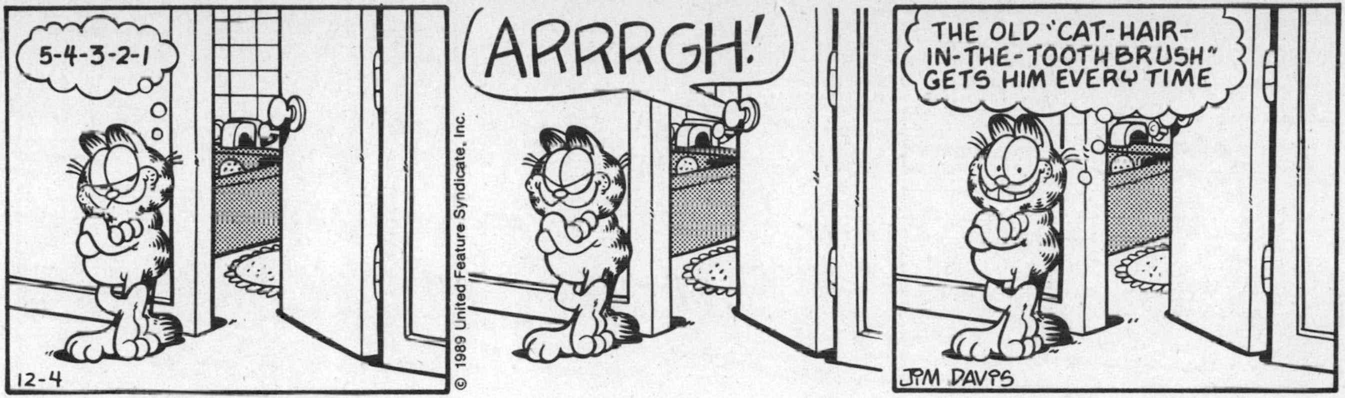
5-4-3-2-1
ARRRGH!
THE OLD "CAT-HAIR-IN-THE-TOOTHBRUSH" GETS HIM EVERY TIME
12-4
© 1989 United Feature Syndicate, Inc.
JIM DAVIS

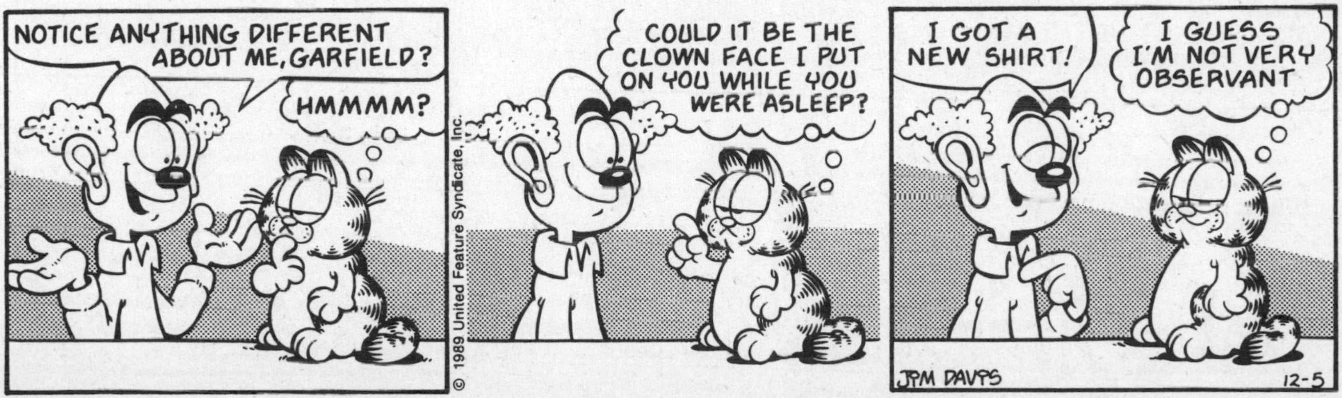
NOTICE ANYTHING DIFFERENT ABOUT ME, GARFIELD?
HMMMM?
COULD IT BE THE CLOWN FACE I PUT ON YOU WHILE YOU WERE ASLEEP?
I GOT A NEW SHIRT!
I GUESS I'M NOT VERY OBSERVANT
© 1989 United Feature Syndicate, Inc.
JIM DAVIS
12-5

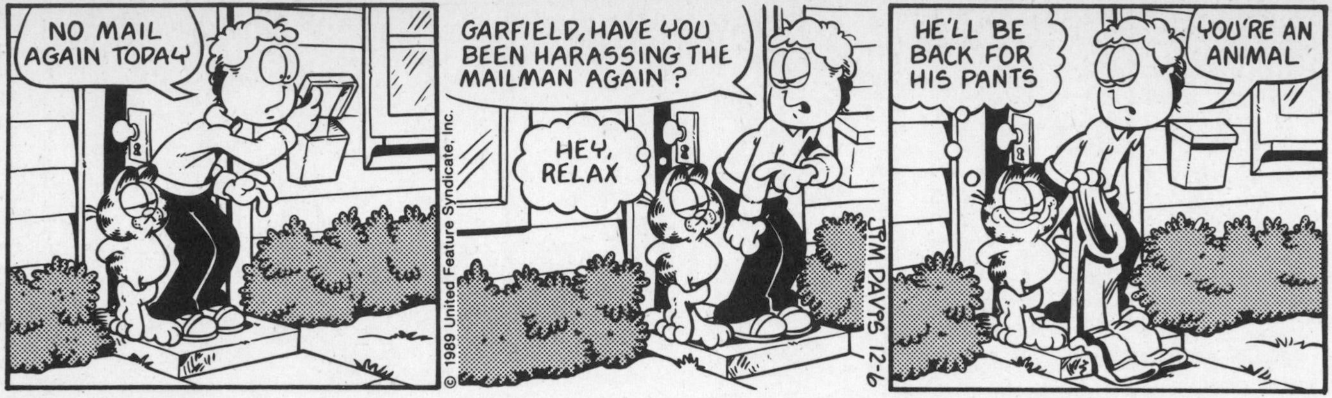
NO MAIL AGAIN TODAY
GARFIELD, HAVE YOU BEEN HARASSING THE MAILMAN AGAIN?
HEY, RELAX
© 1989 United Feature Syndicate, Inc.
JIM DAVIS 12-6
HE'LL BE BACK FOR HIS PANTS
YOU'RE AN ANIMAL

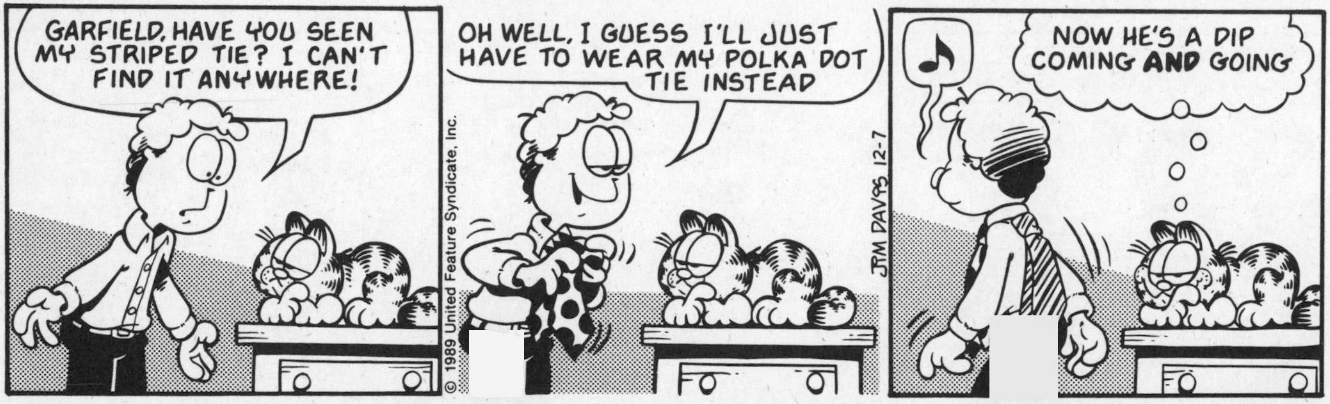
GARFIELD, HAVE YOU SEEN MY STRIPED TIE? I CAN'T FIND IT ANYWHERE!
© 1989 United Feature Syndicate, Inc.
OH WELL, I GUESS I'LL JUST HAVE TO WEAR MY POLKA DOT TIE INSTEAD
JIM DAVIS 12-7
♪
NOW HE'S A DIP COMING AND GOING

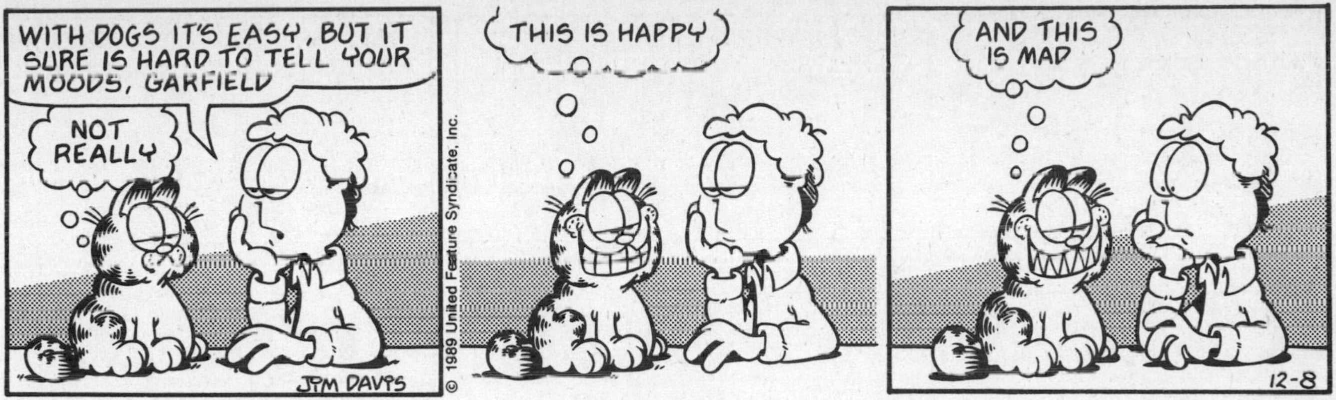
WITH DOGS IT'S EASY, BUT IT SURE IS HARD TO TELL YOUR MOODS, GARFIELD
NOT REALLY
JIM DAVIS
© 1989 United Feature Syndicate, Inc.
THIS IS HAPPY
AND THIS IS MAD
12-8

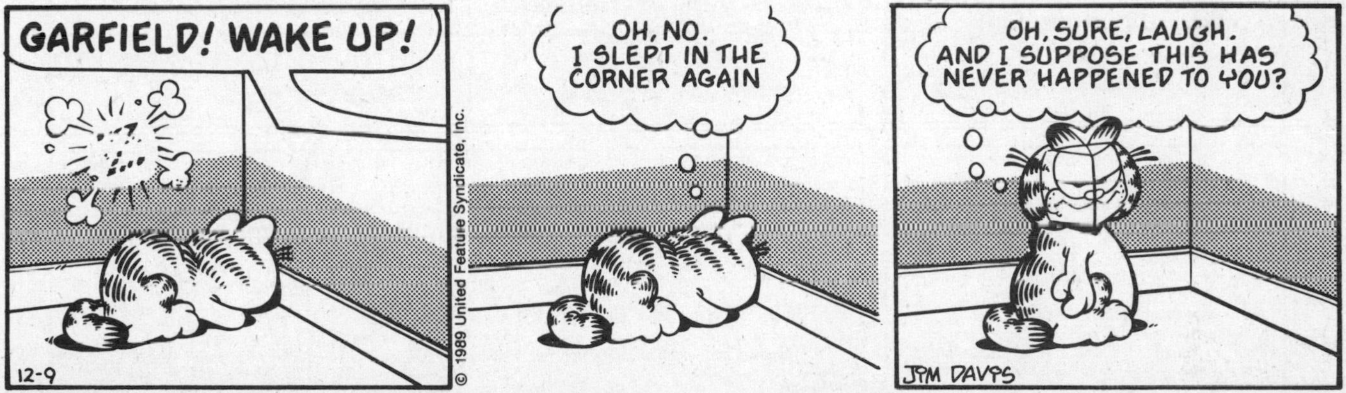
GARFIELD! WAKE UP!
12-9
© 1989 United Feature Syndicate, Inc.
OH, NO. I SLEPT IN THE CORNER AGAIN
OH, SURE, LAUGH. AND I SUPPOSE THIS HAS NEVER HAPPENED TO YOU?
JIM DAVIS

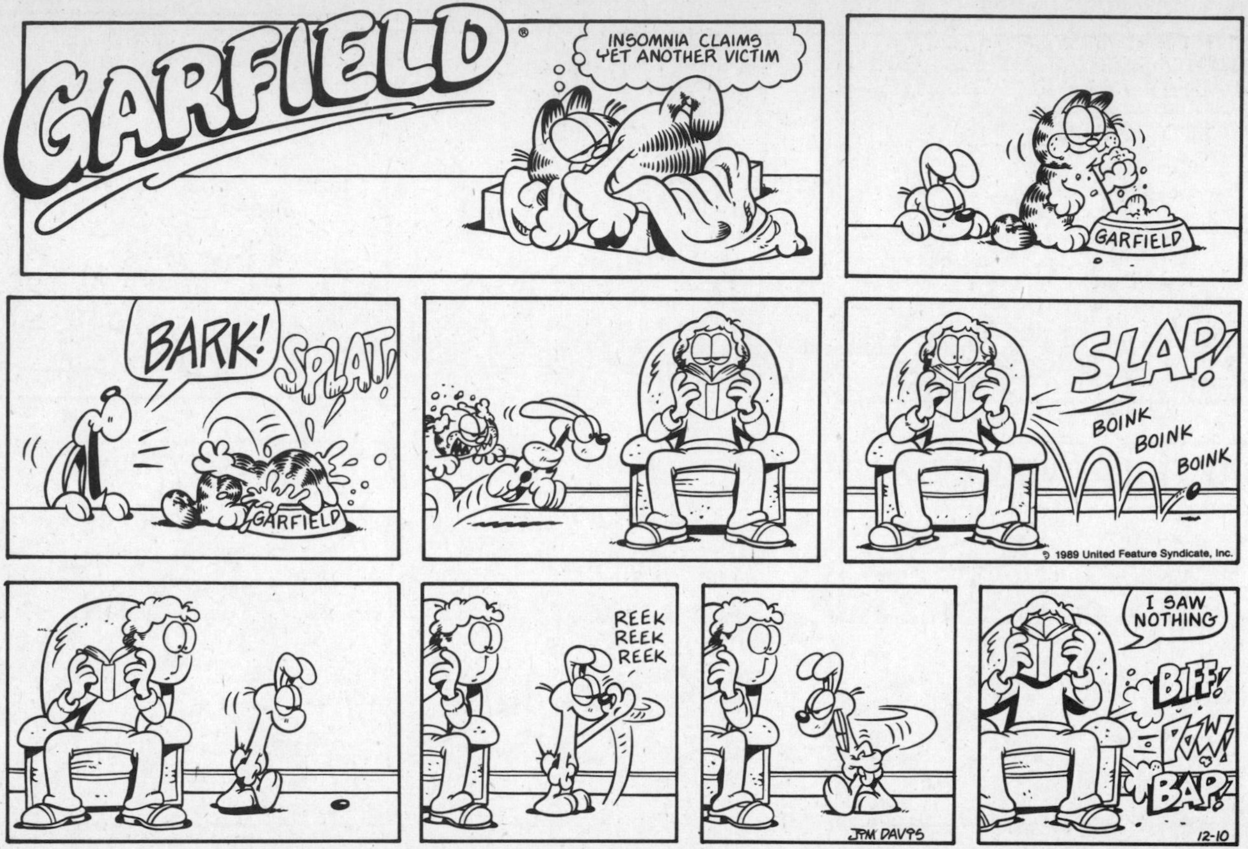

GARFIELD®
INSOMNIA CLAIMS YET ANOTHER VICTIM
GARFIELD
BARK!
SPLAT!
GARFIELD
SLAP!
BOINK
BOINK
BOINK
© 1989 United Feature Syndicate, Inc.
REEK
REEK
REEK
JIM DAVIS
I SAW NOTHING
BIFF!
POW!
BAP!
12-10

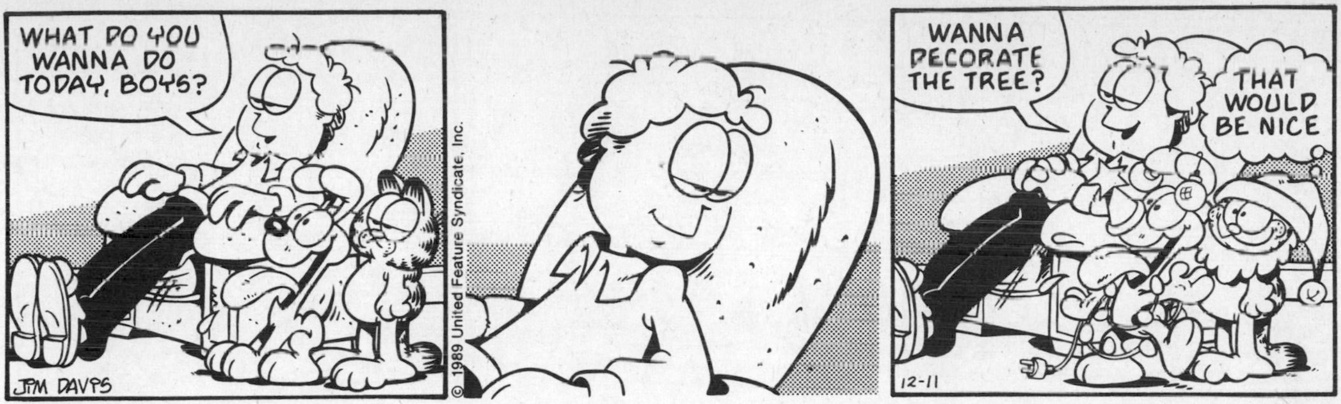
WHAT DO YOU WANNA DO TODAY, BOYS?
JIM DAVIS
© 1989 United Feature Syndicate, Inc.
WANNA DECORATE THE TREE?
THAT WOULD BE NICE
12-11

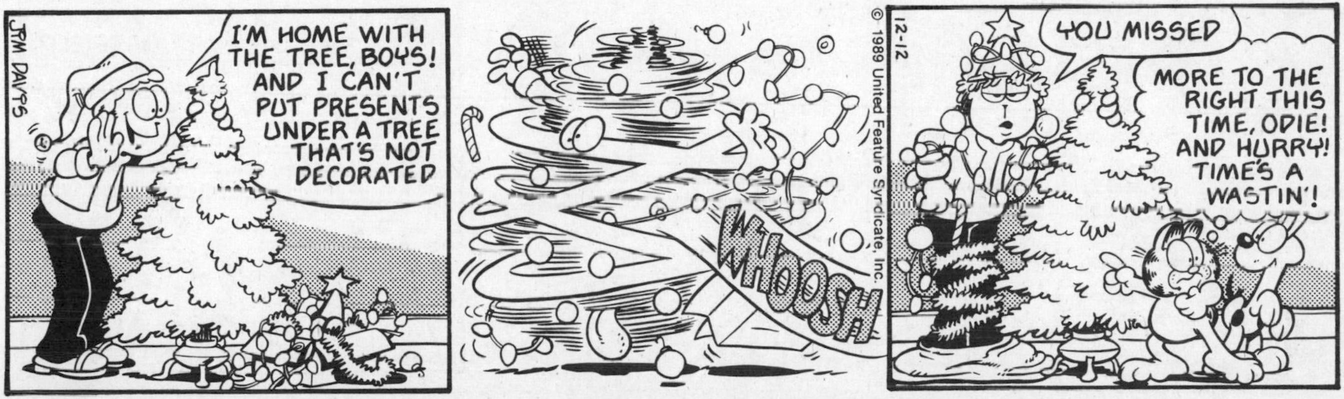
JIM DAVIS
I'M HOME WITH THE TREE, BOYS! AND I CAN'T PUT PRESENTS UNDER A TREE THAT'S NOT DECORATED
WHOOSH
© 1989 United Feature Syndicate, Inc.
12-12
YOU MISSED
MORE TO THE RIGHT THIS TIME, ODIE! AND HURRY! TIME'S A WASTIN'!

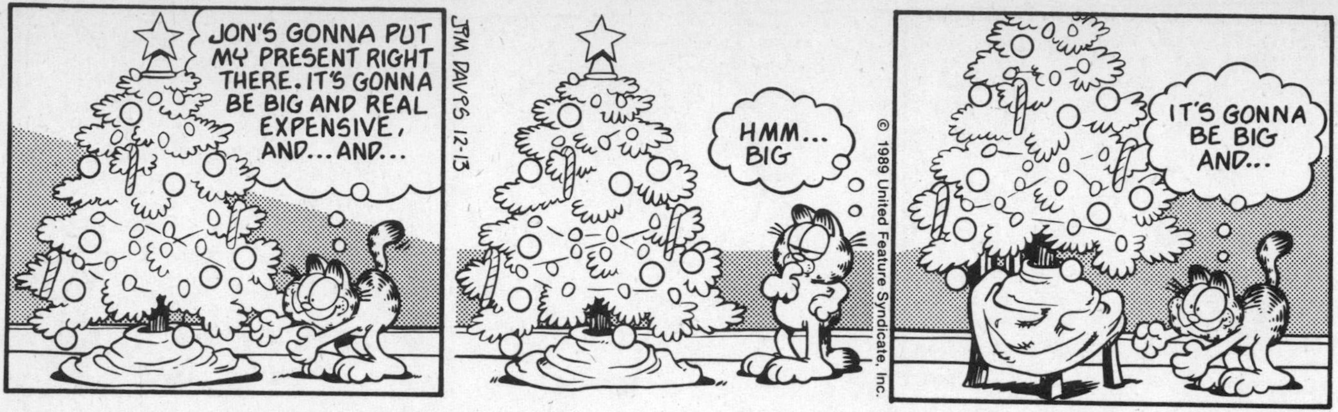
JON'S GONNA PUT MY PRESENT RIGHT THERE. IT'S GONNA BE BIG AND REAL EXPENSIVE, AND... AND...
JIM DAVIS 12-13
HMM... BIG
© 1989 United Feature Syndicate, Inc.
IT'S GONNA BE BIG AND...

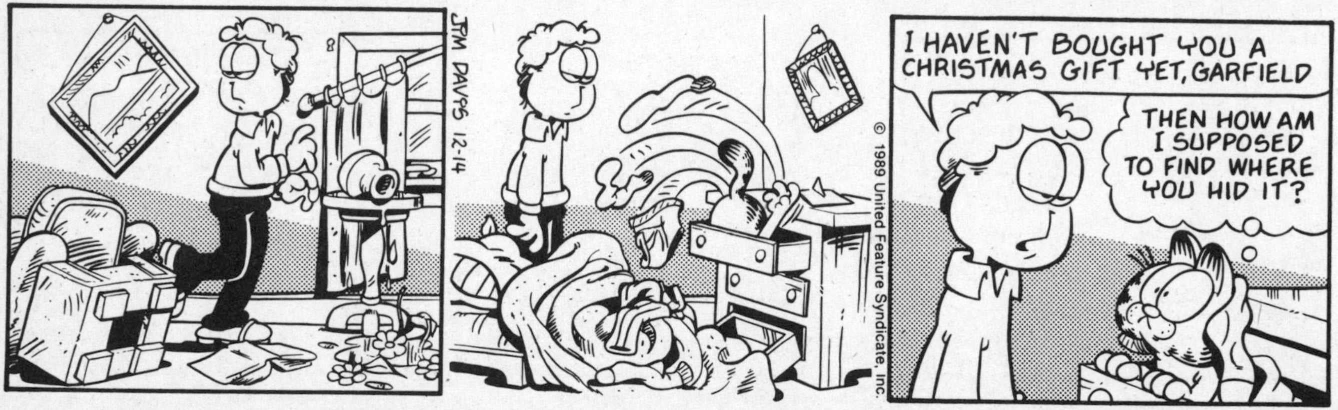
JIM DAVIS 12-14
© 1989 United Feature Syndicate, Inc.
I HAVEN'T BOUGHT YOU A CHRISTMAS GIFT YET, GARFIELD
THEN HOW AM I SUPPOSED TO FIND WHERE YOU HID IT?

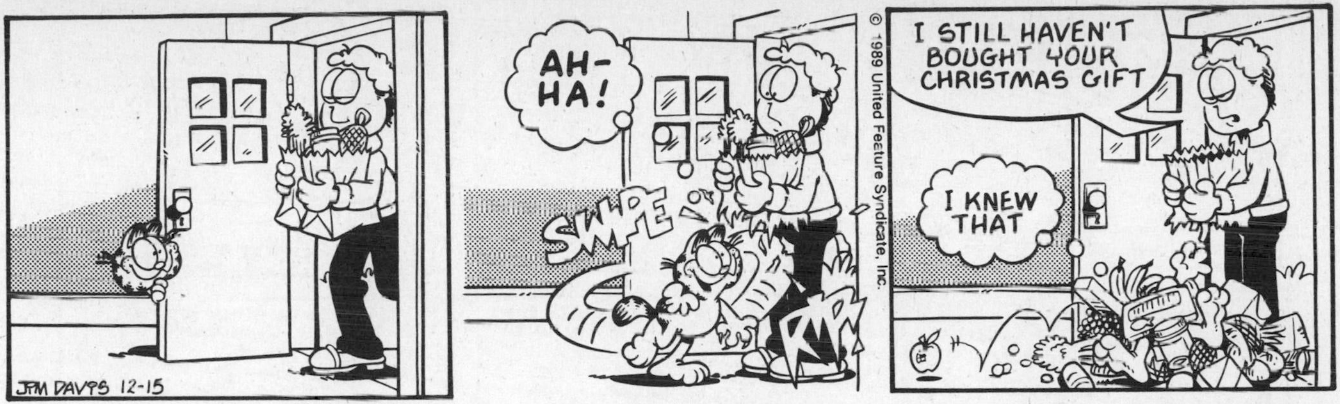
JIM DAVIS 12-15
AH-HA!
SWIPE
RIP
© 1989 United Feature Syndicate, Inc.
I STILL HAVEN'T BOUGHT YOUR CHRISTMAS GIFT
I KNEW THAT

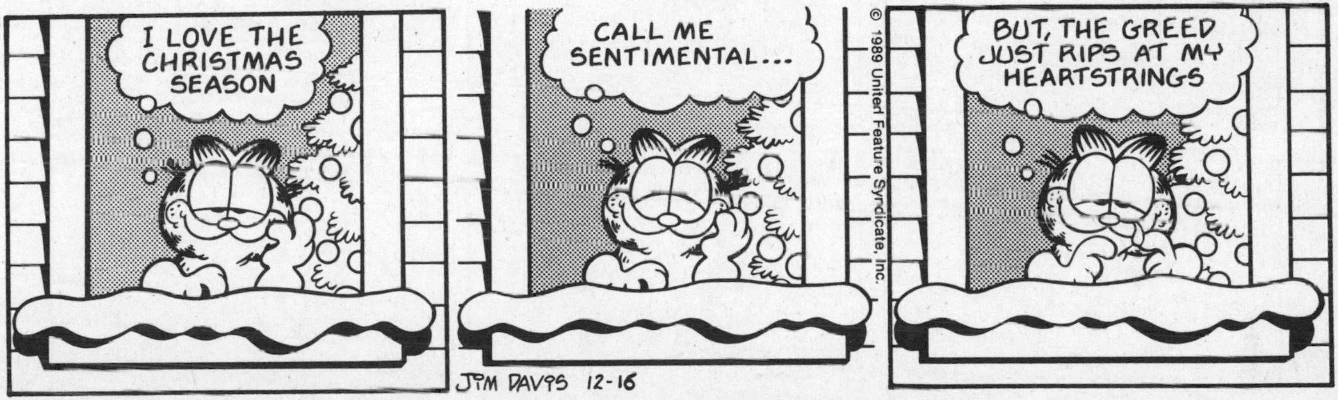
I LOVE THE CHRISTMAS SEASON
CALL ME SENTIMENTAL...
© 1989 United Feature Syndicate, Inc.
BUT, THE GREED JUST RIPS AT MY HEARTSTRINGS
JIM DAVIS 12-16

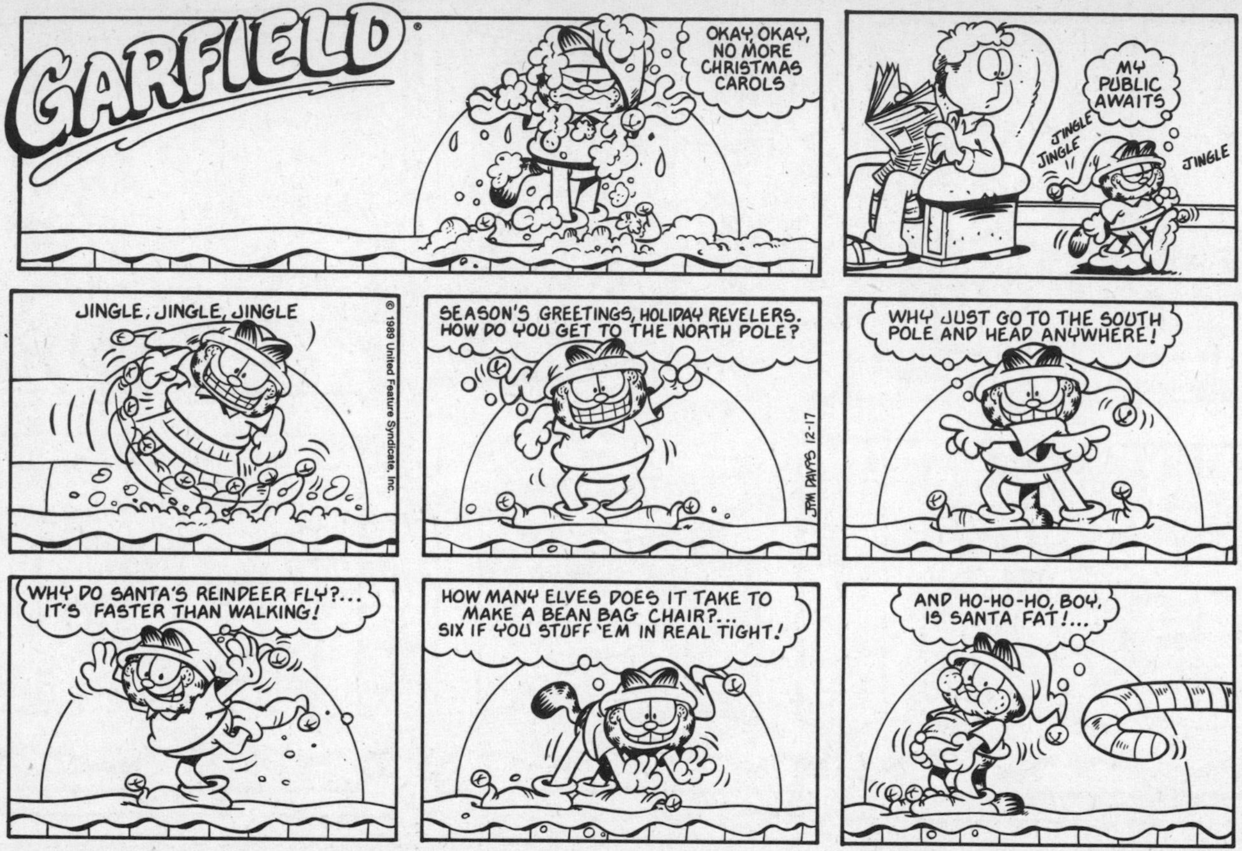
GARFIELD
OKAY, OKAY, NO MORE CHRISTMAS CAROLS
MY PUBLIC AWAITS
JINGLE
JINGLE
JINGLE
JINGLE, JINGLE, JINGLE
© 1989 United Feature Syndicate, Inc.
SEASON'S GREETINGS, HOLIDAY REVELERS. HOW DO YOU GET TO THE NORTH POLE?
JPM DAVIS 12-17
WHY JUST GO TO THE SOUTH POLE AND HEAD ANYWHERE!
WHY DO SANTA'S REINDEER FLY?... IT'S FASTER THAN WALKING!
HOW MANY ELVES DOES IT TAKE TO MAKE A BEAN BAG CHAIR?... SIX IF YOU STUFF 'EM IN REAL TIGHT!
AND HO-HO-HO, BOY, IS SANTA FAT!...

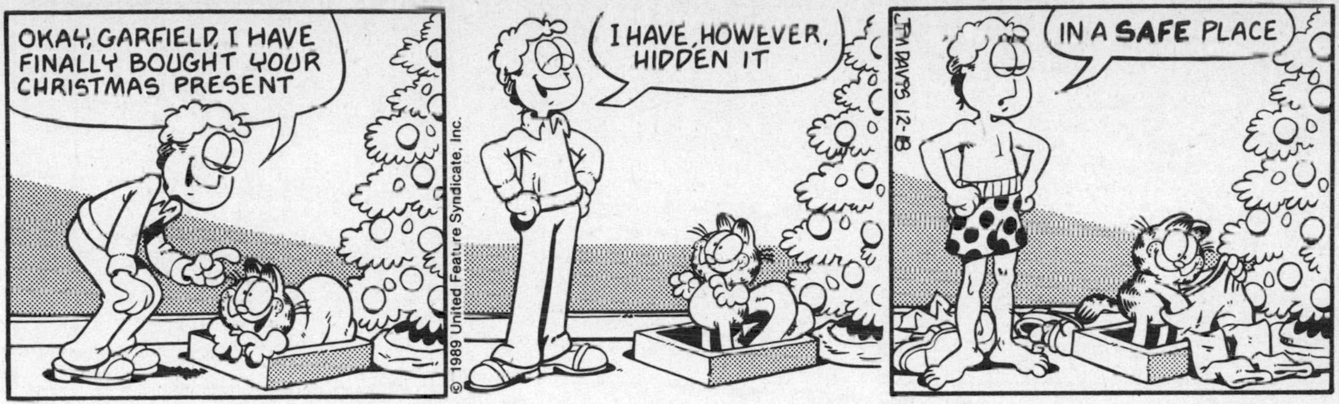
OKAY, GARFIELD, I HAVE FINALLY BOUGHT YOUR CHRISTMAS PRESENT
© 1989 United Feature Syndicate, Inc.
I HAVE, HOWEVER, HIDDEN IT
JIM DAVIS 12-18
IN A **SAFE** PLACE

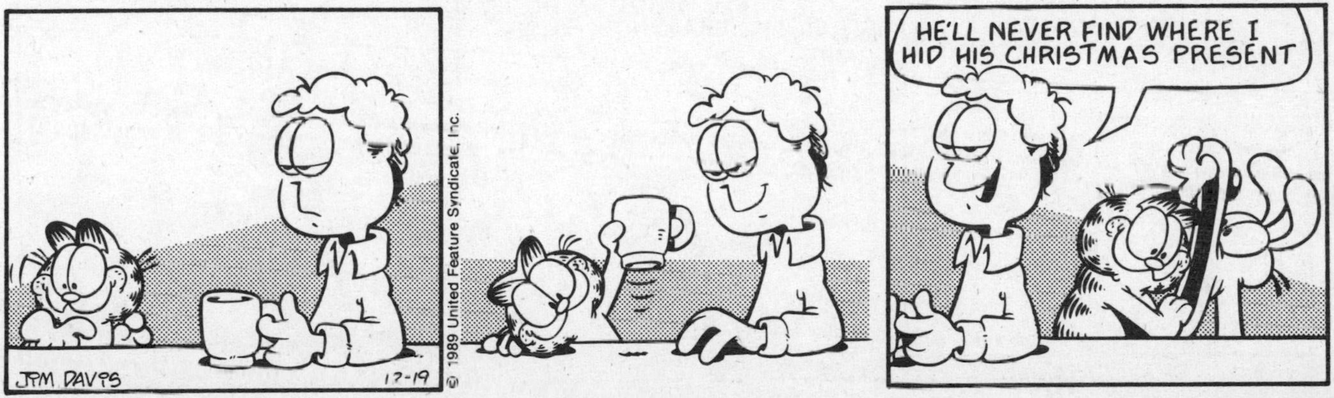
JIM DAVIS 12-19
© 1989 United Feature Syndicate, Inc.
HE'LL NEVER FIND WHERE I HID HIS CHRISTMAS PRESENT

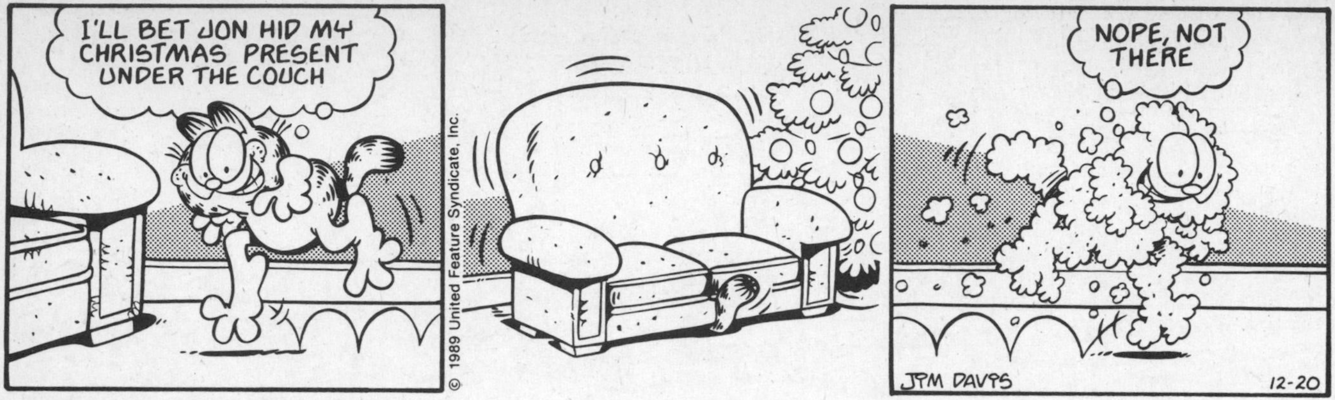
I'LL BET JON HID MY CHRISTMAS PRESENT UNDER THE COUCH
© 1989 United Feature Syndicate, Inc.
NOPE, NOT THERE
JIM DAVIS
12-20

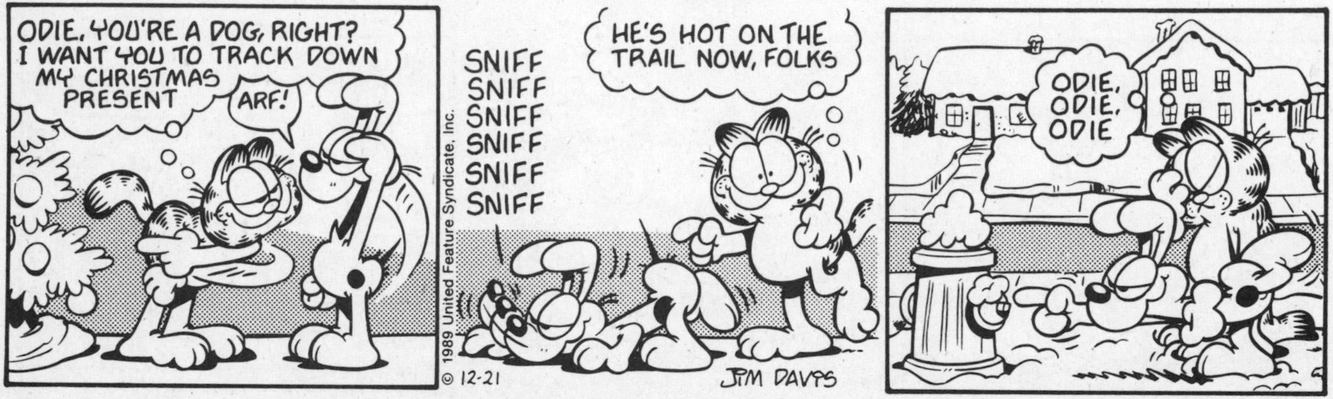
ODIE, YOU'RE A DOG, RIGHT? I WANT YOU TO TRACK DOWN MY CHRISTMAS PRESENT
ARF!
© 1989 United Feature Syndicate, Inc.
12-21
SNIFF
SNIFF
SNIFF
SNIFF
SNIFF
SNIFF
HE'S HOT ON THE TRAIL NOW, FOLKS
JIM DAVIS
ODIE, ODIE, ODIE

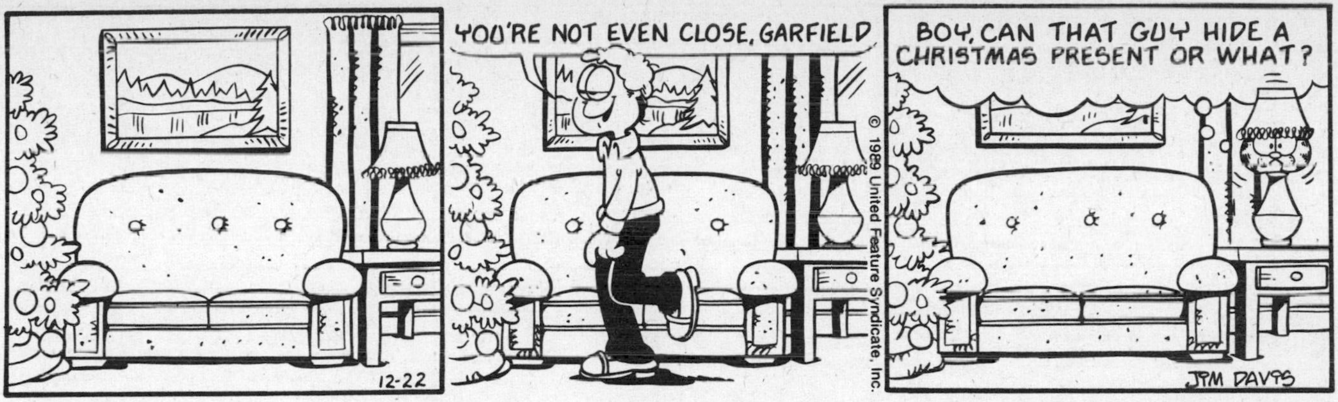
12-22
YOU'RE NOT EVEN CLOSE, GARFIELD
© 1989 United Feature Syndicate, Inc.
BOY, CAN THAT GUY HIDE A CHRISTMAS PRESENT OR WHAT?
JIM DAVIS

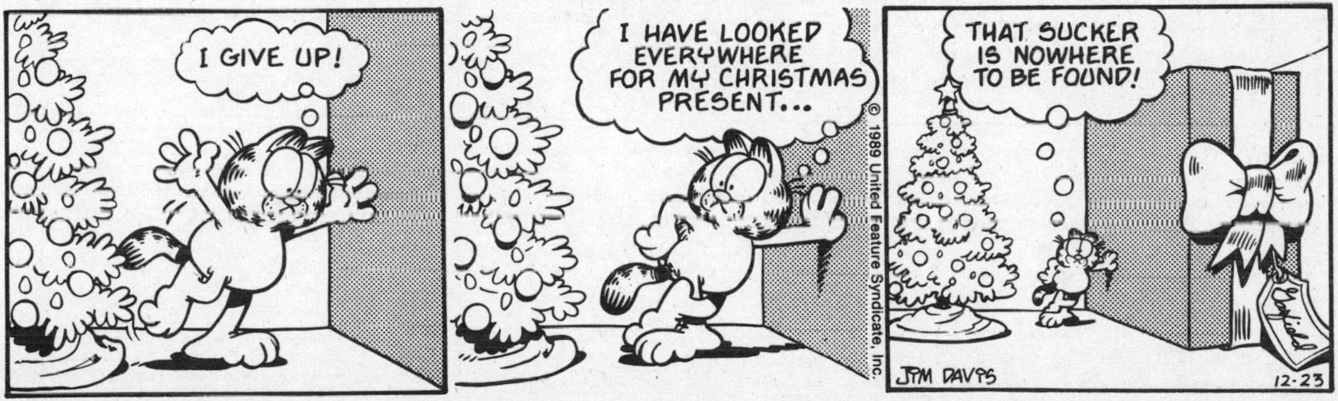
I GIVE UP!
I HAVE LOOKED EVERYWHERE FOR MY CHRISTMAS PRESENT...
© 1989 United Feature Syndicate, Inc.
THAT SUCKER IS NOWHERE TO BE FOUND!
JIM DAVIS
12-23

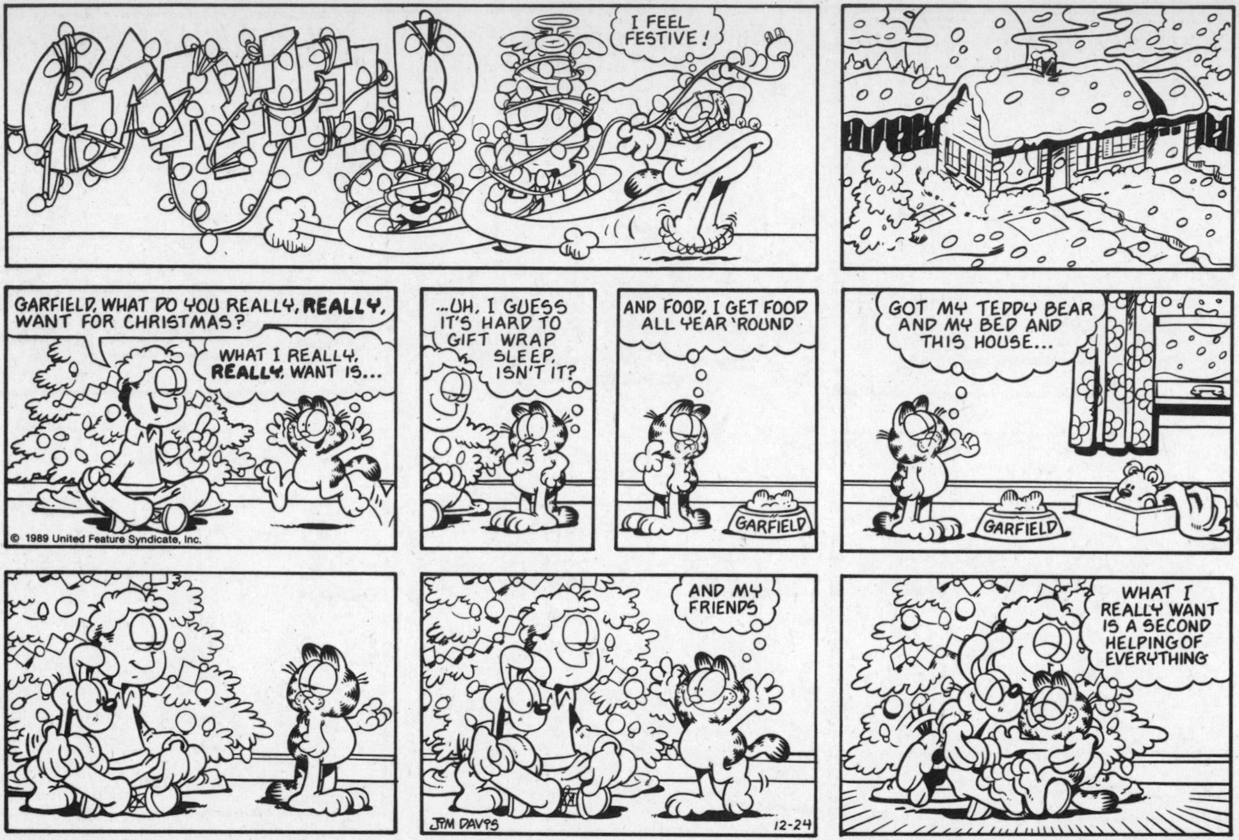

I FEEL FESTIVE!
GARFIELD, WHAT DO YOU REALLY, REALLY, WANT FOR CHRISTMAS?
WHAT I REALLY, REALLY, WANT IS...
...UH, I GUESS IT'S HARD TO GIFT WRAP SLEEP, ISN'T IT?
AND FOOD, I GET FOOD ALL YEAR 'ROUND
GOT MY TEDDY BEAR AND MY BED AND THIS HOUSE...
GARFIELD
GARFIELD
AND MY FRIENDS
WHAT I REALLY WANT IS A SECOND HELPING OF EVERYTHING
JPM DAVIS
12-24

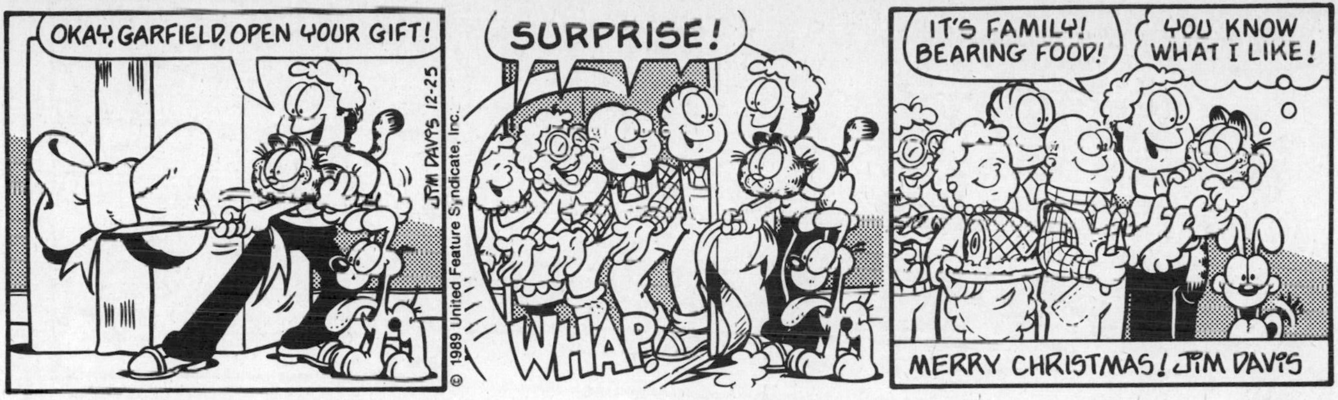
OKAY, GARFIELD, OPEN YOUR GIFT!
JIM DAVIS 12-25
© 1989 United Feature Syndicate, Inc.
SURPRISE!
WHAP!
IT'S FAMILY! BEARING FOOD!
YOU KNOW WHAT I LIKE!
MERRY CHRISTMAS! JIM DAVIS

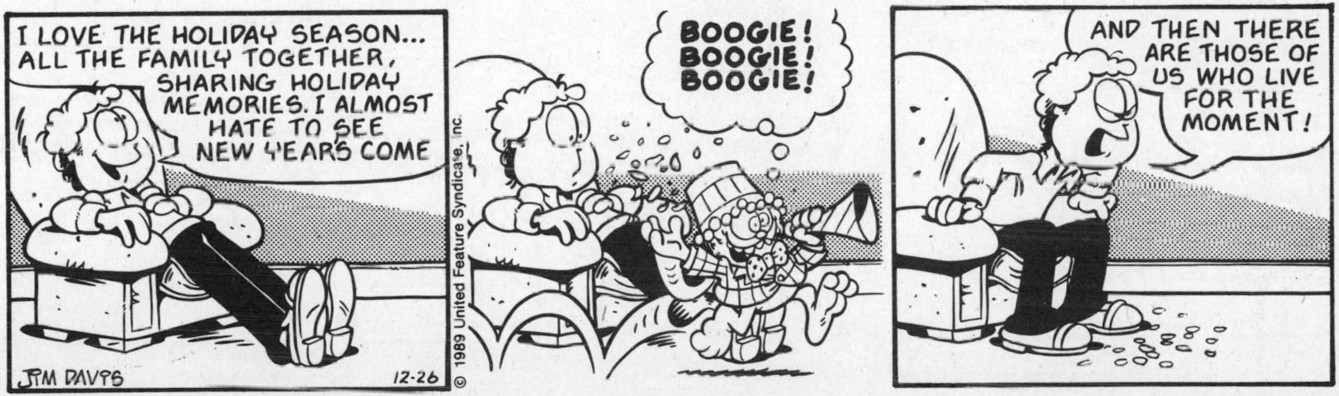
I LOVE THE HOLIDAY SEASON... ALL THE FAMILY TOGETHER, SHARING HOLIDAY MEMORIES. I ALMOST HATE TO SEE NEW YEAR'S COME
JIM DAVIS
12-26
© 1989 United Feature Syndicate, Inc.
BOOGIE! BOOGIE! BOOGIE!
AND THEN THERE ARE THOSE OF US WHO LIVE FOR THE MOMENT!

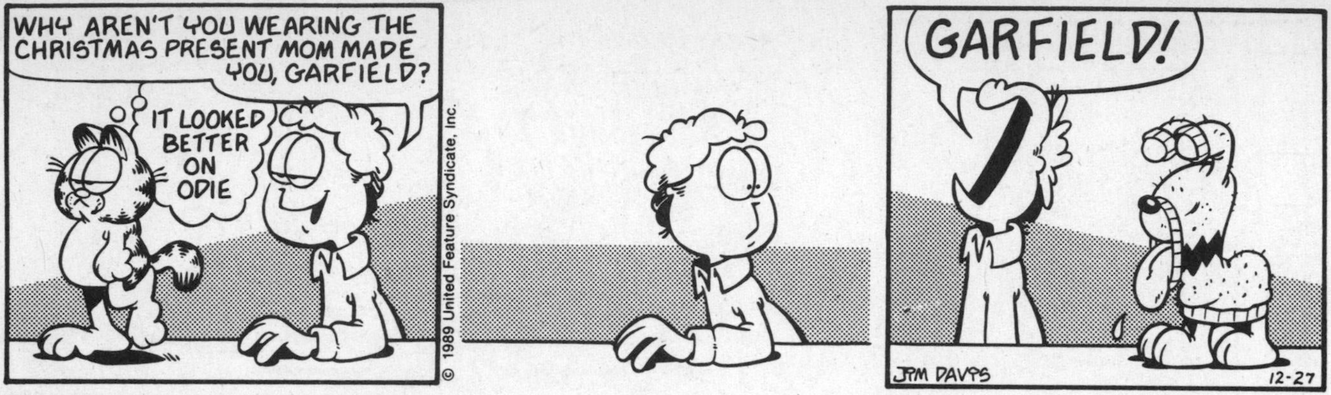
WHY AREN'T YOU WEARING THE CHRISTMAS PRESENT MOM MADE YOU, GARFIELD?
IT LOOKED BETTER ON ODIE
GARFIELD!
© 1989 United Feature Syndicate, Inc.
JIM DAVIS
12-27

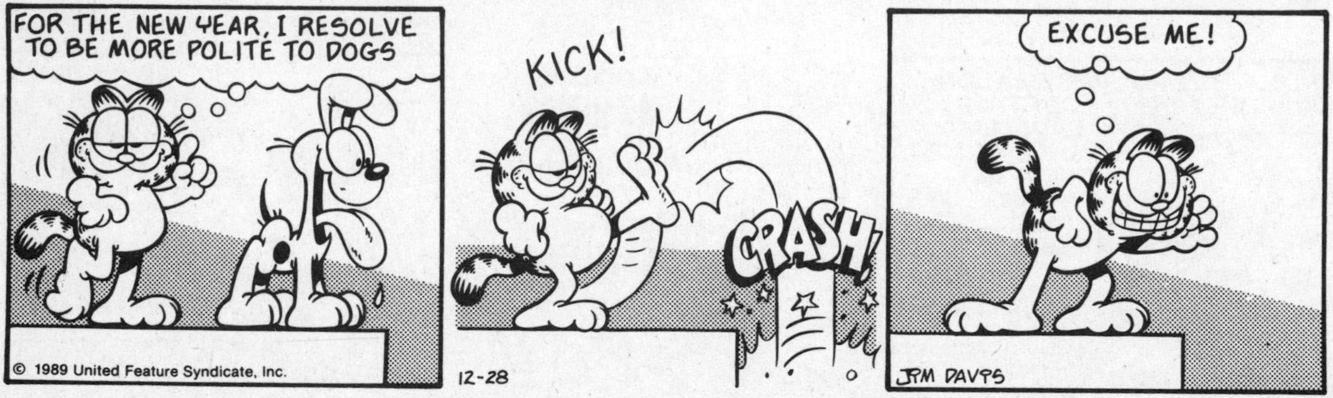
FOR THE NEW YEAR, I RESOLVE TO BE MORE POLITE TO DOGS
KICK!
CRASH!
EXCUSE ME!
© 1989 United Feature Syndicate, Inc.
12-28
JIM DAVIS

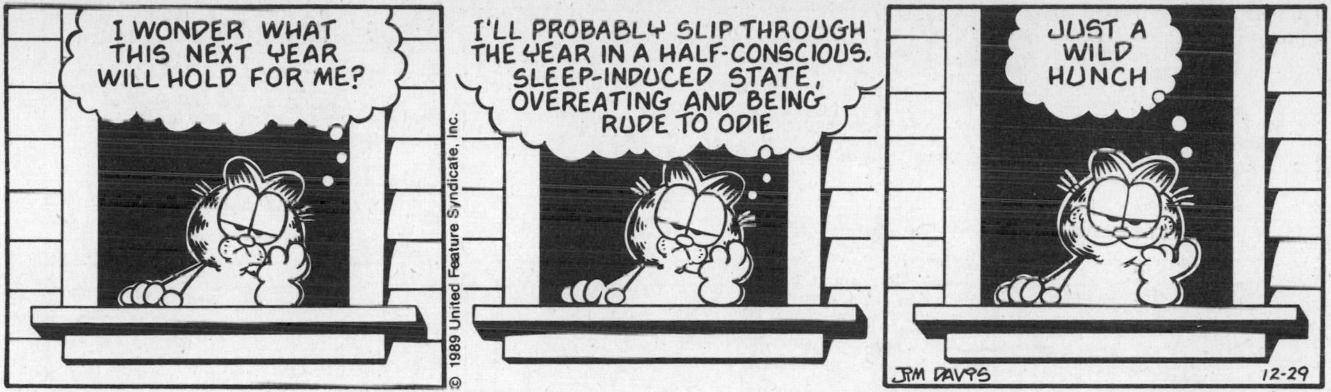
I WONDER WHAT THIS NEXT YEAR WILL HOLD FOR ME?
I'LL PROBABLY SLIP THROUGH THE YEAR IN A HALF-CONSCIOUS, SLEEP-INDUCED STATE, OVEREATING AND BEING RUDE TO ODIE
JUST A WILD HUNCH
© 1989 United Feature Syndicate, Inc.
JIM DAVIS
12-29

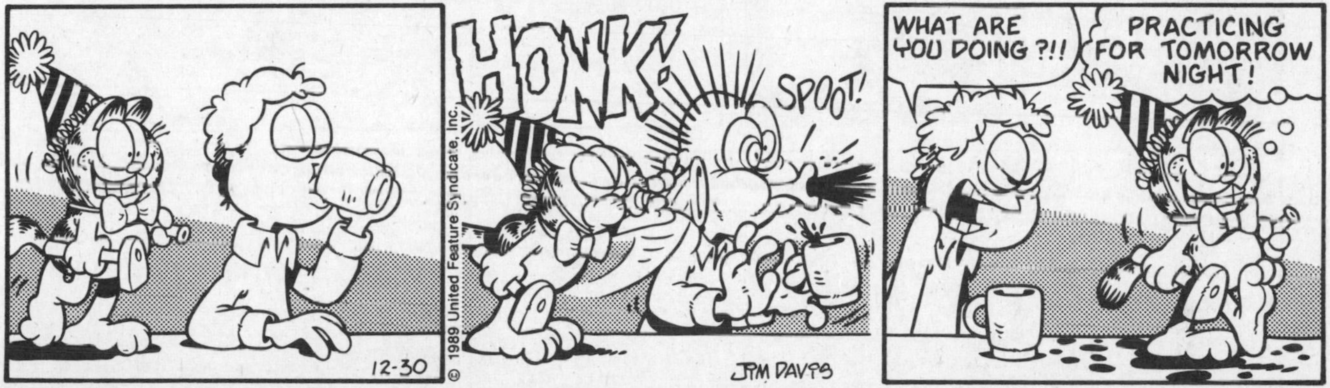
HONK!
SPOOT!
WHAT ARE YOU DOING ?!!
PRACTICING FOR TOMORROW NIGHT!
© 1989 United Feature Syndicate, Inc.
JIM DAVIS
12-30

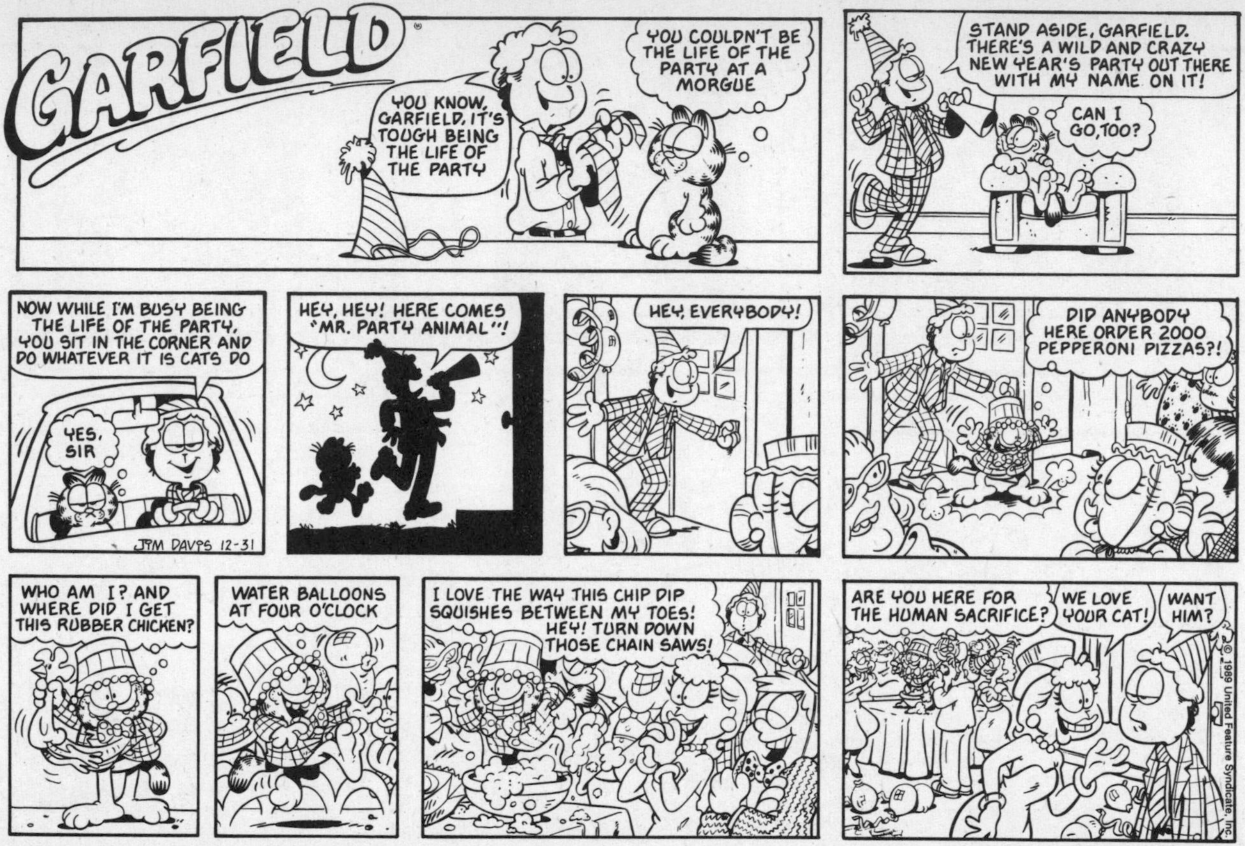
GARFIELD
YOU KNOW, GARFIELD, IT'S TOUGH BEING THE LIFE OF THE PARTY
YOU COULDN'T BE THE LIFE OF THE PARTY AT A MORGUE
STAND ASIDE, GARFIELD. THERE'S A WILD AND CRAZY NEW YEAR'S PARTY OUT THERE WITH MY NAME ON IT!
CAN I GO, TOO?
NOW WHILE I'M BUSY BEING THE LIFE OF THE PARTY, YOU SIT IN THE CORNER AND DO WHATEVER IT IS CATS DO
YES, SIR
JIM DAVIS 12-31
HEY, HEY! HERE COMES "MR. PARTY ANIMAL"!
HEY, EVERYBODY!
DID ANYBODY HERE ORDER 2000 PEPPERONI PIZZAS?!
WHO AM I? AND WHERE DID I GET THIS RUBBER CHICKEN?
WATER BALLOONS AT FOUR O'CLOCK
I LOVE THE WAY THIS CHIP DIP SQUISHES BETWEEN MY TOES!
HEY! TURN DOWN THOSE CHAIN SAWS!
ARE YOU HERE FOR THE HUMAN SACRIFICE?
WE LOVE YOUR CAT!
WANT HIM?
© 1989 United Feature Syndicate, Inc.

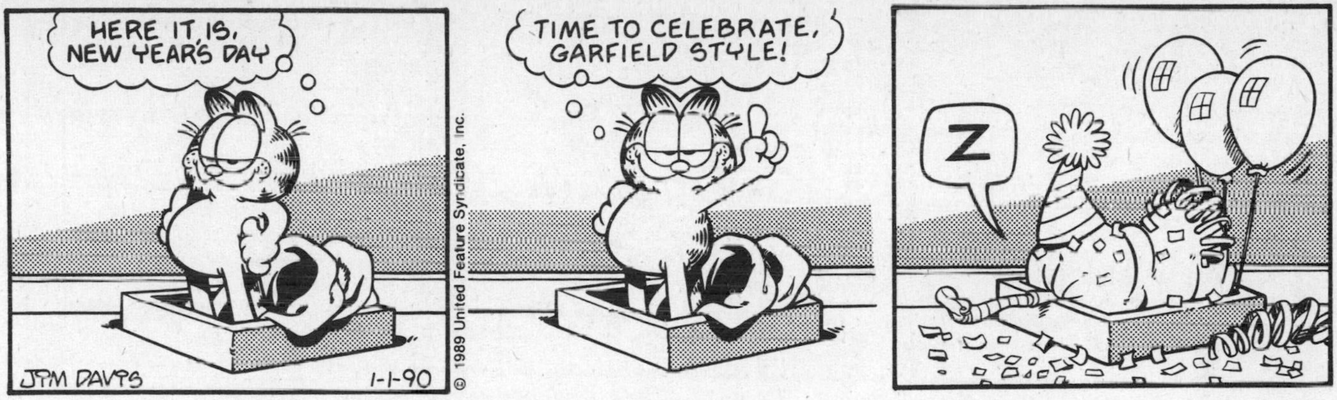
HERE IT IS, NEW YEAR'S DAY
TIME TO CELEBRATE, GARFIELD STYLE!
Z
JIM DAVIS
1-1-90
© 1989 United Feature Syndicate, Inc.

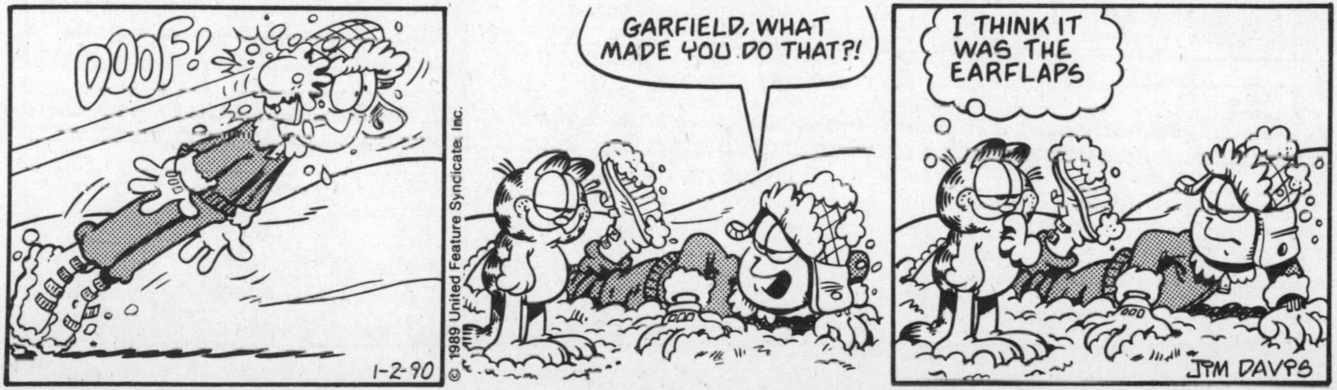
DOOF!
GARFIELD, WHAT MADE YOU DO THAT?!
I THINK IT WAS THE EARFLAPS
1-2-90
© 1989 United Feature Syndicate, Inc.
JIM DAVIS

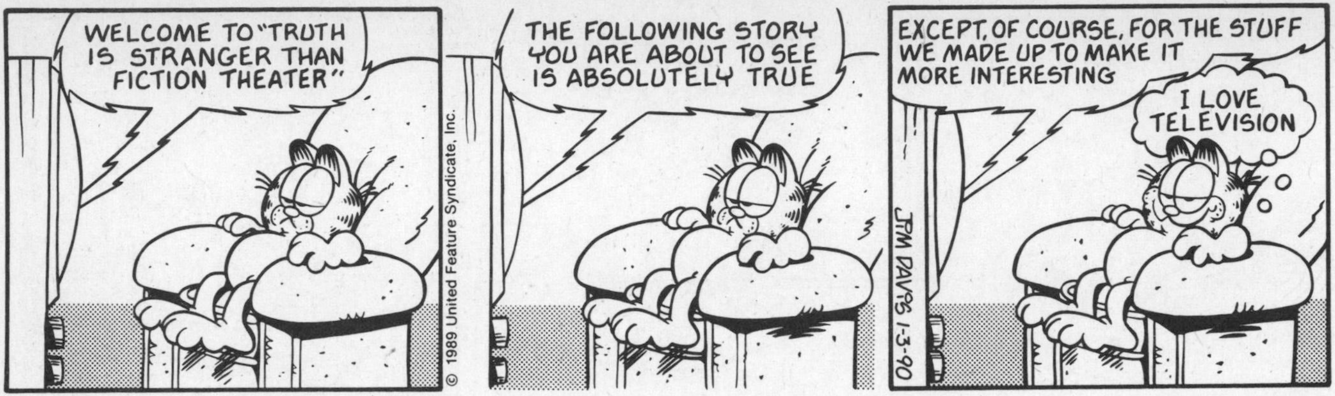
WELCOME TO "TRUTH IS STRANGER THAN FICTION THEATER"
© 1989 United Feature Syndicate, Inc.
THE FOLLOWING STORY YOU ARE ABOUT TO SEE IS ABSOLUTELY TRUE
JIM DAVIS 1-3-90
EXCEPT, OF COURSE, FOR THE STUFF WE MADE UP TO MAKE IT MORE INTERESTING
I LOVE TELEVISION

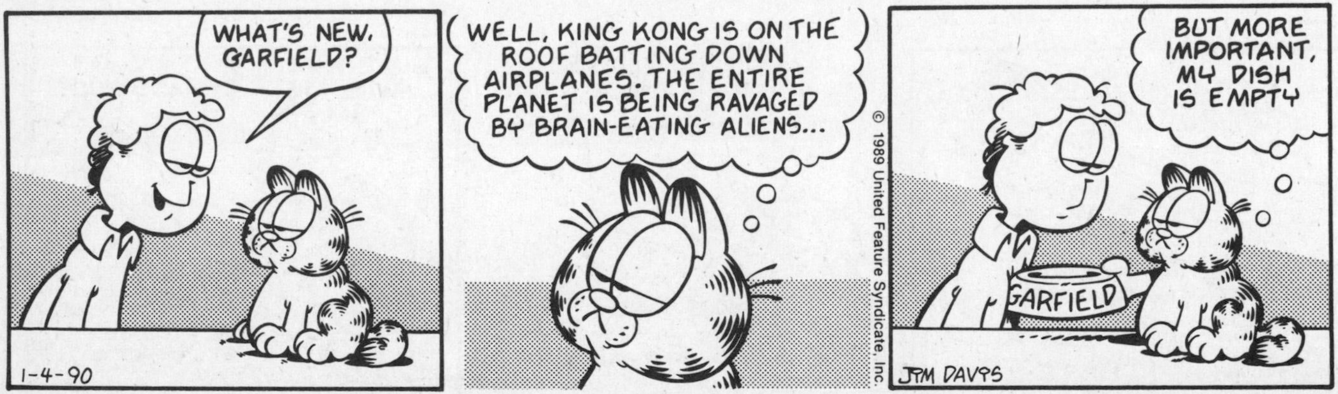
WHAT'S NEW, GARFIELD?
1-4-90
WELL, KING KONG IS ON THE ROOF BATTING DOWN AIRPLANES. THE ENTIRE PLANET IS BEING RAVAGED BY BRAIN-EATING ALIENS...
© 1989 United Feature Syndicate, Inc.
BUT MORE IMPORTANT, MY DISH IS EMPTY
GARFIELD
JIM DAVIS

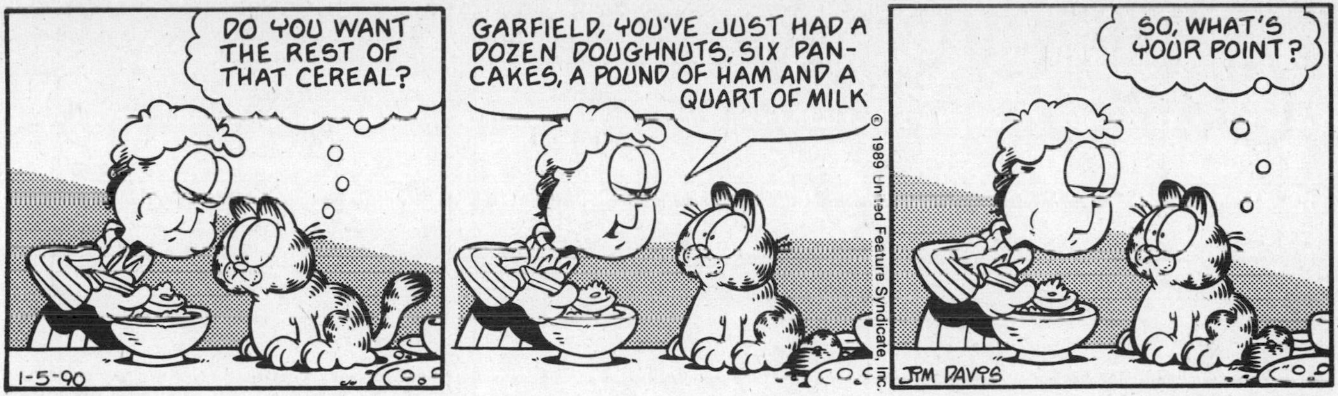
DO YOU WANT THE REST OF THAT CEREAL?
1-5-90
GARFIELD, YOU'VE JUST HAD A DOZEN DOUGHNUTS, SIX PANCAKES, A POUND OF HAM AND A QUART OF MILK
© 1989 United Feature Syndicate, Inc.
SO, WHAT'S YOUR POINT?
JIM DAVIS

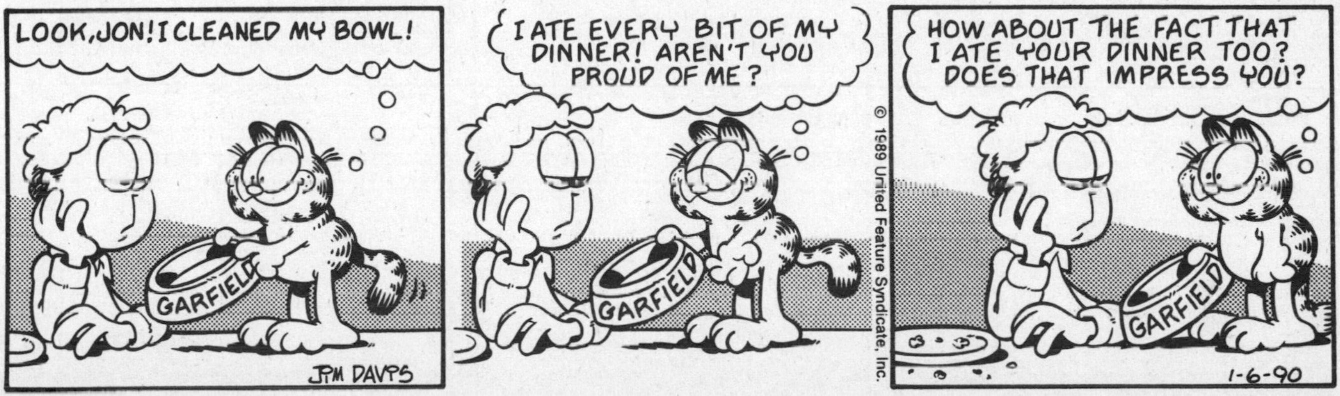
LOOK, JON! I CLEANED MY BOWL!
GARFIELD
JIM DAVIS
I ATE EVERY BIT OF MY DINNER! AREN'T YOU PROUD OF ME?
GARFIELD
© 1989 United Feature Syndicate, Inc.
HOW ABOUT THE FACT THAT I ATE YOUR DINNER TOO? DOES THAT IMPRESS YOU?
GARFIELD
1-6-90

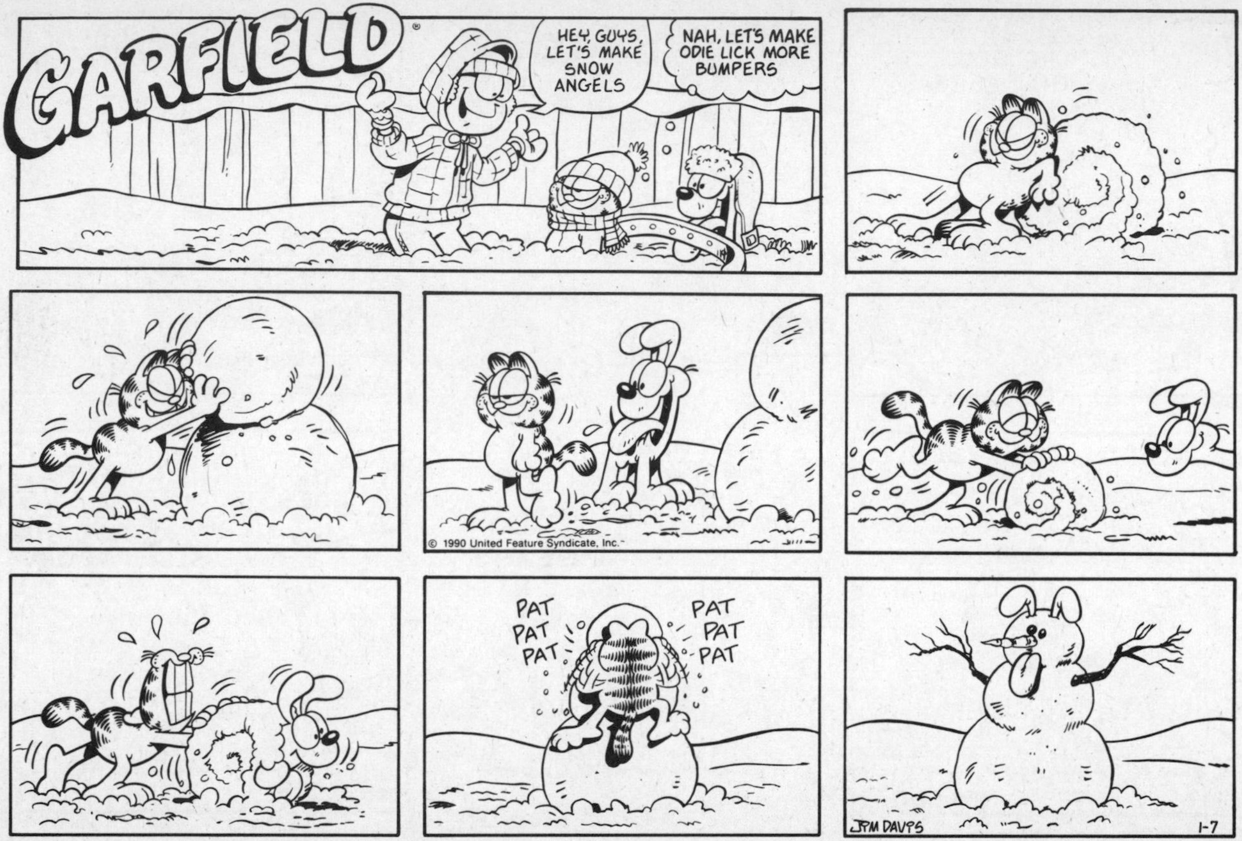
GARFIELD®
HEY, GUYS, LET'S MAKE SNOW ANGELS
NAH, LET'S MAKE ODIE LICK MORE BUMPERS
© 1990 United Feature Syndicate, Inc.
PAT PAT PAT
PAT PAT PAT
JPM DAVIS
1-7

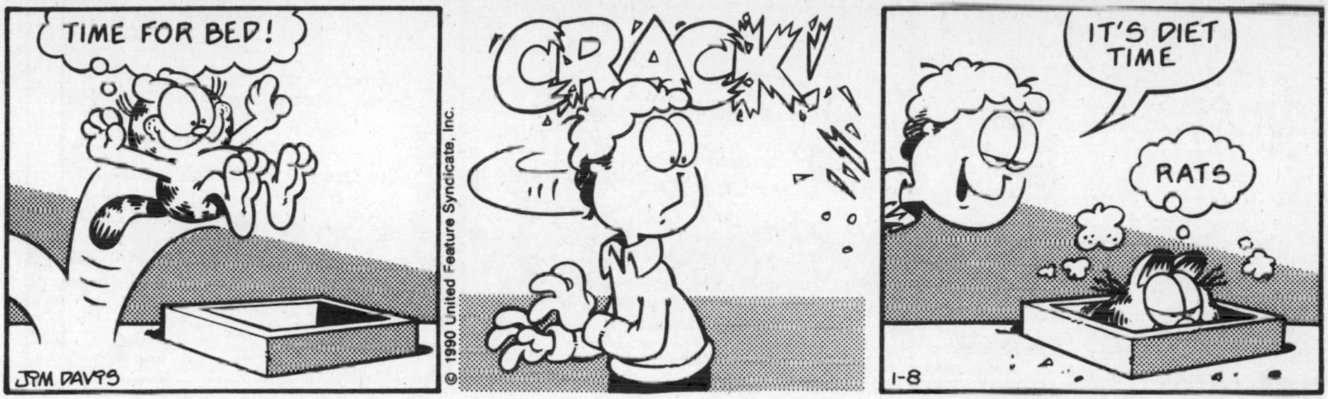
TIME FOR BED!
JIM DAVIS
© 1990 United Feature Syndicate, Inc.
CRACK!
IT'S DIET TIME
RATS
1-8

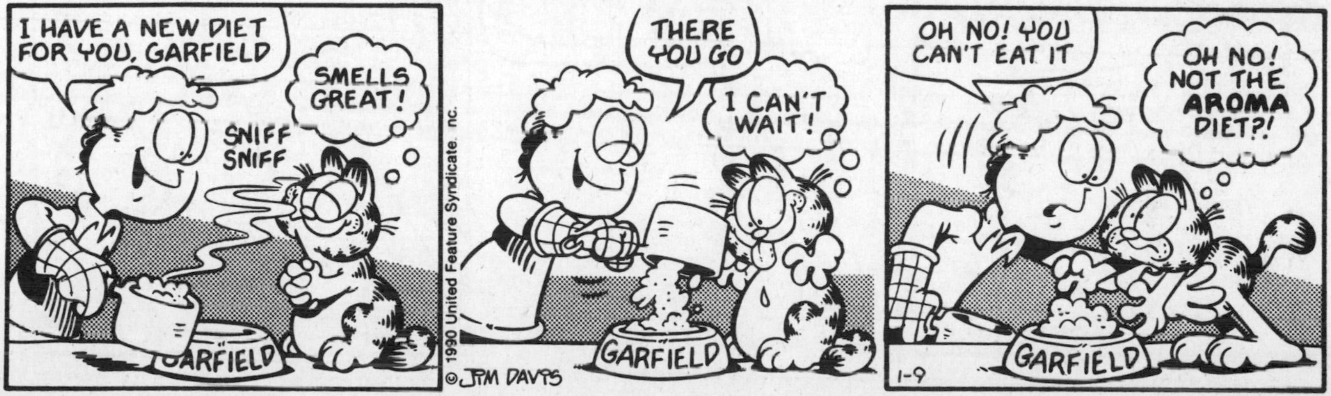
I HAVE A NEW DIET FOR YOU, GARFIELD
SMELLS GREAT!
SNIFF SNIFF
GARFIELD
© 1990 United Feature Syndicate, Inc.
JIM DAVIS
THERE YOU GO
I CAN'T WAIT!
GARFIELD
OH NO! YOU CAN'T EAT IT
OH NO! NOT THE AROMA DIET?!
GARFIELD
1-9

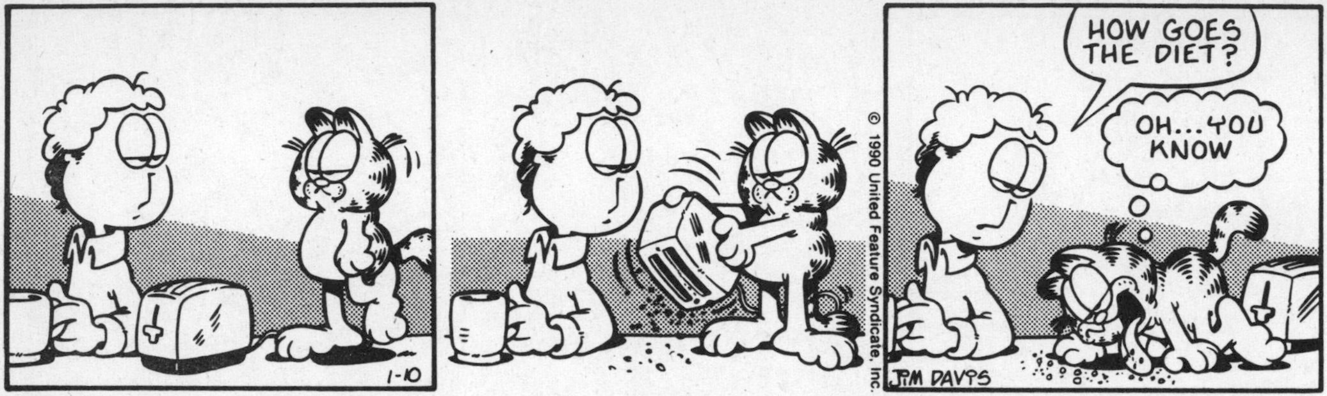
1-10
HOW GOES THE DIET?
OH... YOU KNOW
JIM DAVIS
© 1990 United Feature Syndicate, Inc.

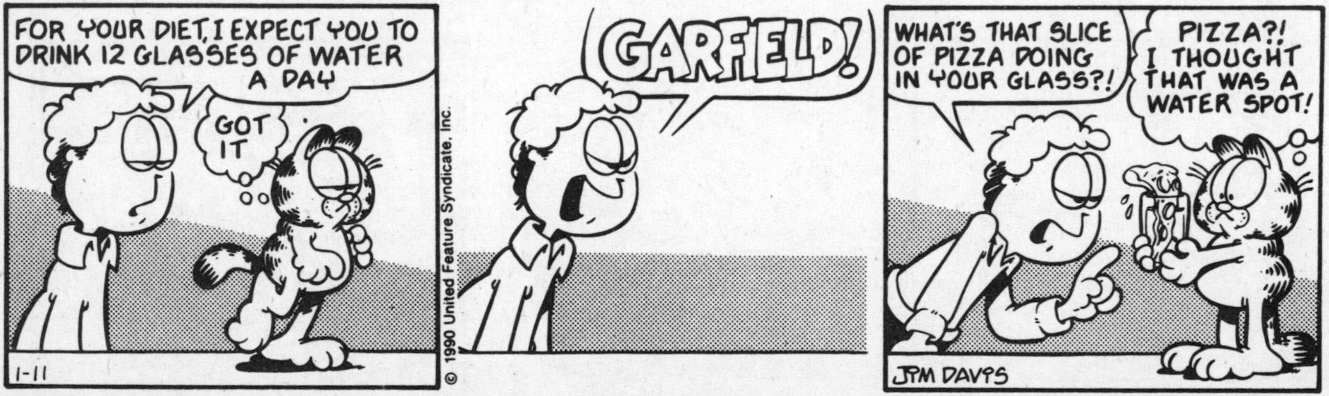
FOR YOUR DIET, I EXPECT YOU TO DRINK 12 GLASSES OF WATER A DAY
GOT IT
1-11
GARFIELD!
WHAT'S THAT SLICE OF PIZZA DOING IN YOUR GLASS?!
PIZZA?! I THOUGHT THAT WAS A WATER SPOT!
JIM DAVIS
© 1990 United Feature Syndicate, Inc.

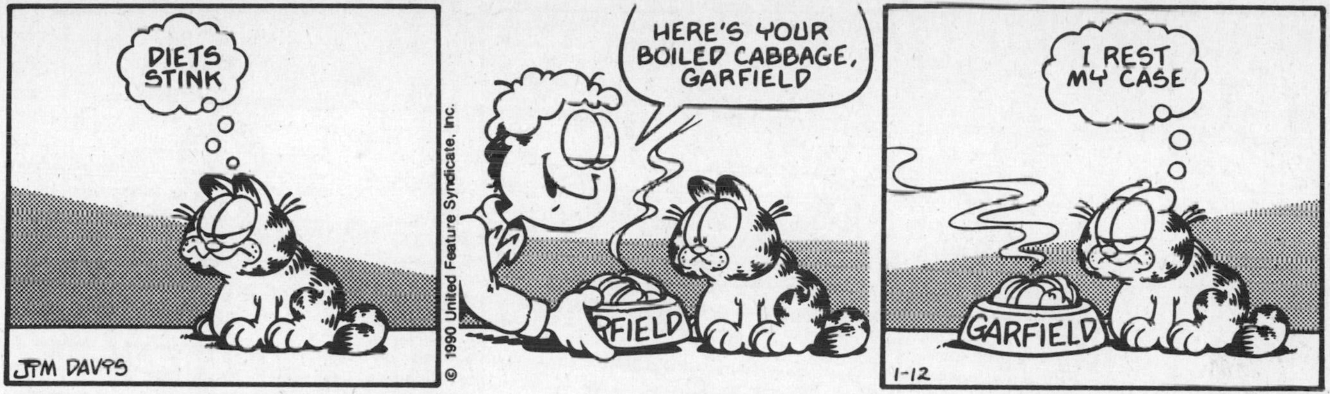

DIETS STINK
HERE'S YOUR BOILED CABBAGE, GARFIELD
I REST MY CASE
JIM DAVIS
© 1990 United Feature Syndicate, Inc.
1-12

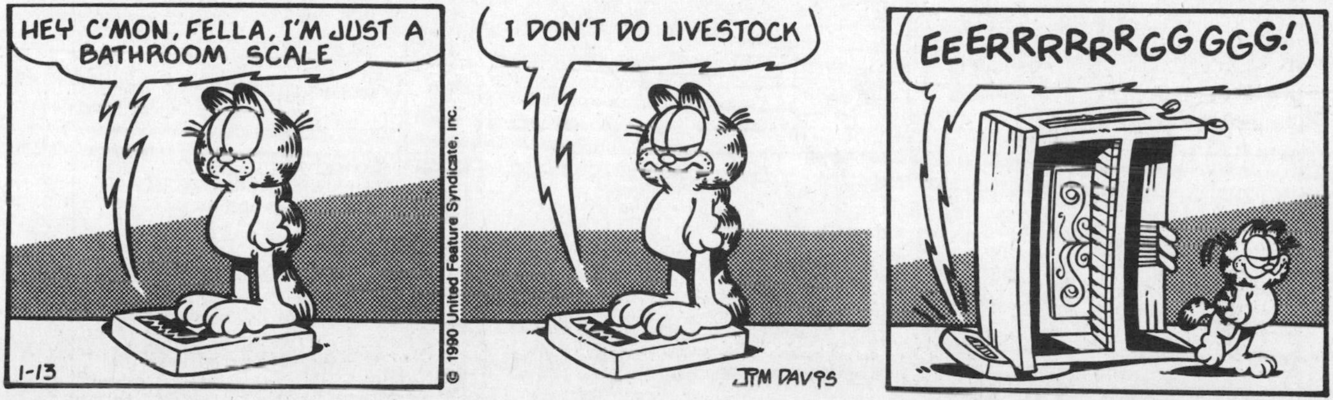

HEY C'MON, FELLA, I'M JUST A BATHROOM SCALE
I DON'T DO LIVESTOCK
EEERRRRRRGGGGG!
1-13
© 1990 United Feature Syndicate, Inc.
JIM DAVIS

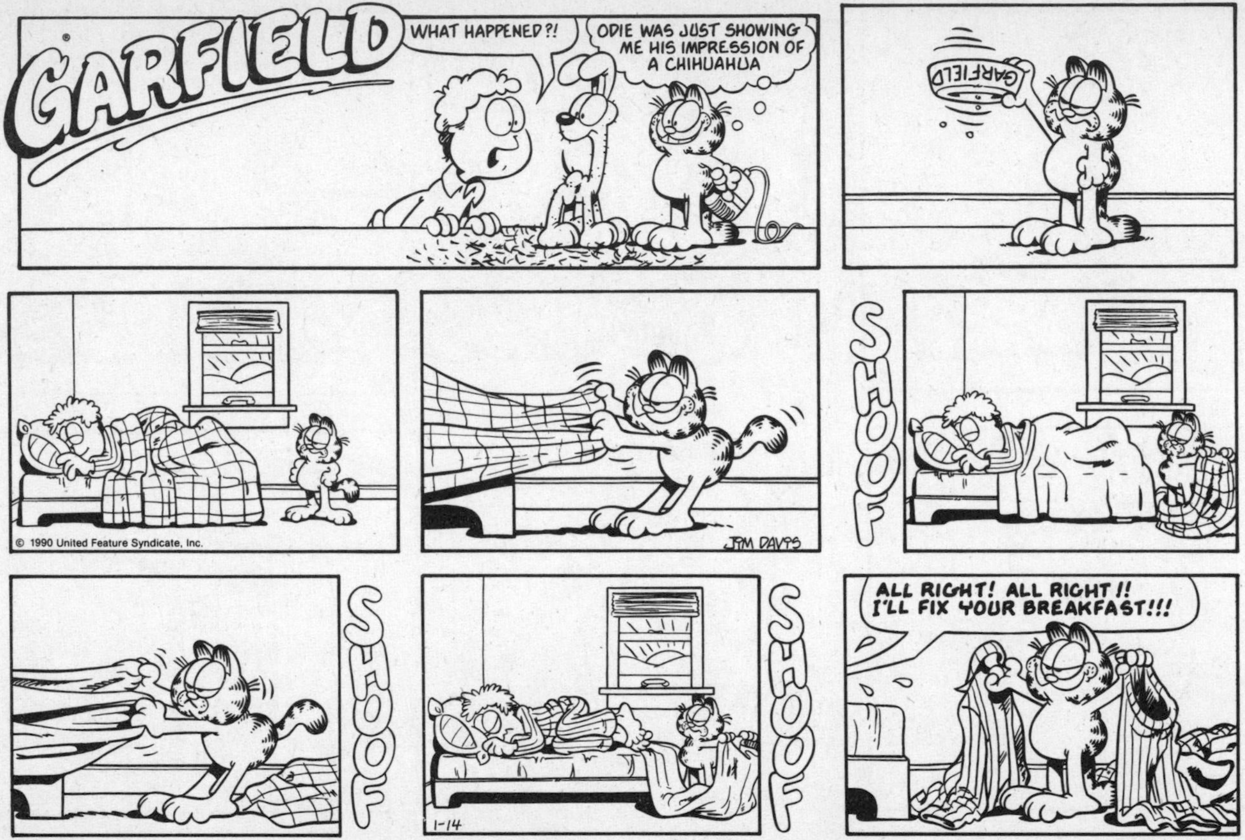
GARFIELD
WHAT HAPPENED?!
ODIE WAS JUST SHOWING ME HIS IMPRESSION OF A CHIHUAHUA
GARFIELD
© 1990 United Feature Syndicate, Inc.
JIM DAVIS
SHOOF
SHOOF
1-14
SHOOF
ALL RIGHT! ALL RIGHT!! I'LL FIX YOUR BREAKFAST!!!

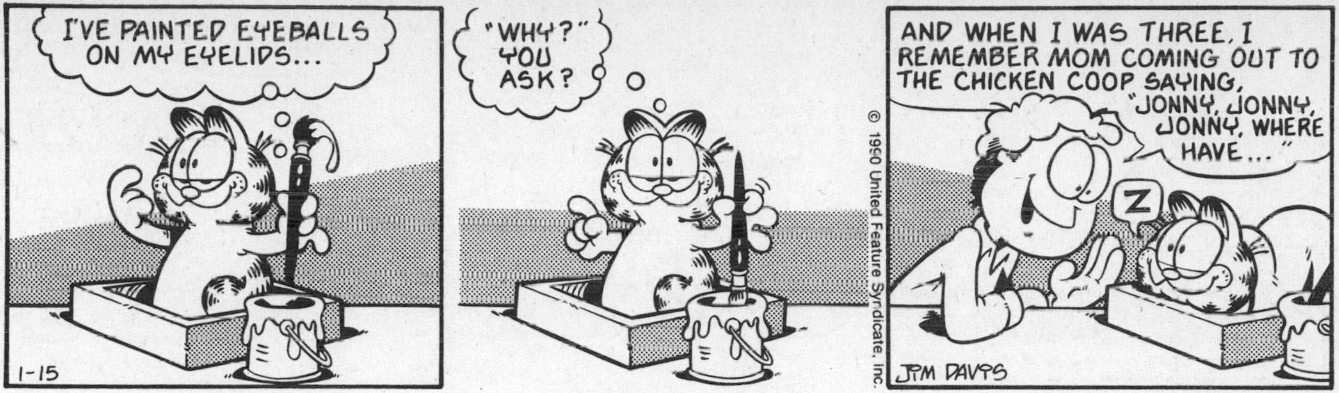
I'VE PAINTED EYEBALLS ON MY EYELIDS...
1-15
"WHY?" YOU ASK?
AND WHEN I WAS THREE, I REMEMBER MOM COMING OUT TO THE CHICKEN COOP SAYING, "JONNY, JONNY, JONNY, WHERE HAVE..."
Z
JIM DAVIS
© 1990 United Feature Syndicate, Inc.

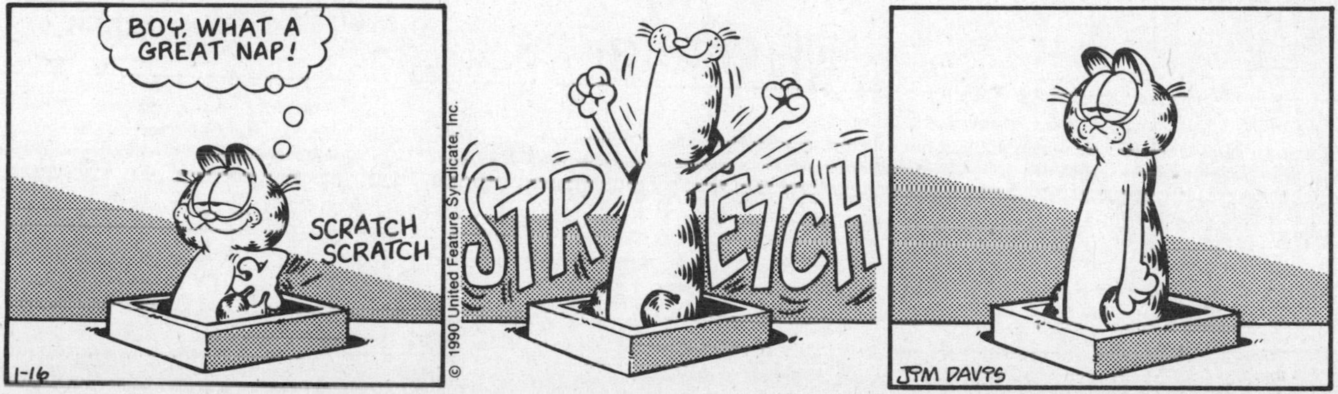
BOY, WHAT A GREAT NAP!
SCRATCH SCRATCH
1-16
© 1990 United Feature Syndicate, Inc.
STRETCH
JIM DAVIS

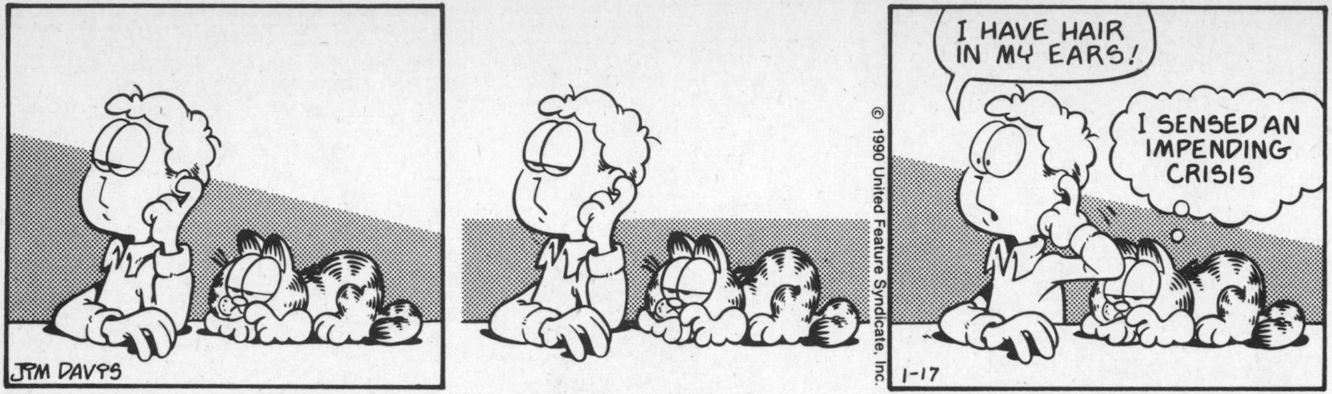
JIM DAVIS
I HAVE HAIR IN MY EARS!
I SENSED AN IMPENDING CRISIS
1-17

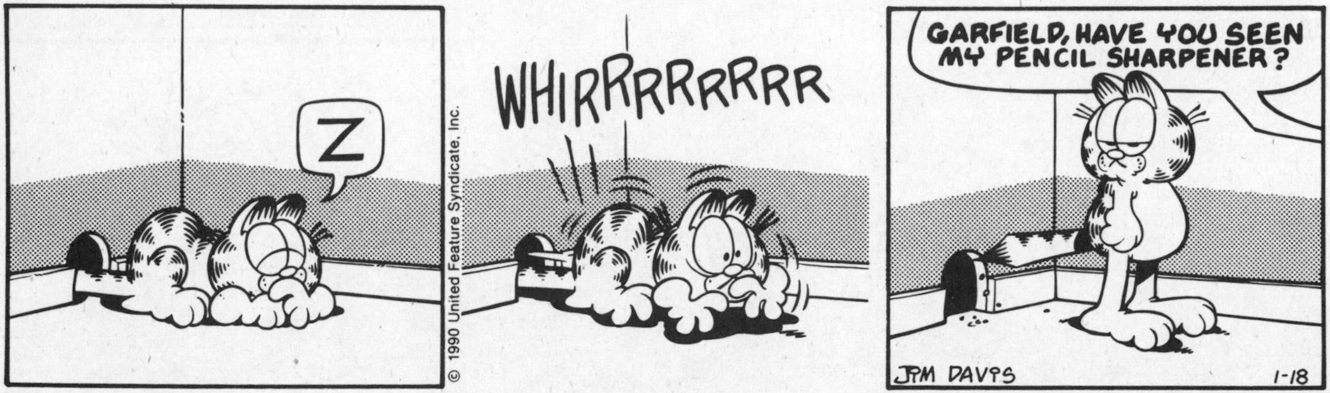
Z
WHIRRRRRRRR
GARFIELD, HAVE YOU SEEN MY PENCIL SHARPENER?
JIM DAVIS
1-18

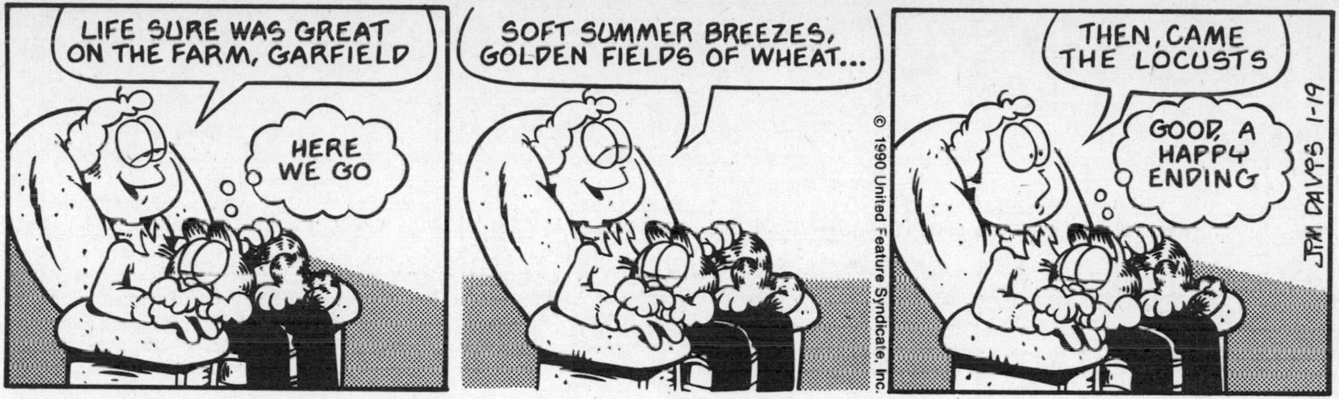
LIFE SURE WAS GREAT ON THE FARM, GARFIELD
HERE WE GO
SOFT SUMMER BREEZES, GOLDEN FIELDS OF WHEAT...
THEN, CAME THE LOCUSTS
GOOD, A HAPPY ENDING
© 1990 United Feature Syndicate, Inc.
JIM DAVIS 1-19

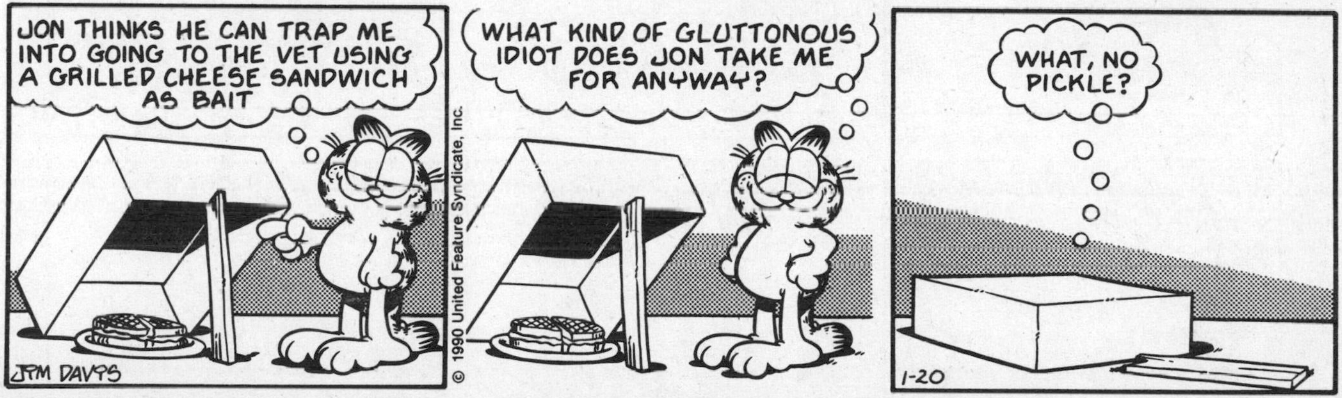
JON THINKS HE CAN TRAP ME INTO GOING TO THE VET USING A GRILLED CHEESE SANDWICH AS BAIT
WHAT KIND OF GLUTTONOUS IDIOT DOES JON TAKE ME FOR ANYWAY?
WHAT, NO PICKLE?
© 1990 United Feature Syndicate, Inc.
JIM DAVIS
1-20

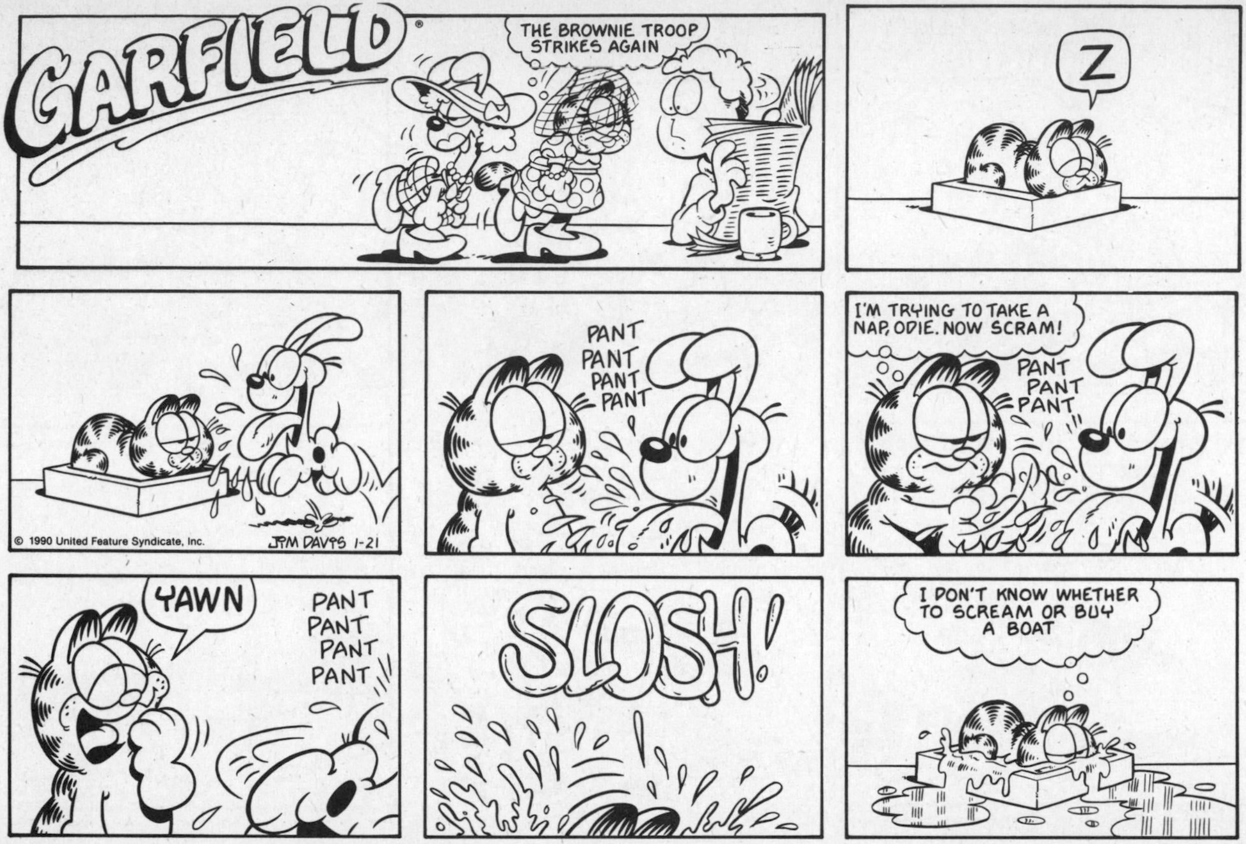
GARFIELD
THE BROWNIE TROOP STRIKES AGAIN
Z
© 1990 United Feature Syndicate, Inc.
JIM DAVIS 1-21
PANT PANT PANT PANT
I'M TRYING TO TAKE A NAP, ODIE. NOW SCRAM!
PANT PANT PANT
YAWN
PANT PANT PANT PANT PANT
SLOSH!
I DON'T KNOW WHETHER TO SCREAM OR BUY A BOAT

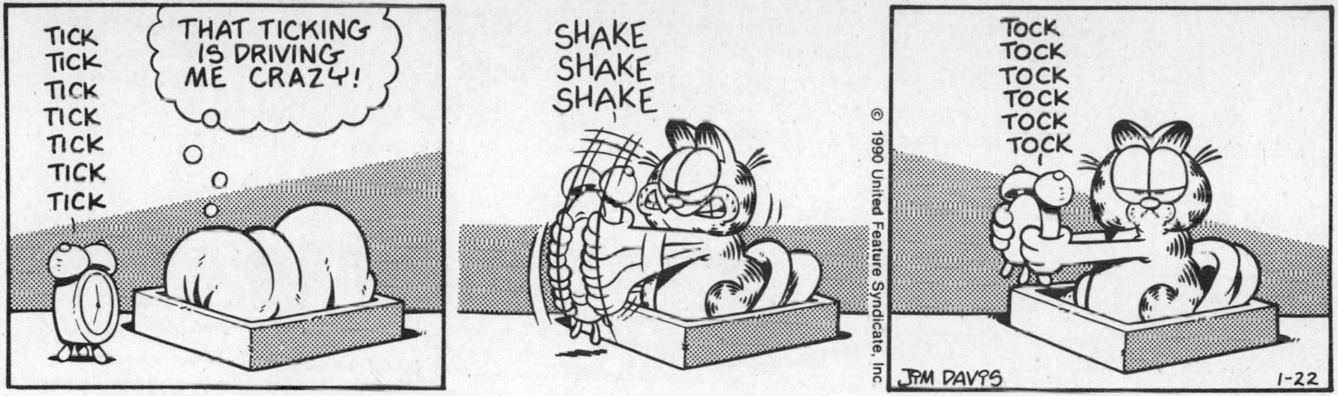
TICK
TICK
TICK
TICK
TICK
TICK
TICK
THAT TICKING IS DRIVING ME CRAZY!
SHAKE
SHAKE
SHAKE
TOCK
TOCK
TOCK
TOCK
TOCK
TOCK
JIM DAVIS
1-22

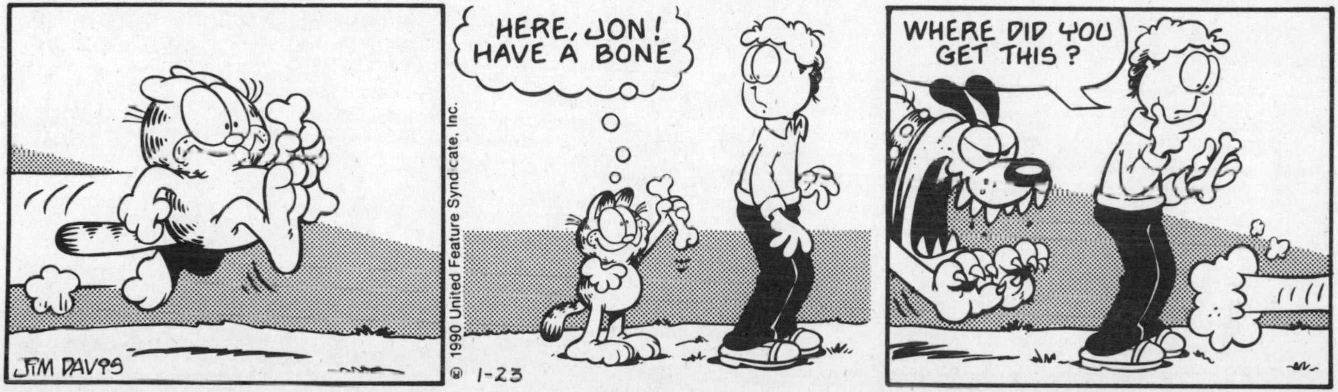
JIM DAVIS
HERE, JON! HAVE A BONE
1-23
WHERE DID YOU GET THIS?

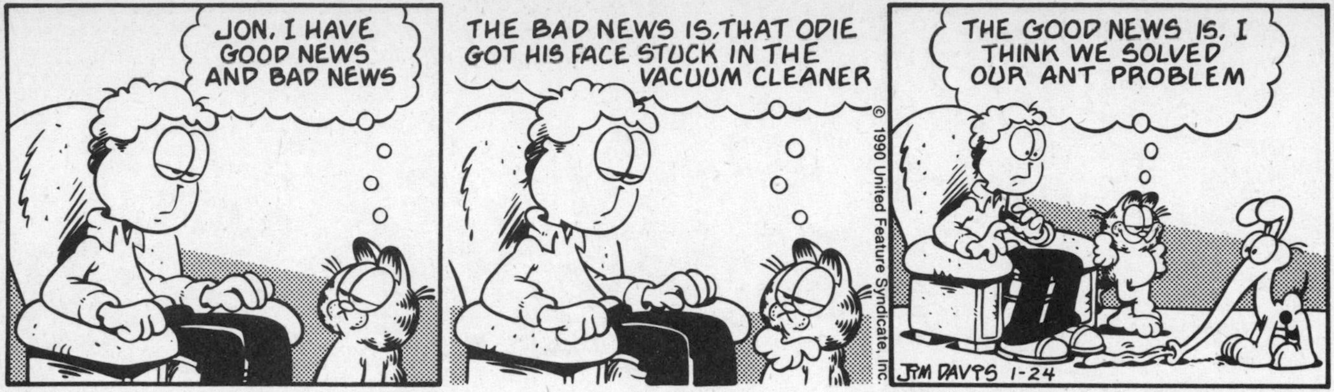
JON, I HAVE GOOD NEWS AND BAD NEWS
THE BAD NEWS IS, THAT ODIE GOT HIS FACE STUCK IN THE VACUUM CLEANER
THE GOOD NEWS IS, I THINK WE SOLVED OUR ANT PROBLEM
© 1990 United Feature Syndicate, Inc.
JIM DAVIS 1-24

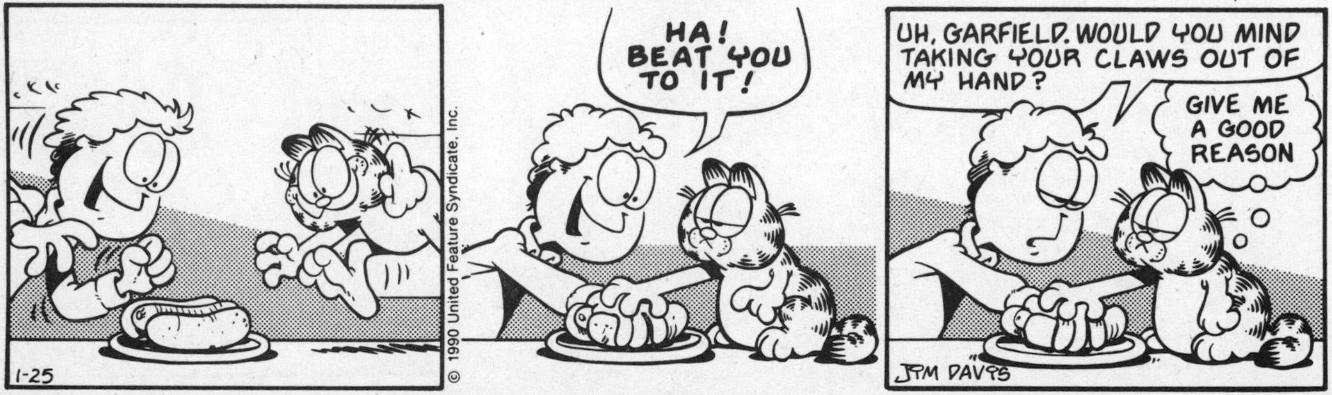
1-25
© 1990 United Feature Syndicate, Inc.
HA! BEAT YOU TO IT!
UH, GARFIELD. WOULD YOU MIND TAKING YOUR CLAWS OUT OF MY HAND?
GIVE ME A GOOD REASON
JIM DAVIS

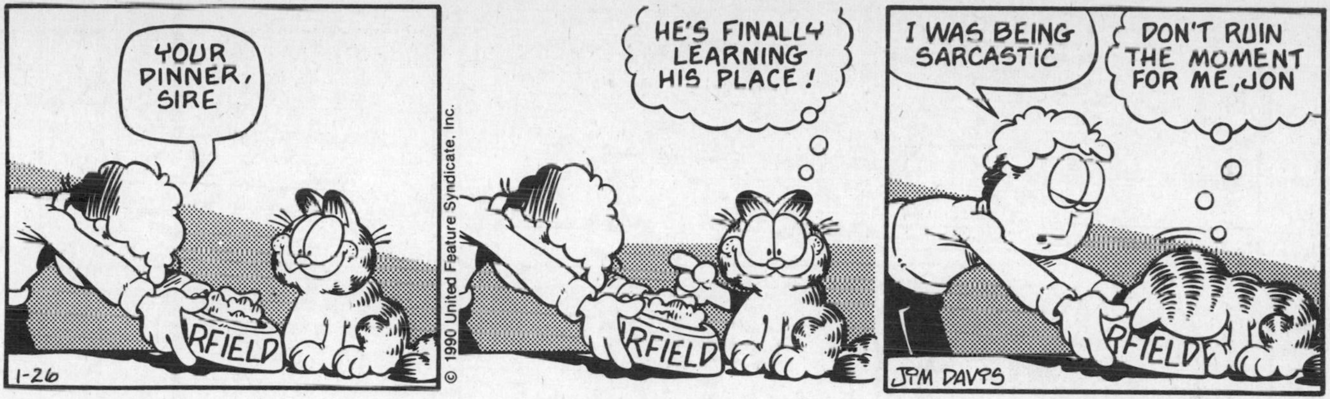
YOUR DINNER, SIRE
HE'S FINALLY LEARNING HIS PLACE!
I WAS BEING SARCASTIC
DON'T RUIN THE MOMENT FOR ME, JON
RFIELD
1-26
JIM DAVIS
© 1990 United Feature Syndicate, Inc.

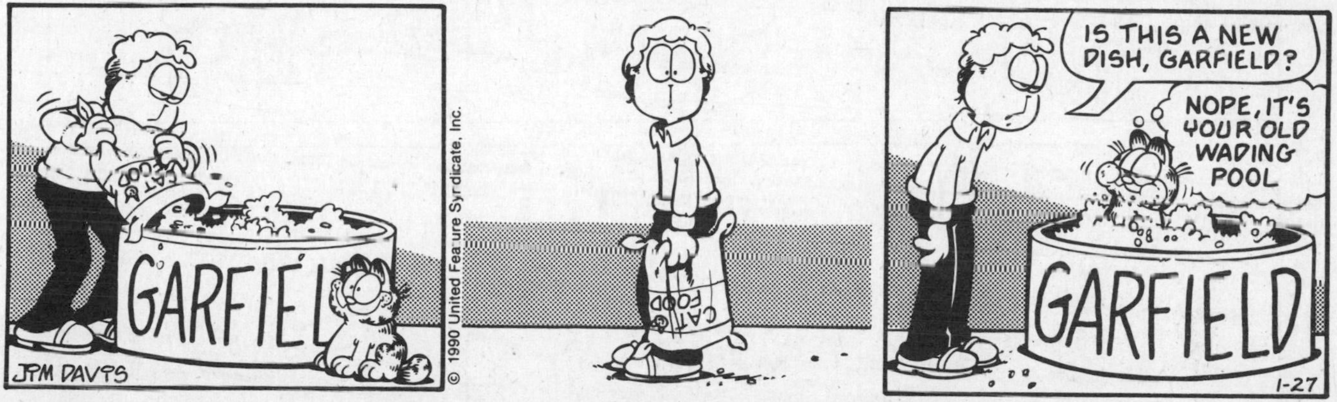
CAT FOOD
GARFIEL
IS THIS A NEW DISH, GARFIELD?
NOPE, IT'S YOUR OLD WADING POOL
GARFIELD
1-27
JIM DAVIS
© 1990 United Feature Syndicate, Inc.

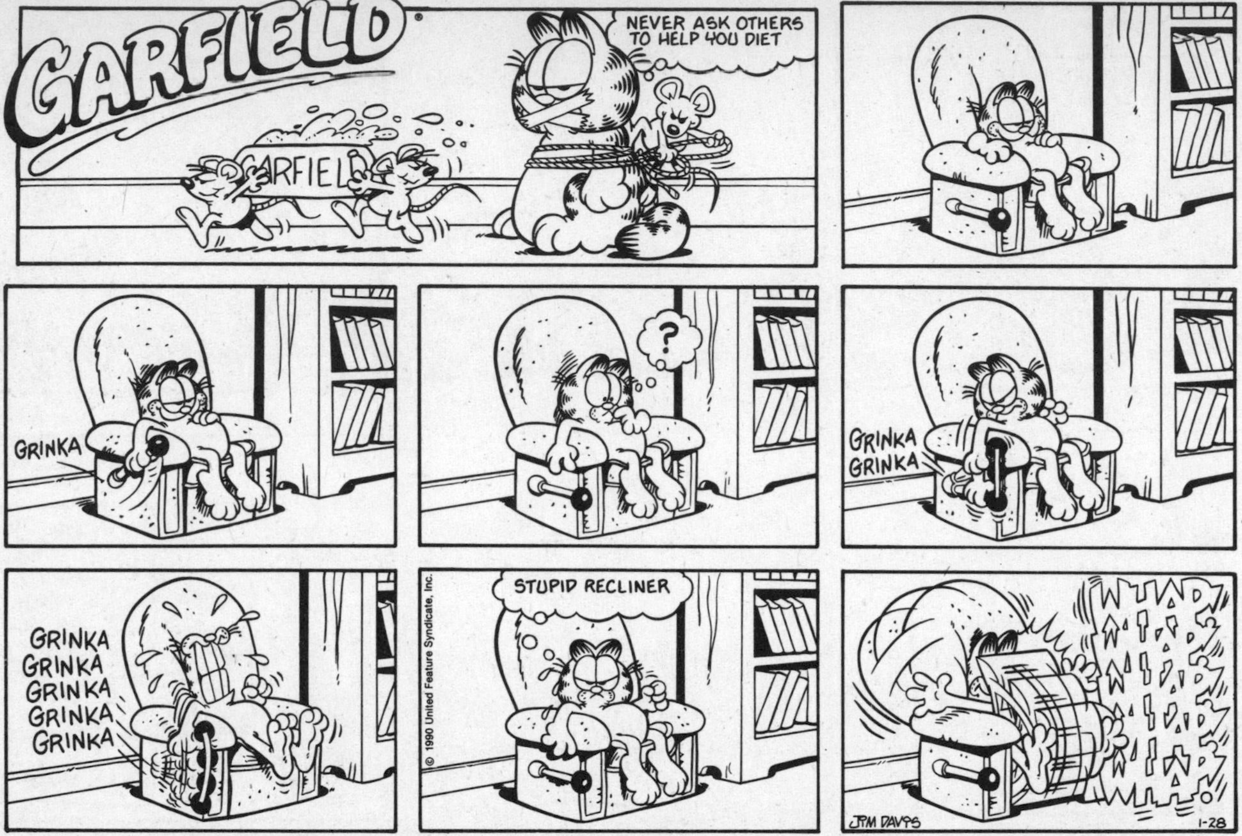
GARFIELD
GARFIELD
NEVER ASK OTHERS TO HELP YOU DIET
GRINKA
?
GRINKA GRINKA
GRINKA GRINKA GRINKA GRINKA GRINKA
© 1990 United Feature Syndicate, Inc.
STUPID RECLINER
WHAP! WHAP! WHAP! WHAP! WHAP!
JIM DAVIS
1-28

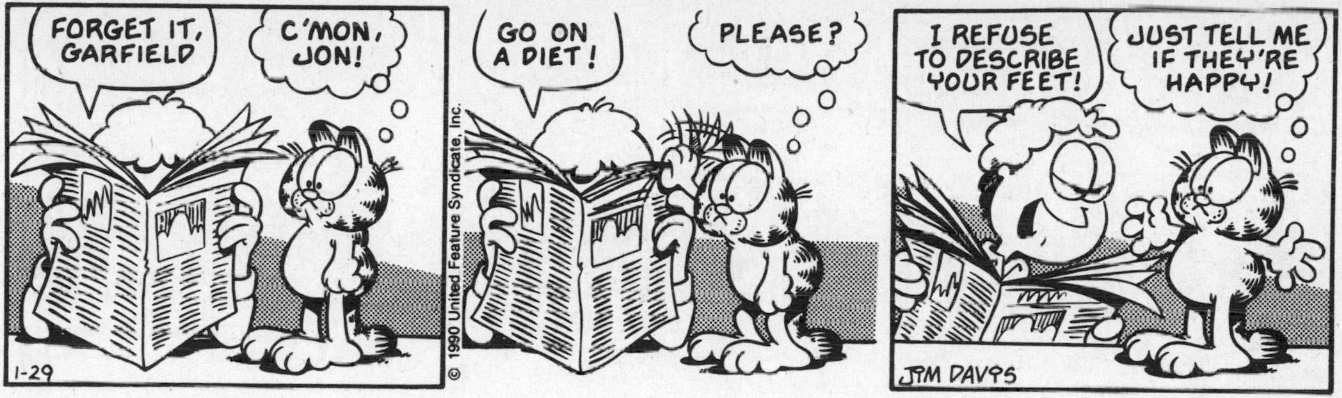
FORGET IT, GARFIELD
C'MON, JON!
GO ON A DIET!
PLEASE?
I REFUSE TO DESCRIBE YOUR FEET!
JUST TELL ME IF THEY'RE HAPPY!
1-29
© 1990 United Feature Syndicate, Inc.
JIM DAVIS

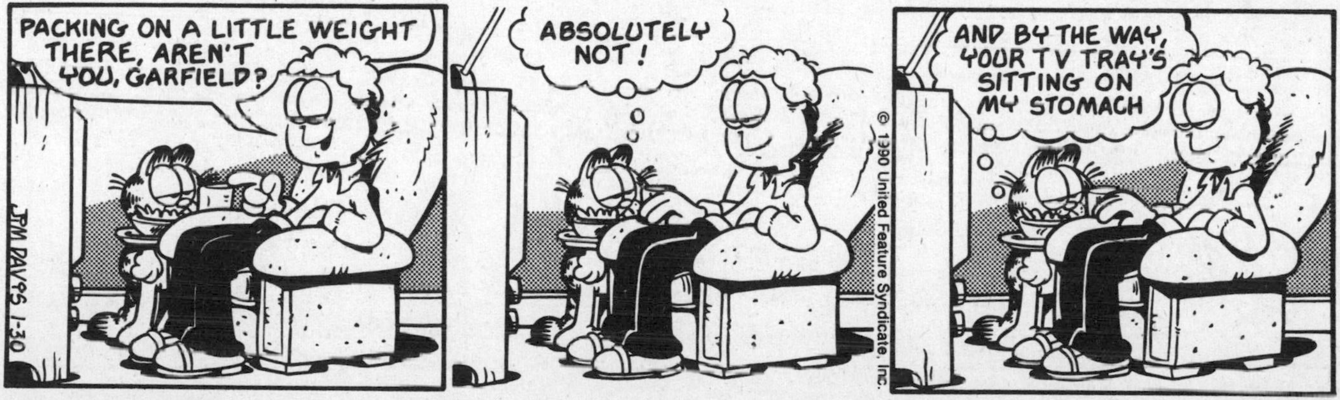
PACKING ON A LITTLE WEIGHT THERE, AREN'T YOU, GARFIELD?
ABSOLUTELY NOT!
AND BY THE WAY, YOUR TV TRAY'S SITTING ON MY STOMACH
JIM DAVIS 1-30
© 1990 United Feature Syndicate, Inc.

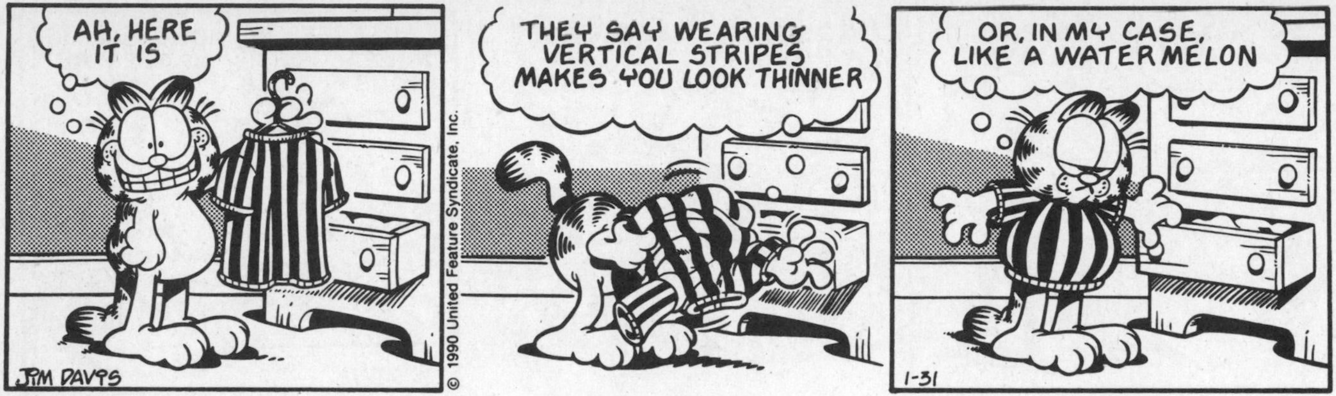
AH, HERE IT IS
JIM DAVIS
© 1990 United Feature Syndicate, Inc.
THEY SAY WEARING VERTICAL STRIPES MAKES YOU LOOK THINNER
OR, IN MY CASE, LIKE A WATERMELON
1-31

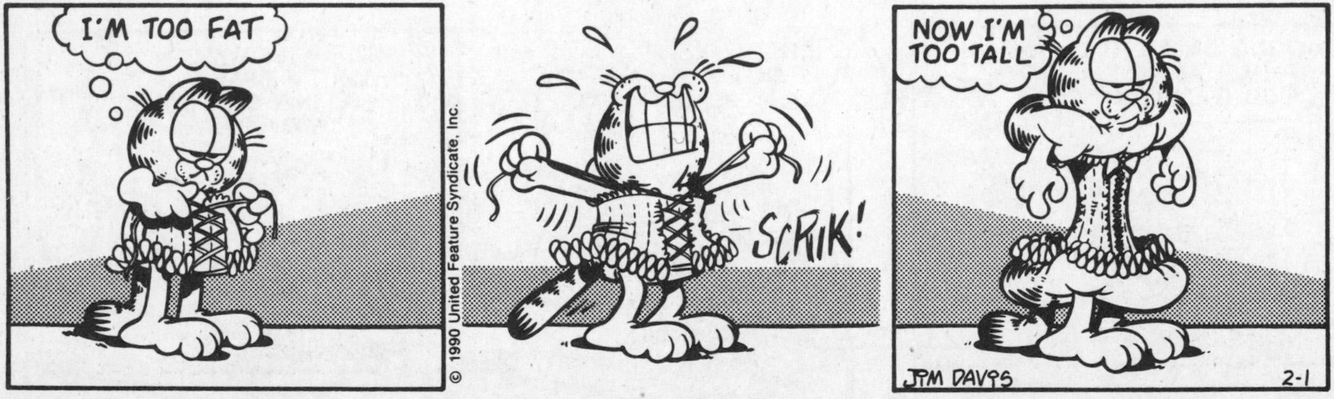
I'M TOO FAT
© 1990 United Feature Syndicate, Inc.
SCRIK!
NOW I'M TOO TALL
JIM DAVIS
2-1

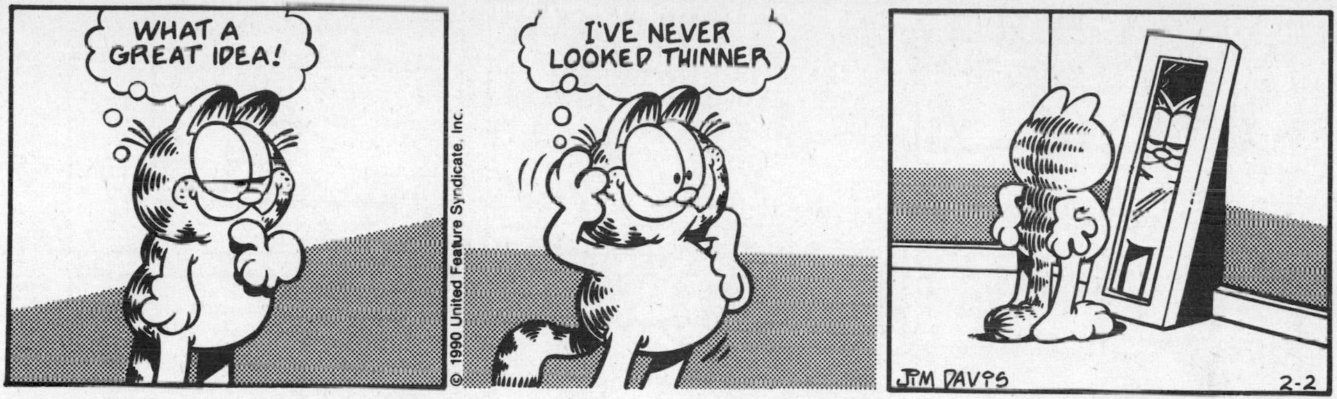
WHAT A GREAT IDEA!
I'VE NEVER LOOKED THINNER
© 1990 United Feature Syndicate, Inc.
JIM DAVIS
2-2

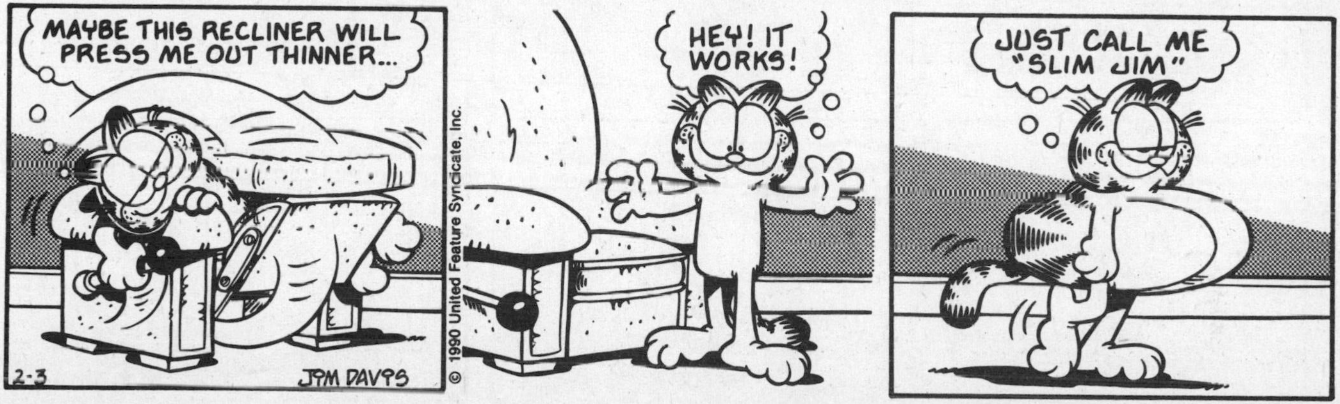
MAYBE THIS RECLINER WILL PRESS ME OUT THINNER...
2-3
JIM DAVIS
© 1990 United Feature Syndicate, Inc.
HEY! IT WORKS!
JUST CALL ME "SLIM JIM"

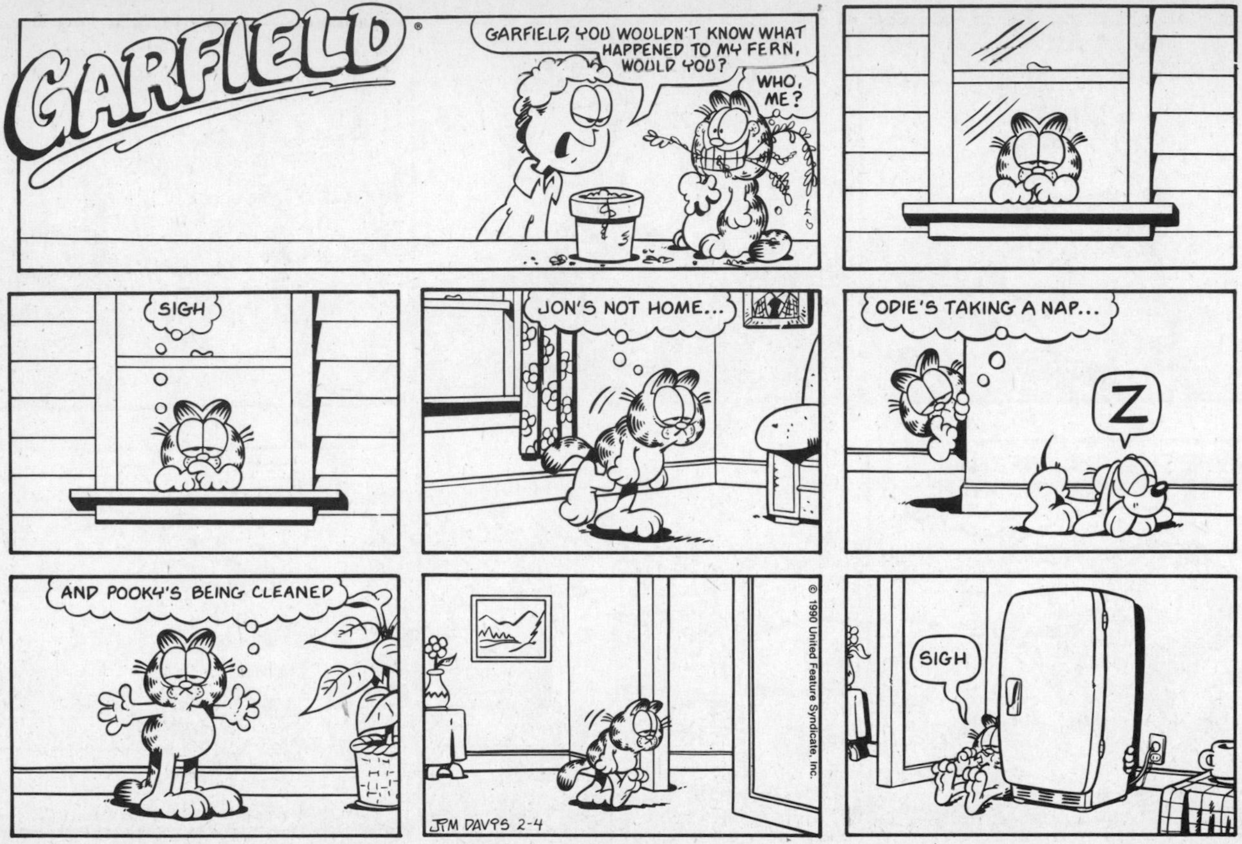
GARFIELD
GARFIELD, YOU WOULDN'T KNOW WHAT HAPPENED TO MY FERN, WOULD YOU?
WHO, ME?
SIGH
JON'S NOT HOME...
ODIE'S TAKING A NAP...
Z
AND POOKY'S BEING CLEANED
JPM DAVPS 2-4
© 1990 United Feature Syndicate, Inc.
SIGH

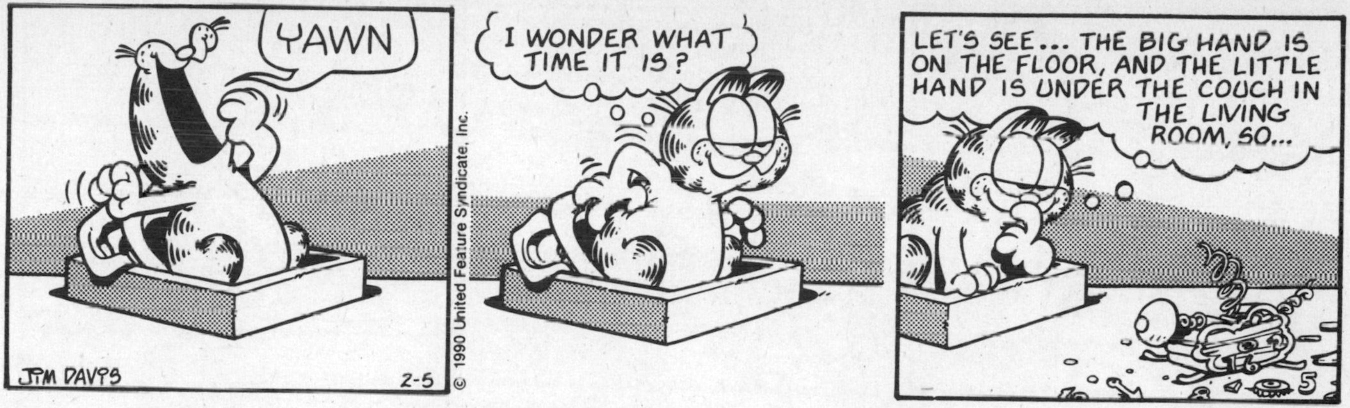
YAWN
I WONDER WHAT TIME IT IS?
LET'S SEE... THE BIG HAND IS ON THE FLOOR, AND THE LITTLE HAND IS UNDER THE COUCH IN THE LIVING ROOM, SO...
5
JIM DAVIS
2-5
© 1990 United Feature Syndicate, Inc.

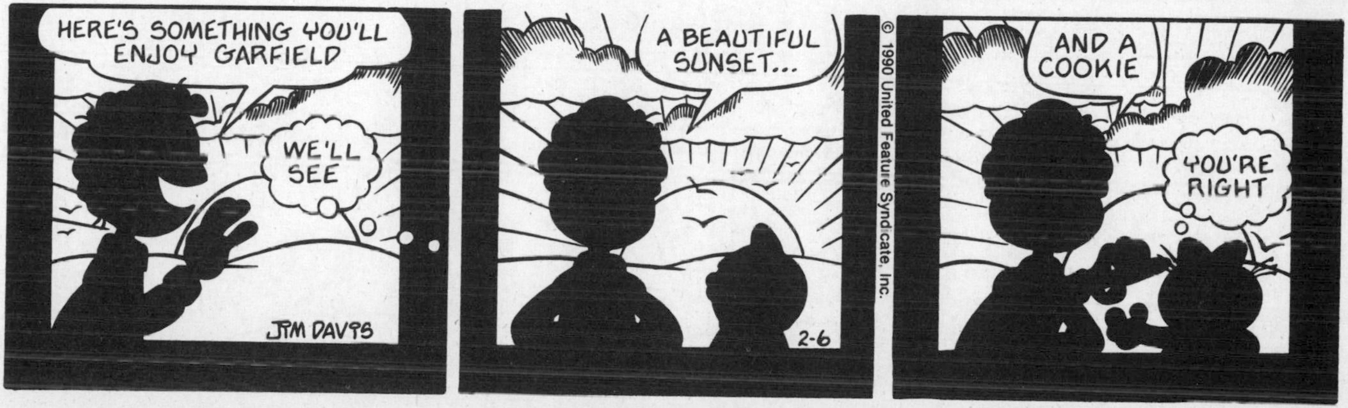
HERE'S SOMETHING YOU'LL ENJOY GARFIELD
WE'LL SEE
A BEAUTIFUL SUNSET...
AND A COOKIE
YOU'RE RIGHT
JIM DAVIS
2-6
© 1990 United Feature Syndicate, Inc.

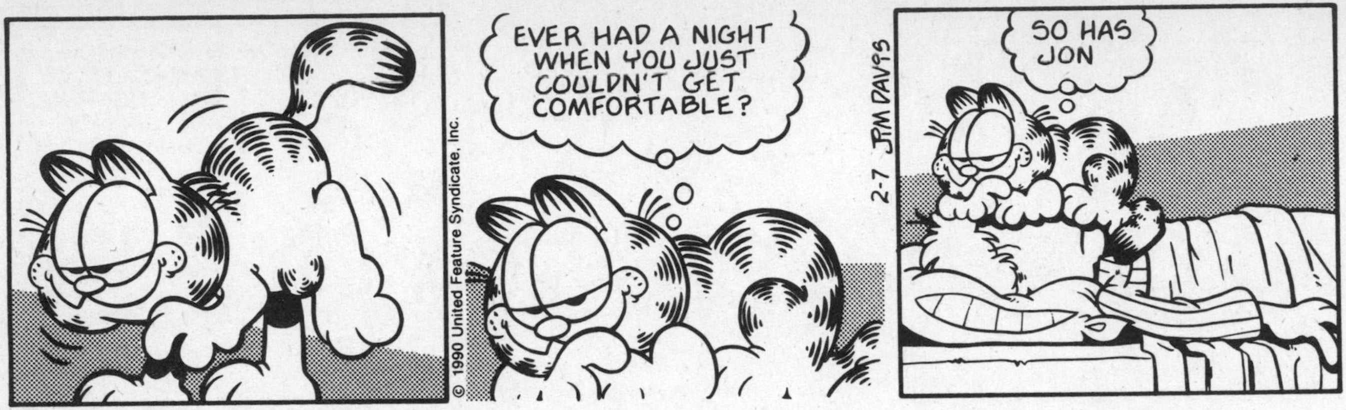
EVER HAD A NIGHT WHEN YOU JUST COULDN'T GET COMFORTABLE?
SO HAS JON
© 1990 United Feature Syndicate, Inc.
JIM DAVIS 2-7

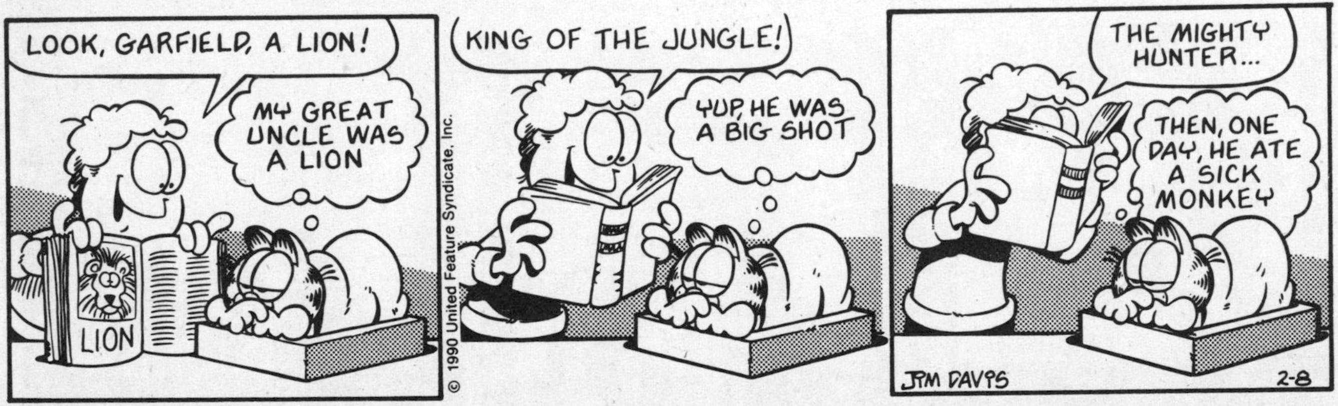
LOOK, GARFIELD, A LION!
MY GREAT UNCLE WAS A LION
LION
KING OF THE JUNGLE!
YUP, HE WAS A BIG SHOT
THE MIGHTY HUNTER...
THEN, ONE DAY, HE ATE A SICK MONKEY
© 1990 United Feature Syndicate, Inc.
JIM DAVIS
2-8

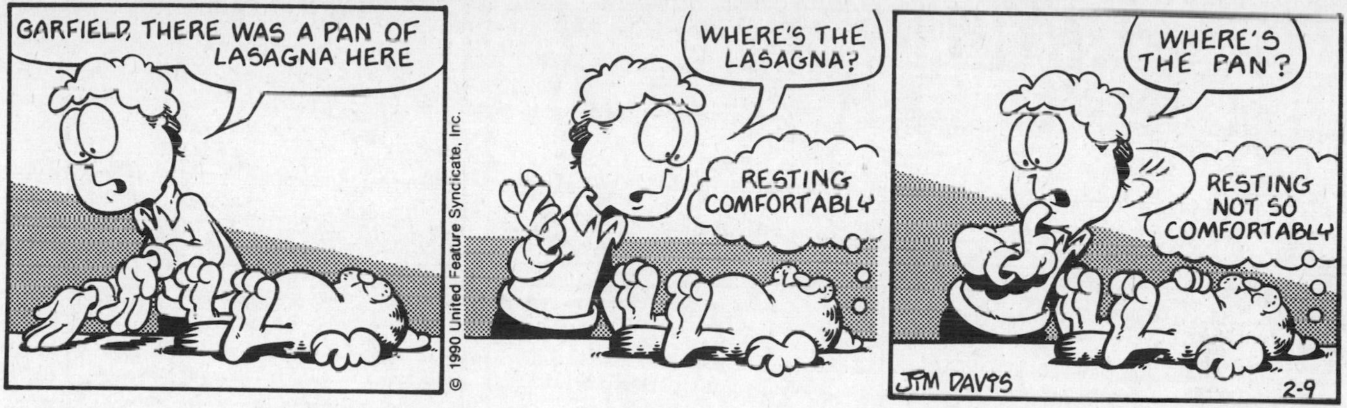
GARFIELD, THERE WAS A PAN OF LASAGNA HERE
WHERE'S THE LASAGNA?
RESTING COMFORTABLY
WHERE'S THE PAN?
RESTING NOT SO COMFORTABLY
© 1990 United Feature Syndicate, Inc.
JIM DAVIS
2-9

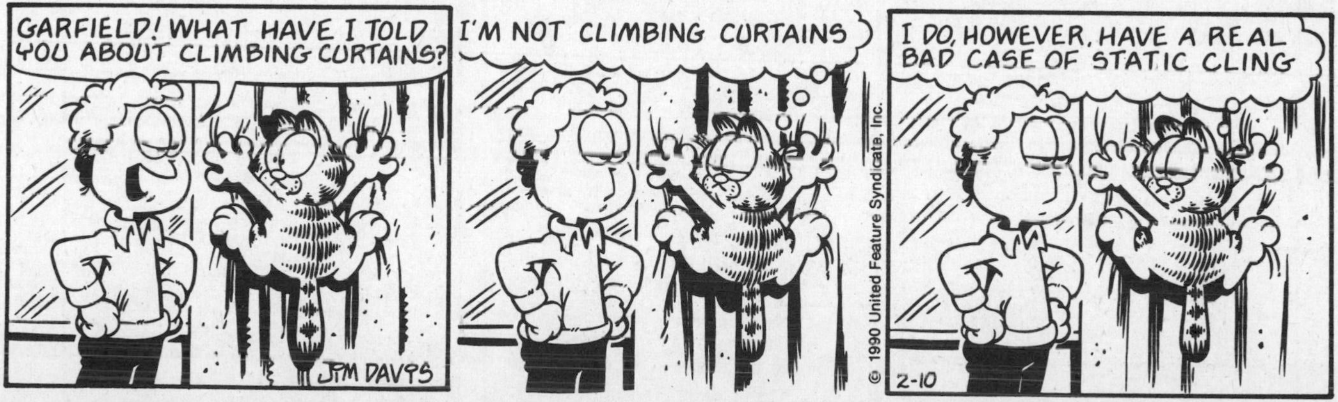
GARFIELD! WHAT HAVE I TOLD YOU ABOUT CLIMBING CURTAINS?
I'M NOT CLIMBING CURTAINS
I DO, HOWEVER, HAVE A REAL BAD CASE OF STATIC CLING
JIM DAVIS
© 1990 United Feature Syndicate, Inc.
2-10

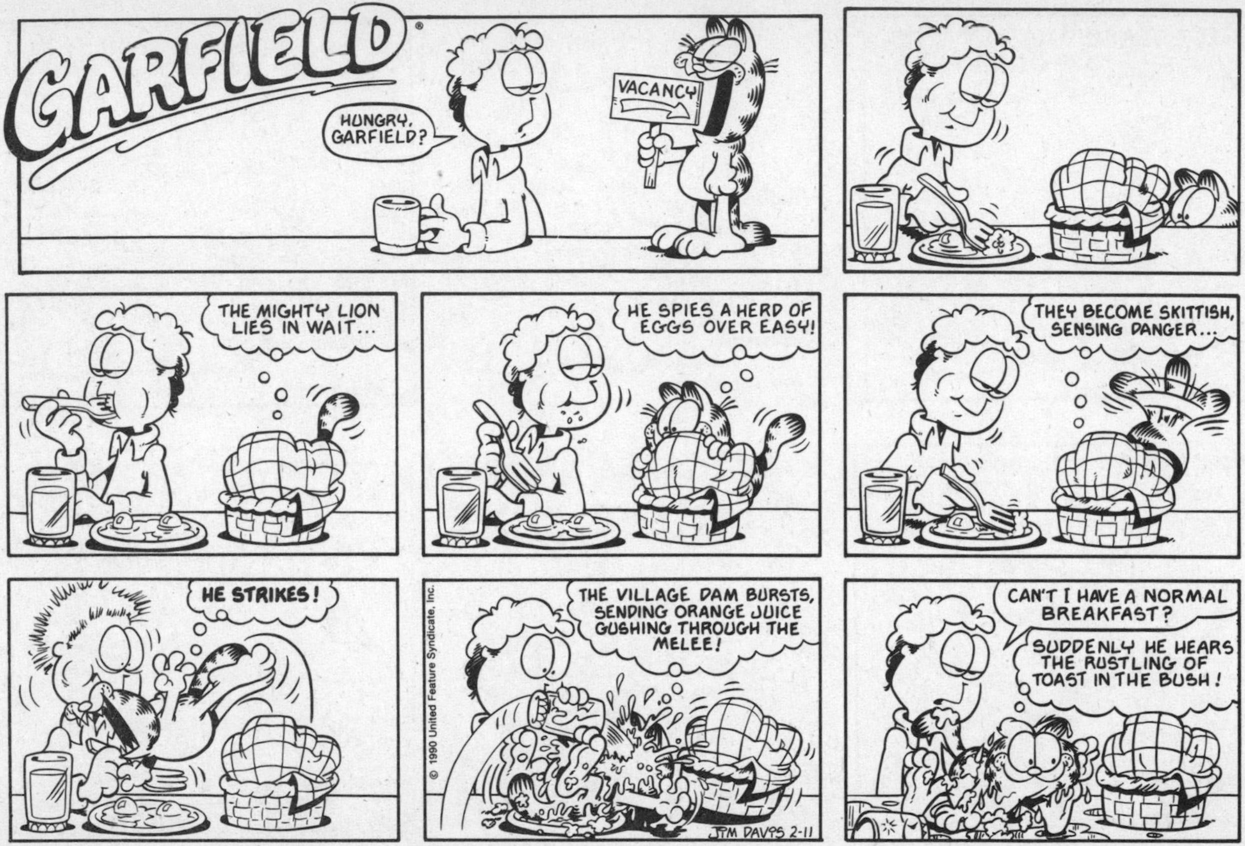
GARFIELD
HUNGRY, GARFIELD?
VACANCY
THE MIGHTY LION LIES IN WAIT...
HE SPIES A HERD OF EGGS OVER EASY!
THEY BECOME SKITTISH, SENSING DANGER...
HE STRIKES!
THE VILLAGE DAM BURSTS, SENDING ORANGE JUICE GUSHING THROUGH THE MELEE!
CAN'T I HAVE A NORMAL BREAKFAST?
SUDDENLY HE HEARS THE RUSTLING OF TOAST IN THE BUSH!
© 1990 United Feature Syndicate, Inc.
JIM DAVIS 2-11

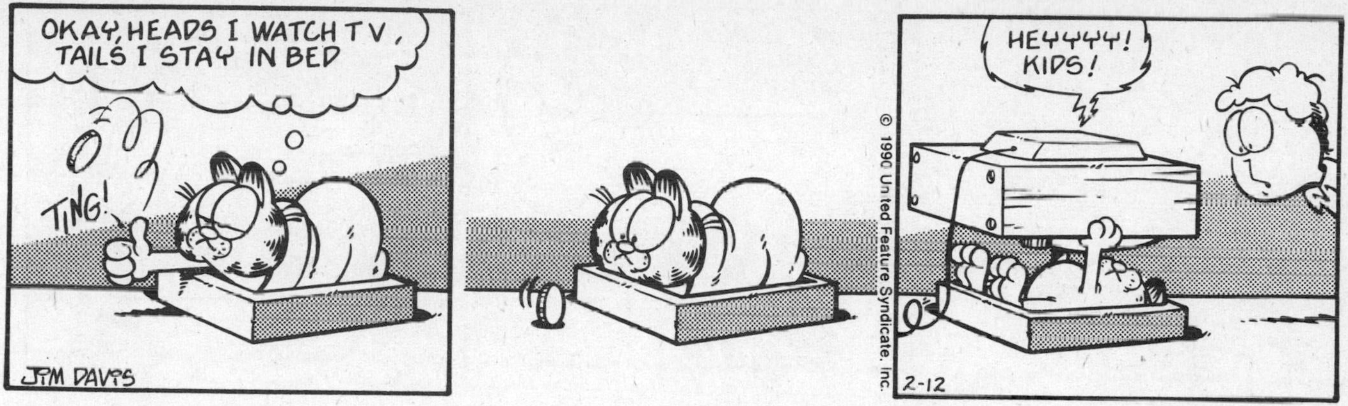
OKAY, HEADS I WATCH TV, TAILS I STAY IN BED
TING!
JIM DAVIS
© 1990 United Feature Syndicate, Inc.
HEYYYY! KIDS!
2-12

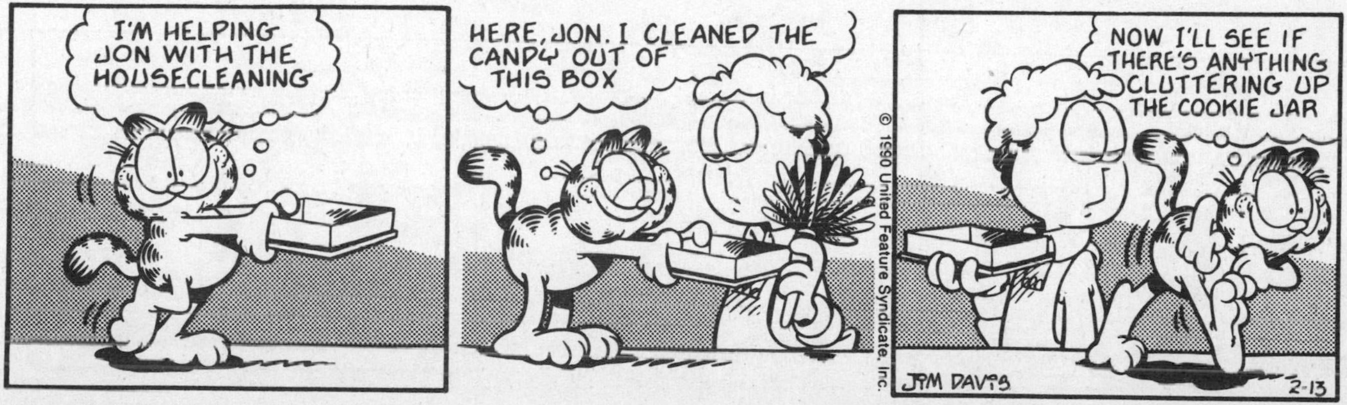
I'M HELPING JON WITH THE HOUSECLEANING
HERE, JON. I CLEANED THE CANDY OUT OF THIS BOX
© 1990 United Feature Syndicate, Inc.
NOW I'LL SEE IF THERE'S ANYTHING CLUTTERING UP THE COOKIE JAR
JIM DAVIS
2-13

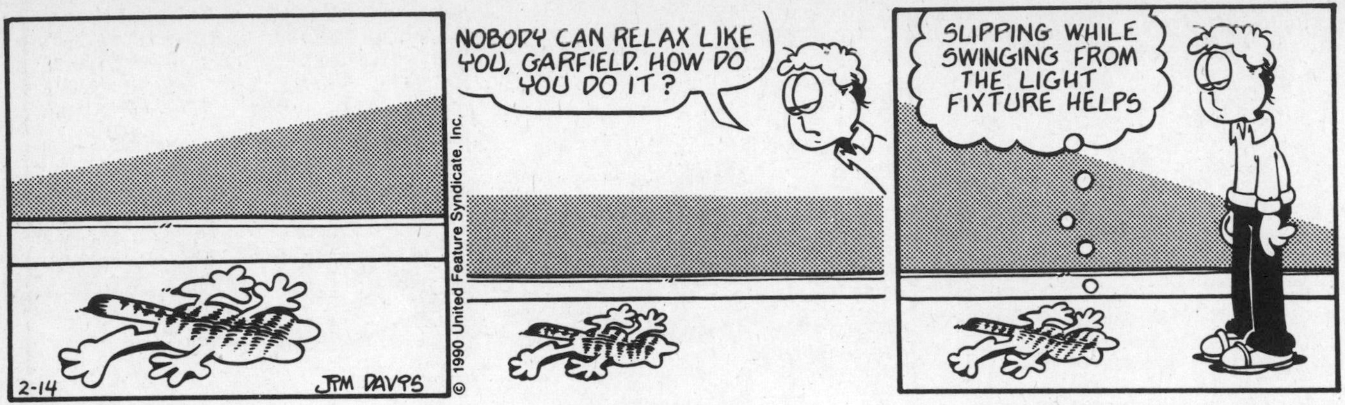
2-14
JIM DAVIS
NOBODY CAN RELAX LIKE YOU, GARFIELD. HOW DO YOU DO IT?
SLIPPING WHILE SWINGING FROM THE LIGHT FIXTURE HELPS

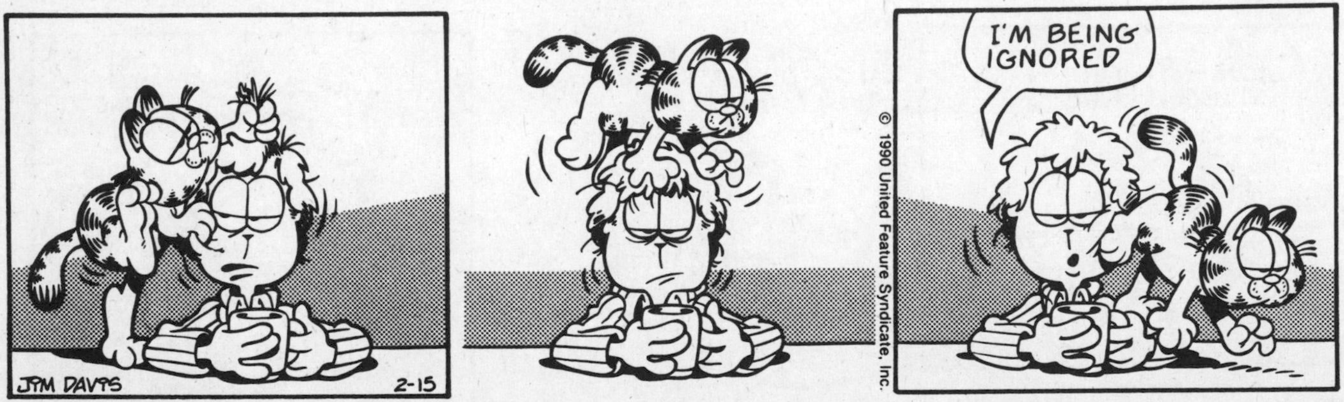
JIM DAVIS
2-15
I'M BEING IGNORED

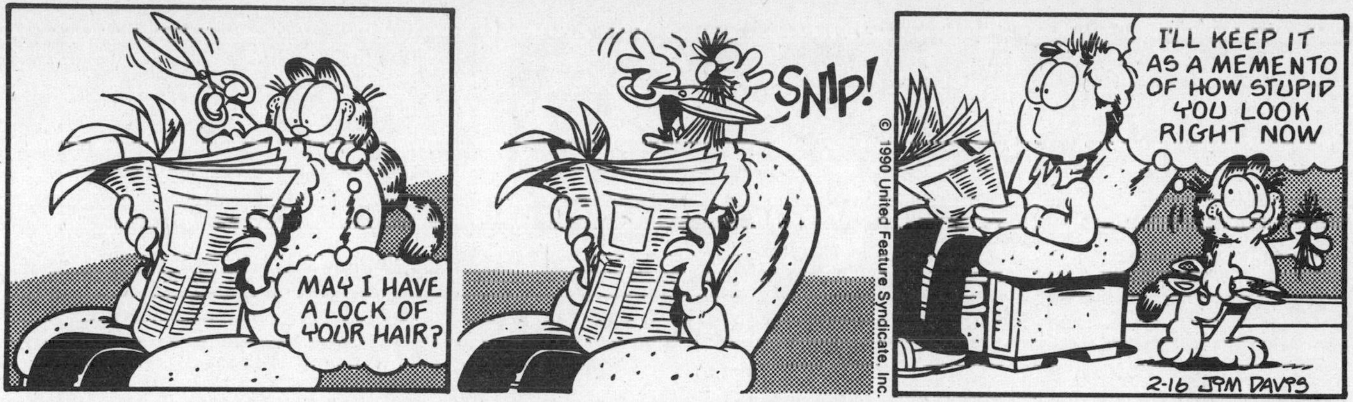
MAY I HAVE A LOCK OF YOUR HAIR?
SNIP!
I'LL KEEP IT AS A MEMENTO OF HOW STUPID YOU LOOK RIGHT NOW
© 1990 United Feature Syndicate, Inc.
2-16 JIM DAVIS

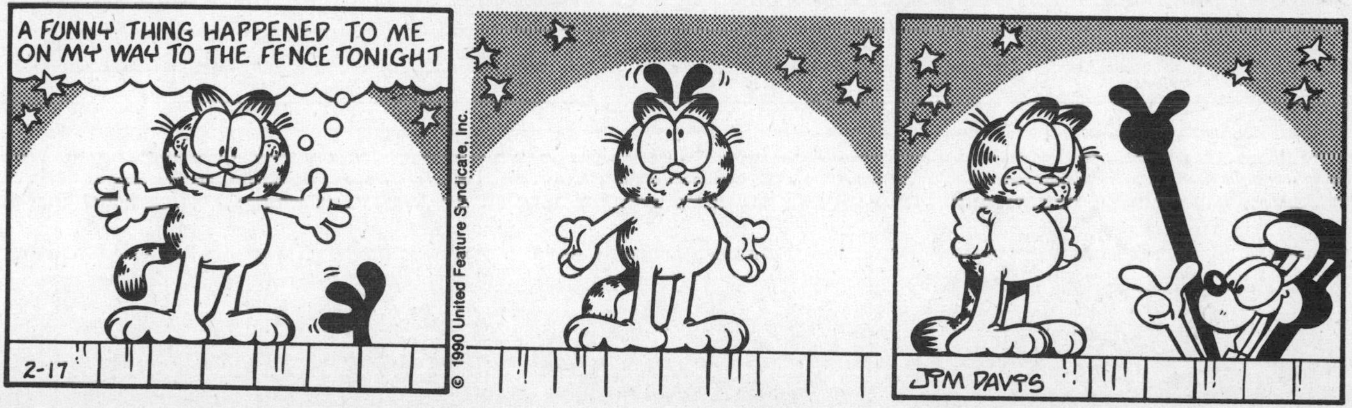
A FUNNY THING HAPPENED TO ME ON MY WAY TO THE FENCE TONIGHT
2-17
© 1990 United Feature Syndicate, Inc.
JIM DAVIS

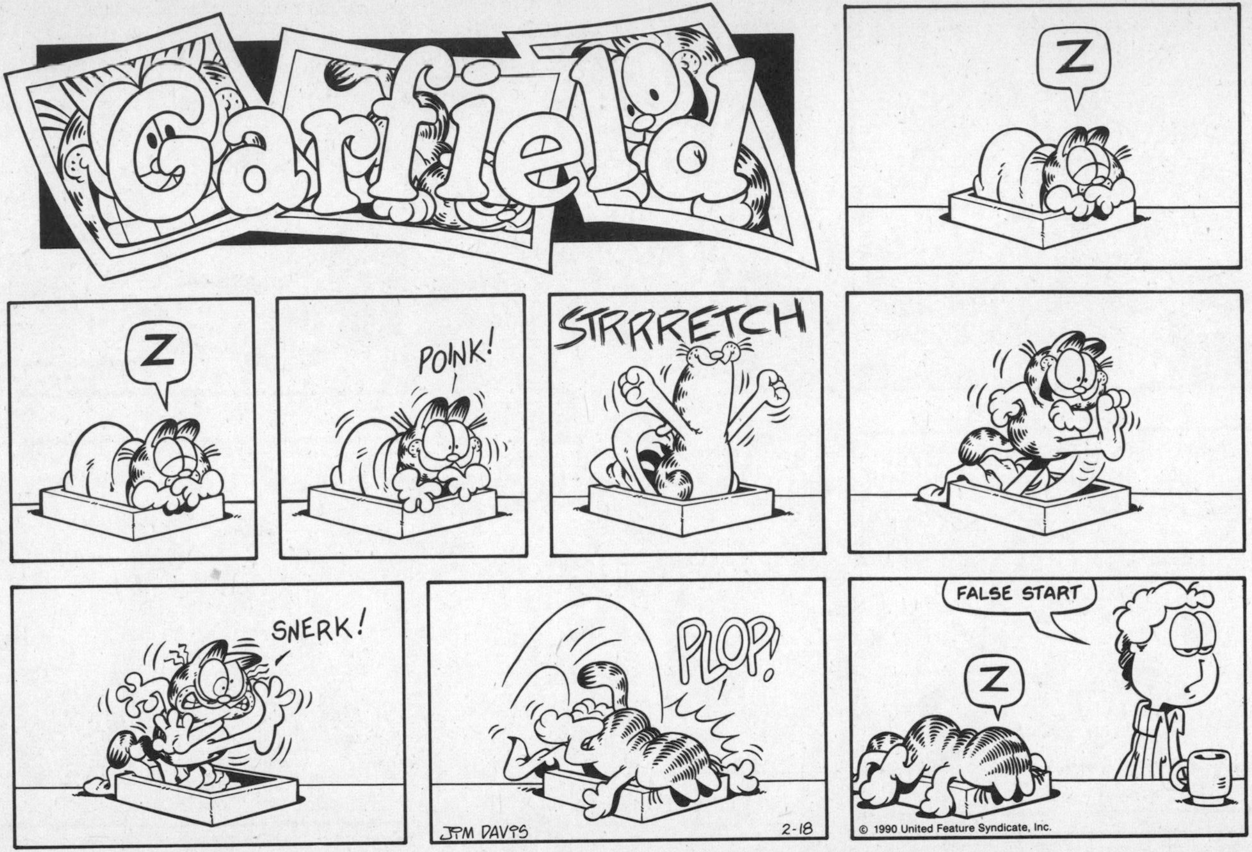
Garfield
Z
Z
POINK!
STRRRETCH
SNERK!
PLOP!
FALSE START
Z
JIM DAVIS
2-18

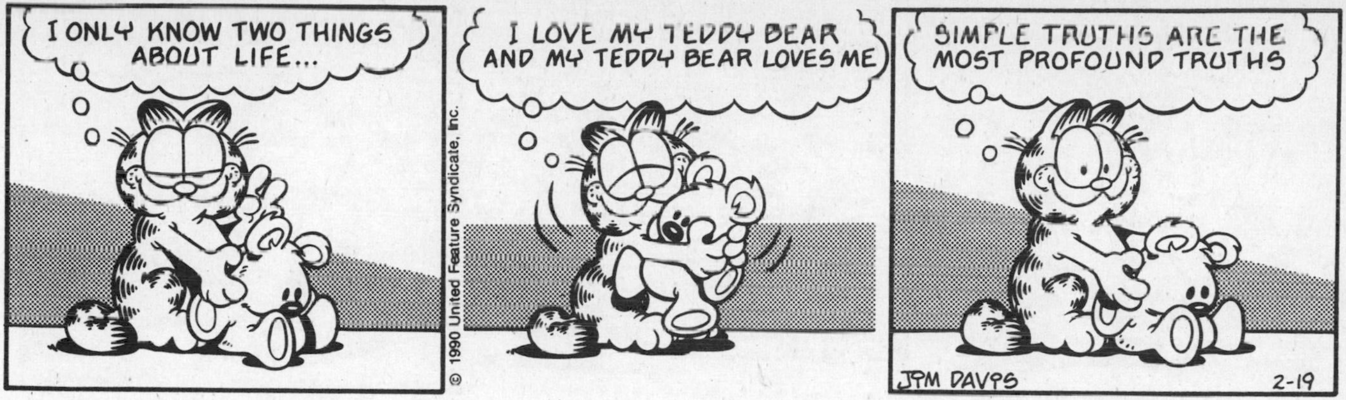
I ONLY KNOW TWO THINGS ABOUT LIFE...
I LOVE MY TEDDY BEAR AND MY TEDDY BEAR LOVES ME
SIMPLE TRUTHS ARE THE MOST PROFOUND TRUTHS
© 1990 United Feature Syndicate, Inc.
JIM DAVIS
2-19

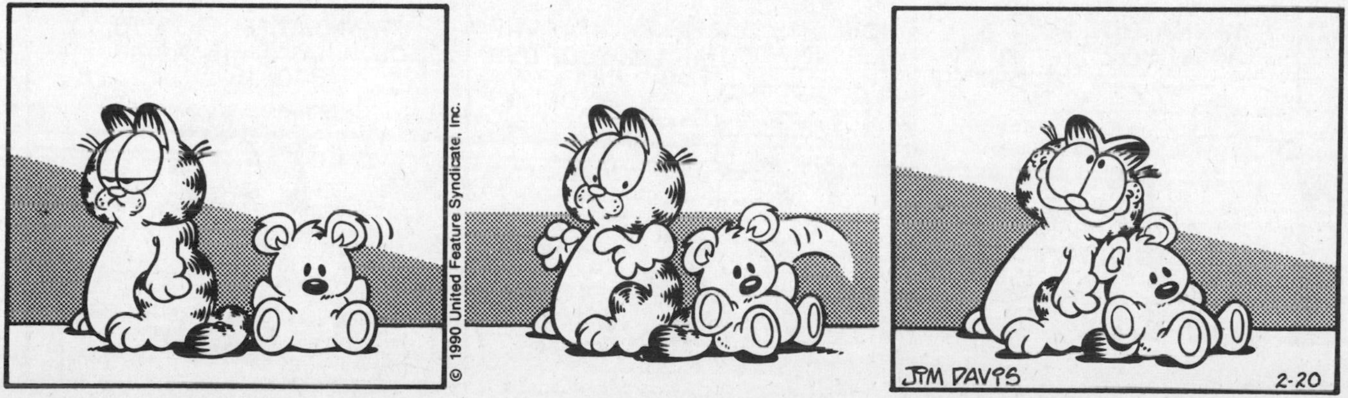
© 1990 United Feature Syndicate, Inc.
JIM DAVIS
2-20

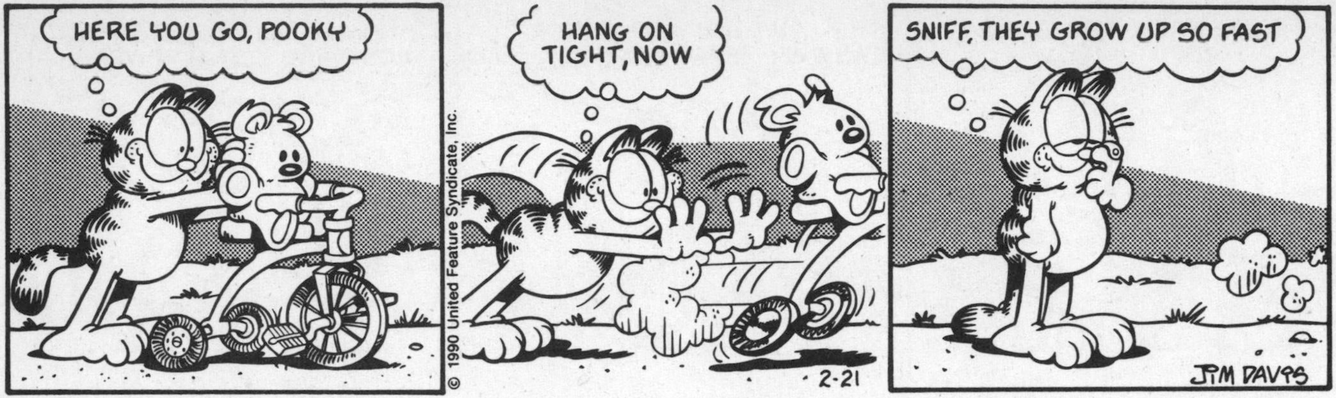
HERE YOU GO, POOKY
HANG ON TIGHT, NOW
SNIFF, THEY GROW UP SO FAST
JIM DAVIS
2-21
© 1990 United Feature Syndicate, Inc.

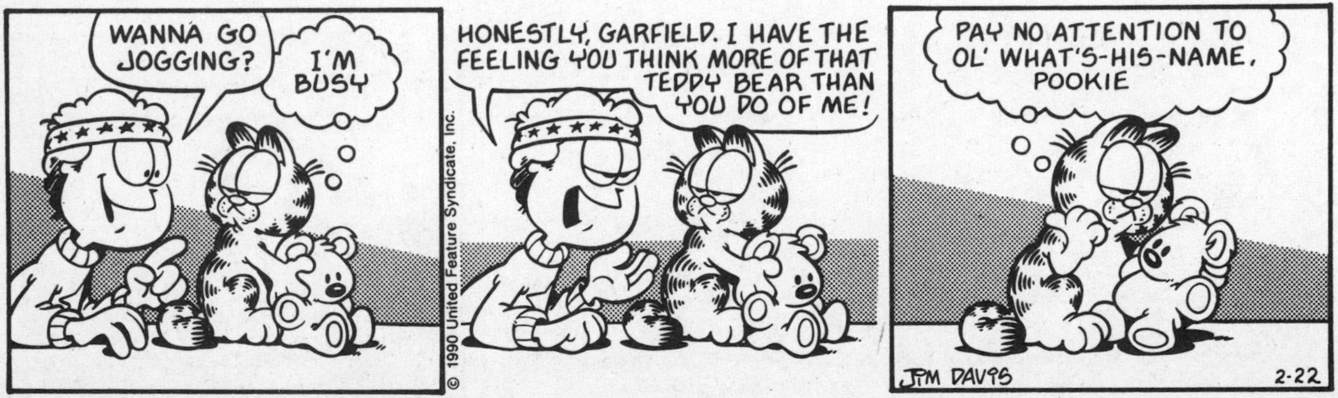
WANNA GO JOGGING?
I'M BUSY
HONESTLY, GARFIELD. I HAVE THE FEELING YOU THINK MORE OF THAT TEDDY BEAR THAN YOU DO OF ME!
PAY NO ATTENTION TO OL' WHAT'S-HIS-NAME, POOKIE
JIM DAVIS
2-22
© 1990 United Feature Syndicate, Inc.

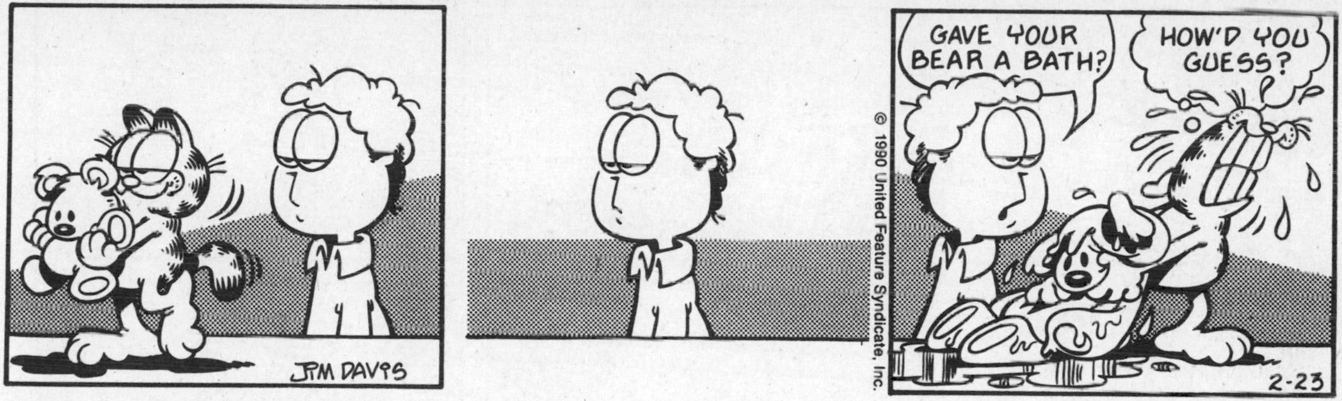
JIM DAVIS
GAVE YOUR BEAR A BATH?
HOW'D YOU GUESS?
© 1990 United Feature Syndicate, Inc.
2-23

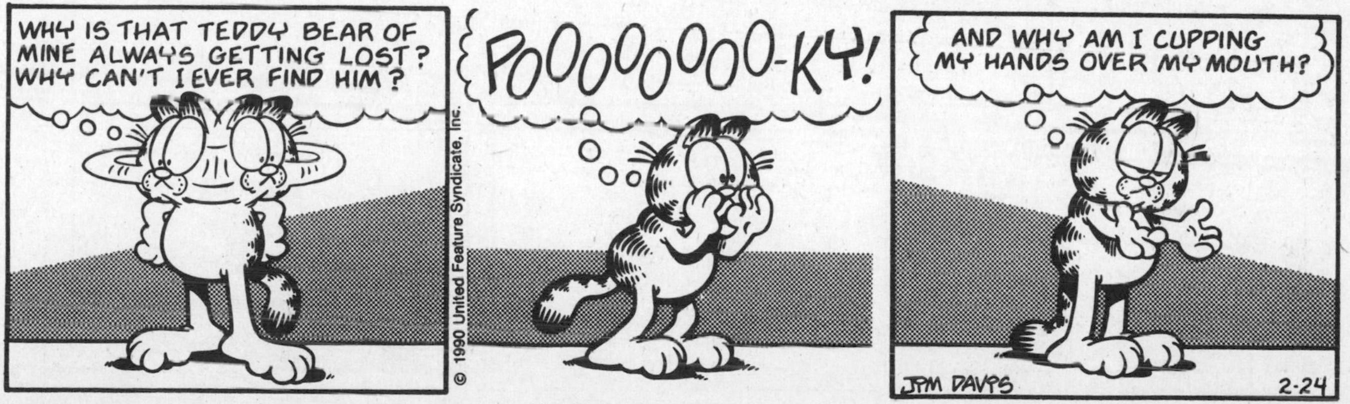
WHY IS THAT TEDDY BEAR OF MINE ALWAYS GETTING LOST? WHY CAN'T I EVER FIND HIM?
© 1990 United Feature Syndicate, Inc.
POOOOOOOOO-KY!
AND WHY AM I CUPPING MY HANDS OVER MY MOUTH?
JIM DAVIS
2-24

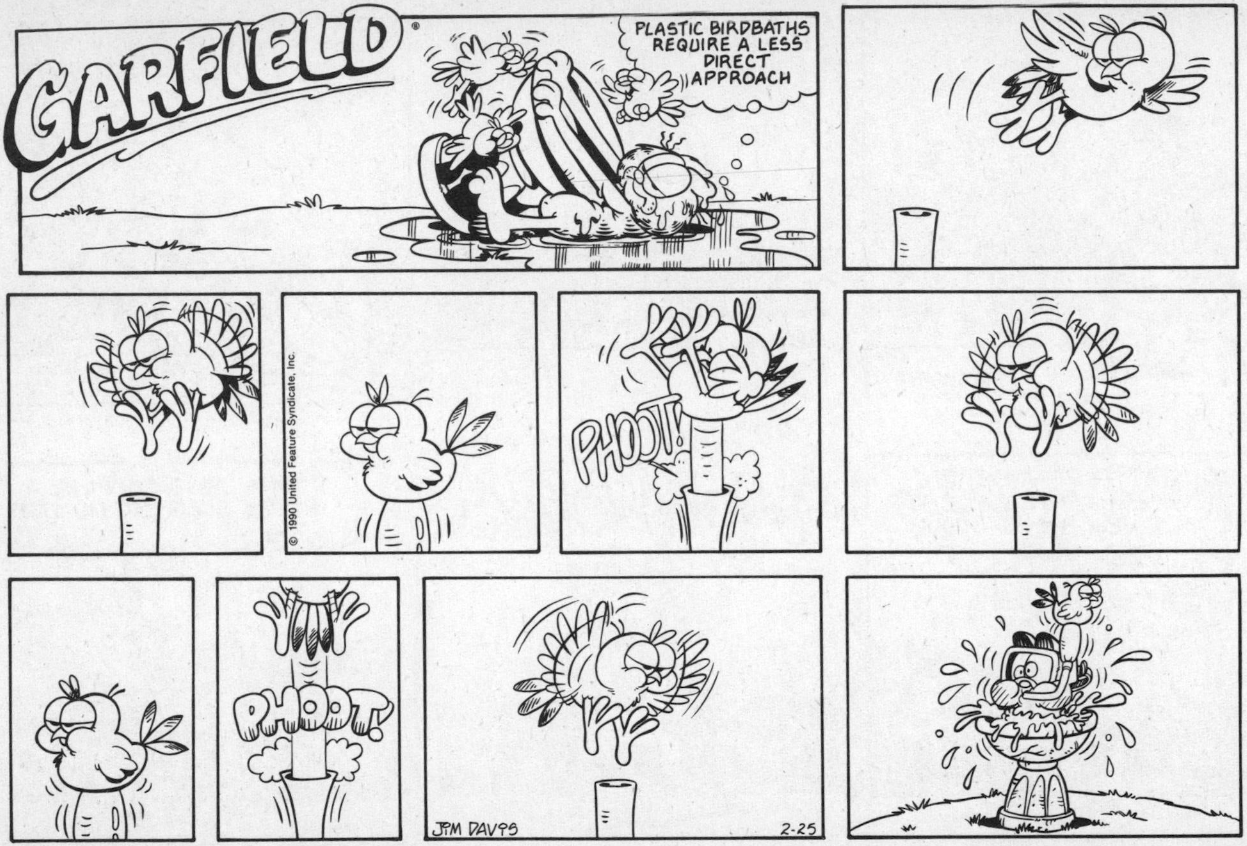
GARFIELD
PLASTIC BIRDBATHS REQUIRE A LESS DIRECT APPROACH
© 1990 United Feature Syndicate, Inc.
PHOOT!
PHOOT!
JPM DAVPS
2-25

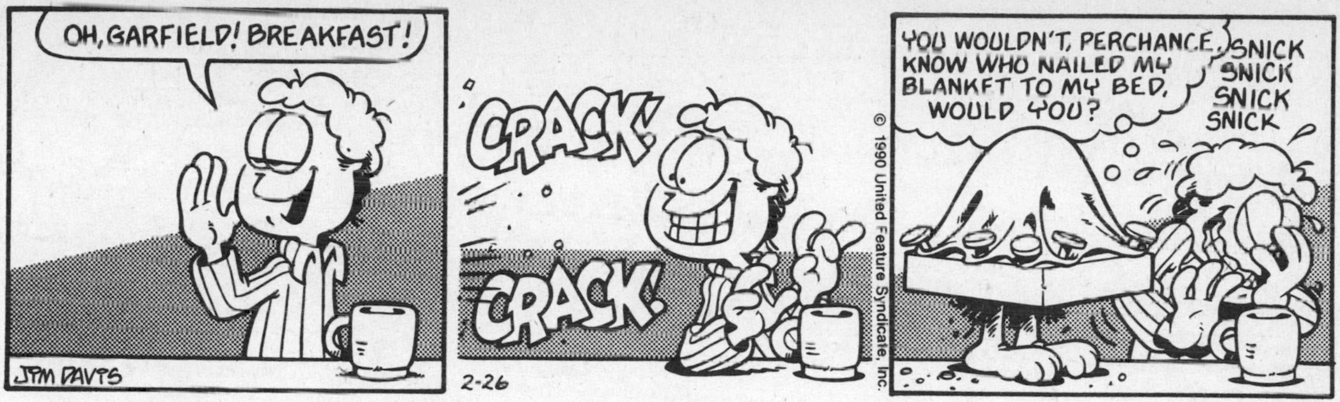

OH, GARFIELD! BREAKFAST!
CRACK!
CRACK!
JIM DAVIS
2-26
© 1990 United Feature Syndicate, Inc.
YOU WOULDN'T, PERCHANCE, KNOW WHO NAILED MY BLANKET TO MY BED, WOULD YOU?
SNICK SNICK SNICK SNICK

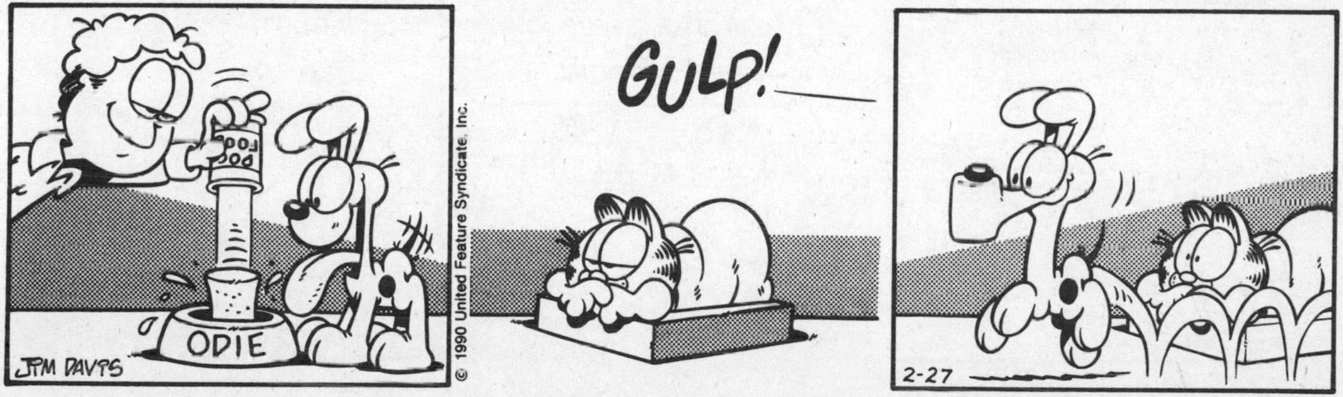

ODIE
JIM DAVIS
© 1990 United Feature Syndicate, Inc.
GULP!
2-27

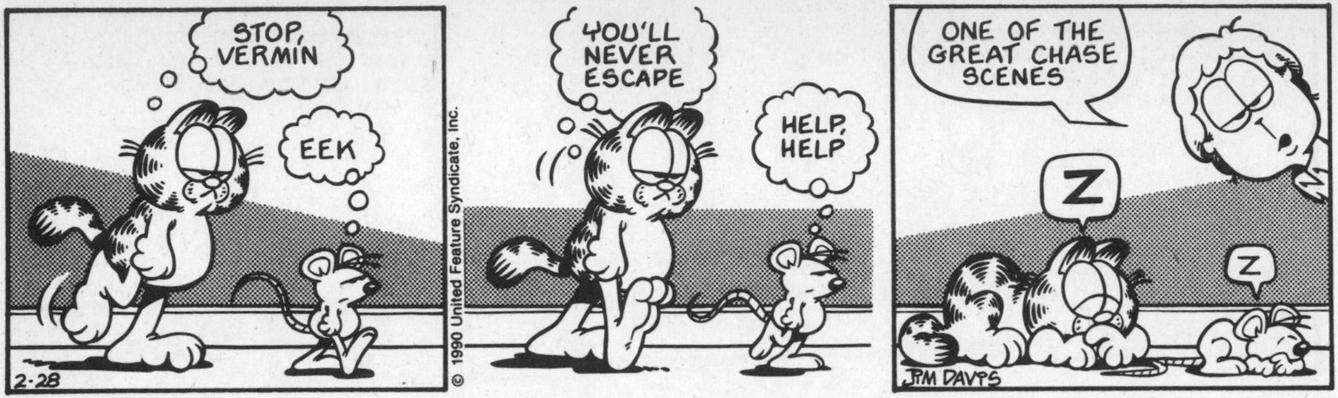
STOP, VERMIN
EEK
2-28
© 1990 United Feature Syndicate, Inc.
YOU'LL NEVER ESCAPE
HELP, HELP
ONE OF THE GREAT CHASE SCENES
Z
Z
JIM DAVIS

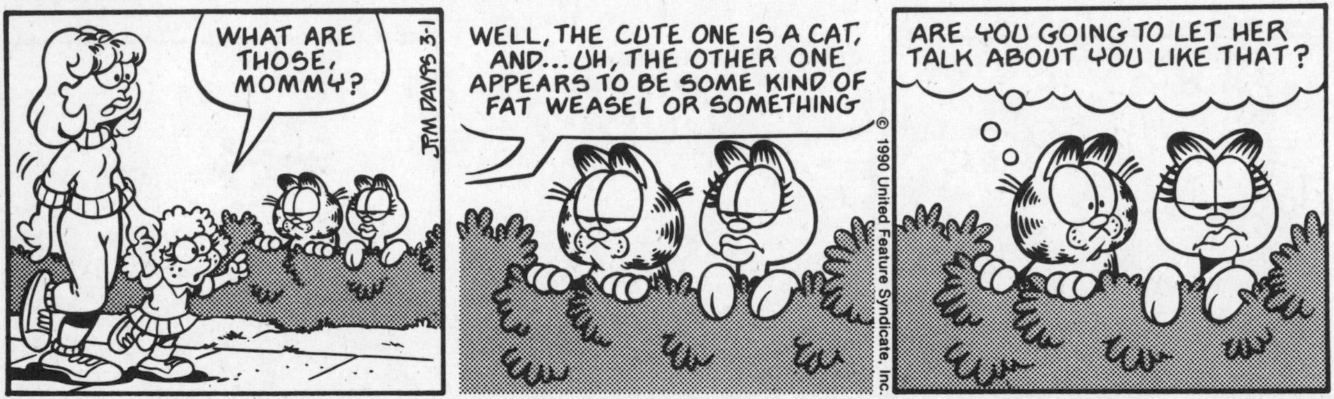
WHAT ARE THOSE, MOMMY?
JIM DAVIS 3-1
WELL, THE CUTE ONE IS A CAT, AND... UH, THE OTHER ONE APPEARS TO BE SOME KIND OF FAT WEASEL OR SOMETHING
© 1990 United Feature Syndicate, Inc.
ARE YOU GOING TO LET HER TALK ABOUT YOU LIKE THAT?

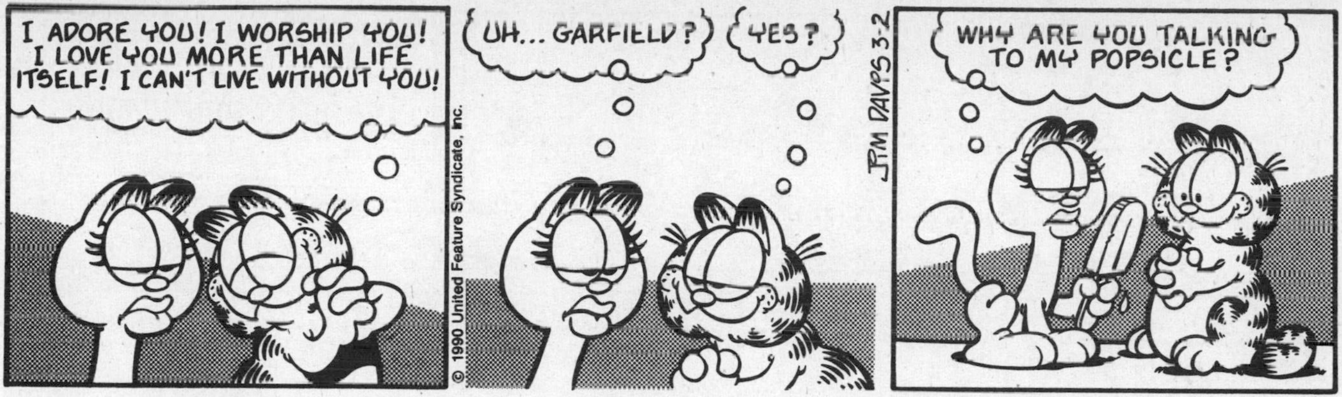
I ADORE YOU! I WORSHIP YOU! I LOVE YOU MORE THAN LIFE ITSELF! I CAN'T LIVE WITHOUT YOU!
UH... GARFIELD?
YES?
WHY ARE YOU TALKING TO MY POPSICLE?
© 1990 United Feature Syndicate, Inc.
JIM DAVIS 3-2

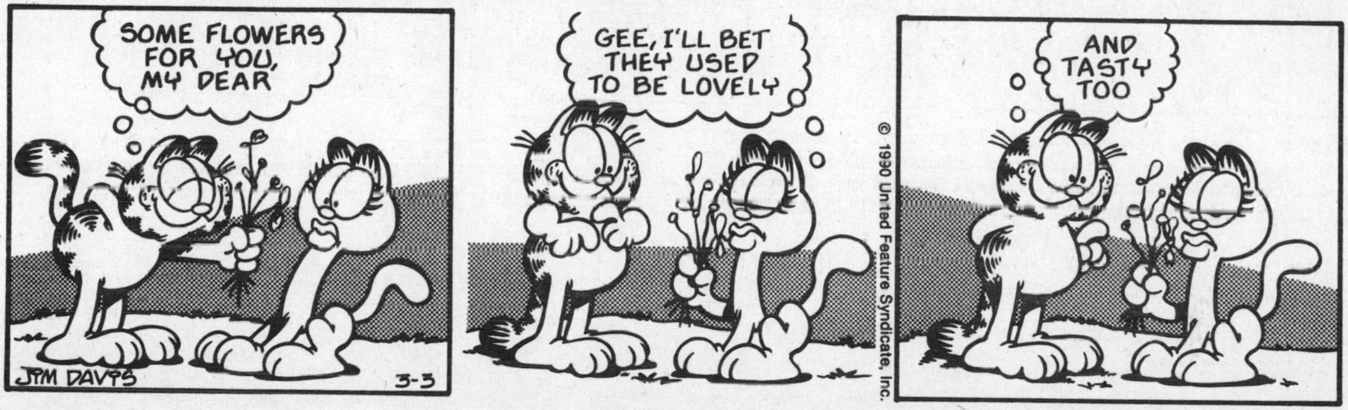
SOME FLOWERS FOR YOU, MY DEAR
GEE, I'LL BET THEY USED TO BE LOVELY
AND TASTY TOO
JIM DAVIS 3-3
© 1990 United Feature Syndicate, Inc.

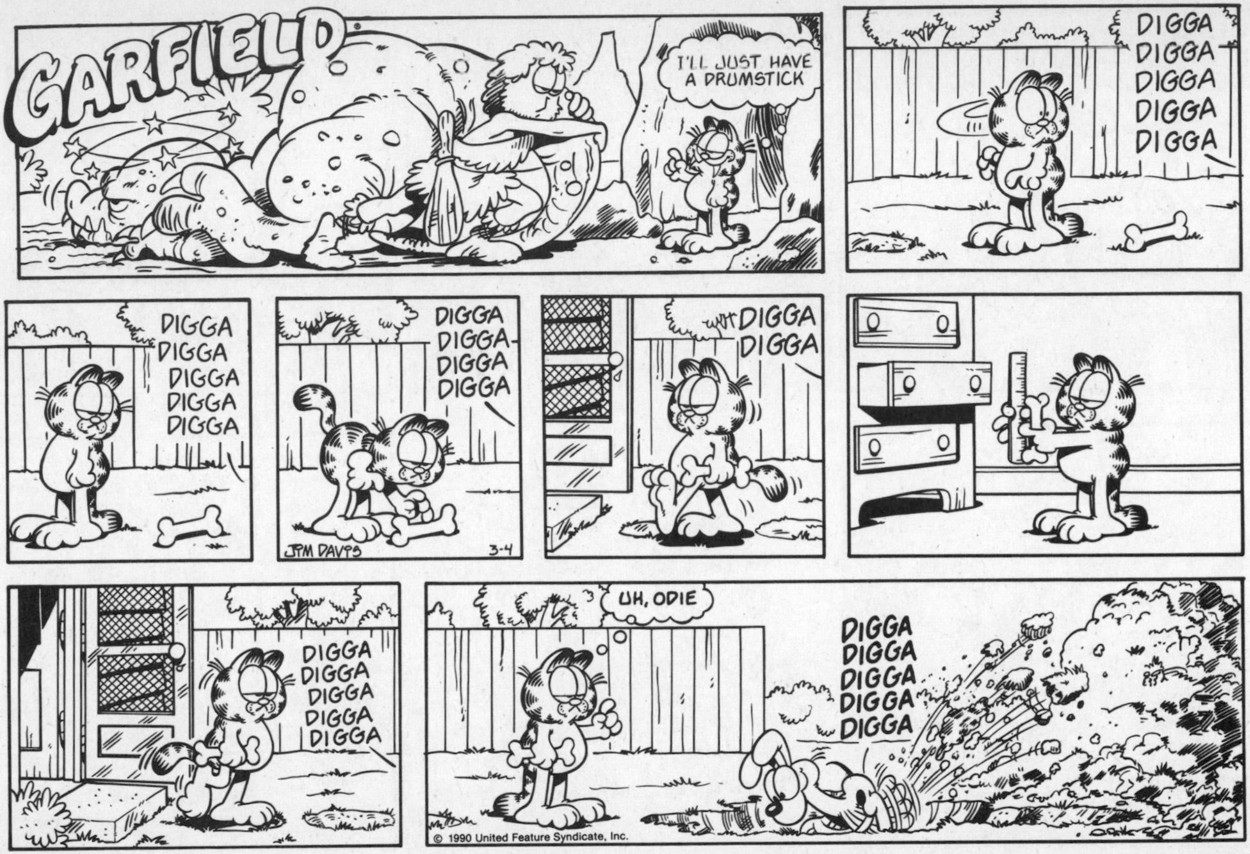
GARFIELD
I'LL JUST HAVE A DRUMSTICK
DIGGA DIGGA DIGGA DIGGA DIGGA
DIGGA DIGGA DIGGA DIGGA DIGGA
DIGGA DIGGA DIGGA DIGGA
JIM DAVIS 3-4
DIGGA DIGGA
DIGGA DIGGA DIGGA DIGGA DIGGA
UH, ODIE
DIGGA DIGGA DIGGA DIGGA DIGGA
© 1990 United Feature Syndicate, Inc.

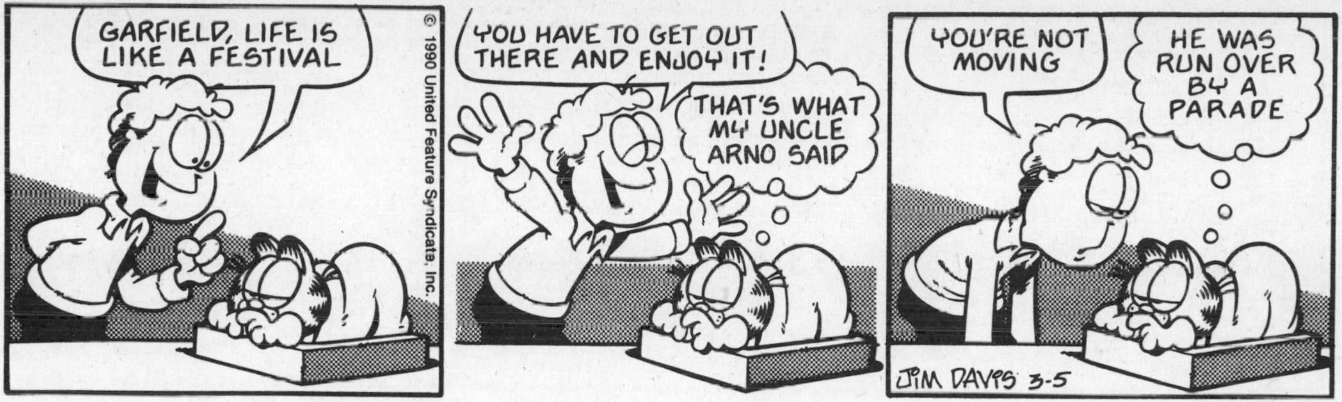
GARFIELD, LIFE IS LIKE A FESTIVAL
© 1990 United Feature Syndicate, Inc.
YOU HAVE TO GET OUT THERE AND ENJOY IT!
THAT'S WHAT MY UNCLE ARNO SAID
YOU'RE NOT MOVING
HE WAS RUN OVER BY A PARADE
JIM DAVIS 3-5

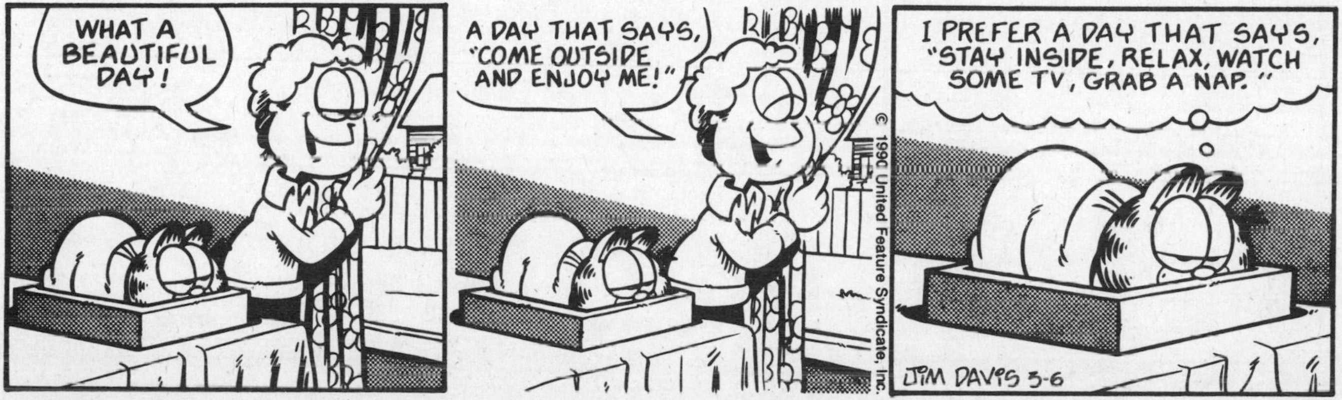
WHAT A BEAUTIFUL DAY!
A DAY THAT SAYS, "COME OUTSIDE AND ENJOY ME!"
© 1990 United Feature Syndicate, Inc.
I PREFER A DAY THAT SAYS, "STAY INSIDE, RELAX, WATCH SOME TV, GRAB A NAP."
JIM DAVIS 3-6

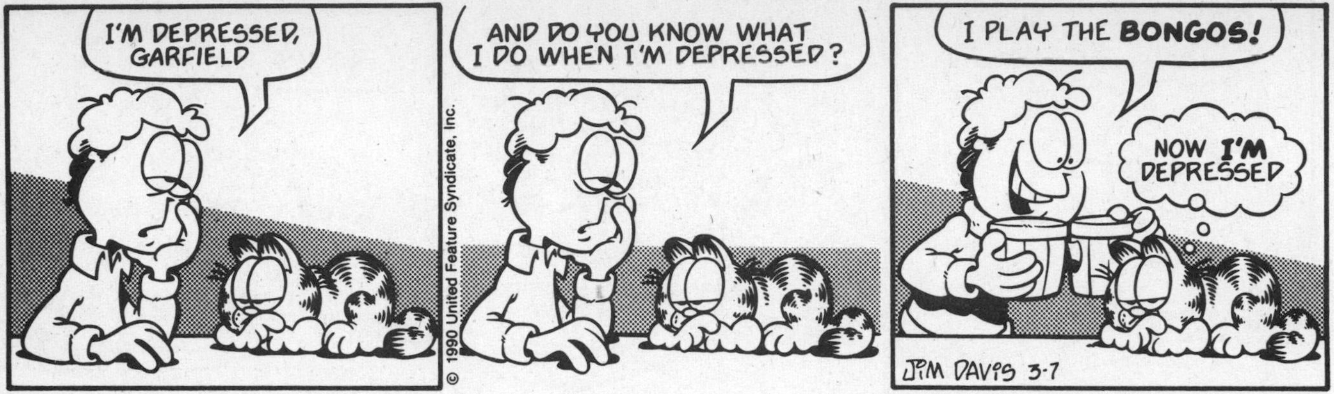
I'M DEPRESSED, GARFIELD
AND DO YOU KNOW WHAT I DO WHEN I'M DEPRESSED?
I PLAY THE **BONGOS!**
NOW **I'M** DEPRESSED
JIM DAVIS 3-7

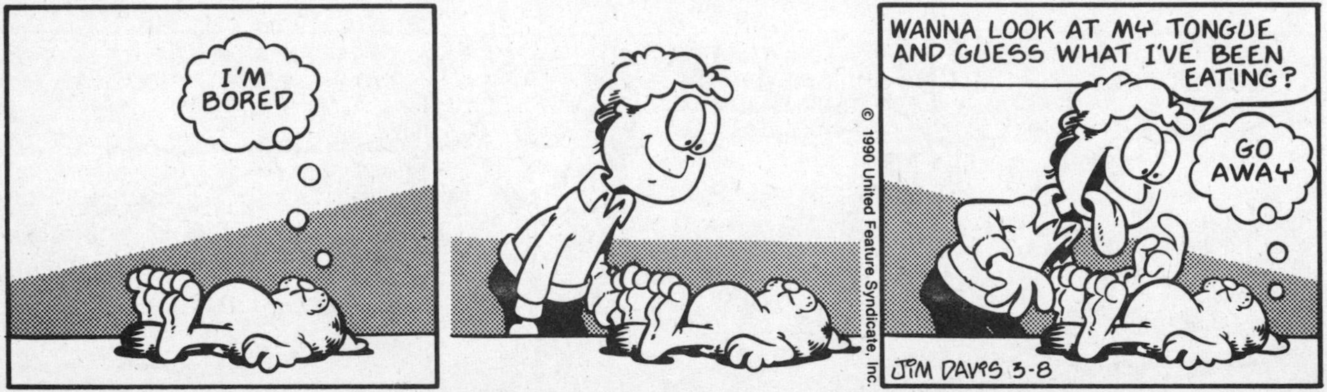
I'M BORED
WANNA LOOK AT MY TONGUE AND GUESS WHAT I'VE BEEN EATING?
GO AWAY
JIM DAVIS 3-8

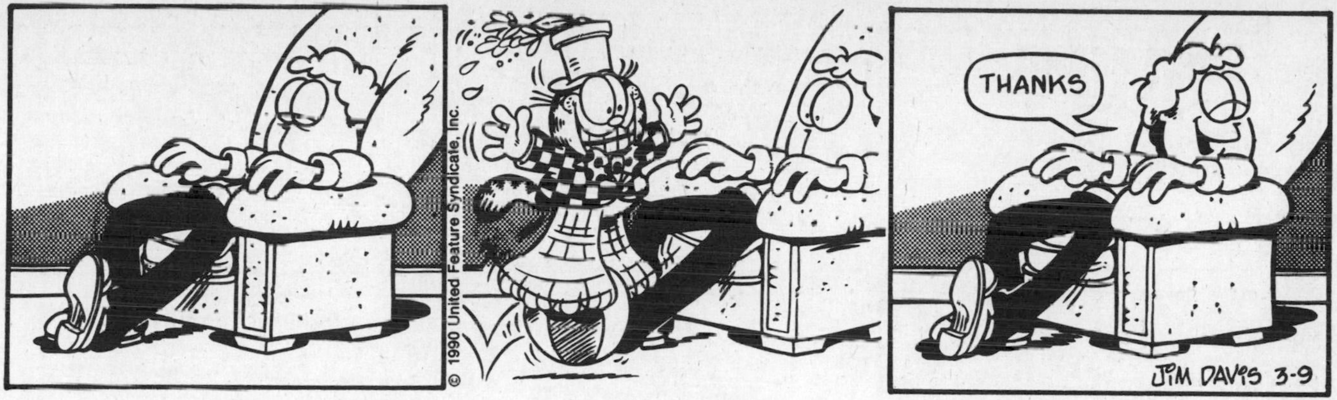
© 1990 United Feature Syndicate, Inc.
THANKS
JIM DAVIS 3-9

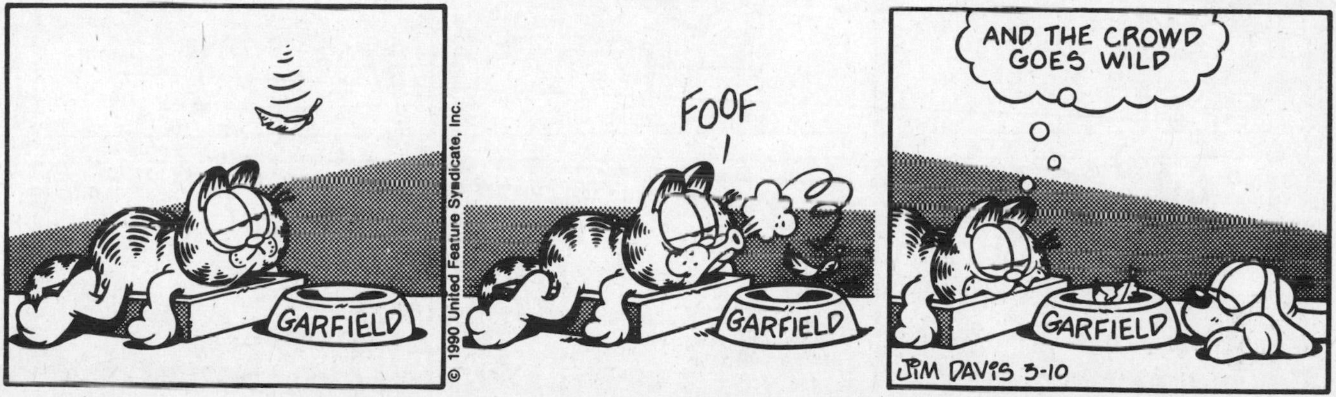
© 1990 United Feature Syndicate, Inc.
GARFIELD
FOOF
GARFIELD
AND THE CROWD GOES WILD
GARFIELD
JIM DAVIS 3-10

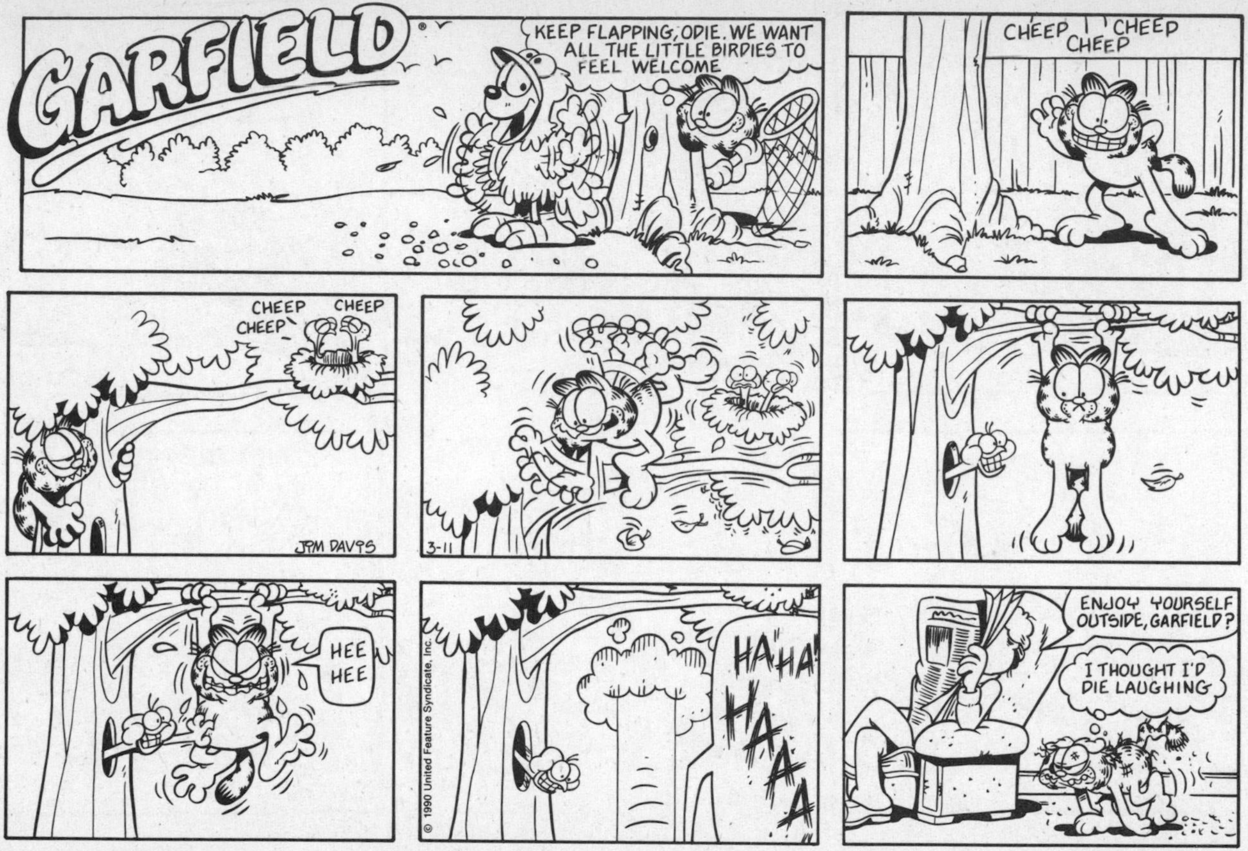
GARFIELD
KEEP FLAPPING, ODIE. WE WANT ALL THE LITTLE BIRDIES TO FEEL WELCOME
CHEEP CHEEP CHEEP
CHEEP CHEEP CHEEP
JIM DAVIS
3-11
HEE HEE
© 1990 United Feature Syndicate, Inc.
HA HA HA HAAA
ENJOY YOURSELF OUTSIDE, GARFIELD?
I THOUGHT I'D DIE LAUGHING

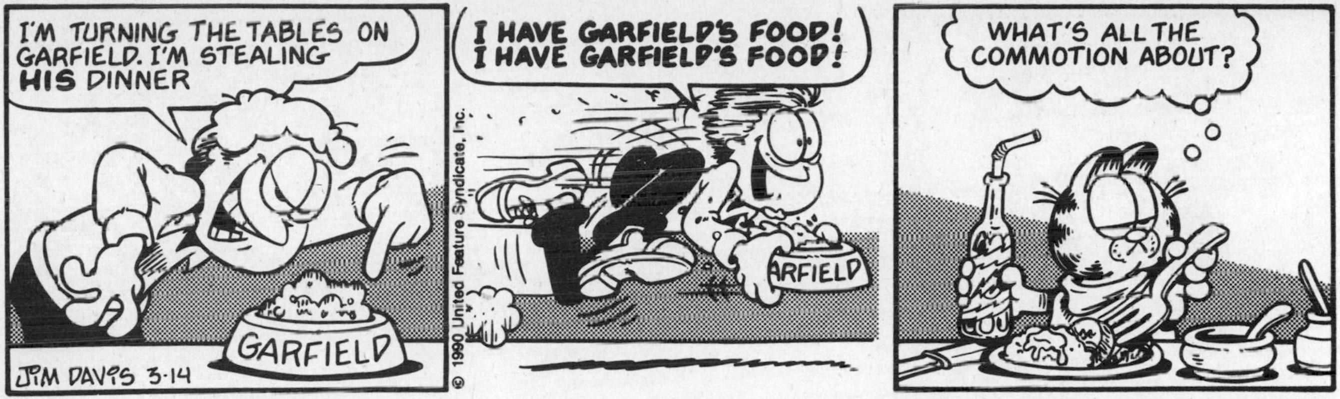
I'M TURNING THE TABLES ON GARFIELD. I'M STEALING **HIS** DINNER
GARFIELD
JIM DAVIS 3-14
© 1990 United Feature Syndicate, Inc.
I HAVE GARFIELD'S FOOD! I HAVE GARFIELD'S FOOD!
ARFIELD
WHAT'S ALL THE COMMOTION ABOUT?

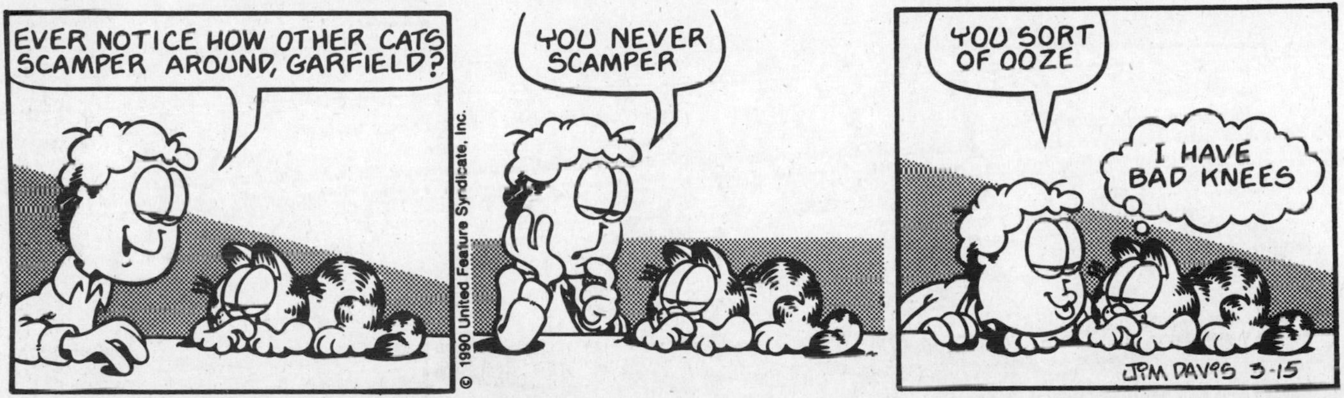
EVER NOTICE HOW OTHER CATS SCAMPER AROUND, GARFIELD?
© 1990 United Feature Syndicate, Inc.
YOU NEVER SCAMPER
YOU SORT OF OOZE
I HAVE BAD KNEES
JIM DAVIS 3-15

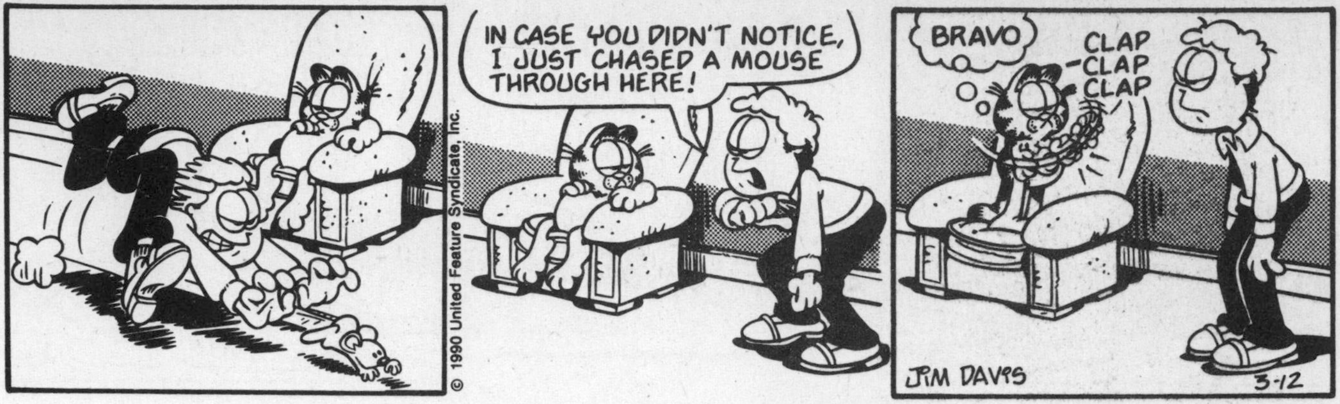
IN CASE YOU DIDN'T NOTICE, I JUST CHASED A MOUSE THROUGH HERE!
BRAVO
CLAP
CLAP
CLAP
© 1990 United Feature Syndicate, Inc.
JIM DAVIS
3-12

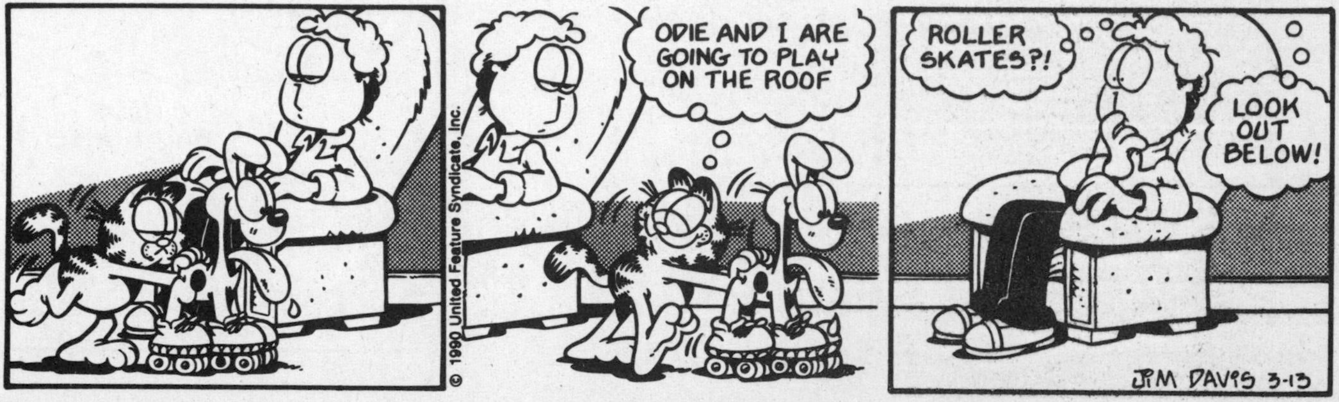
ODIE AND I ARE GOING TO PLAY ON THE ROOF
ROLLER SKATES?!
LOOK OUT BELOW!
© 1990 United Feature Syndicate, Inc.
JIM DAVIS 3-13

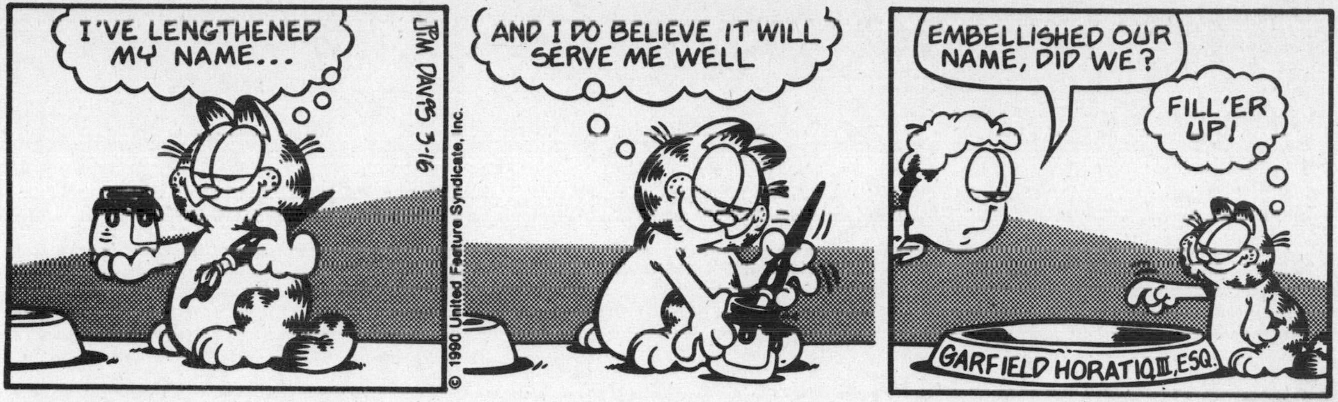
I'VE LENGTHENED MY NAME...
JIM DAVIS 3-16
© 1990 United Feature Syndicate, Inc.
AND I DO BELIEVE IT WILL SERVE ME WELL
EMBELLISHED OUR NAME, DID WE?
FILL'ER UP!
GARFIELD HORATIO III, ESQ.

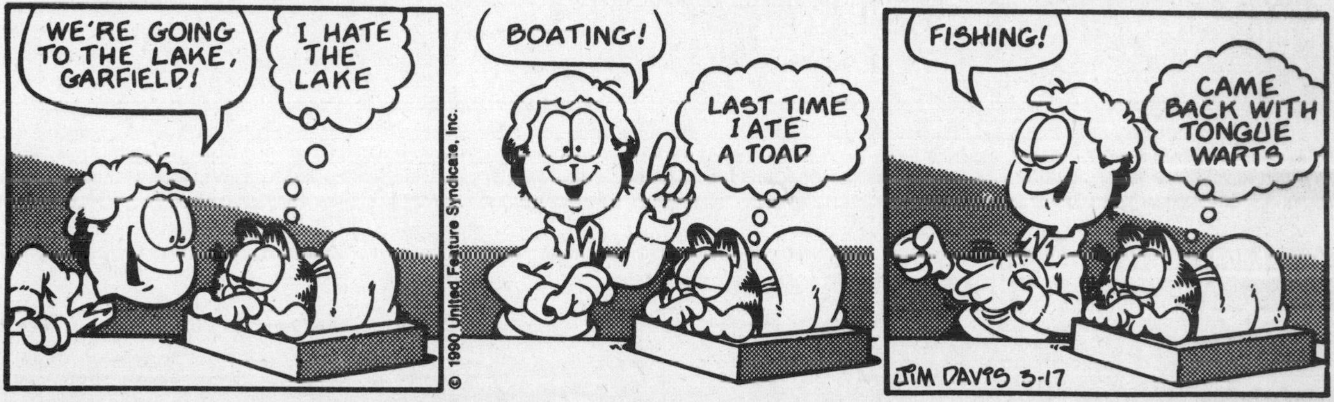
WE'RE GOING TO THE LAKE, GARFIELD!
I HATE THE LAKE
© 1990 United Feature Syndicate, Inc.
BOATING!
LAST TIME I ATE A TOAD
FISHING!
CAME BACK WITH TONGUE WARTS
JIM DAVIS 3-17

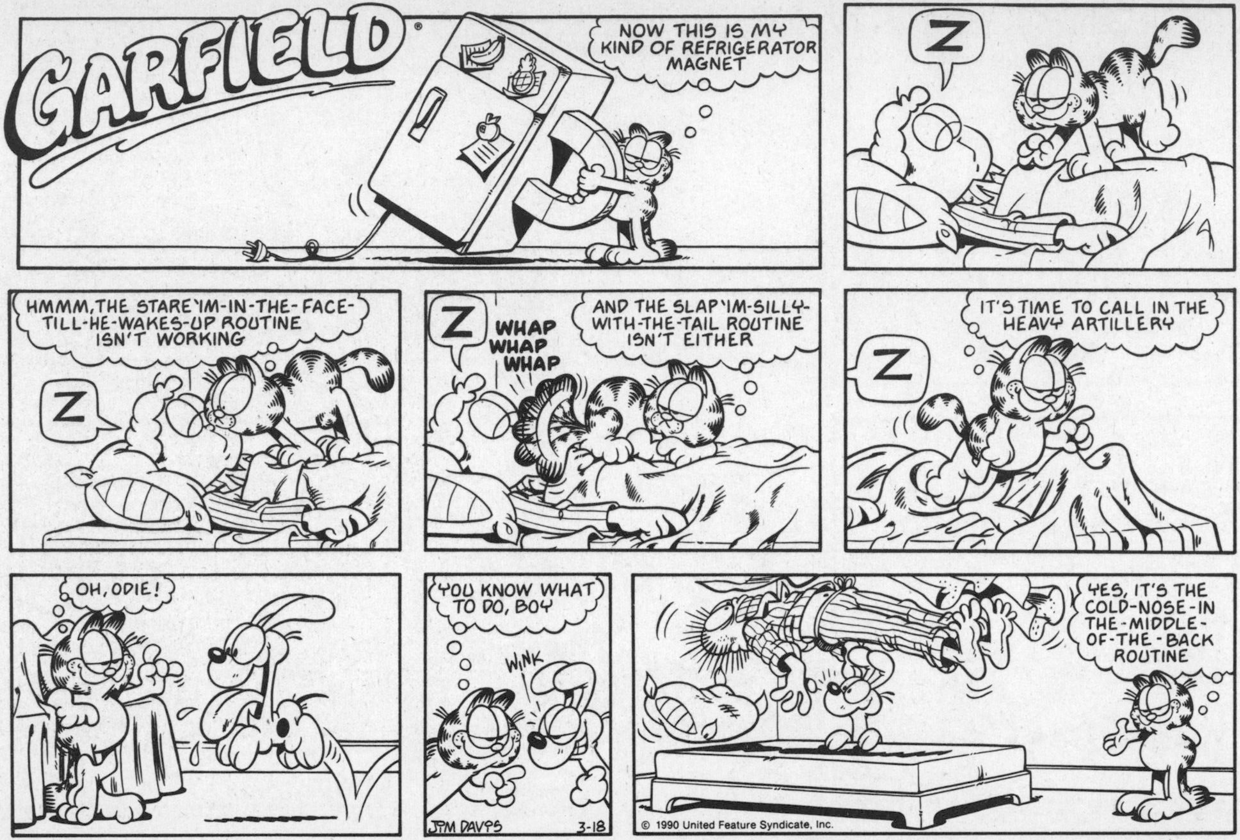
GARFIELD
NOW THIS IS MY KIND OF REFRIGERATOR MAGNET
Z
HMMM, THE STARE 'IM-IN-THE-FACE-TILL-HE-WAKES-UP ROUTINE ISN'T WORKING
Z
Z
WHAP WHAP WHAP
AND THE SLAP 'IM-SILLY-WITH-THE-TAIL ROUTINE ISN'T EITHER
Z
IT'S TIME TO CALL IN THE HEAVY ARTILLERY
OH, ODIE!
YOU KNOW WHAT TO DO, BOY
WINK
JIM DAVIS 3-18
YES, IT'S THE COLD-NOSE-IN THE-MIDDLE-OF-THE-BACK ROUTINE
© 1990 United Feature Syndicate, Inc.

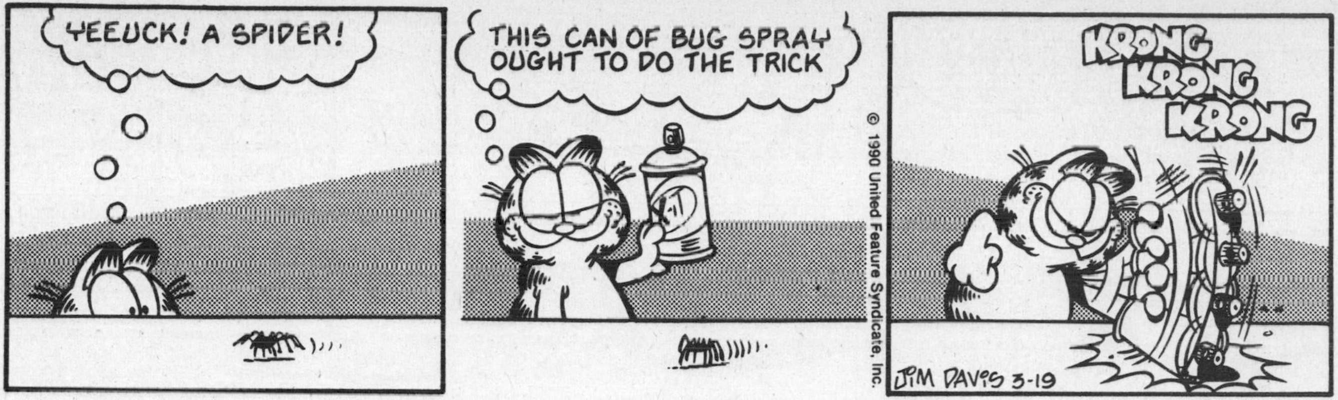
YEEUCK! A SPIDER!
THIS CAN OF BUG SPRAY OUGHT TO DO THE TRICK
© 1990 United Feature Syndicate, Inc.
KRONG
KRONG
KRONG
JIM DAVIS 3-19

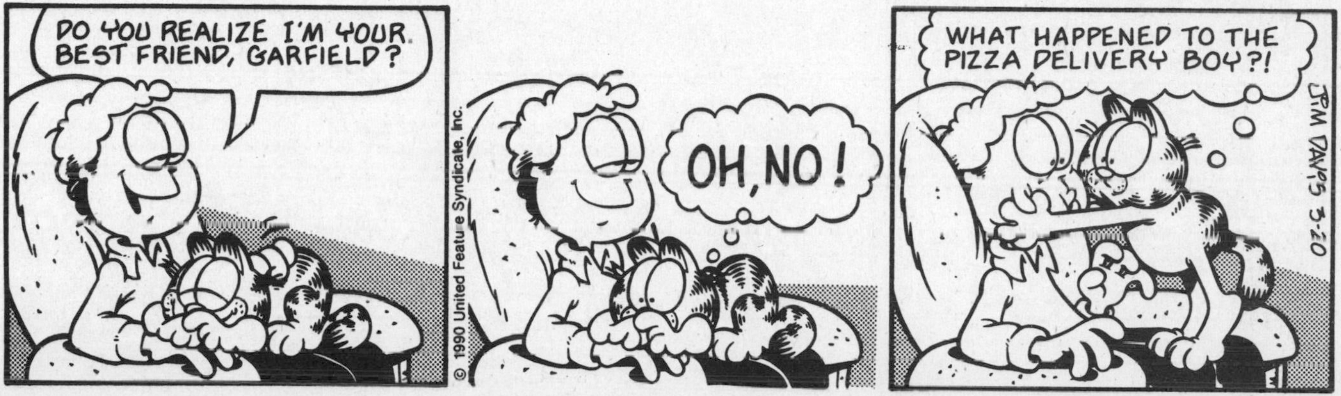
DO YOU REALIZE I'M YOUR BEST FRIEND, GARFIELD?
© 1990 United Feature Syndicate, Inc.
OH, NO!
WHAT HAPPENED TO THE PIZZA DELIVERY BOY?!
JIM DAVIS 3-20

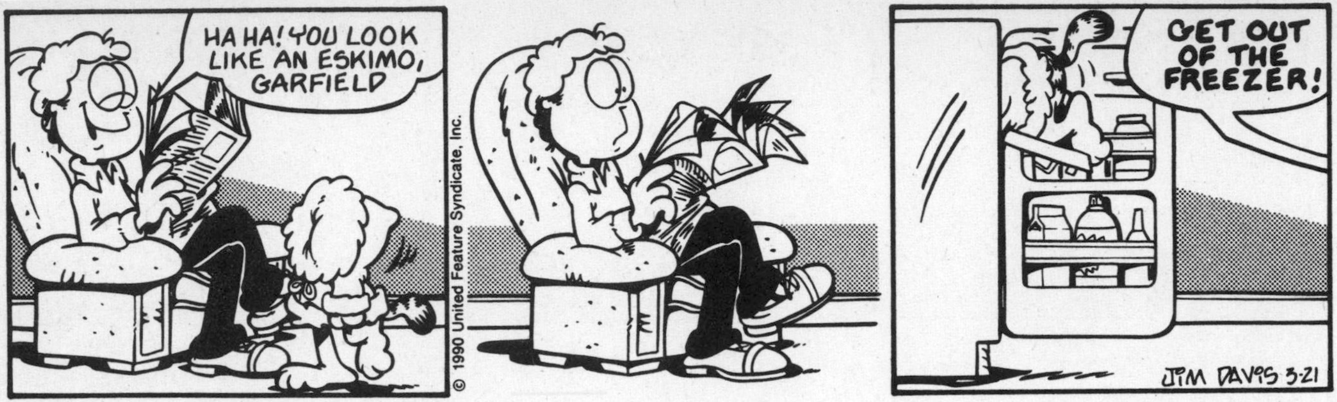
HA HA! YOU LOOK LIKE AN ESKIMO, GARFIELD
GET OUT OF THE FREEZER!
JIM DAVIS 3-21
© 1990 United Feature Syndicate, Inc.

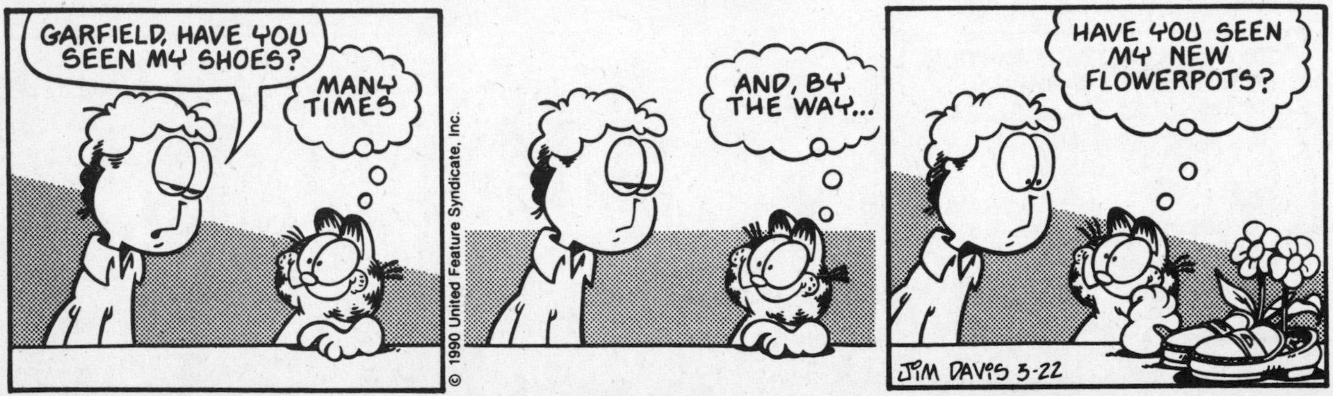
GARFIELD, HAVE YOU SEEN MY SHOES?
MANY TIMES
AND, BY THE WAY...
HAVE YOU SEEN MY NEW FLOWERPOTS?
JIM DAVIS 3-22
© 1990 United Feature Syndicate, Inc.

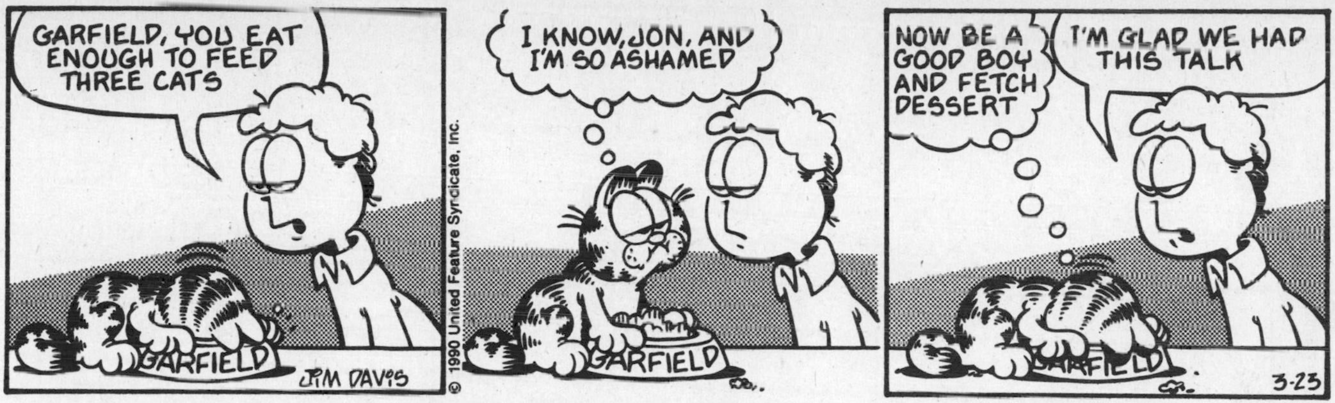
GARFIELD, YOU EAT ENOUGH TO FEED THREE CATS
GARFIELD
JIM DAVIS
© 1990 United Feature Syndicate, Inc.
I KNOW, JON, AND I'M SO ASHAMED
GARFIELD
NOW BE A GOOD BOY AND FETCH DESSERT
I'M GLAD WE HAD THIS TALK
GARFIELD
3-23

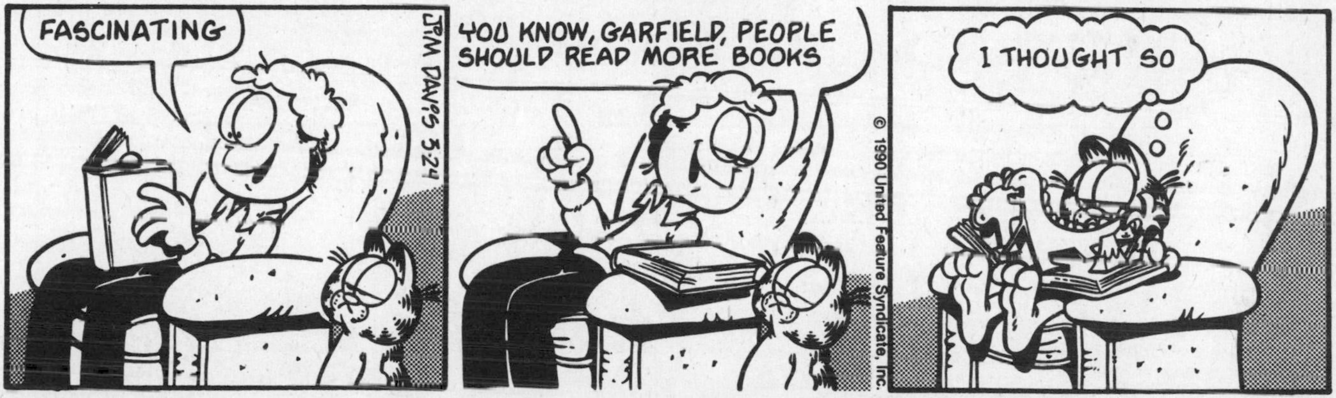
FASCINATING
JIM DAVIS 3-24
YOU KNOW, GARFIELD, PEOPLE SHOULD READ MORE BOOKS
© 1990 United Feature Syndicate, Inc.
I THOUGHT SO

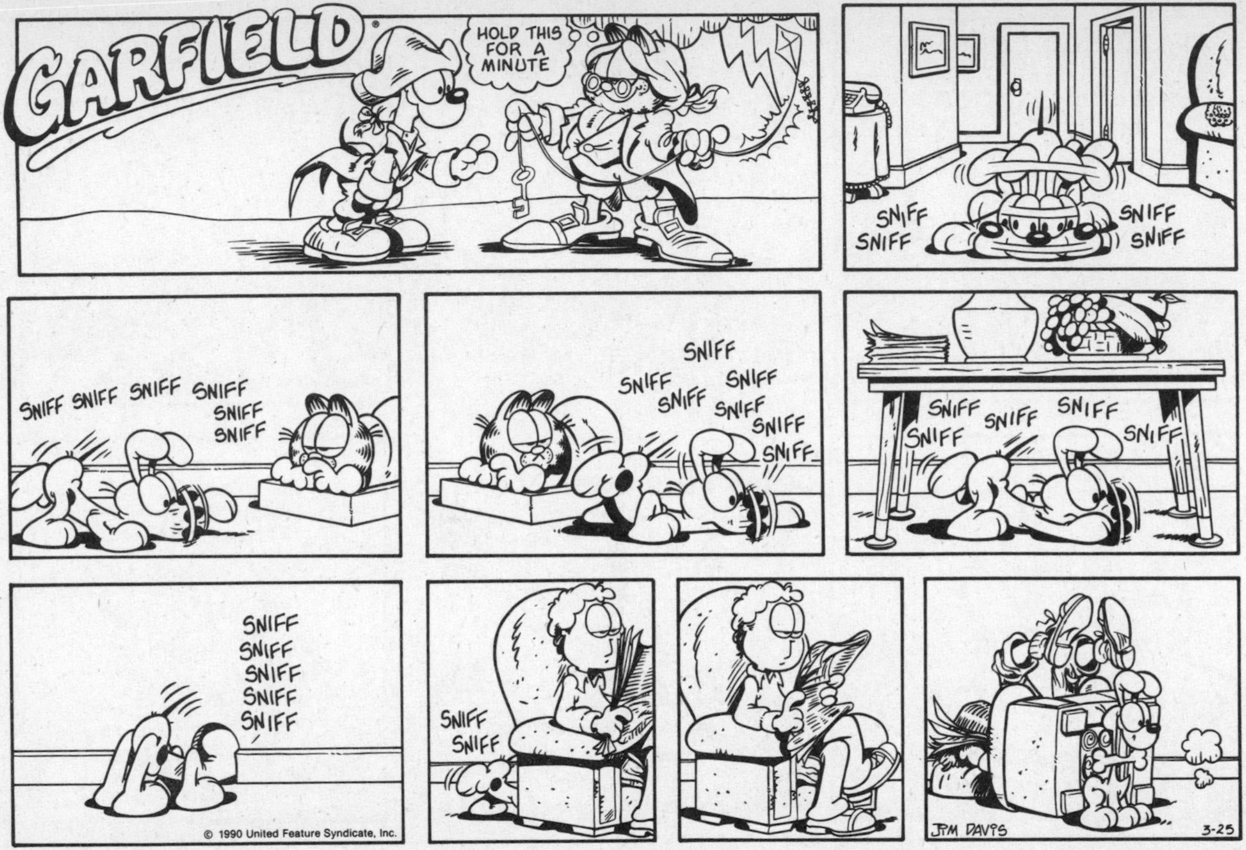
GARFIELD
HOLD THIS FOR A MINUTE
SNIFF SNIFF
SNIFF SNIFF
SNIFF SNIFF SNIFF SNIFF SNIFF SNIFF
SNIFF SNIFF SNIFF SNIFF SNIFF SNIFF SNIFF
SNIFF SNIFF SNIFF SNIFF SNIFF
SNIFF SNIFF SNIFF SNIFF SNIFF
© 1990 United Feature Syndicate, Inc.
SNIFF SNIFF
JPM DAVIS
3-25

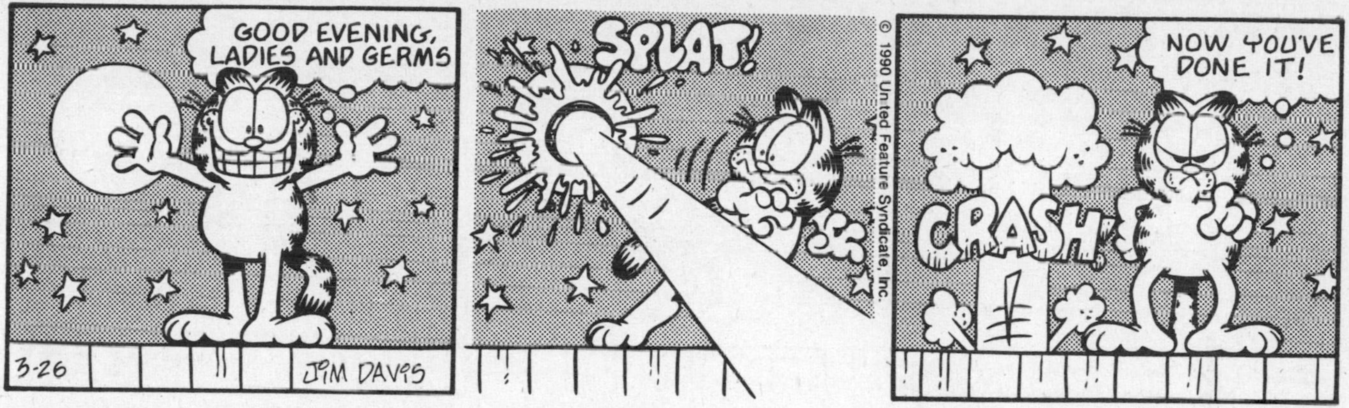
GOOD EVENING, LADIES AND GERMS
3-26
JIM DAVIS
SPLAT!
© 1990 United Feature Syndicate, Inc.
CRASH!
NOW YOU'VE DONE IT!

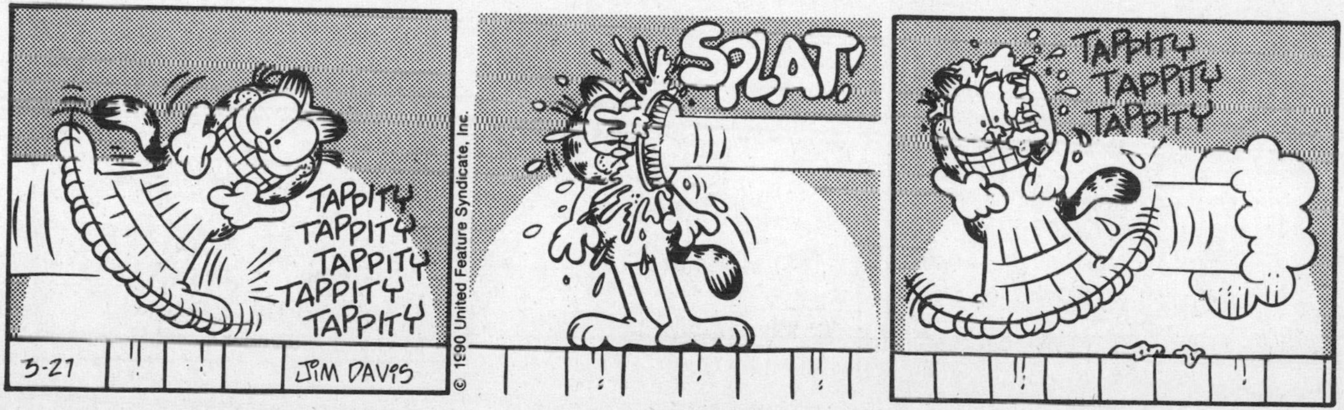
TAPPITY
TAPPITY
TAPPITY
TAPPITY
TAPPITY
3-27
JIM DAVIS
© 1990 United Feature Syndicate, Inc.
SPLAT!
TAPPITY
TAPPITY
TAPPITY

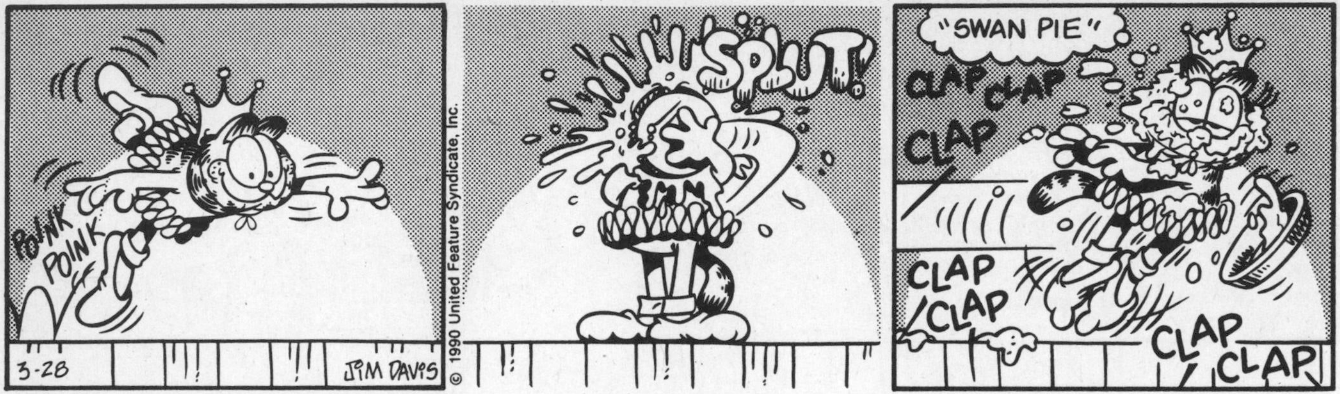
POINK
POINK
SPLUT!
"SWAN PIE"
CLAP CLAP
CLAP
CLAP
CLAP
CLAP
CLAP
3-28
JIM DAVIS
© 1990 United Feature Syndicate, Inc.

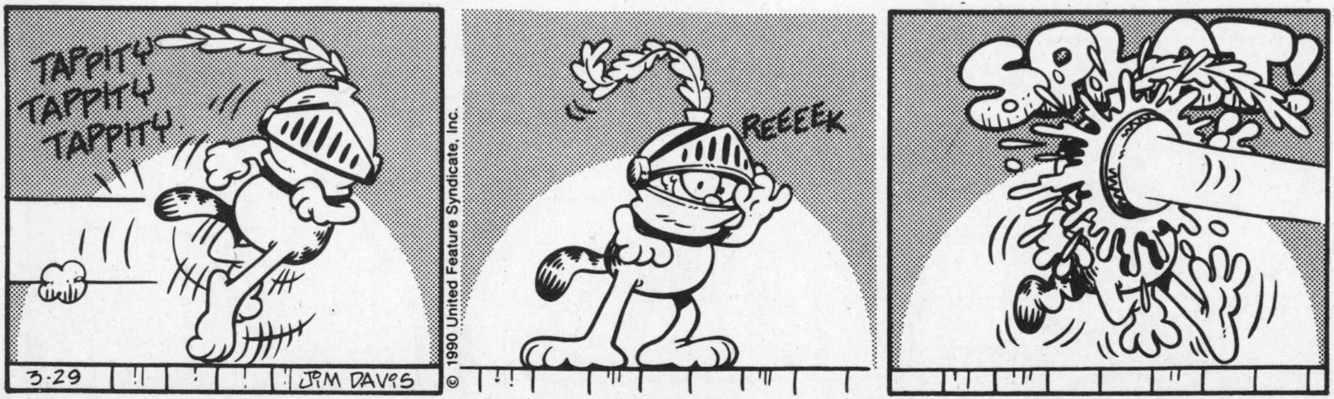
TAPPITY
TAPPITY
TAPPITY
REEEEK
SPLAT!
3-29
JIM DAVIS
© 1990 United Feature Syndicate, Inc.

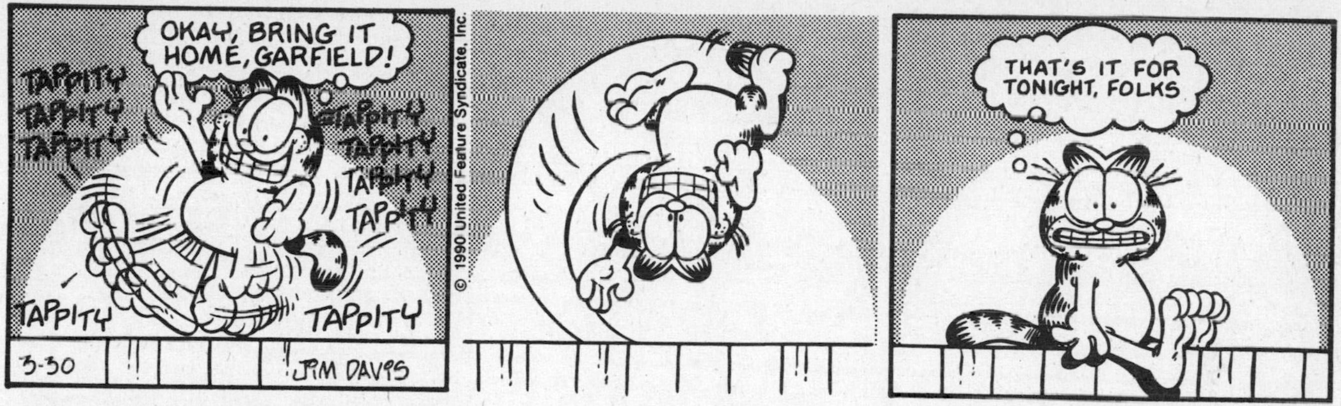
OKAY, BRING IT HOME, GARFIELD!
TAPPITY TAPPITY TAPPITY
TAPPITY TAPPITY TAPPITY TAPPITY
TAPPITY
TAPPITY
3-30
JIM DAVIS
© 1990 United Feature Syndicate, Inc.
THAT'S IT FOR TONIGHT, FOLKS

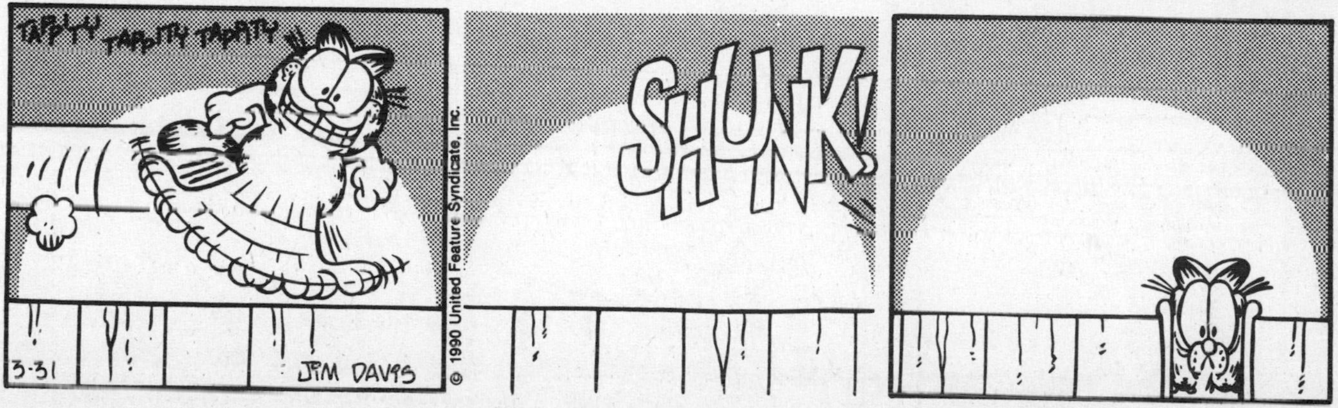
TAPPITY TAPPITY TAPPITY
3-31
JIM DAVIS
© 1990 United Feature Syndicate, Inc.
SHUNK!

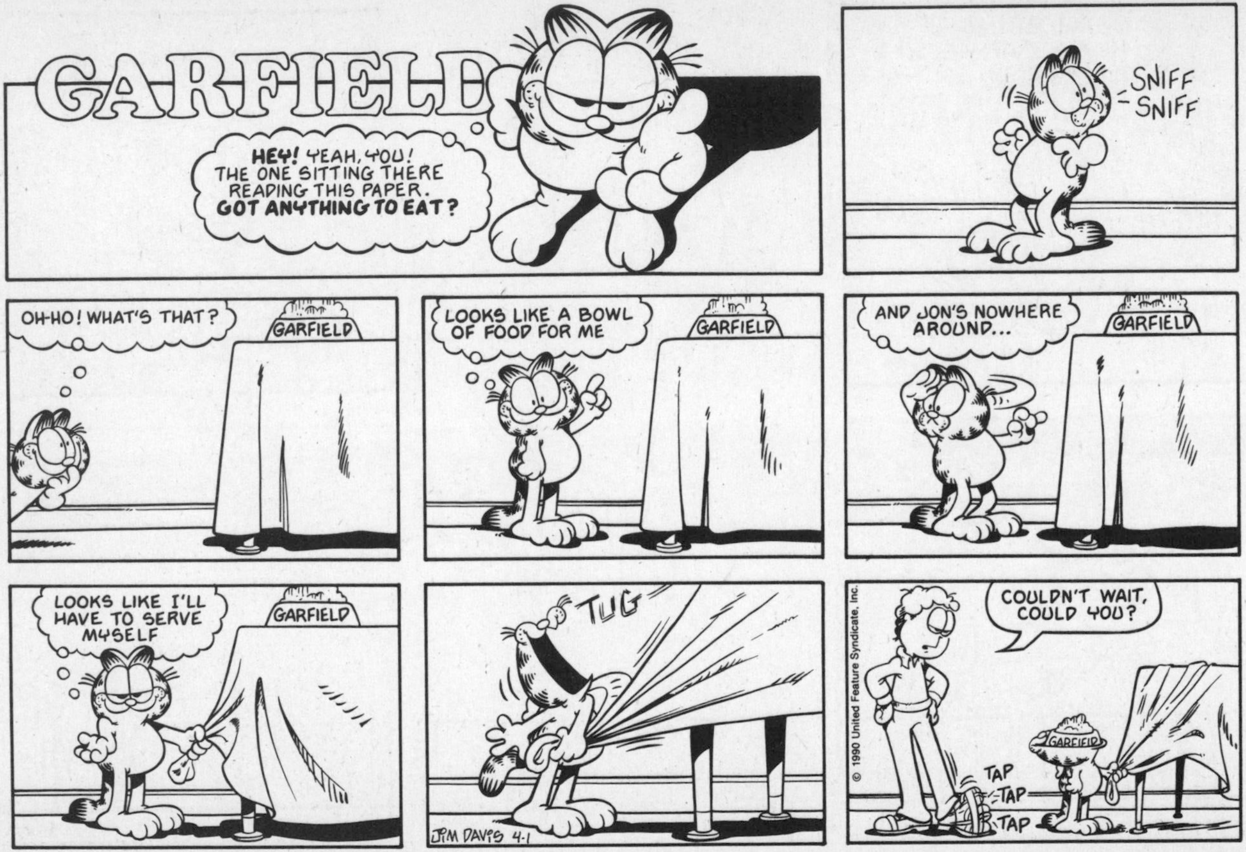
GARFIELD
HEY! YEAH, YOU! THE ONE SITTING THERE READING THIS PAPER. GOT ANYTHING TO EAT?
SNIFF SNIFF
OH-HO! WHAT'S THAT?
GARFIELD
LOOKS LIKE A BOWL OF FOOD FOR ME
GARFIELD
AND JON'S NOWHERE AROUND...
GARFIELD
LOOKS LIKE I'LL HAVE TO SERVE MYSELF
GARFIELD
TUG
JIM DAVIS 4-1
© 1990 United Feature Syndicate, Inc.
COULDN'T WAIT, COULD YOU?
TAP TAP TAP
GARFIELD

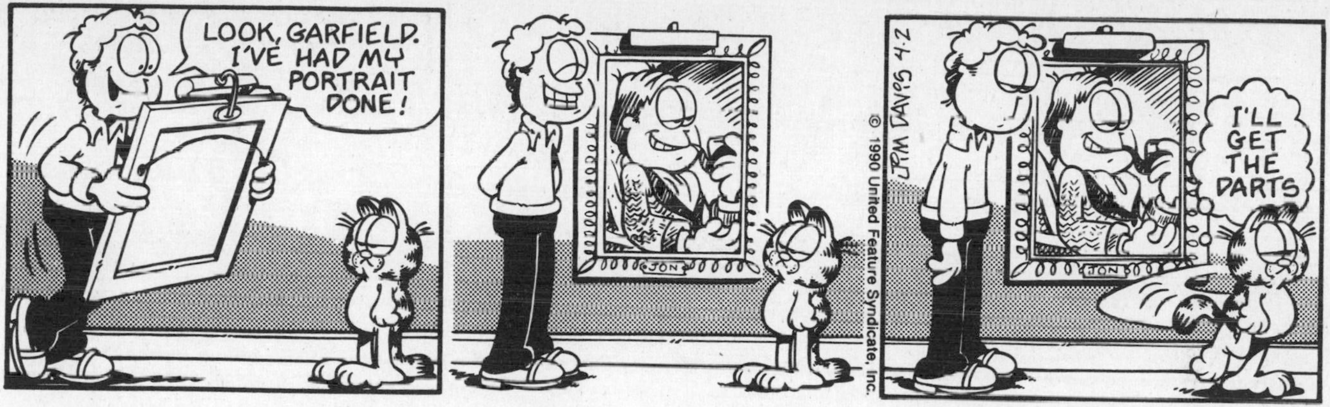
LOOK, GARFIELD. I'VE HAD MY PORTRAIT DONE!
JON
JON
JIM DAVIS 4-2
© 1990 United Feature Syndicate, Inc.
I'LL GET THE DARTS

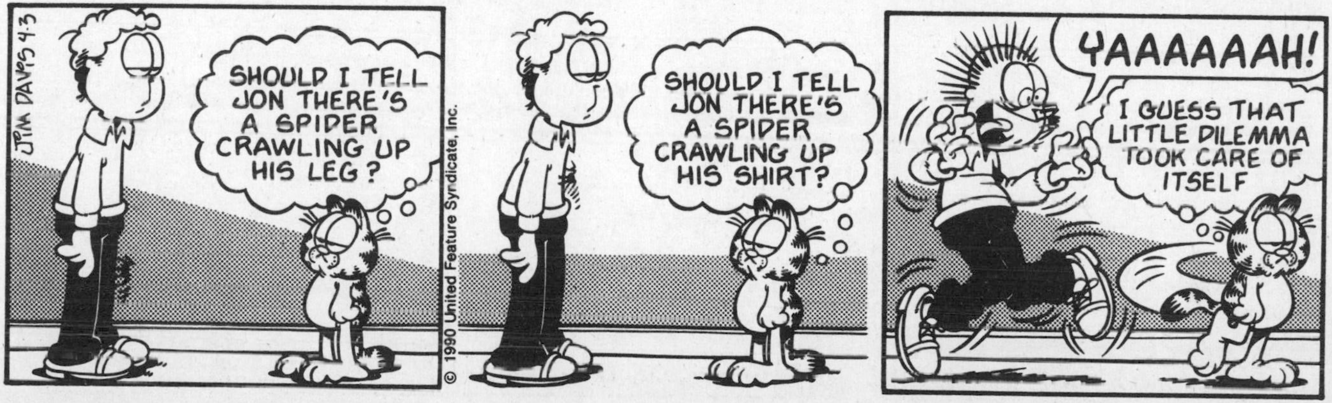
JIM DAVIS 4-3
SHOULD I TELL JON THERE'S A SPIDER CRAWLING UP HIS LEG?
© 1990 United Feature Syndicate, Inc.
SHOULD I TELL JON THERE'S A SPIDER CRAWLING UP HIS SHIRT?
YAAAAAAH!
I GUESS THAT LITTLE DILEMMA TOOK CARE OF ITSELF

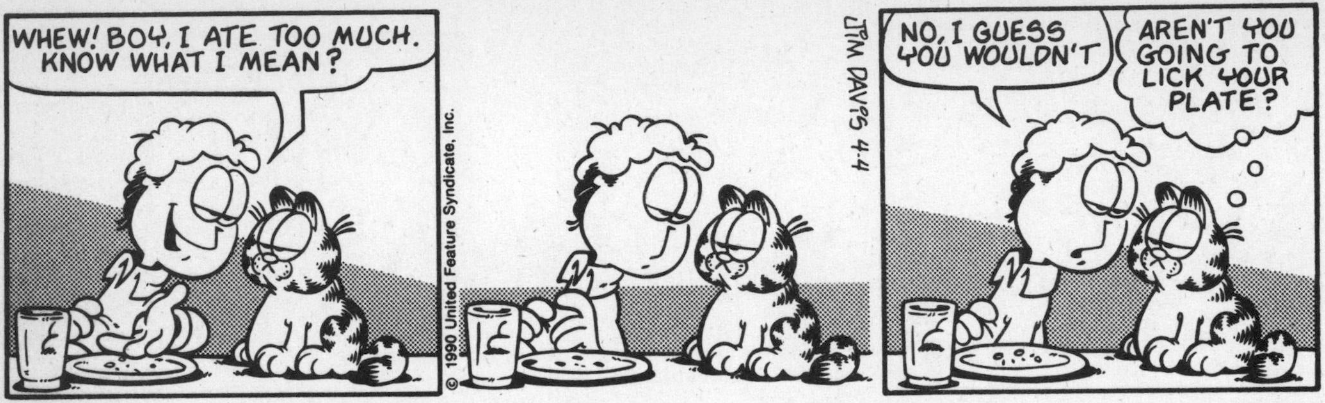
WHEW! BOY, I ATE TOO MUCH. KNOW WHAT I MEAN?
© 1990 United Feature Syndicate, Inc.
JIM DAVIS 4-4
NO, I GUESS YOU WOULDN'T
AREN'T YOU GOING TO LICK YOUR PLATE?

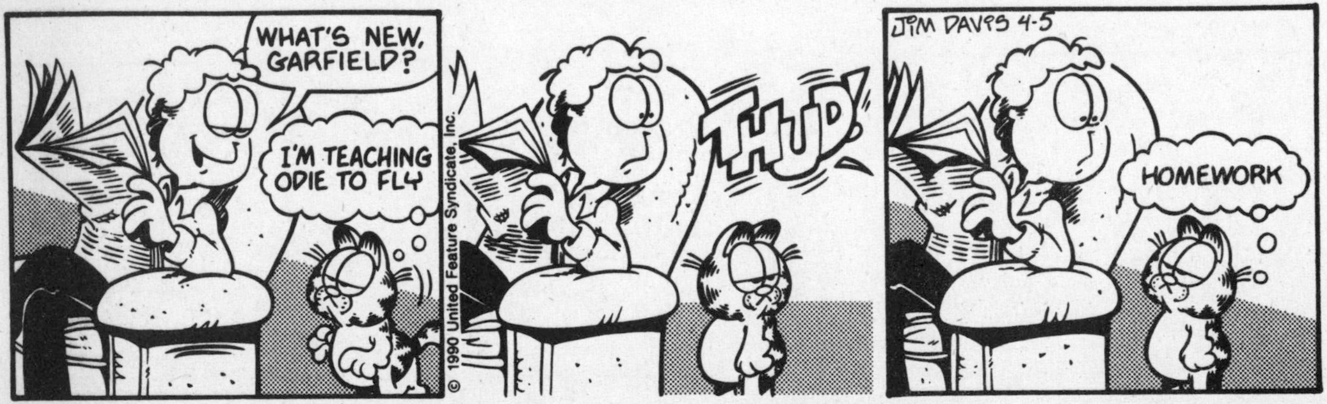
WHAT'S NEW, GARFIELD?
I'M TEACHING ODIE TO FLY
© 1990 United Feature Syndicate, Inc.
THUD!
JIM DAVIS 4-5
HOMEWORK

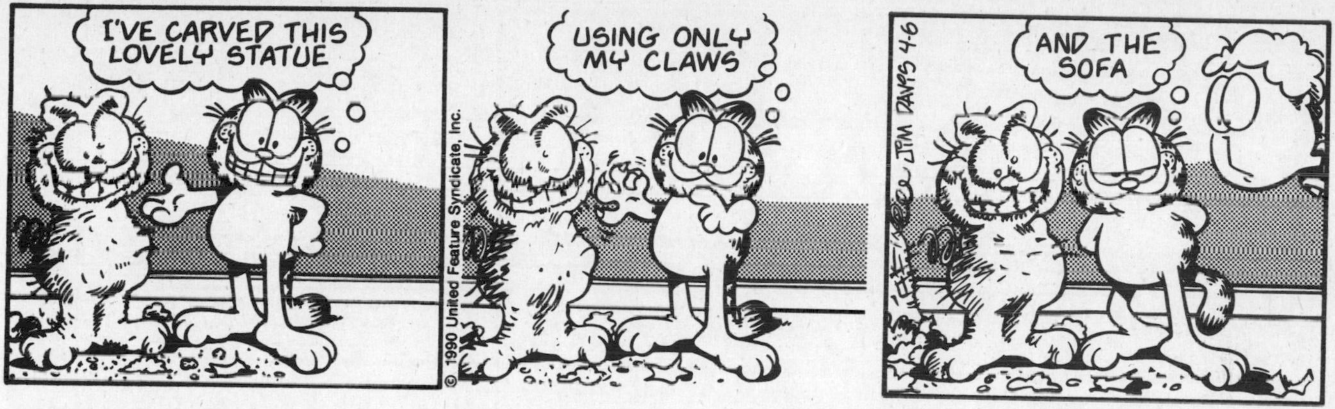
I'VE CARVED THIS LOVELY STATUE
USING ONLY MY CLAWS
© 1990 United Feature Syndicate, Inc.
AND THE SOFA
JIM DAVIS 4-6

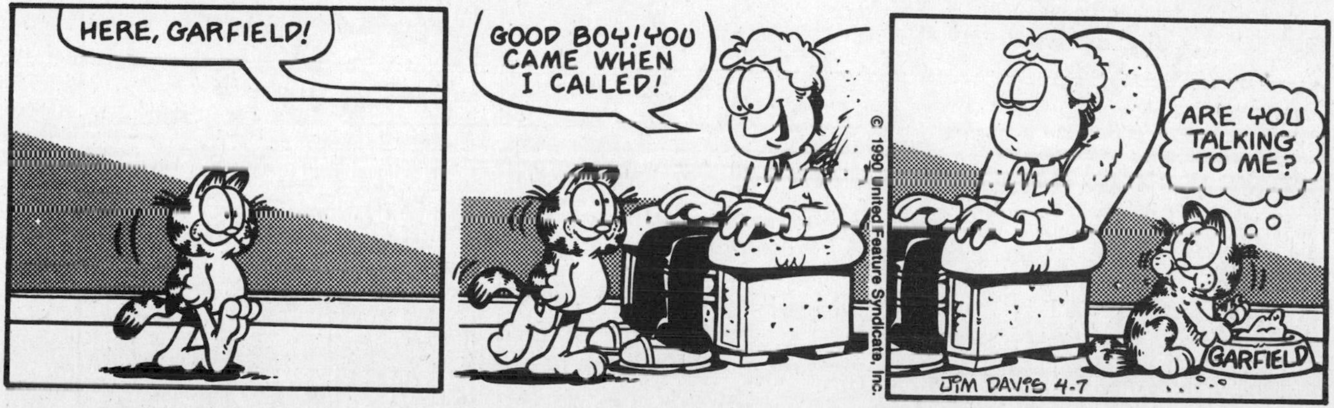
HERE, GARFIELD!
GOOD BOY! YOU CAME WHEN I CALLED!
© 1990 United Feature Syndicate, Inc.
ARE YOU TALKING TO ME?
GARFIELD
JIM DAVIS 4-7

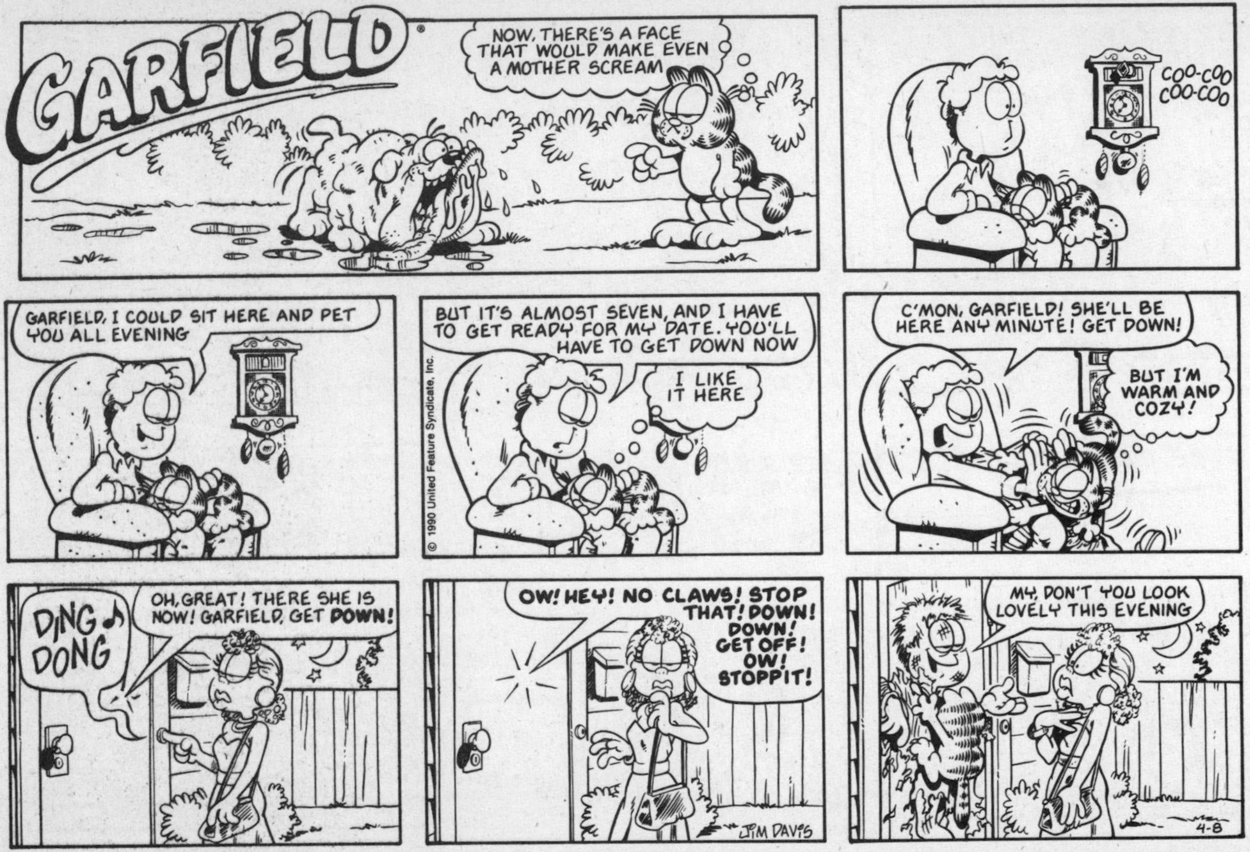
GARFIELD®
NOW, THERE'S A FACE THAT WOULD MAKE EVEN A MOTHER SCREAM
COO-COO COO-COO
GARFIELD, I COULD SIT HERE AND PET YOU ALL EVENING
BUT IT'S ALMOST SEVEN, AND I HAVE TO GET READY FOR MY DATE. YOU'LL HAVE TO GET DOWN NOW
I LIKE IT HERE
© 1990 United Feature Syndicate, Inc.
C'MON, GARFIELD! SHE'LL BE HERE ANY MINUTE! GET DOWN!
BUT I'M WARM AND COZY!
DING DONG
OH, GREAT! THERE SHE IS NOW! GARFIELD, GET DOWN!
OW! HEY! NO CLAWS! STOP THAT! DOWN! DOWN! GET OFF! OW! STOPPIT!
JIM DAVIS
MY, DON'T YOU LOOK LOVELY THIS EVENING
4-8

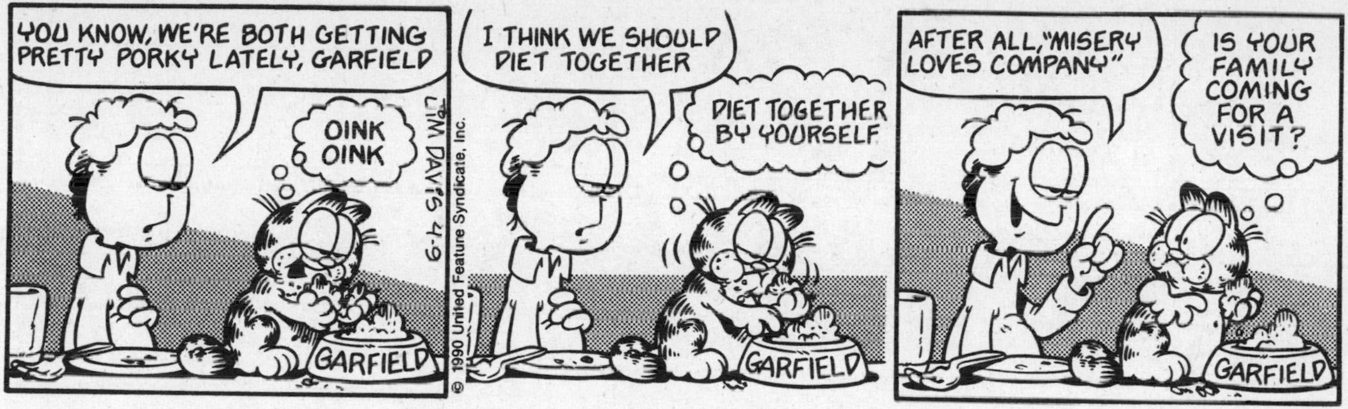
YOU KNOW, WE'RE BOTH GETTING PRETTY PORKY LATELY, GARFIELD
OINK OINK
JIM DAVIS 4-9
© 1990 United Feature Syndicate, Inc.
I THINK WE SHOULD DIET TOGETHER
DIET TOGETHER BY YOURSELF
AFTER ALL, "MISERY LOVES COMPANY"
IS YOUR FAMILY COMING FOR A VISIT?
GARFIELD

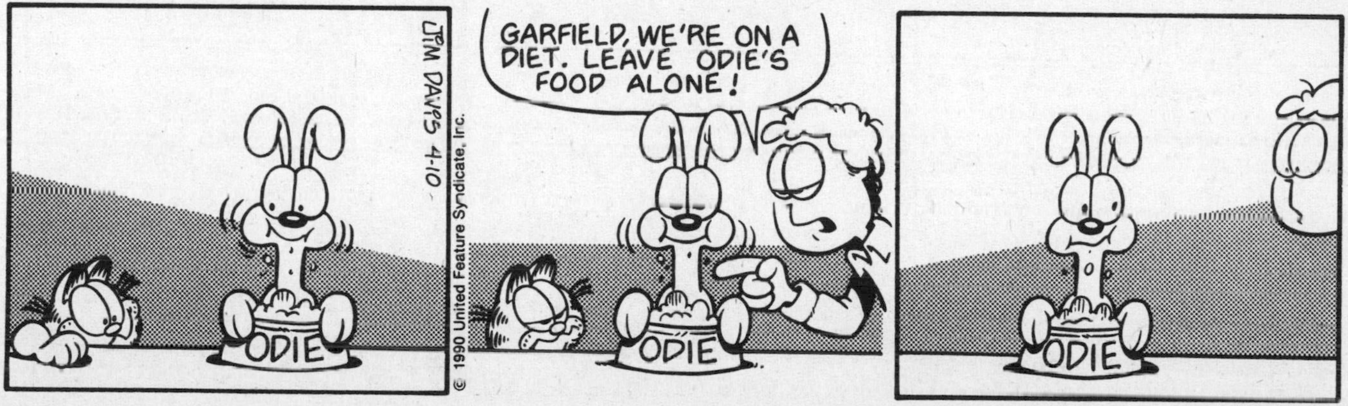
JIM DAVIS 4-10
© 1990 United Feature Syndicate, Inc.
GARFIELD, WE'RE ON A DIET. LEAVE ODIE'S FOOD ALONE!
ODIE

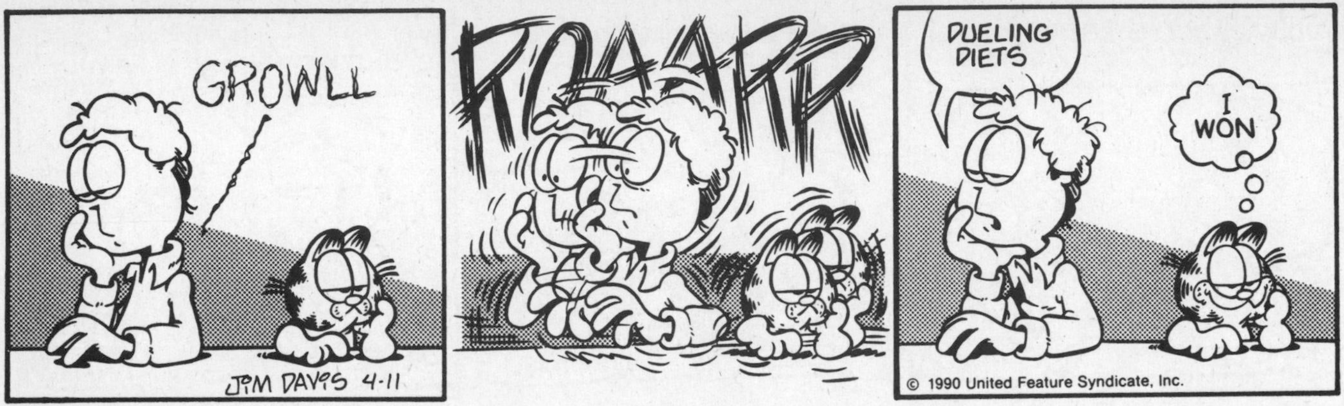
GROWLL
JIM DAVIS 4-11
ROAARR
DUELING DIETS
I WON
© 1990 United Feature Syndicate, Inc.

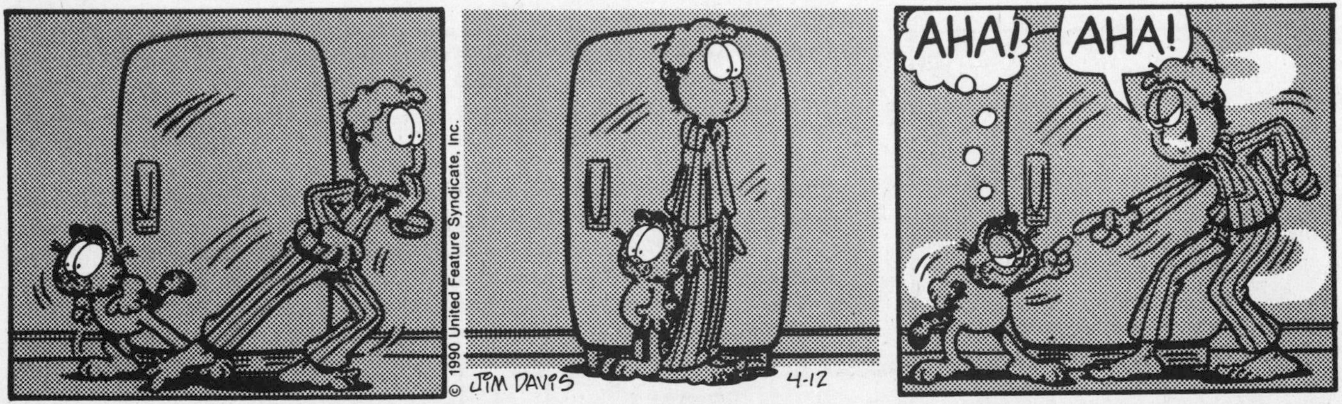
© 1990 United Feature Syndicate, Inc.
JIM DAVIS
4-12
AHA!
AHA!

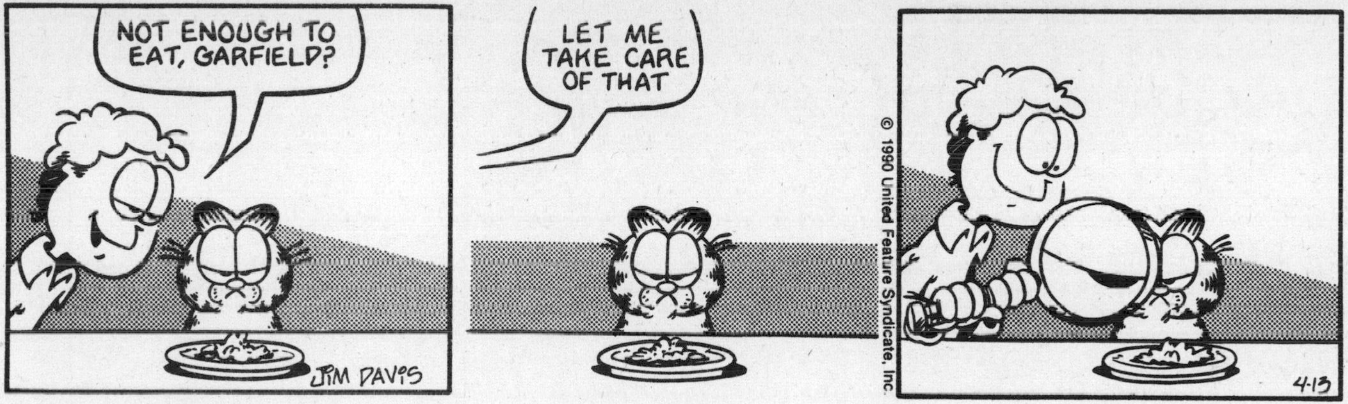
NOT ENOUGH TO EAT, GARFIELD?
JIM DAVIS
LET ME TAKE CARE OF THAT
© 1990 United Feature Syndicate, Inc.
4-13

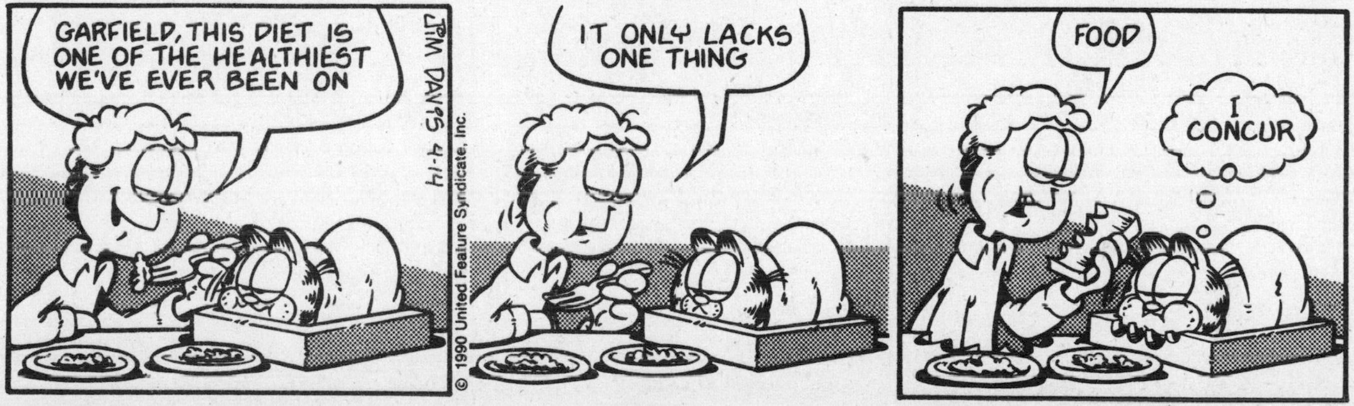
GARFIELD, THIS DIET IS ONE OF THE HEALTHIEST WE'VE EVER BEEN ON
JIM DAVIS 4-14
© 1990 United Feature Syndicate, Inc.
IT ONLY LACKS ONE THING
FOOD
I CONCUR

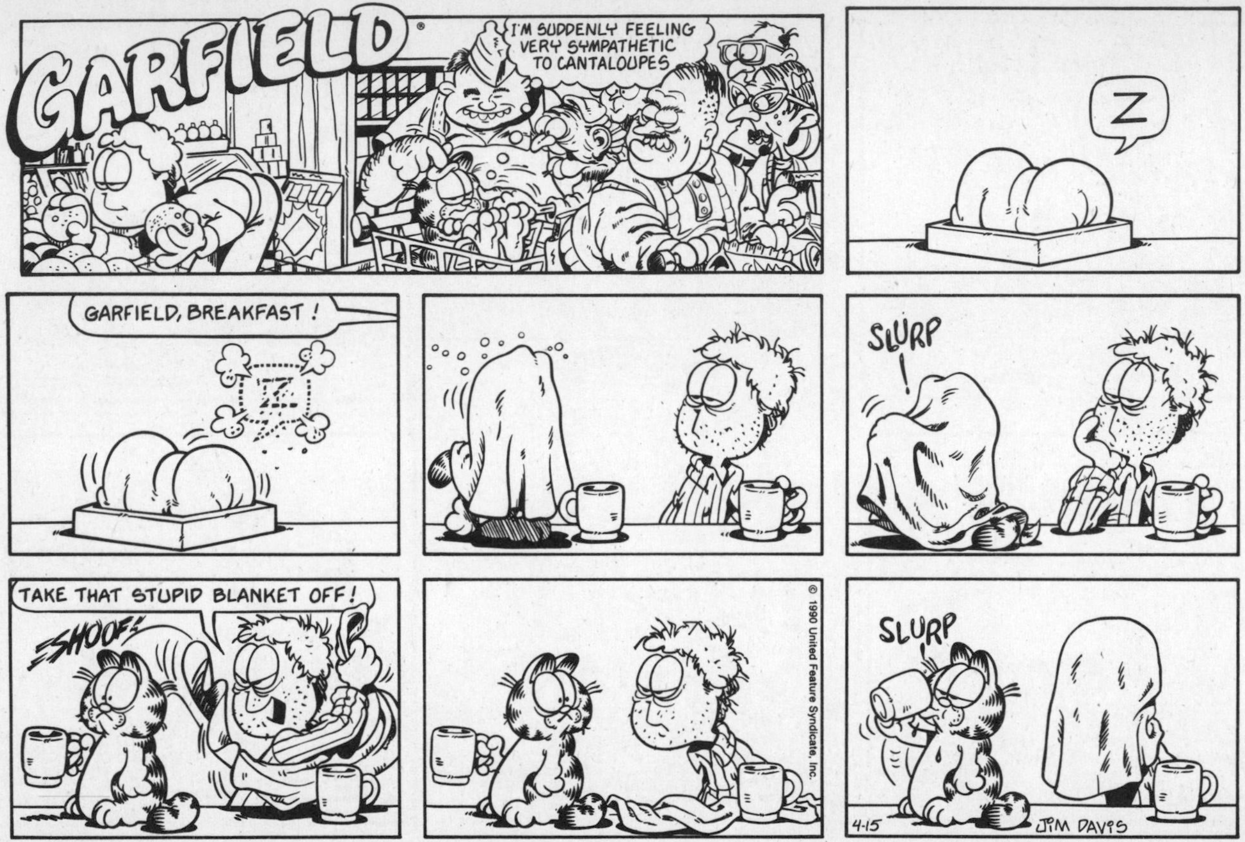
GARFIELD
I'M SUDDENLY FEELING VERY SYMPATHETIC TO CANTALOUPES
Z
GARFIELD, BREAKFAST!
SLURP
TAKE THAT STUPID BLANKET OFF!
SHOOF!
SLURP
© 1990 United Feature Syndicate, Inc.
4-15
JIM DAVIS

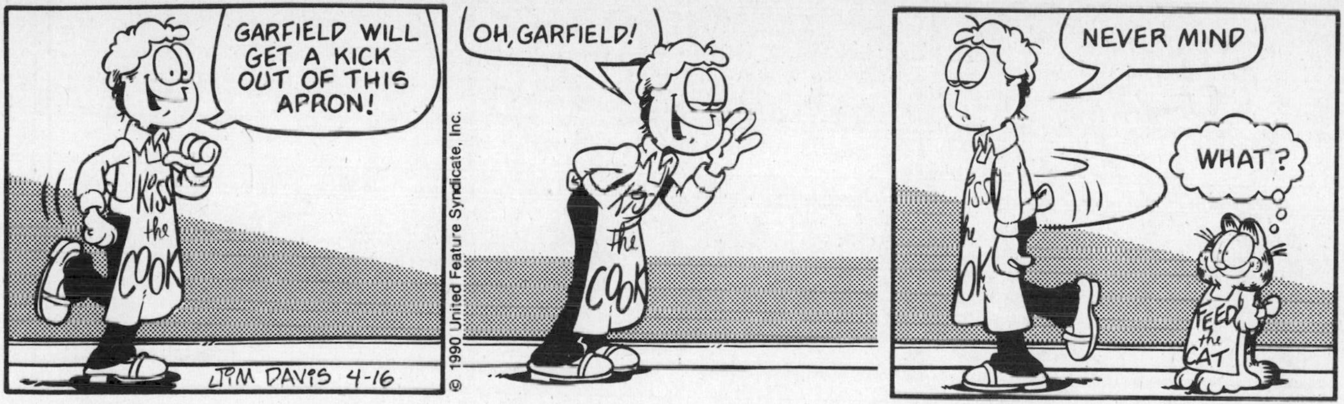
GARFIELD WILL GET A KICK OUT OF THIS APRON!
KISS the COOK
JIM DAVIS 4-16
© 1990 United Feature Syndicate, Inc.
OH, GARFIELD!
NEVER MIND
WHAT?
FEED the CAT

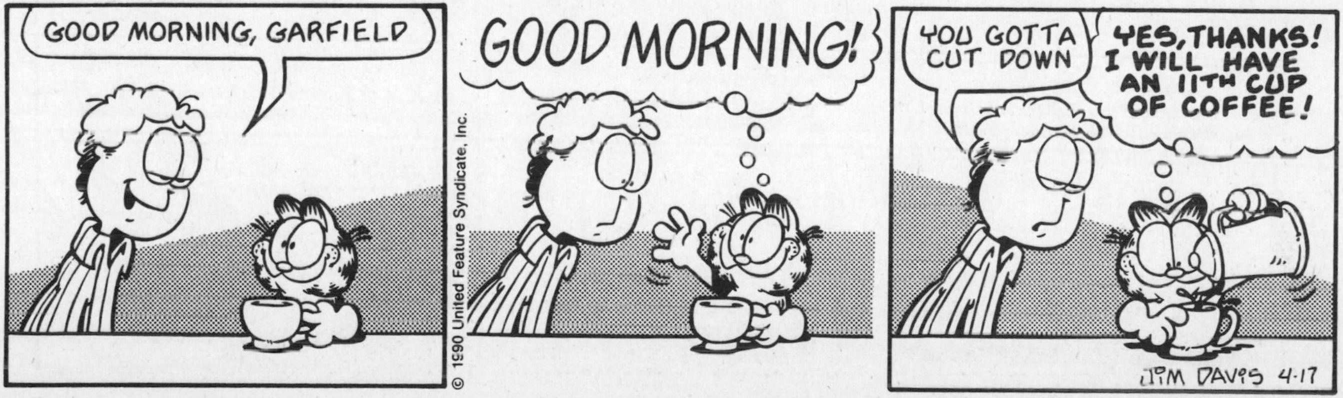
GOOD MORNING, GARFIELD
© 1990 United Feature Syndicate, Inc.
GOOD MORNING!
YOU GOTTA CUT DOWN
YES, THANKS! I WILL HAVE AN 11TH CUP OF COFFEE!
JIM DAVIS 4-17

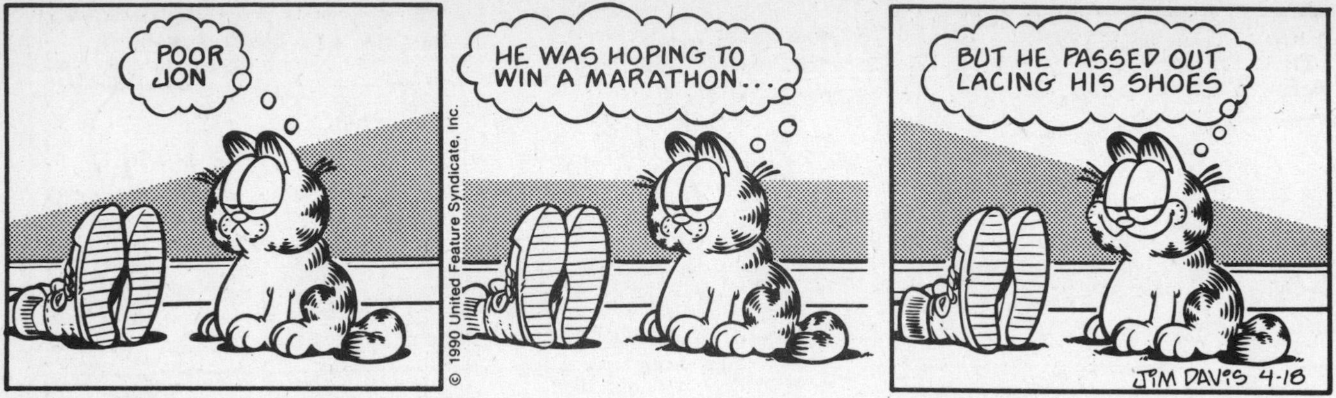
POOR JON
HE WAS HOPING TO WIN A MARATHON...
BUT HE PASSED OUT LACING HIS SHOES
JIM DAVIS 4-18
© 1990 United Feature Syndicate, Inc.

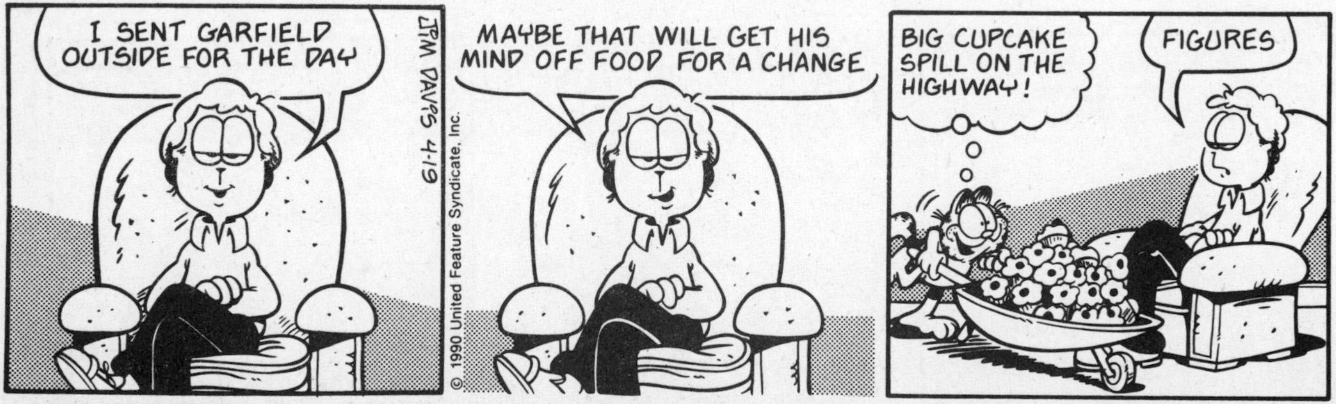
I SENT GARFIELD OUTSIDE FOR THE DAY
JIM DAVIS 4-19
© 1990 United Feature Syndicate, Inc.
MAYBE THAT WILL GET HIS MIND OFF FOOD FOR A CHANGE
BIG CUPCAKE SPILL ON THE HIGHWAY!
FIGURES

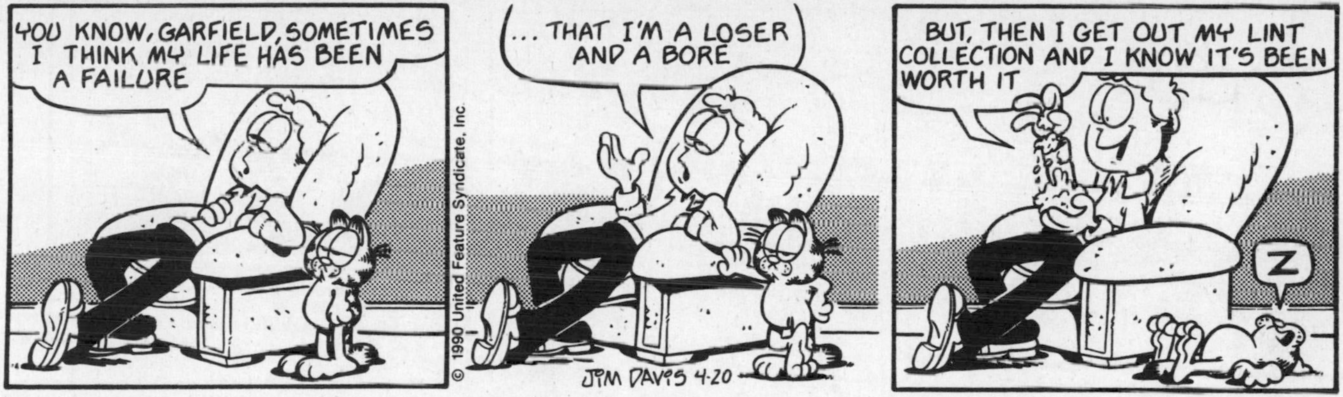
YOU KNOW, GARFIELD, SOMETIMES I THINK MY LIFE HAS BEEN A FAILURE
... THAT I'M A LOSER AND A BORE
BUT, THEN I GET OUT MY LINT COLLECTION AND I KNOW IT'S BEEN WORTH IT
Z
JIM DAVIS 4-20
© 1990 United Feature Syndicate, Inc.

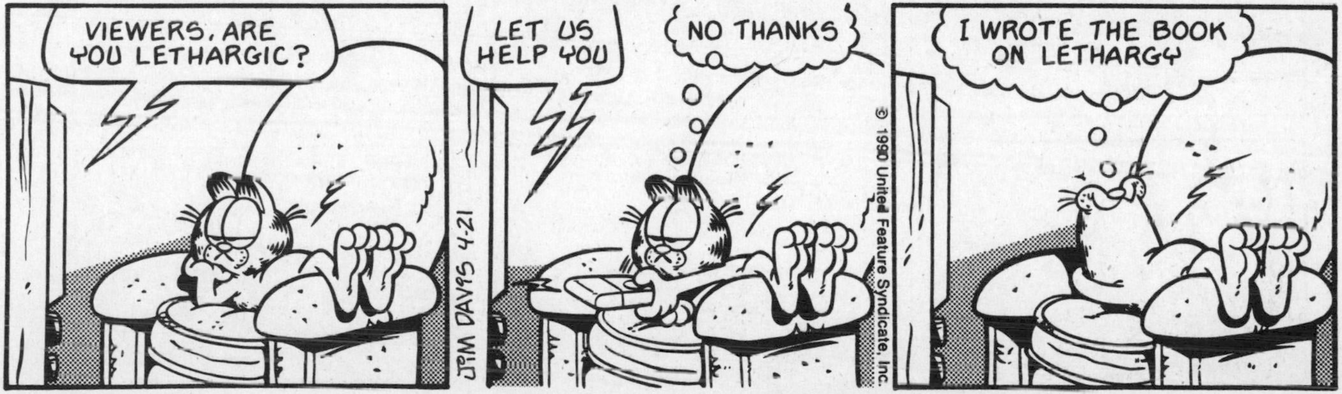
VIEWERS, ARE YOU LETHARGIC?
LET US HELP YOU
NO THANKS
I WROTE THE BOOK ON LETHARGY
JIM DAVIS 4-21
© 1990 United Feature Syndicate, Inc.

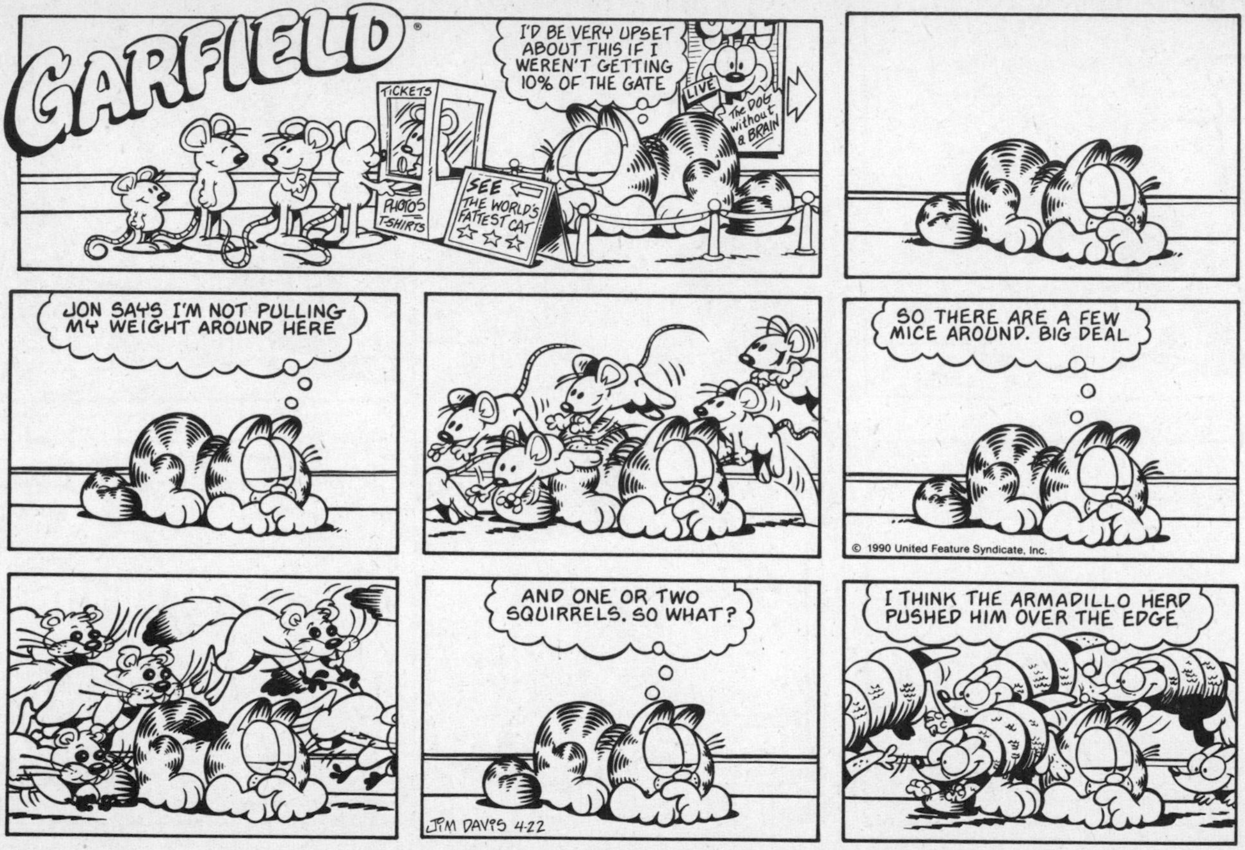
GARFIELD
TICKETS
PHOTOS
T-SHIRTS
SEE THE WORLD'S FATTEST CAT
I'D BE VERY UPSET ABOUT THIS IF I WEREN'T GETTING 10% OF THE GATE
LIVE
The DOG without a BRAIN
JON SAYS I'M NOT PULLING MY WEIGHT AROUND HERE
SO THERE ARE A FEW MICE AROUND. BIG DEAL
© 1990 United Feature Syndicate, Inc.
AND ONE OR TWO SQUIRRELS. SO WHAT?
JIM DAVIS 4-22
I THINK THE ARMADILLO HERD PUSHED HIM OVER THE EDGE

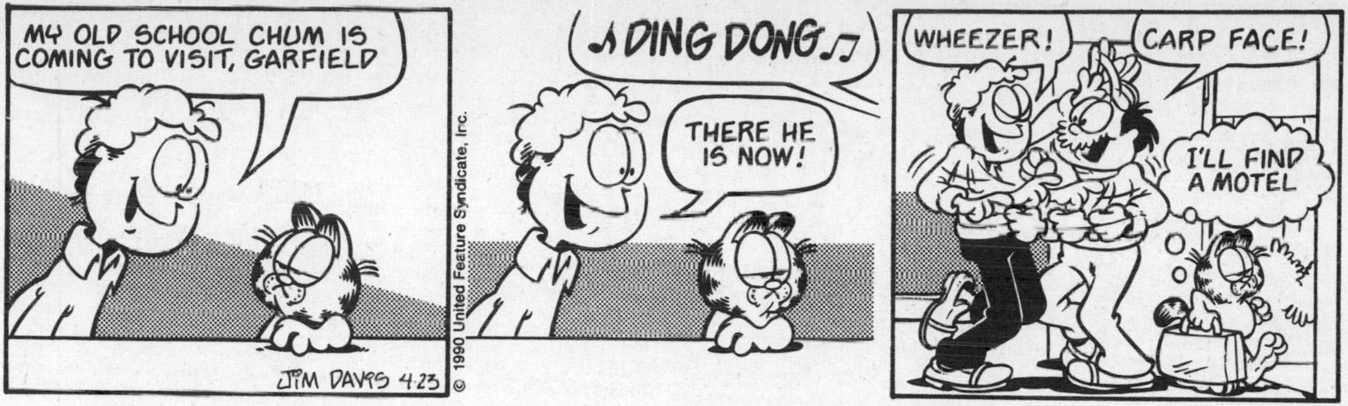

MY OLD SCHOOL CHUM IS COMING TO VISIT, GARFIELD
JIM DAVIS 4·23
© 1990 United Feature Syndicate, Inc.
DING DONG
THERE HE IS NOW!
WHEEZER!
CARP FACE!
I'LL FIND A MOTEL

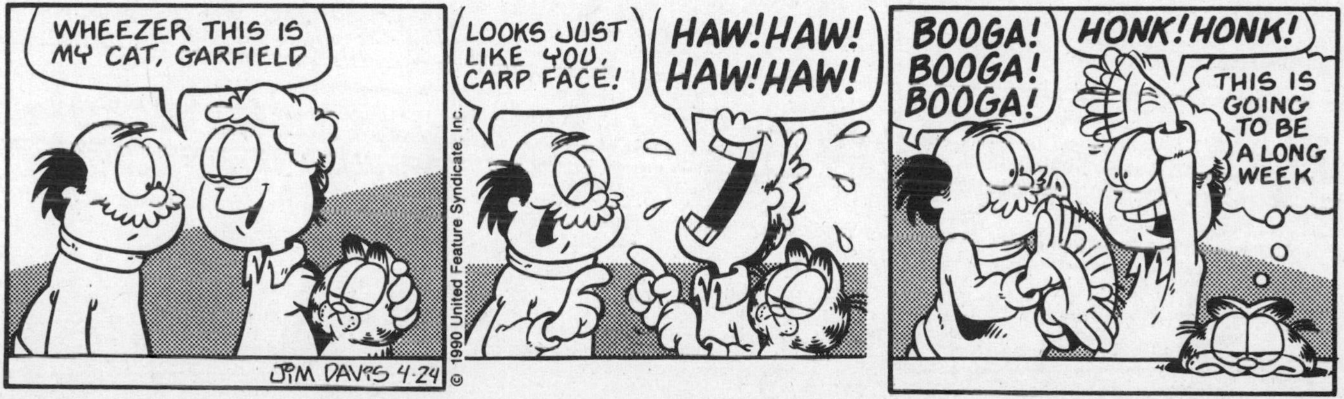

WHEEZER THIS IS MY CAT, GARFIELD
JIM DAVIS 4·24
© 1990 United Feature Syndicate, Inc.
LOOKS JUST LIKE YOU, CARP FACE!
HAW! HAW! HAW! HAW!
BOOGA! BOOGA! BOOGA!
HONK! HONK!
THIS IS GOING TO BE A LONG WEEK

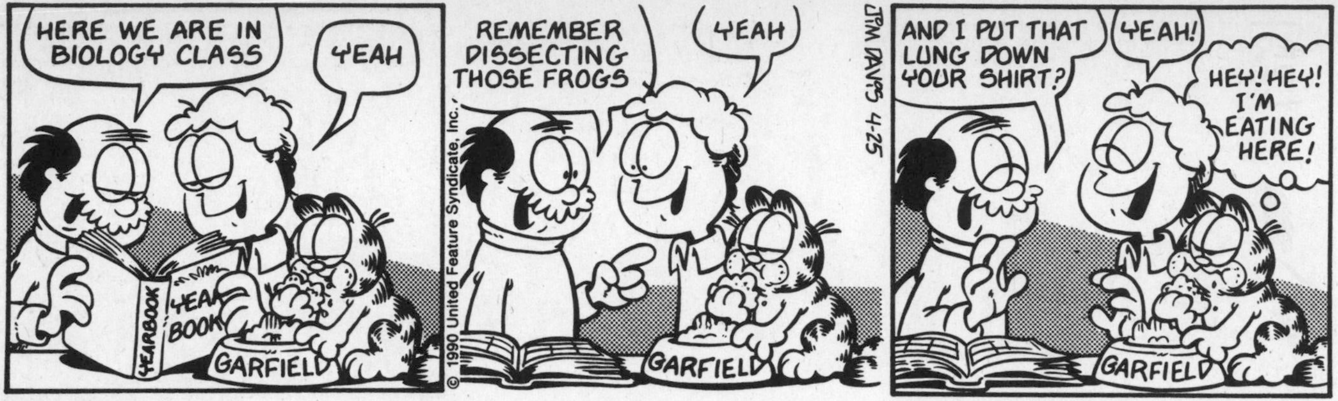
HERE WE ARE IN BIOLOGY CLASS
YEAH
YEARBOOK
YEAR BOOK
GARFIELD
© 1990 United Feature Syndicate, Inc.
REMEMBER DISSECTING THOSE FROGS
YEAH
GARFIELD
JIM DAVIS 4-25
AND I PUT THAT LUNG DOWN YOUR SHIRT?
YEAH!
HEY! HEY! I'M EATING HERE!
GARFIELD

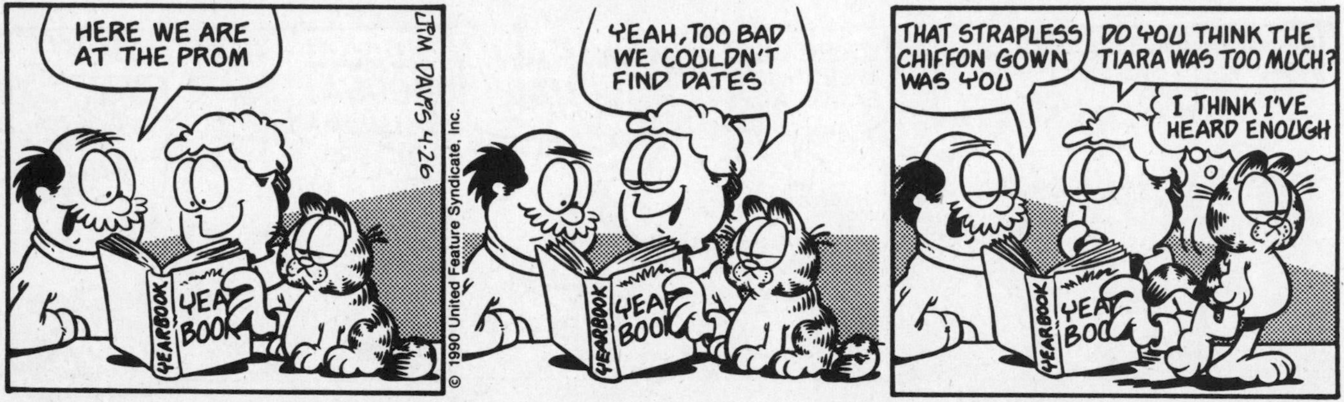
HERE WE ARE AT THE PROM
YEARBOOK
YEAR BOOK
JIM DAVIS 4-26
© 1990 United Feature Syndicate, Inc.
YEAH, TOO BAD WE COULDN'T FIND DATES
YEARBOOK
THAT STRAPLESS CHIFFON GOWN WAS YOU
DO YOU THINK THE TIARA WAS TOO MUCH?
I THINK I'VE HEARD ENOUGH
YEARBOOK

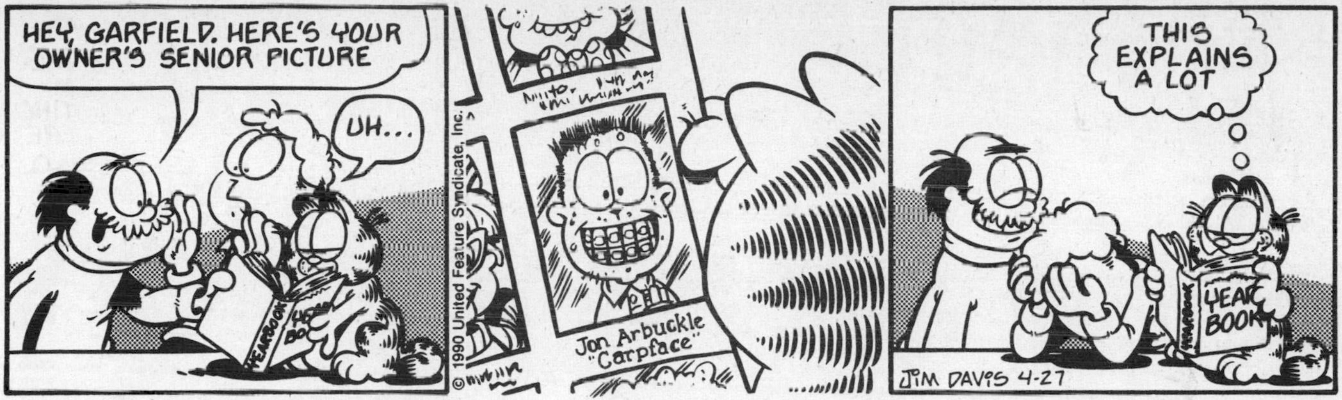
HEY, GARFIELD. HERE'S YOUR OWNER'S SENIOR PICTURE
UH...
YEARBOOK
Jon Arbuckle "Carpface"
THIS EXPLAINS A LOT
YEAR BOOK
© 1990 United Feature Syndicate, Inc.
JIM DAVIS 4-27

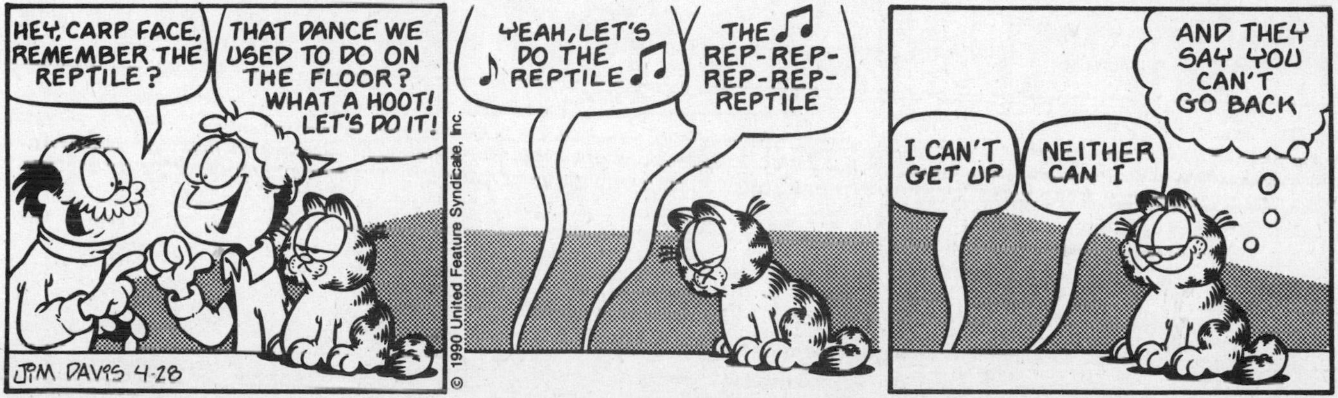
HEY, CARP FACE, REMEMBER THE REPTILE?
THAT DANCE WE USED TO DO ON THE FLOOR? WHAT A HOOT! LET'S DO IT!
YEAH, LET'S DO THE REPTILE
THE REP-REP-REP-REP-REPTILE
I CAN'T GET UP
NEITHER CAN I
AND THEY SAY YOU CAN'T GO BACK
© 1990 United Feature Syndicate, Inc.
JIM DAVIS 4-28

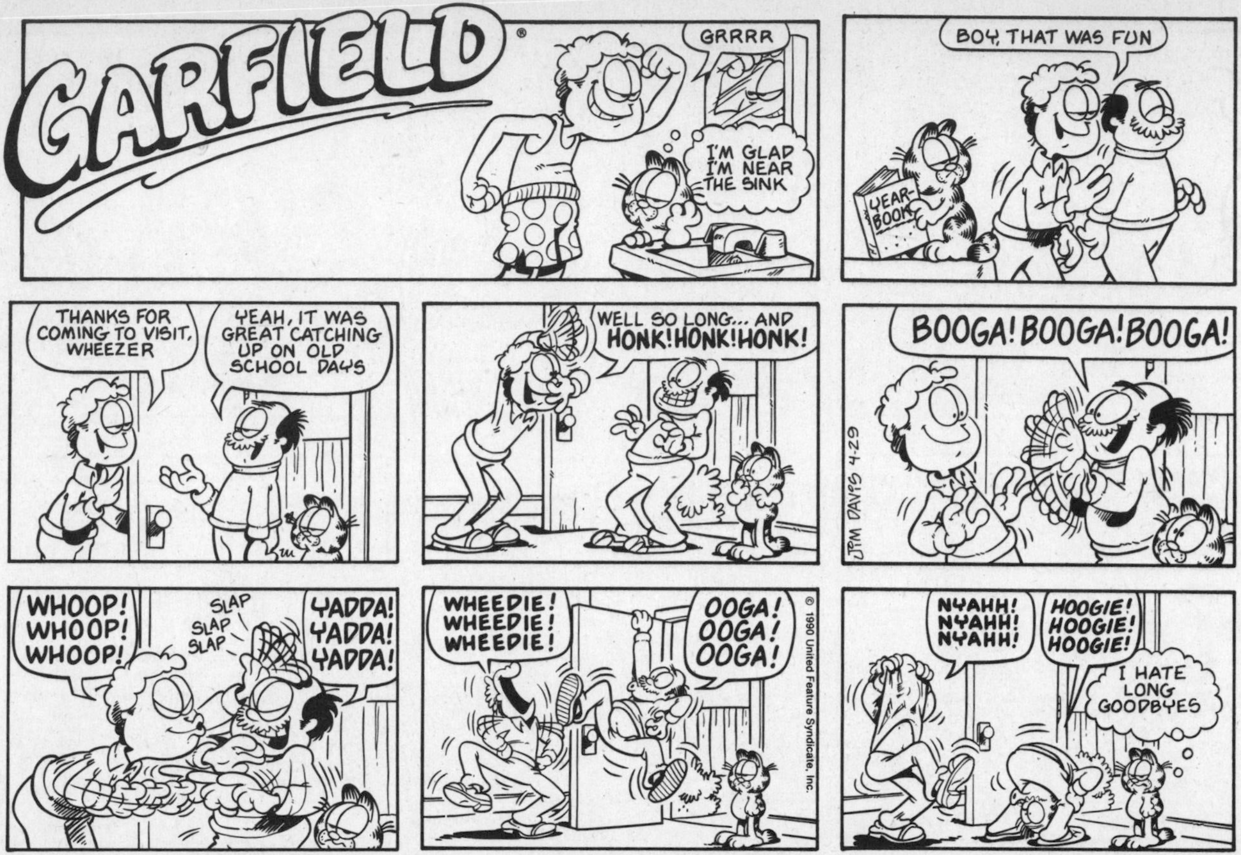
GARFIELD®
GRRRR
I'M GLAD I'M NEAR THE SINK
BOY, THAT WAS FUN
YEAR-BOOK
THANKS FOR COMING TO VISIT, WHEEZER
YEAH, IT WAS GREAT CATCHING UP ON OLD SCHOOL DAYS
WELL SO LONG... AND HONK! HONK! HONK!
BOOGA! BOOGA! BOOGA!
JIM DAVIS 4-29
WHOOP! WHOOP! WHOOP!
SLAP SLAP SLAP
YADDA! YADDA! YADDA!
WHEEDIE! WHEEDIE! WHEEDIE!
OOGA! OOGA! OOGA!
© 1990 United Feature Syndicate, Inc.
NYAHH! NYAHH! NYAHH!
HOOGIE! HOOGIE! HOOGIE!
I HATE LONG GOODBYES

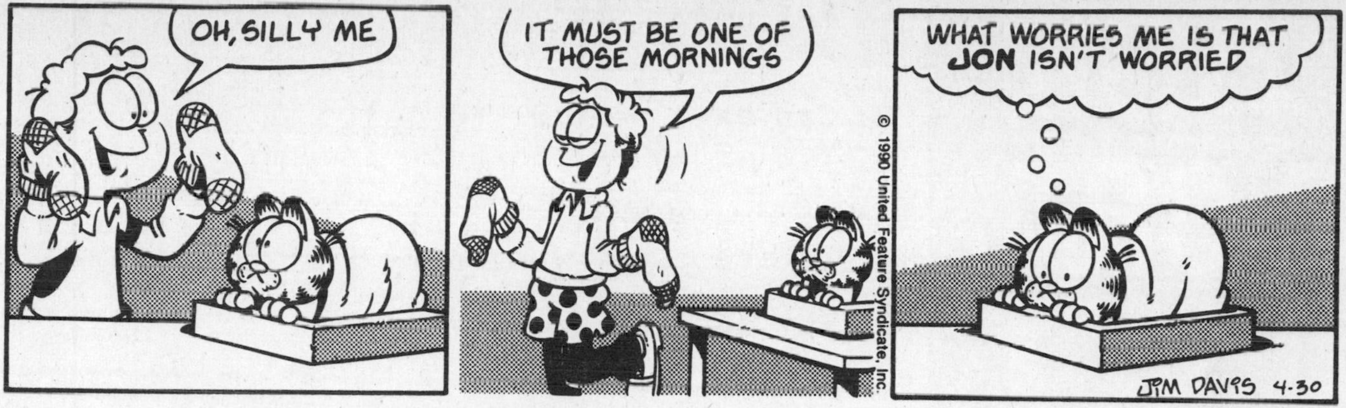
OH, SILLY ME
IT MUST BE ONE OF THOSE MORNINGS
WHAT WORRIES ME IS THAT **JON** ISN'T WORRIED
JIM DAVIS 4-30
© 1990 United Feature Syndicate, Inc.

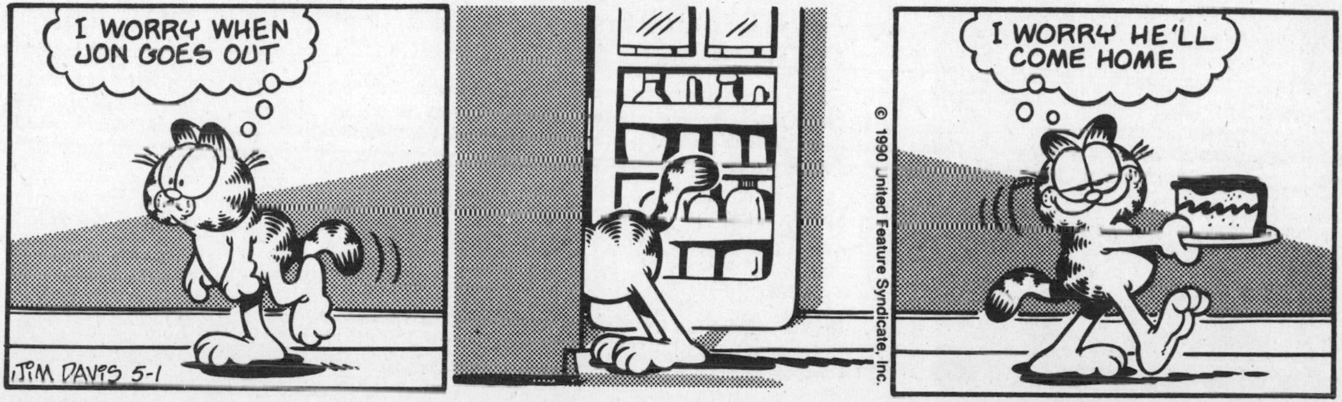
I WORRY WHEN JON GOES OUT
I WORRY HE'LL COME HOME
JIM DAVIS 5-1
© 1990 United Feature Syndicate, Inc.

Ask a cat.

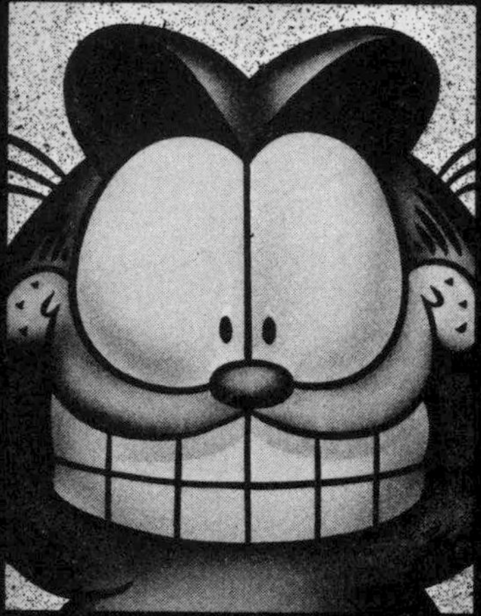

Q: Why does a cat always land on its feet?
A: Because it beats landing on its face.

Q: Can cats see in the dark?
A: Yes. They see a whole lot of dark.

Q: Is there more than one way to skin a cat?
A: I have given your name to the authorities.

Q: Why do cats eat plants?
A: To get rid of that mouse aftertaste.

Q: How often should I take my cat to the vet?
A: As often as you would like to have your lips ripped off.

Q: Should I have my cat fixed?
A: Why? Is it broken?

Q: Why do cats spend so much time napping?
A: To rest up for bedtime.

Q: How much food should my cat eat?
A: How much have you got?

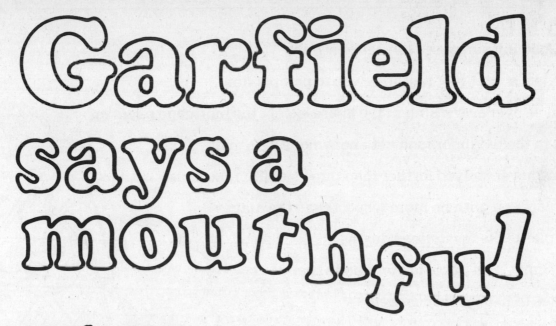

Garfield says a mouthful

BY: JIM DAVIS

Top Ten Signs That Your Cat is a "Garfield"

10. Your food bill surpasses the national debt
9. He gets a court order requiring you to pamper him
8. He takes over everything in the house except the mortgage payment
7. Dogs in the neighborhood get anonymous hate mail
6. He has never strayed farther than three feet from the house
5. He treats you with no more respect than the drapes
4. Your plants die mysterious deaths
3. He's sometimes mistaken for Rhode Island
2. He tries to have *you* declawed
1. Can't tell if he's sleeping or dead

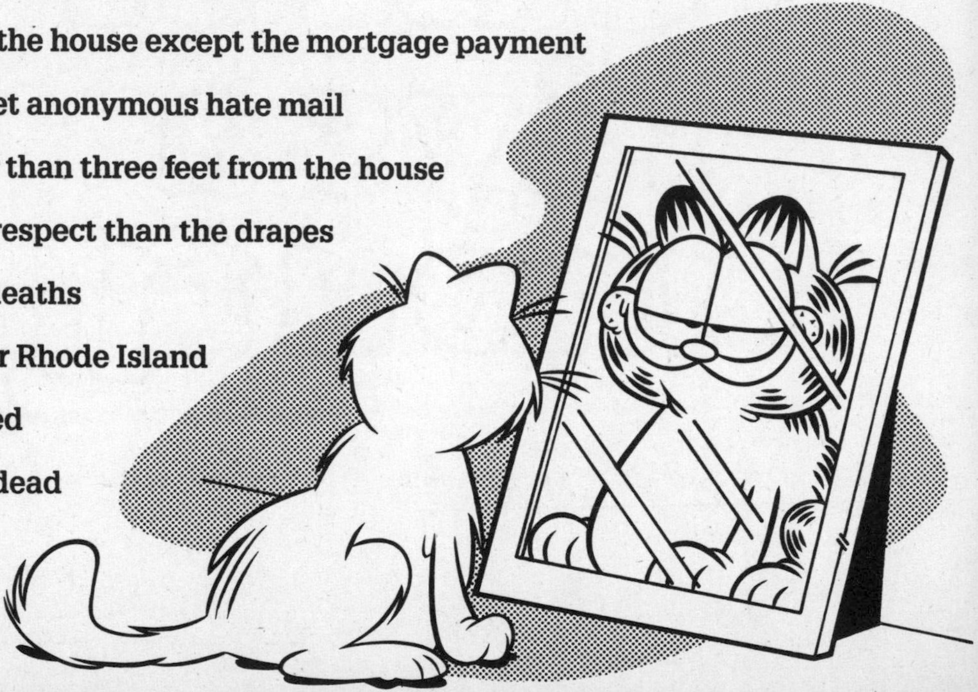

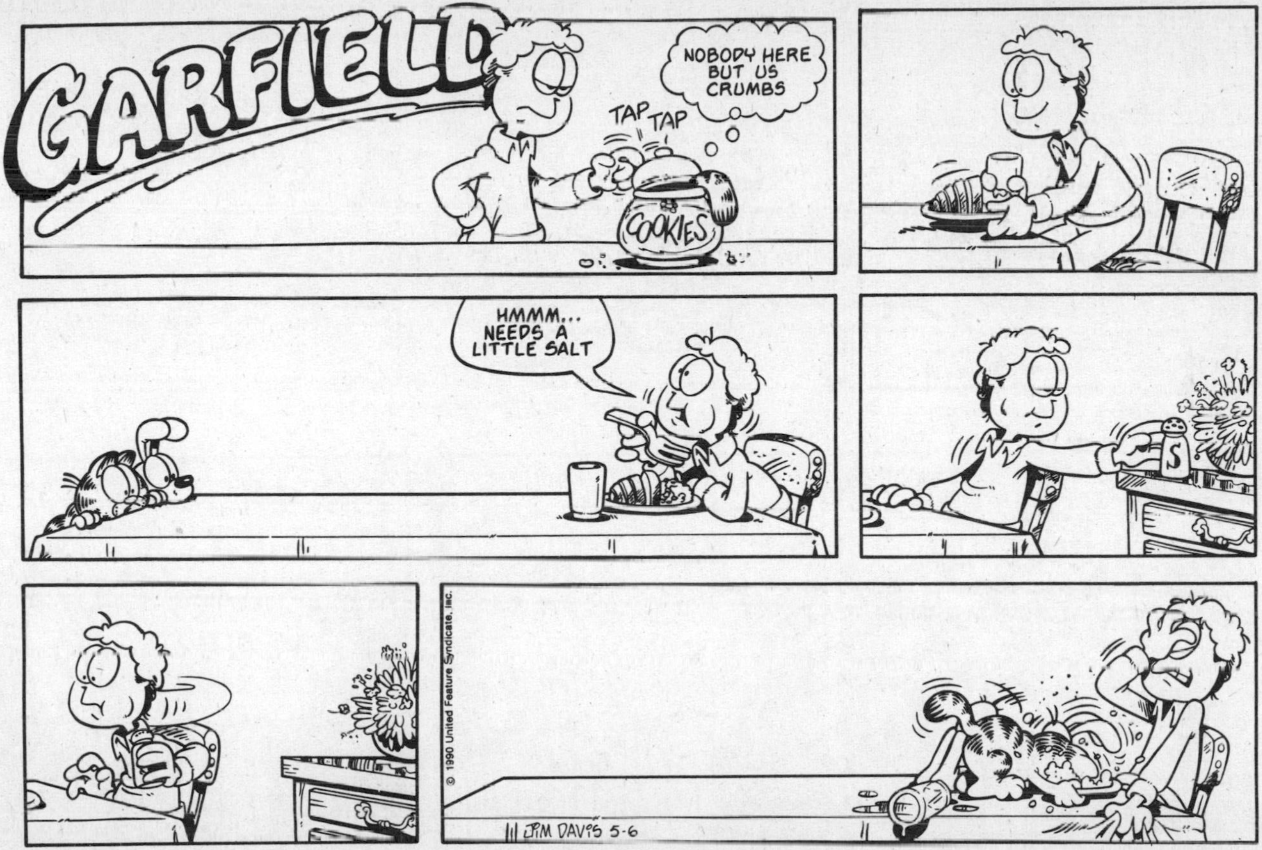
GARFIELD
NOBODY HERE BUT US CRUMBS
TAP TAP
COOKIES
HMMM... NEEDS A LITTLE SALT
S
© 1990 United Feature Syndicate, Inc.
JIM DAVIS 5-6

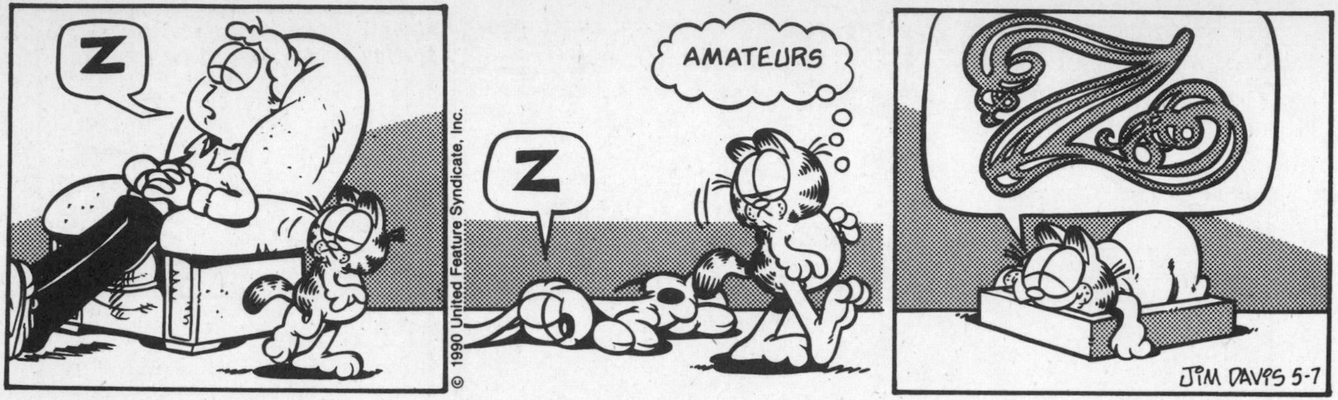
Z
Z
AMATEURS
© 1990 United Feature Syndicate, Inc.
JIM DAVIS 5-7

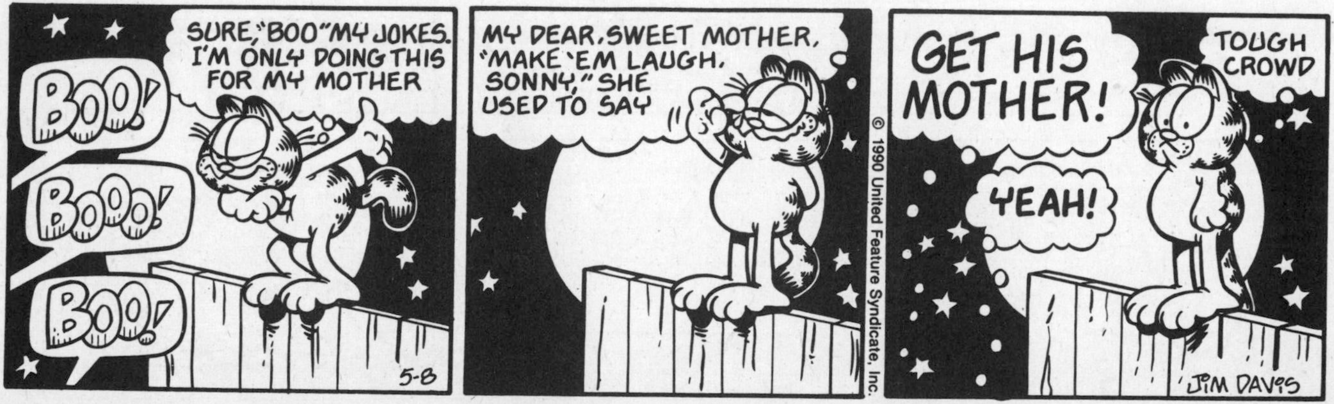
BOO!
BOOO!
BOO!
SURE, "BOO" MY JOKES. I'M ONLY DOING THIS FOR MY MOTHER
5-8
MY DEAR, SWEET MOTHER. "MAKE 'EM LAUGH, SONNY," SHE USED TO SAY
© 1990 United Feature Syndicate, Inc.
GET HIS MOTHER!
YEAH!
TOUGH CROWD
JIM DAVIS

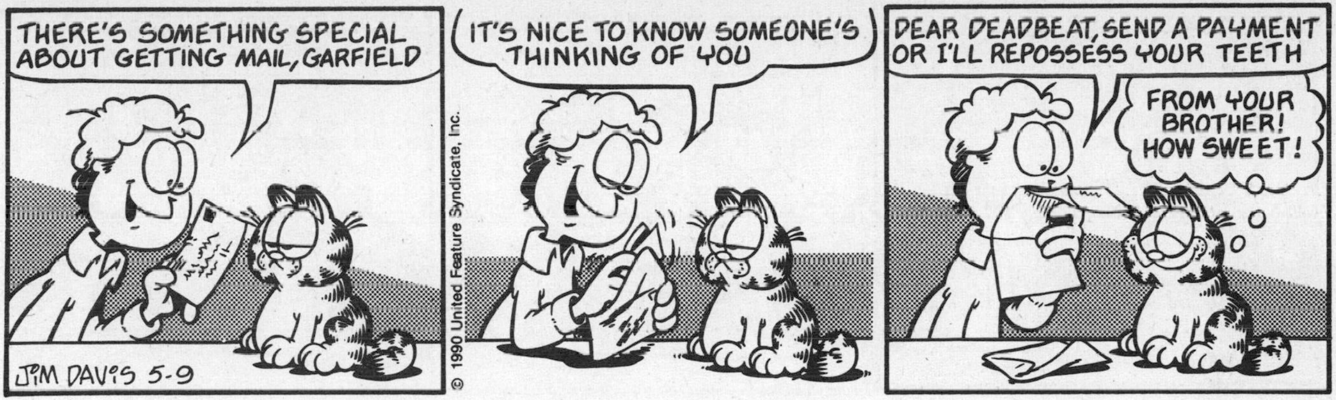
THERE'S SOMETHING SPECIAL ABOUT GETTING MAIL, GARFIELD
JIM DAVIS 5-9
© 1990 United Feature Syndicate, Inc.
IT'S NICE TO KNOW SOMEONE'S THINKING OF YOU
DEAR DEADBEAT, SEND A PAYMENT OR I'LL REPOSSESS YOUR TEETH
FROM YOUR BROTHER! HOW SWEET!

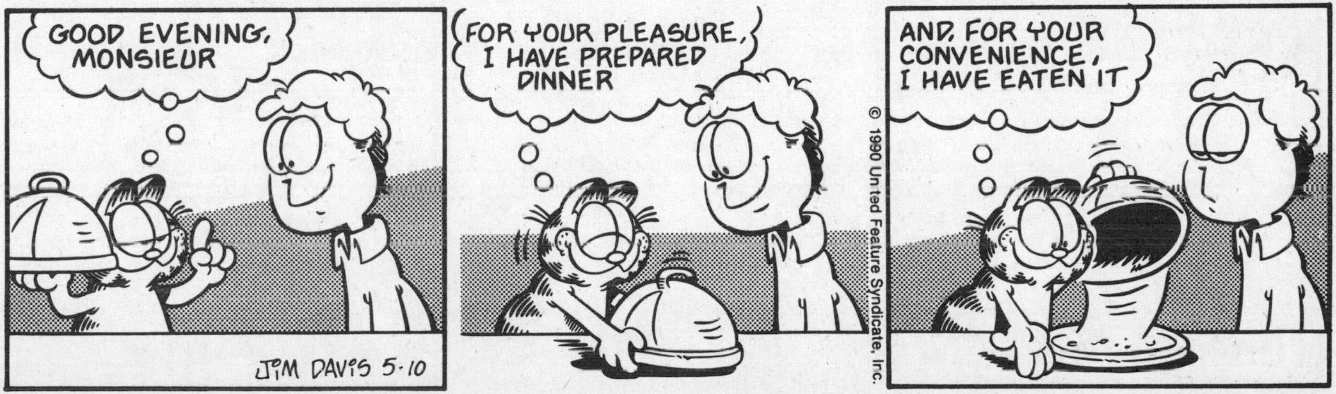
GOOD EVENING, MONSIEUR
JIM DAVIS 5-10
FOR YOUR PLEASURE, I HAVE PREPARED DINNER
© 1990 United Feature Syndicate, Inc.
AND, FOR YOUR CONVENIENCE, I HAVE EATEN IT

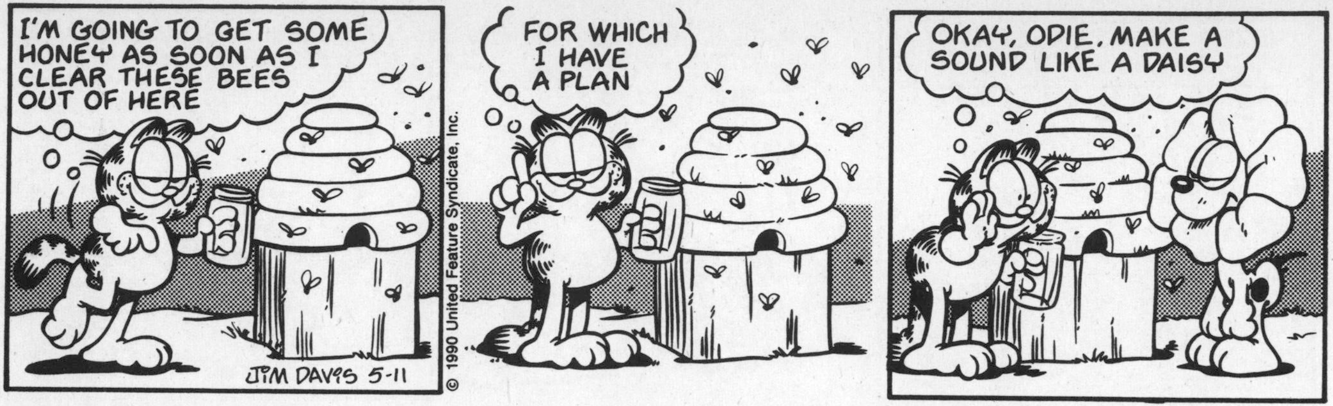
I'M GOING TO GET SOME HONEY AS SOON AS I CLEAR THESE BEES OUT OF HERE
FOR WHICH I HAVE A PLAN
OKAY, ODIE, MAKE A SOUND LIKE A DAISY
JIM DAVIS 5-11
© 1990 United Feature Syndicate, Inc.

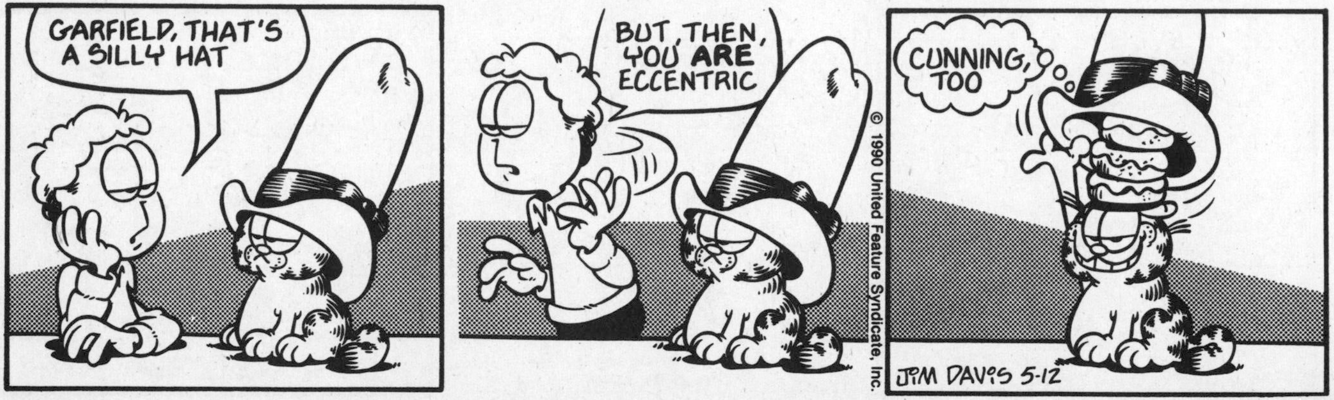
GARFIELD, THAT'S A SILLY HAT
BUT, THEN, YOU **ARE** ECCENTRIC
CUNNING, TOO
JIM DAVIS 5-12
© 1990 United Feature Syndicate, Inc.

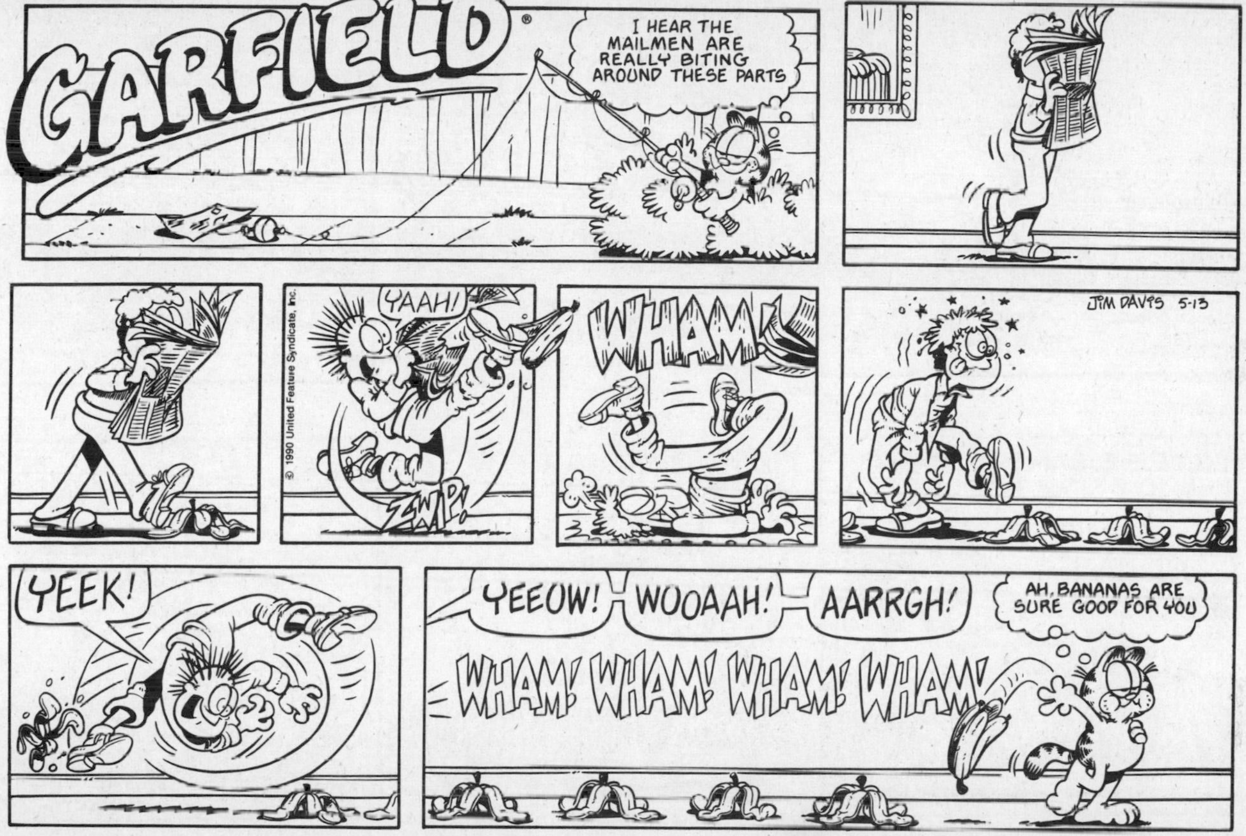
GARFIELD®
I HEAR THE MAILMEN ARE REALLY BITING AROUND THESE PARTS
© 1990 United Feature Syndicate, Inc.
YAAH!
ZWIP!
WHAM!
JIM DAVIS 5-13
YEEK!
YEEOW!
WOOAAH!
AARRGH!
WHAM! WHAM! WHAM! WHAM!
AH, BANANAS ARE SURE GOOD FOR YOU

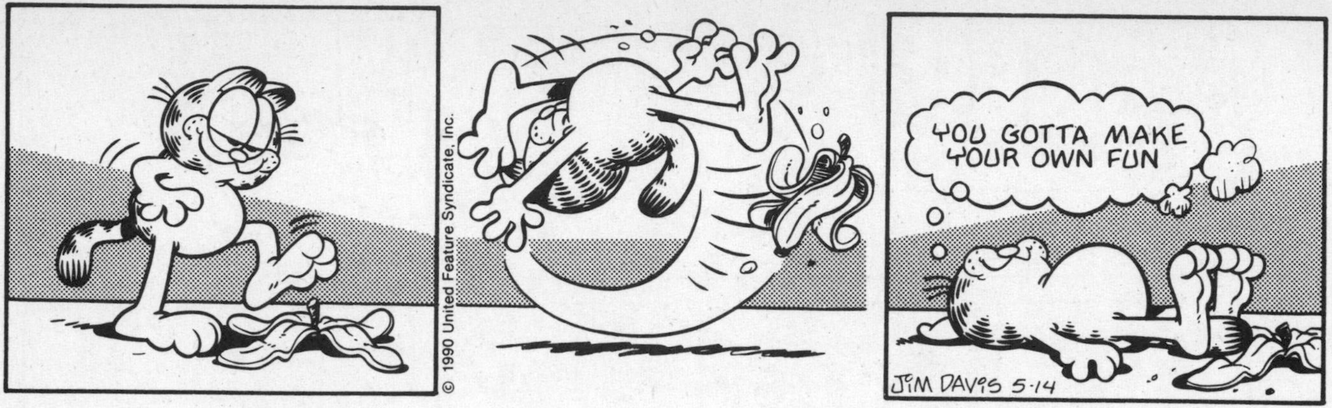

YOU GOTTA MAKE YOUR OWN FUN
JIM DAVIS 5-14

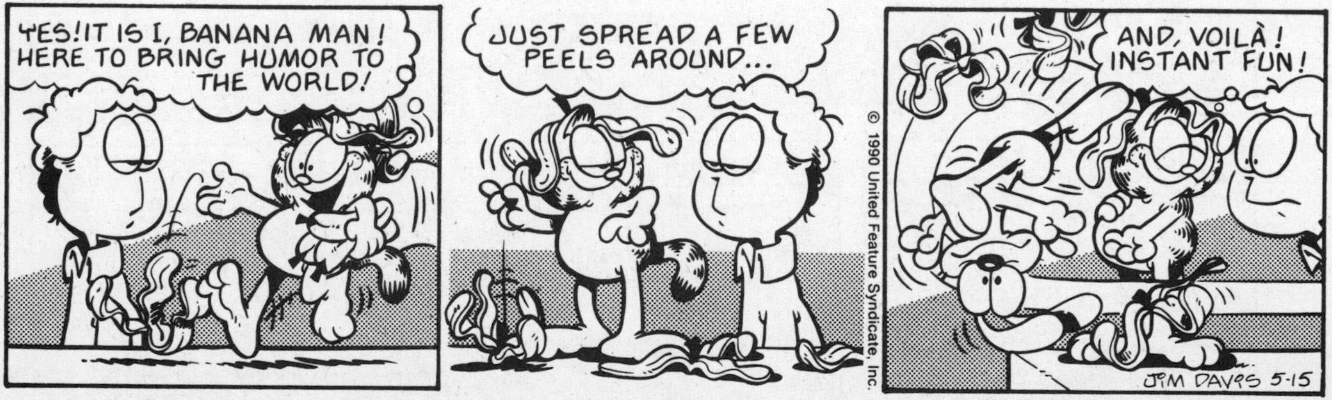

YES! IT IS I, BANANA MAN! HERE TO BRING HUMOR TO THE WORLD!
JUST SPREAD A FEW PEELS AROUND...
AND, VOILÀ! INSTANT FUN!
JIM DAVIS 5-15

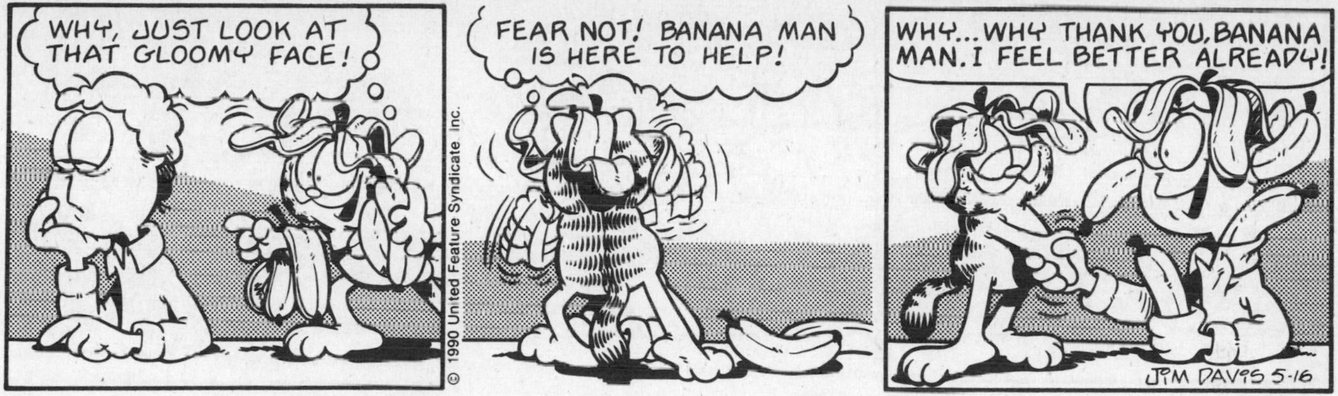
WHY, JUST LOOK AT THAT GLOOMY FACE!
FEAR NOT! BANANA MAN IS HERE TO HELP!
WHY...WHY THANK YOU, BANANA MAN. I FEEL BETTER ALREADY!
© 1990 United Feature Syndicate, Inc.
JIM DAVIS 5-16

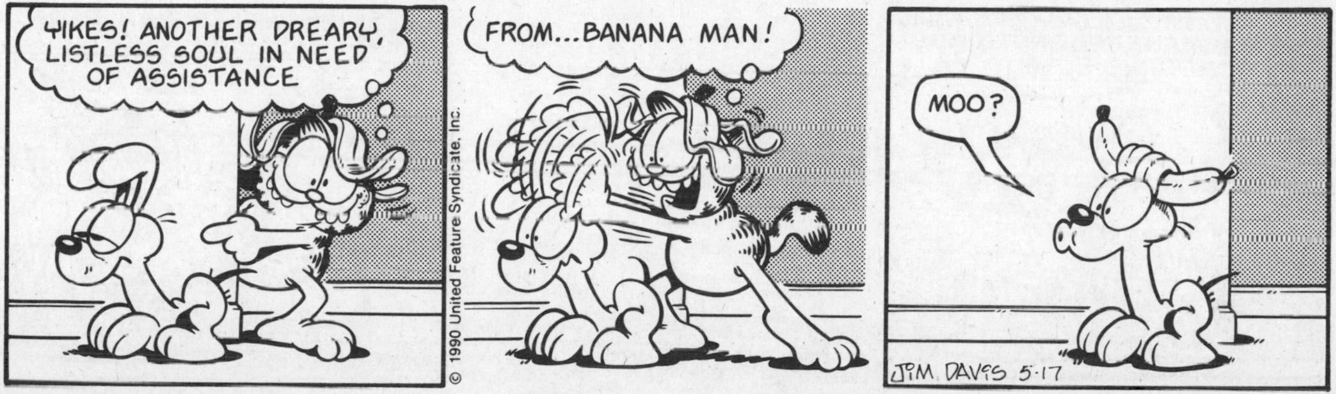
YIKES! ANOTHER DREARY, LISTLESS SOUL IN NEED OF ASSISTANCE
FROM...BANANA MAN!
MOO?
© 1990 United Feature Syndicate, Inc.
JIM DAVIS 5-17

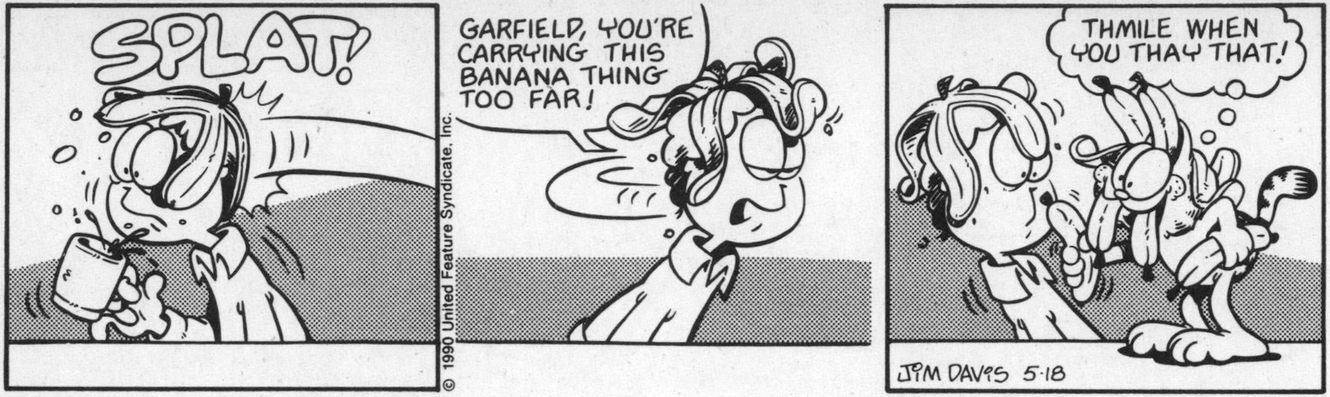
SPLAT!
GARFIELD, YOU'RE CARRYING THIS BANANA THING TOO FAR!
THMILE WHEN YOU THAY THAT!
JIM DAVIS 5·18
© 1990 United Feature Syndicate, Inc.

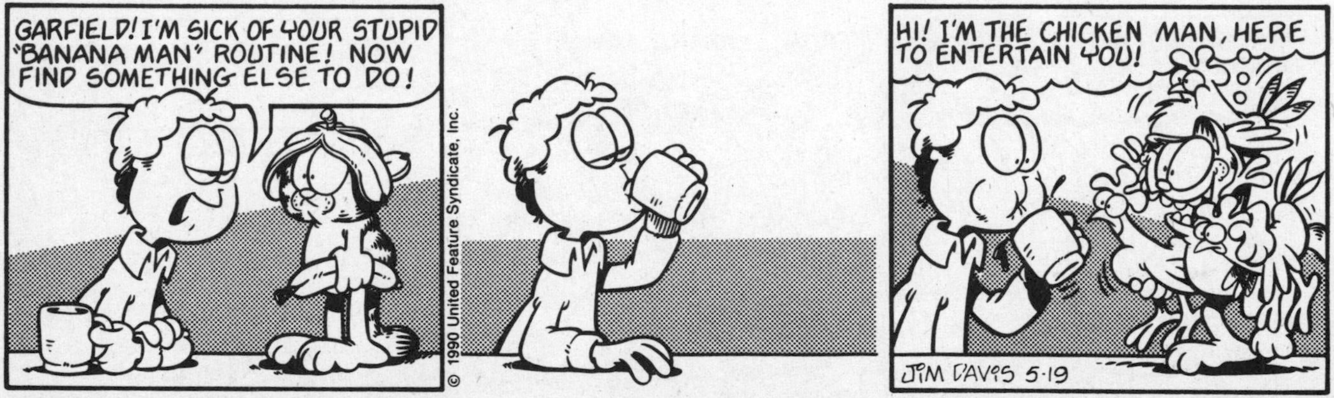
GARFIELD! I'M SICK OF YOUR STUPID "BANANA MAN" ROUTINE! NOW FIND SOMETHING ELSE TO DO!
HI! I'M THE CHICKEN MAN, HERE TO ENTERTAIN YOU!
JIM DAVIS 5·19
© 1990 United Feature Syndicate, Inc.

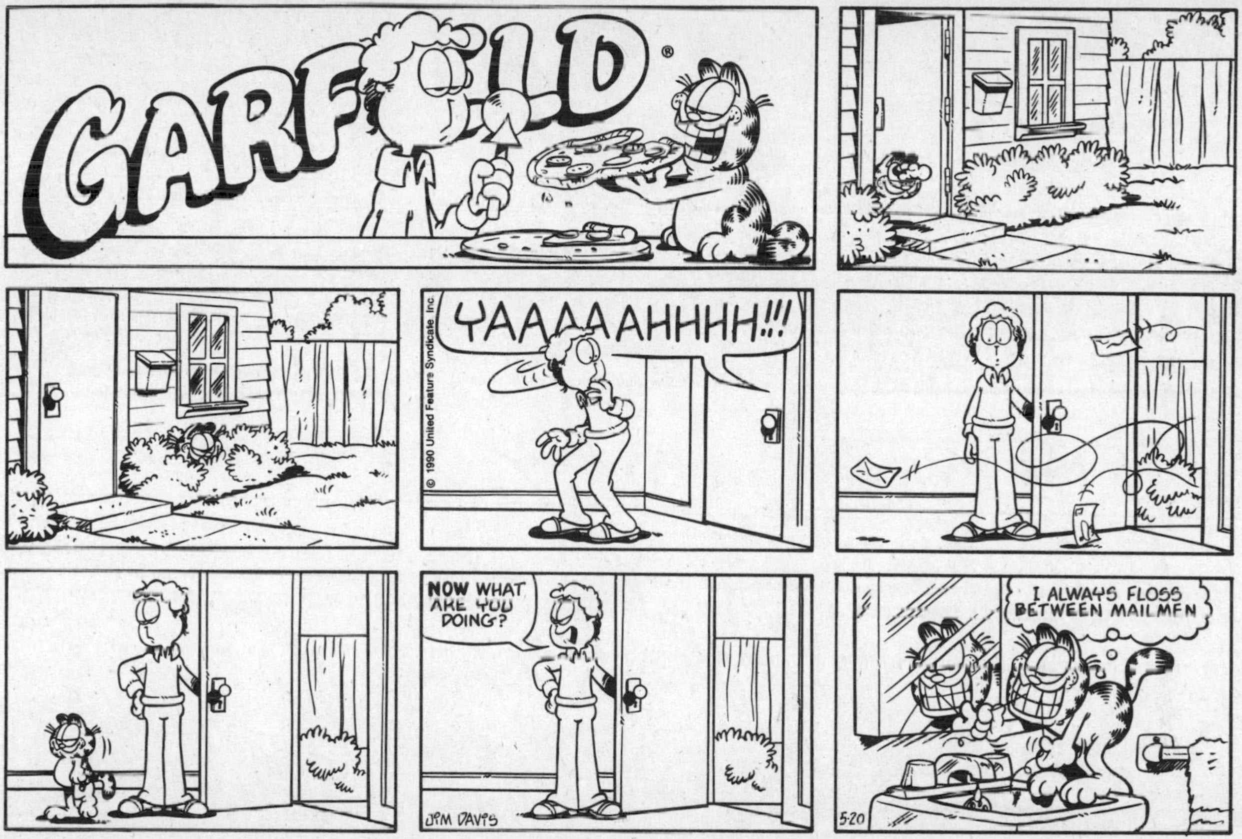
GARFIELD®
© 1990 United Feature Syndicate, Inc.
YAAAAAHHHH!!!
NOW WHAT ARE YOU DOING?
JIM DAVIS
I ALWAYS FLOSS BETWEEN MAILMEN
5-20

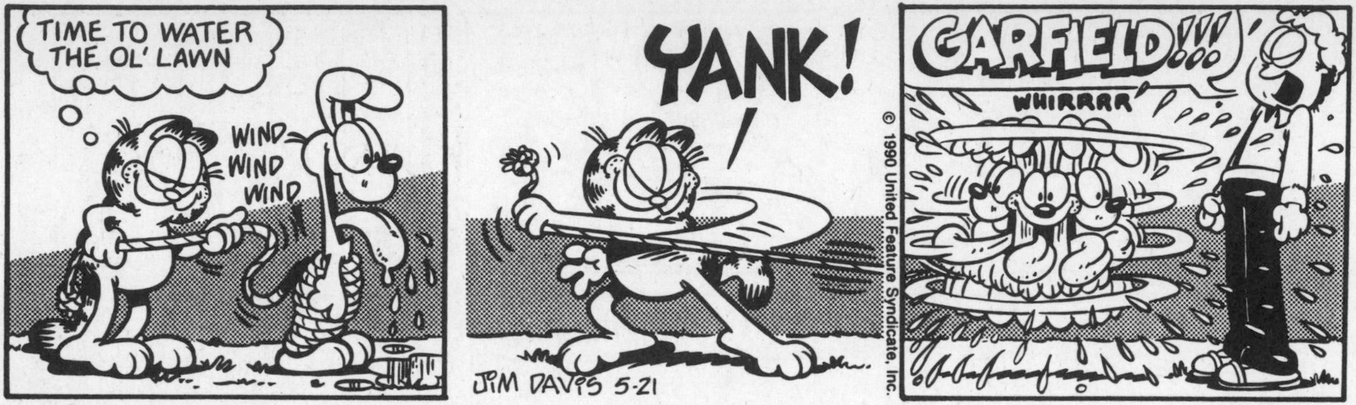
TIME TO WATER THE OL' LAWN
WIND WIND WIND
YANK!
JIM DAVIS 5-21
© 1990 United Feature Syndicate, Inc.
GARFIELD!!!
WHIRRRR

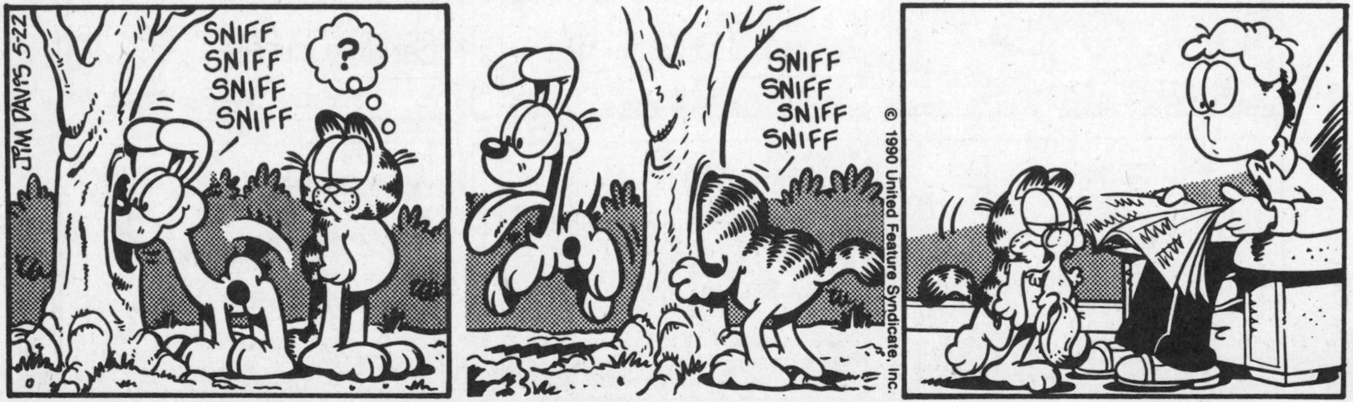
JIM DAVIS 5-22
SNIFF SNIFF SNIFF SNIFF
?
SNIFF SNIFF SNIFF SNIFF
© 1990 United Feature Syndicate, Inc.

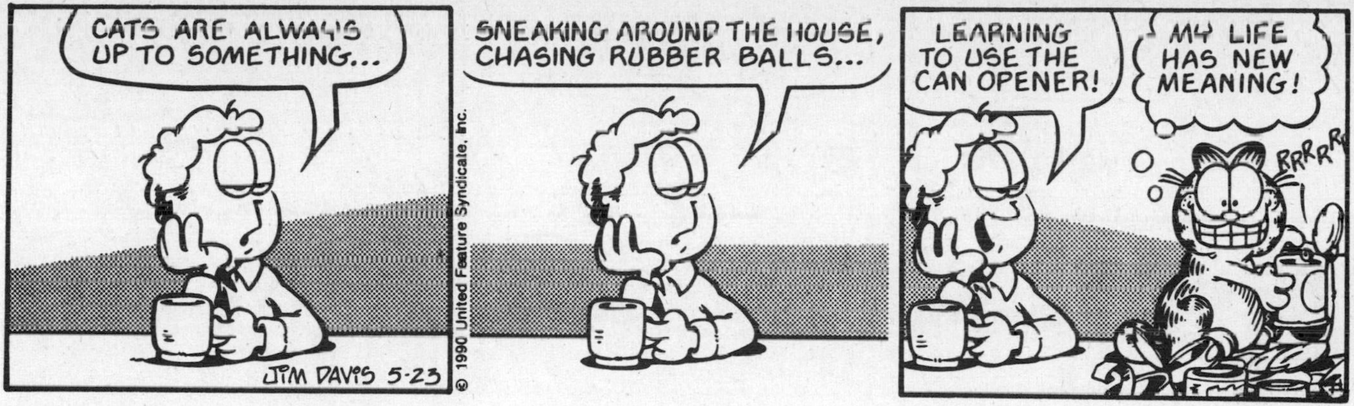
CATS ARE ALWAYS UP TO SOMETHING...
JIM DAVIS 5-23
© 1990 United Feature Syndicate, Inc.
SNEAKING AROUND THE HOUSE, CHASING RUBBER BALLS...
LEARNING TO USE THE CAN OPENER!
MY LIFE HAS NEW MEANING!

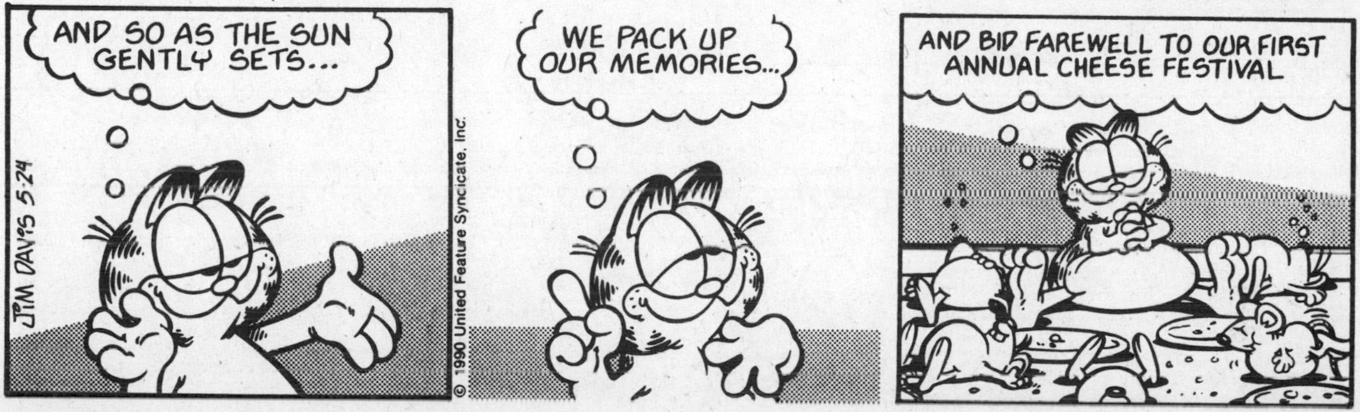
JIM DAVIS 5-24
AND SO AS THE SUN GENTLY SETS...
© 1990 United Feature Syndicate, Inc.
WE PACK UP OUR MEMORIES...
AND BID FAREWELL TO OUR FIRST ANNUAL CHEESE FESTIVAL

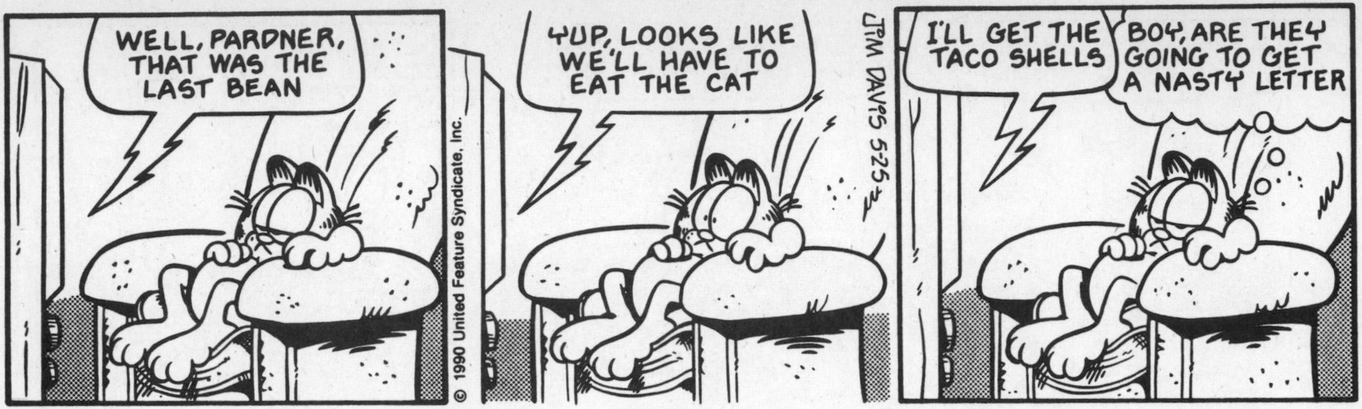
WELL, PARDNER, THAT WAS THE LAST BEAN
YUP, LOOKS LIKE WE'LL HAVE TO EAT THE CAT
JIM DAVIS 5-25
© 1990 United Feature Syndicate, Inc.
I'LL GET THE TACO SHELLS
BOY, ARE THEY GOING TO GET A NASTY LETTER

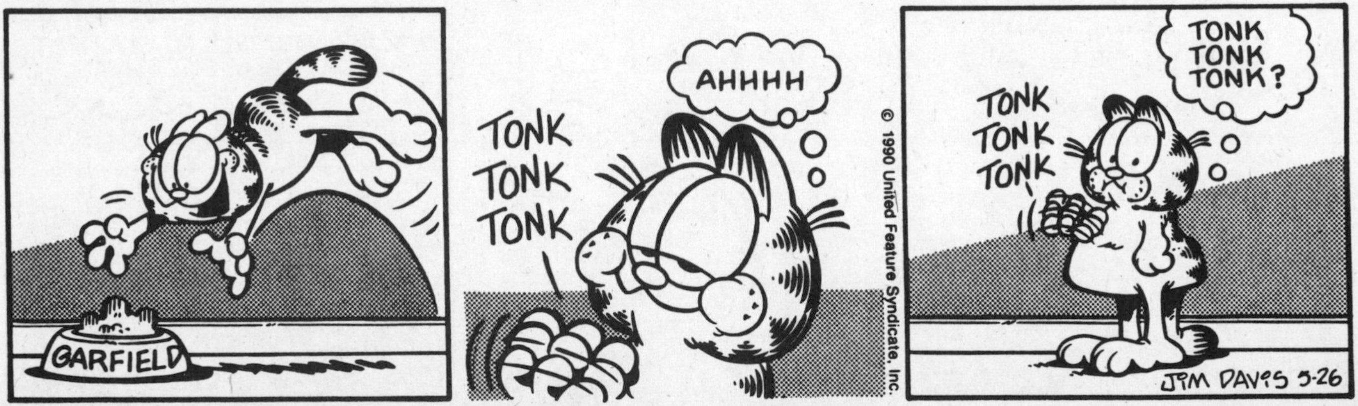
GARFIELD
TONK
TONK
TONK
AHHHH
© 1990 United Feature Syndicate, Inc.
TONK
TONK
TONK
TONK
TONK
TONK?
JIM DAVIS 5-26

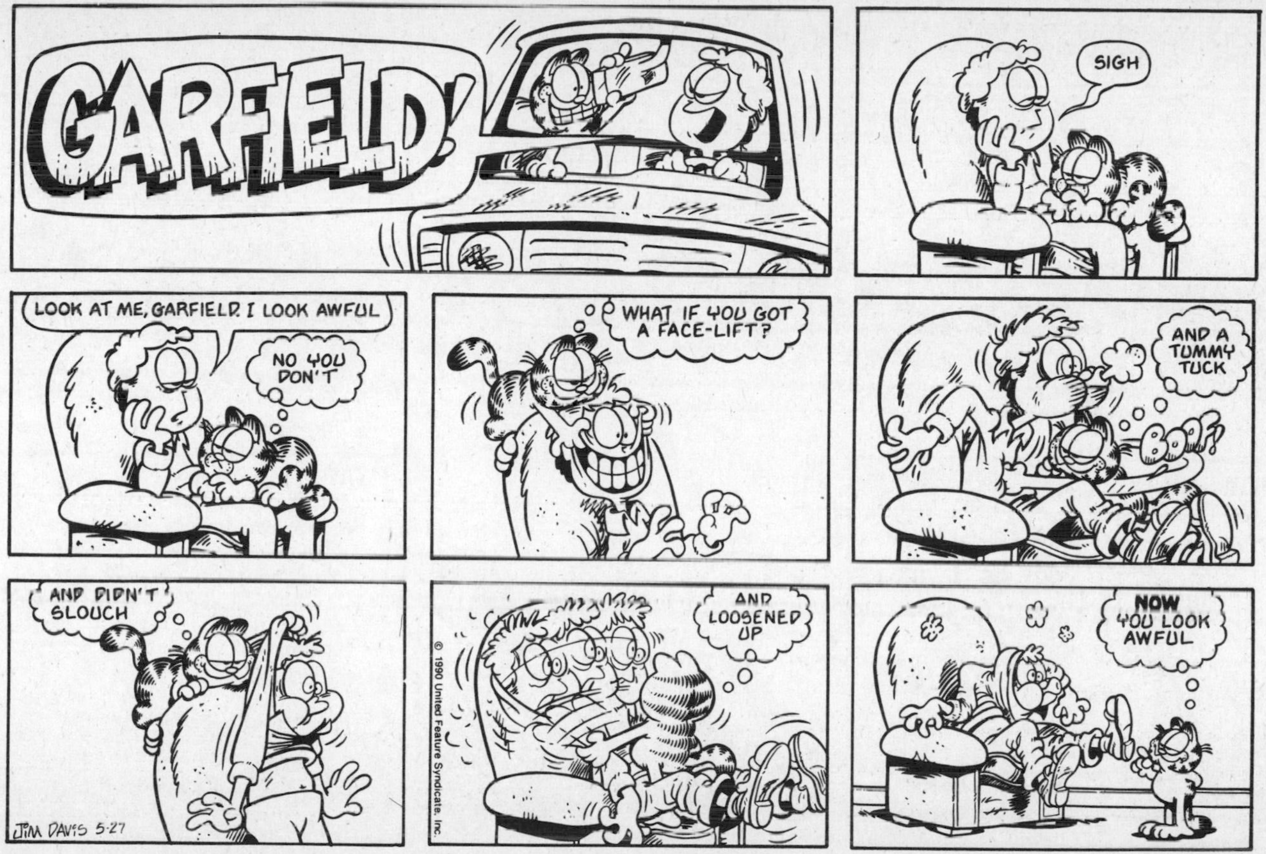
GARFIELD
SIGH
LOOK AT ME, GARFIELD. I LOOK AWFUL
NO YOU DON'T
WHAT IF YOU GOT A FACE-LIFT?
AND A TUMMY TUCK
BOOF!
AND DIDN'T SLOUCH
JIM DAVIS 5-27
AND LOOSENED UP
© 1990 United Feature Syndicate, Inc.
NOW YOU LOOK AWFUL

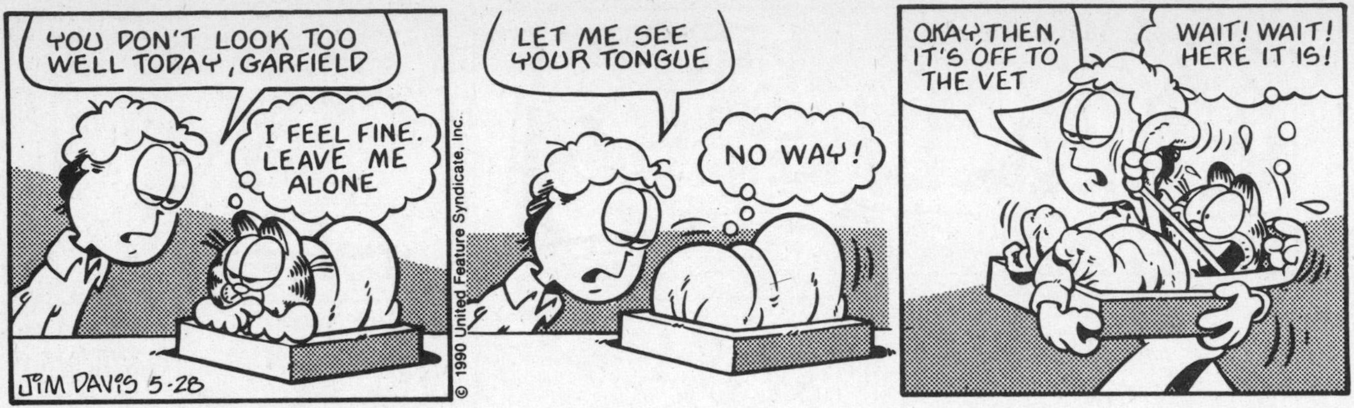

YOU DON'T LOOK TOO WELL TODAY, GARFIELD
I FEEL FINE. LEAVE ME ALONE
LET ME SEE YOUR TONGUE
NO WAY!
OKAY, THEN, IT'S OFF TO THE VET
WAIT! WAIT! HERE IT IS!
JIM DAVIS 5-28
© 1990 United Feature Syndicate, Inc.

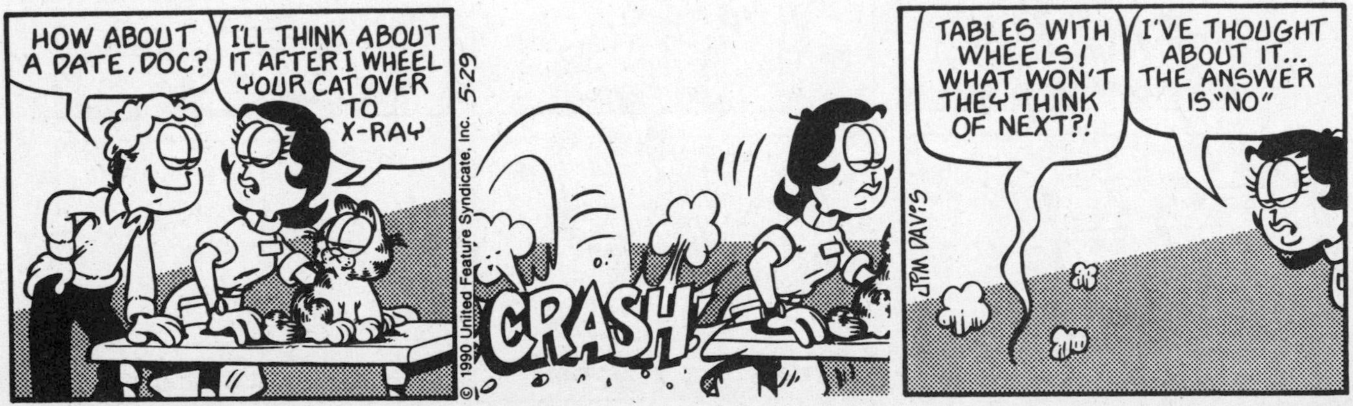

HOW ABOUT A DATE, DOC?
I'LL THINK ABOUT IT AFTER I WHEEL YOUR CAT OVER TO X-RAY
5-29
© 1990 United Feature Syndicate, Inc.
CRASH
TABLES WITH WHEELS! WHAT WON'T THEY THINK OF NEXT?!
I'VE THOUGHT ABOUT IT... THE ANSWER IS "NO"
JIM DAVIS

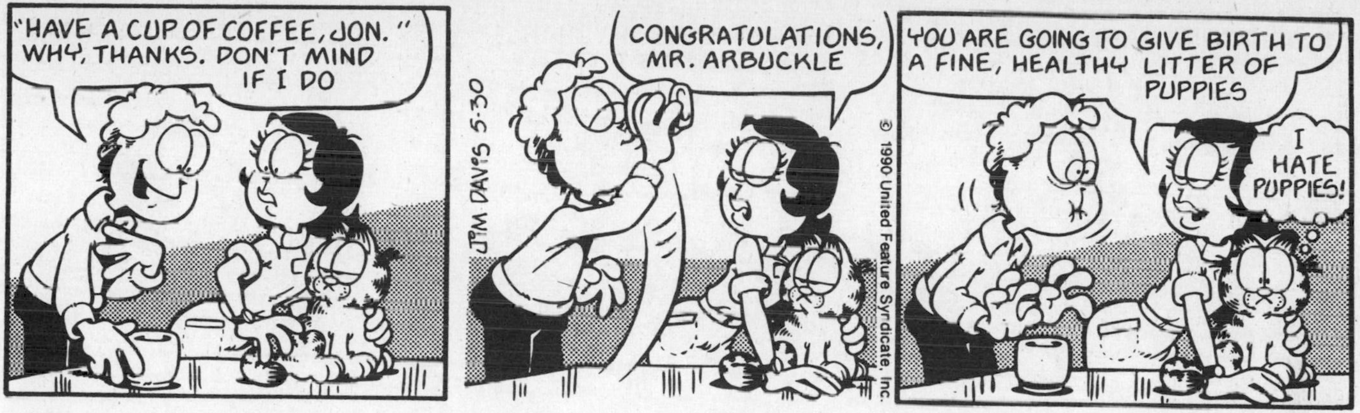
"HAVE A CUP OF COFFEE, JON." WHY, THANKS. DON'T MIND IF I DO
JIM DAVIS 5-30
CONGRATULATIONS, MR. ARBUCKLE
YOU ARE GOING TO GIVE BIRTH TO A FINE, HEALTHY LITTER OF PUPPIES
I HATE PUPPIES!
© 1990 United Feature Syndicate, Inc.

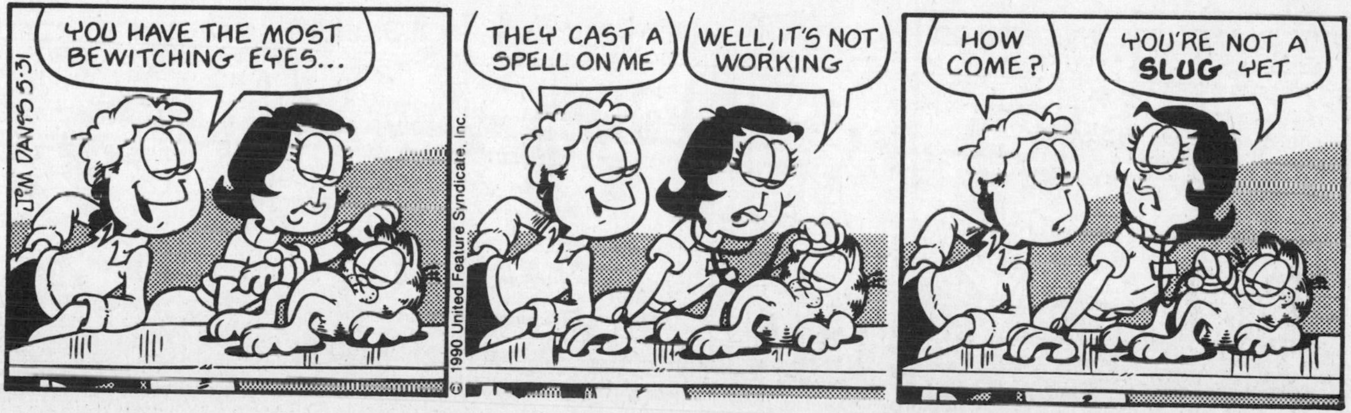
JIM DAVIS 5-31
YOU HAVE THE MOST BEWITCHING EYES...
THEY CAST A SPELL ON ME
WELL, IT'S NOT WORKING
HOW COME?
YOU'RE NOT A **SLUG** YET
© 1990 United Feature Syndicate, Inc.

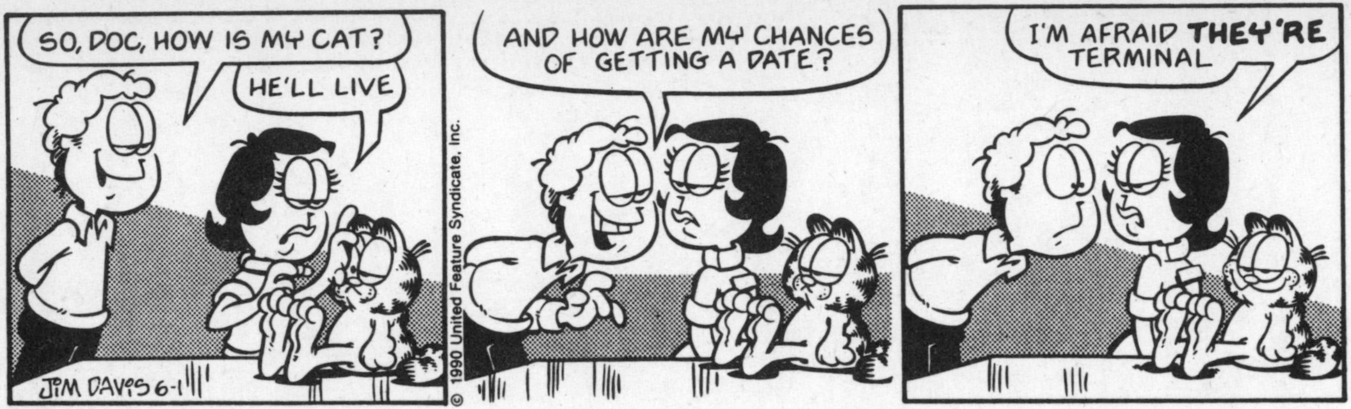
SO, DOC, HOW IS MY CAT?
HE'LL LIVE
JIM DAVIS 6-1
© 1990 United Feature Syndicate, Inc.
AND HOW ARE MY CHANCES OF GETTING A DATE?
I'M AFRAID **THEY'RE** TERMINAL

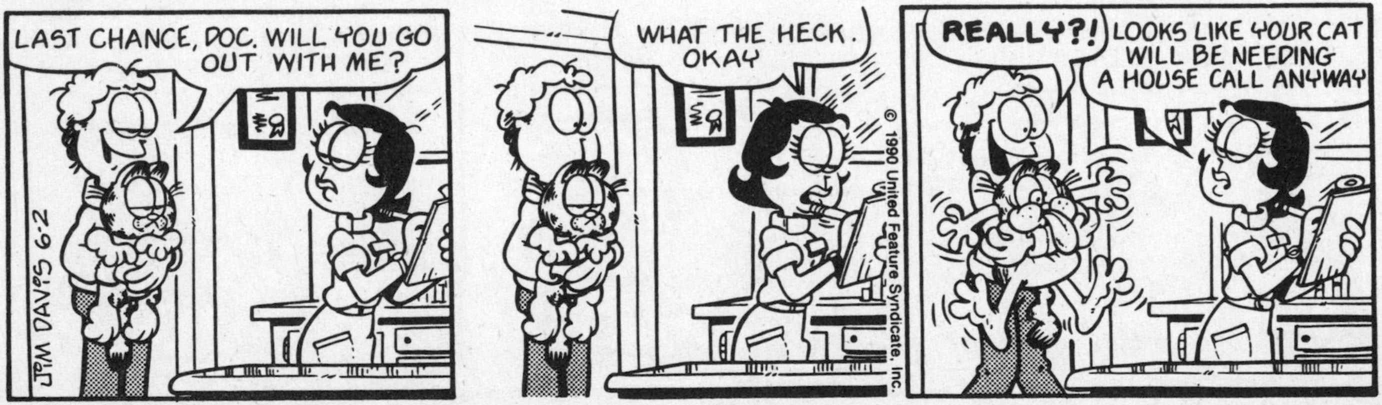
LAST CHANCE, DOC. WILL YOU GO OUT WITH ME?
JIM DAVIS 6-2
WHAT THE HECK. OKAY
© 1990 United Feature Syndicate, Inc.
REALLY?!
LOOKS LIKE YOUR CAT WILL BE NEEDING A HOUSE CALL ANYWAY

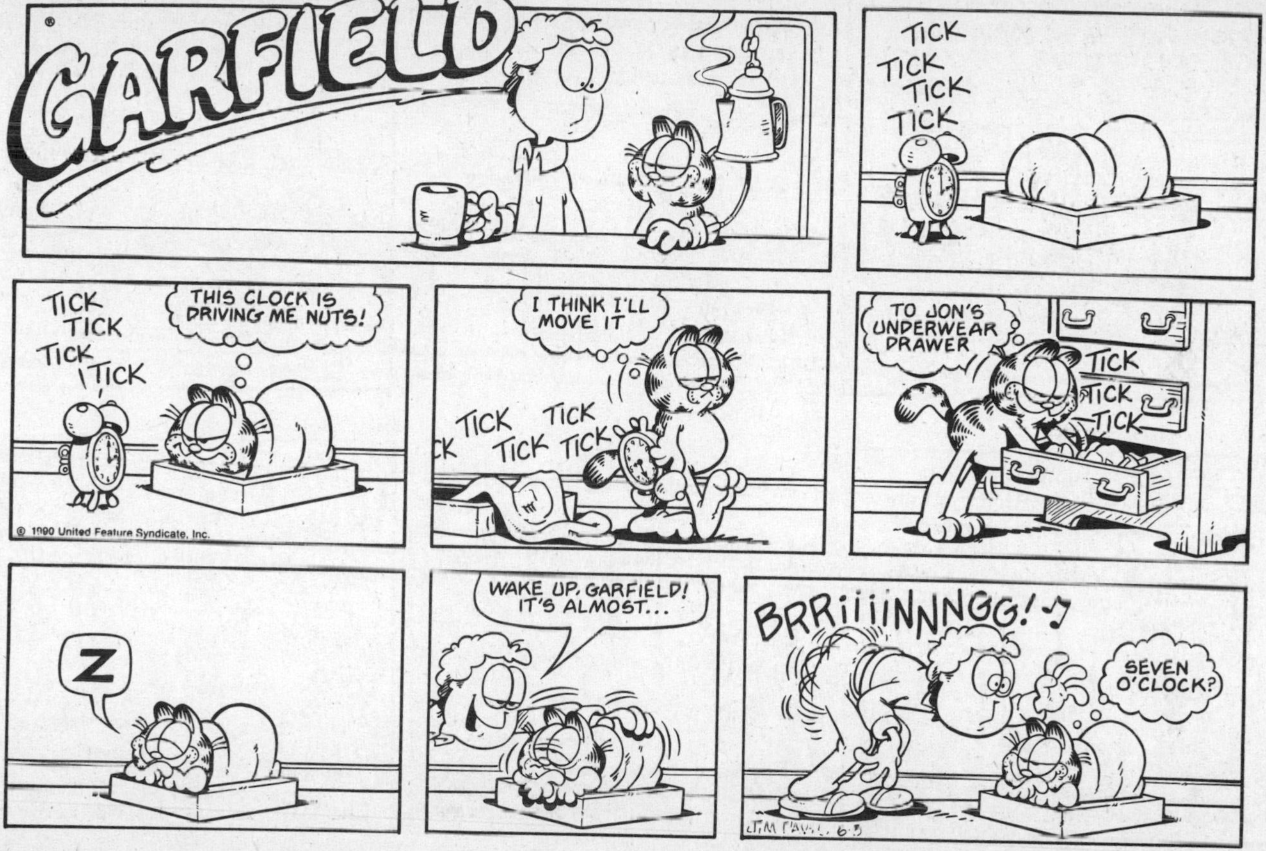
GARFIELD
TICK TICK TICK TICK
TICK TICK TICK TICK
THIS CLOCK IS DRIVING ME NUTS!
© 1990 United Feature Syndicate, Inc.
I THINK I'LL MOVE IT
CK TICK TICK TICK TICK
TO JON'S UNDERWEAR DRAWER
TICK TICK TICK
Z
WAKE UP, GARFIELD! IT'S ALMOST...
BRRiiiiNNNGG!
SEVEN O'CLOCK?
JIM DAVIS 6-3

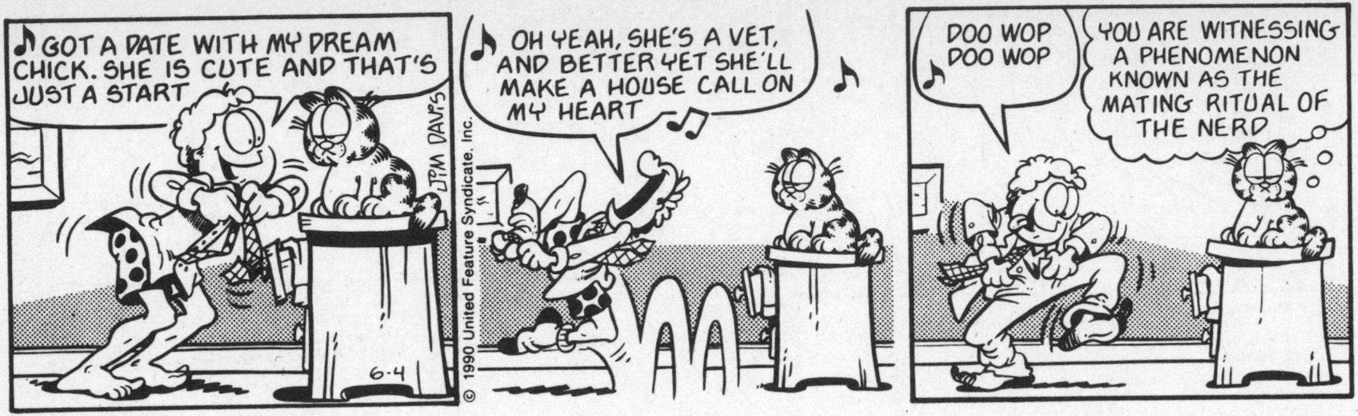
GOT A DATE WITH MY DREAM CHICK. SHE IS CUTE AND THAT'S JUST A START
JIM DAVIS
6-4
© 1990 United Feature Syndicate, Inc.
OH YEAH, SHE'S A VET, AND BETTER YET SHE'LL MAKE A HOUSE CALL ON MY HEART
DOO WOP DOO WOP
YOU ARE WITNESSING A PHENOMENON KNOWN AS THE MATING RITUAL OF THE NERD

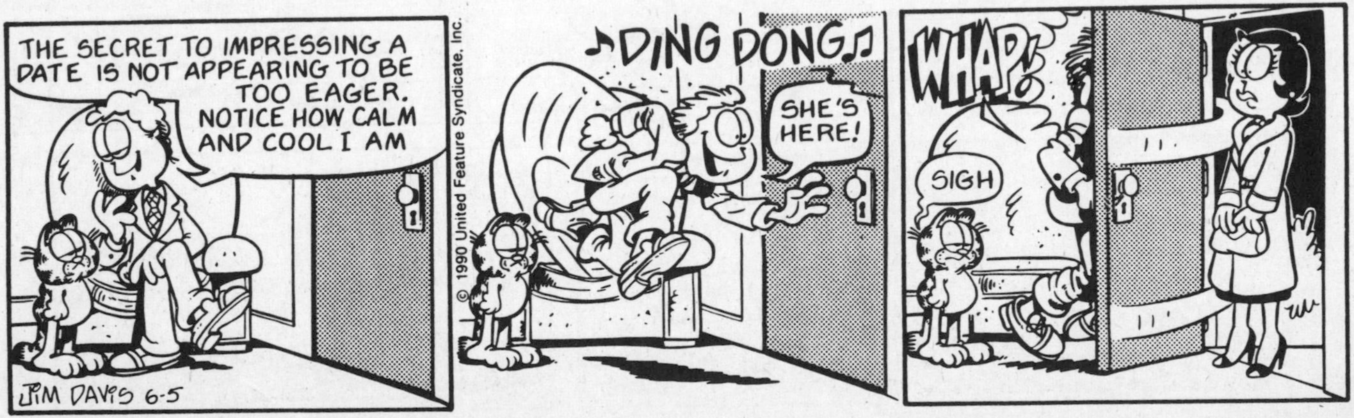
THE SECRET TO IMPRESSING A DATE IS NOT APPEARING TO BE TOO EAGER. NOTICE HOW CALM AND COOL I AM
JIM DAVIS 6-5
© 1990 United Feature Syndicate, Inc.
DING DONG
SHE'S HERE!
WHAP!
SIGH

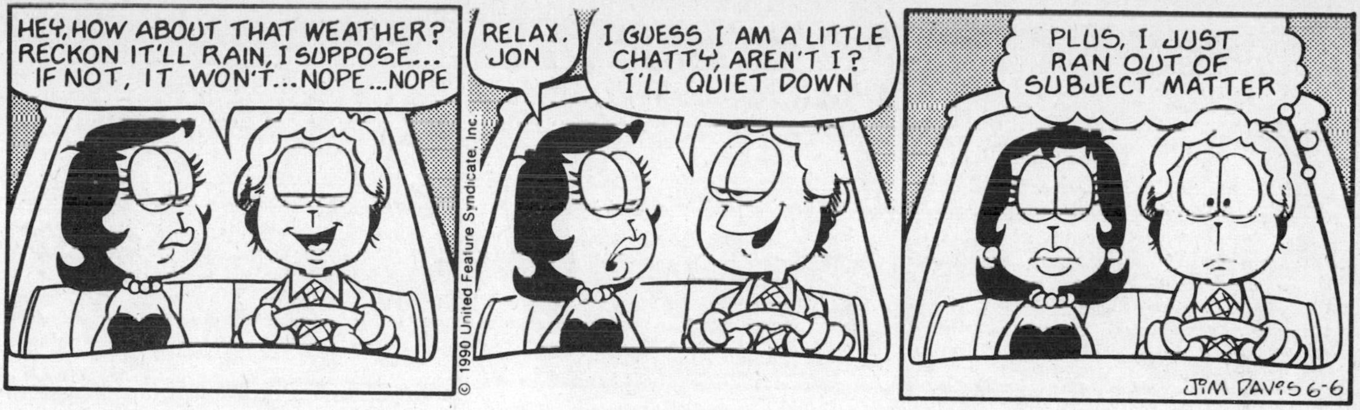
HEY, HOW ABOUT THAT WEATHER? RECKON IT'LL RAIN, I SUPPOSE... IF NOT, IT WON'T...NOPE...NOPE
RELAX, JON
I GUESS I AM A LITTLE CHATTY, AREN'T I? I'LL QUIET DOWN
PLUS, I JUST RAN OUT OF SUBJECT MATTER
© 1990 United Feature Syndicate, Inc.
JIM DAVIS 6-6

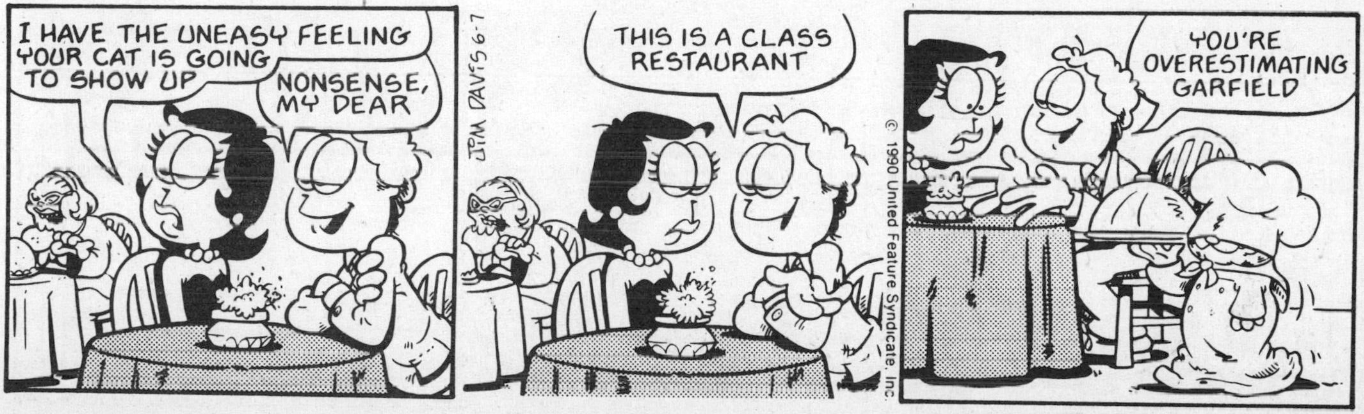
I HAVE THE UNEASY FEELING YOUR CAT IS GOING TO SHOW UP
NONSENSE, MY DEAR
JIM DAVIS 6-7
THIS IS A CLASS RESTAURANT
YOU'RE OVERESTIMATING GARFIELD
© 1990 United Feature Syndicate, Inc.

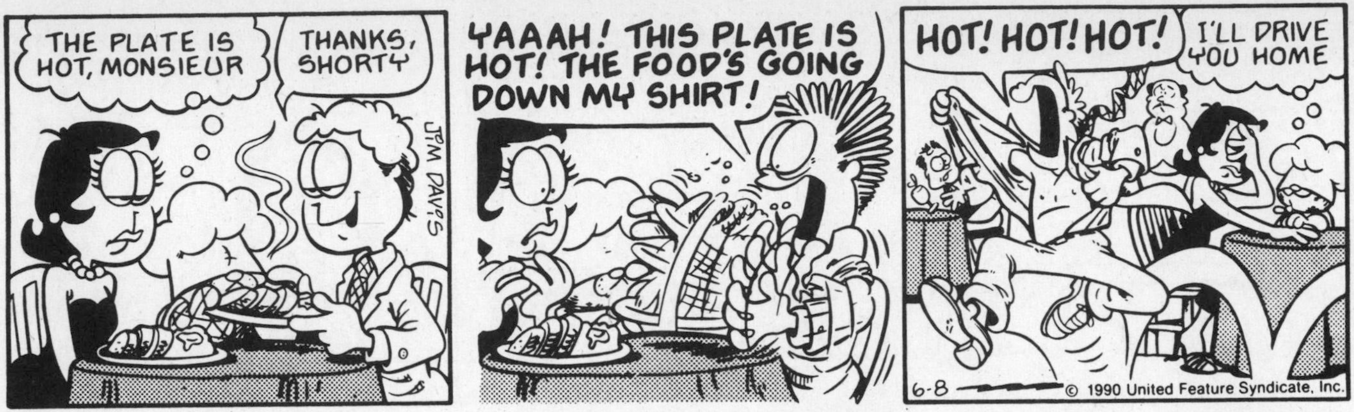
THE PLATE IS HOT, MONSIEUR
THANKS, SHORTY
JIM DAVIS
YAAAH! THIS PLATE IS HOT! THE FOOD'S GOING DOWN MY SHIRT!
HOT! HOT! HOT!
I'LL DRIVE YOU HOME
6-8
© 1990 United Feature Syndicate, Inc.

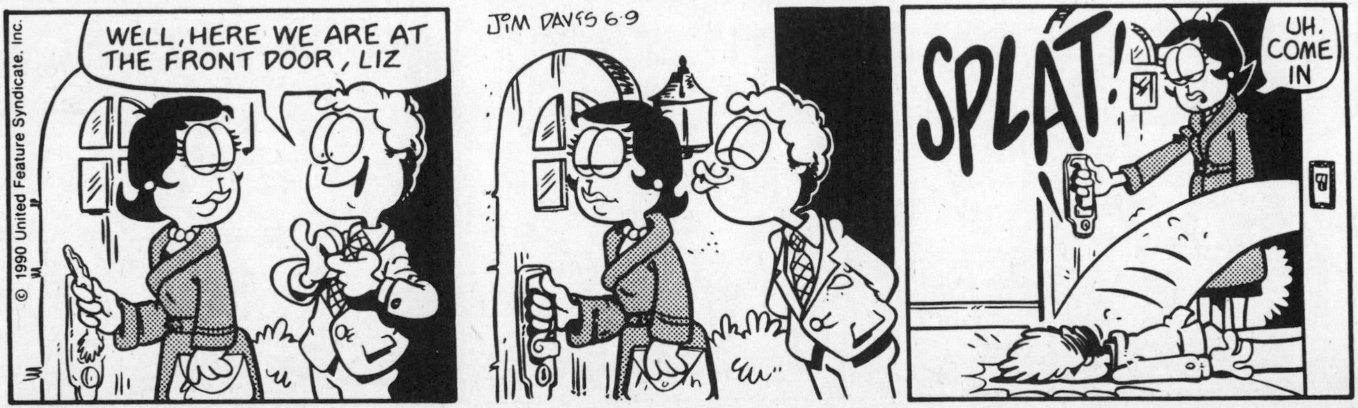
© 1990 United Feature Syndicate, Inc.
WELL, HERE WE ARE AT THE FRONT DOOR, LIZ
JIM DAVIS 6-9
SPLAT!
UH. COME IN

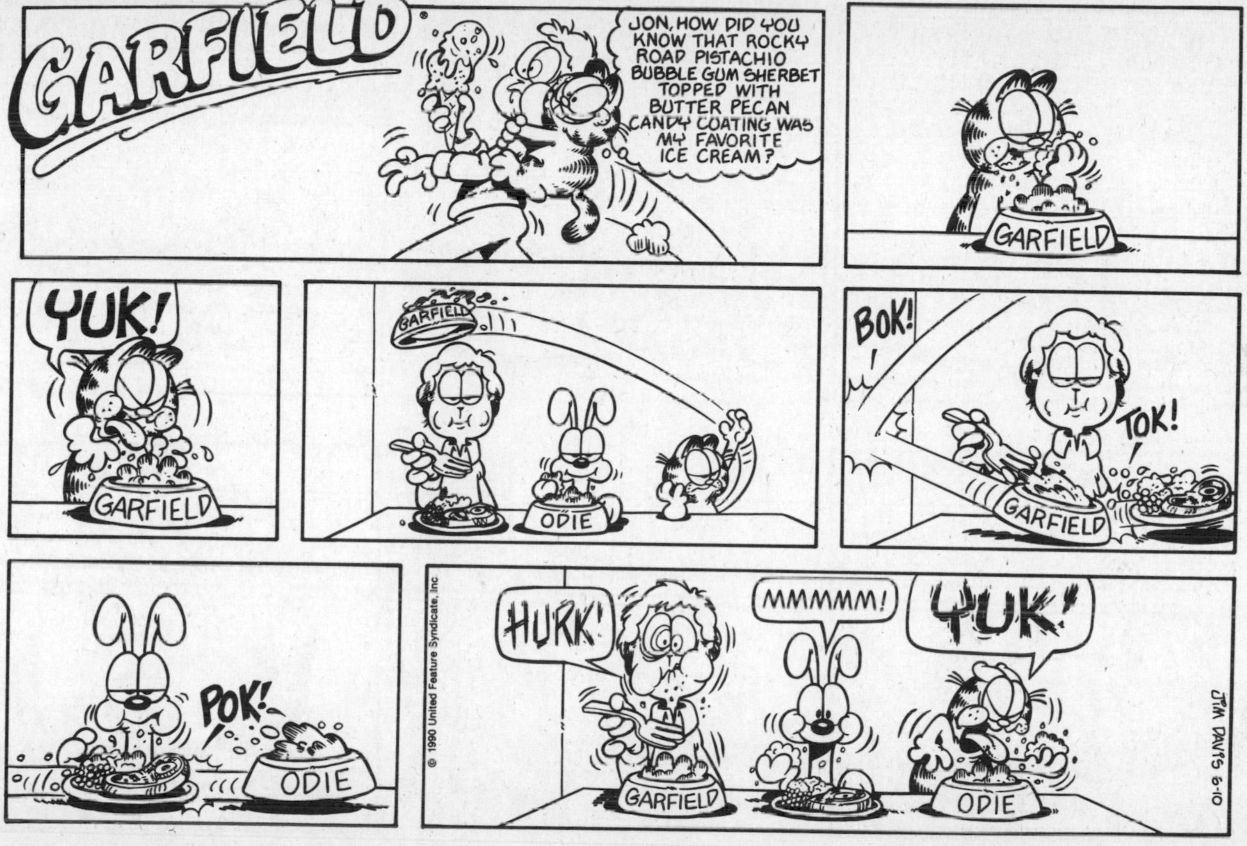
GARFIELD®
JON, HOW DID YOU KNOW THAT ROCKY ROAD PISTACHIO BUBBLE GUM SHERBET TOPPED WITH BUTTER PECAN CANDY COATING WAS MY FAVORITE ICE CREAM?
GARFIELD
YUK!
GARFIELD
GARFIELD
ODIE
BOK!
TOK!
GARFIELD
POK!
ODIE
© 1990 United Feature Syndicate, Inc.
HURK!
MMMMM!
YUK!
GARFIELD
ODIE
JIM DAVIS 6-10

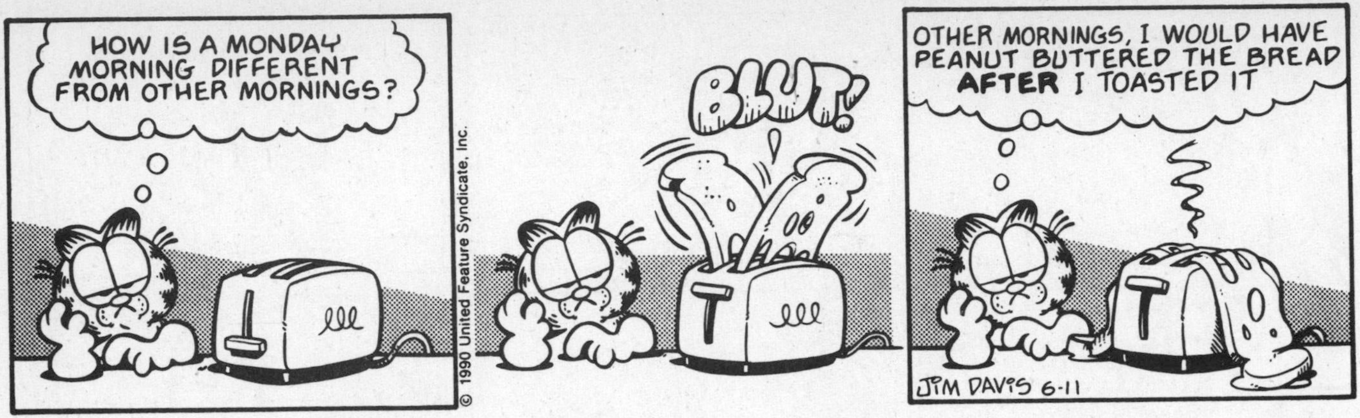
HOW IS A MONDAY MORNING DIFFERENT FROM OTHER MORNINGS?
© 1990 United Feature Syndicate, Inc.
BLUT!
OTHER MORNINGS, I WOULD HAVE PEANUT BUTTERED THE BREAD **AFTER** I TOASTED IT
JIM DAVIS 6-11

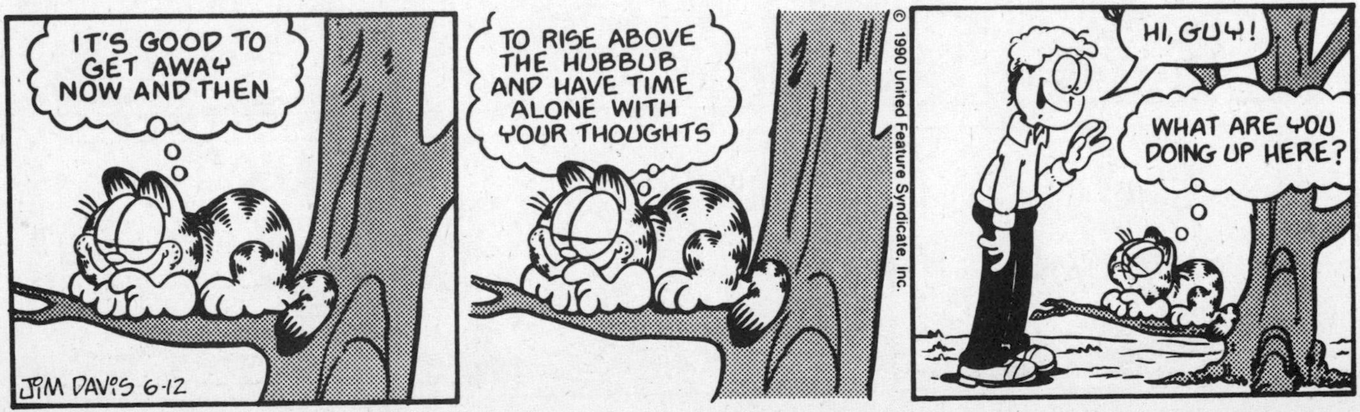
IT'S GOOD TO GET AWAY NOW AND THEN
JIM DAVIS 6-12
TO RISE ABOVE THE HUBBUB AND HAVE TIME ALONE WITH YOUR THOUGHTS
© 1990 United Feature Syndicate, Inc.
HI, GUY!
WHAT ARE YOU DOING UP HERE?

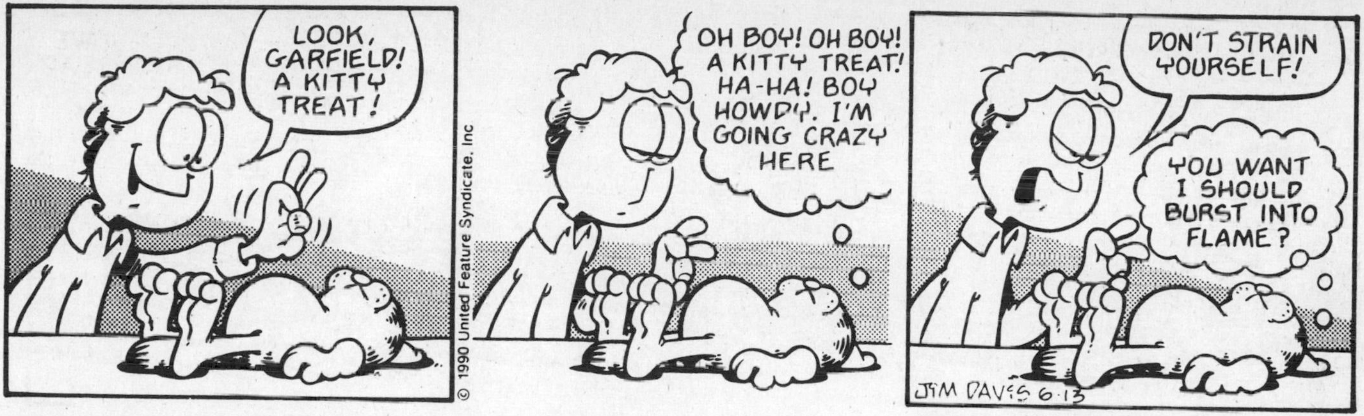
LOOK, GARFIELD! A KITTY TREAT!
OH BOY! OH BOY! A KITTY TREAT! HA-HA! BOY HOWDY. I'M GOING CRAZY HERE
DON'T STRAIN YOURSELF!
YOU WANT I SHOULD BURST INTO FLAME?
JIM DAVIS 6·13
© 1990 United Feature Syndicate, Inc

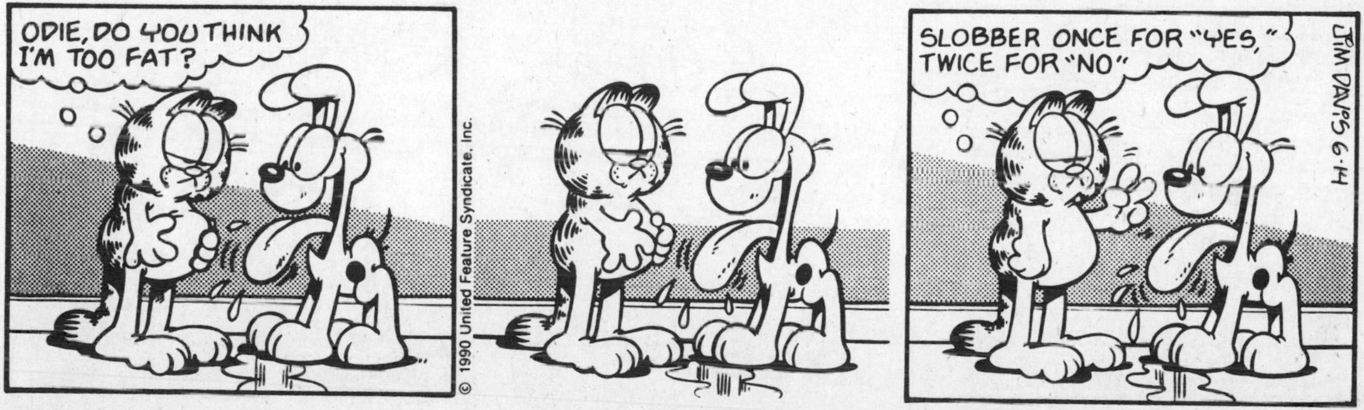
ODIE, DO YOU THINK I'M TOO FAT?
SLOBBER ONCE FOR "YES," TWICE FOR "NO"
JIM DAVIS 6·14
© 1990 United Feature Syndicate, Inc.

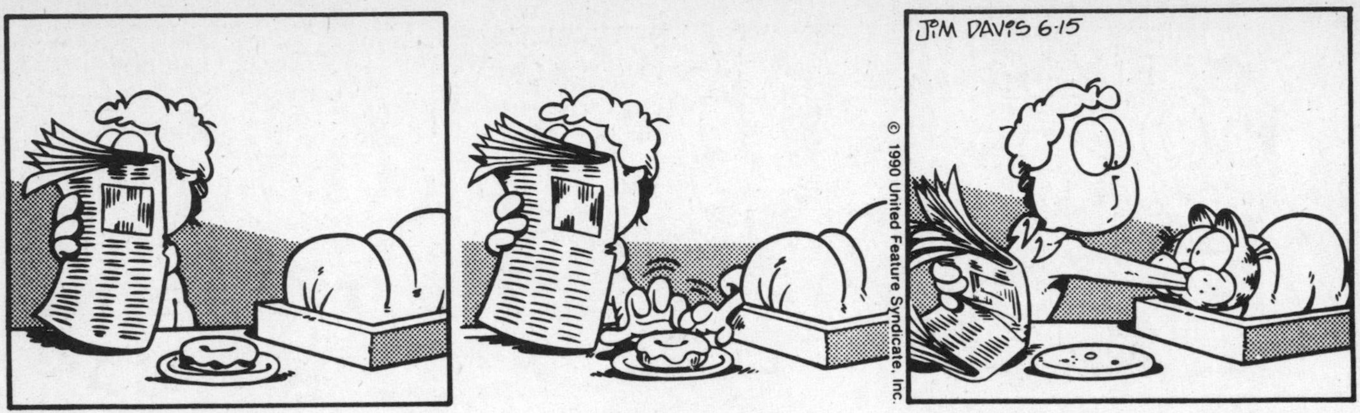
JIM DAVIS 6-15
© 1990 United Feature Syndicate, Inc.

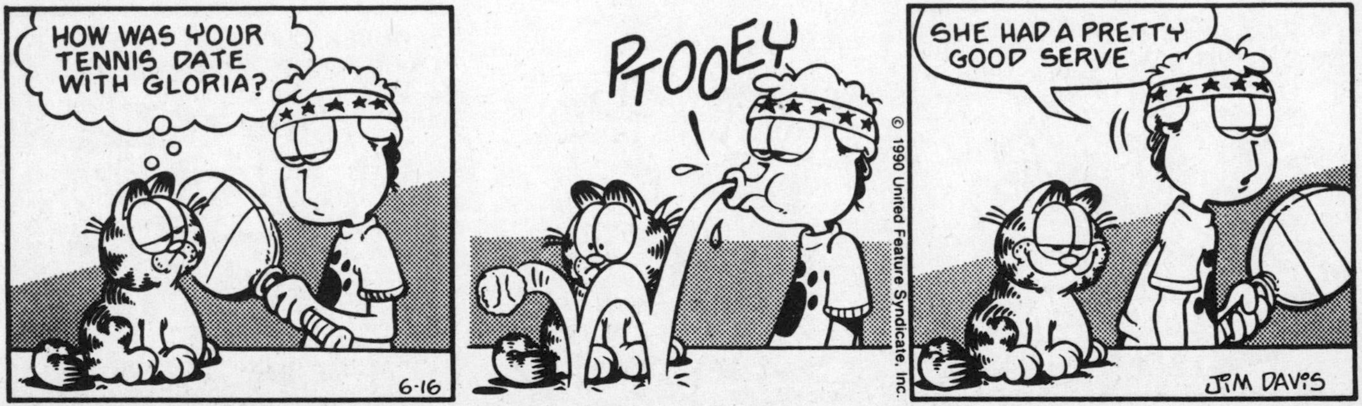
HOW WAS YOUR TENNIS DATE WITH GLORIA?
6-16
PTOOEY
© 1990 United Feature Syndicate, Inc.
SHE HAD A PRETTY GOOD SERVE
JIM DAVIS

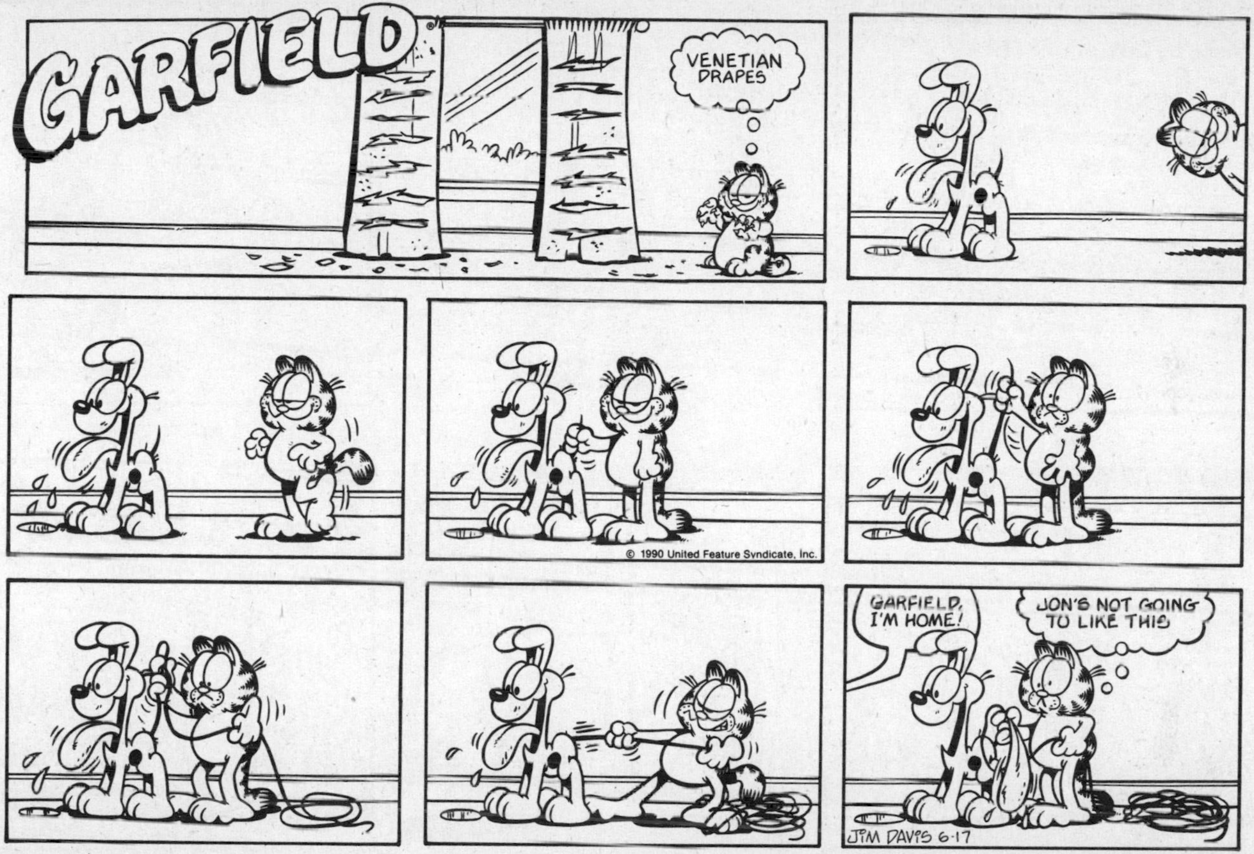
GARFIELD
VENETIAN DRAPES
© 1990 United Feature Syndicate, Inc.
GARFIELD, I'M HOME!
JON'S NOT GOING TO LIKE THIS
JIM DAVIS 6-17

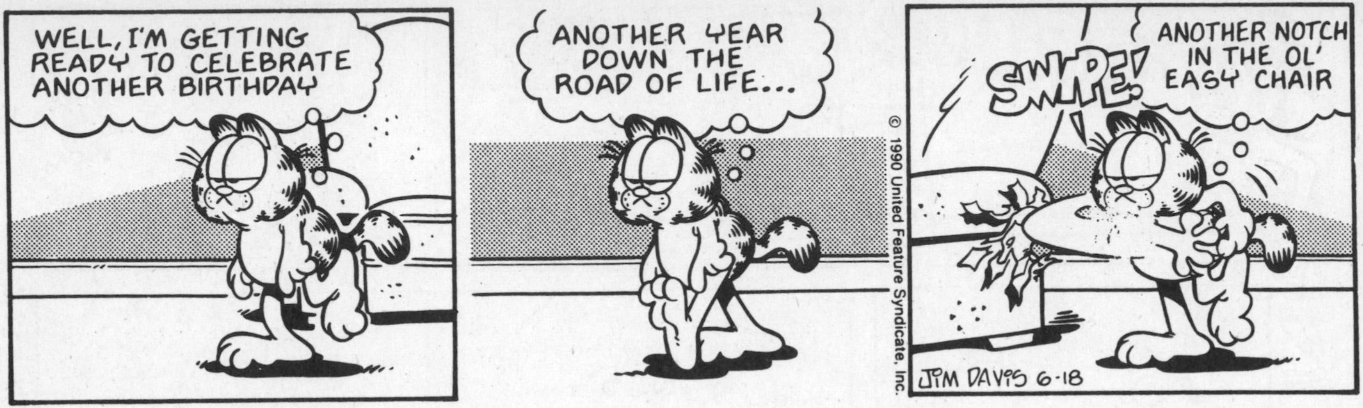
WELL, I'M GETTING READY TO CELEBRATE ANOTHER BIRTHDAY
ANOTHER YEAR DOWN THE ROAD OF LIFE...
SWIPE!
ANOTHER NOTCH IN THE OL' EASY CHAIR
© 1990 United Feature Syndicate, Inc.
JIM DAVIS 6-18

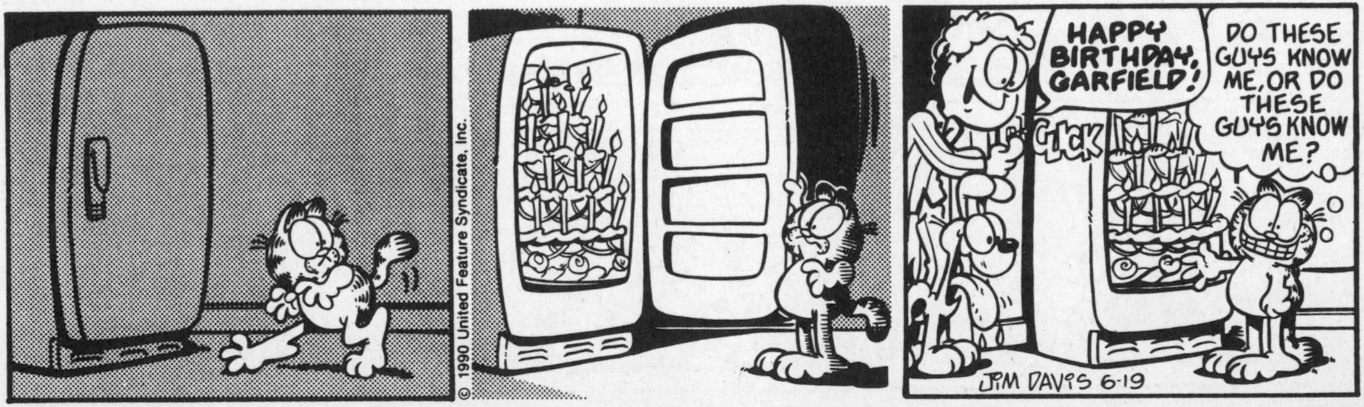
© 1990 United Feature Syndicate, Inc.
HAPPY BIRTHDAY, GARFIELD!
CLICK
DO THESE GUYS KNOW ME, OR DO THESE GUYS KNOW ME?
JIM DAVIS 6-19

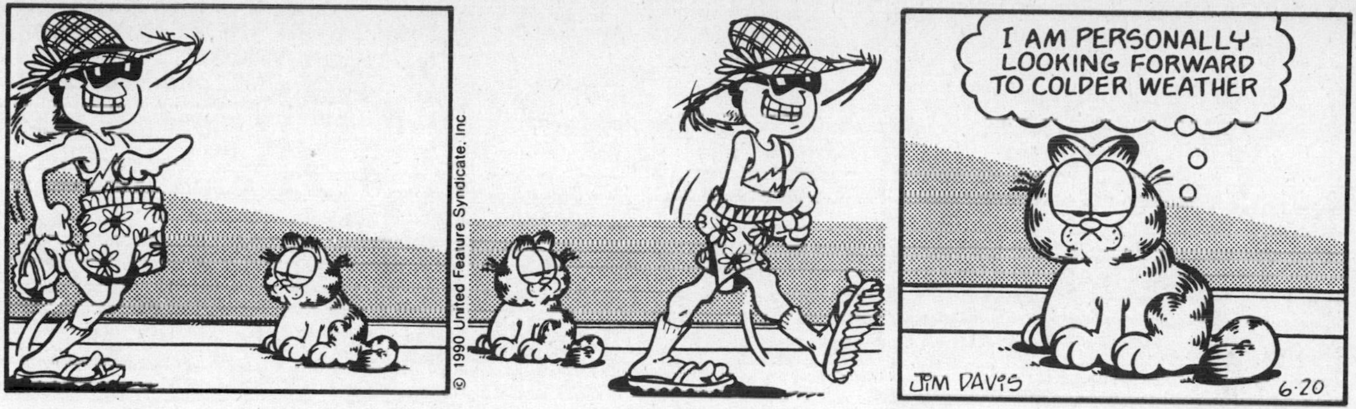

© 1990 United Feature Syndicate, Inc
I AM PERSONALLY LOOKING FORWARD TO COLDER WEATHER
JIM DAVIS
6·20

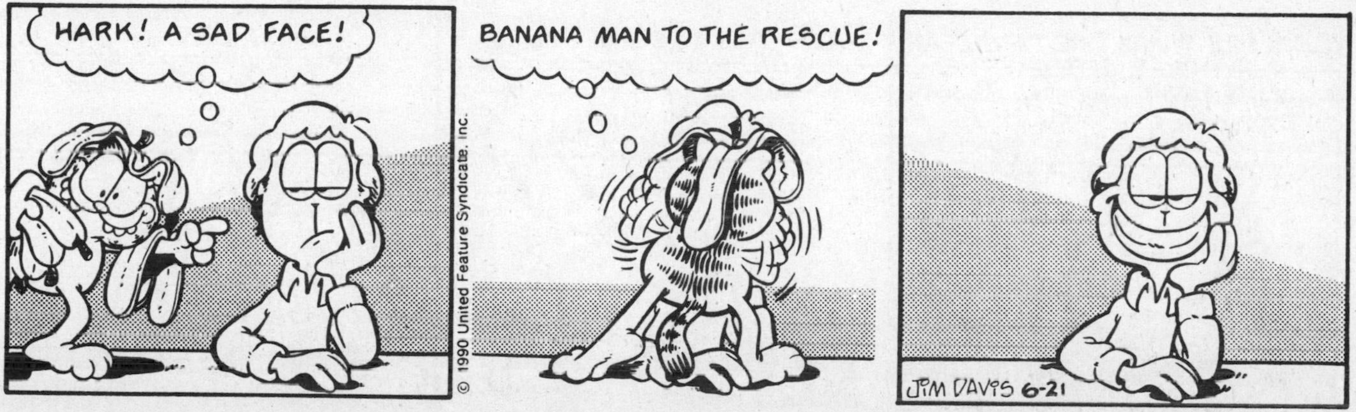

HARK! A SAD FACE!
© 1990 United Feature Syndicate, Inc.
BANANA MAN TO THE RESCUE!
JIM DAVIS 6-21

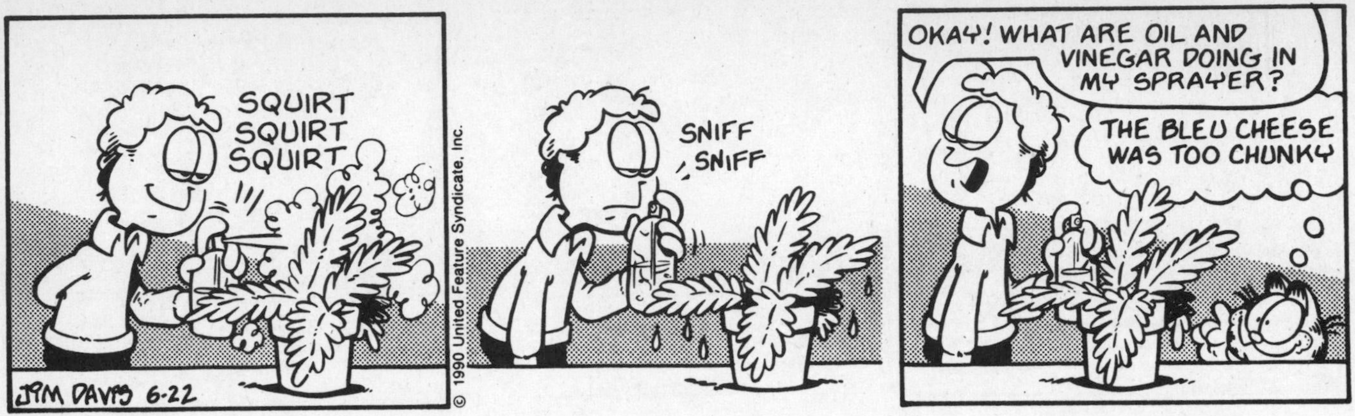
SQUIRT
SQUIRT
SQUIRT
JIM DAVIS 6-22
© 1990 United Feature Syndicate, Inc.
SNIFF
SNIFF
OKAY! WHAT ARE OIL AND VINEGAR DOING IN MY SPRAYER?
THE BLEU CHEESE WAS TOO CHUNKY

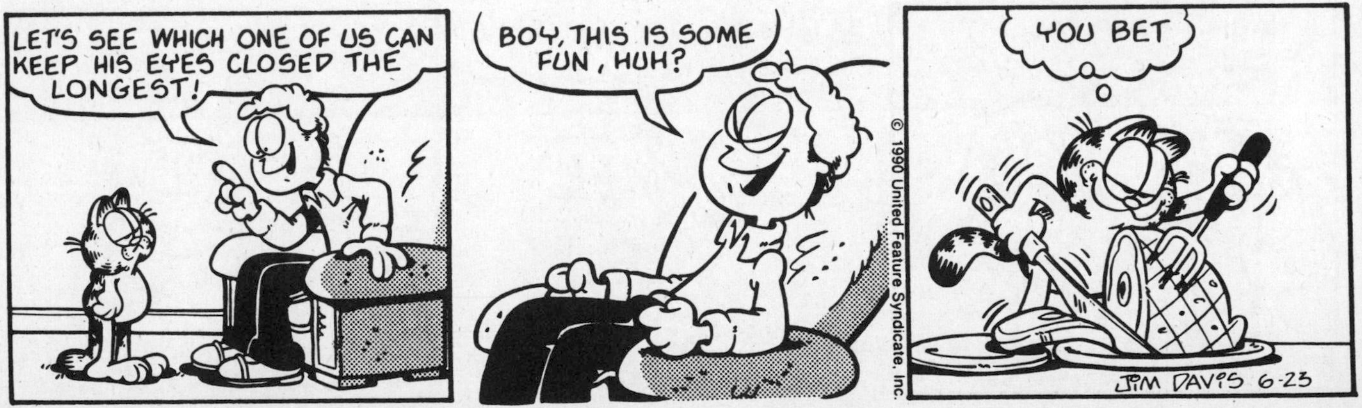
LET'S SEE WHICH ONE OF US CAN KEEP HIS EYES CLOSED THE LONGEST!
BOY, THIS IS SOME FUN, HUH?
© 1990 United Feature Syndicate, Inc.
YOU BET
JIM DAVIS 6-23

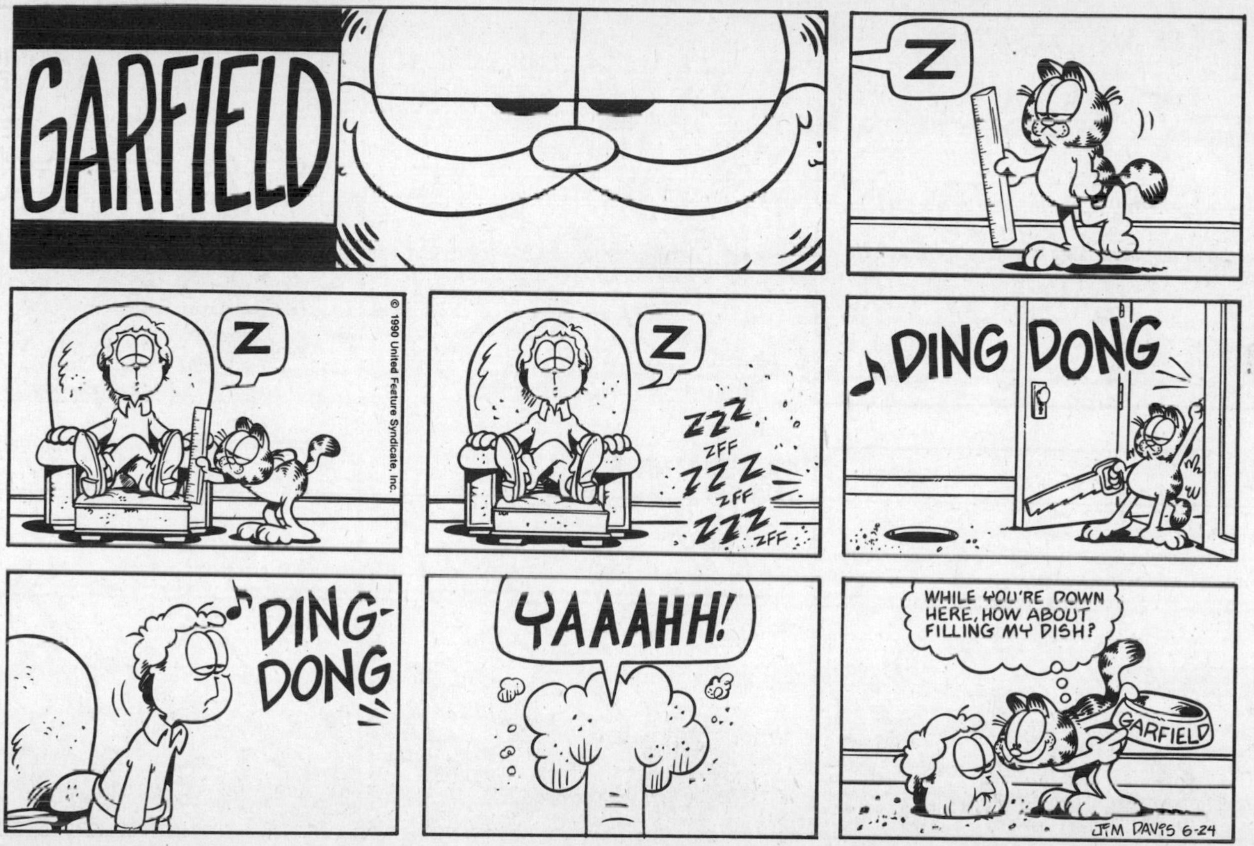
GARFIELD
Z
© 1990 United Feature Syndicate, Inc.
Z
Z
ZZZ
ZFF
ZZZ
ZFF
ZZZ
ZFF
DING DONG
DING-
DONG
YAAAHH!
WHILE YOU'RE DOWN HERE, HOW ABOUT FILLING MY DISH?
GARFIELD
JIM DAVIS 6-24

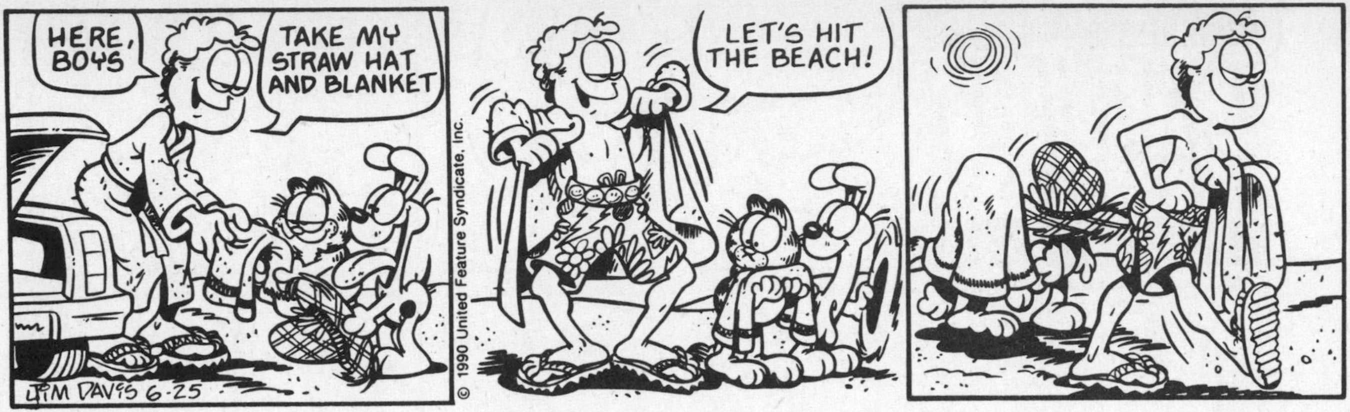
HERE, BOYS
TAKE MY STRAW HAT AND BLANKET
JIM DAVIS 6-25
© 1990 United Feature Syndicate, Inc.
LET'S HIT THE BEACH!

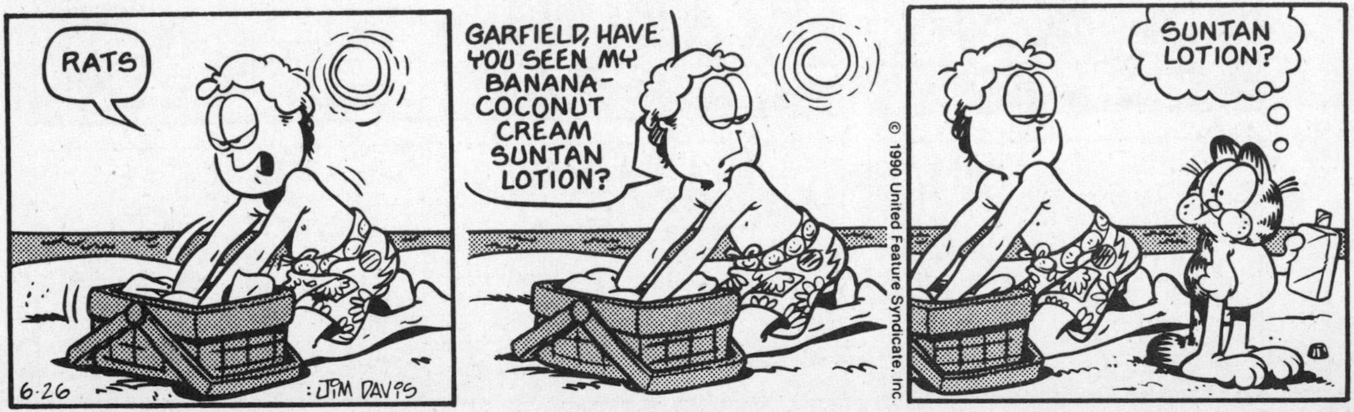
RATS
6-26
JIM DAVIS
GARFIELD, HAVE YOU SEEN MY BANANA-COCONUT CREAM SUNTAN LOTION?
© 1990 United Feature Syndicate, Inc.
SUNTAN LOTION?

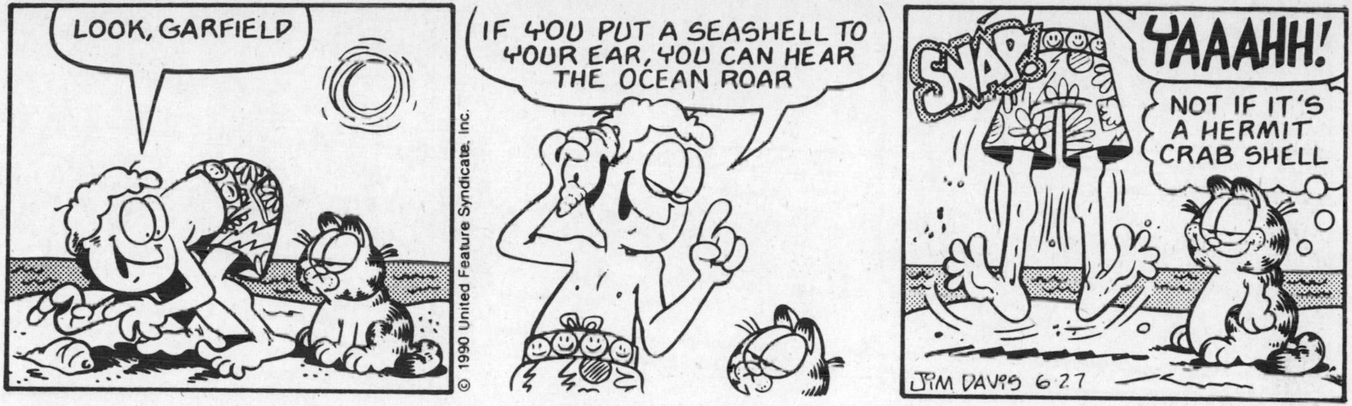
LOOK, GARFIELD
IF YOU PUT A SEASHELL TO YOUR EAR, YOU CAN HEAR THE OCEAN ROAR
SNAP!
YAAAHH!
NOT IF IT'S A HERMIT CRAB SHELL
JIM DAVIS 6-27
© 1990 United Feature Syndicate, Inc.

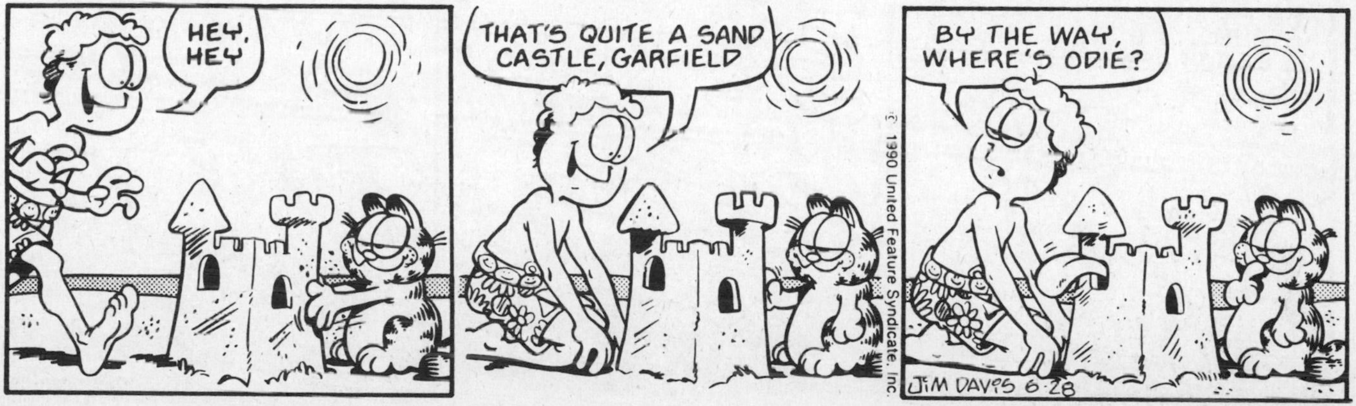
HEY, HEY
THAT'S QUITE A SAND CASTLE, GARFIELD
BY THE WAY, WHERE'S ODIE?
JIM DAVIS 6-28
© 1990 United Feature Syndicate, Inc.

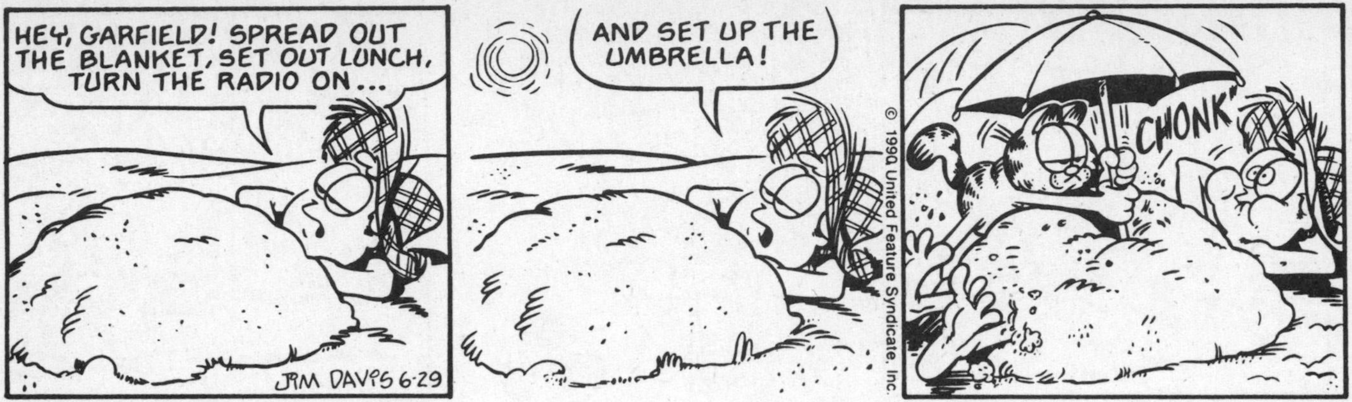
HEY, GARFIELD! SPREAD OUT THE BLANKET, SET OUT LUNCH, TURN THE RADIO ON...
AND SET UP THE UMBRELLA!
CHONK
JIM DAVIS 6-29
© 1990 United Feature Syndicate, Inc.

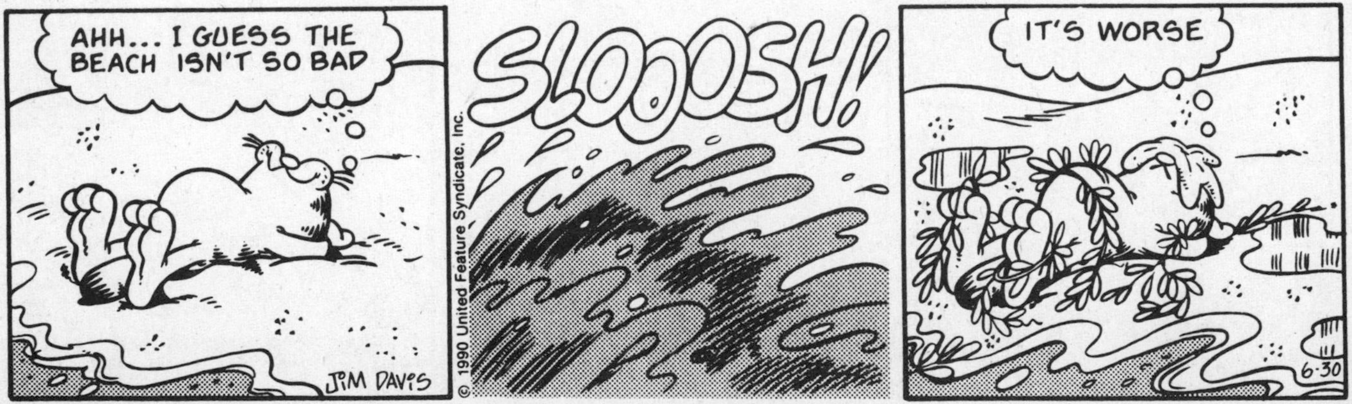
AHH... I GUESS THE BEACH ISN'T SO BAD
SLOOOOSH!
IT'S WORSE
JIM DAVIS
6-30
© 1990 United Feature Syndicate, Inc.

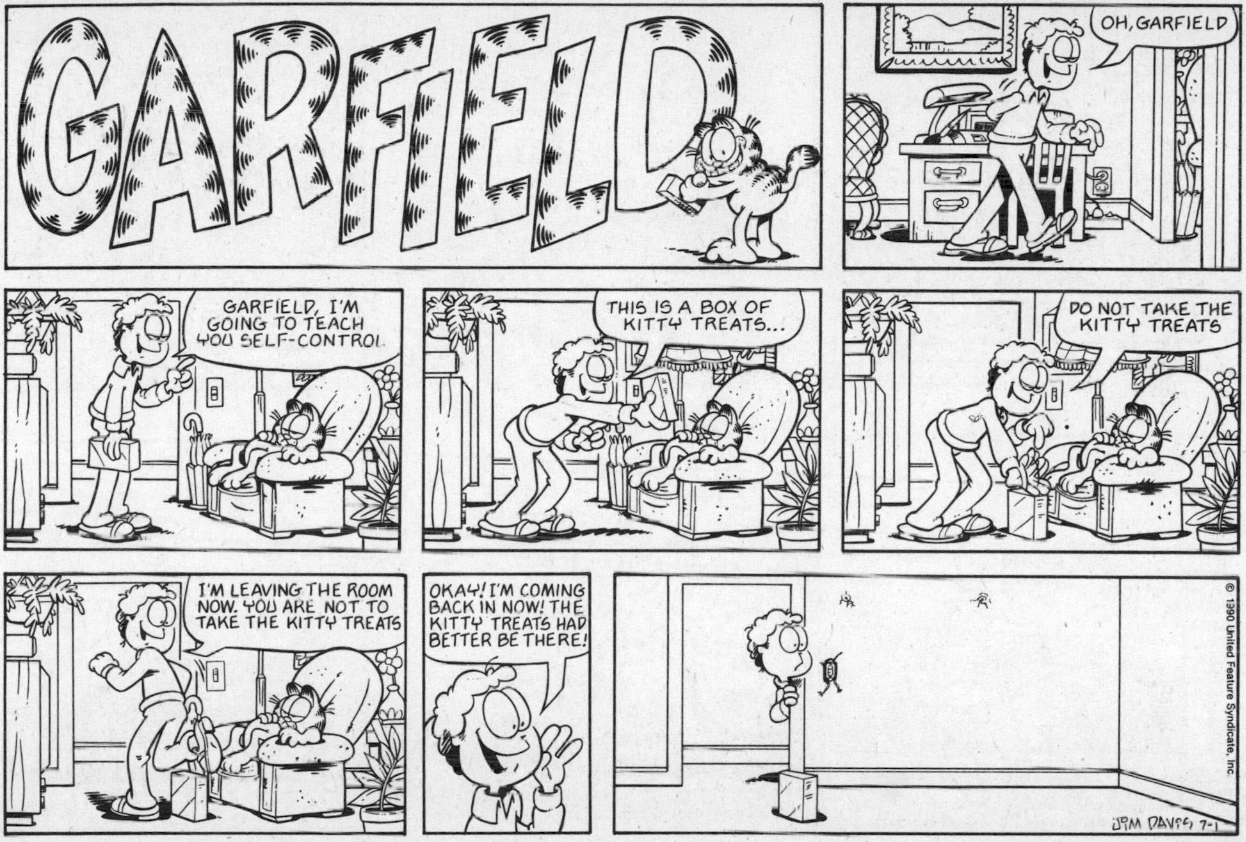
GARFIELD
OH, GARFIELD
GARFIELD, I'M GOING TO TEACH YOU SELF-CONTROL
THIS IS A BOX OF KITTY TREATS...
DO NOT TAKE THE KITTY TREATS
I'M LEAVING THE ROOM NOW. YOU ARE NOT TO TAKE THE KITTY TREATS
OKAY! I'M COMING BACK IN NOW! THE KITTY TREATS HAD BETTER BE THERE!
© 1990 United Feature Syndicate, Inc.
JIM DAVIS 7-1

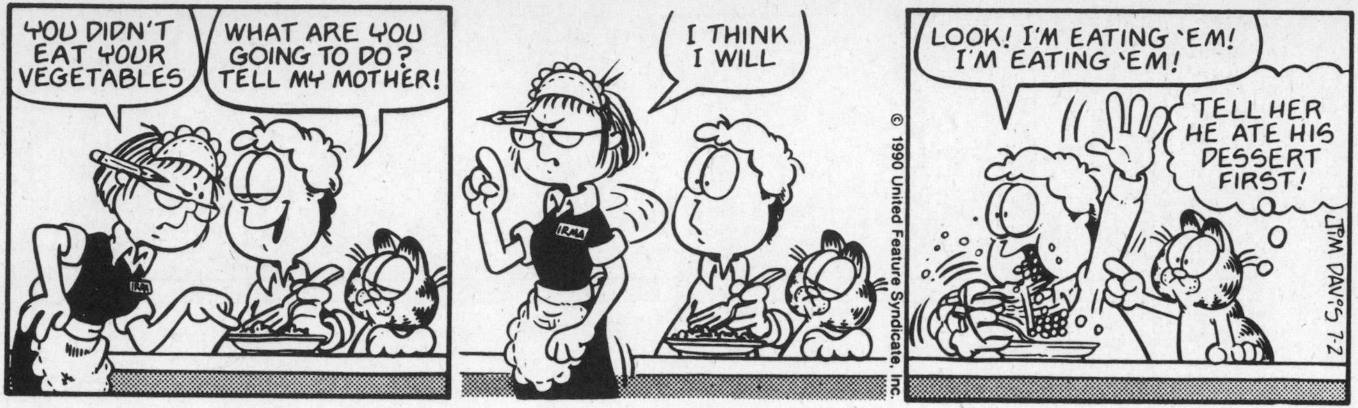
YOU DIDN'T EAT YOUR VEGETABLES
WHAT ARE YOU GOING TO DO? TELL MY MOTHER!
IRMA
I THINK I WILL
© 1990 United Feature Syndicate, Inc.
LOOK! I'M EATING 'EM! I'M EATING 'EM!
TELL HER HE ATE HIS DESSERT FIRST!
JIM DAVIS 7-2

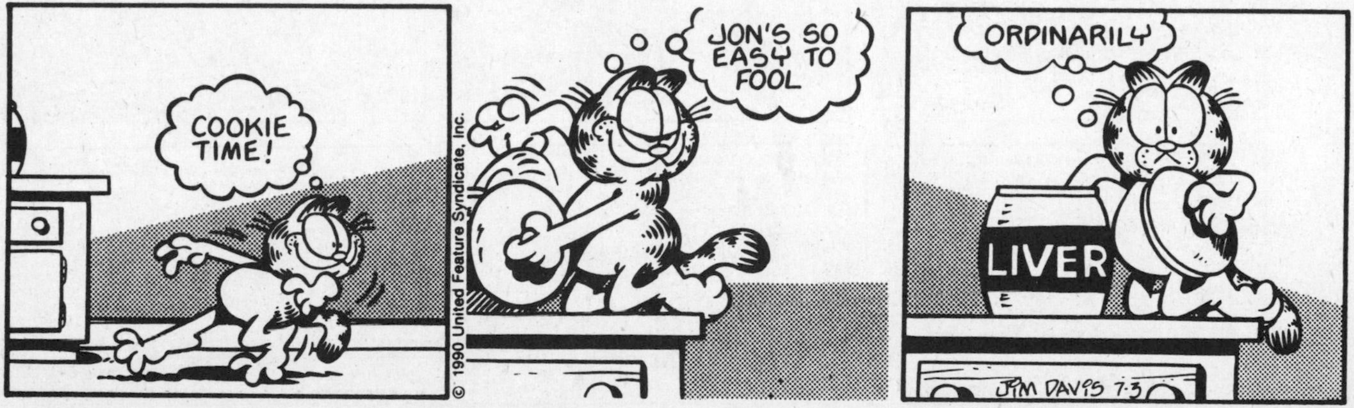
COOKIE TIME!
© 1990 United Feature Syndicate, Inc.
JON'S SO EASY TO FOOL
ORDINARILY
LIVER
JIM DAVIS 7-3

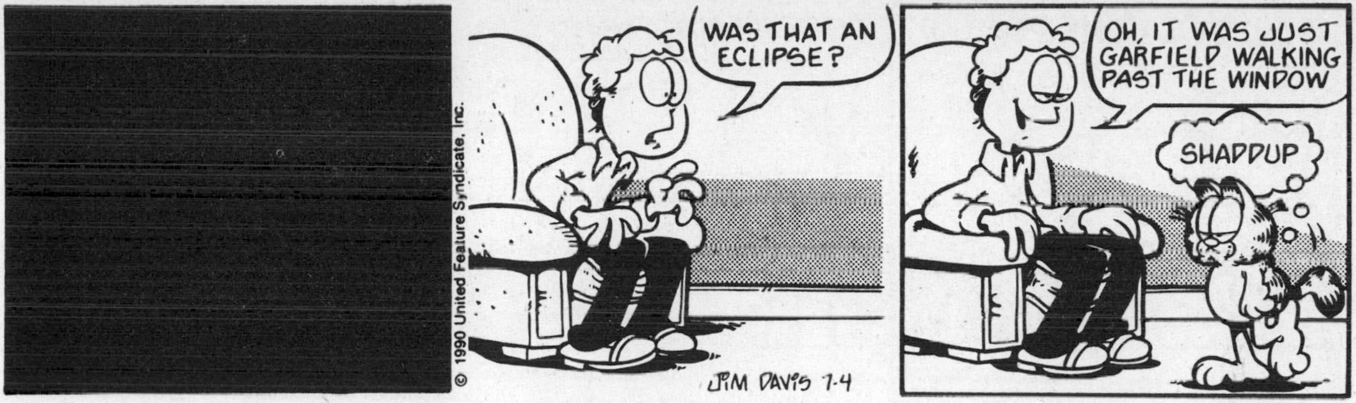
WAS THAT AN ECLIPSE?
© 1990 United Feature Syndicate, Inc.
JIM DAVIS 7-4
OH, IT WAS JUST GARFIELD WALKING PAST THE WINDOW
SHADDUP

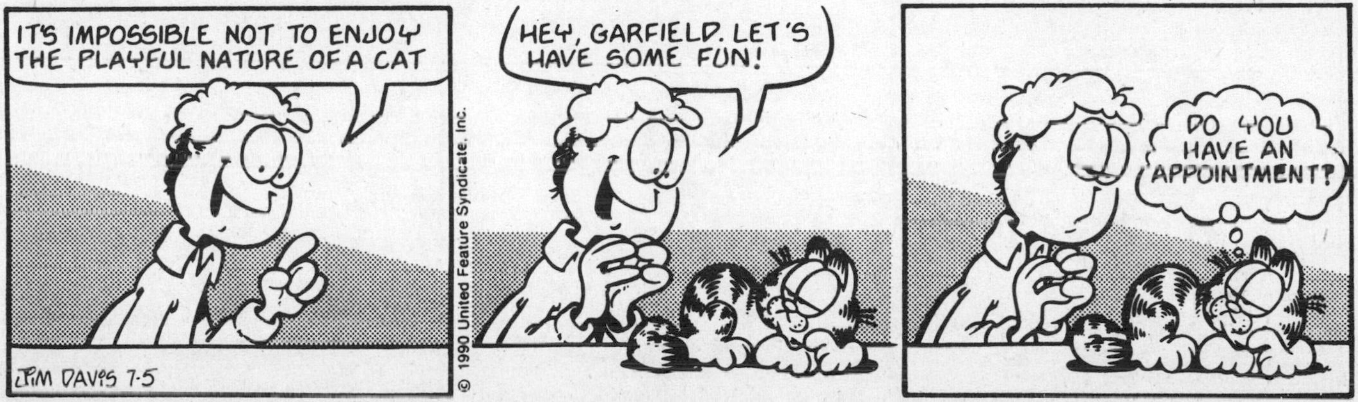
IT'S IMPOSSIBLE NOT TO ENJOY THE PLAYFUL NATURE OF A CAT
JIM DAVIS 7-5
© 1990 United Feature Syndicate, Inc.
HEY, GARFIELD. LET'S HAVE SOME FUN!
DO YOU HAVE AN APPOINTMENT?

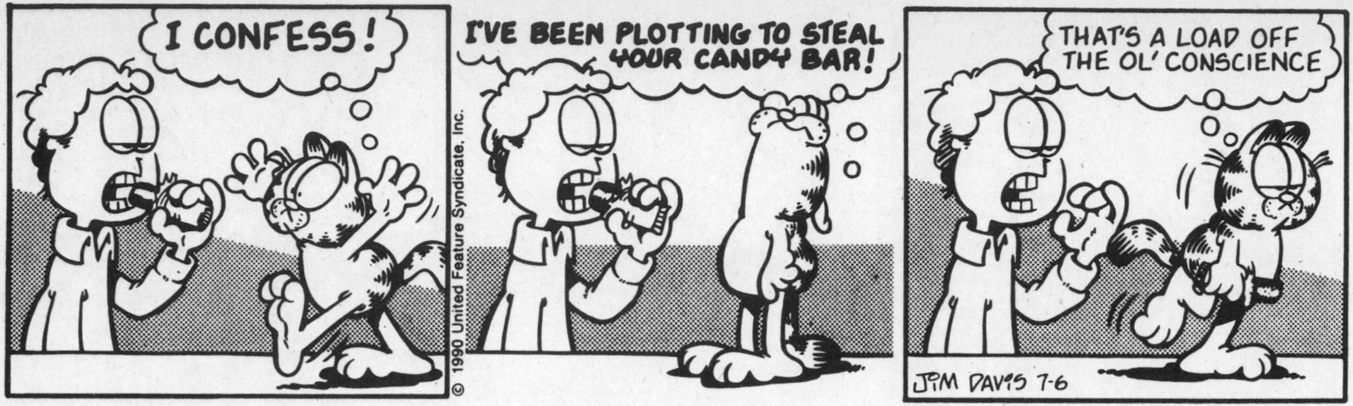
I CONFESS!
I'VE BEEN PLOTTING TO STEAL YOUR CANDY BAR!
THAT'S A LOAD OFF THE OL' CONSCIENCE
© 1990 United Feature Syndicate, Inc.
JIM DAVIS 7-6

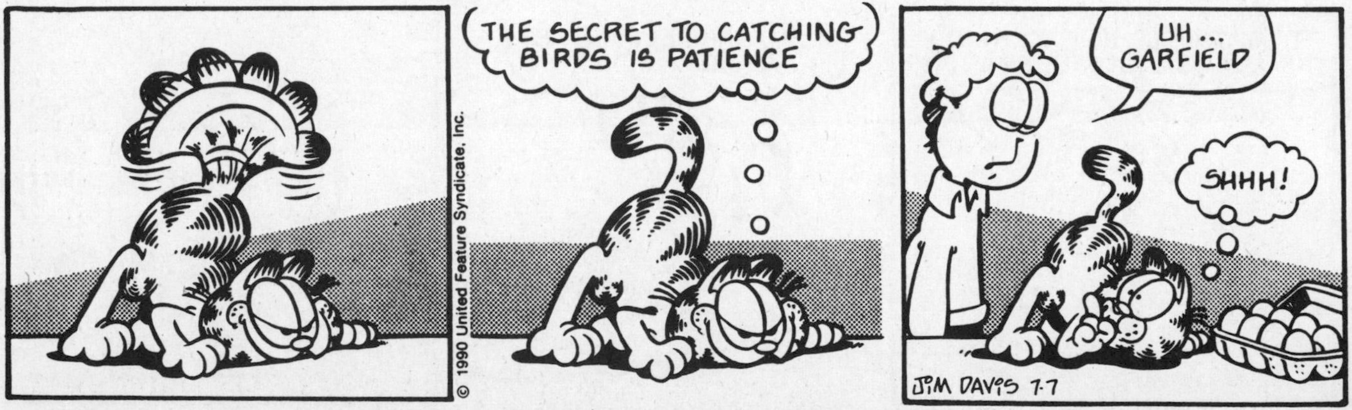
THE SECRET TO CATCHING BIRDS IS PATIENCE
UH... GARFIELD
SHHH!
© 1990 United Feature Syndicate, Inc.
JIM DAVIS 7-7

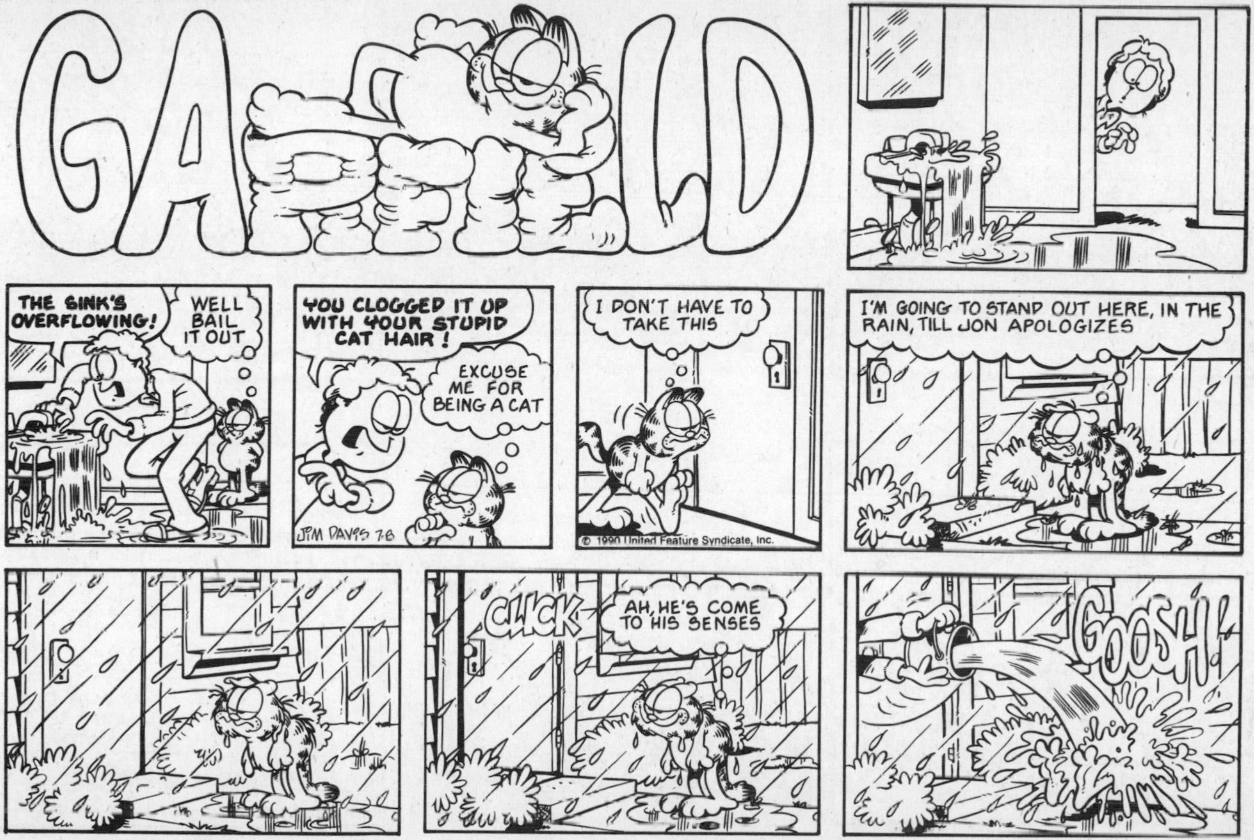
GARFIELD
THE SINK'S OVERFLOWING!
WELL BAIL IT OUT
YOU CLOGGED IT UP WITH YOUR STUPID CAT HAIR!
EXCUSE ME FOR BEING A CAT
JIM DAVIS 7-8
I DON'T HAVE TO TAKE THIS
© 1990 United Feature Syndicate, Inc.
I'M GOING TO STAND OUT HERE, IN THE RAIN, TILL JON APOLOGIZES
CLICK
AH, HE'S COME TO HIS SENSES
GOOSH!

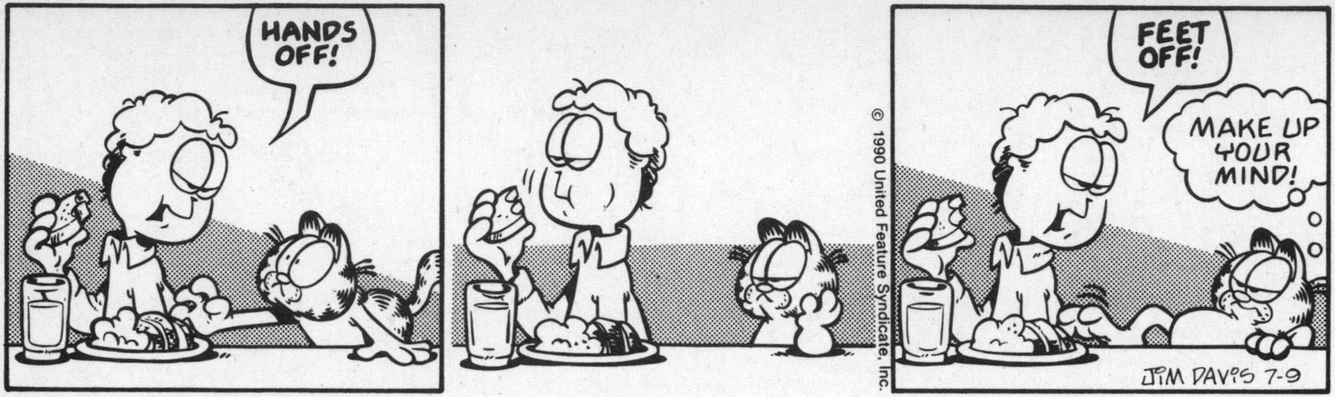
HANDS OFF!
FEET OFF!
MAKE UP YOUR MIND!
© 1990 United Feature Syndicate, Inc.
JIM DAVIS 7-9

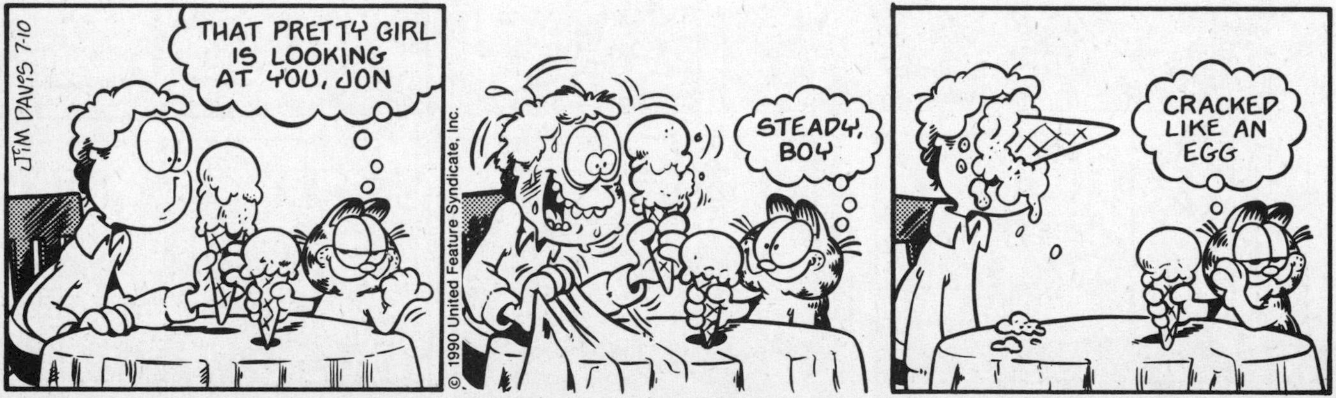
JIM DAVIS 7-10
THAT PRETTY GIRL IS LOOKING AT YOU, JON
© 1990 United Feature Syndicate, Inc.
STEADY, BOY
CRACKED LIKE AN EGG

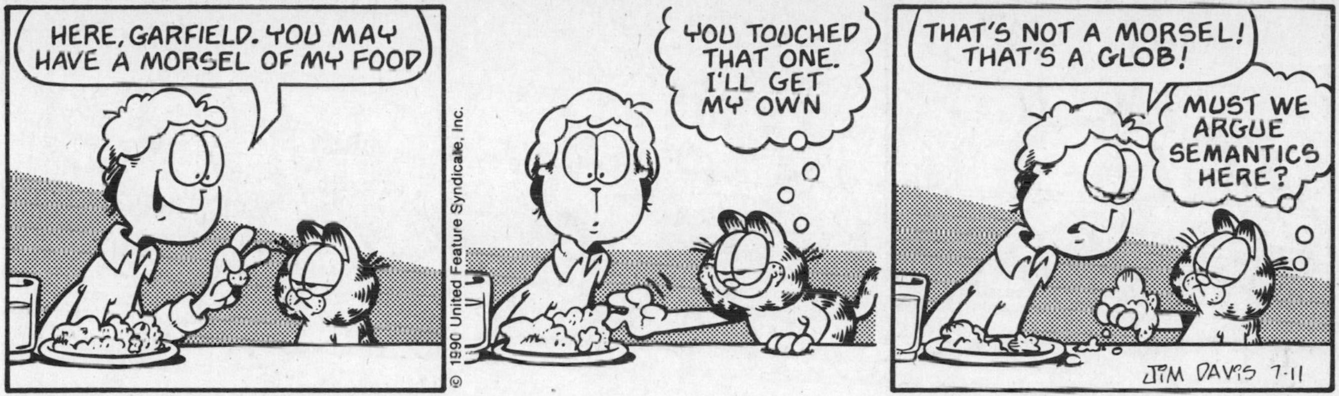
HERE, GARFIELD. YOU MAY HAVE A MORSEL OF MY FOOD
© 1990 United Feature Syndicate, Inc.
YOU TOUCHED THAT ONE. I'LL GET MY OWN
THAT'S NOT A MORSEL! THAT'S A GLOB!
MUST WE ARGUE SEMANTICS HERE?
JIM DAVIS 7-11

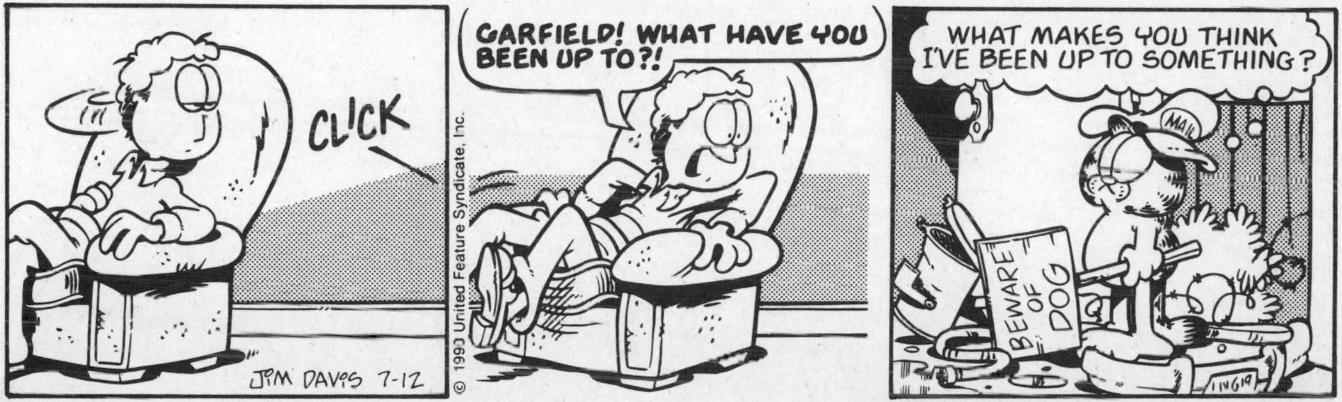
CLICK
JIM DAVIS 7-12
© 1990 United Feature Syndicate, Inc.
GARFIELD! WHAT HAVE YOU BEEN UP TO?!
WHAT MAKES YOU THINK I'VE BEEN UP TO SOMETHING?
MAIL
BEWARE OF DOG

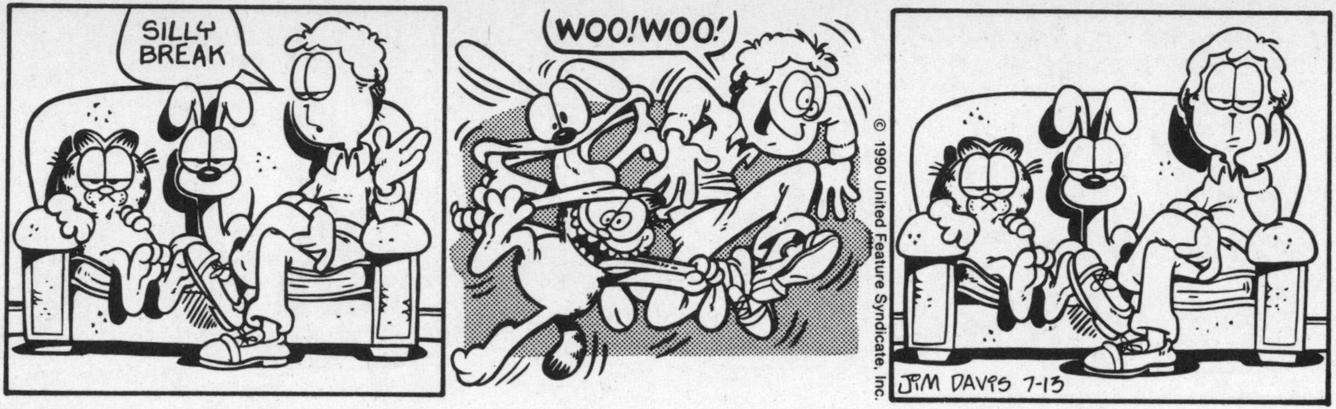
SILLY BREAK
WOO! WOO!
© 1990 United Feature Syndicate, Inc.
JIM DAVIS 7-13

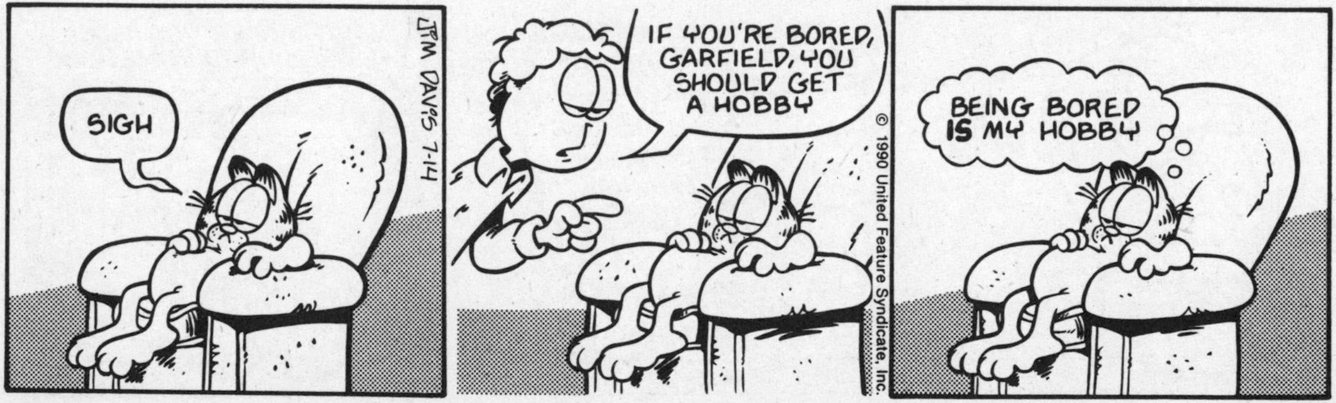
SIGH
JIM DAVIS 7-14
IF YOU'RE BORED, GARFIELD, YOU SHOULD GET A HOBBY
© 1990 United Feature Syndicate, Inc.
BEING BORED IS MY HOBBY

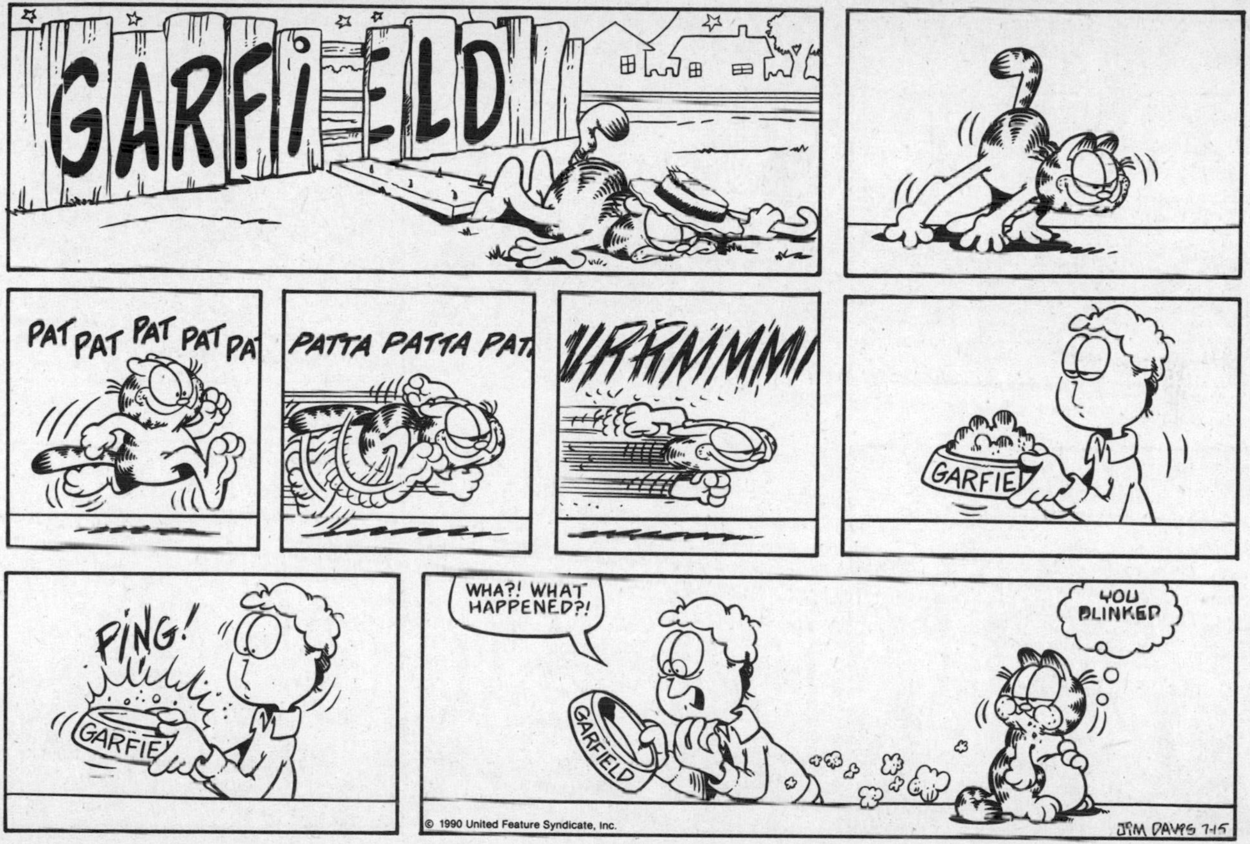
GARFIELD
PAT PAT PAT PAT PA
PATTA PATTA PAT
GARFIE
PING!
GARFIE
WHA?! WHAT HAPPENED?!
GARFIELD
YOU BLINKED
JIM DAVIS 7-15

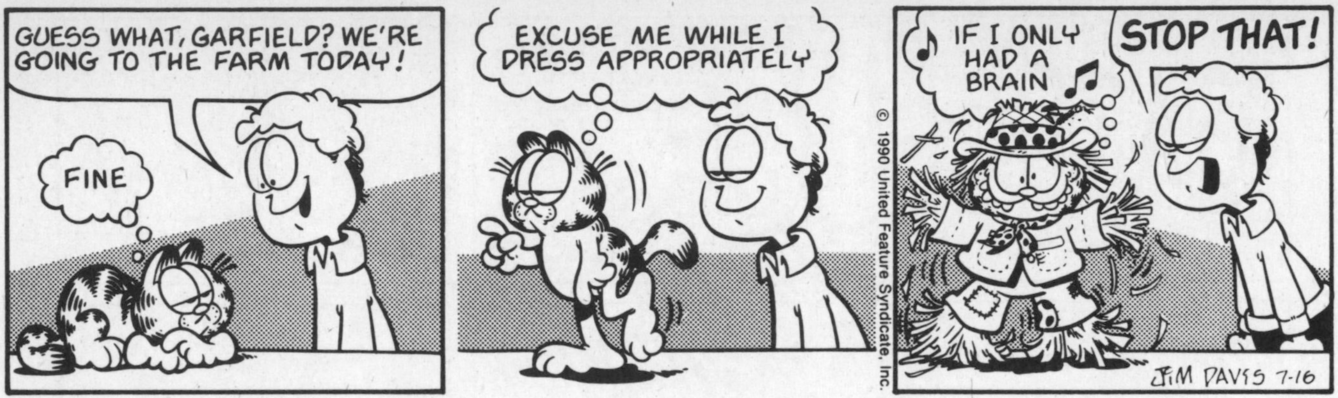
GUESS WHAT, GARFIELD? WE'RE GOING TO THE FARM TODAY!
FINE
EXCUSE ME WHILE I DRESS APPROPRIATELY
IF I ONLY HAD A BRAIN
STOP THAT!
JIM DAVIS 7-16
© 1990 United Feature Syndicate, Inc.

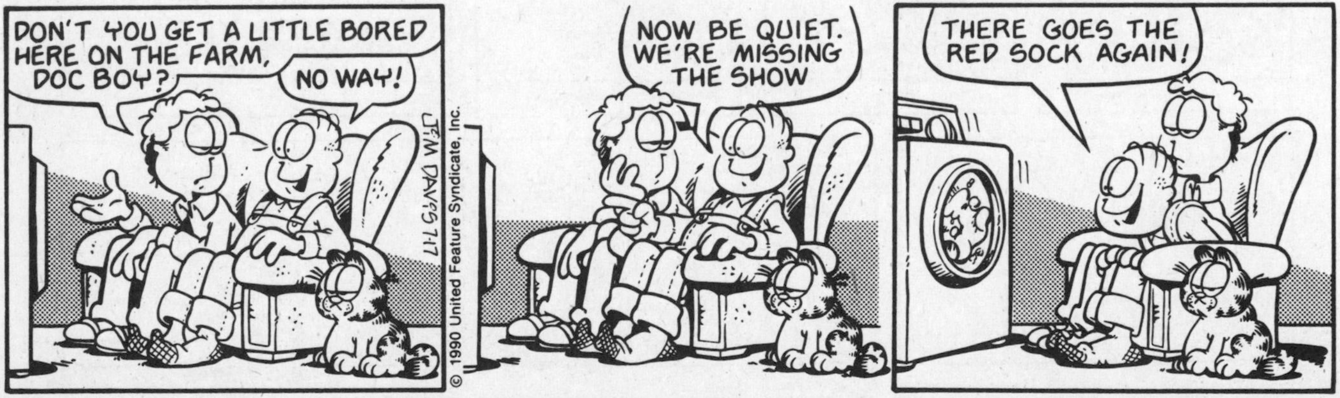
DON'T YOU GET A LITTLE BORED HERE ON THE FARM, DOC BOY?
NO WAY!
JIM DAVIS 7-17
© 1990 United Feature Syndicate, Inc.
NOW BE QUIET. WE'RE MISSING THE SHOW
THERE GOES THE RED SOCK AGAIN!

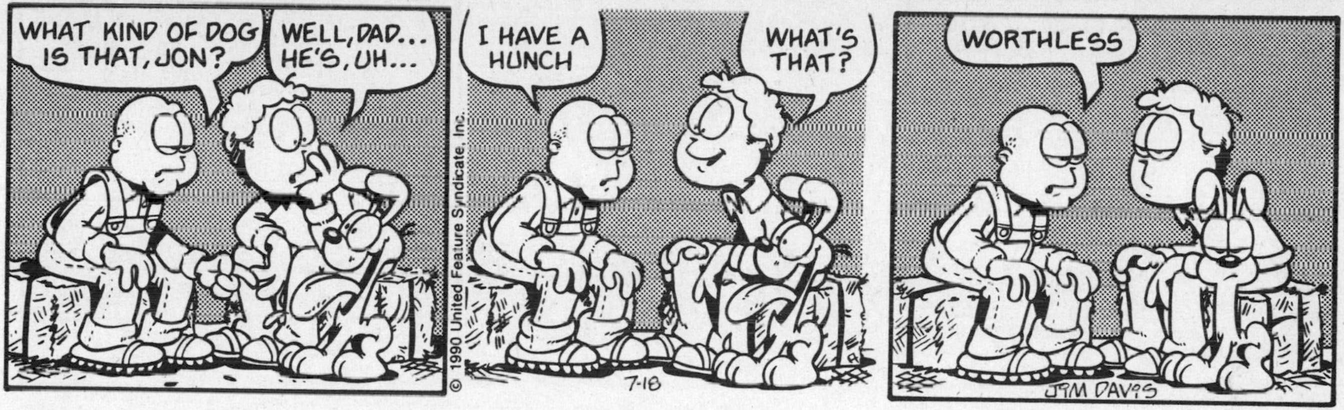
WHAT KIND OF DOG IS THAT, JON?
WELL, DAD... HE'S, UH...
I HAVE A HUNCH
WHAT'S THAT?
WORTHLESS
© 1990 United Feature Syndicate, Inc.
7-18
JIM DAVIS

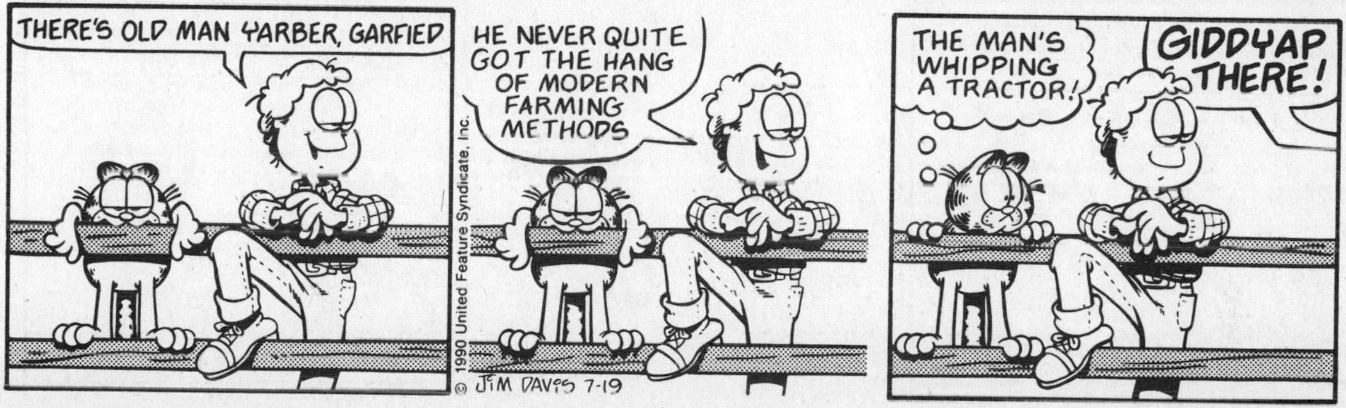
THERE'S OLD MAN YARBER, GARFIED
HE NEVER QUITE GOT THE HANG OF MODERN FARMING METHODS
THE MAN'S WHIPPING A TRACTOR!
GIDDYAP THERE!
© 1990 United Feature Syndicate, Inc.
JIM DAVIS 7-19

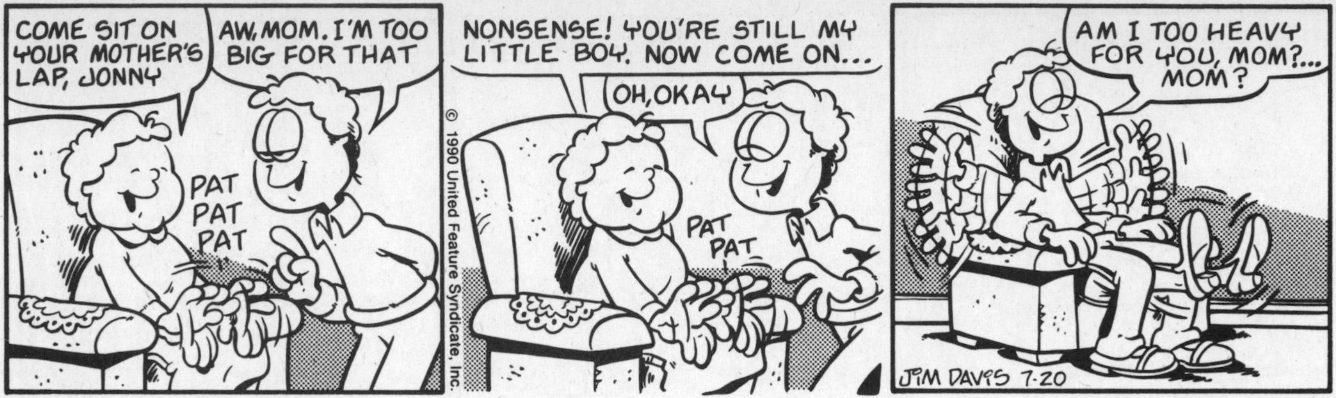
COME SIT ON YOUR MOTHER'S LAP, JONNY
AW, MOM. I'M TOO BIG FOR THAT
PAT PAT PAT
© 1990 United Feature Syndicate, Inc.
NONSENSE! YOU'RE STILL MY LITTLE BOY. NOW COME ON...
OH, OKAY
PAT PAT
AM I TOO HEAVY FOR YOU, MOM?... MOM?
JIM DAVIS 7-20

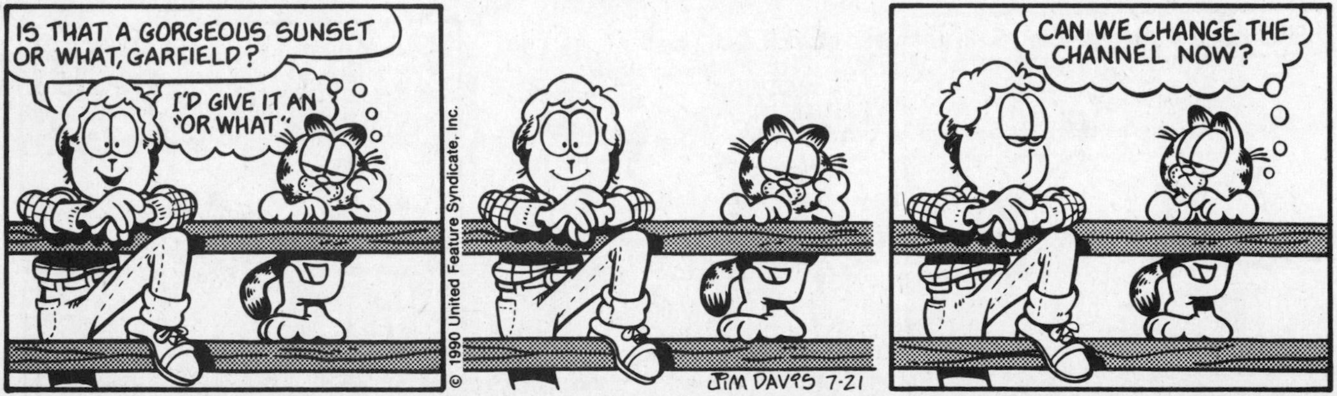
IS THAT A GORGEOUS SUNSET OR WHAT, GARFIELD?
I'D GIVE IT AN "OR WHAT"
© 1990 United Feature Syndicate, Inc.
JIM DAVIS 7-21
CAN WE CHANGE THE CHANNEL NOW?

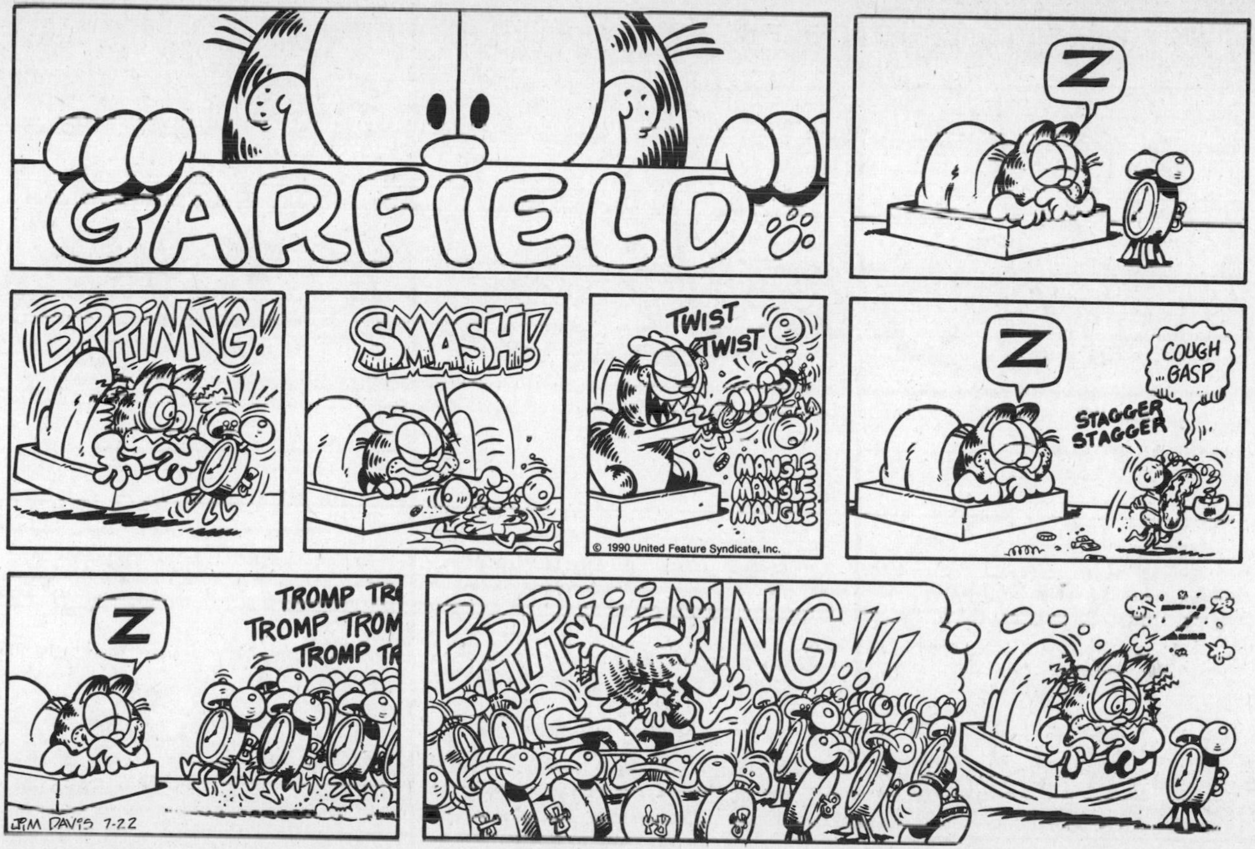
GARFIELD
Z
BRRINNG!
SMASH!
TWIST
TWIST
MANGLE
MANGLE
MANGLE
© 1990 United Feature Syndicate, Inc.
Z
COUGH
...GASP
STAGGER
STAGGER
Z
TROMP TR
TROMP TROM
TROMP TR
JIM DAVIS 7-22
BRRiiiNNG!!!
Z

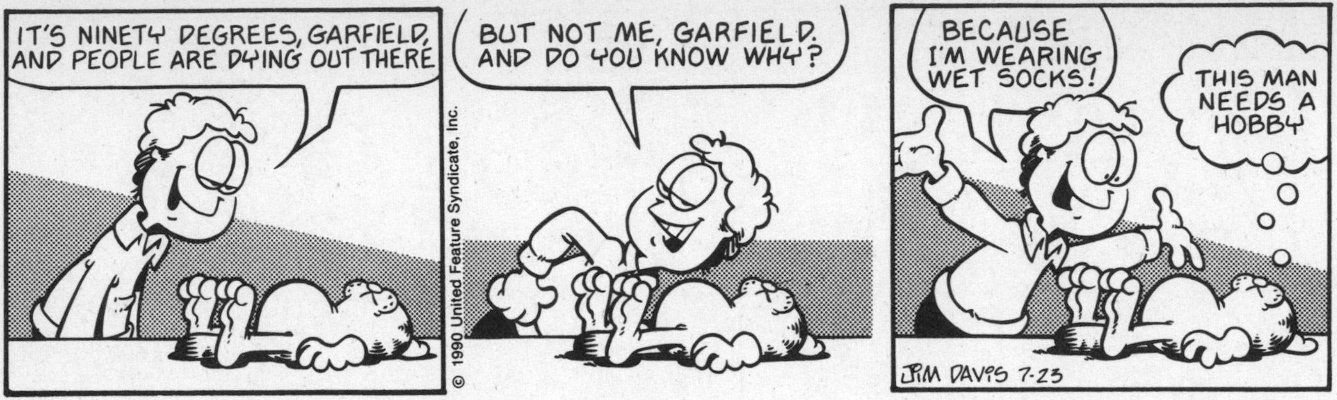
IT'S NINETY DEGREES, GARFIELD, AND PEOPLE ARE DYING OUT THERE
BUT NOT ME, GARFIELD. AND DO YOU KNOW WHY?
BECAUSE I'M WEARING WET SOCKS!
THIS MAN NEEDS A HOBBY
JIM DAVIS 7-23
© 1990 United Feature Syndicate, Inc.

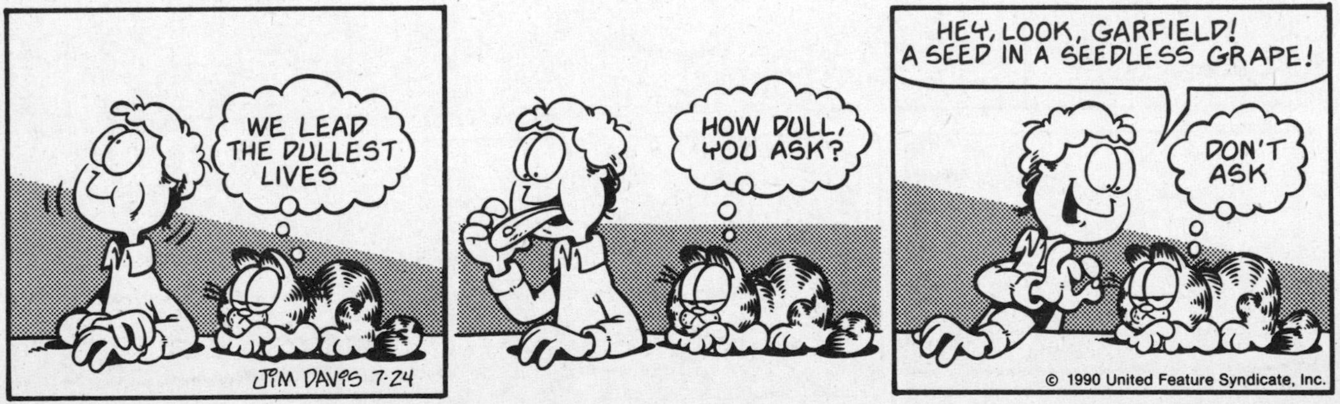
WE LEAD THE DULLEST LIVES
JIM DAVIS 7-24
HOW DULL, YOU ASK?
HEY, LOOK, GARFIELD! A SEED IN A SEEDLESS GRAPE!
DON'T ASK
© 1990 United Feature Syndicate, Inc.

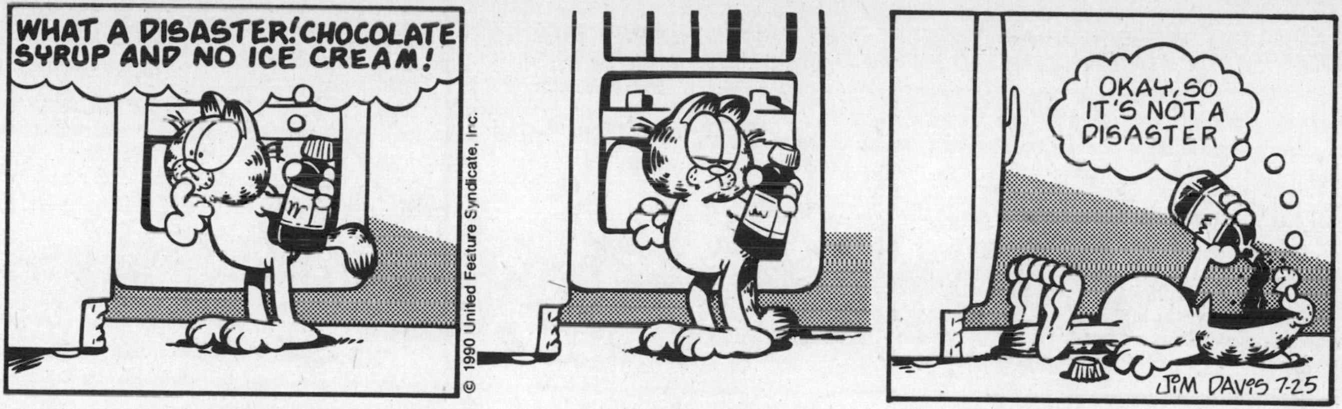
WHAT A DISASTER! CHOCOLATE SYRUP AND NO ICE CREAM!
OKAY, SO IT'S NOT A DISASTER
JIM DAVIS 7-25

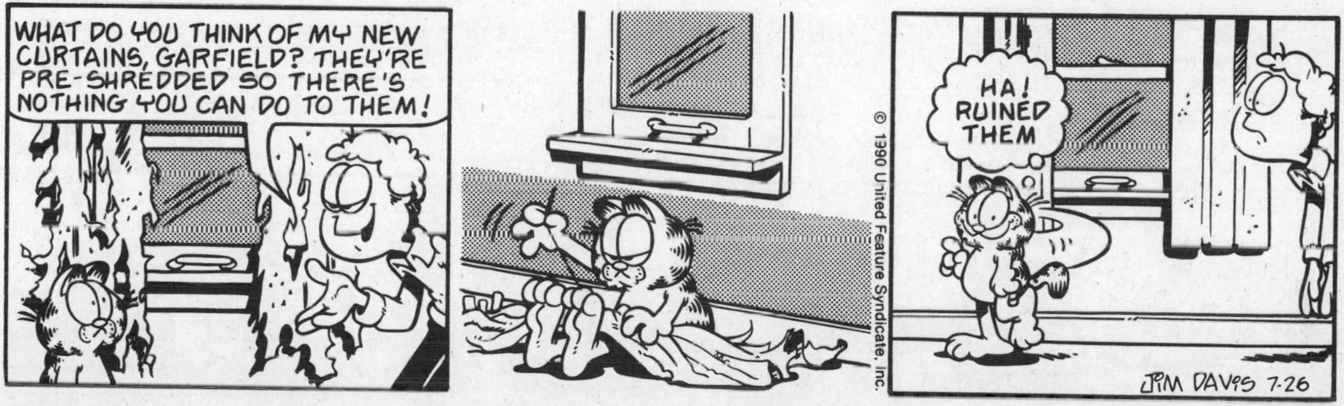
WHAT DO YOU THINK OF MY NEW CURTAINS, GARFIELD? THEY'RE PRE-SHREDDED SO THERE'S NOTHING YOU CAN DO TO THEM!
HA! RUINED THEM
JIM DAVIS 7-26

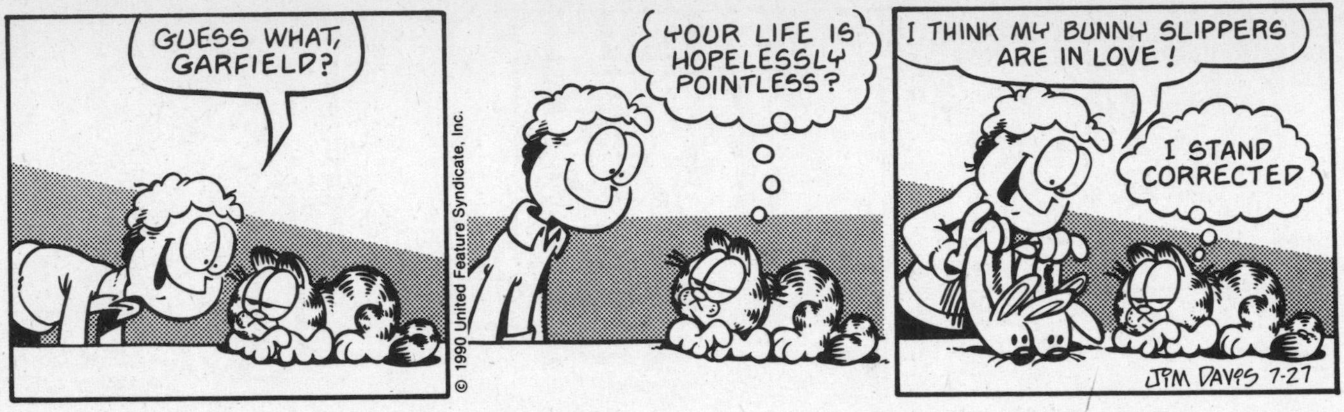
GUESS WHAT, GARFIELD?
YOUR LIFE IS HOPELESSLY POINTLESS?
I THINK MY BUNNY SLIPPERS ARE IN LOVE!
I STAND CORRECTED
JIM DAVIS 7-27

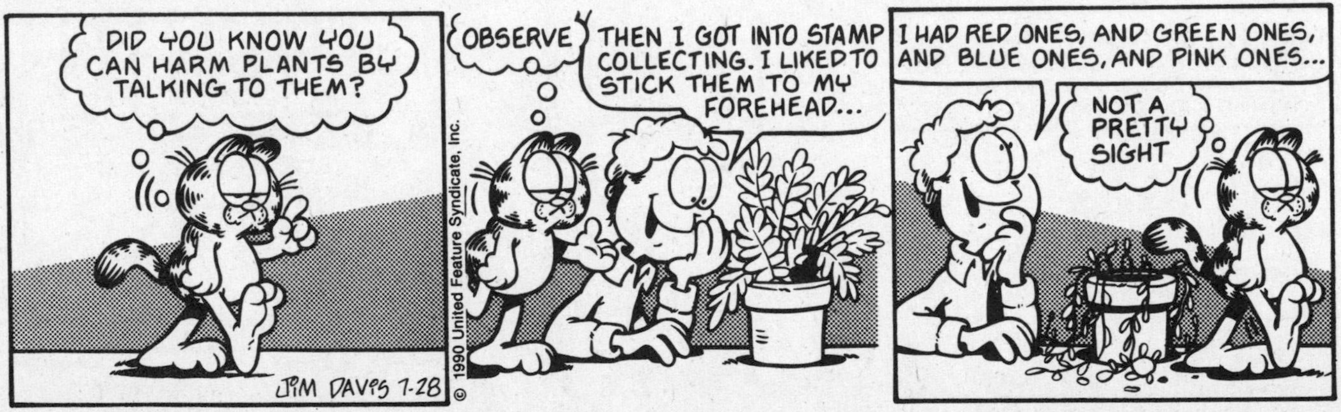
DID YOU KNOW YOU CAN HARM PLANTS BY TALKING TO THEM?
JIM DAVIS 7-28
OBSERVE
THEN I GOT INTO STAMP COLLECTING. I LIKED TO STICK THEM TO MY FOREHEAD...
I HAD RED ONES, AND GREEN ONES, AND BLUE ONES, AND PINK ONES...
NOT A PRETTY SIGHT

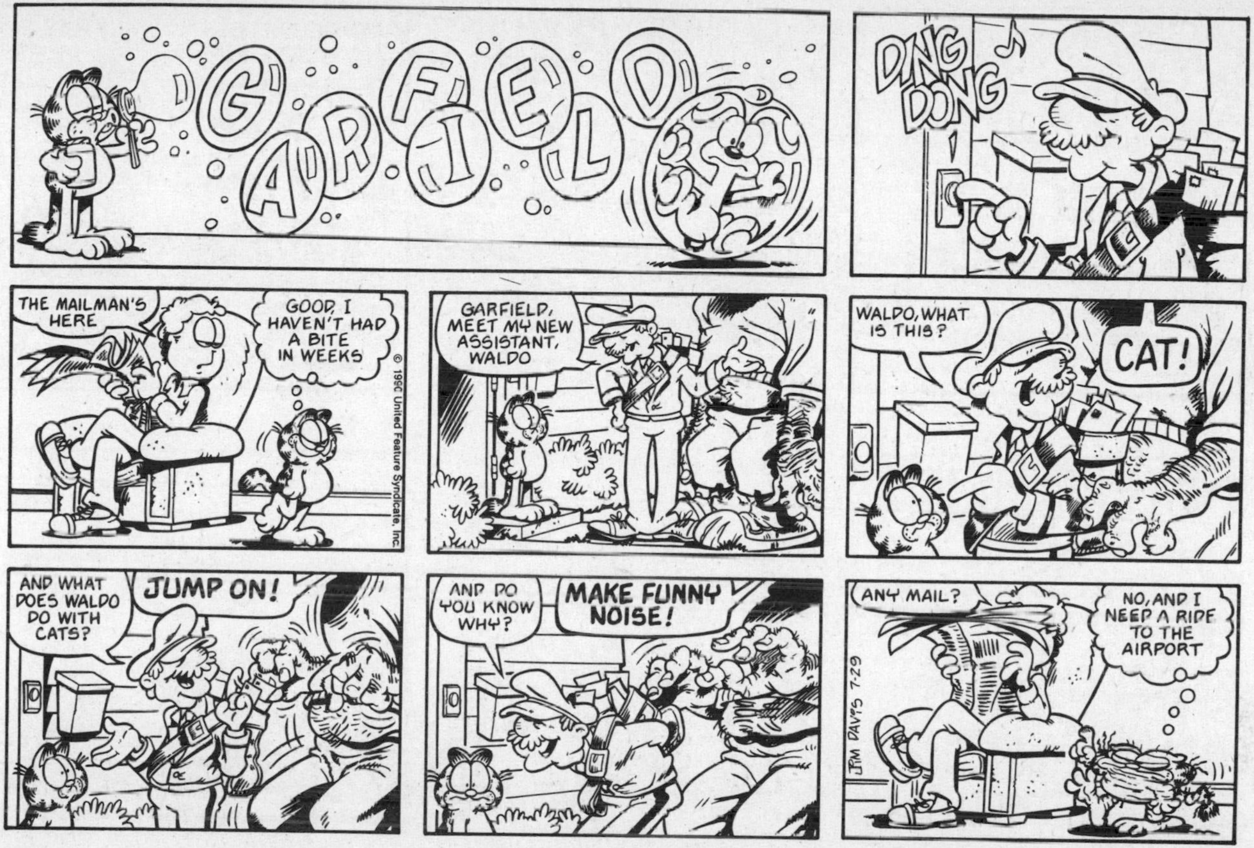
GARFIELD
DING DONG
THE MAILMAN'S HERE
GOOD, I HAVEN'T HAD A BITE IN WEEKS
© 1990 United Feature Syndicate, Inc.
GARFIELD, MEET MY NEW ASSISTANT, WALDO
WALDO, WHAT IS THIS?
CAT!
AND WHAT DOES WALDO DO WITH CATS?
JUMP ON!
AND DO YOU KNOW WHY?
MAKE FUNNY NOISE!
JIM DAVIS 7-29
ANY MAIL?
NO, AND I NEED A RIDE TO THE AIRPORT

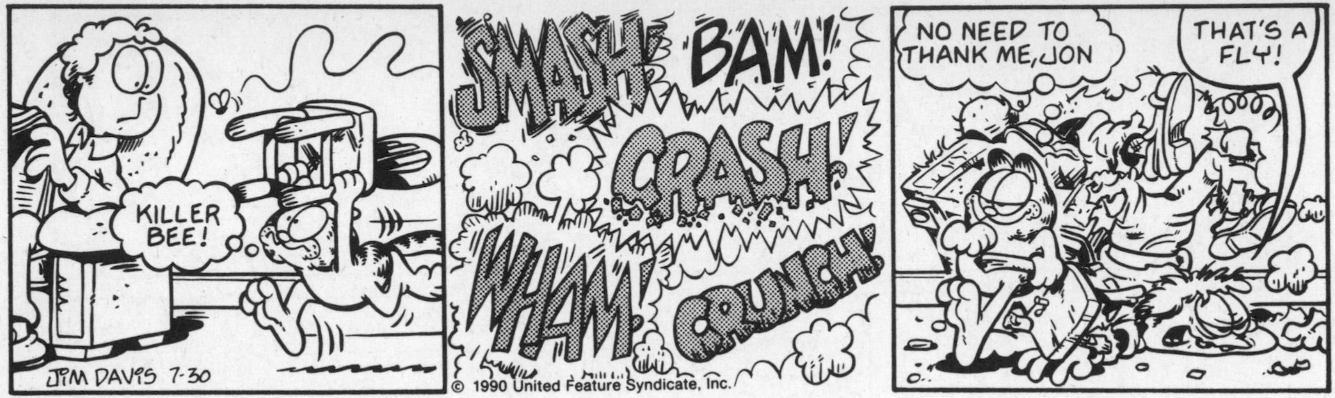
KILLER BEE!
JIM DAVIS 7-30
SMASH!
BAM!
CRASH!
WHAM!
CRUNCH!
© 1990 United Feature Syndicate, Inc.
NO NEED TO THANK ME, JON
THAT'S A FLY!

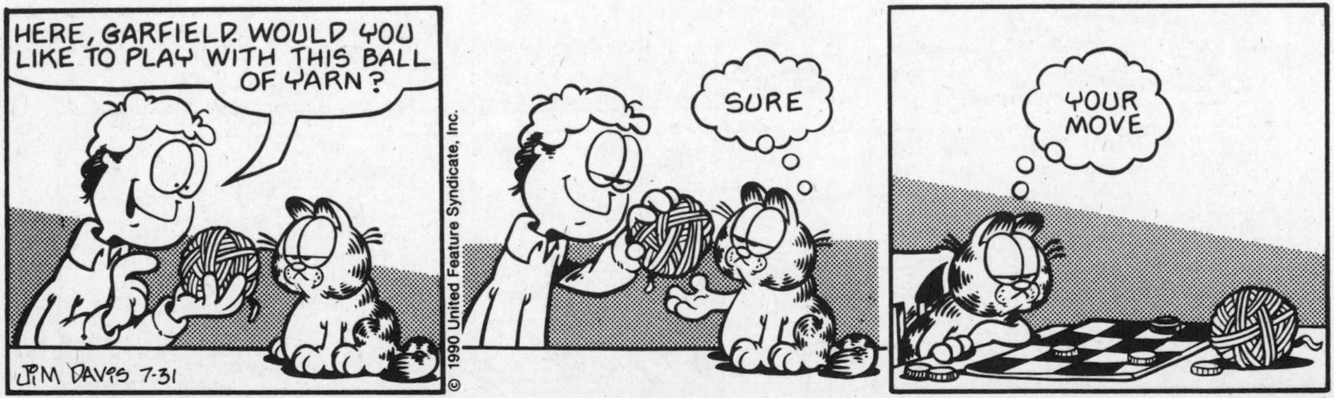
HERE, GARFIELD. WOULD YOU LIKE TO PLAY WITH THIS BALL OF YARN?
JIM DAVIS 7-31
© 1990 United Feature Syndicate, Inc.
SURE
YOUR MOVE

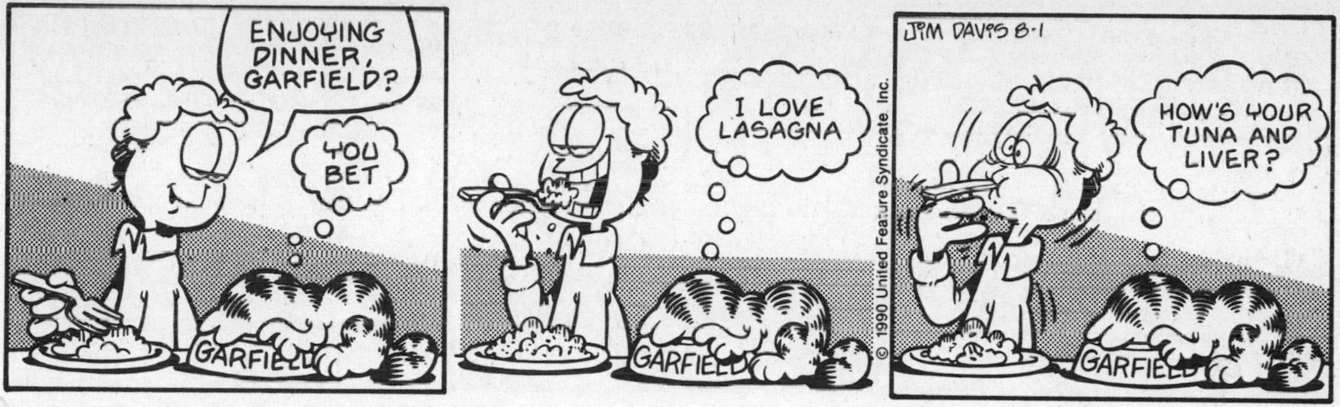
ENJOYING DINNER, GARFIELD?
YOU BET
I LOVE LASAGNA
© 1990 United Feature Syndicate, Inc.
JIM DAVIS 8-1
HOW'S YOUR TUNA AND LIVER?
GARFIELD

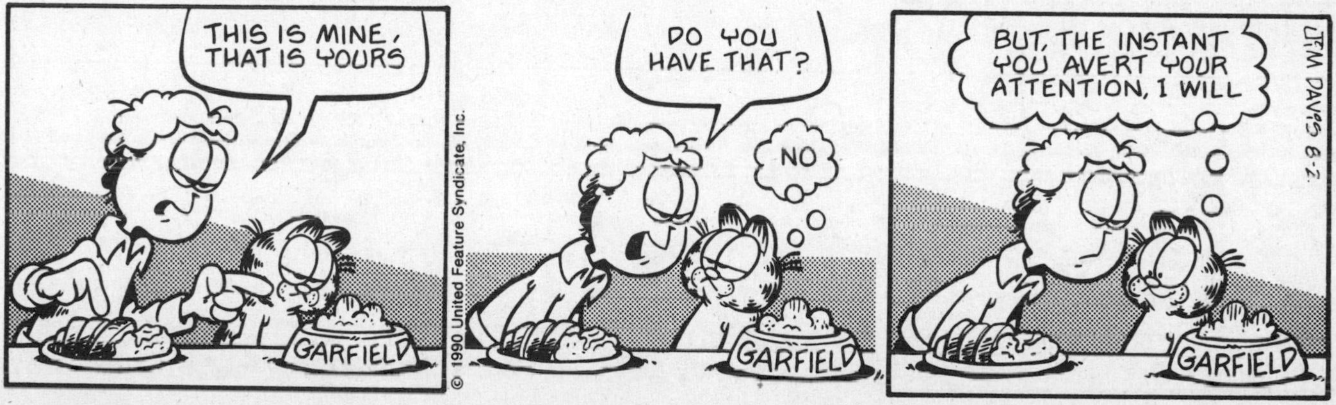
THIS IS MINE, THAT IS YOURS
GARFIELD
© 1990 United Feature Syndicate, Inc.
DO YOU HAVE THAT?
NO
BUT, THE INSTANT YOU AVERT YOUR ATTENTION, I WILL
JIM DAVIS 8-2

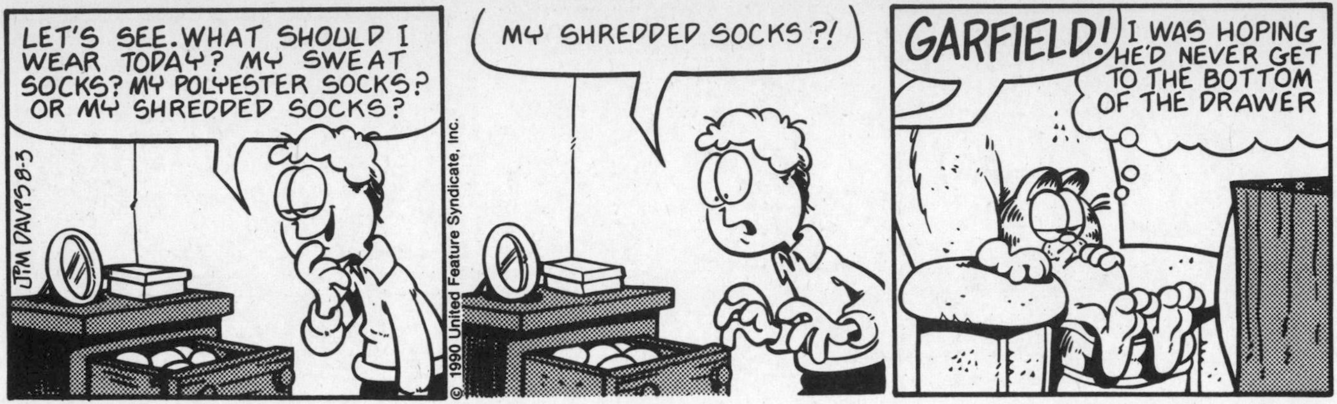
LET'S SEE. WHAT SHOULD I WEAR TODAY? MY SWEAT SOCKS? MY POLYESTER SOCKS? OR MY SHREDDED SOCKS?
JIM DAVIS 8-3
© 1990 United Feature Syndicate, Inc.
MY SHREDDED SOCKS?!
GARFIELD!
I WAS HOPING HE'D NEVER GET TO THE BOTTOM OF THE DRAWER

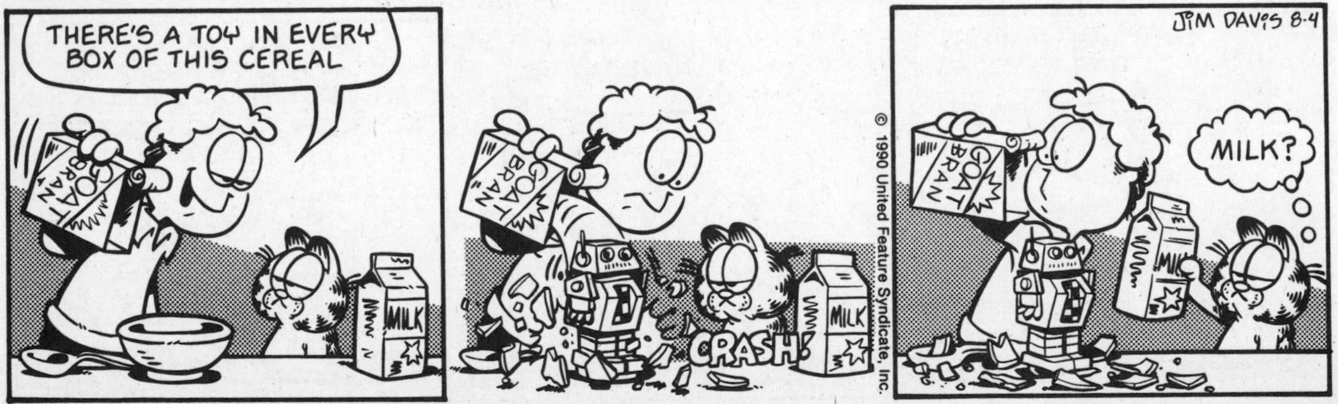
THERE'S A TOY IN EVERY BOX OF THIS CEREAL
GOAT BRAN
MILK
CRASH!
© 1990 United Feature Syndicate, Inc.
JIM DAVIS 8-4
MILK?

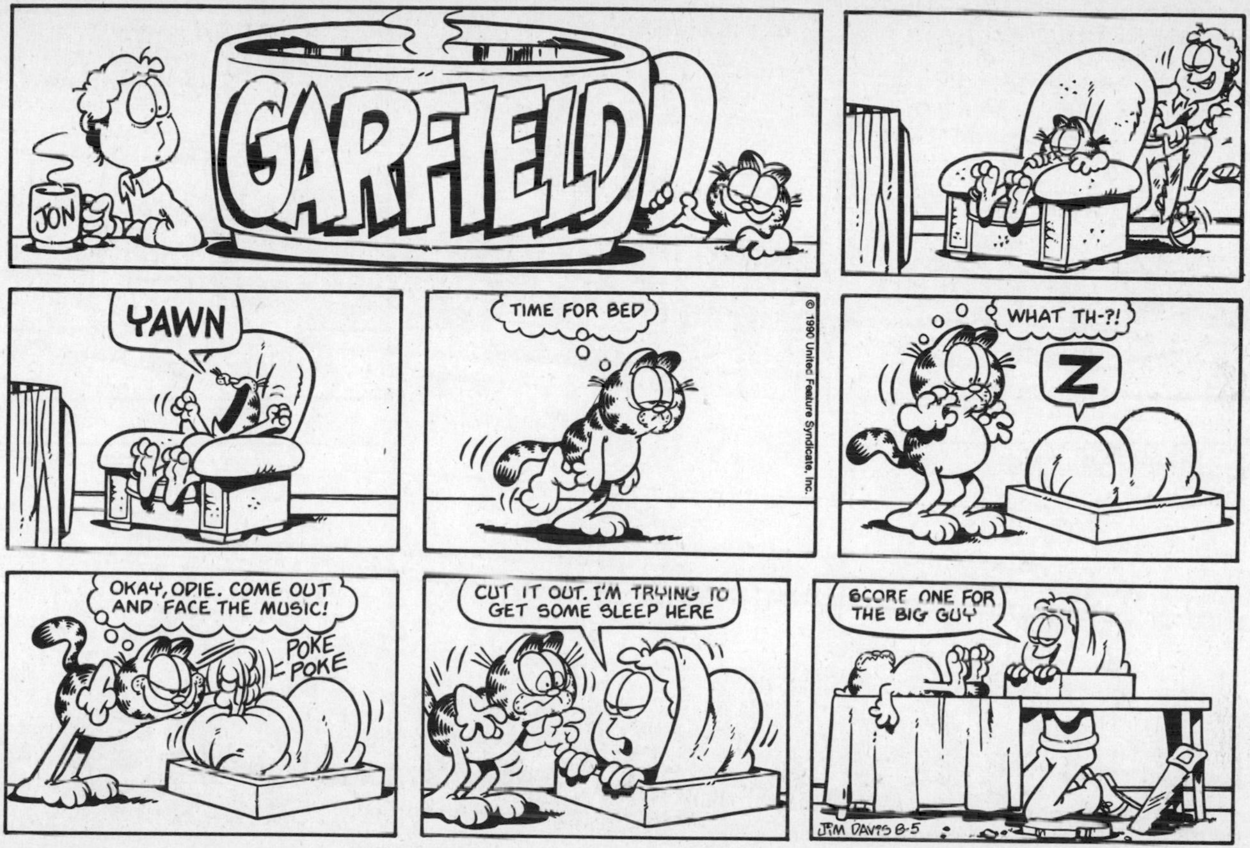
JON
GARFIELD
YAWN
TIME FOR BED
WHAT TH-?!
Z
OKAY, ODIE. COME OUT AND FACE THE MUSIC!
POKE POKE
CUT IT OUT. I'M TRYING TO GET SOME SLEEP HERE
SCORE ONE FOR THE BIG GUY
JIM DAVIS 8-5
© 1990 United Feature Syndicate, Inc.

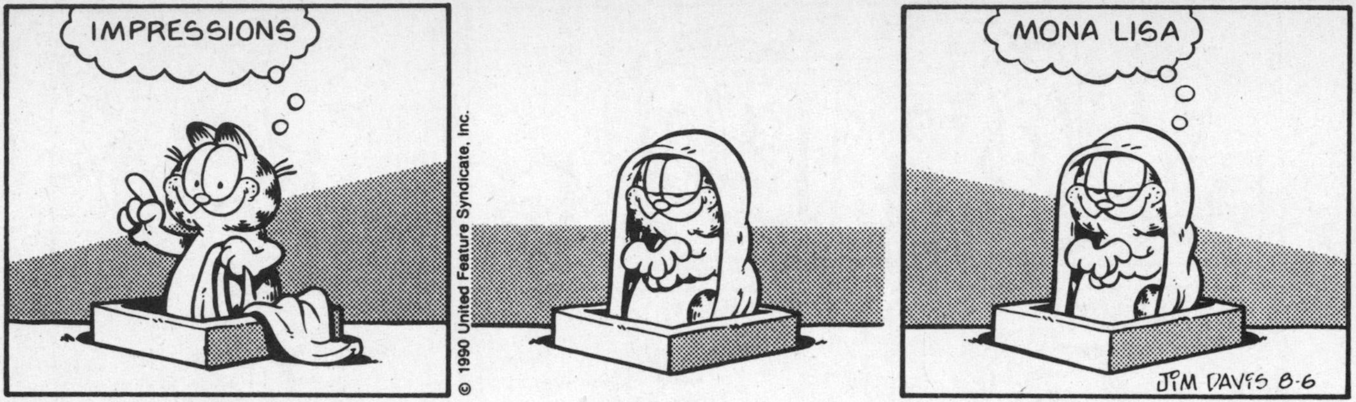
IMPRESSIONS
© 1990 United Feature Syndicate, Inc.
MONA LISA
JIM DAVIS 8-6

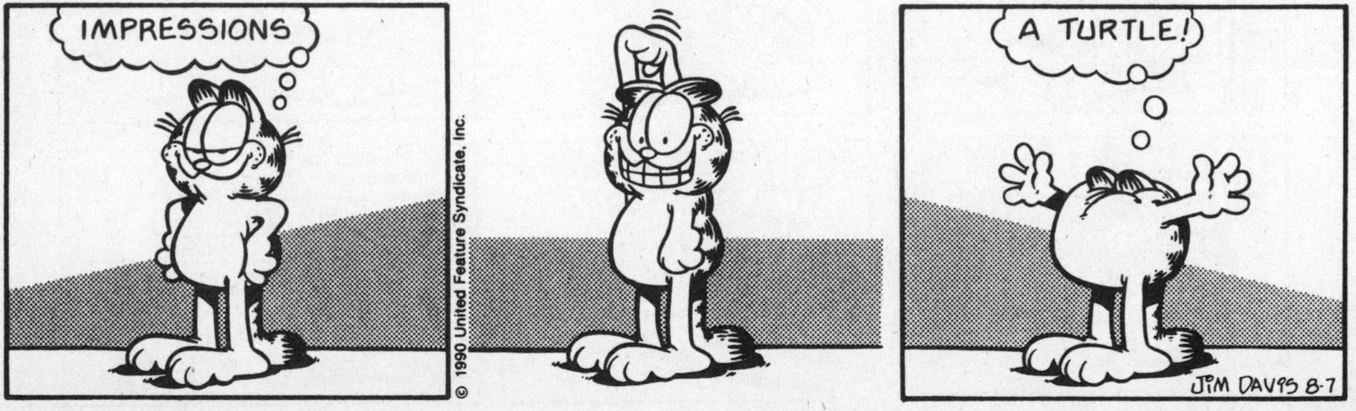
IMPRESSIONS
© 1990 United Feature Syndicate, Inc.
A TURTLE!
JIM DAVIS 8-7

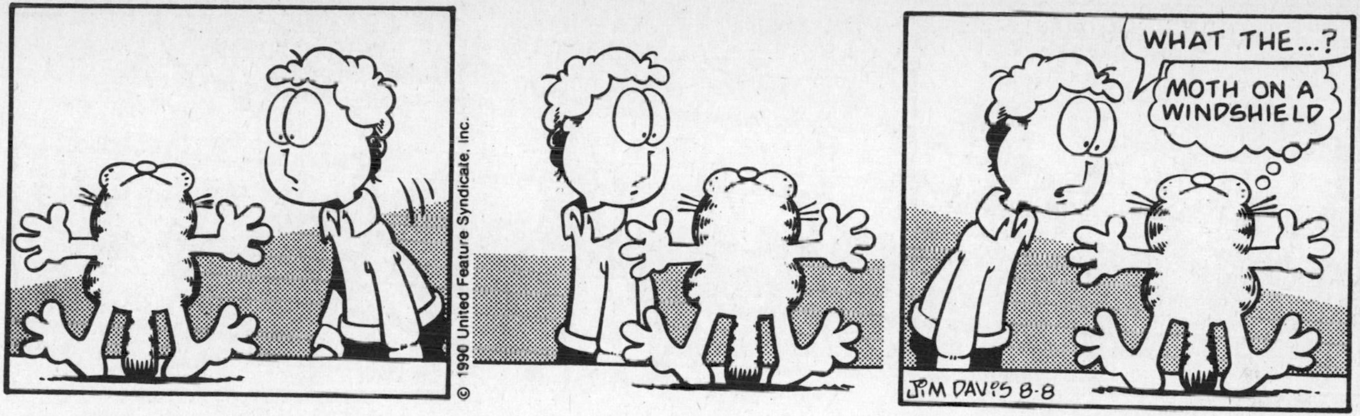
© 1990 United Feature Syndicate, Inc.
WHAT THE...?
MOTH ON A WINDSHIELD
JIM DAVIS 8-8

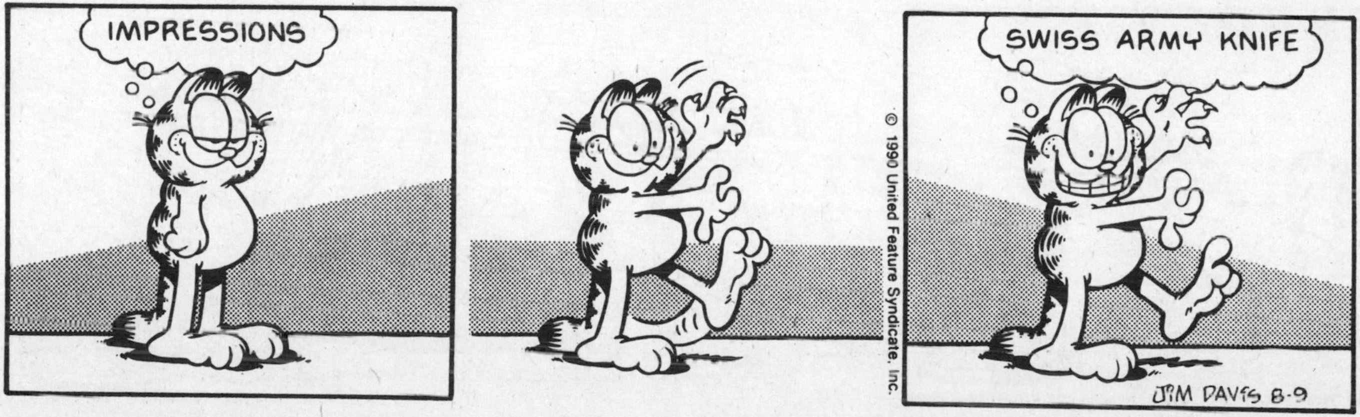
IMPRESSIONS
© 1990 United Feature Syndicate, Inc.
SWISS ARMY KNIFE
JIM DAVIS 8-9

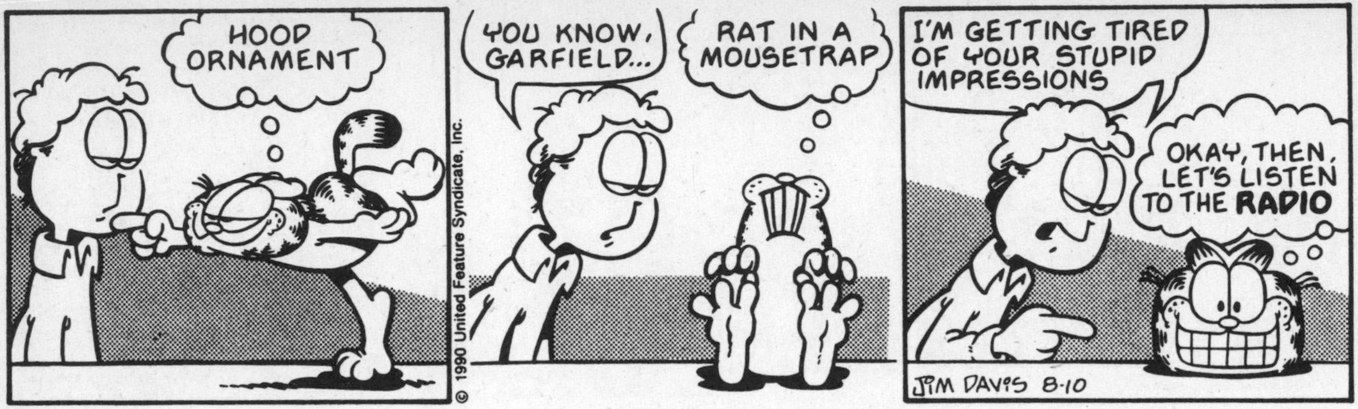
HOOD ORNAMENT
YOU KNOW, GARFIELD...
RAT IN A MOUSETRAP
I'M GETTING TIRED OF YOUR STUPID IMPRESSIONS
OKAY, THEN, LET'S LISTEN TO THE **RADIO**
JIM DAVIS 8-10
© 1990 United Feature Syndicate, Inc.

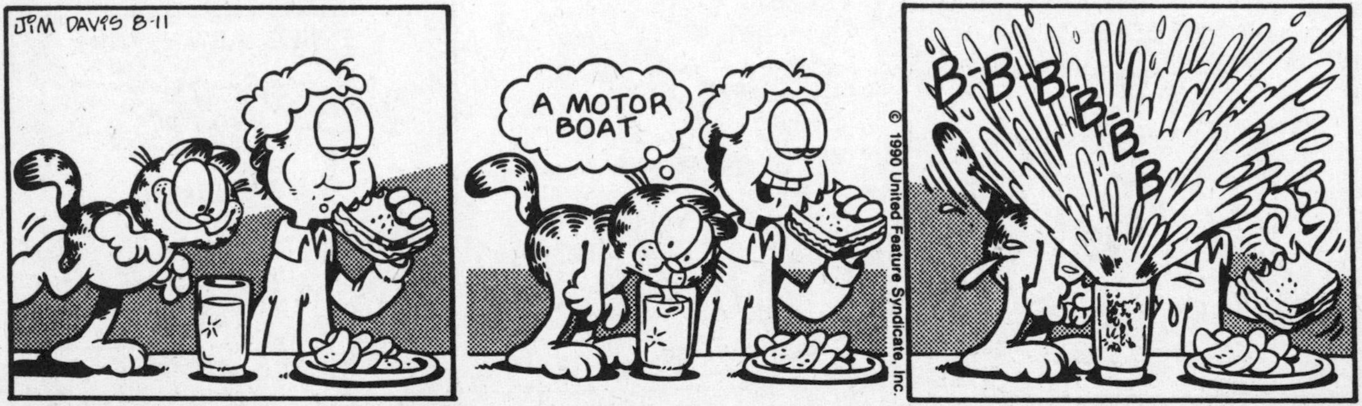
JIM DAVIS 8-11
A MOTOR BOAT
B-B-B-B-B-B
© 1990 United Feature Syndicate, Inc.

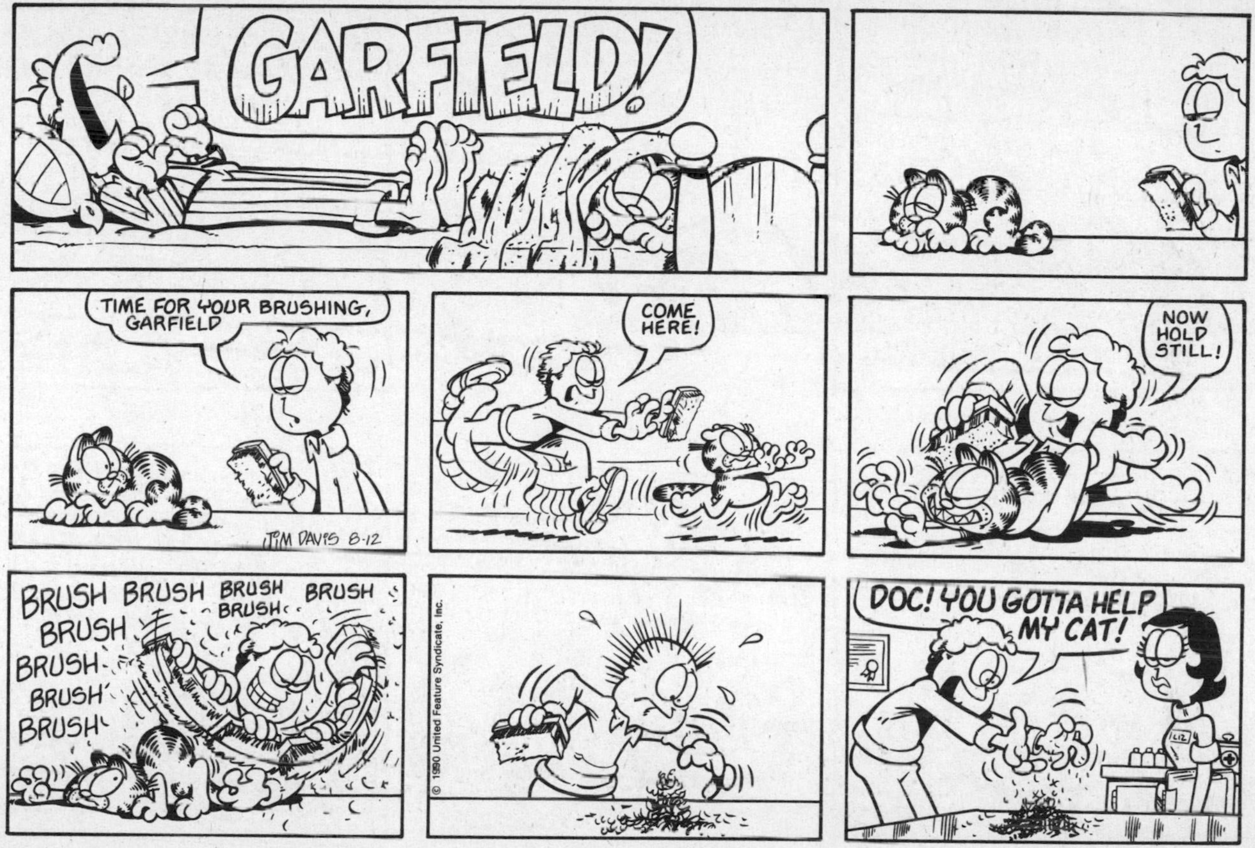
GARFIELD!
TIME FOR YOUR BRUSHING, GARFIELD
JIM DAVIS 8-12
COME HERE!
NOW HOLD STILL!
BRUSH BRUSH BRUSH BRUSH BRUSH BRUSH BRUSH BRUSH BRUSH BRUSH
© 1990 United Feature Syndicate, Inc.
DOC! YOU GOTTA HELP MY CAT!
LIZ

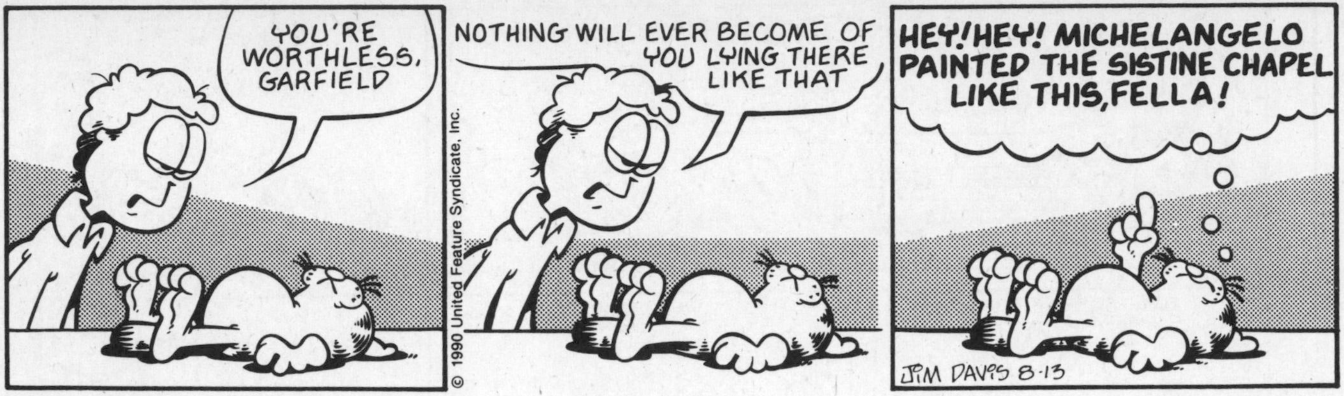
YOU'RE WORTHLESS, GARFIELD
© 1990 United Feature Syndicate, Inc.
NOTHING WILL EVER BECOME OF YOU LYING THERE LIKE THAT
HEY! HEY! MICHELANGELO PAINTED THE SISTINE CHAPEL LIKE THIS, FELLA!
JIM DAVIS 8-13

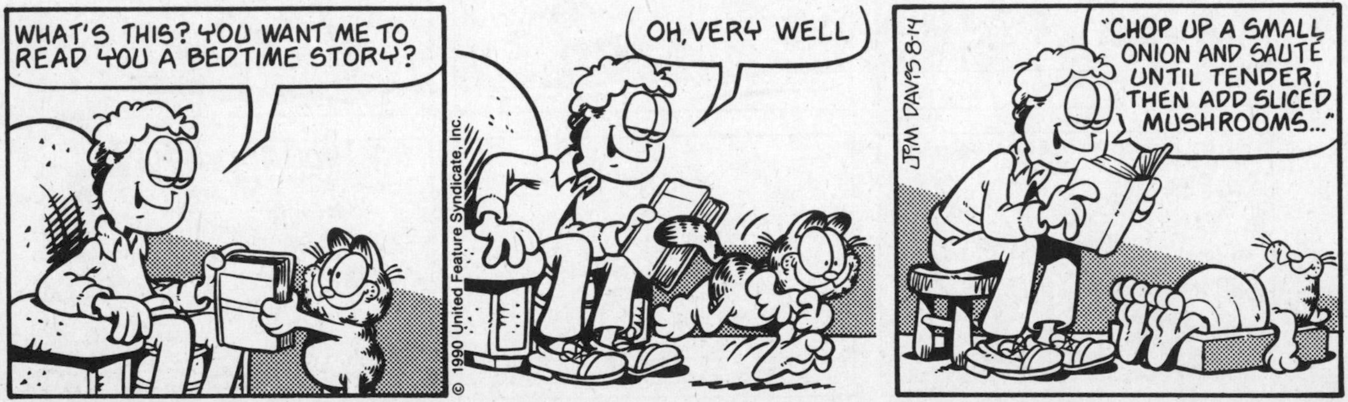
WHAT'S THIS? YOU WANT ME TO READ YOU A BEDTIME STORY?
© 1990 United Feature Syndicate, Inc.
OH, VERY WELL
JIM DAVIS 8-14
"CHOP UP A SMALL ONION AND SAUTÉ UNTIL TENDER, THEN ADD SLICED MUSHROOMS..."

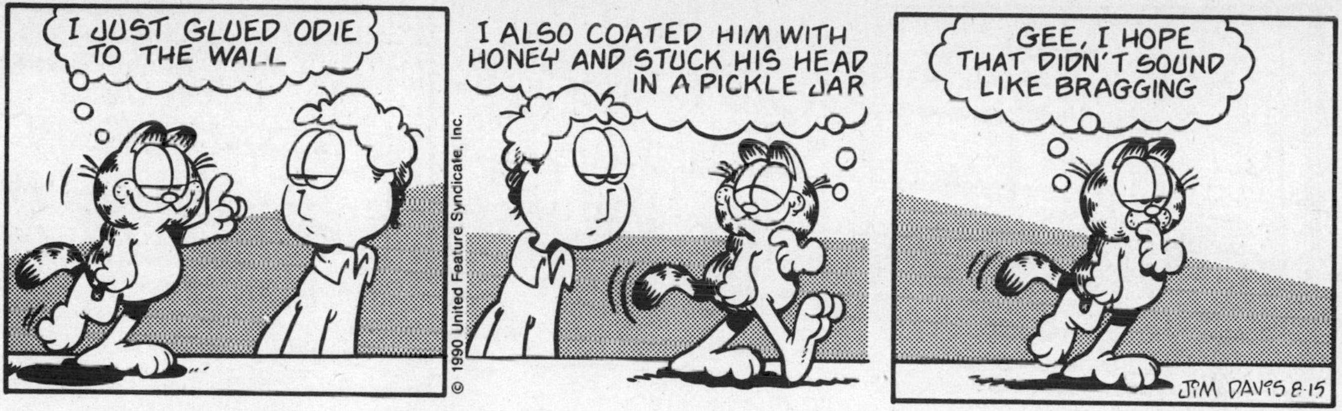
I JUST GLUED ODIE TO THE WALL
I ALSO COATED HIM WITH HONEY AND STUCK HIS HEAD IN A PICKLE JAR
GEE, I HOPE THAT DIDN'T SOUND LIKE BRAGGING
JIM DAVIS 8-15
© 1990 United Feature Syndicate, Inc.

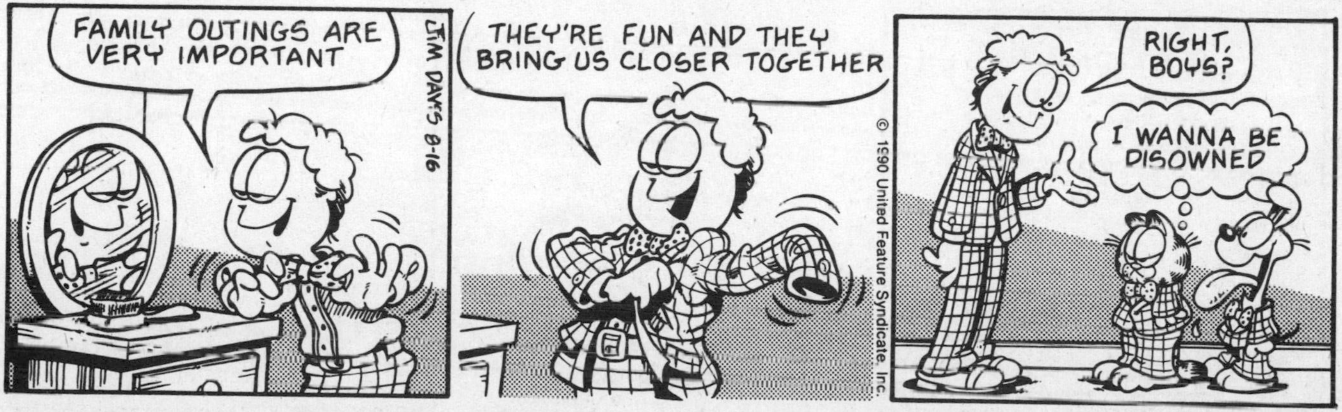
FAMILY OUTINGS ARE VERY IMPORTANT
JIM DAVIS 8-16
THEY'RE FUN AND THEY BRING US CLOSER TOGETHER
RIGHT, BOYS?
I WANNA BE DISOWNED
© 1990 United Feature Syndicate, Inc.

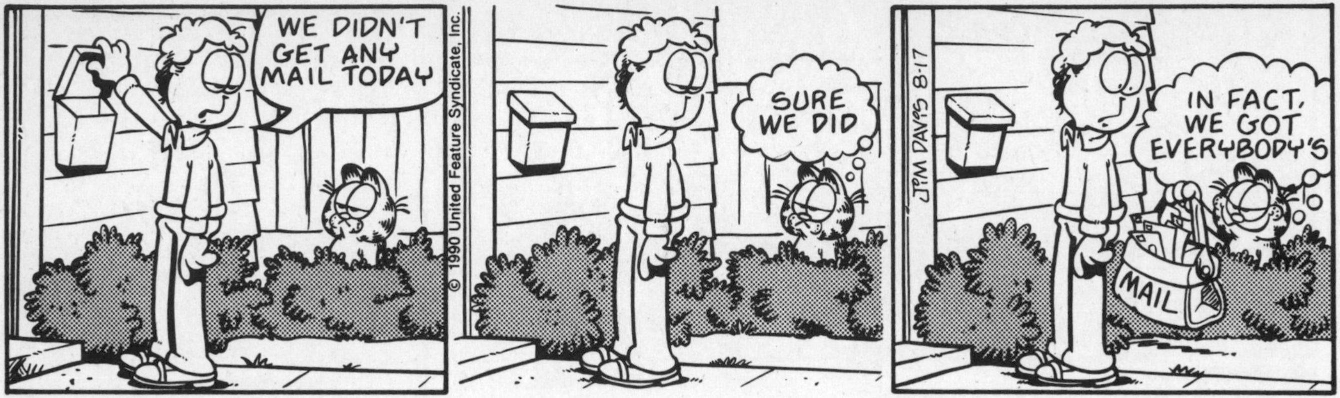
WE DIDN'T GET ANY MAIL TODAY
SURE WE DID
IN FACT, WE GOT EVERYBODY'S
MAIL
JIM DAVIS 8-17
© 1990 United Feature Syndicate, Inc.

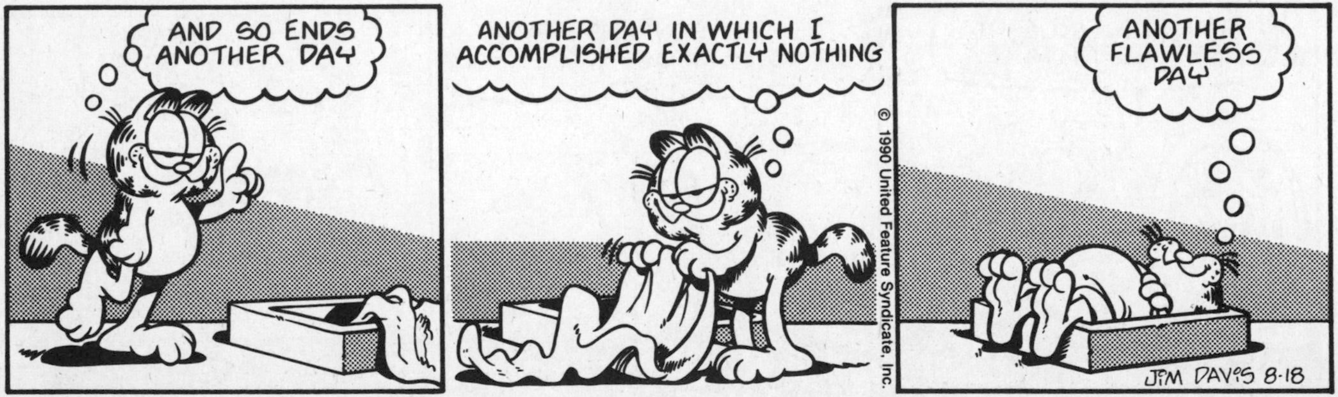
AND SO ENDS ANOTHER DAY
ANOTHER DAY IN WHICH I ACCOMPLISHED EXACTLY NOTHING
ANOTHER FLAWLESS DAY
JIM DAVIS 8-18
© 1990 United Feature Syndicate, Inc.

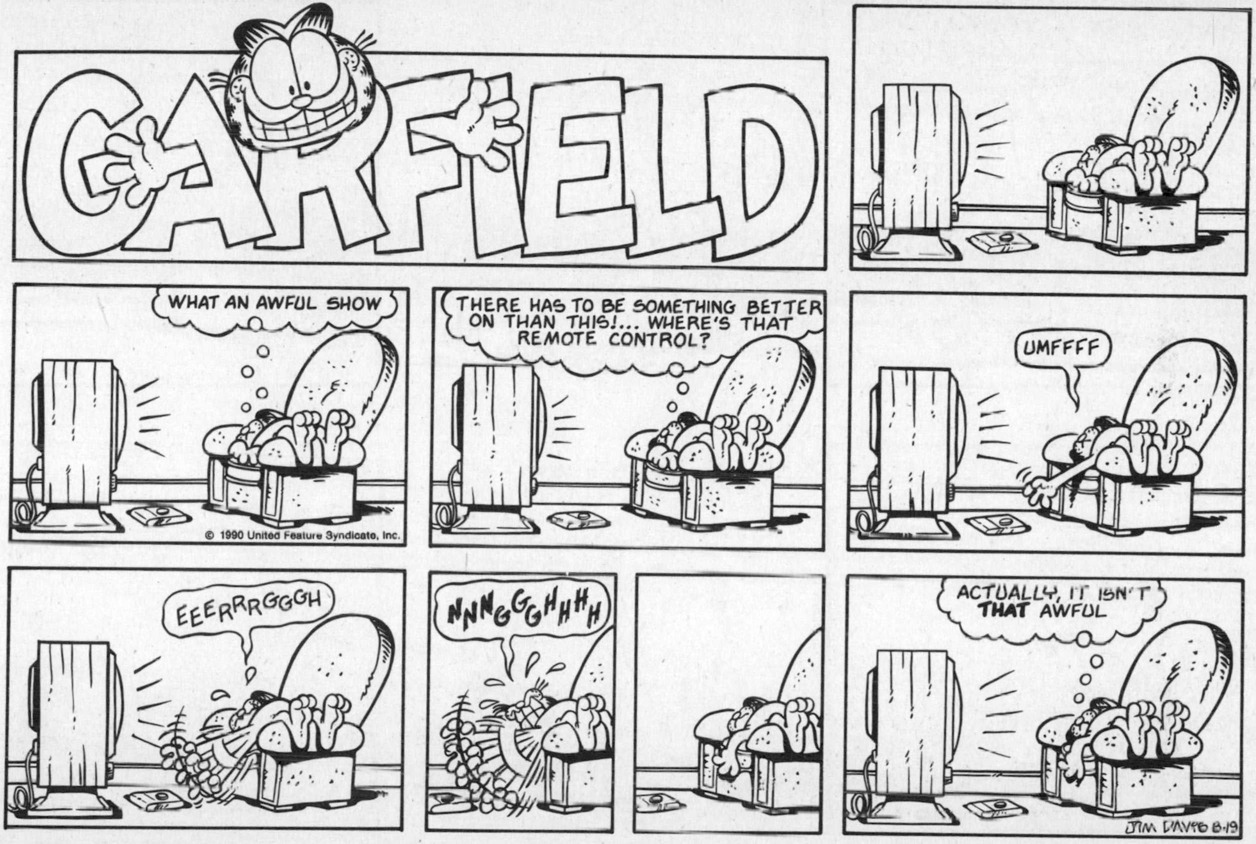
GARFIELD
WHAT AN AWFUL SHOW
© 1990 United Feature Syndicate, Inc.
THERE HAS TO BE SOMETHING BETTER ON THAN THIS!... WHERE'S THAT REMOTE CONTROL?
UMFFFF
EEERRRRGGGH
NNNGGGHHHH
ACTUALLY, IT ISN'T **THAT** AWFUL
JIM DAVIS 8-19

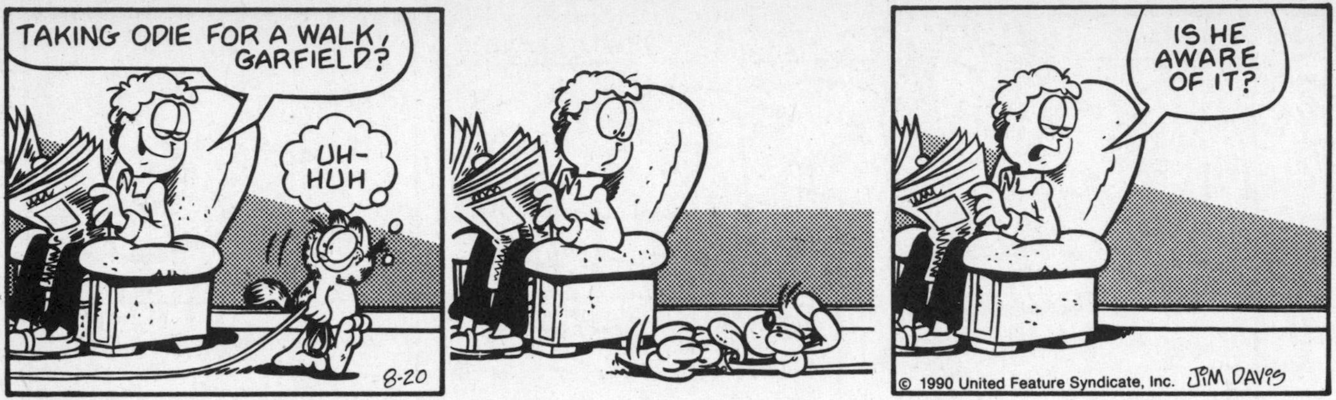
TAKING ODIE FOR A WALK, GARFIELD?
UH-HUH
8-20
IS HE AWARE OF IT?
© 1990 United Feature Syndicate, Inc. JIM DAVIS

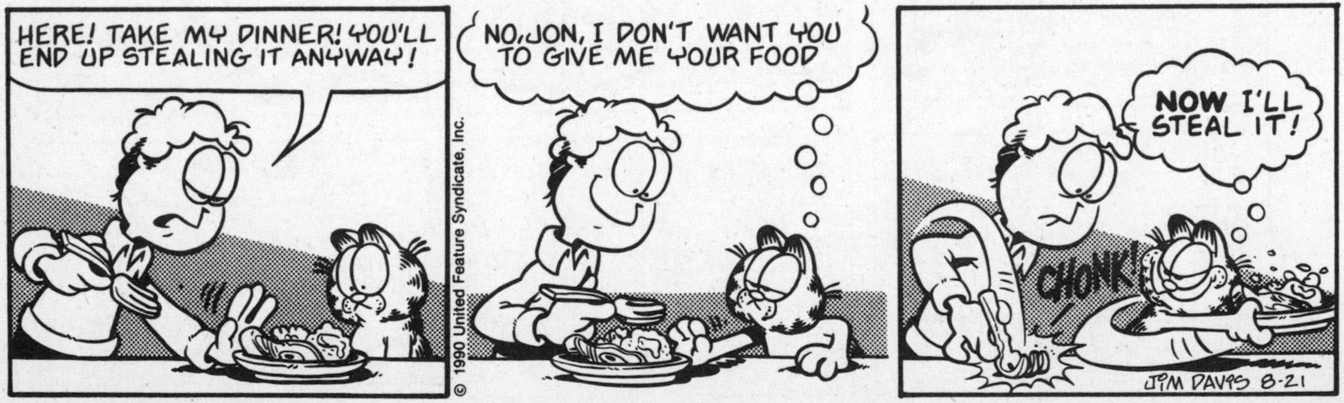
HERE! TAKE MY DINNER! YOU'LL END UP STEALING IT ANYWAY!
© 1990 United Feature Syndicate, Inc.
NO, JON, I DON'T WANT YOU TO GIVE ME YOUR FOOD
NOW I'LL STEAL IT!
CHONK!
JIM DAVIS 8-21

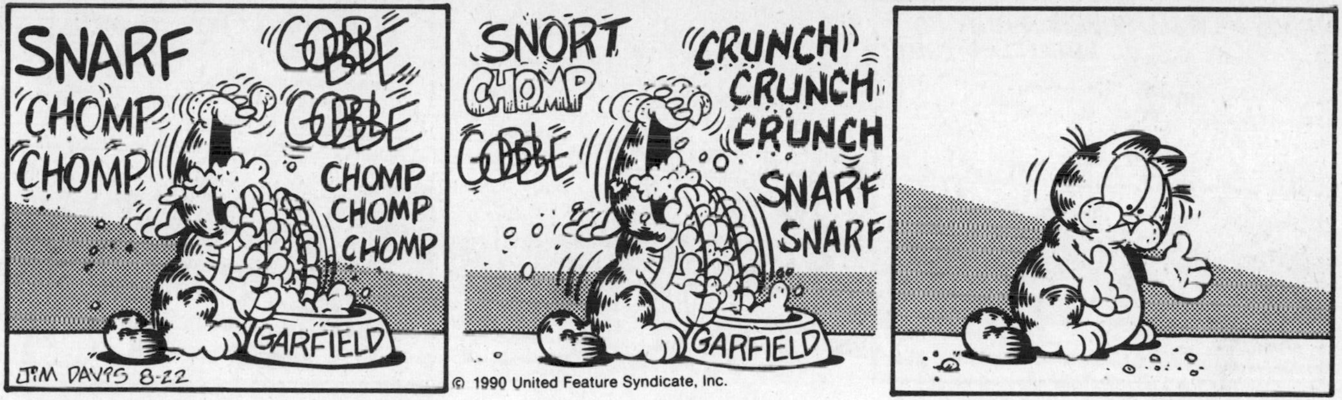
SNARF
GOBBLE
CHOMP
GOBBLE
CHOMP
CHOMP
CHOMP
CHOMP
JIM DAVIS 8-22
SNORT
CHOMP
GOBBLE
CRUNCH
CRUNCH
CRUNCH
SNARF
SNARF

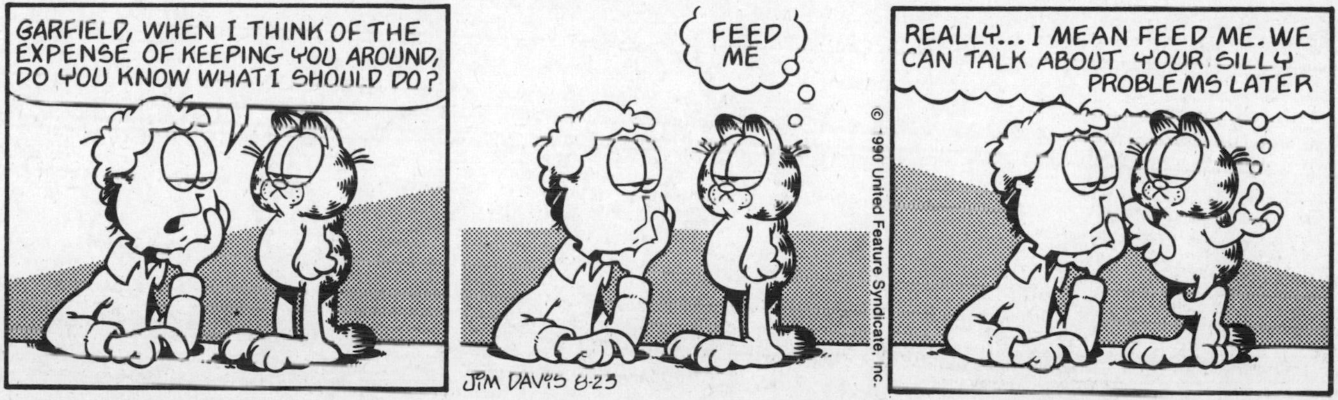
GARFIELD, WHEN I THINK OF THE EXPENSE OF KEEPING YOU AROUND, DO YOU KNOW WHAT I SHOULD DO?
FEED ME
JIM DAVIS 8-23
REALLY... I MEAN FEED ME. WE CAN TALK ABOUT YOUR SILLY PROBLEMS LATER

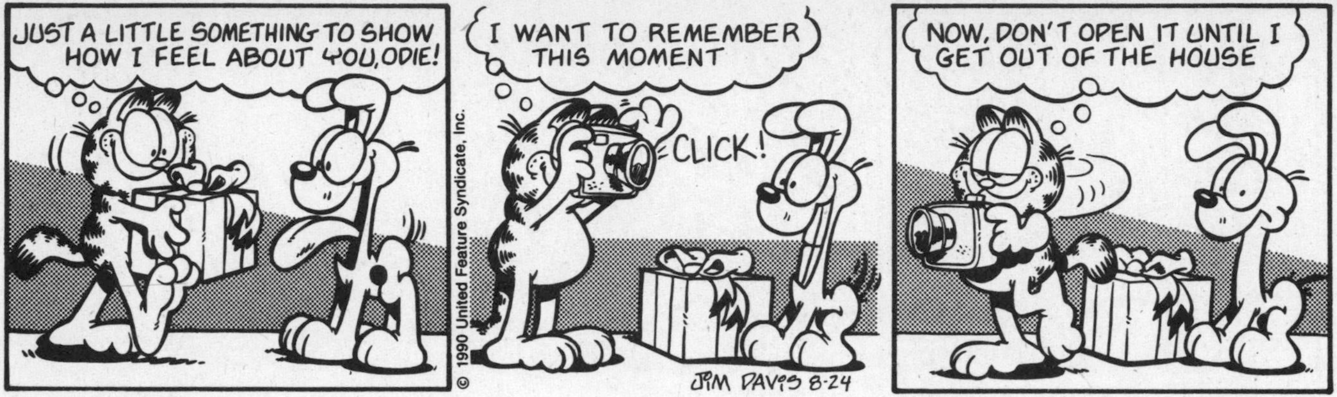
JUST A LITTLE SOMETHING TO SHOW HOW I FEEL ABOUT YOU, ODIE!
I WANT TO REMEMBER THIS MOMENT
CLICK!
NOW, DON'T OPEN IT UNTIL I GET OUT OF THE HOUSE
JIM DAVIS 8-24
© 1990 United Feature Syndicate, Inc.

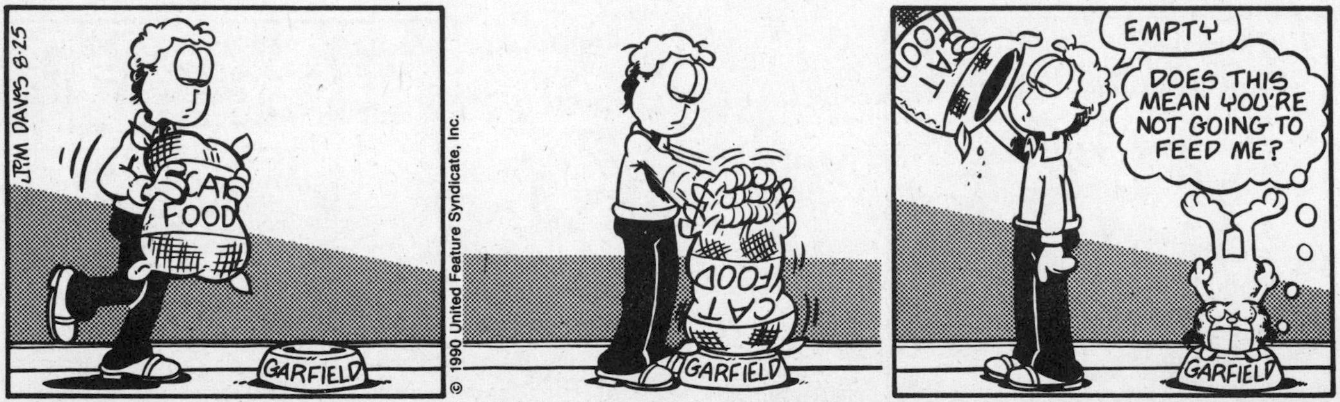
JIM DAVIS 8-25
CAT FOOD
GARFIELD
CAT FOOD
GARFIELD
CAT FOOD
EMPTY
DOES THIS MEAN YOU'RE NOT GOING TO FEED ME?
GARFIELD
© 1990 United Feature Syndicate, Inc.

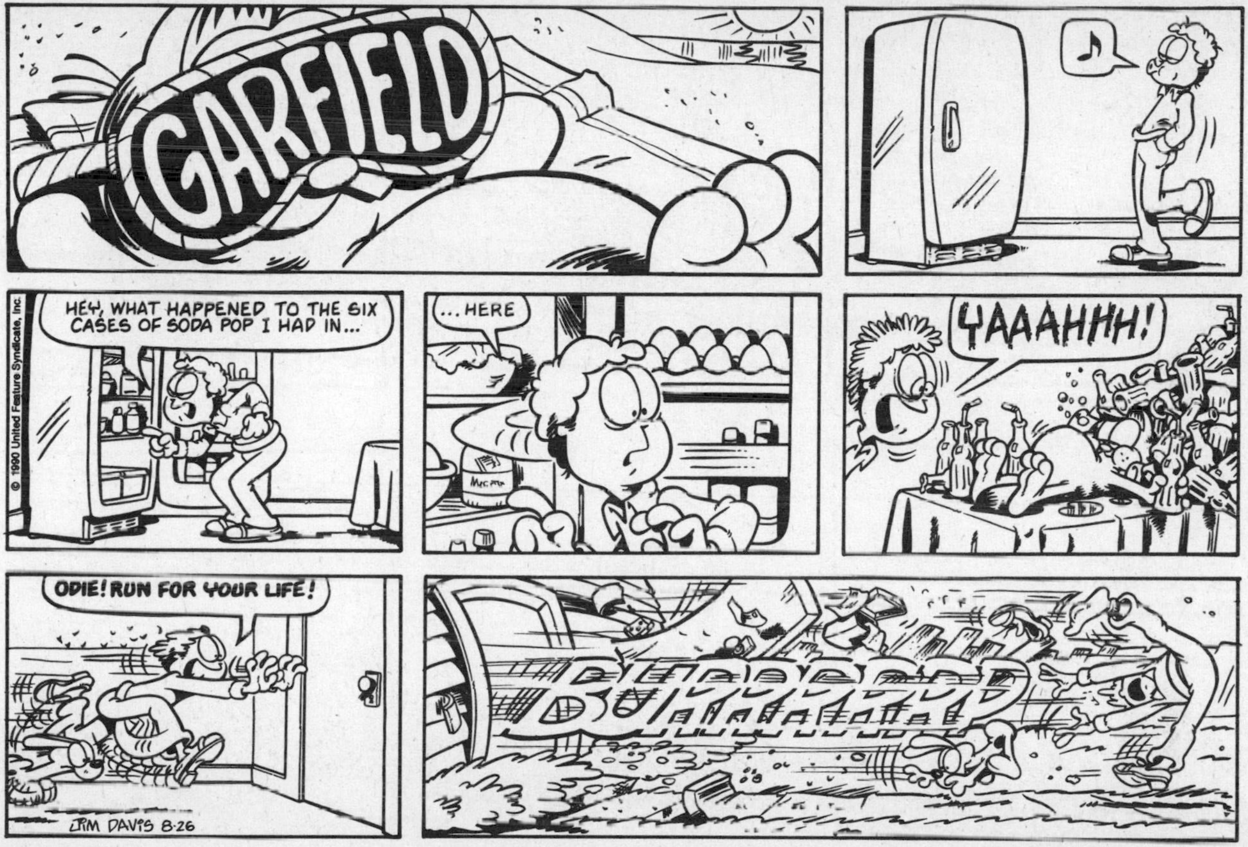
GARFIELD
HEY, WHAT HAPPENED TO THE SIX CASES OF SODA POP I HAD IN...
... HERE
YAAAHHH!
ODIE! RUN FOR YOUR LIFE!
BURRRRRP
© 1990 United Feature Syndicate, Inc.
JIM DAVIS 8-26

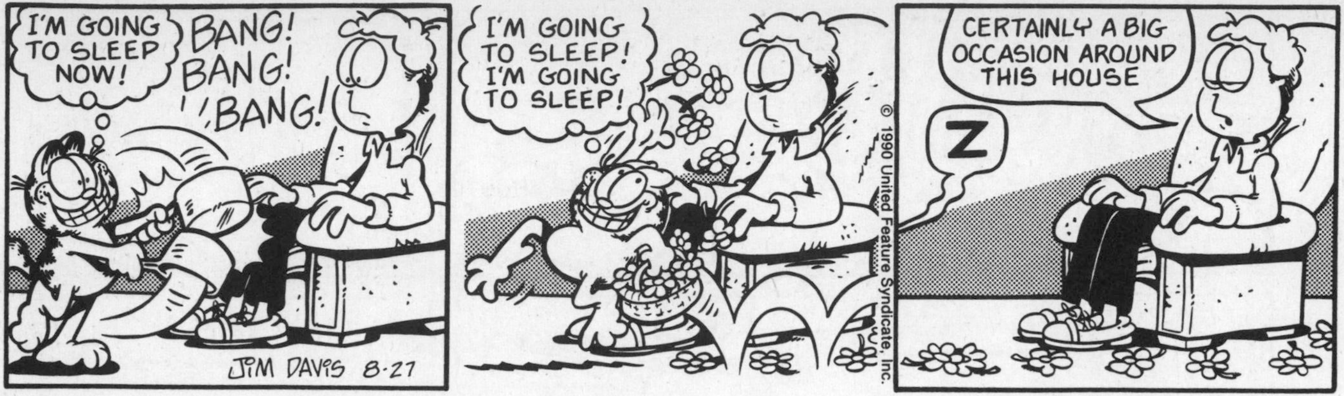
I'M GOING TO SLEEP NOW!
BANG! BANG! BANG!
JIM DAVIS 8-27
I'M GOING TO SLEEP! I'M GOING TO SLEEP!
© 1990 United Feature Syndicate, Inc.
CERTAINLY A BIG OCCASION AROUND THIS HOUSE
Z

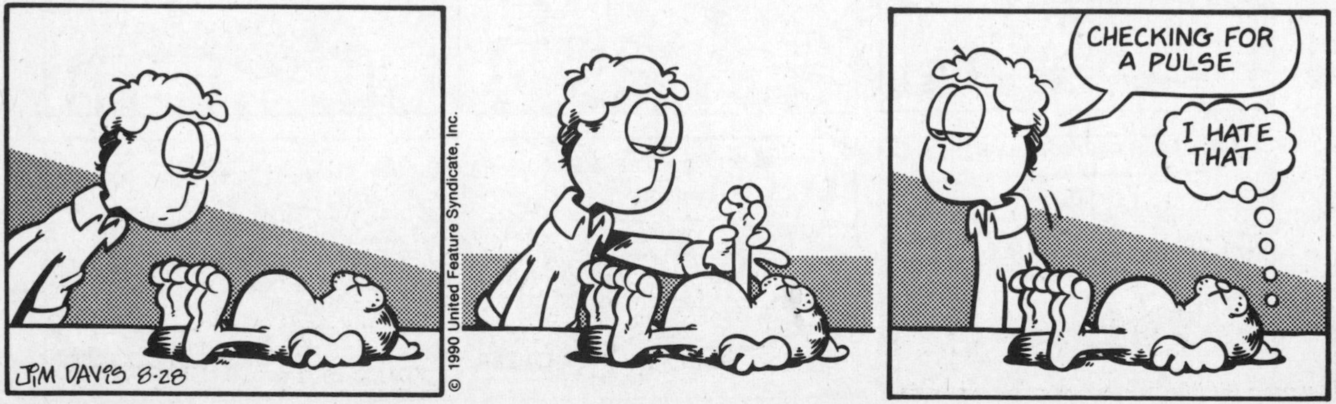
JIM DAVIS 8-28
© 1990 United Feature Syndicate, Inc.
CHECKING FOR A PULSE
I HATE THAT

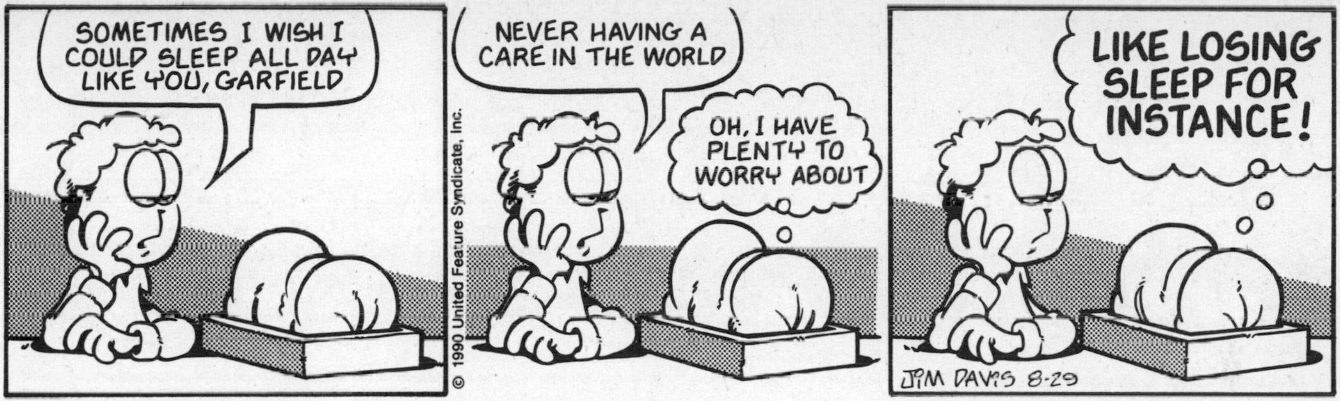
SOMETIMES I WISH I COULD SLEEP ALL DAY LIKE YOU, GARFIELD
NEVER HAVING A CARE IN THE WORLD
OH, I HAVE PLENTY TO WORRY ABOUT
LIKE LOSING SLEEP FOR INSTANCE!
JIM DAVIS 8-29
© 1990 United Feature Syndicate, Inc.

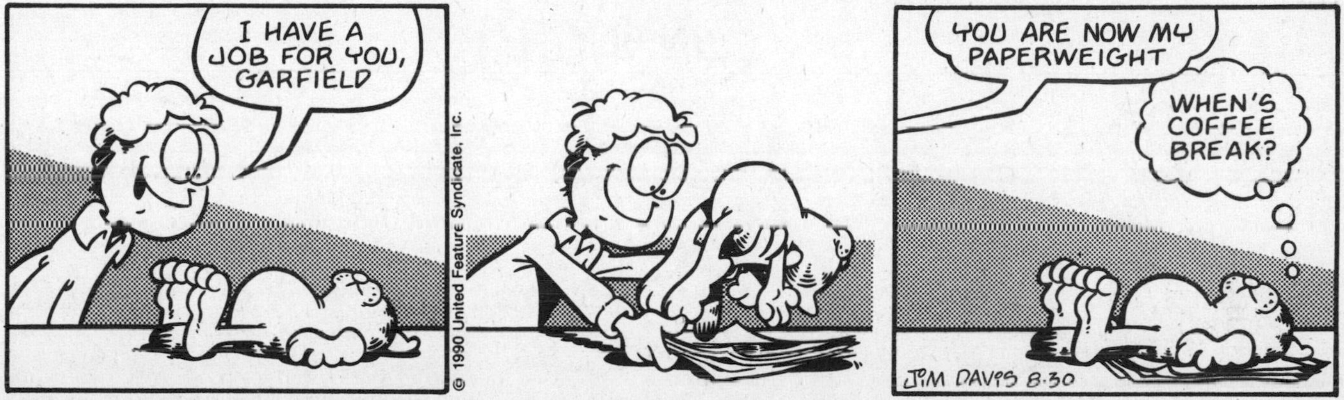
I HAVE A JOB FOR YOU, GARFIELD
YOU ARE NOW MY PAPERWEIGHT
WHEN'S COFFEE BREAK?
JIM DAVIS 8-30
© 1990 United Feature Syndicate, Inc.

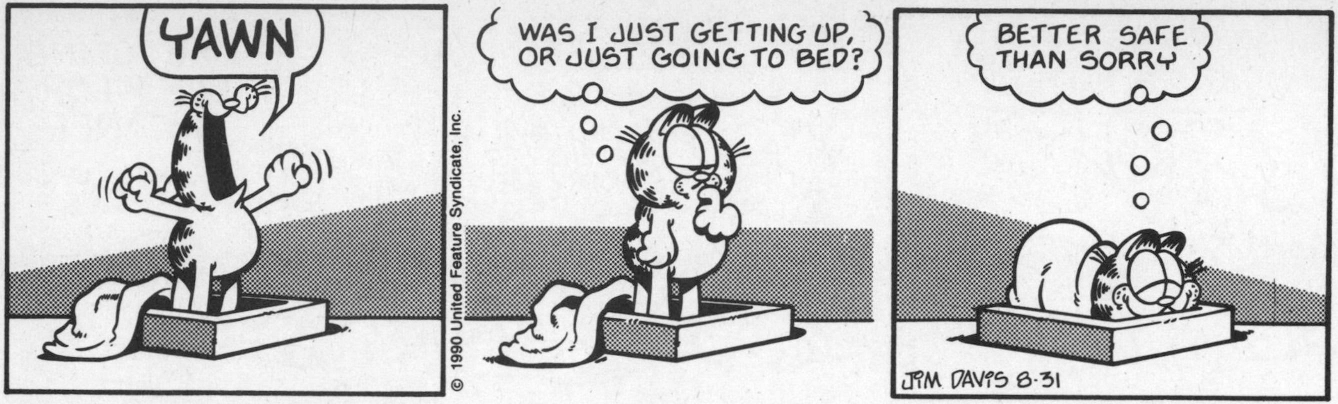
YAWN
© 1990 United Feature Syndicate, Inc.
WAS I JUST GETTING UP, OR JUST GOING TO BED?
BETTER SAFE THAN SORRY
JIM DAVIS 8-31

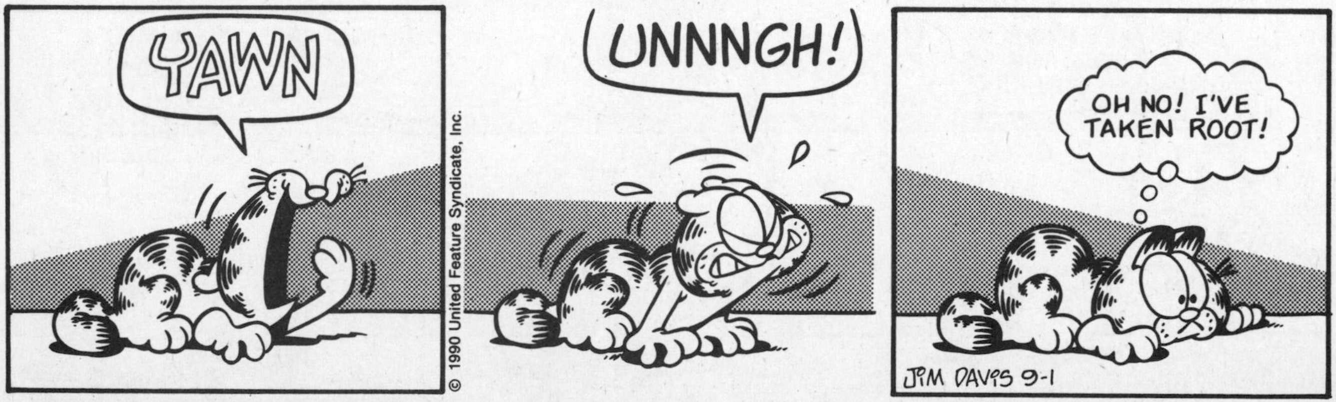
YAWN
© 1990 United Feature Syndicate, Inc.
UNNNGH!
OH NO! I'VE TAKEN ROOT!
JIM DAVIS 9-1

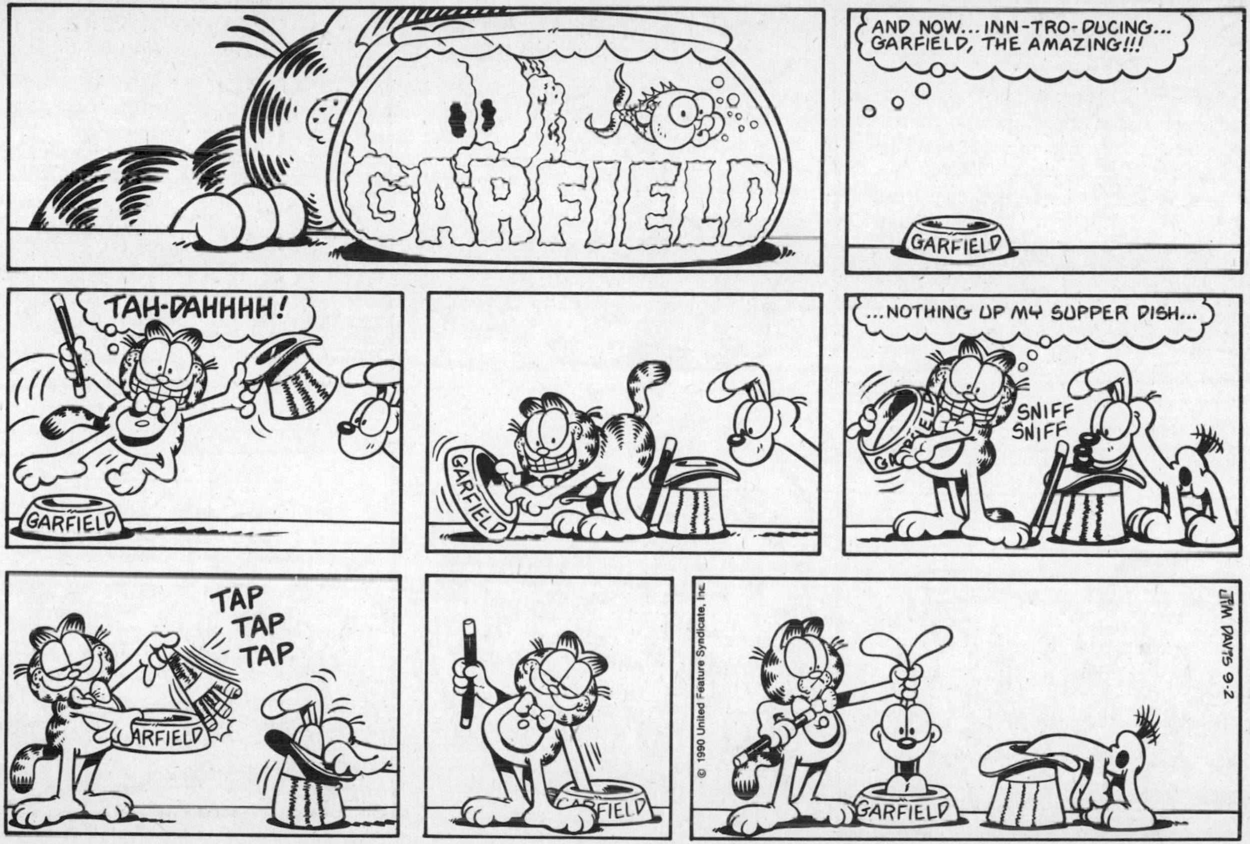
GARFIELD
AND NOW... INN-TRO-DUCING... GARFIELD, THE AMAZING!!!
GARFIELD
TAH-DAHHHH!
GARFIELD
GARFIELD
...NOTHING UP MY SUPPER DISH...
SNIFF SNIFF
TAP TAP TAP
ARFIELD
ARFIELD
© 1990 United Feature Syndicate, Inc.
JIM DAVIS 9-2
GARFIELD

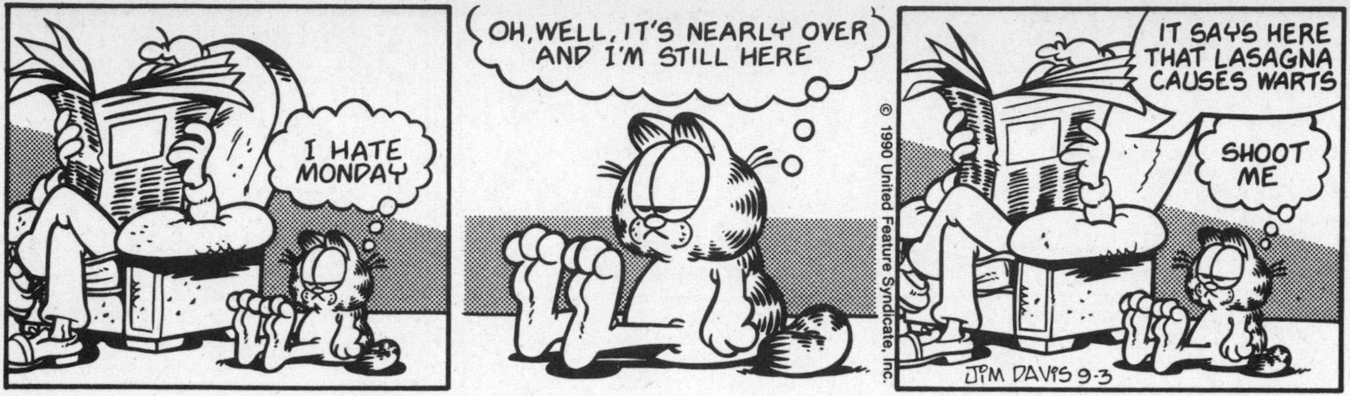
I HATE MONDAY
OH, WELL, IT'S NEARLY OVER AND I'M STILL HERE
© 1990 United Feature Syndicate, Inc.
IT SAYS HERE THAT LASAGNA CAUSES WARTS
SHOOT ME
JIM DAVIS 9-3

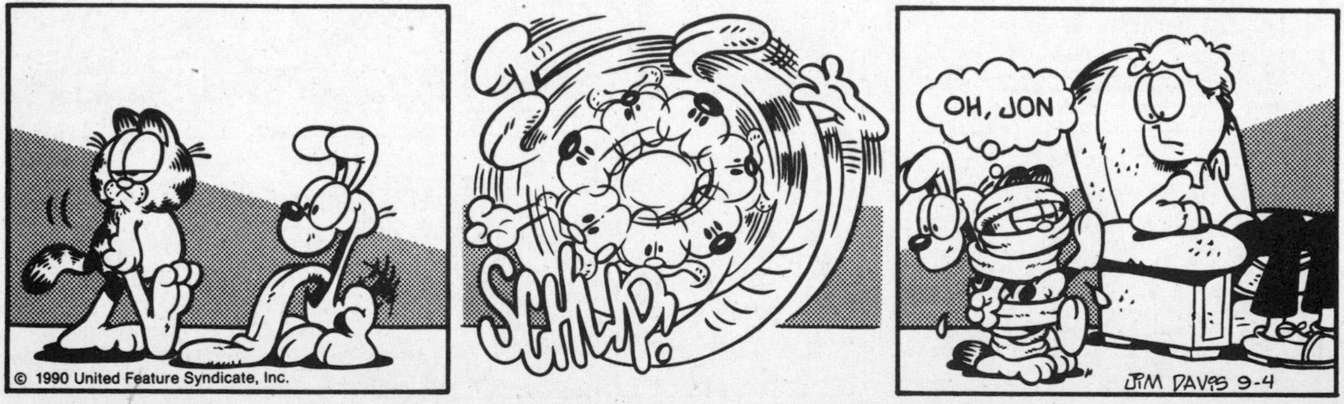
© 1990 United Feature Syndicate, Inc.
SCHLUP!
OH, JON
JIM DAVIS 9-4

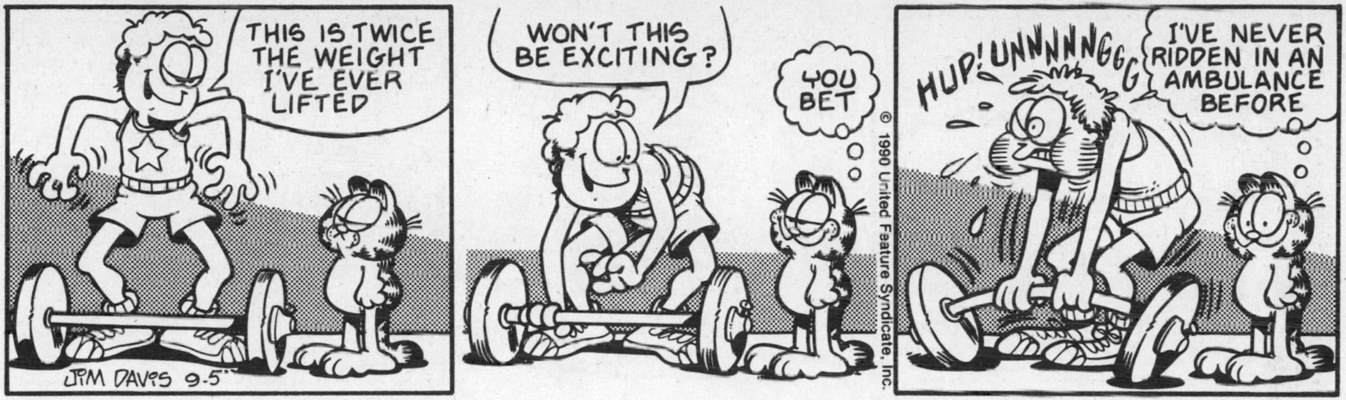
THIS IS TWICE THE WEIGHT I'VE EVER LIFTED
JIM DAVIS 9-5
WON'T THIS BE EXCITING?
YOU BET
© 1990 United Feature Syndicate, Inc.
HUP! UNNNNNGGG
I'VE NEVER RIDDEN IN AN AMBULANCE BEFORE

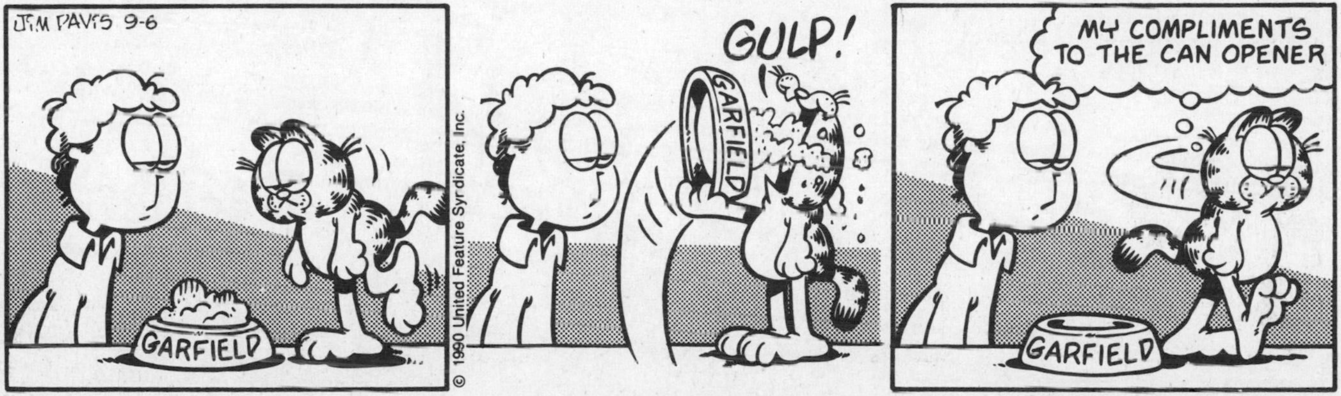
JIM DAVIS 9-6
GARFIELD
© 1990 United Feature Syndicate, Inc.
GULP!
GARFIELD
MY COMPLIMENTS TO THE CAN OPENER
GARFIELD

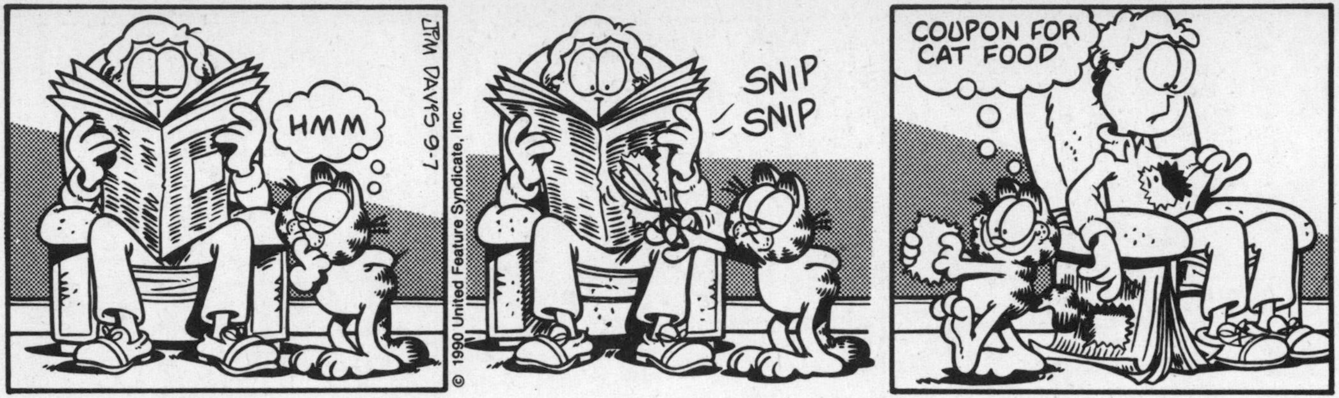
HMM
JIM DAVIS 9-7
© 1990 United Feature Syndicate, Inc.
SNIP
SNIP
COUPON FOR CAT FOOD

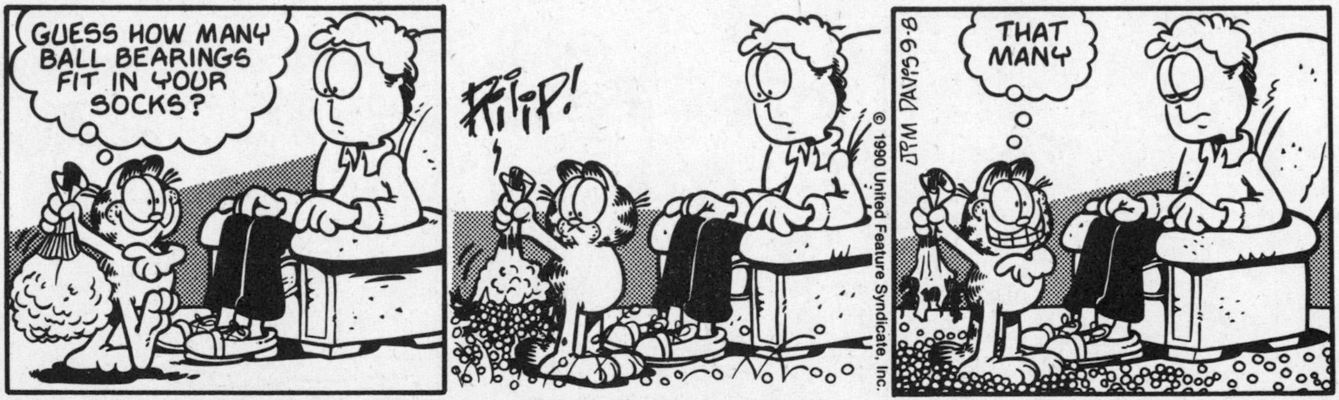
GUESS HOW MANY BALL BEARINGS FIT IN YOUR SOCKS?
© 1990 United Feature Syndicate, Inc.
JIM DAVIS 9-8
THAT MANY

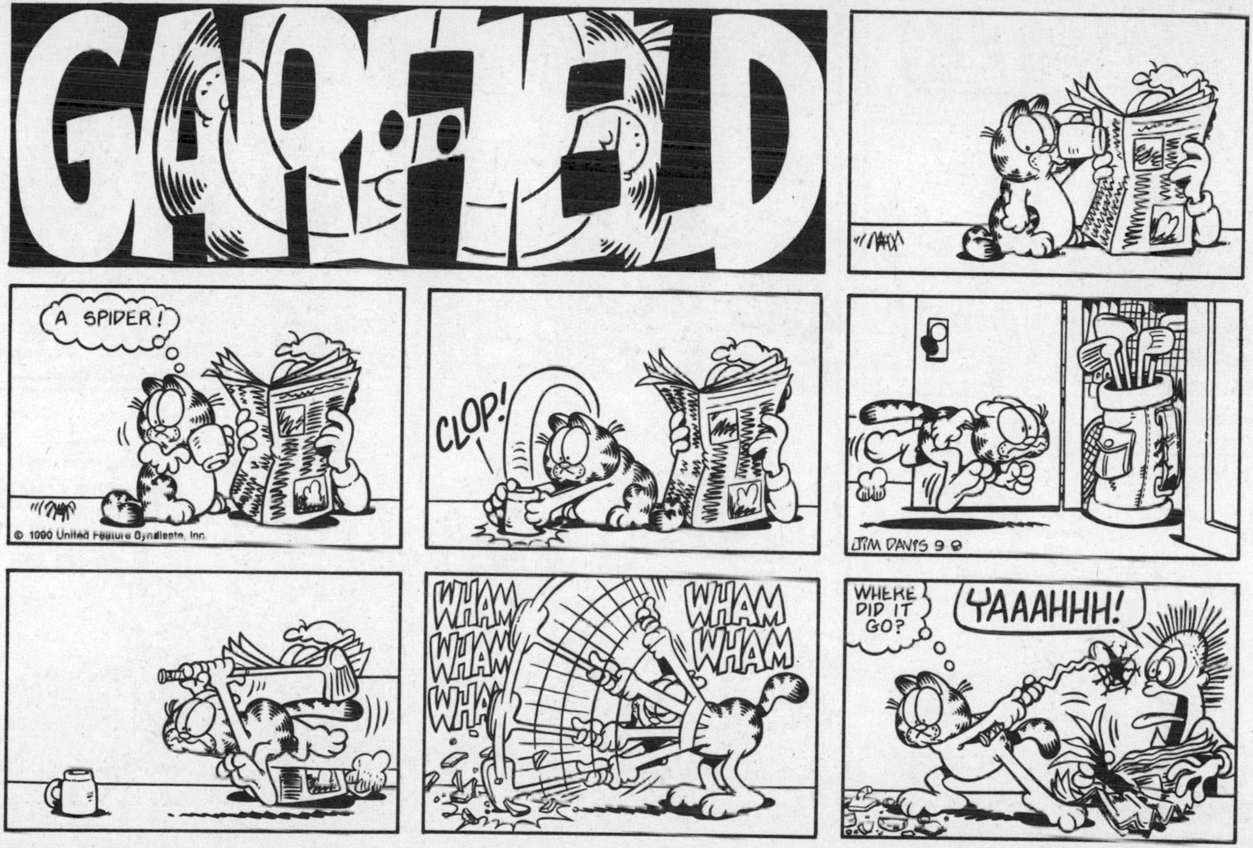
GARFIELD
A SPIDER!
© 1990 United Feature Syndicate, Inc.
CLOP!
JIM DAVIS 9-9
WHAM
WHAM
WHAM
WHAM
WHAM
WHERE DID IT GO?
YAAAHHH!

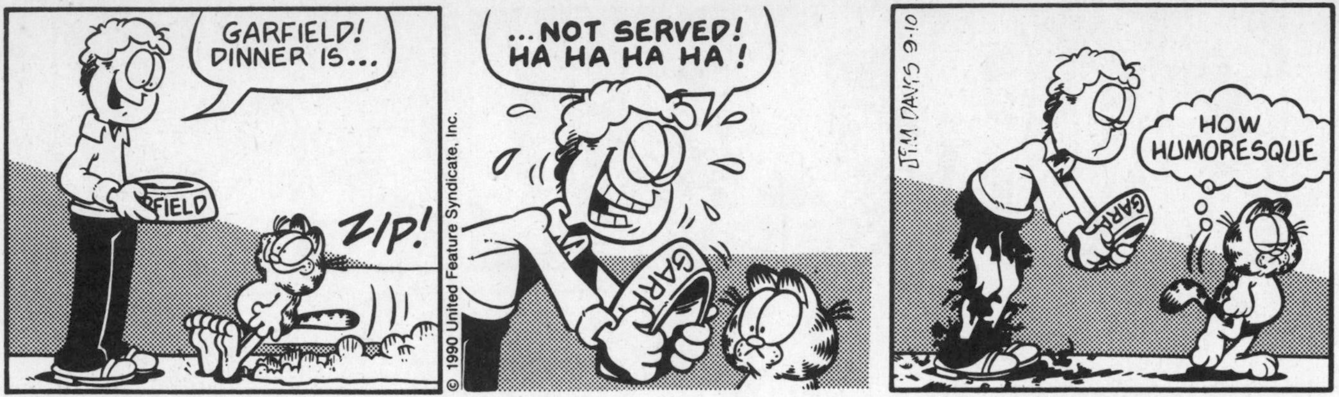
GARFIELD! DINNER IS...
FIELD
ZIP!
...NOT SERVED! HA HA HA HA !
GARF
GARF
HOW HUMORESQUE
JIM DAVIS 9·10
© 1990 United Feature Syndicate, Inc.

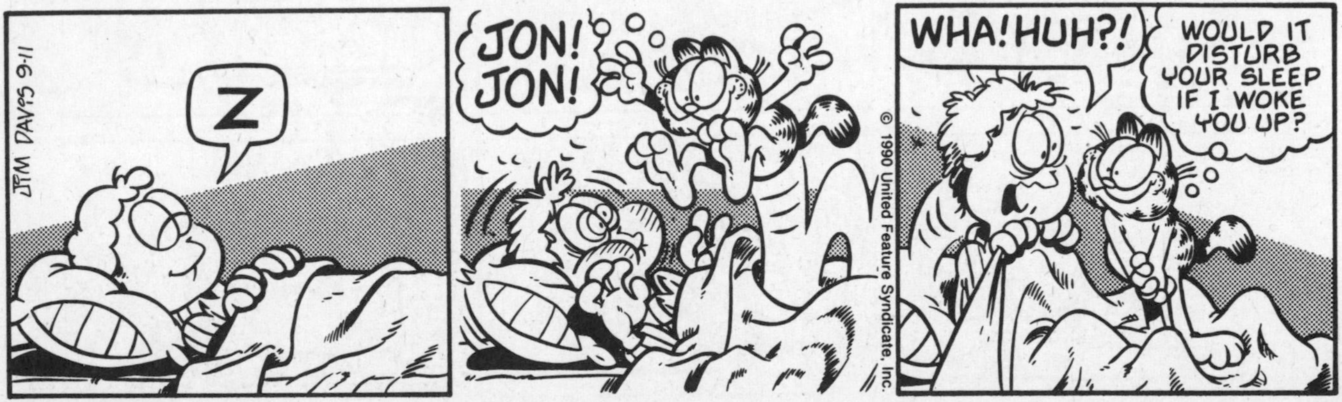
JIM DAVIS 9·11
Z
JON! JON!
WHA! HUH?!
WOULD IT DISTURB YOUR SLEEP IF I WOKE YOU UP?
© 1990 United Feature Syndicate, Inc.

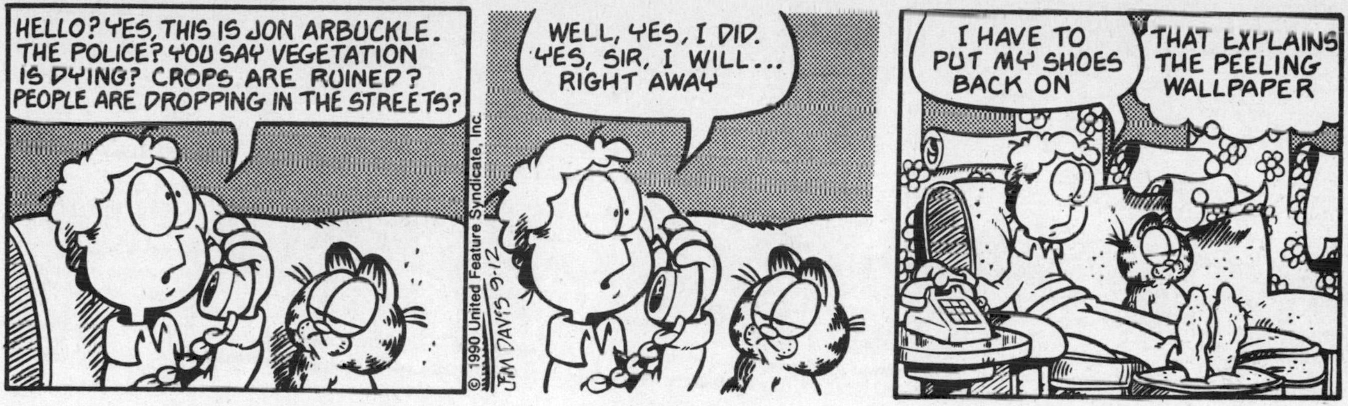
HELLO? YES, THIS IS JON ARBUCKLE. THE POLICE? YOU SAY VEGETATION IS DYING? CROPS ARE RUINED? PEOPLE ARE DROPPING IN THE STREETS?
WELL, YES, I DID. YES, SIR, I WILL... RIGHT AWAY
I HAVE TO PUT MY SHOES BACK ON
THAT EXPLAINS THE PEELING WALLPAPER
© 1990 United Feature Syndicate, Inc.
JIM DAVIS 9-12

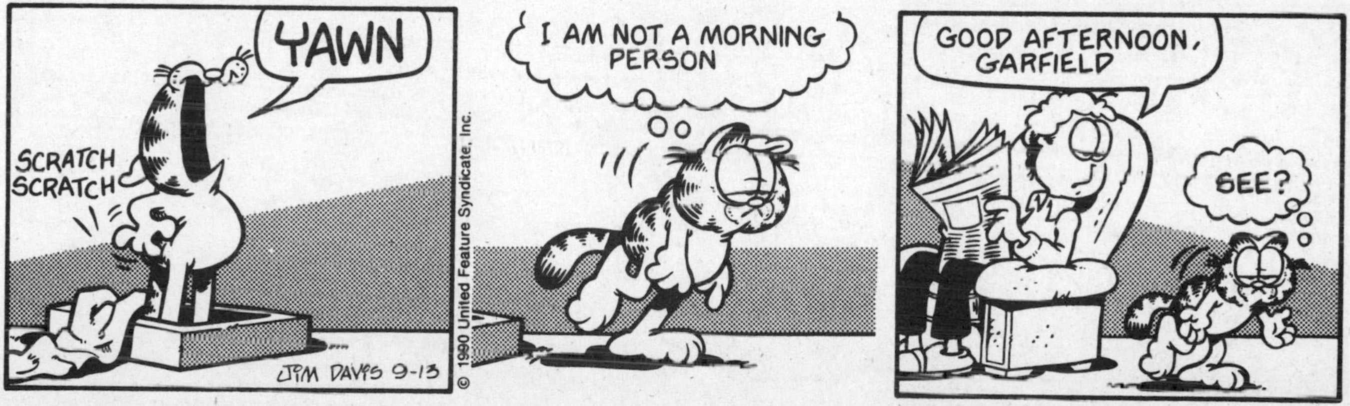
SCRATCH SCRATCH
YAWN
I AM NOT A MORNING PERSON
GOOD AFTERNOON, GARFIELD
SEE?
© 1990 United Feature Syndicate, Inc.
JIM DAVIS 9-13

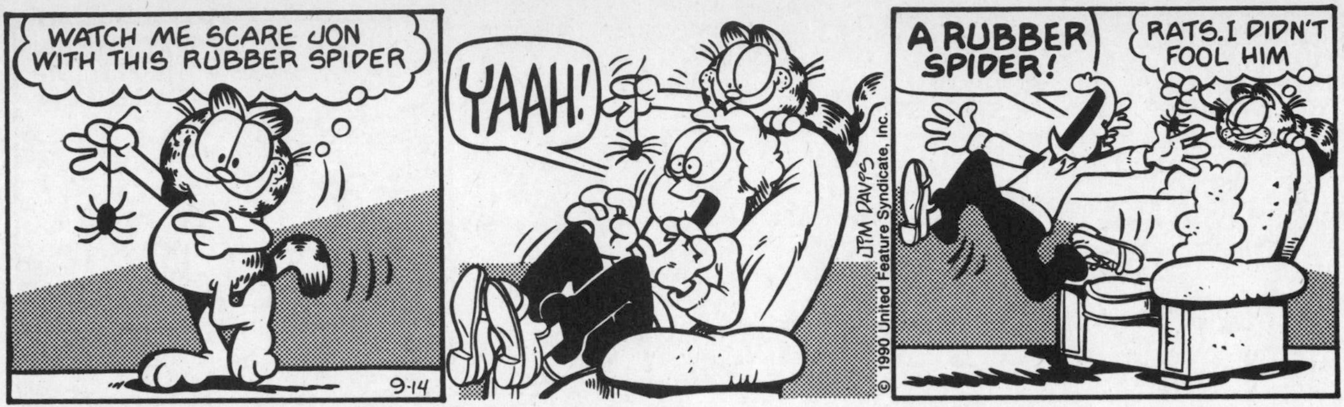
WATCH ME SCARE JON WITH THIS RUBBER SPIDER
9·14
YAAH!
JIM DAVIS
© 1990 United Feature Syndicate, Inc.
A RUBBER SPIDER!
RATS. I DIDN'T FOOL HIM

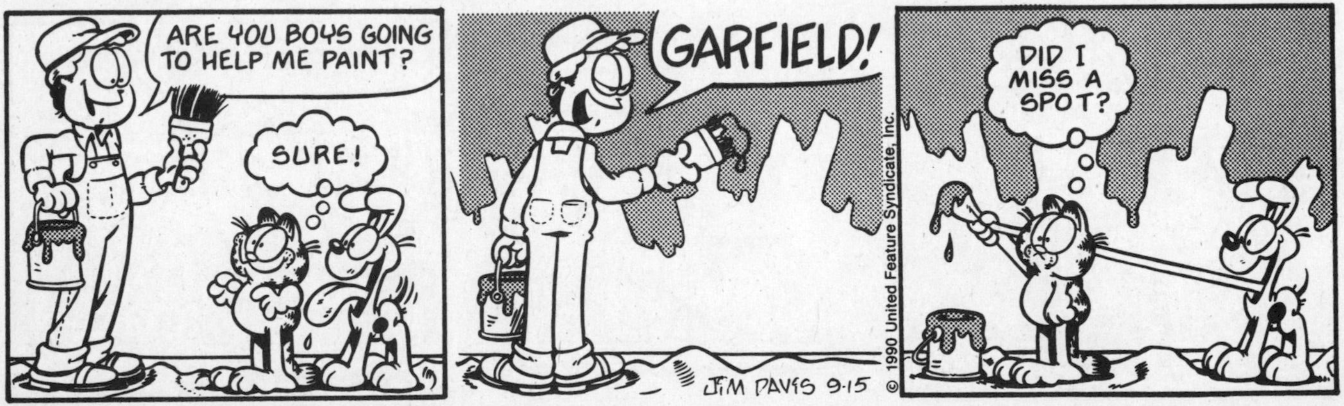
ARE YOU BOYS GOING TO HELP ME PAINT?
SURE!
GARFIELD!
JIM DAVIS 9·15
© 1990 United Feature Syndicate, Inc.
DID I MISS A SPOT?

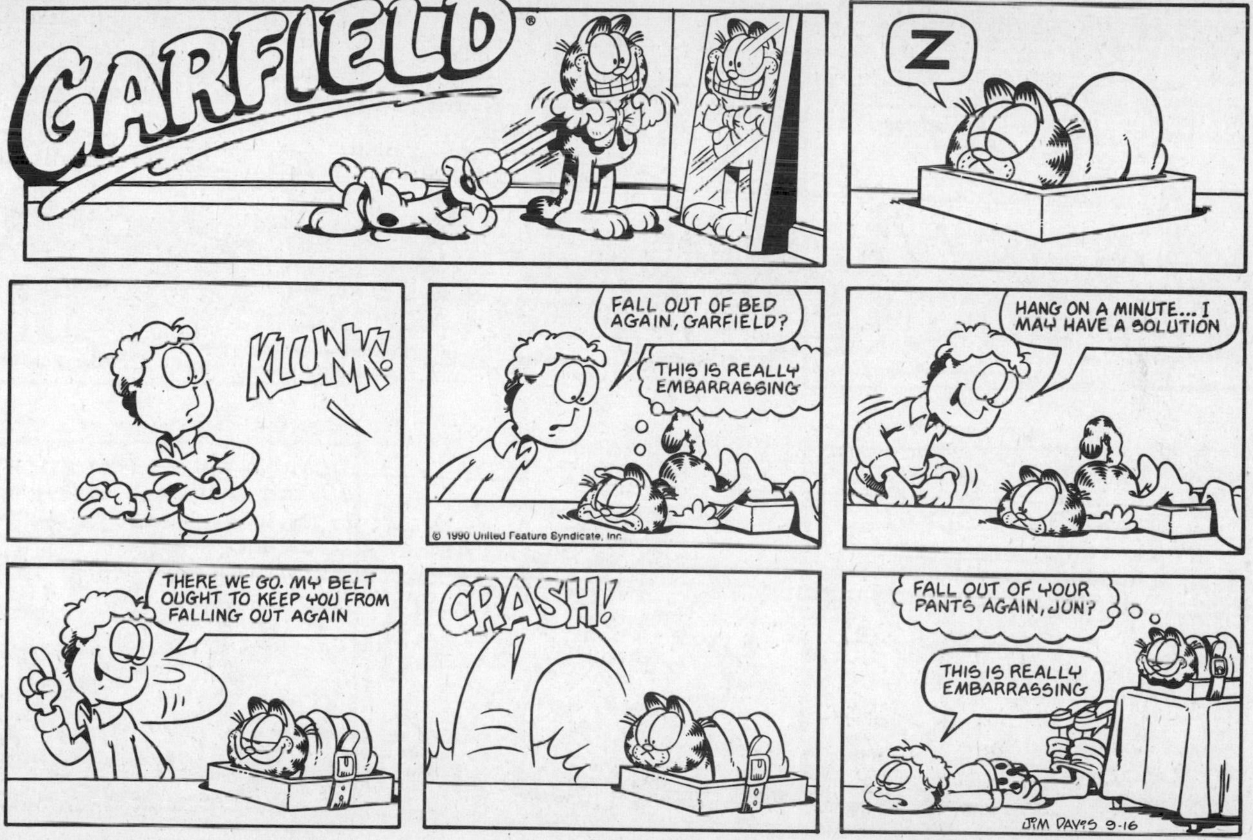
GARFIELD®
Z
KLUNK!
FALL OUT OF BED AGAIN, GARFIELD?
THIS IS REALLY EMBARRASSING
© 1990 United Feature Syndicate, Inc.
HANG ON A MINUTE... I MAY HAVE A SOLUTION
THERE WE GO. MY BELT OUGHT TO KEEP YOU FROM FALLING OUT AGAIN
CRASH!
FALL OUT OF YOUR PANTS AGAIN, JON?
THIS IS REALLY EMBARRASSING
JIM DAVIS 9-16

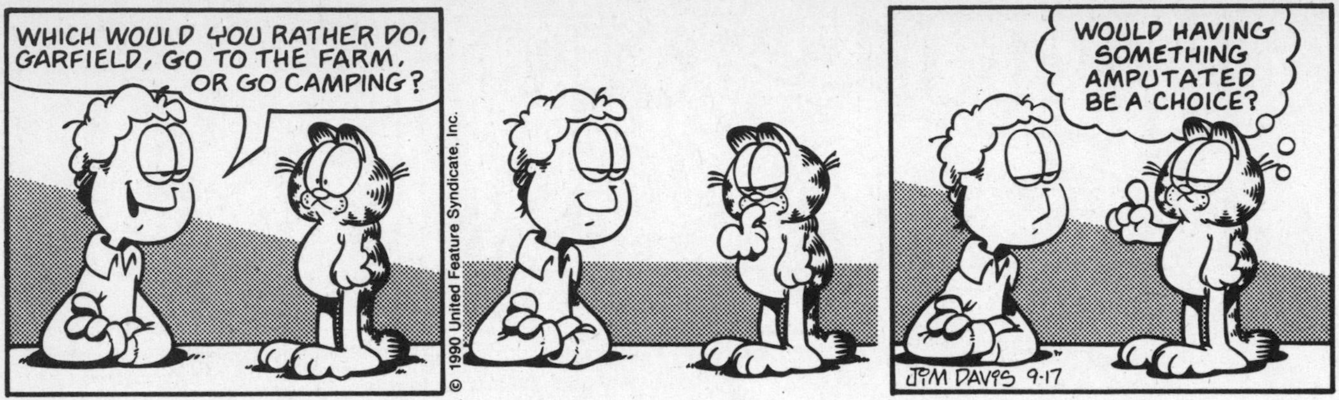
WHICH WOULD YOU RATHER DO, GARFIELD, GO TO THE FARM, OR GO CAMPING?
© 1990 United Feature Syndicate, Inc.
WOULD HAVING SOMETHING AMPUTATED BE A CHOICE?
JIM DAVIS 9-17

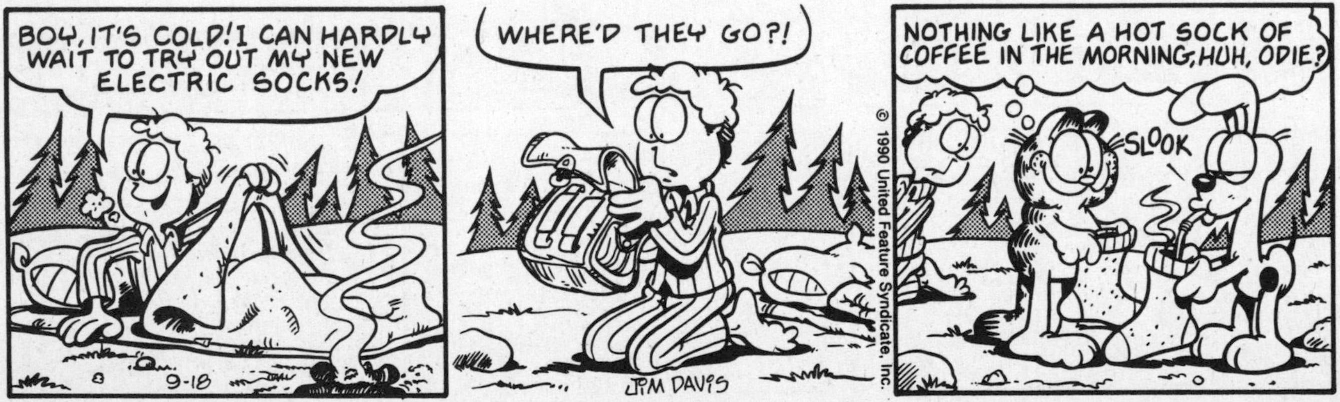
BOY, IT'S COLD! I CAN HARDLY WAIT TO TRY OUT MY NEW ELECTRIC SOCKS!
9-18
WHERE'D THEY GO?!
JIM DAVIS
© 1990 United Feature Syndicate, Inc.
NOTHING LIKE A HOT SOCK OF COFFEE IN THE MORNING, HUH, ODIE?
SLOOK

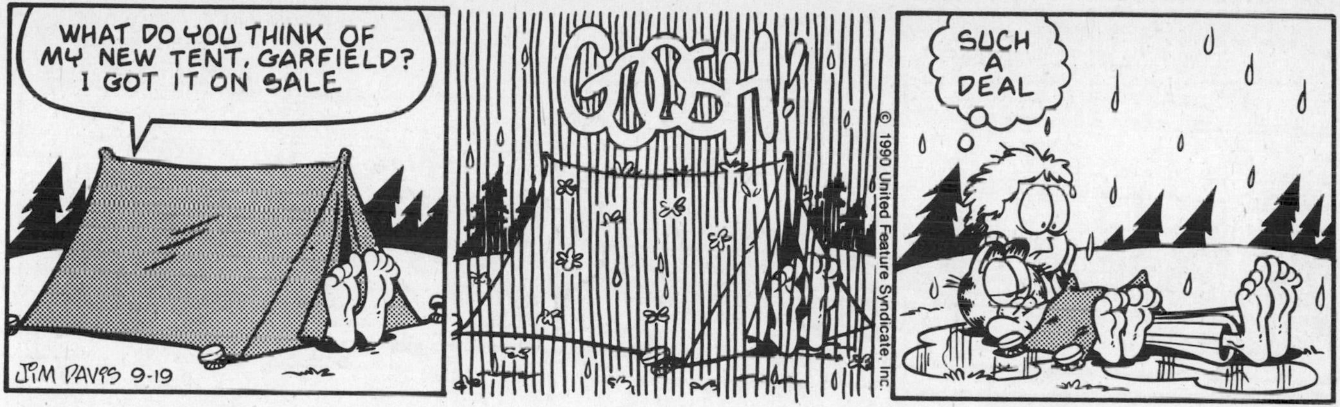

WHAT DO YOU THINK OF MY NEW TENT, GARFIELD? I GOT IT ON SALE
JIM DAVIS 9-19
GOOSH!
© 1990 United Feature Syndicate, Inc.
SUCH A DEAL

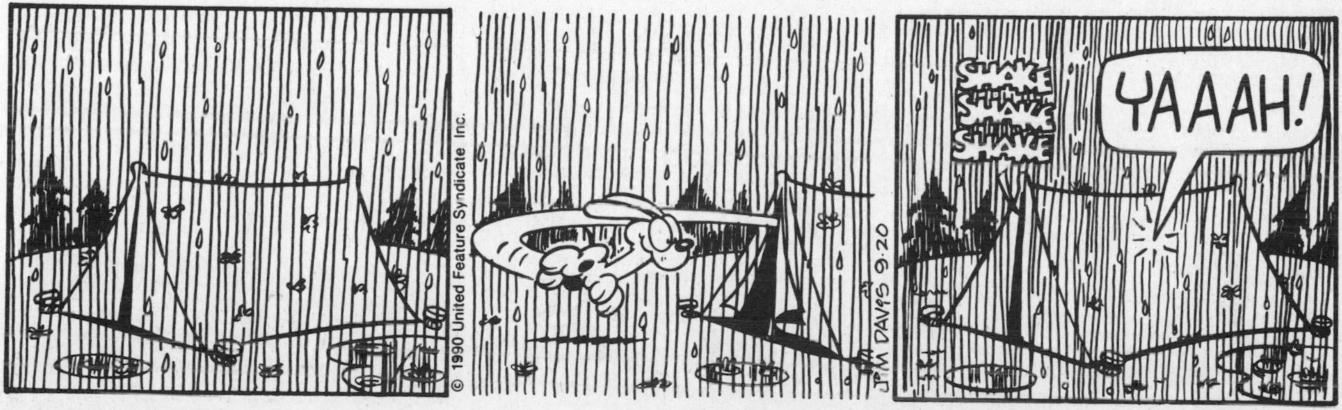

© 1990 United Feature Syndicate Inc.
JIM DAVIS 9-20
SHAKE
SHAKE
SHAKE
YAAAH!

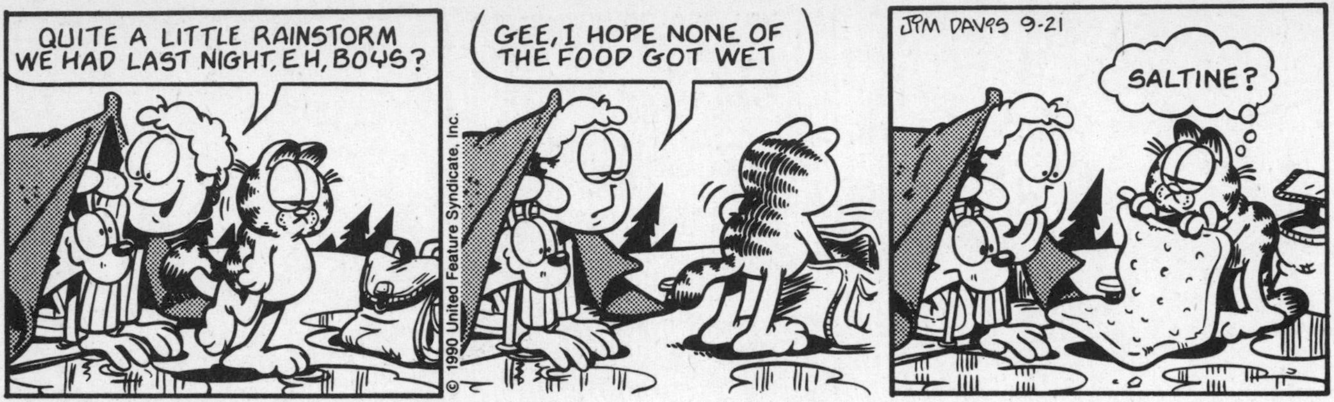
QUITE A LITTLE RAINSTORM WE HAD LAST NIGHT, EH, BOYS?
© 1990 United Feature Syndicate, Inc.
GEE, I HOPE NONE OF THE FOOD GOT WET
JIM DAVIS 9-21
SALTINE?

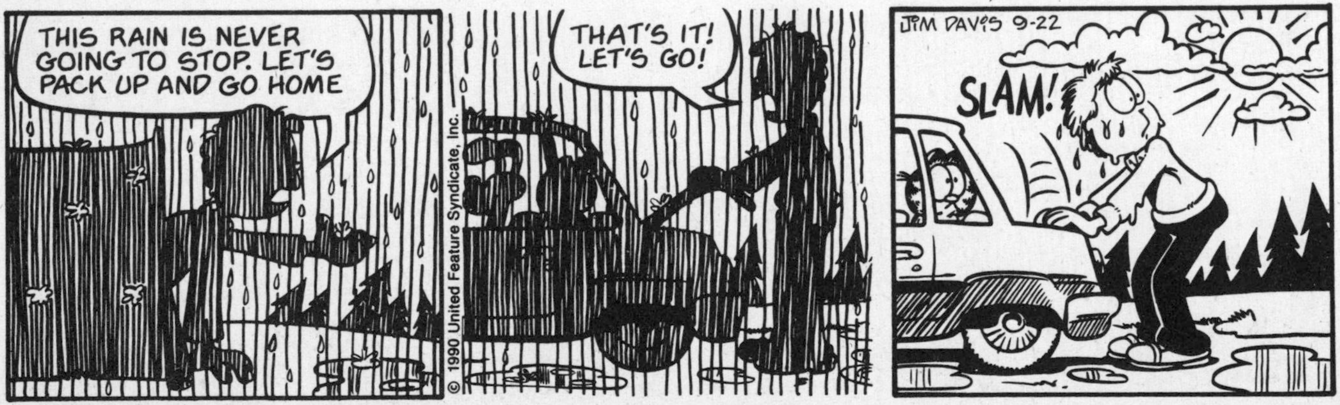
THIS RAIN IS NEVER GOING TO STOP. LET'S PACK UP AND GO HOME
© 1990 United Feature Syndicate, Inc.
THAT'S IT! LET'S GO!
JIM DAVIS 9-22
SLAM!

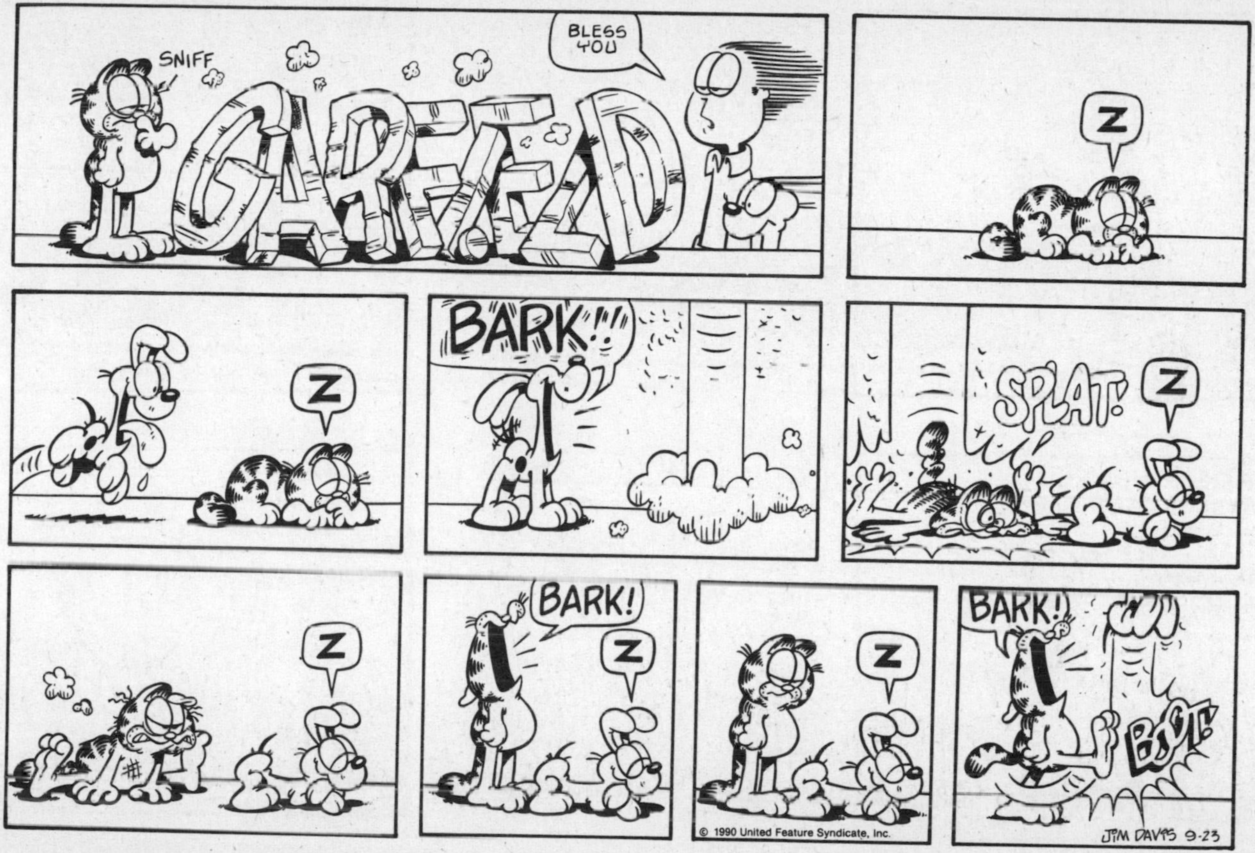
SNIFF
GARFIELD
BLESS YOU
Z
Z
BARK!!!
SPLAT!
Z
Z
BARK!
Z
Z
BARK!
BOOT!
© 1990 United Feature Syndicate, Inc.
JIM DAVIS 9-23

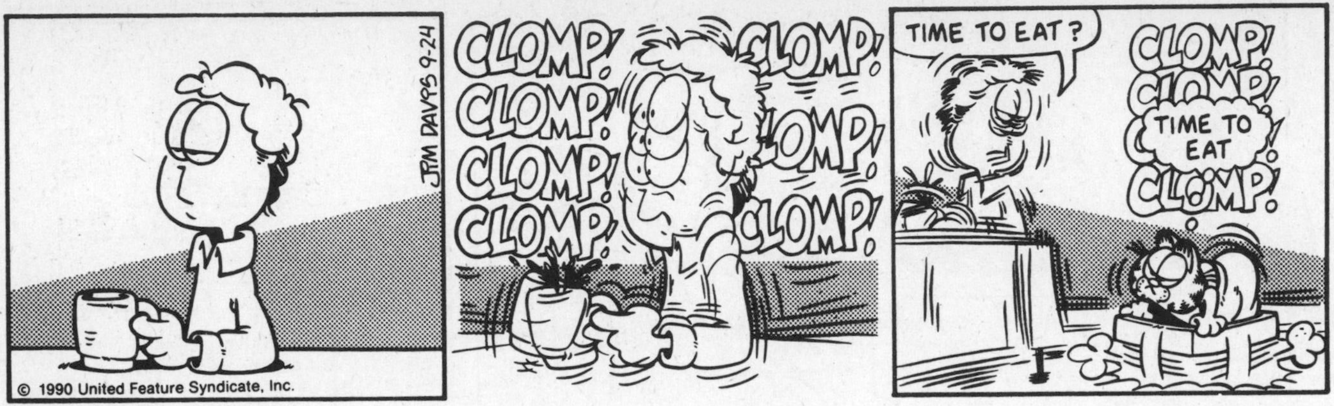

JPM DAVPS 9-24
© 1990 United Feature Syndicate, Inc.
CLOMP! CLOMP! CLOMP! CLOMP!
CLOMP! CLOMP! CLOMP!
TIME TO EAT?
CLOMP! CLOMP!
TIME TO EAT
CLOMP!

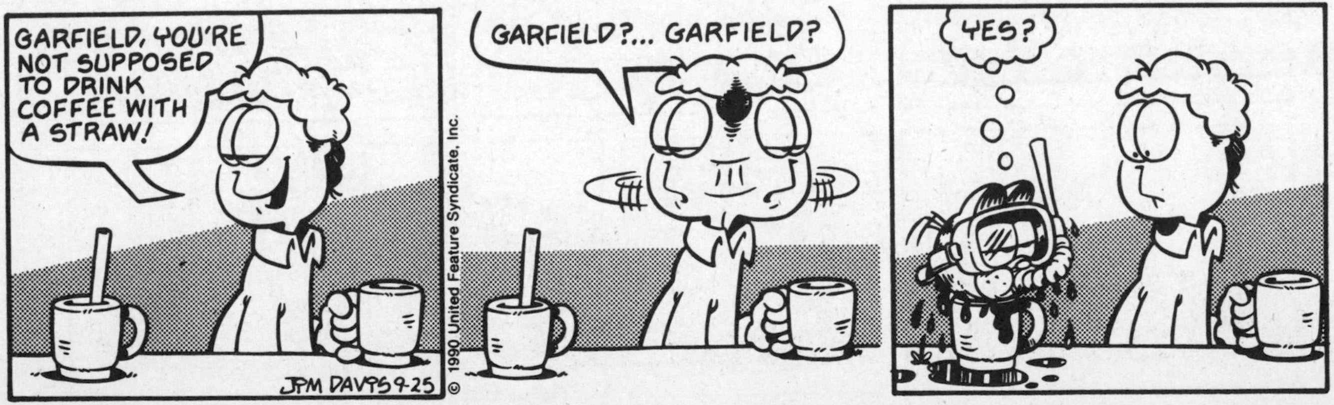

GARFIELD, YOU'RE NOT SUPPOSED TO DRINK COFFEE WITH A STRAW!
JPM DAVPS 9-25
© 1990 United Feature Syndicate, Inc.
GARFIELD?... GARFIELD?
YES?

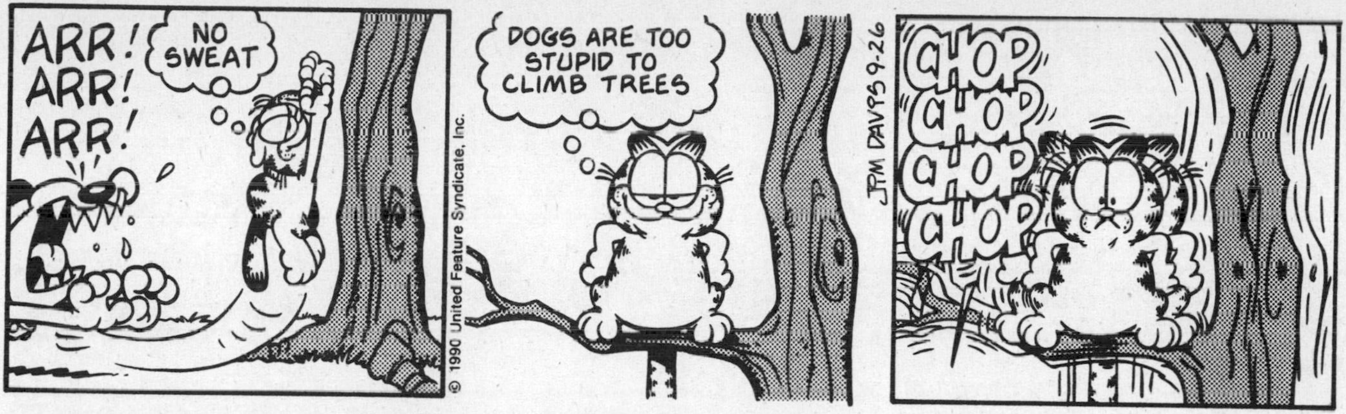
ARR! ARR! ARR!
NO SWEAT
© 1990 United Feature Syndicate, Inc.
DOGS ARE TOO STUPID TO CLIMB TREES
JPM DAVPS 9-26
CHOP CHOP CHOP CHOP

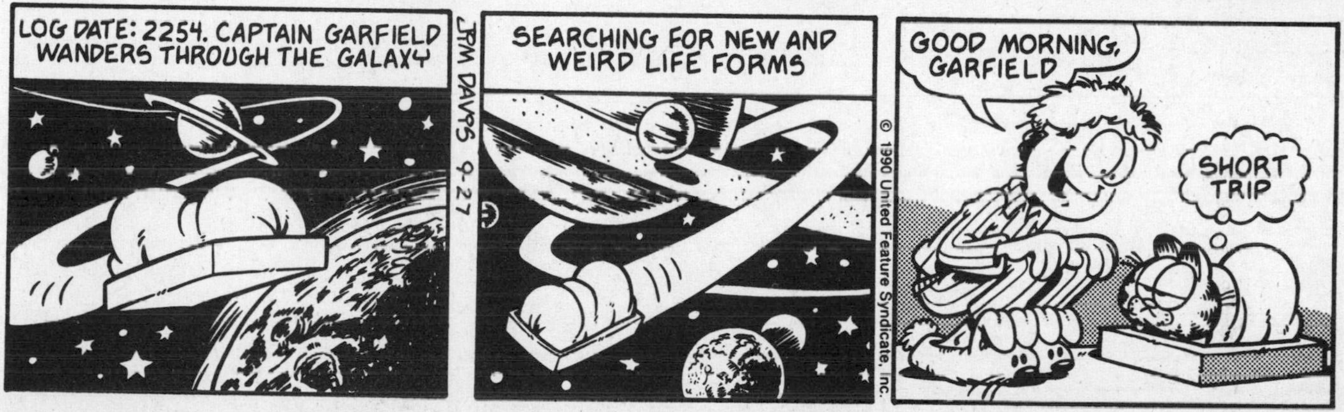
LOG DATE: 2254. CAPTAIN GARFIELD WANDERS THROUGH THE GALAXY
JPM DAVPS 9-27
SEARCHING FOR NEW AND WEIRD LIFE FORMS
© 1990 United Feature Syndicate, Inc.
GOOD MORNING, GARFIELD
SHORT TRIP

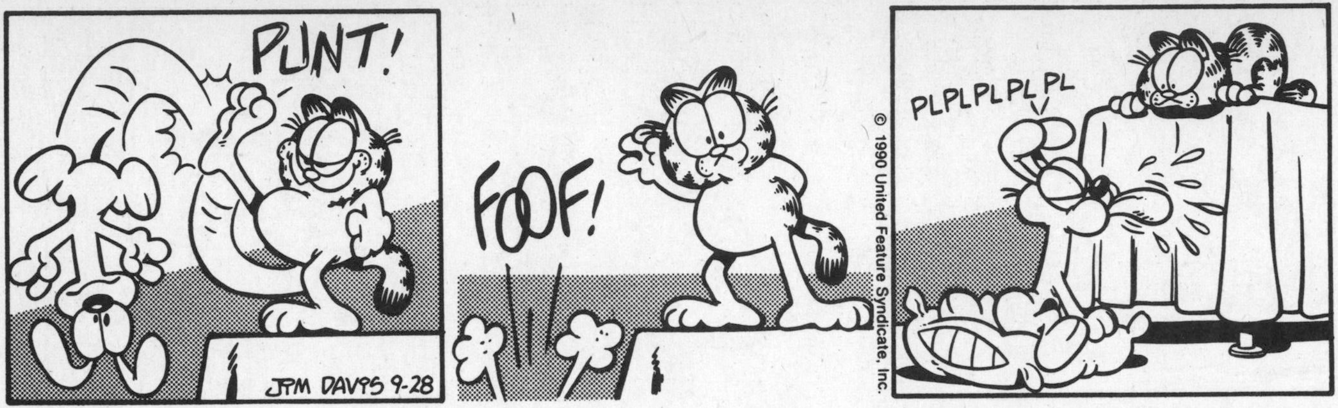
PUNT!
JIM DAVIS 9-28
FOOF!
© 1990 United Feature Syndicate, Inc.
PLPLPLPLPL

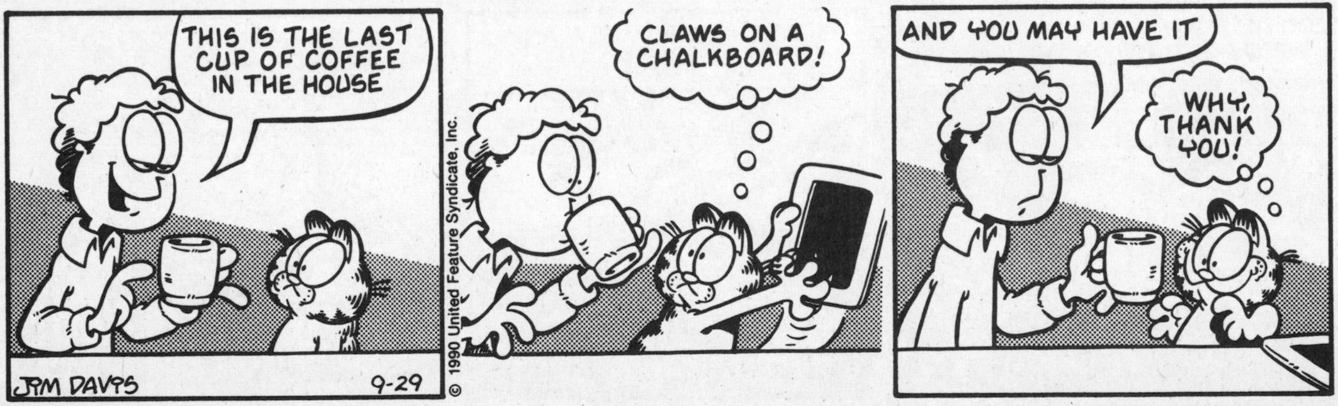
THIS IS THE LAST CUP OF COFFEE IN THE HOUSE
JIM DAVIS 9-29
© 1990 United Feature Syndicate, Inc.
CLAWS ON A CHALKBOARD!
AND YOU MAY HAVE IT
WHY, THANK YOU!

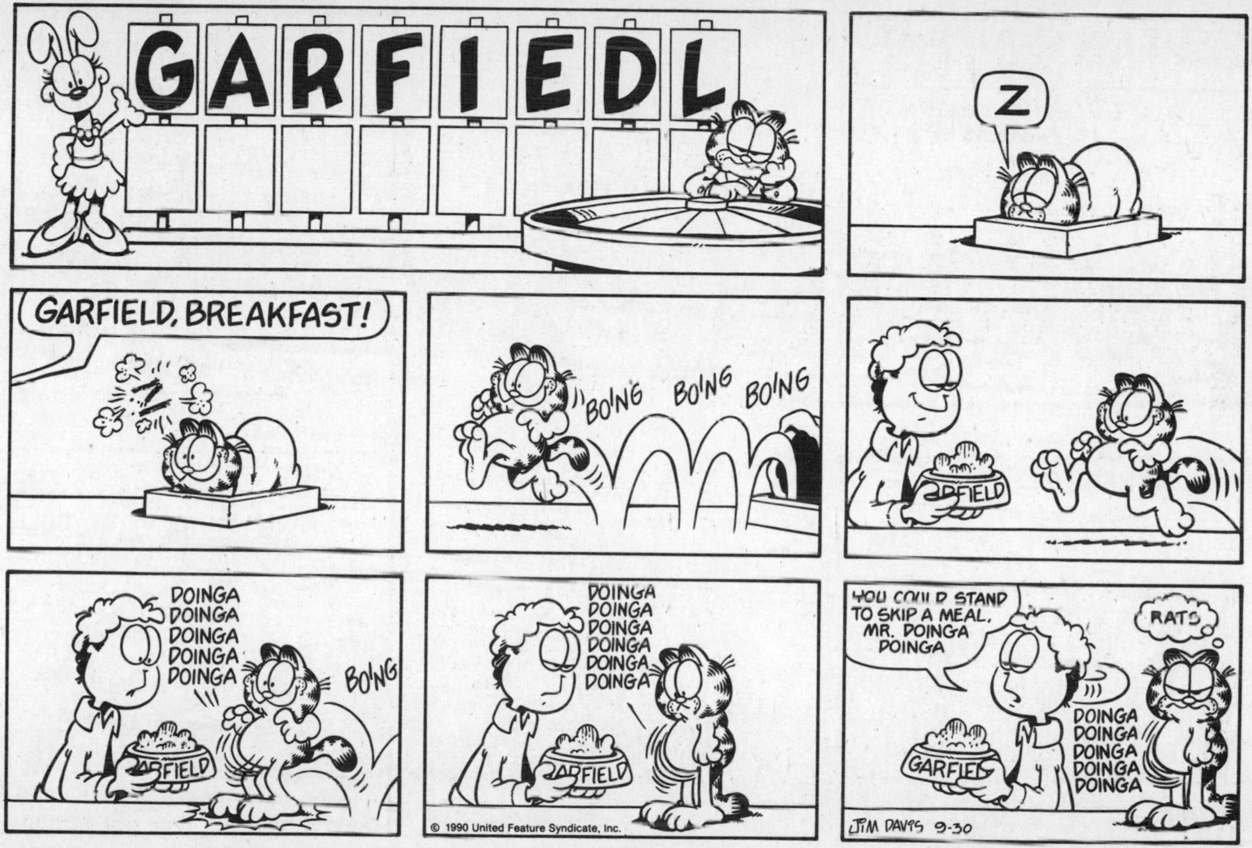

GARFIEDL
Z
GARFIELD, BREAKFAST!
Z
BOING BOING BOING
GARFIELD
DOINGA
DOINGA
DOINGA
DOINGA
DOINGA
BOING
GARFIELD
DOINGA
DOINGA
DOINGA
DOINGA
DOINGA
DOINGA
GARFIELD
YOU COULD STAND TO SKIP A MEAL, MR. DOINGA DOINGA
RATS
DOINGA
DOINGA
DOINGA
DOINGA
DOINGA
GARFIELD
JIM DAVIS 9-30
© 1990 United Feature Syndicate, Inc.

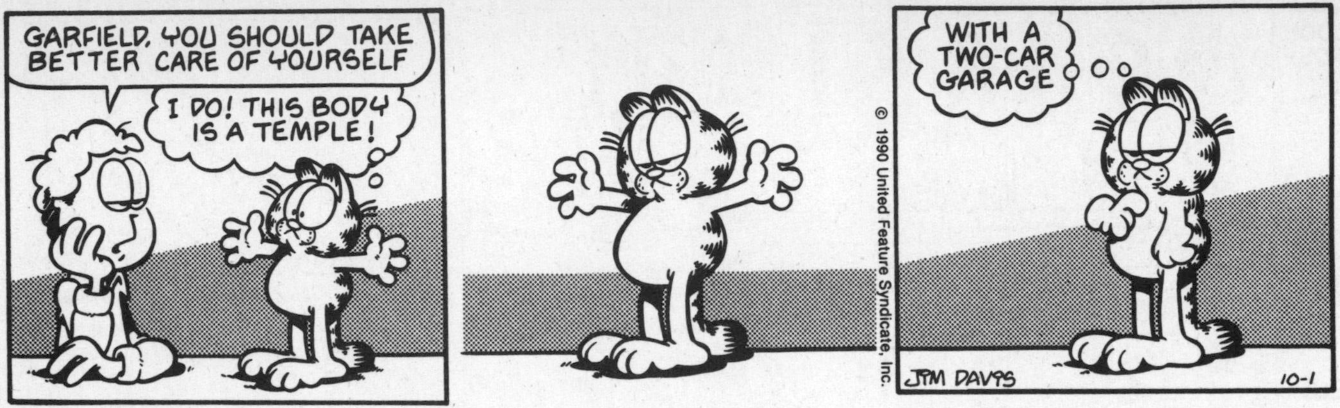
GARFIELD, YOU SHOULD TAKE BETTER CARE OF YOURSELF
I DO! THIS BODY IS A TEMPLE!
WITH A TWO-CAR GARAGE
JIM DAVIS
10-1

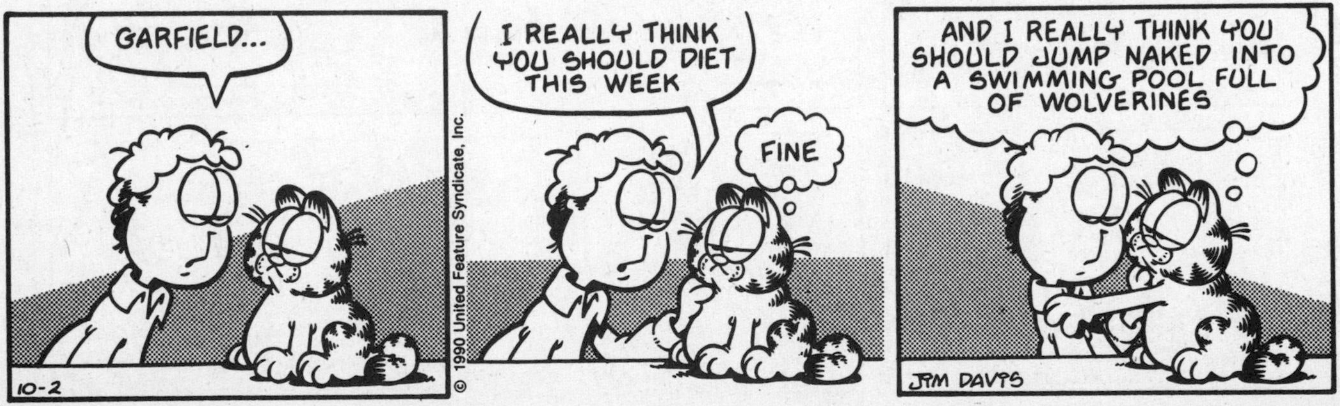
GARFIELD...
10-2
I REALLY THINK YOU SHOULD DIET THIS WEEK
FINE
AND I REALLY THINK YOU SHOULD JUMP NAKED INTO A SWIMMING POOL FULL OF WOLVERINES
JIM DAVIS

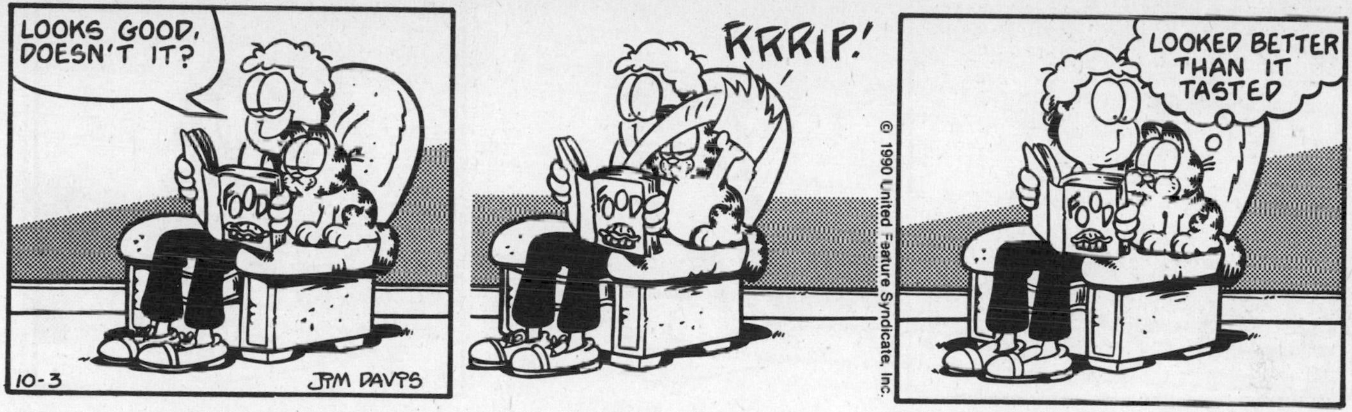
LOOKS GOOD, DOESN'T IT?
FOOD
10-3
JIM DAVIS
KRRIP!
FOOD
© 1990 United Feature Syndicate, Inc.
LOOKED BETTER THAN IT TASTED
FOOD

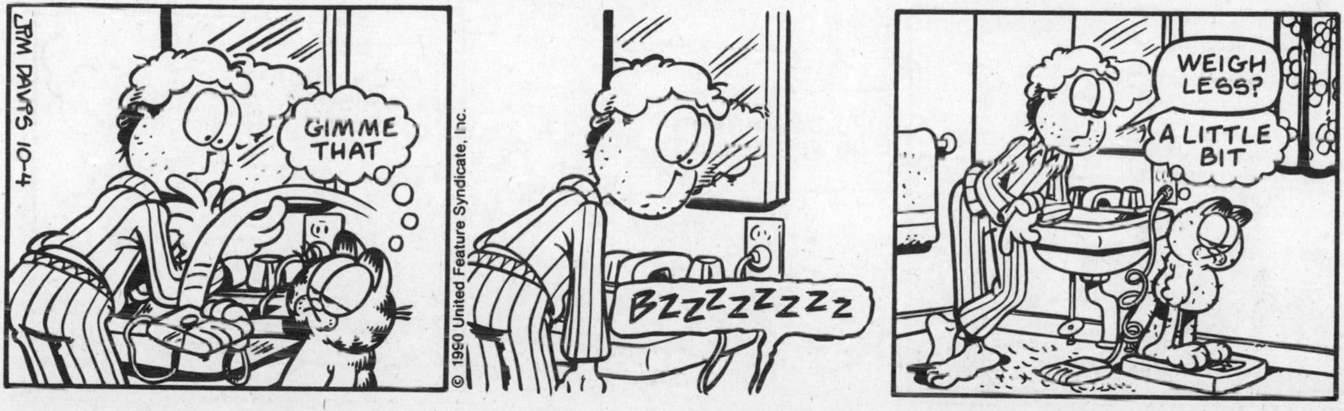
JIM DAVIS 10-4
GIMME THAT
© 1990 United Feature Syndicate, Inc.
BZZZZZZZZZ
WEIGH LESS?
A LITTLE BIT

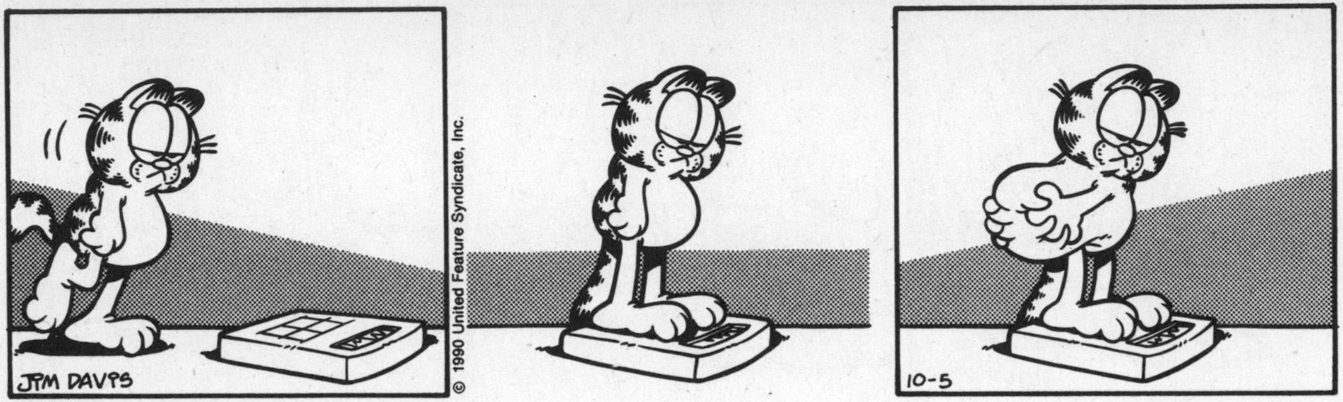
JIM DAVIS
10-5

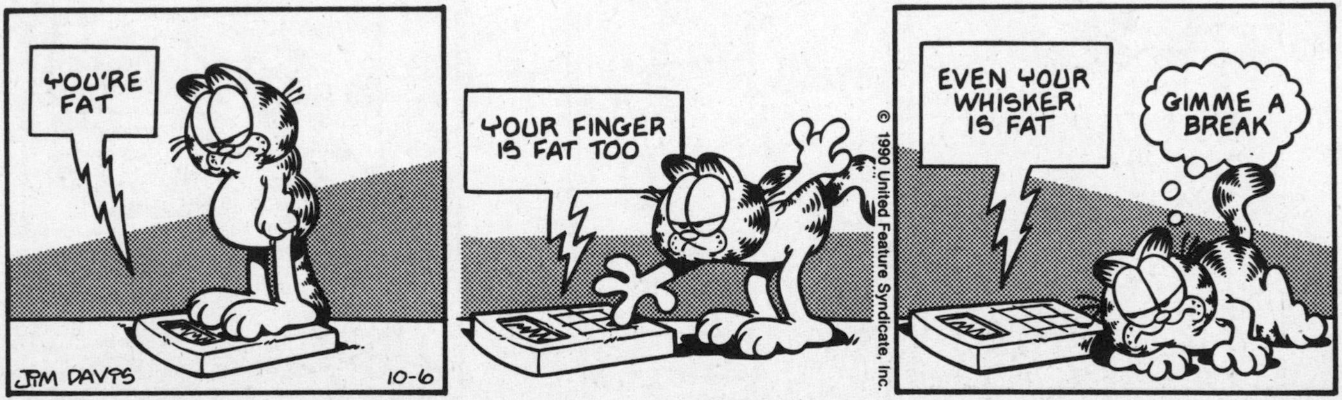
YOU'RE FAT
JIM DAVIS
10-6
YOUR FINGER IS FAT TOO
EVEN YOUR WHISKER IS FAT
GIMME A BREAK

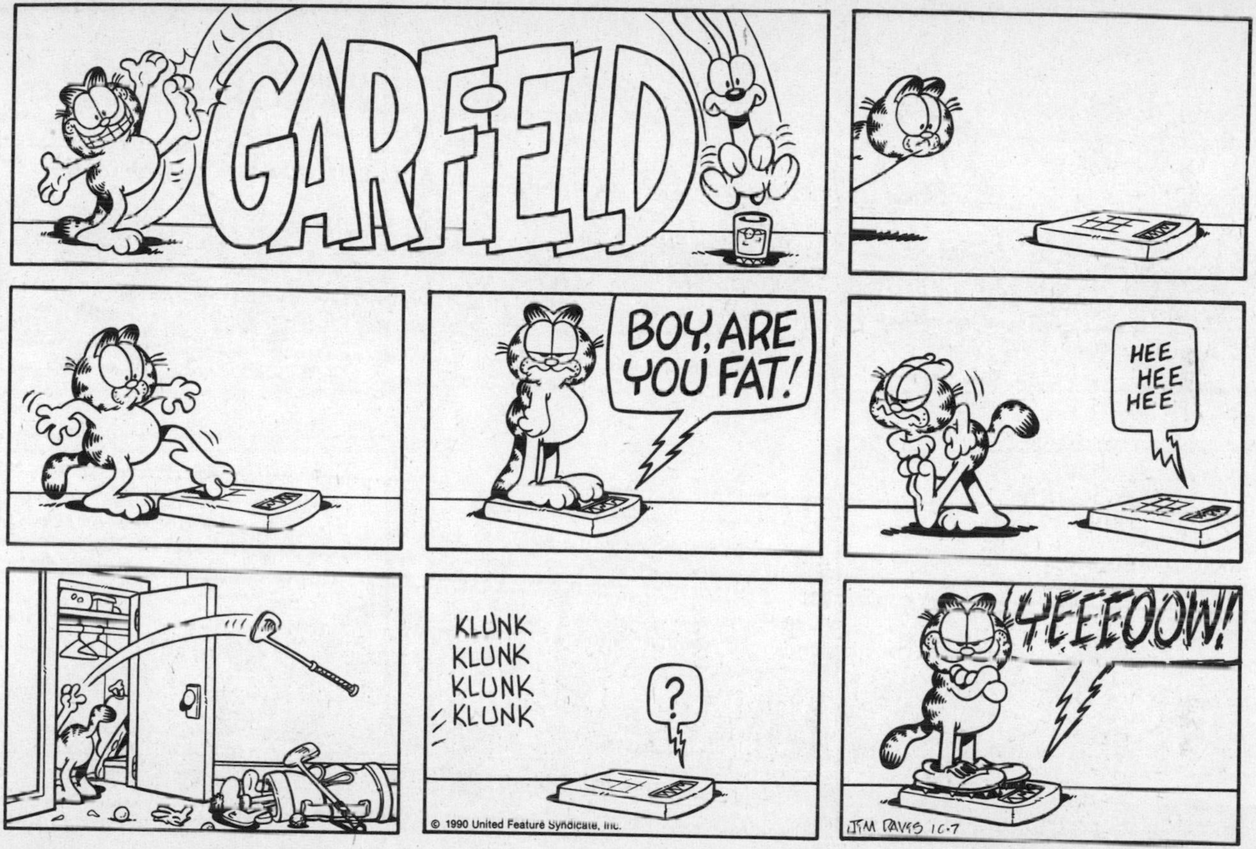
GARFIELD
BOY, ARE YOU FAT!
HEE HEE HEE
KLUNK KLUNK KLUNK KLUNK
?
YEEEOOW!
© 1990 United Feature Syndicate, Inc.
JIM DAVIS 10-7

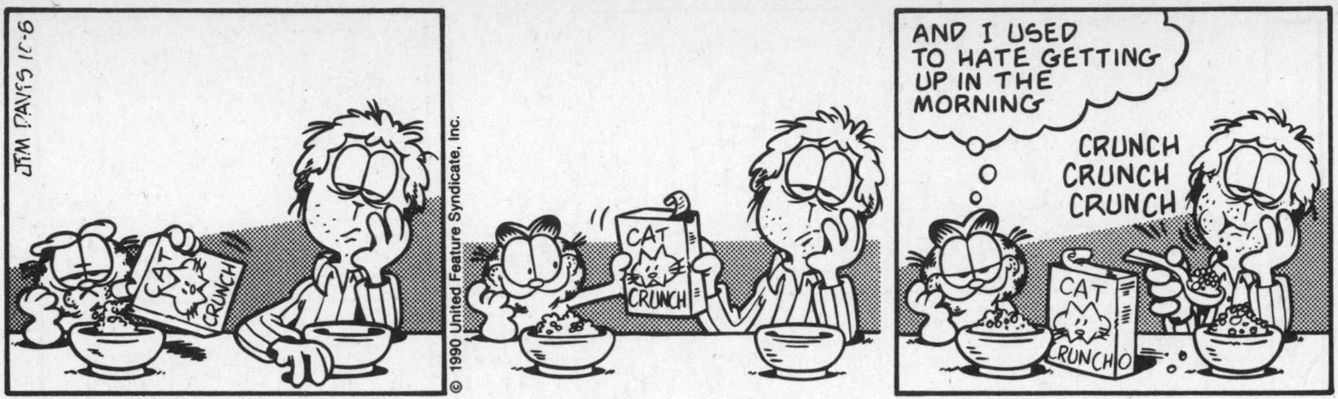
JIM DAVIS 10-6
CAT CRUNCH
© 1990 United Feature Syndicate, Inc.
CAT CRUNCH
AND I USED TO HATE GETTING UP IN THE MORNING
CRUNCH CRUNCH CRUNCH
CAT CRUNCHO

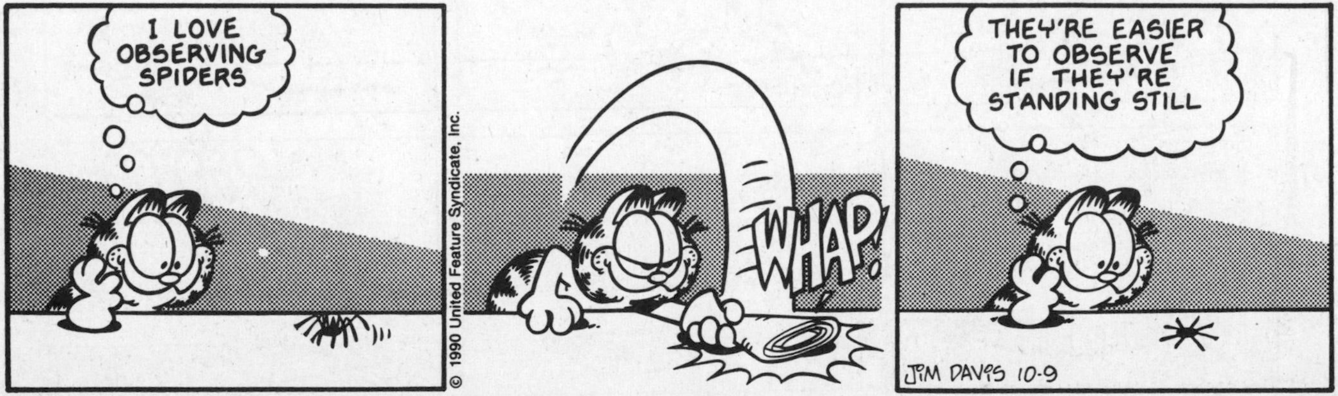
I LOVE OBSERVING SPIDERS
© 1990 United Feature Syndicate, Inc.
WHAP!
THEY'RE EASIER TO OBSERVE IF THEY'RE STANDING STILL
JIM DAVIS 10-9

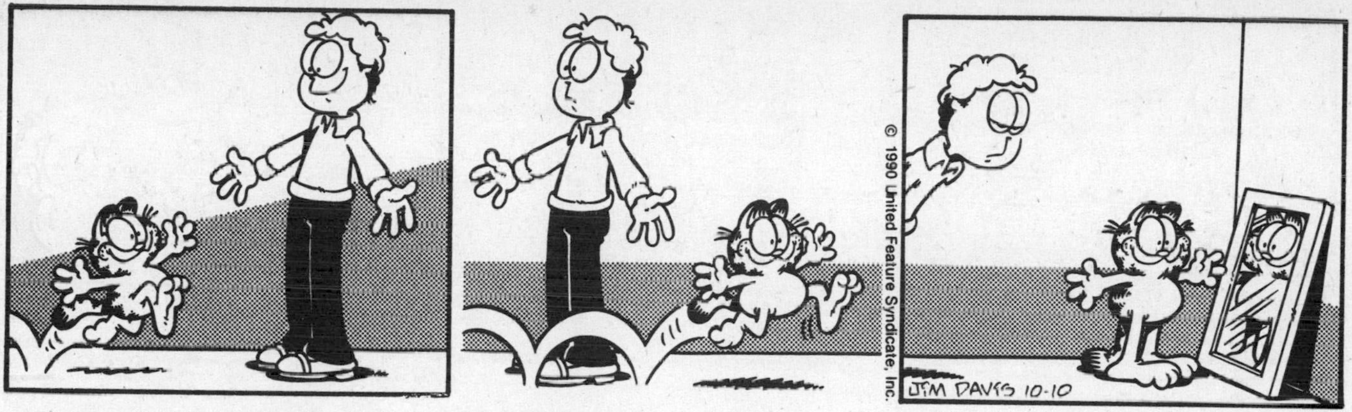
© 1990 United Feature Syndicate, Inc.
JIM DAVIS 10-10

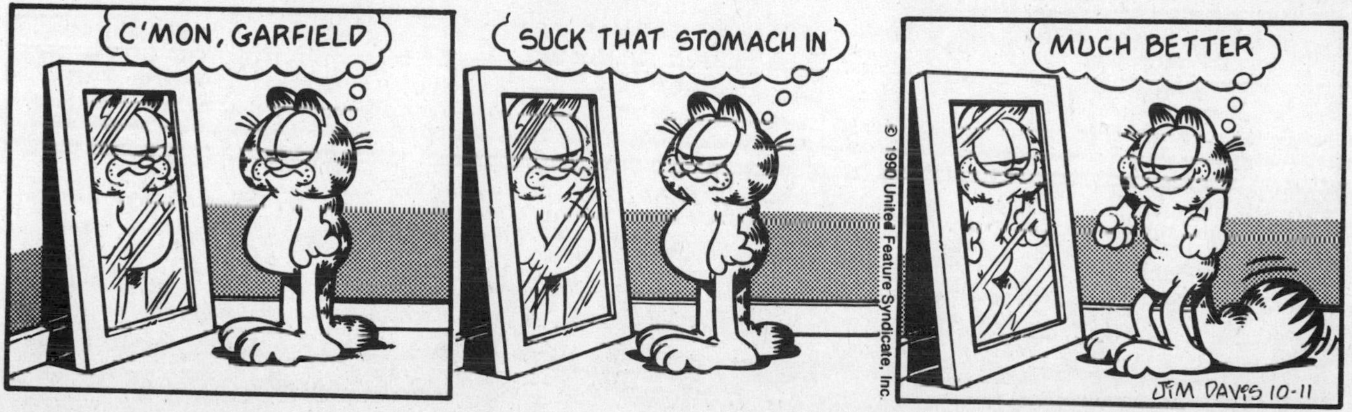
C'MON, GARFIELD
SUCK THAT STOMACH IN
MUCH BETTER
© 1990 United Feature Syndicate, Inc.
JIM DAVIS 10-11

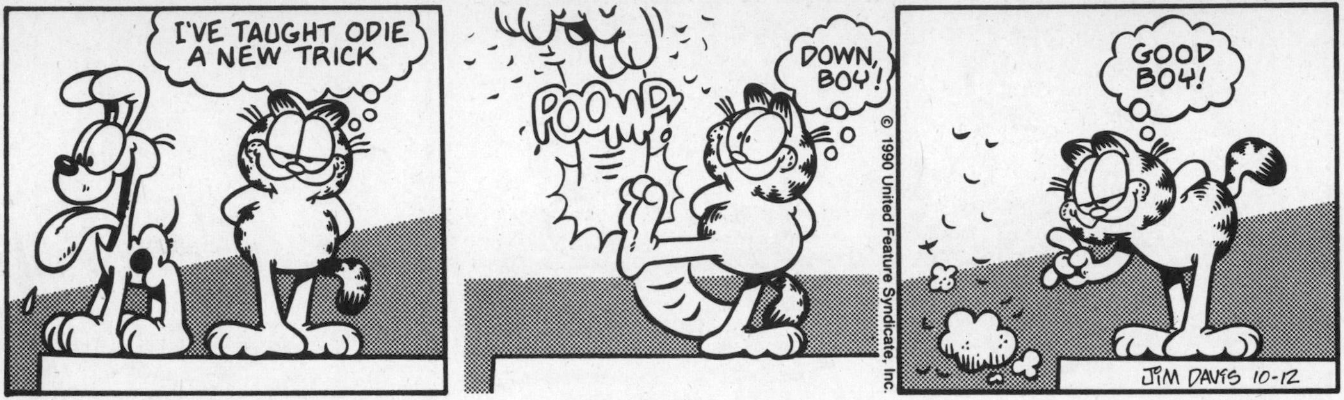
I'VE TAUGHT ODIE A NEW TRICK
POOMP!
DOWN, BOY!
GOOD BOY!
JIM DAVIS 10-12
© 1990 United Feature Syndicate, Inc.

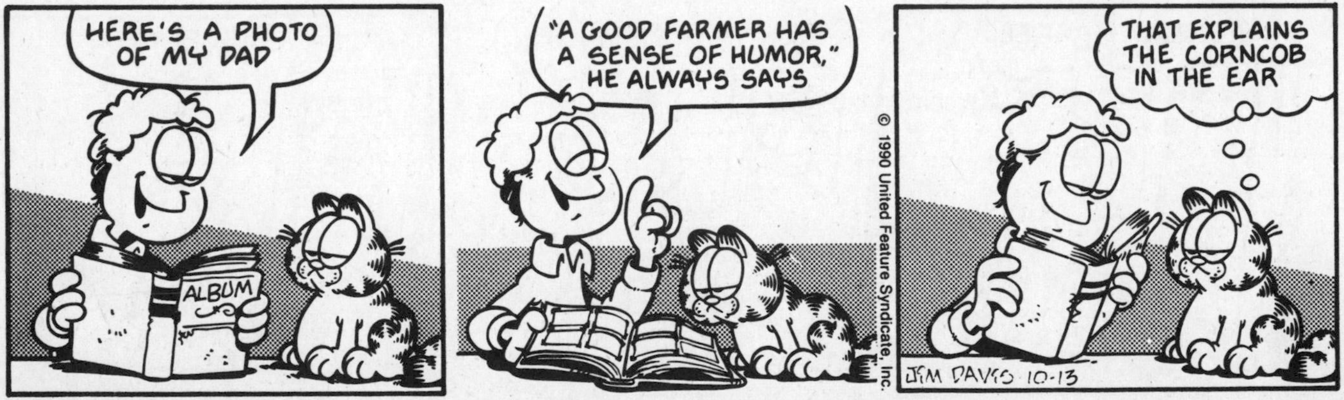
HERE'S A PHOTO OF MY DAD
ALBUM
"A GOOD FARMER HAS A SENSE OF HUMOR," HE ALWAYS SAYS
THAT EXPLAINS THE CORNCOB IN THE EAR
JIM DAVIS 10-13
© 1990 United Feature Syndicate, Inc.

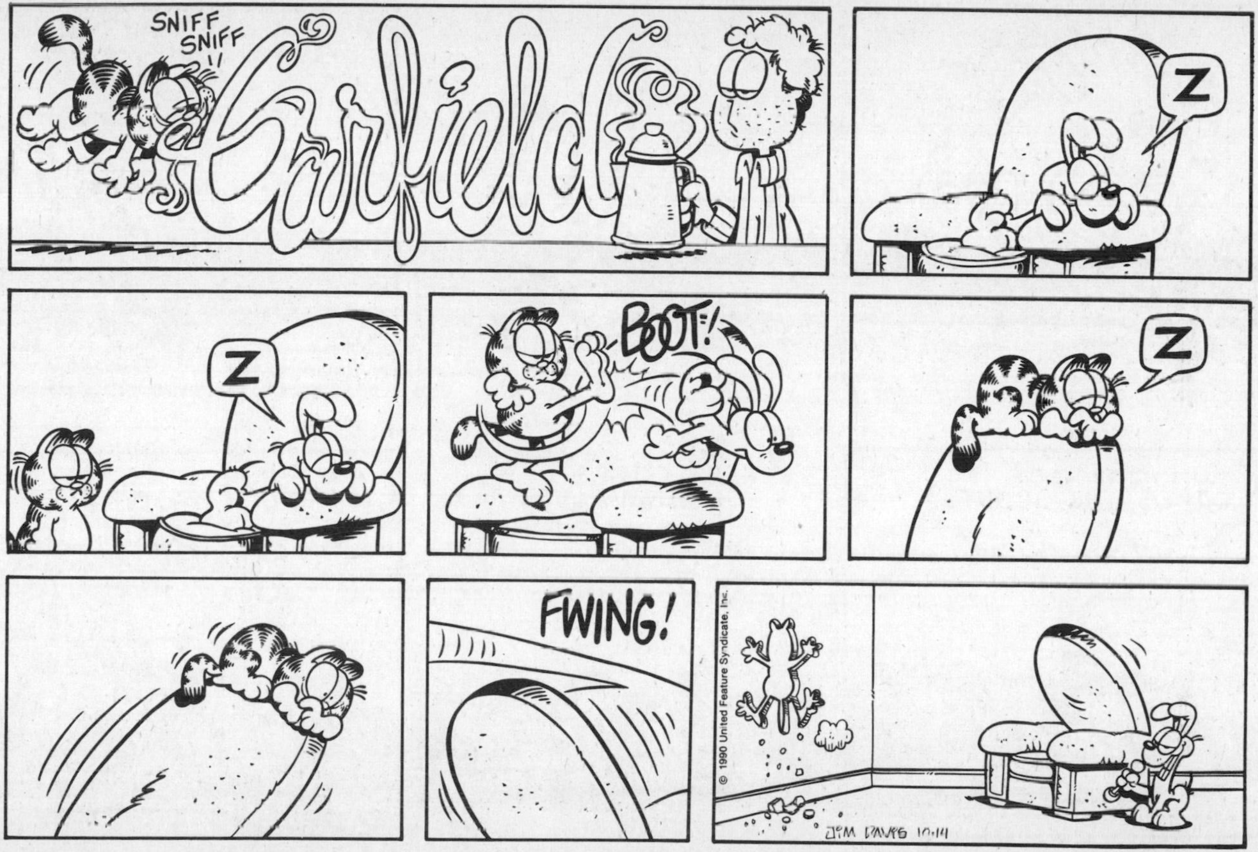

SNIFF SNIFF
Garfield
Z
Z
BOOT!
Z
FWING!
© 1990 United Feature Syndicate, Inc.
JIM DAVIS 10-14

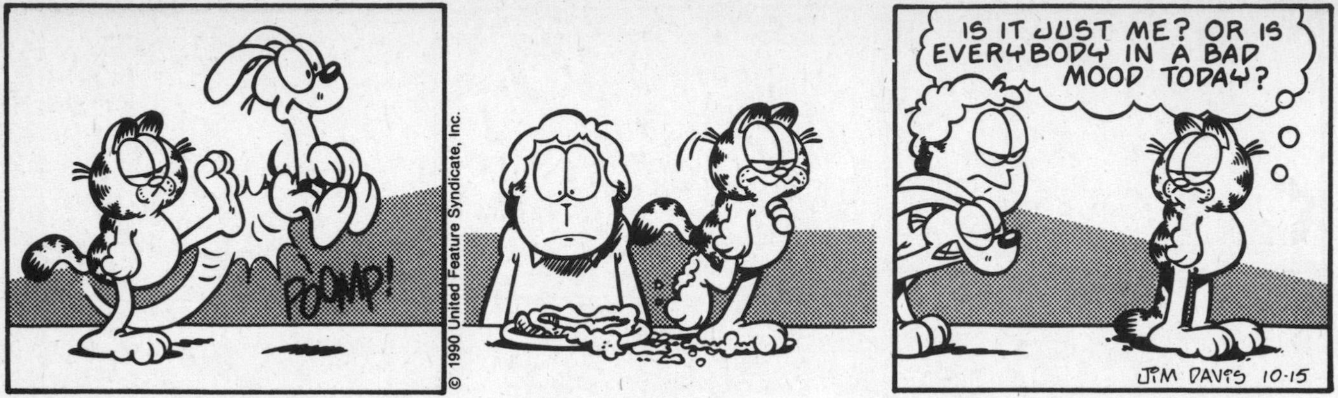
POOMP!
© 1990 United Feature Syndicate, Inc.
IS IT JUST ME? OR IS EVERYBODY IN A BAD MOOD TODAY?
JIM DAVIS 10-15

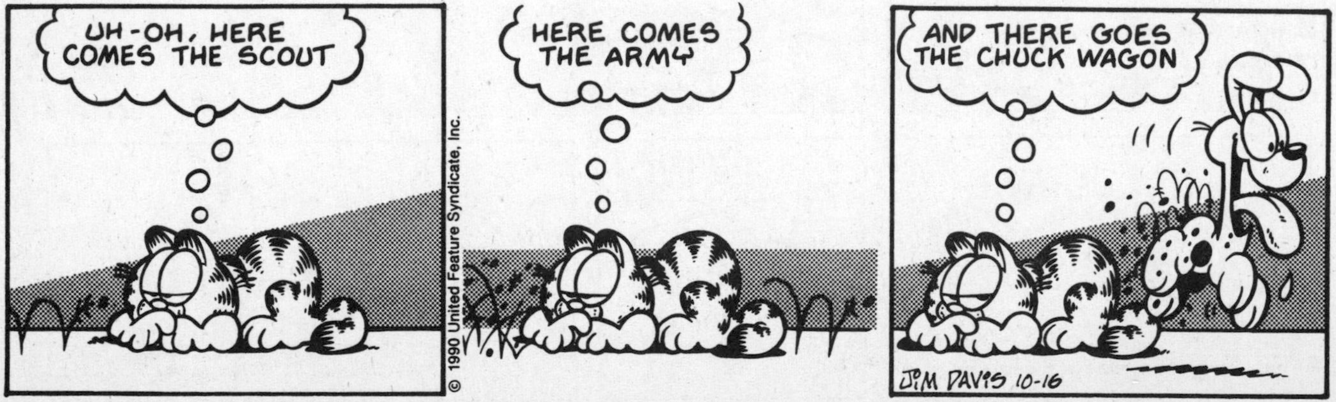
UH-OH, HERE COMES THE SCOUT
© 1990 United Feature Syndicate, Inc.
HERE COMES THE ARMY
AND THERE GOES THE CHUCK WAGON
JIM DAVIS 10-16

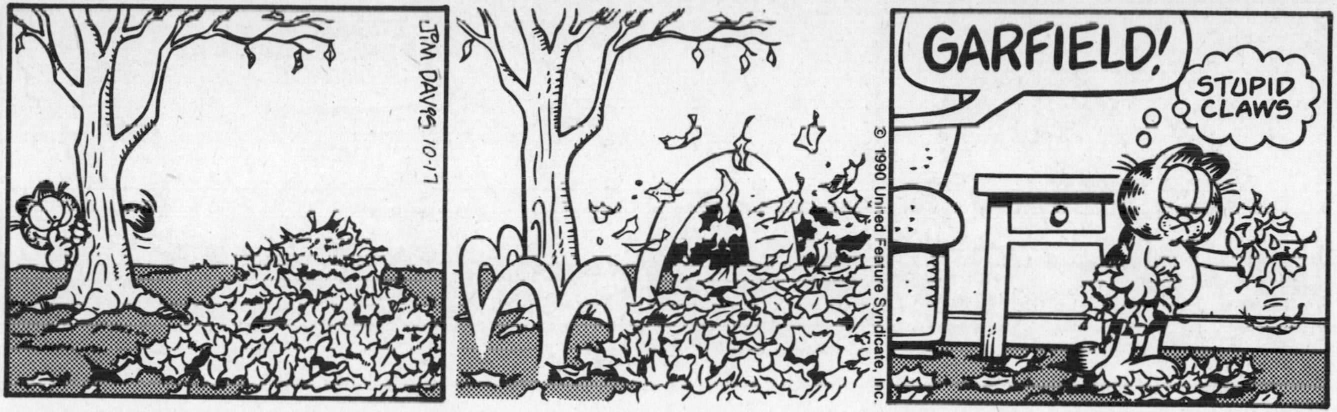
JIM DAVIS 10-17
© 1990 United Feature Syndicate, Inc.
GARFIELD!
STUPID CLAWS

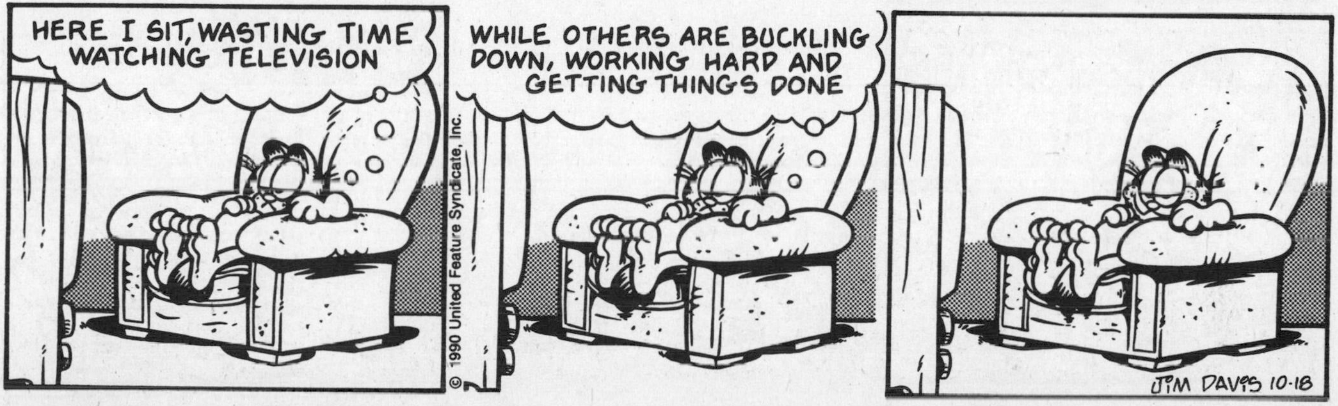
HERE I SIT, WASTING TIME WATCHING TELEVISION
© 1990 United Feature Syndicate, Inc.
WHILE OTHERS ARE BUCKLING DOWN, WORKING HARD AND GETTING THINGS DONE
JIM DAVIS 10-18

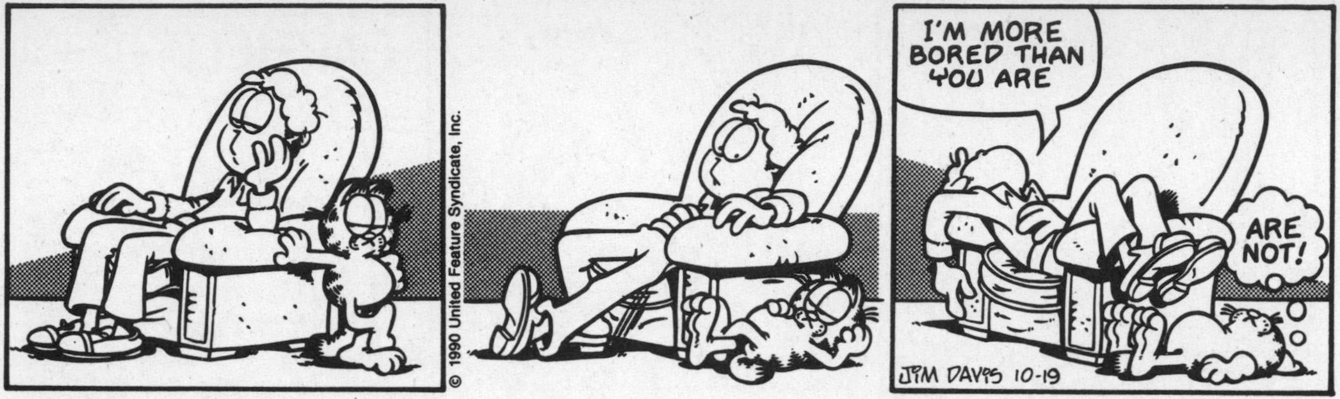
© 1990 United Feature Syndicate, Inc.
I'M MORE BORED THAN YOU ARE
ARE NOT!
JIM DAVIS 10-19

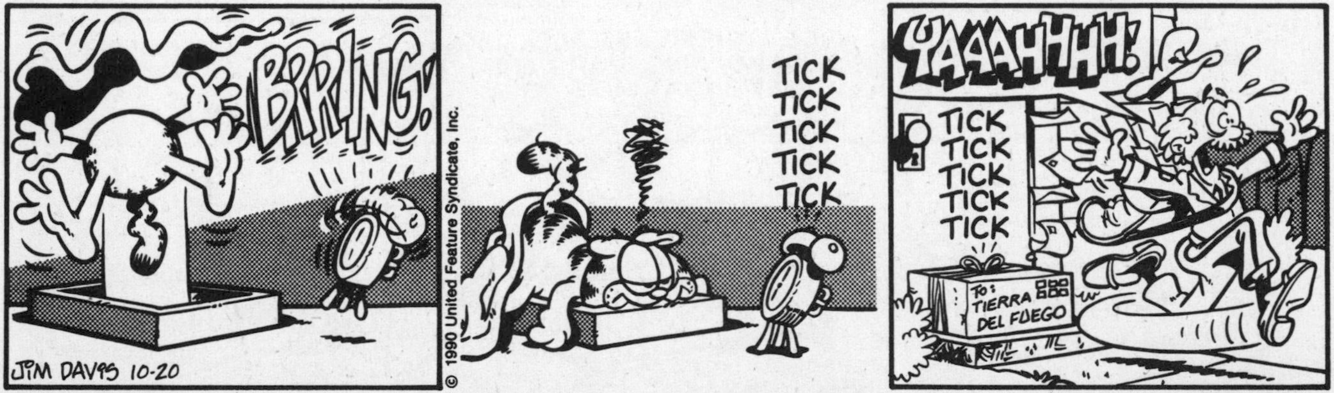
BRRING!
JIM DAVIS 10-20
© 1990 United Feature Syndicate, Inc.
TICK TICK TICK TICK TICK
YAAAHHHH!
TICK TICK TICK TICK TICK
TO: TIERRA DEL FUEGO

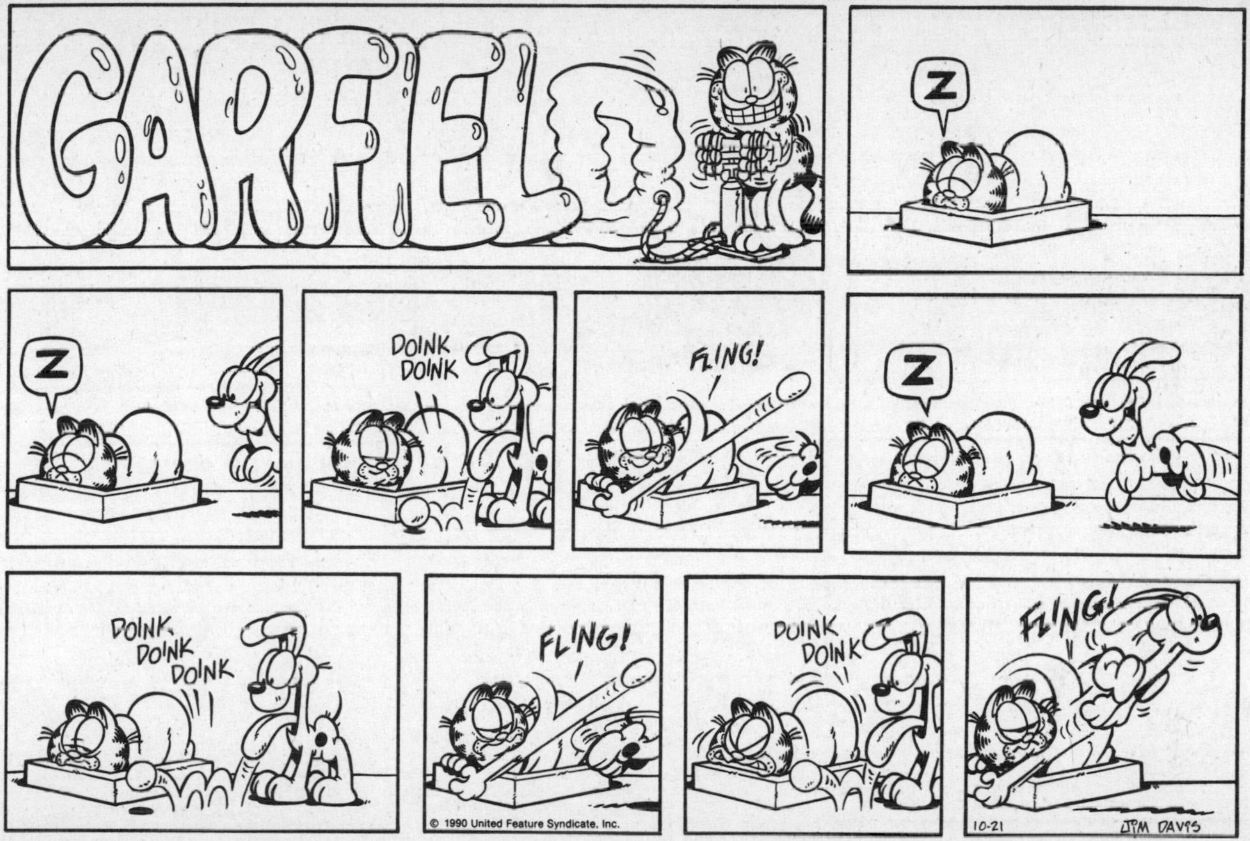
GARFIELD
Z
Z
DOINK DOINK
FLING!
Z
DOINK DOINK DOINK
FLING!
DOINK DOINK
FLING!
© 1990 United Feature Syndicate, Inc.
10-21
JIM DAVIS

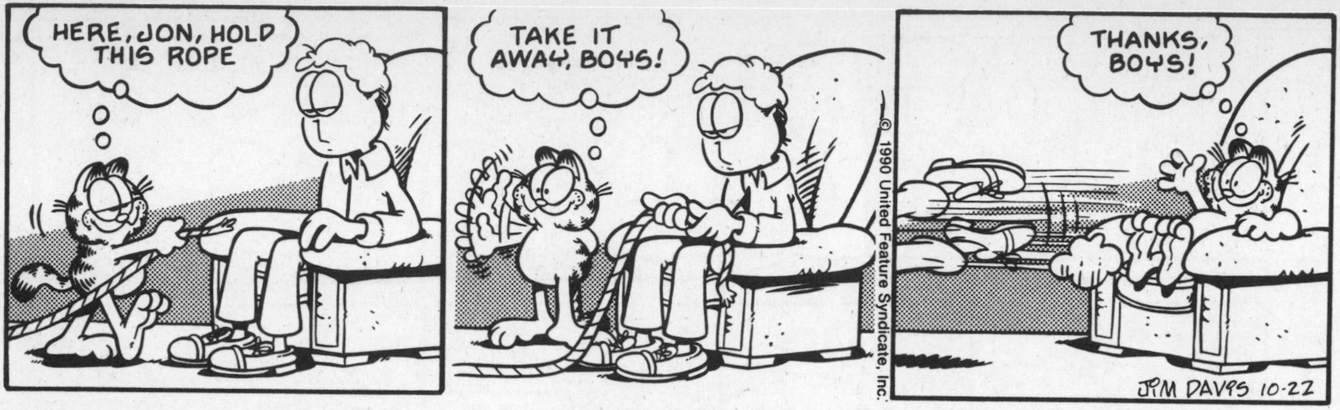
HERE, JON, HOLD THIS ROPE
TAKE IT AWAY, BOYS!
© 1990 United Feature Syndicate, Inc.
THANKS, BOYS!
JIM DAVIS 10-22

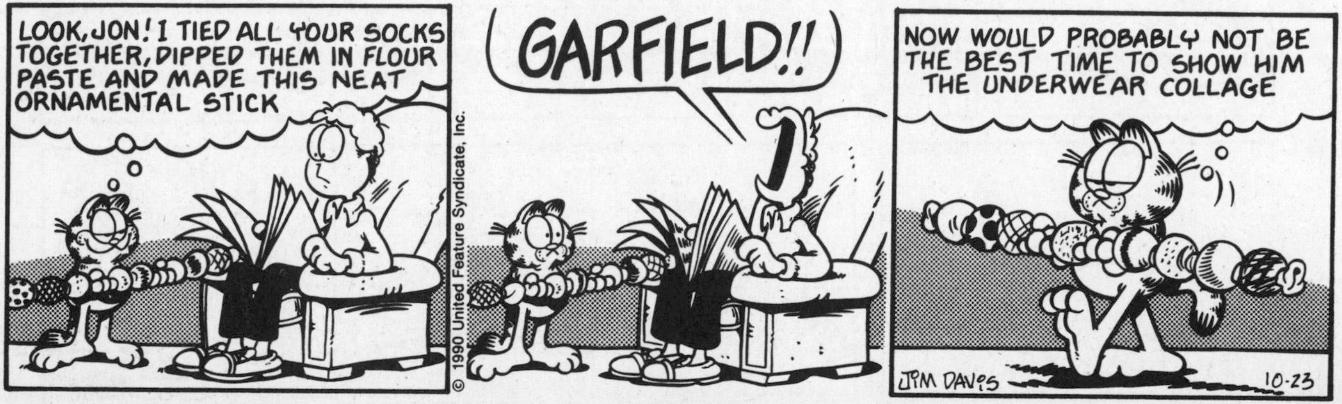
LOOK, JON! I TIED ALL YOUR SOCKS TOGETHER, DIPPED THEM IN FLOUR PASTE AND MADE THIS NEAT ORNAMENTAL STICK
© 1990 United Feature Syndicate, Inc.
GARFIELD!!
NOW WOULD PROBABLY NOT BE THE BEST TIME TO SHOW HIM THE UNDERWEAR COLLAGE
JIM DAVIS 10-23

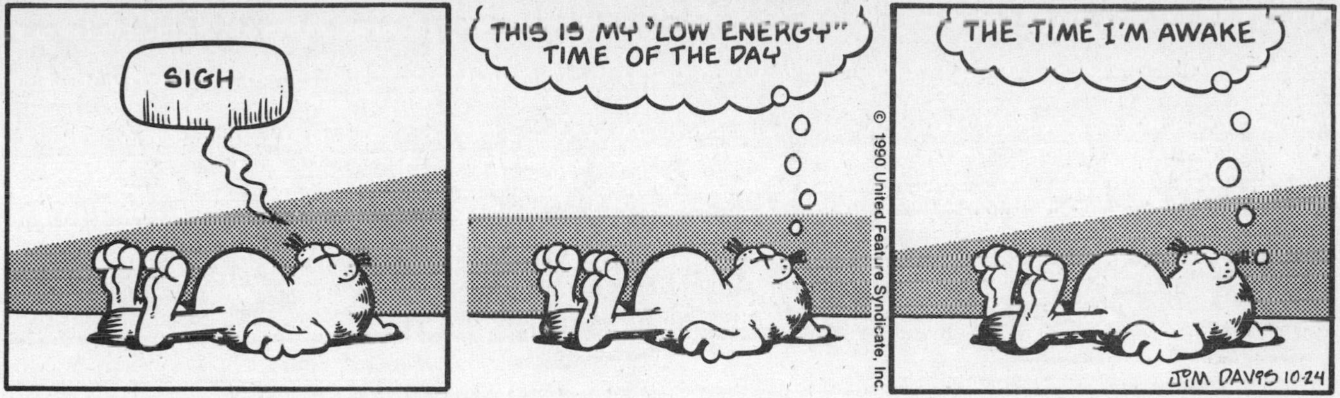

SIGH
THIS IS MY "LOW ENERGY" TIME OF THE DAY
THE TIME I'M AWAKE
JIM DAVIS 10-24

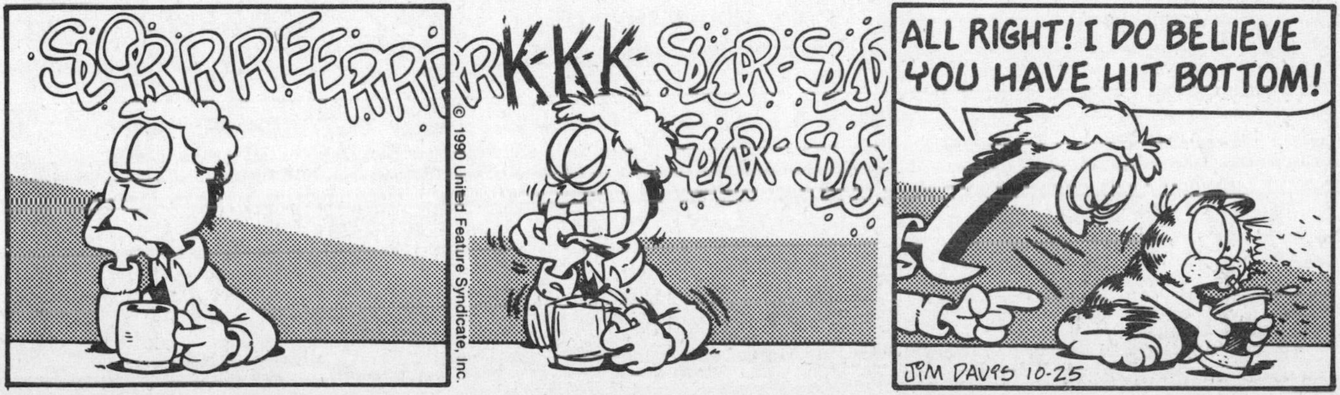

ALL RIGHT! I DO BELIEVE YOU HAVE HIT BOTTOM!
JIM DAVIS 10-25

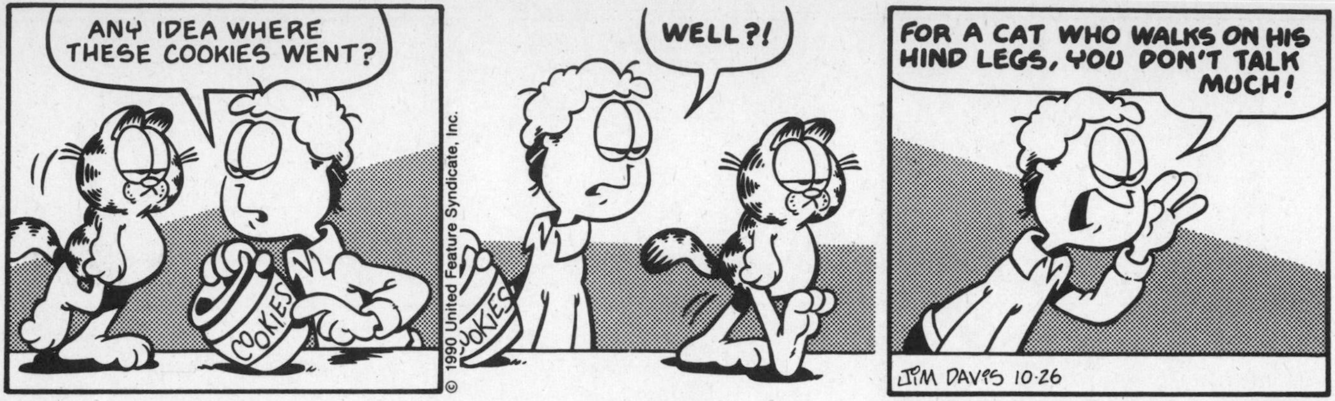

ANY IDEA WHERE THESE COOKIES WENT?
COOKIES
WELL?!
COOKIES
FOR A CAT WHO WALKS ON HIS HIND LEGS, YOU DON'T TALK MUCH!
JIM DAVIS 10·26

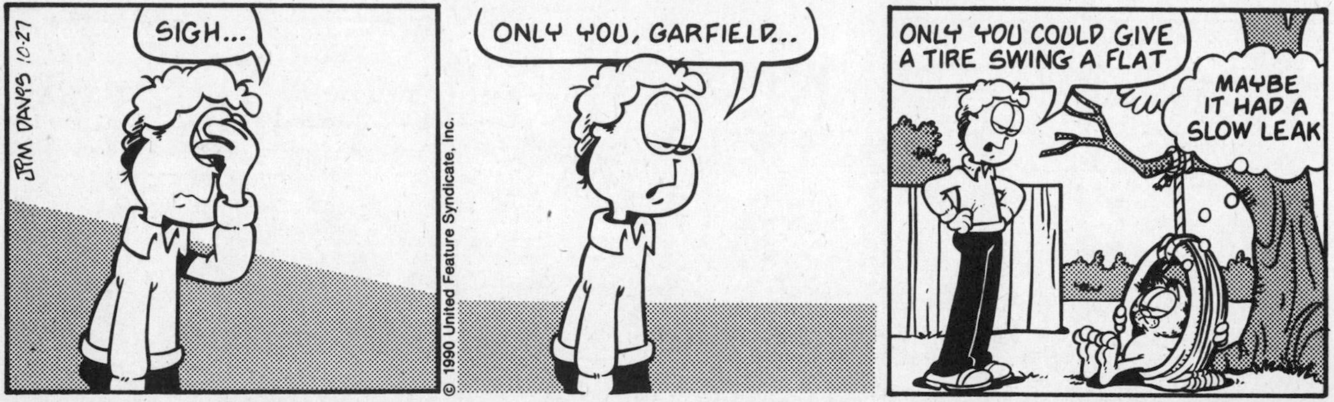

JIM DAVIS 10·27
SIGH...
ONLY YOU, GARFIELD...
ONLY YOU COULD GIVE A TIRE SWING A FLAT
MAYBE IT HAD A SLOW LEAK

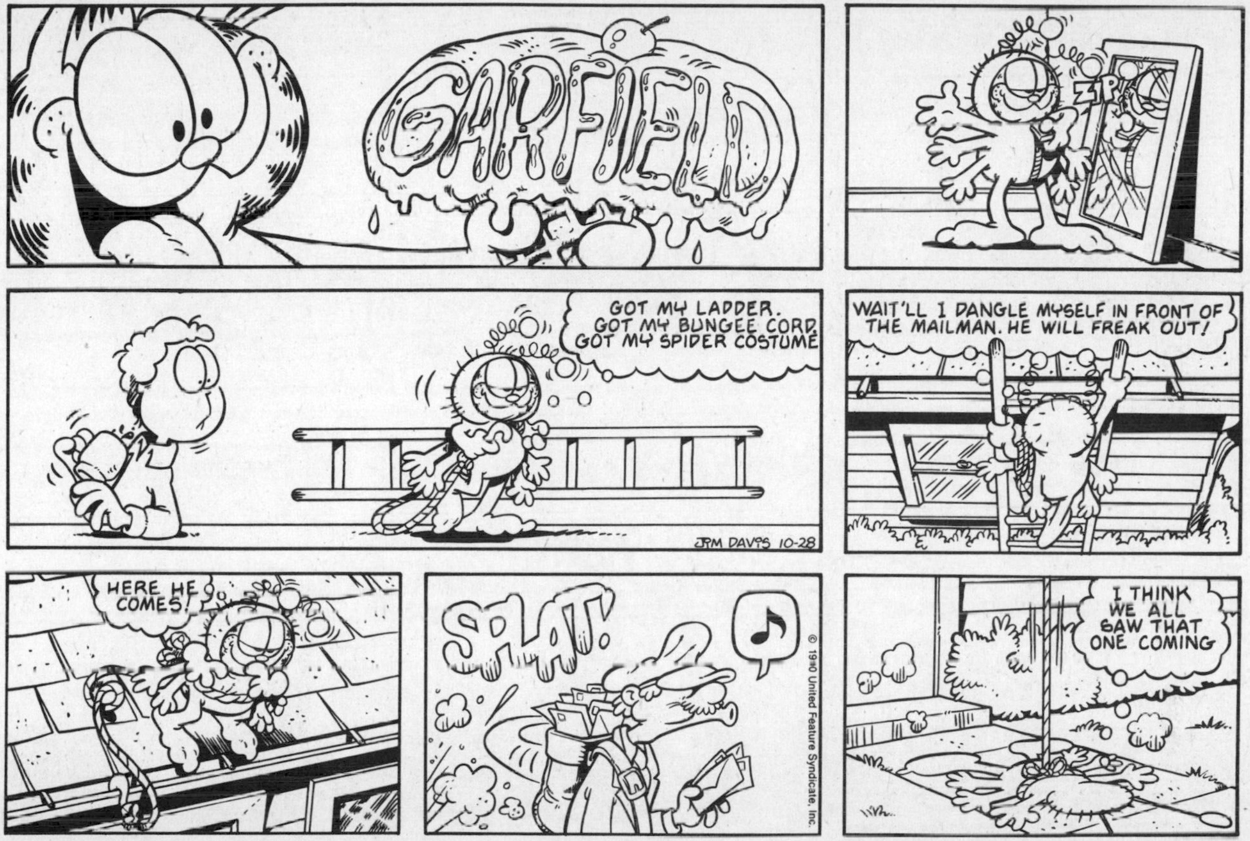
GARFIELD
ZIP
GOT MY LADDER. GOT MY BUNGEE CORD. GOT MY SPIDER COSTUME.
JPM DAVIS 10-28
WAIT'LL I DANGLE MYSELF IN FRONT OF THE MAILMAN. HE WILL FREAK OUT!
HERE HE COMES!
SPLAT!
© 1990 United Feature Syndicate, Inc.
I THINK WE ALL SAW THAT ONE COMING

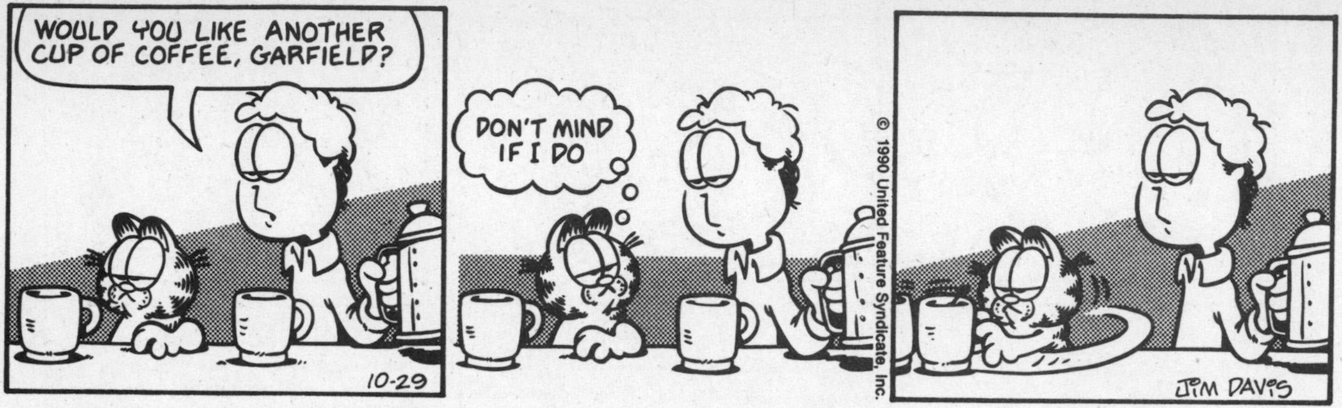
WOULD YOU LIKE ANOTHER CUP OF COFFEE, GARFIELD?
10-29
DON'T MIND IF I DO
© 1990 United Feature Syndicate, Inc.
JIM DAVIS

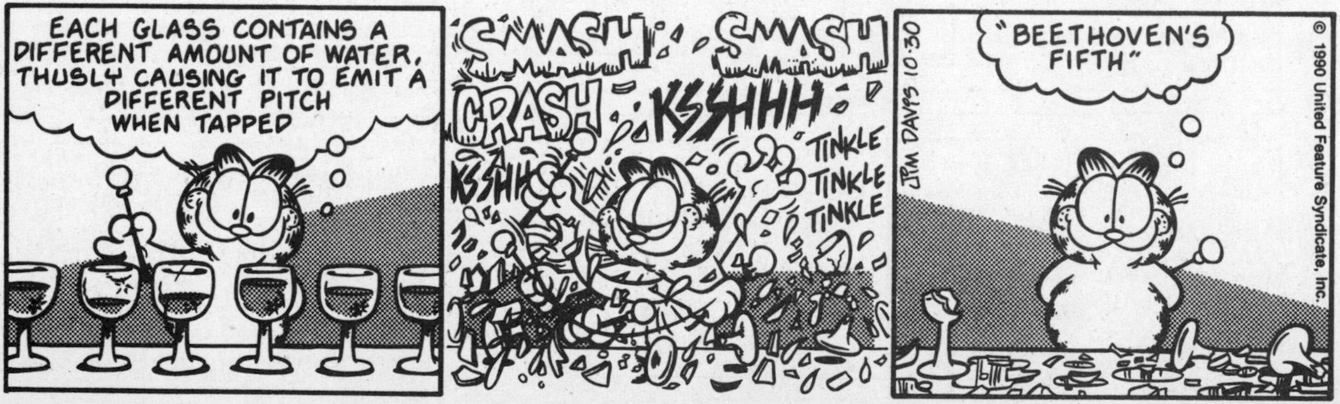
EACH GLASS CONTAINS A DIFFERENT AMOUNT OF WATER, THUSLY CAUSING IT TO EMIT A DIFFERENT PITCH WHEN TAPPED
SMASH
SMASH
CRASH
KSSHHH
KSSHH
TINKLE
TINKLE
TINKLE
JIM DAVIS 10-30
"BEETHOVEN'S FIFTH"
© 1990 United Feature Syndicate, Inc.

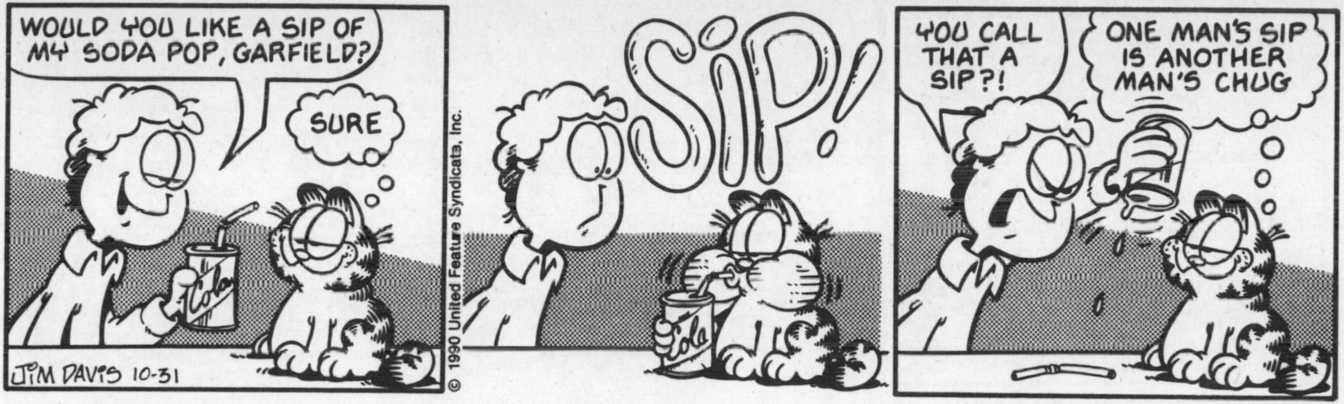
WOULD YOU LIKE A SIP OF MY SODA POP, GARFIELD?
SURE
JIM DAVIS 10-31
© 1990 United Feature Syndicate, Inc.
SIP!
YOU CALL THAT A SIP?!
ONE MAN'S SIP IS ANOTHER MAN'S CHUG

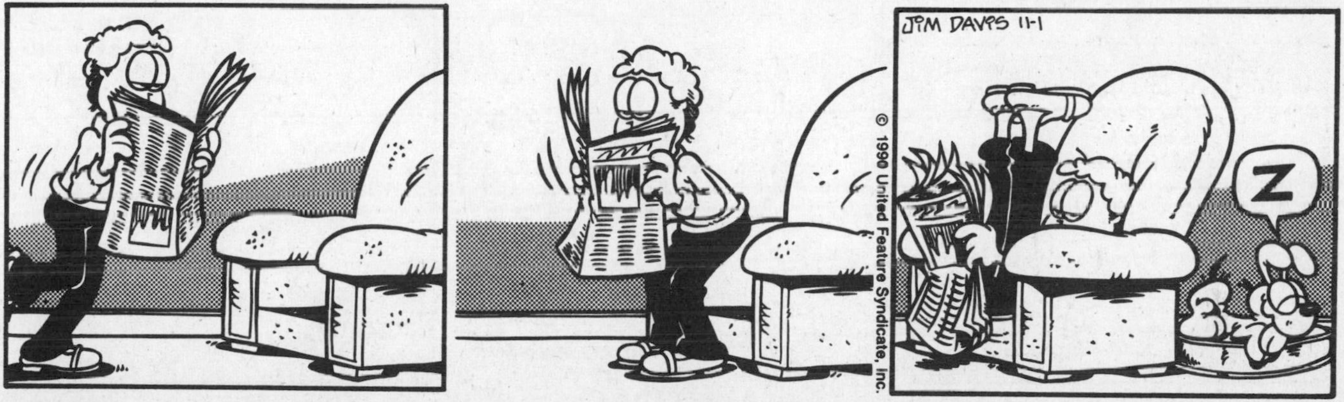
© 1990 United Feature Syndicate, Inc.
JIM DAVIS 11-1
Z

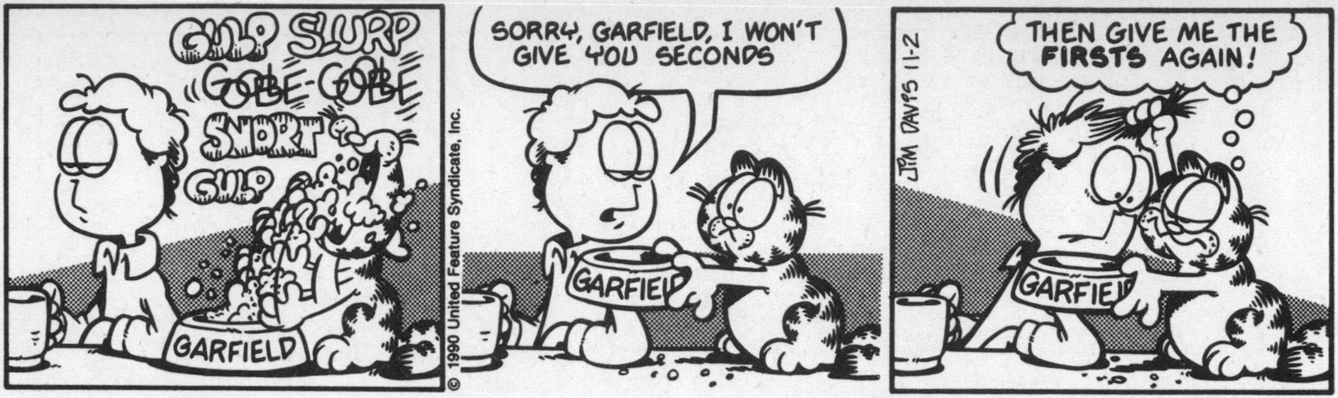
GULP SLURP
GOBBLE-GOBBLE
SNORT
GULP
GARFIELD
© 1990 United Feature Syndicate, Inc.
SORRY, GARFIELD, I WON'T GIVE YOU SECONDS
GARFIELD
JIM DAVIS 11-2
THEN GIVE ME THE **FIRSTS** AGAIN!
GARFIELD

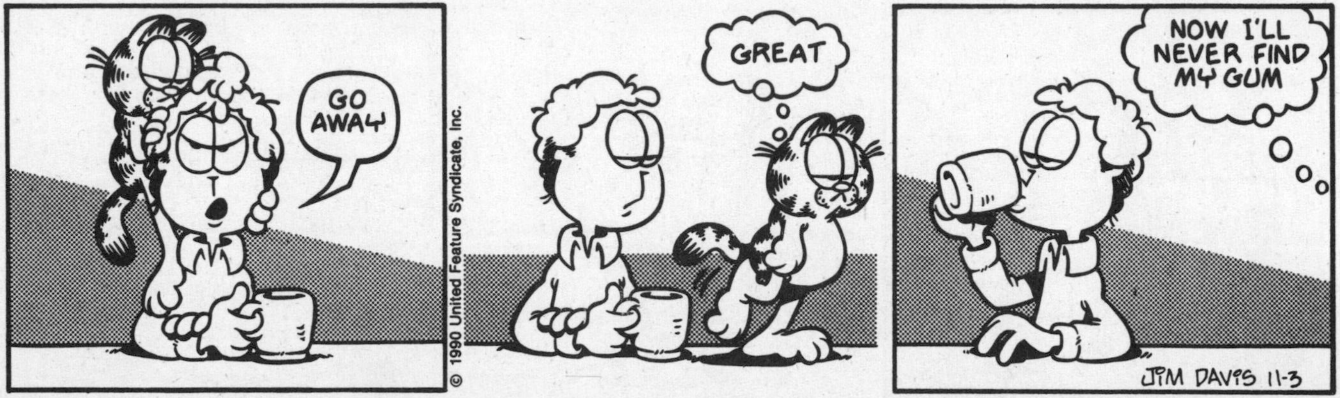
GO AWAY
© 1990 United Feature Syndicate, Inc.
GREAT
NOW I'LL NEVER FIND MY GUM
JIM DAVIS 11-3

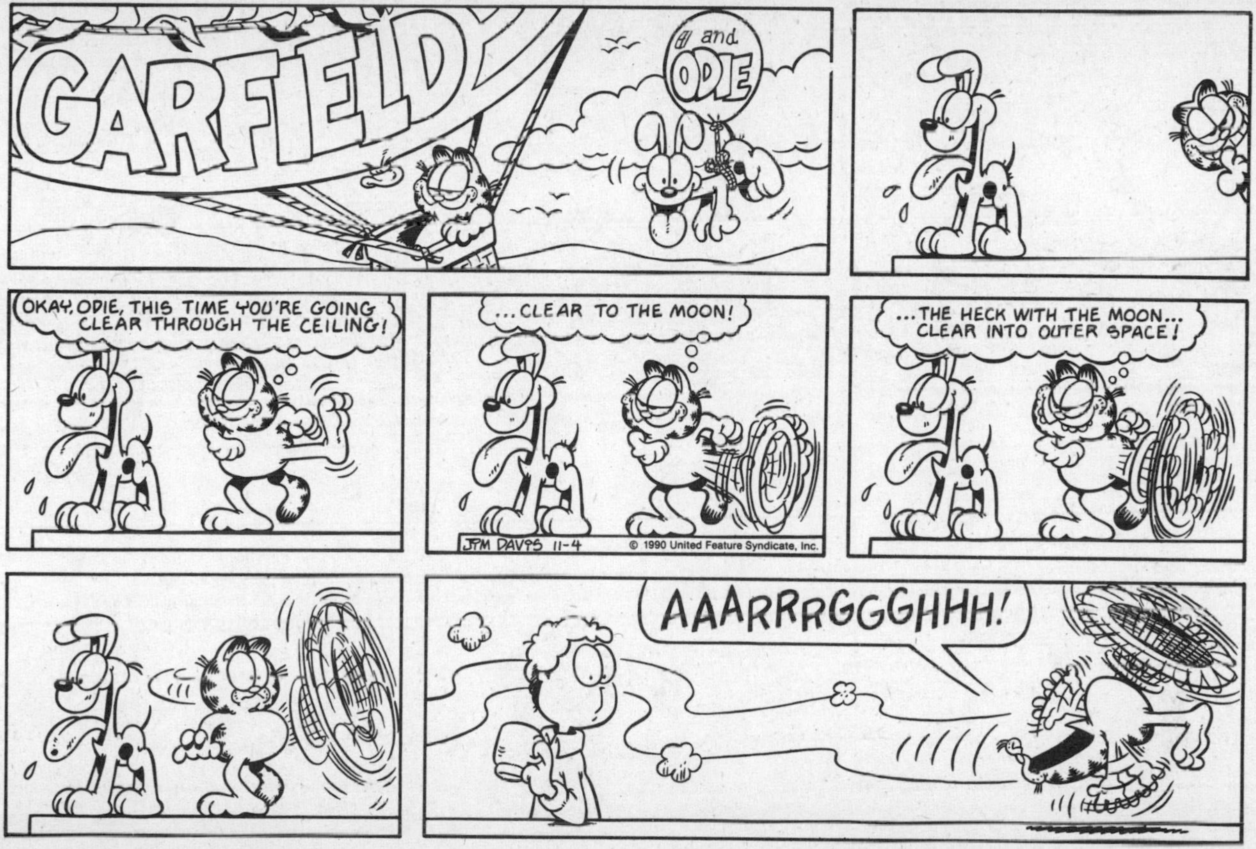
GARFIELD
and
ODIE
OKAY, ODIE, THIS TIME YOU'RE GOING CLEAR THROUGH THE CEILING!
...CLEAR TO THE MOON!
JIM DAVIS 11-4
© 1990 United Feature Syndicate, Inc.
...THE HECK WITH THE MOON... CLEAR INTO OUTER SPACE!
AAARRRGGGHHH!

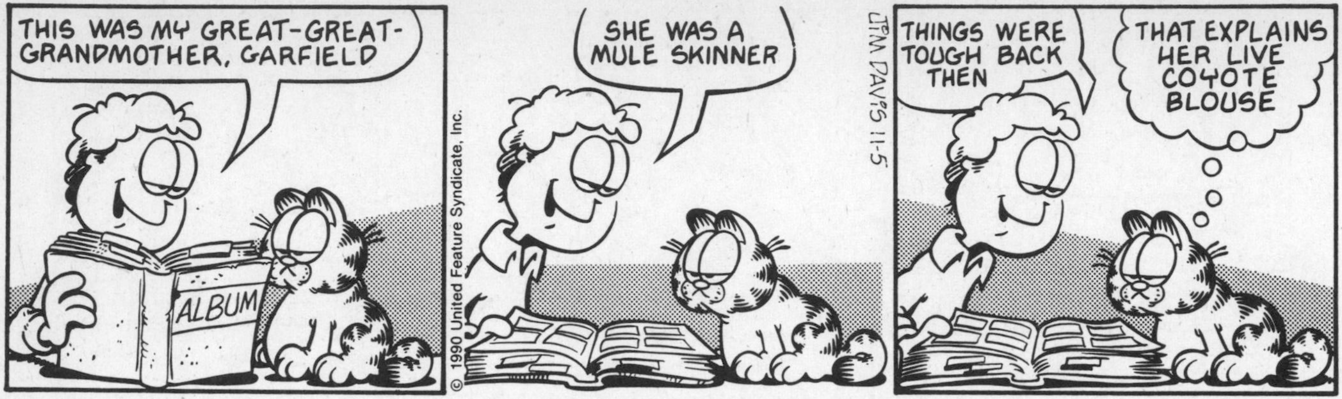
THIS WAS MY GREAT-GREAT-GRANDMOTHER, GARFIELD
© 1990 United Feature Syndicate, Inc.
SHE WAS A MULE SKINNER
JIM DAVIS 11-5
THINGS WERE TOUGH BACK THEN
THAT EXPLAINS HER LIVE COYOTE BLOUSE

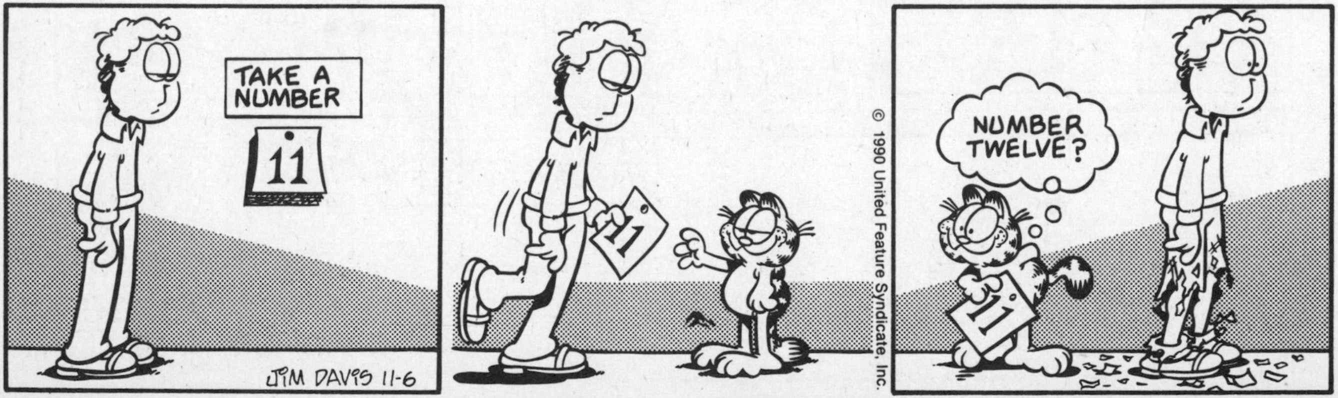
TAKE A NUMBER
11
JIM DAVIS 11-6
11
© 1990 United Feature Syndicate, Inc.
NUMBER TWELVE?
11

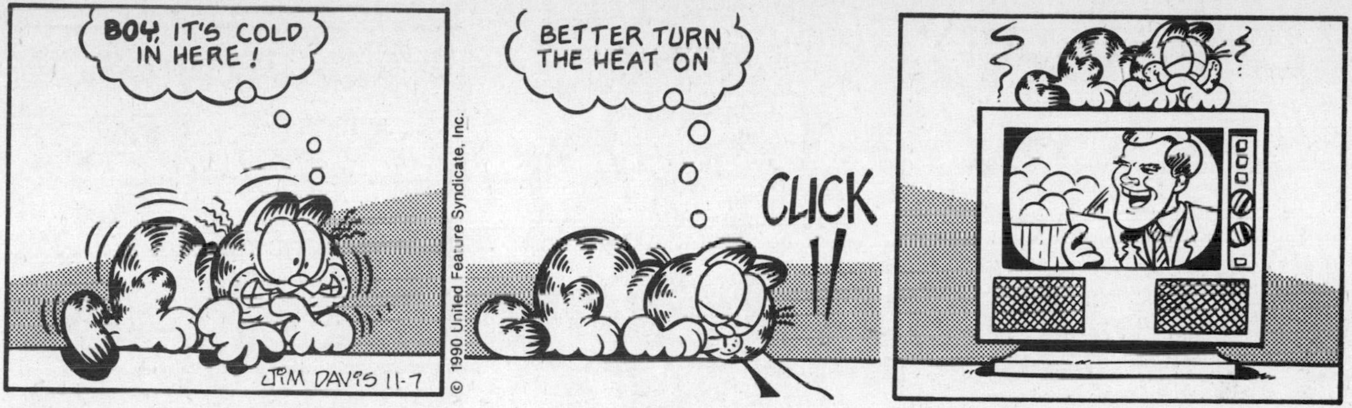
BOY, IT'S COLD IN HERE!
JIM DAVIS 11-7
© 1990 United Feature Syndicate, Inc.
BETTER TURN THE HEAT ON
CLICK

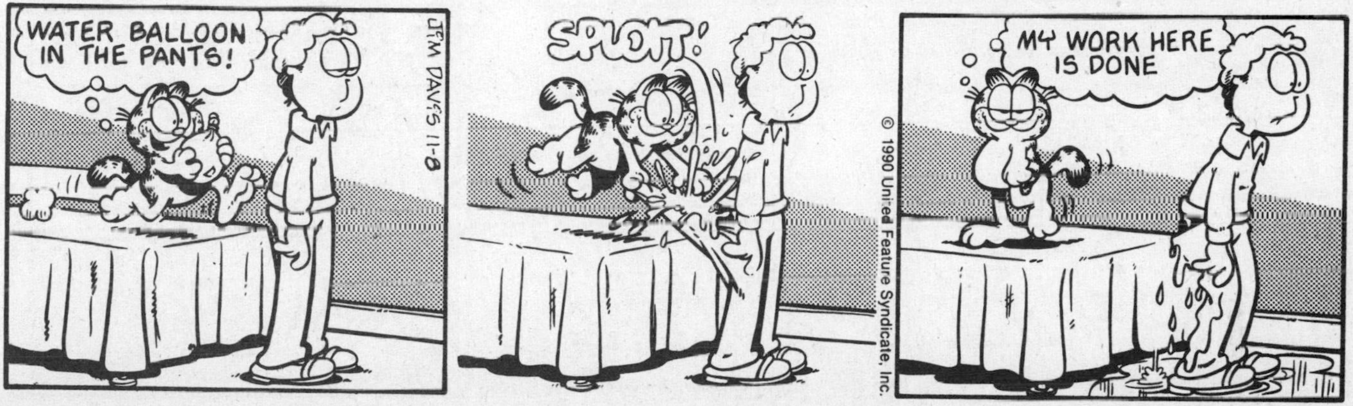
WATER BALLOON IN THE PANTS!
JIM DAVIS 11-8
SPLOIT!
© 1990 United Feature Syndicate, Inc.
MY WORK HERE IS DONE

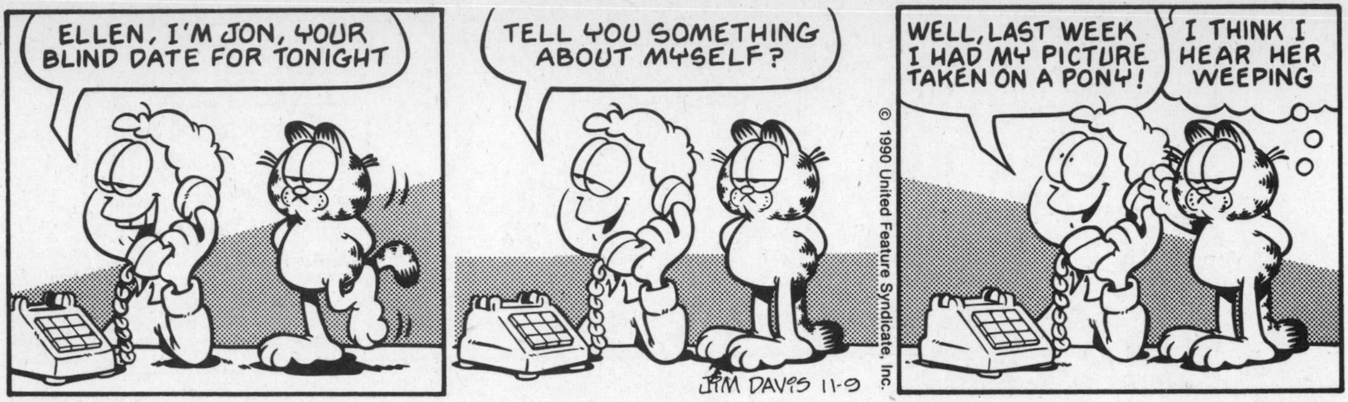
ELLEN, I'M JON, YOUR BLIND DATE FOR TONIGHT
TELL YOU SOMETHING ABOUT MYSELF?
JIM DAVIS 11-9
© 1990 United Feature Syndicate, Inc.
WELL, LAST WEEK I HAD MY PICTURE TAKEN ON A PONY!
I THINK I HEAR HER WEEPING

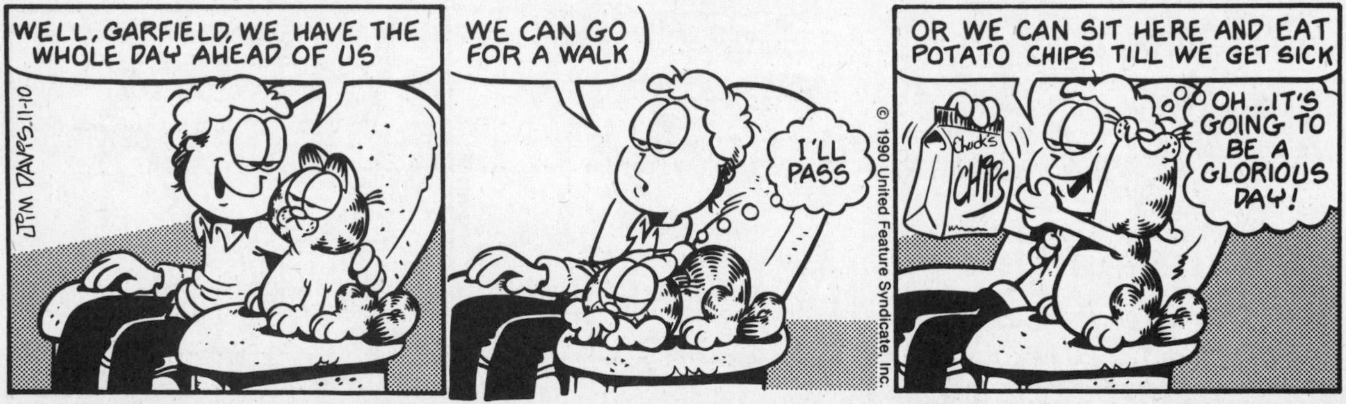
WELL, GARFIELD, WE HAVE THE WHOLE DAY AHEAD OF US
JIM DAVIS 11-10
WE CAN GO FOR A WALK
I'LL PASS
© 1990 United Feature Syndicate, Inc.
OR WE CAN SIT HERE AND EAT POTATO CHIPS TILL WE GET SICK
Chuck's
CHIPS
OH...IT'S GOING TO BE A GLORIOUS DAY!

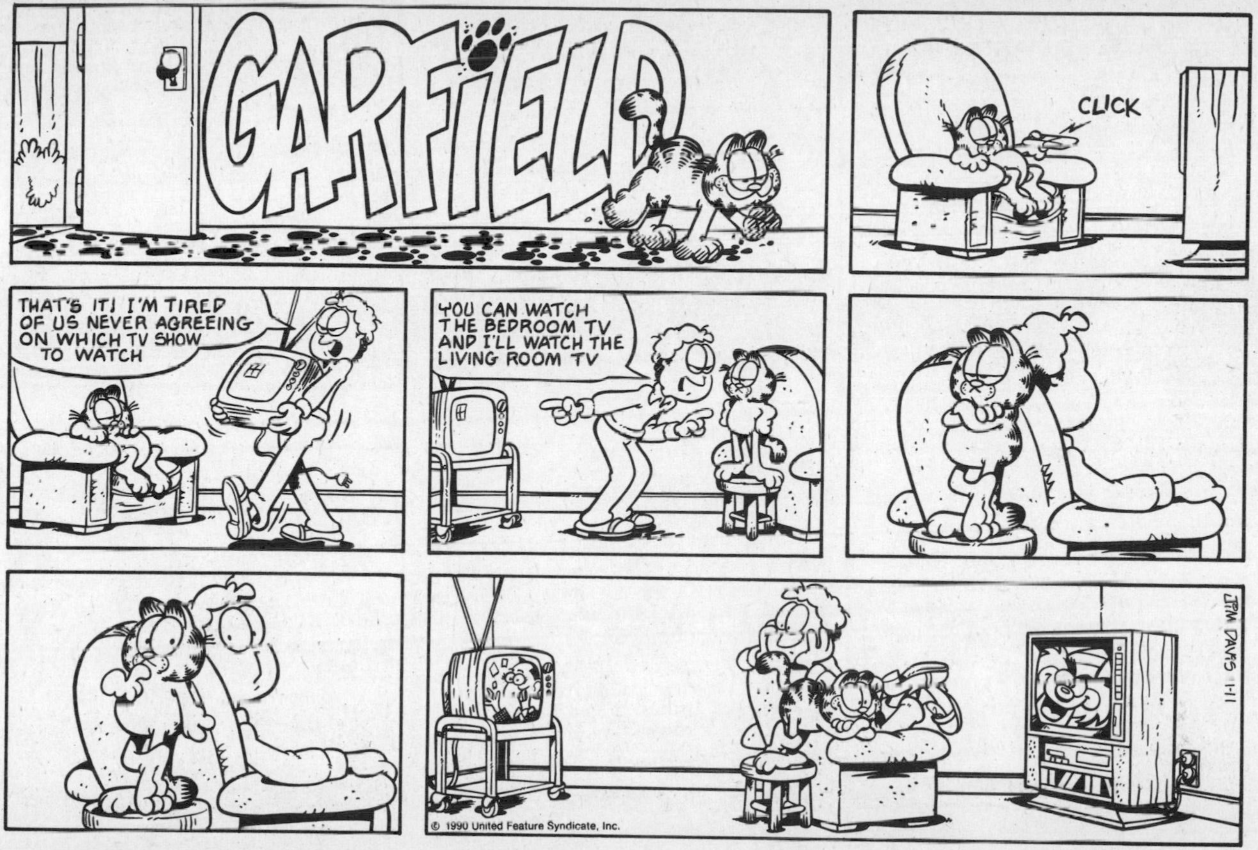
GARFIELD
CLICK
THAT'S IT! I'M TIRED OF US NEVER AGREEING ON WHICH TV SHOW TO WATCH
YOU CAN WATCH THE BEDROOM TV AND I'LL WATCH THE LIVING ROOM TV
JPM DAVIS 11-11
© 1990 United Feature Syndicate, Inc.

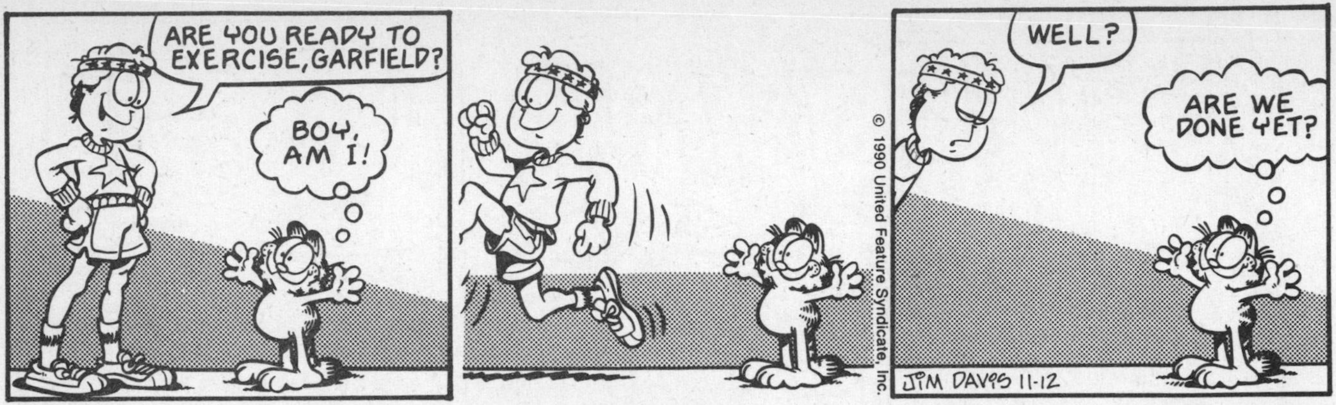
ARE YOU READY TO EXERCISE, GARFIELD?
BOY, AM I!
© 1990 United Feature Syndicate, Inc.
WELL?
ARE WE DONE YET?
JIM DAVIS 11-12

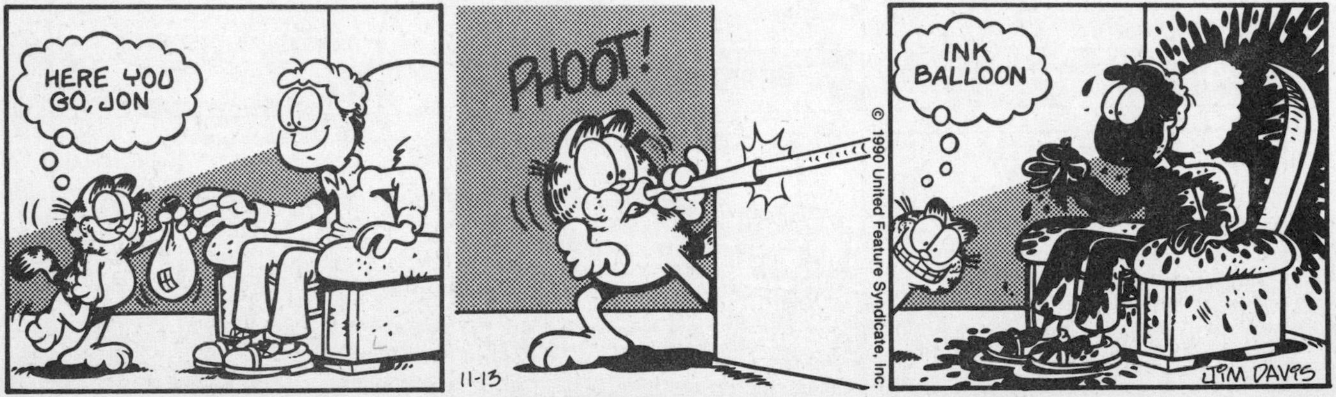
HERE YOU GO, JON
JIM DAVIS
11-13
PHOOT!
© 1990 United Feature Syndicate, Inc.
INK BALLOON
JIM DAVIS

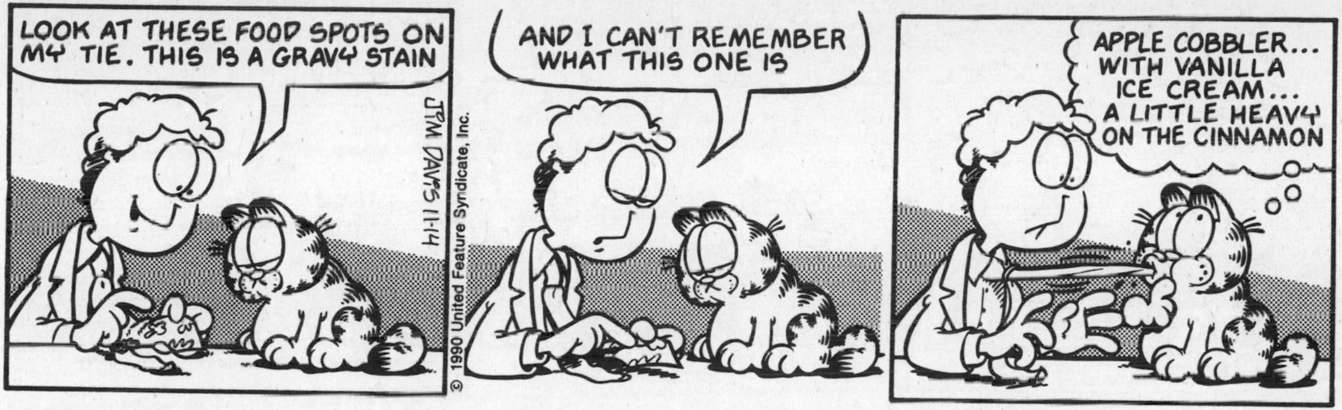
LOOK AT THESE FOOD SPOTS ON MY TIE. THIS IS A GRAVY STAIN
AND I CAN'T REMEMBER WHAT THIS ONE IS
APPLE COBBLER... WITH VANILLA ICE CREAM... A LITTLE HEAVY ON THE CINNAMON
JIM DAVIS 11-14
© 1990 United Feature Syndicate, Inc.

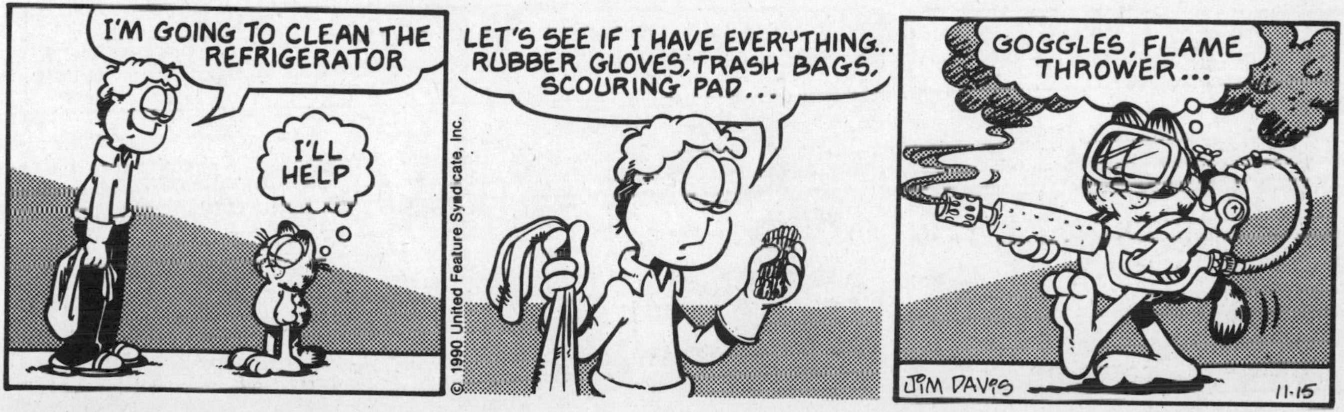
I'M GOING TO CLEAN THE REFRIGERATOR
I'LL HELP
LET'S SEE IF I HAVE EVERYTHING... RUBBER GLOVES, TRASH BAGS, SCOURING PAD...
GOGGLES, FLAME THROWER...
© 1990 United Feature Syndicate, Inc.
JIM DAVIS 11-15

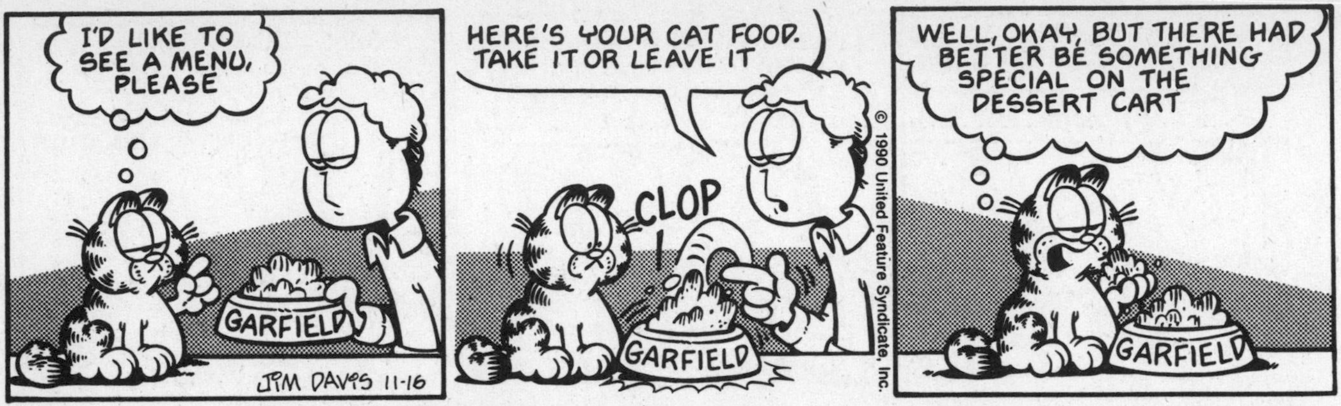
I'D LIKE TO SEE A MENU, PLEASE
JIM DAVIS 11-16
HERE'S YOUR CAT FOOD. TAKE IT OR LEAVE IT
CLOP
GARFIELD
© 1990 United Feature Syndicate, Inc.
WELL, OKAY, BUT THERE HAD BETTER BE SOMETHING SPECIAL ON THE DESSERT CART

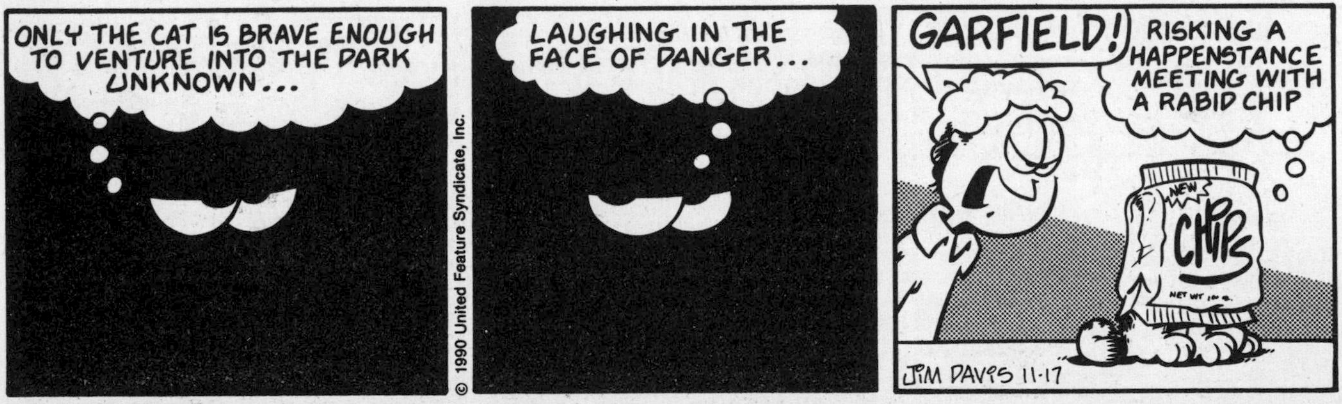
ONLY THE CAT IS BRAVE ENOUGH TO VENTURE INTO THE DARK UNKNOWN...
© 1990 United Feature Syndicate, Inc.
LAUGHING IN THE FACE OF DANGER...
GARFIELD!
RISKING A HAPPENSTANCE MEETING WITH A RABID CHIP
NEW
CHIPS
JIM DAVIS 11-17

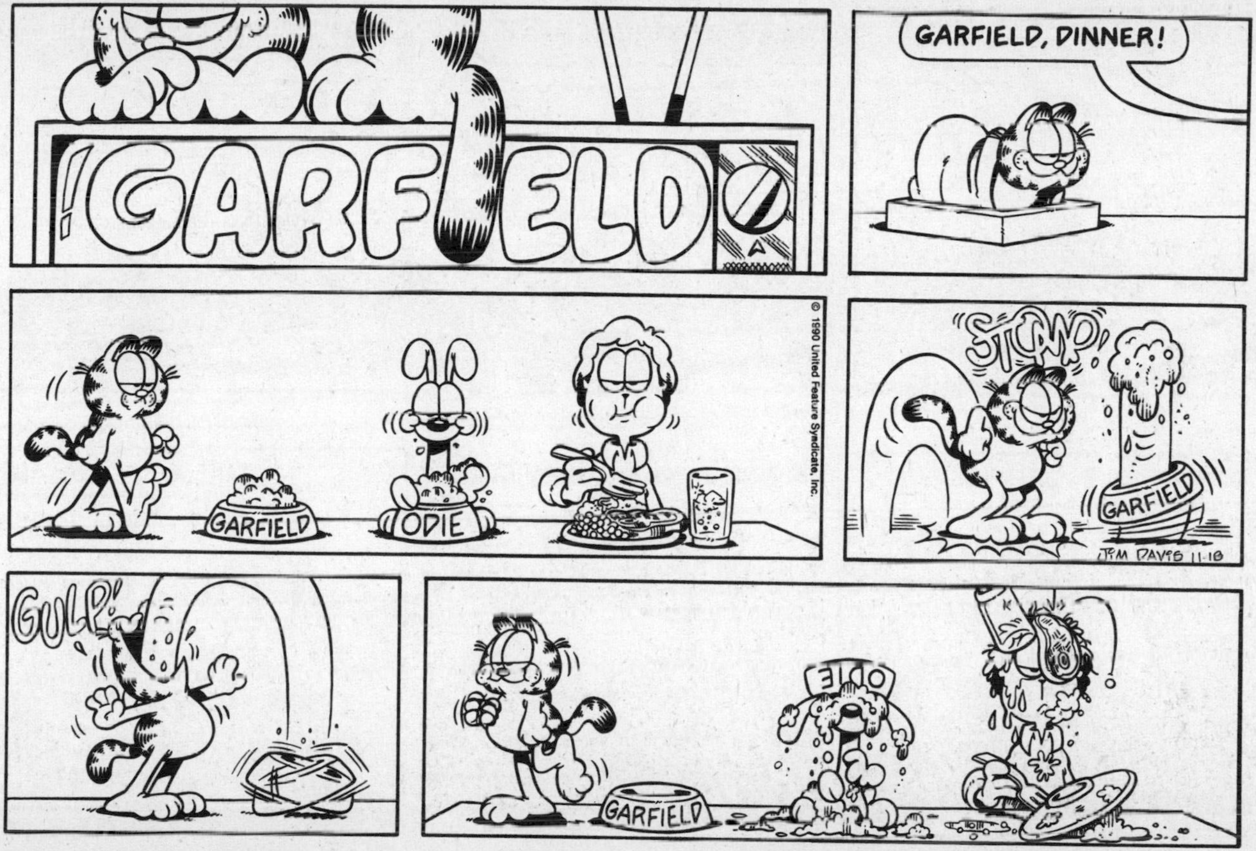
GARFIELD
GARFIELD, DINNER!
GARFIELD
ODIE
© 1990 United Feature Syndicate, Inc.
STOMP!
GARFIELD
JIM DAVIS 11-18
GULP!
GARFIELD
ODIE

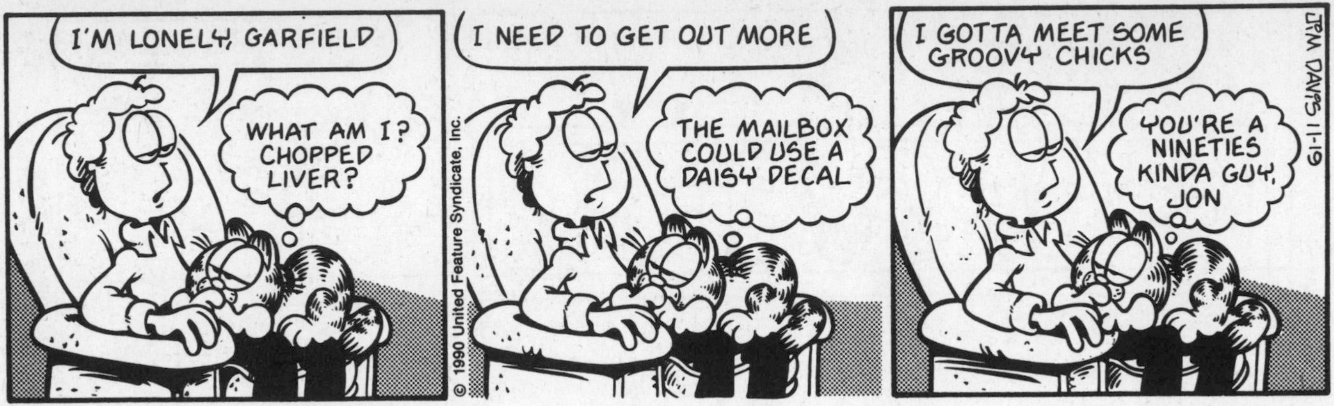
I'M LONELY, GARFIELD
WHAT AM I? CHOPPED LIVER?
© 1990 United Feature Syndicate, Inc.
I NEED TO GET OUT MORE
THE MAILBOX COULD USE A DAISY DECAL
I GOTTA MEET SOME GROOVY CHICKS
YOU'RE A NINETIES KINDA GUY, JON
JIM DAVIS 11-19

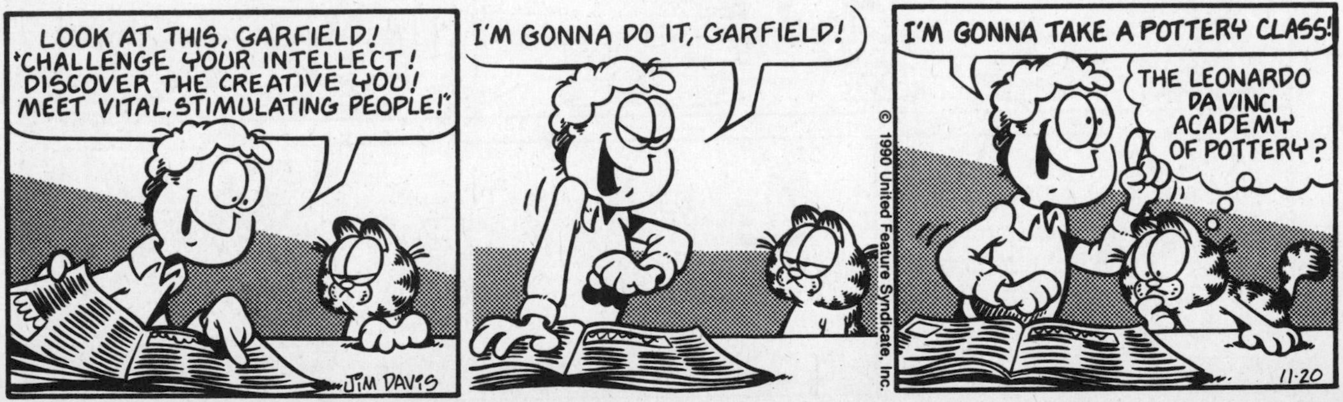
LOOK AT THIS, GARFIELD! "CHALLENGE YOUR INTELLECT! DISCOVER THE CREATIVE YOU! MEET VITAL, STIMULATING PEOPLE!"
JIM DAVIS
I'M GONNA DO IT, GARFIELD!
© 1990 United Feature Syndicate, Inc.
I'M GONNA TAKE A POTTERY CLASS!
THE LEONARDO DA VINCI ACADEMY OF POTTERY?
11-20

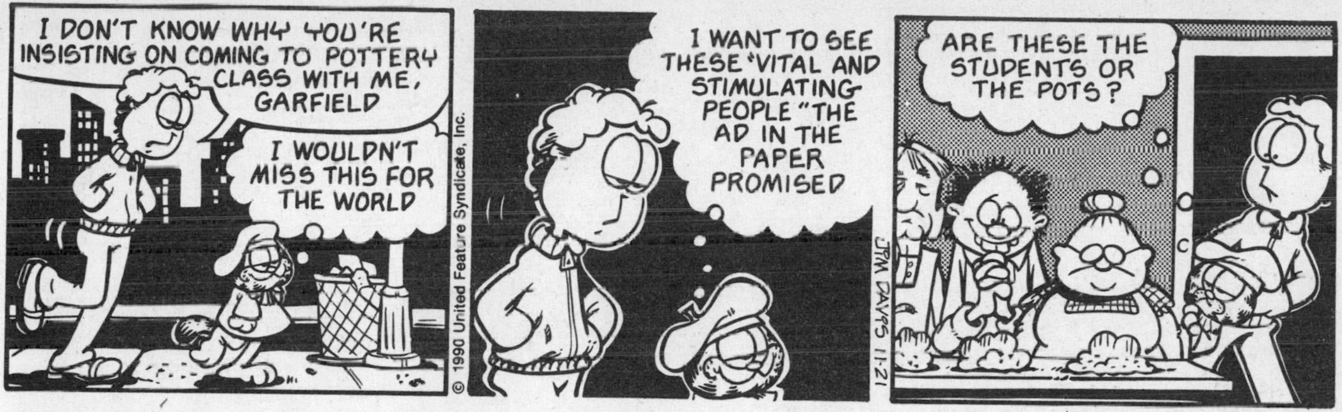
I DON'T KNOW WHY YOU'RE INSISTING ON COMING TO POTTERY CLASS WITH ME, GARFIELD
I WOULDN'T MISS THIS FOR THE WORLD
© 1990 United Feature Syndicate, Inc.
I WANT TO SEE THESE "VITAL AND STIMULATING PEOPLE" THE AD IN THE PAPER PROMISED
JIM DAVIS 11-21
ARE THESE THE STUDENTS OR THE POTS?

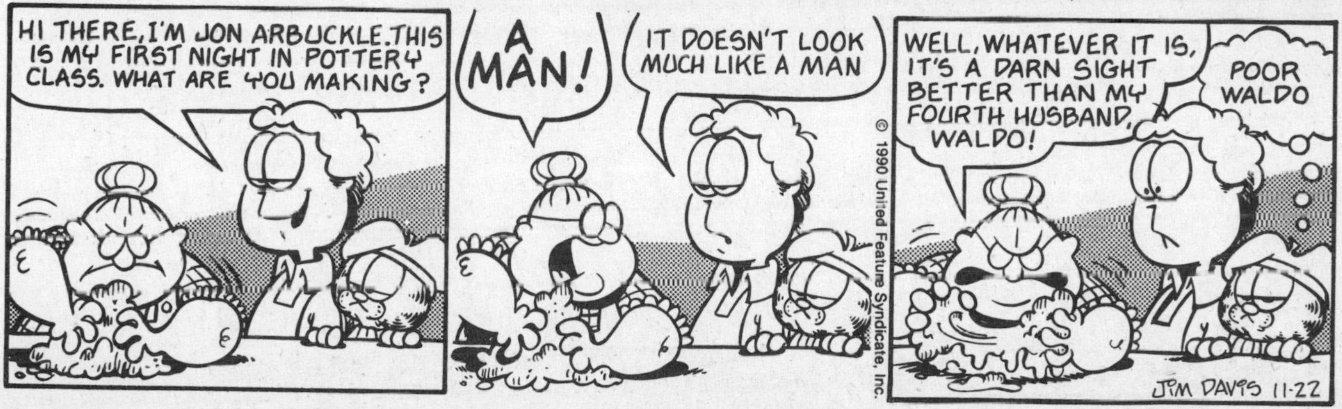
HI THERE, I'M JON ARBUCKLE. THIS IS MY FIRST NIGHT IN POTTERY CLASS. WHAT ARE YOU MAKING?
A MAN!
IT DOESN'T LOOK MUCH LIKE A MAN
© 1990 United Feature Syndicate, Inc.
WELL, WHATEVER IT IS, IT'S A DARN SIGHT BETTER THAN MY FOURTH HUSBAND, WALDO!
POOR WALDO
JIM DAVIS 11-22

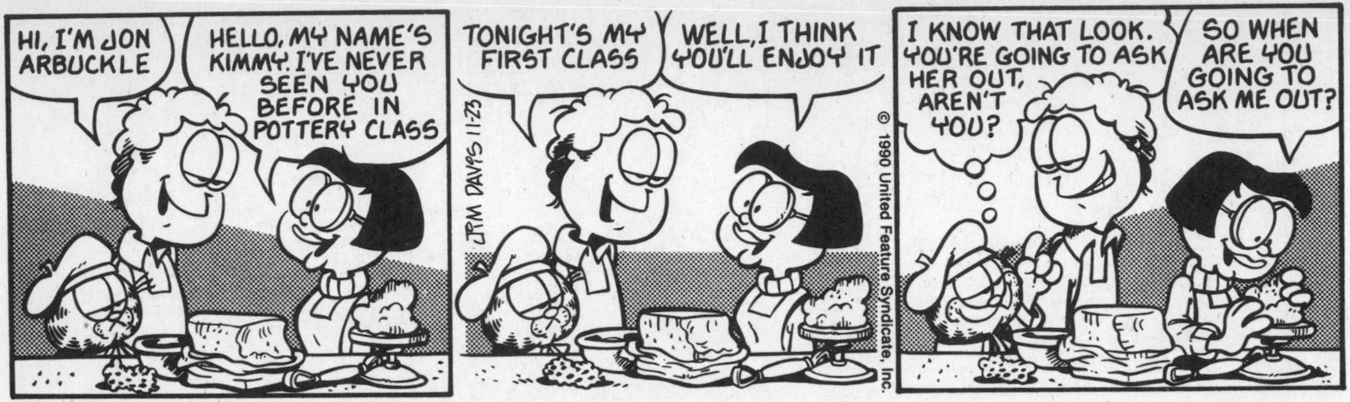
HI, I'M JON ARBUCKLE
HELLO, MY NAME'S KIMMY. I'VE NEVER SEEN YOU BEFORE IN POTTERY CLASS
JIM DAVIS 11-23
TONIGHT'S MY FIRST CLASS
WELL, I THINK YOU'LL ENJOY IT
© 1990 United Feature Syndicate, Inc.
I KNOW THAT LOOK. YOU'RE GOING TO ASK HER OUT, AREN'T YOU?
SO WHEN ARE YOU GOING TO ASK ME OUT?

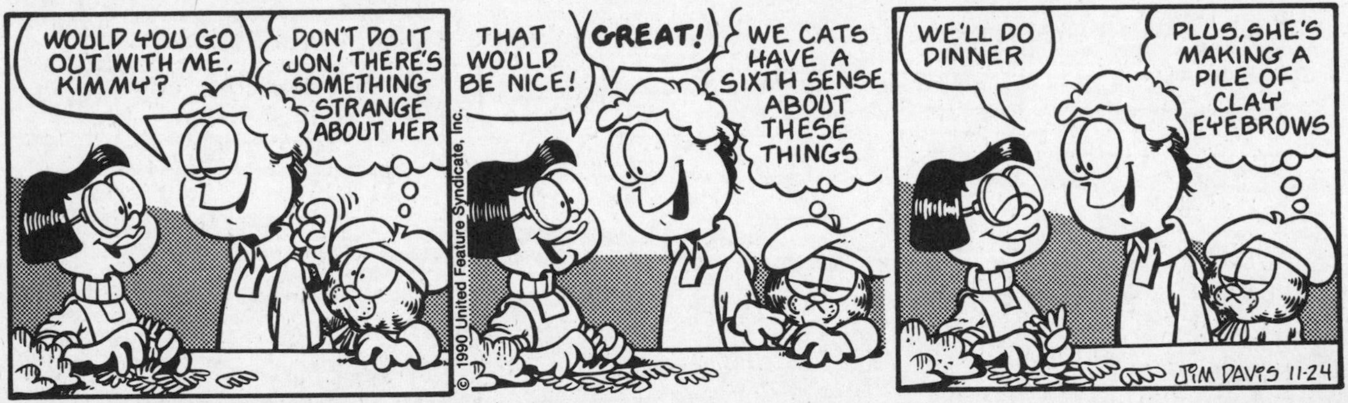
WOULD YOU GO OUT WITH ME, KIMMY?
DON'T DO IT JON! THERE'S SOMETHING STRANGE ABOUT HER
© 1990 United Feature Syndicate, Inc.
THAT WOULD BE NICE!
GREAT!
WE CATS HAVE A SIXTH SENSE ABOUT THESE THINGS
WE'LL DO DINNER
PLUS, SHE'S MAKING A PILE OF CLAY EYEBROWS
JIM DAVIS 11-24

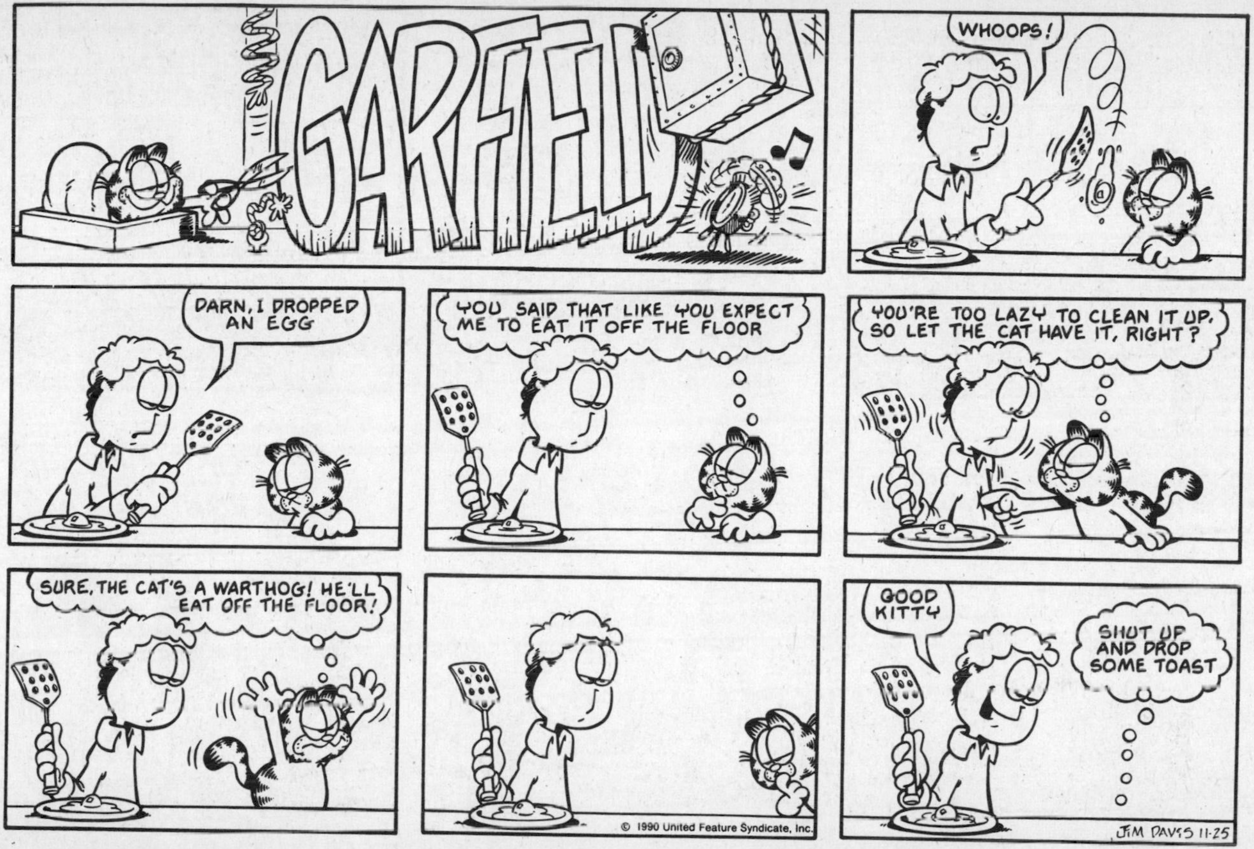
GARFIELD
WHOOPS!
DARN, I DROPPED AN EGG
YOU SAID THAT LIKE YOU EXPECT ME TO EAT IT OFF THE FLOOR
YOU'RE TOO LAZY TO CLEAN IT UP, SO LET THE CAT HAVE IT, RIGHT?
SURE, THE CAT'S A WARTHOG! HE'LL EAT OFF THE FLOOR!
© 1990 United Feature Syndicate, Inc.
GOOD KITTY
SHUT UP AND DROP SOME TOAST
JIM DAVIS 11-25

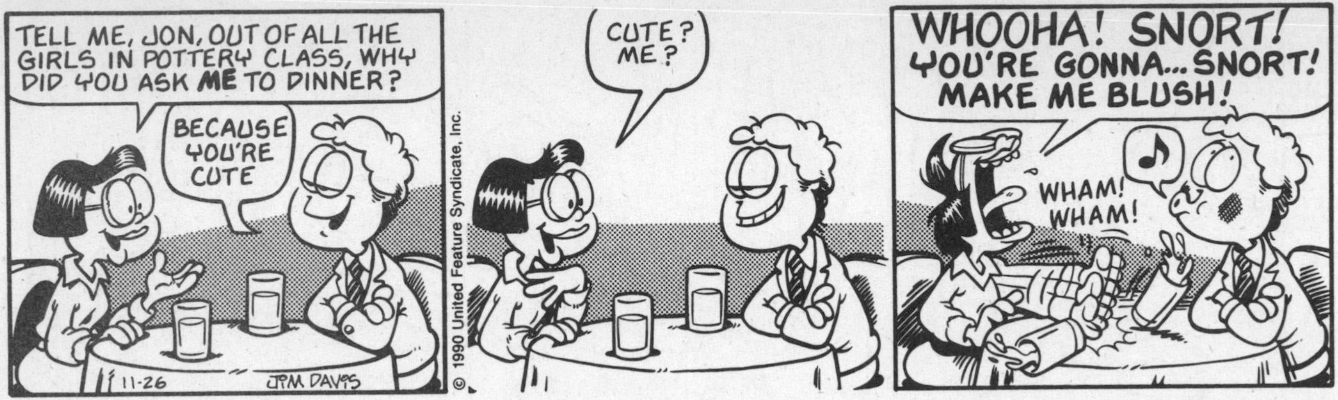
TELL ME, JON, OUT OF ALL THE GIRLS IN POTTERY CLASS, WHY DID YOU ASK **ME** TO DINNER?
BECAUSE YOU'RE CUTE
11-26
JIM DAVIS
© 1990 United Feature Syndicate, Inc.
CUTE? ME?
WHOOHA! SNORT! YOU'RE GONNA... SNORT! MAKE ME BLUSH!
WHAM! WHAM!
♪

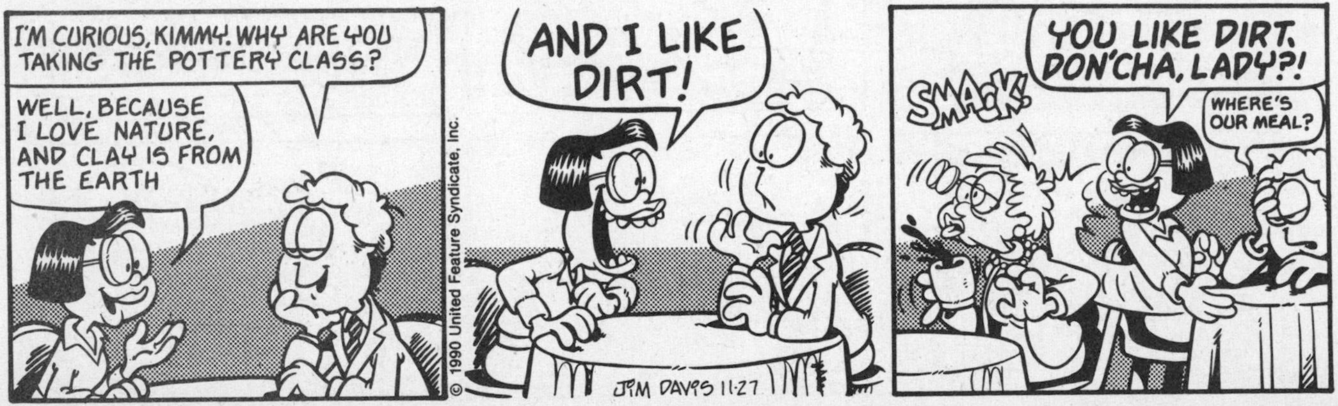
I'M CURIOUS, KIMMY. WHY ARE YOU TAKING THE POTTERY CLASS?
WELL, BECAUSE I LOVE NATURE, AND CLAY IS FROM THE EARTH
© 1990 United Feature Syndicate, Inc.
AND I LIKE DIRT!
JIM DAVIS 11-27
SMACK!
YOU LIKE DIRT, DON'CHA, LADY?!
WHERE'S OUR MEAL?

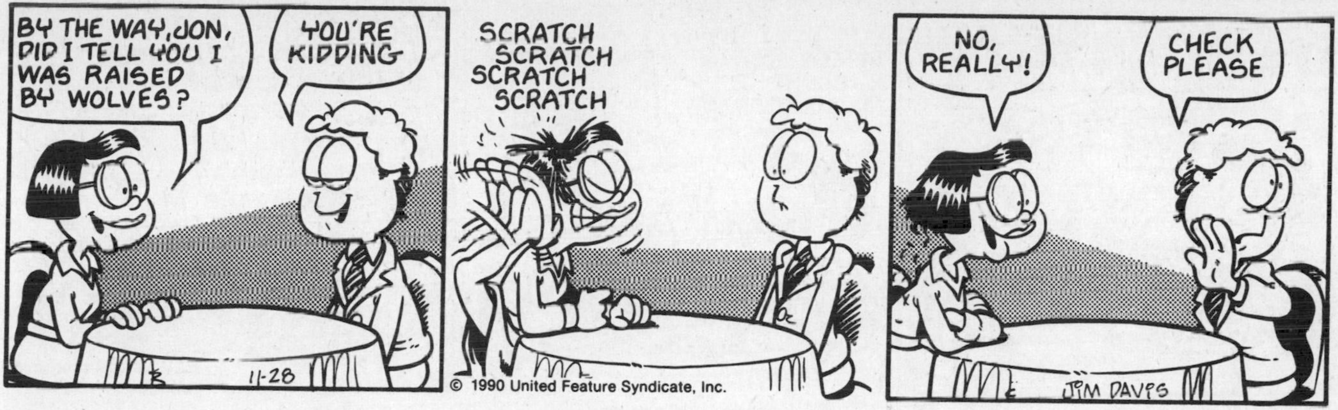
BY THE WAY, JON, DID I TELL YOU I WAS RAISED BY WOLVES?
YOU'RE KIDDING
11-28
SCRATCH SCRATCH SCRATCH SCRATCH
© 1990 United Feature Syndicate, Inc.
NO, REALLY!
CHECK PLEASE
JIM DAVIS

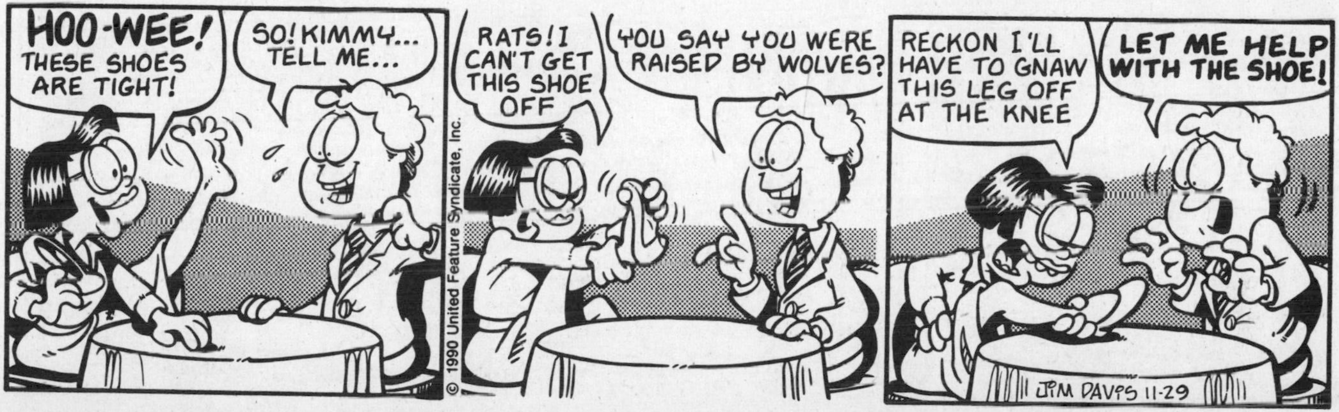
HOO-WEE! THESE SHOES ARE TIGHT!
SO! KIMMY... TELL ME...
© 1990 United Feature Syndicate, Inc.
RATS! I CAN'T GET THIS SHOE OFF
YOU SAY YOU WERE RAISED BY WOLVES?
RECKON I'LL HAVE TO GNAW THIS LEG OFF AT THE KNEE
LET ME HELP WITH THE SHOE!
JIM DAVIS 11-29

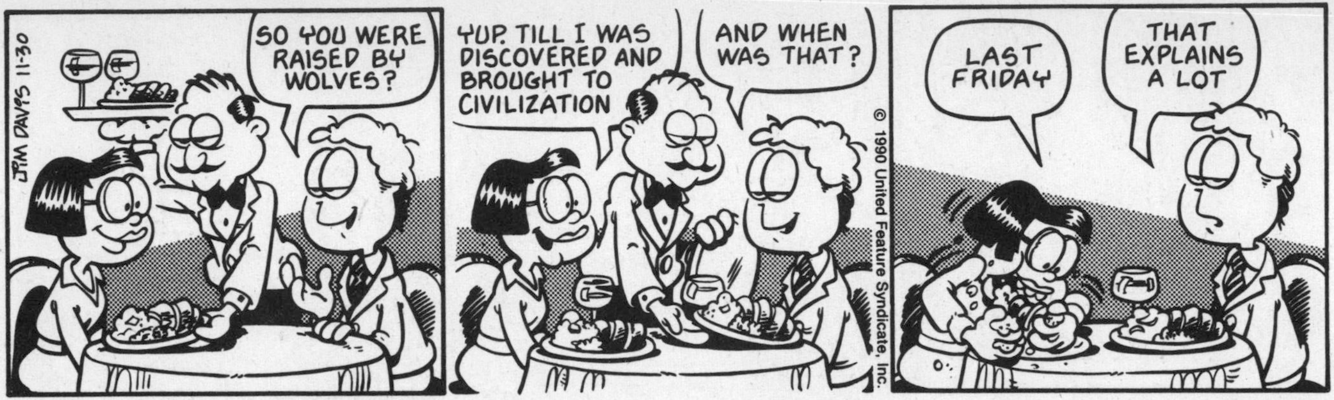
JIM DAVIS 11-30
SO YOU WERE RAISED BY WOLVES?
YUP. TILL I WAS DISCOVERED AND BROUGHT TO CIVILIZATION
AND WHEN WAS THAT?
LAST FRIDAY
THAT EXPLAINS A LOT
© 1990 United Feature Syndicate, Inc.

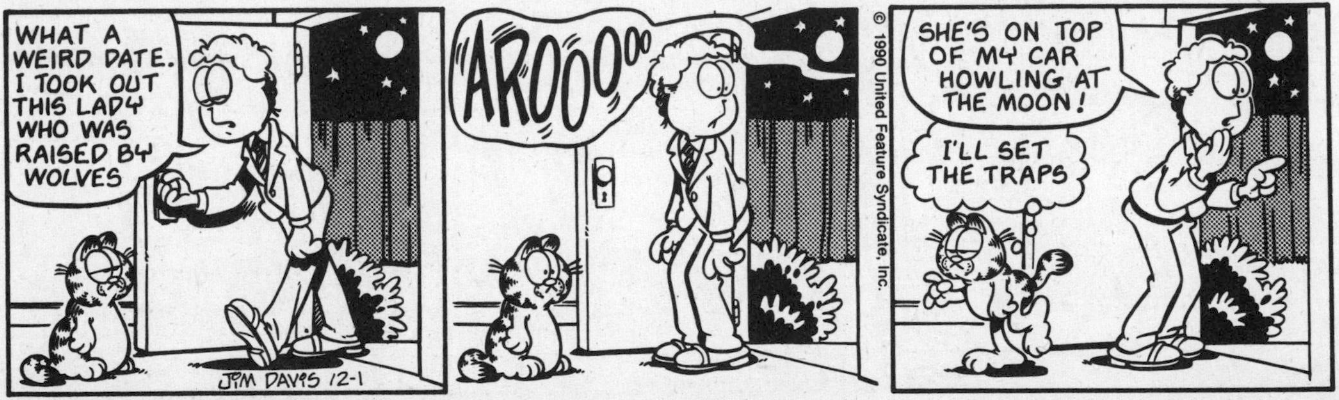
WHAT A WEIRD DATE. I TOOK OUT THIS LADY WHO WAS RAISED BY WOLVES
JIM DAVIS 12-1
AROOOOO
SHE'S ON TOP OF MY CAR HOWLING AT THE MOON!
I'LL SET THE TRAPS
© 1990 United Feature Syndicate, Inc.

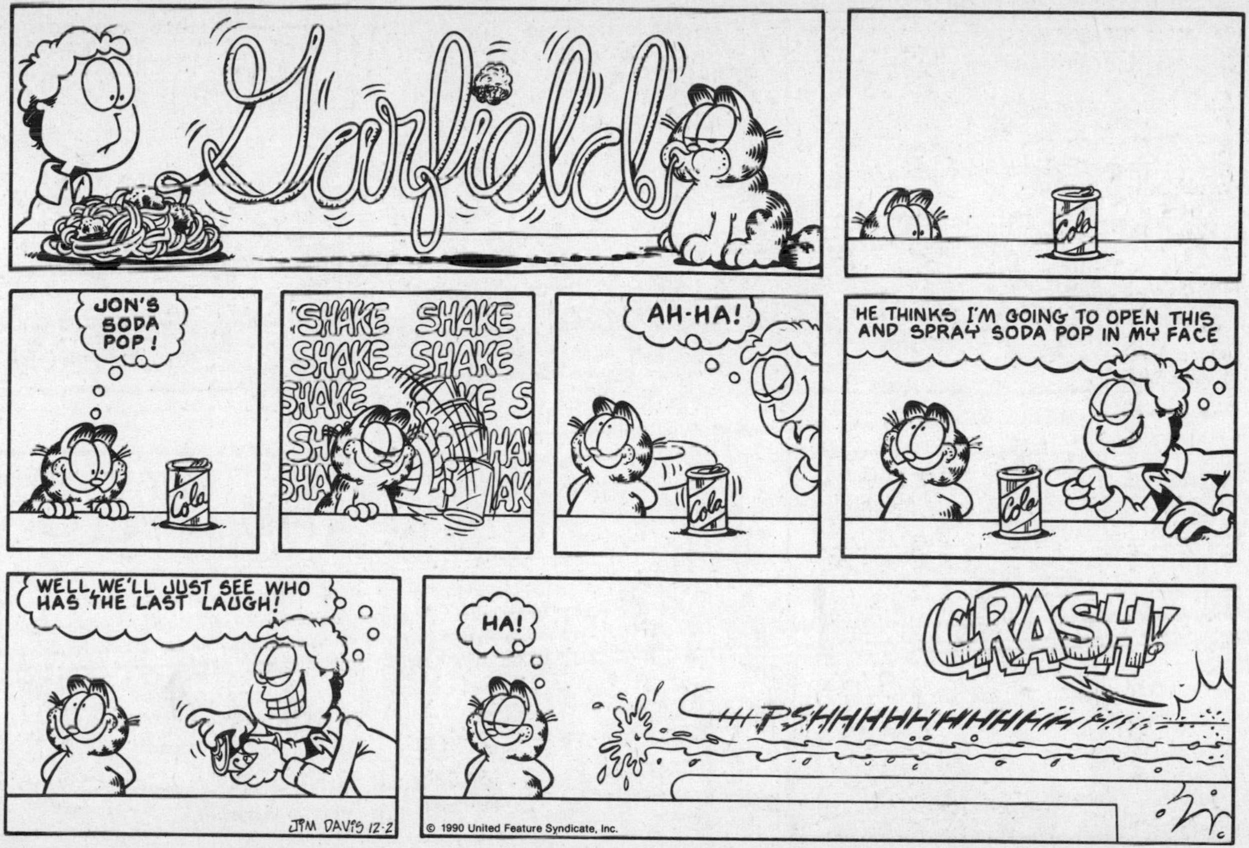

Garfield
JON'S SODA POP!
SHAKE SHAKE SHAKE SHAKE SHAKE
AH-HA!
HE THINKS I'M GOING TO OPEN THIS AND SPRAY SODA POP IN MY FACE
WELL, WE'LL JUST SEE WHO HAS THE LAST LAUGH!
JIM DAVIS 12-2
HA!
CRASH!
PSHHHHHHHHHHH
© 1990 United Feature Syndicate, Inc.

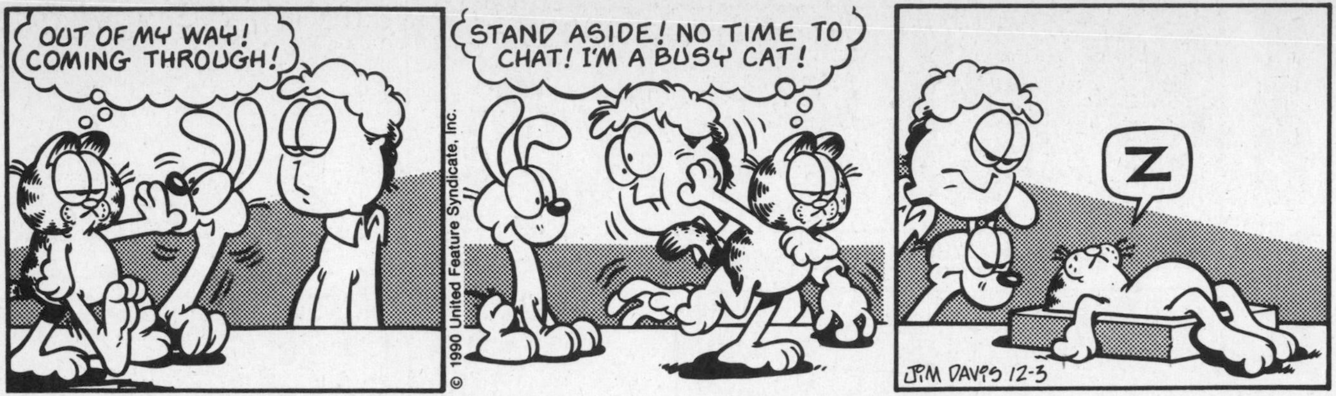
OUT OF MY WAY! COMING THROUGH!
STAND ASIDE! NO TIME TO CHAT! I'M A BUSY CAT!
Z
JIM DAVIS 12-3

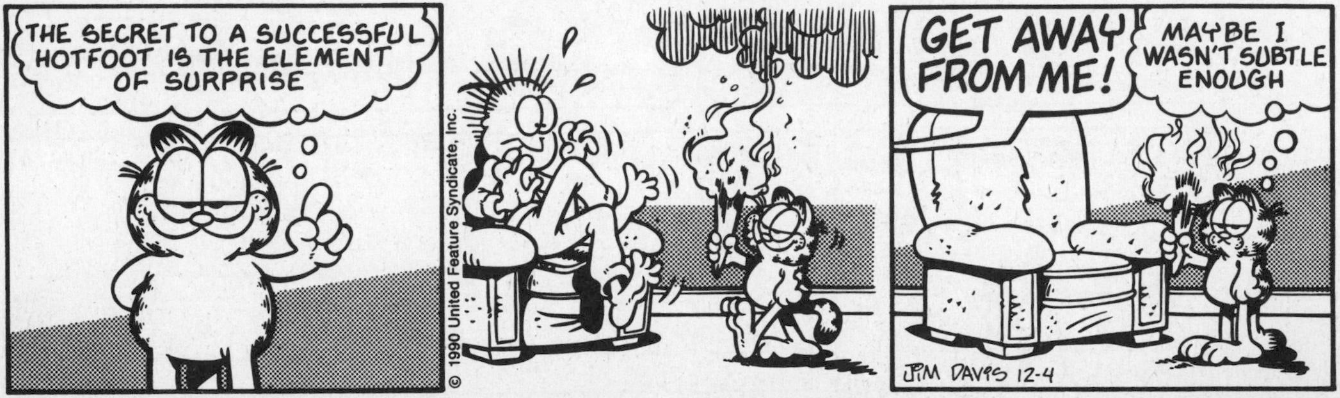
THE SECRET TO A SUCCESSFUL HOTFOOT IS THE ELEMENT OF SURPRISE
GET AWAY FROM ME!
MAYBE I WASN'T SUBTLE ENOUGH
JIM DAVIS 12-4

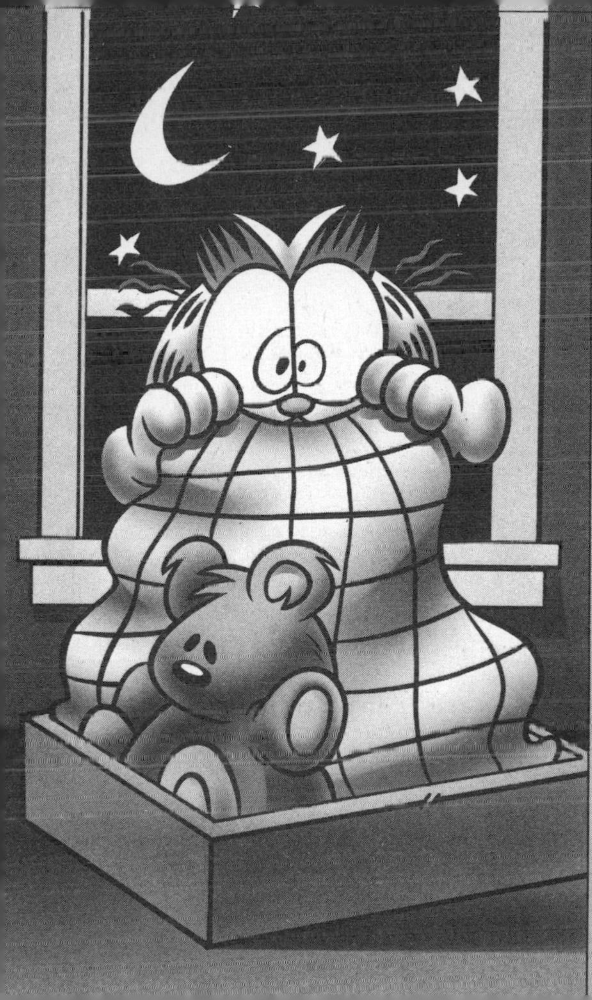

GARFIELD'S TOP TEN NIGHTMARES

10. NERMAL GETS CLONED
9. VET PRESCRIBES "CHAIN SAW THERAPY"
8. FALLS INTO VAT OF ODIE DROOL
7. FLEAS VOTE HIM "MOST BLOODSUCKABLE"
6. MISTAKES JON'S SWEAT SOCK FOR A MATZOH BALL
5. FORCED TO WATCH THE "ALL LASSIE" CHANNEL
4. TRAPPED FOR A WEEK INSIDE HEALTH FOOD STORE
3. CAT FUR BECOMES THE LATEST THING FOR WOMEN'S COATS
2. MEETS HUGE SPIDER WITH AN ATTITUDE
1. DIET MONDAY!

STRIPS, SPECIALS, OR BESTSELLING BOOKS . . .
GARFIELD'S ON EVERYONE'S MENU
Don't miss even one episode in the Tubby Tabby's hilarious series!

__GARFIELD AT LARGE (#1)   32013/$6.95
__GARFIELD GAINS WEIGHT (#2)   32008/$6.95
__GARFIELD BIGGER THAN LIFE (#3)   32007/$6.95
__GARFIELD WEIGHS IN (#4)   32010/$6.95
__GARFIELD TAKES THE CAKE (#5)   32009/$6.95
__GARFIELD EATS HIS HEART OUT (#6)   32018/$6.95
__GARFIELD SITS AROUND THE HOUSE (#7)   32011/$6.95
__GARFIELD TIPS THE SCALES (#8)   33580/$6.95
__GARFIELD LOSES HIS FEET (#9)   31805/$6.95
__GARFIELD MAKES IT BIG (#10)   31928/$6.95
__GARFIELD ROLLS ON (#11)   32634/$6.95
__GARFIELD OUT TO LUNCH (#12)   33118/$6.95
__GARFIELD FOOD FOR THOUGHT (#13)   34129/$6.95
__GARFIELD SWALLOWS HIS PRIDE (#14)   34725/$6.95
__GARFIELD WORLDWIDE (#15)   35158/$6.95
__GARFIELD ROUNDS OUT (#16)   35388/$6.95
__GARFIELD CHEWS THE FAT (#17)   35956/$6.95
__GARFIELD GOES TO WAIST (#18)   36430/$6.95
__GARFIELD HANGS OUT (#19)   36835/$6.95

__GARFIELD TAKES UP SPACE (#20)   37029/$6.95
__GARFIELD SAYS A MOUTHFUL (#21)   37368/$6.95
__GARFIELD BY THE POUND (#22)   37579/$6.95
__GARFIELD KEEPS HIS CHINS UP (#23)   37959/$6.95
__GARFIELD TAKES HIS LICKS (#24)   38170/$6.95
__GARFIELD HITS THE BIG TIME (#25)   38332/$6.95
__GARFIELD PULLS HIS WEIGHT (#26)   38666/$6.95
__GARFIELD DISHES IT OUT (#27)   39287/$6.95
__GARFIELD LIFE IN THE FAT LANE (#28)   39776/$6.95
__GARFIELD TONS OF FUN (#29)   40386/$6.95
__GARFIELD BIGGER AND BETTER (#30)   40770/$6.95
__GARFIELD HAMS IT UP (#31)   41241/$6.95

GARFIELD AT HIS SUNDAY BEST!
__GARFIELD TREASURY   32106/$11.95
__THE SECOND GARFIELD TREASURY   33276/$10.95
__THE THIRD GARFIELD TREASURY   32635/$11.00
__THE FOURTH GARFIELD TREASURY   34726/$10.95
__THE FIFTH GARFIELD TREASURY   36268/$12.00
__THE SIXTH GARFIELD TREASURY   37367/$10.95
__THE SEVENTH GARFIELD TREASURY   38427/$10.95
__THE EIGHTH GARFIELD TREASURY   39778/$12.00

Please send me the BALLANTINE BOOKS I have checked above. I am enclosing $_____. (Please add $2.00 for the first book and $.60 for each additional book for postage and handling and include the appropriate state sales tax.) Send check or money order (no cash or C.O.D.'s) to Ballantine Mail Sales Dept. TA, 400 Hahn Road, Westminster, MD 21157.

To order by phone, call 1-800-733-3000 and use your major credit card.

Prices and numbers are subject to change without notice. Valid in the U.S. only. All orders are subject to availability.

Name_____

Address_____

City_____ State_____ Zip_____

Allow at least 4 weeks for delivery   12/96

BIRTHDAYS, HOLIDAYS, OR ANY DAY . . .

Keep GARFIELD on your calendar all year 'round!

GARFIELD TV SPECIALS
__BABES & BULLETS   36339/$5.95
__GARFIELD GOES HOLLYWOOD   34580/$6.95
__GARFIELD'S HALLOWEEN ADVENTURE   33045/$6.95
  (formerly GARFIELD IN DISGUISE)
__GARFIELD'S FELINE FANTASY   36902/$6.95
__GARFIELD IN PARADISE   33796/$6.95
__GARFIELD IN THE ROUGH   32242/$6.95
__GARFIELD ON THE TOWN   31542/$6.95
__GARFIELD'S THANKSGIVING   35650/$6.95
__HERE COMES GARFIELD   32021/$6.95
__GARFIELD GETS A LIFE   37375/$6.95
__A GARFIELD CHRISTMAS   35368/$5.95

Please send me the BALLANTINE BOOKS I have checked above. I am enclosing $_____. (Please add $2.00 for the first book and $.50 for each additional book for postage and handling and include the appropriate state sales tax.) Send check or money order (no cash or C.O.D.'s) to Ballantine Mail Sales Dept. TA, 400 Hahn Road, Westminster, MD 21157.

To order by phone, call 1-800-733-3000 and use your major credit card.

Prices and numbers are subject to change without notice. Valid in the U.S. only. All orders are subject to availability.

GREETINGS FROM GARFIELD!
GARFIELD POSTCARD BOOKS FOR ALL OCCASIONS.
__GARFIELD THINKING OF YOU   36516/$6.95
__GARFIELD WORDS TO LIVE BY   36679/$6.95
__GARFIELD BIRTHDAY GREETINGS   36771/$7.95
__GARFIELD BE MY VALENTINE   37121/$7.95
__GARFIELD SEASON'S GREETINGS   37435/$8.95
__GARFIELD VACATION GREETINGS   37774/$10.00
__GARFIELD'S THANK YOU POSTCARD BOOK   37893/$10.00
ALSO FROM GARFIELD:
__GARFIELD: HIS NINE LIVES   32061/$9.95
__THE GARFIELD BOOK OF CAT NAMES   35082/$5.95
__THE GARFIELD TRIVIA BOOK   33771/$6.95
__THE UNABRIDGED UNCENSORED
  UNBELIEVABLE GARFIELD   33772/$5.95
__GARFIELD: THE ME BOOK   36545/$7.95
__GARFIELD'S JUDGMENT DAY   36755/$6.95
__THE TRUTH ABOUT CATS   37226/$6.95

Name_____

Address_____

City_____ State_____ Zip_____
30   Allow at least 4 weeks for delivery   7/93 TA-267

Like to get a **COOL CAT**alog stuffed with great **GARFIELD** products? Then just write down the information below, stuff it in an envelope and mail it back to us...or you can fill in the card on our website - **HTTP://www.GARFIELD.com**. We'll get one out to you in two shakes of a cat's tail!

Name:
Address:
City:
State:
Zip:
Phone:
Date of Birth:
Sex:

Please mail your information to:

Artistic Greetings
Dept. #02-7002
Elmira, NY 14925

© PAWS